W9-CZT-044

These United States
The Questions of Our Past

These United States

The Questions of Our Past

THIRD EDITION

Volume I: To 1877

Irwin Unger

New York University

Portraits and *Documents* by Debi Unger

Prentice-Hall, Englewood Cliffs, New Jersey 07632

Library of Congress Cataloging-in-Publication Data

Unger, Irwin.
    These United States.

    Includes bibliographies and index.
    Contents: v. 1. to 1877.
    1. United States—History.   I. Unger, Debi.
II. Title.
E178.1.U54 1986b   973   85-24469
ISBN 0-13-915109-5 (v. 1)

Editorial/production supervision: Marjorie Borden
Interior design: Judith A. Matz-Coniglio
Cover design: Judith A. Matz-Coniglio
Photo research: Barbara Cushing Schultz
Acquisitions editor: Stephen Dalphin
Manufacturing buyer: Barbara Kelly Kittle

Cover photo: Currier & Ives, "The Hudson from West Point," © Francis G. Mayer, Photo Researchers.

© 1986 by Prentice-Hall
A Division of Simon and Schuster, Inc.
Englewood Cliffs, New Jersey 07632

All rights reserved. No part of this book may be
reproduced, in any form or by any means,
without permission in writing from the publisher.

Printed in the United States of America

10 9 8 7 6 5 4 3 2

ISBN 0-13-915109-5   01

Prentice-Hall International (UK) Limited, *London*
Prentice-Hall of Australia Pty. Limited, *Sydney*
Prentice-Hall Canada Inc., *Toronto*
Prentice-Hall Hispanoamericana, S.A., *Mexico*
Prentice-Hall of India Private Limited, *New Delhi*
Prentice-Hall of Japan, Inc., *Tokyo*
Prentice-Hall of Southeast Asia Pte. Ltd., *Singapore*
Editora Prentice-Hall do Brasil, Ltda., *Rio de Janeiro*
Whitehall Books Limited, *Wellington, New Zealand*

To Rita and Mickey, Libby and Arnie,
Phyllis and Jerry, and Norma and David
—with affection.

Contents

6

The Origins of the Constitution: By Popular Demand? *127*

7

The First Party System: What Issues Divided the New Union? *152*

8

The Jeffersonians in Office: How Did Power Affect Republican Ideology? *175*

9

The American Economic Miracle: What Made It Possible? *199*

10

Jacksonian Democracy: What Was It and How Did It Change Political Life? *227*

11

The Mexican War and Expansionism: Greed, Manifest Destiny, or Inevitability? *251*

Preface

The response to the first two editions has made it clear that *These United States* has developed a loyal following among secondary school, college, and university instructors around the country. We hope this new edition will retain these friends and add to them another large contingent.

This hope has informed the preparation of this latest version. We continue to use "questions of our past" as the central organizing principle for each chapter. We have learned from users and reviewers that this format serves as an intellectual challenge and awakens students' interest. As before, the chapters following each "question" attempt to answer it, but not at the expense of "coverage." They provide not just the stimulation and coherence of the question format, but also all of the traditional material of the "core" text. In effect, the student and instructor get "two for the price of one."

As in the past, *These United States* also goes beyond the conventional core text in its coverage of social events and popular culture. We not only cover politics, diplomacy, and battles; we also deal with families, social classes, children, the quality of life, sports, entertainment, the way people worked, health, longevity, living standards, and many other topics that are part of the new social history. While avoiding technical jargon and unnecessary complexity, we discuss economic growth, social mobility, and ideology, in each case attempting to suggest how developments affected the lives of ordinary men and women.

These United States once again tells the story of *all* Americans, not just elites. Black Americans are treated as an essential part of the American story from Chapter 1 on. Women, American Indians, people from other lands besides the British Isles, and men and women from the bottom of the social pyramid are also fully integrated into the text, not merely "tacked on." Yet at the same time, in pursuit of a stylish trend, we do not falsify the record by obscuring the role of political, economic, and social elites. In the process, we have achieved a new synthesis of the old and the new approaches in historical scholarship.

The third edition of *These United States* maintains all of these qualities from previous versions. But it also contains many improvements. We have used the occasion to rewrite extensively. We have added anecdotes and quotations to enliven the text. We have culled out infelicities of style and clarified the language and explanations. The final chapter of volume II has been updated with an extensive discussion of the "Reagan Revolution." The social history has been reinforced. For example, much new material on American Indians has been added to Chapter 19.

One of the biggest changes has been the replacement of the Family Histories by a brief *Portrait* and *Document* in each chapter. We made the change because we learned that many instructors found it difficult to integrate the Family Histories into their courses. Yet we did not want to lose the sense that the American past was constructed out of real people's lives.

The *Portrait* in each chapter is of a representative man or woman whose life or career encapsulates some important event or aspect of that chapter. In many cases, he or she is a figure discussed in the chapter. Thus, in Chapter 14 of Volume I, "The Coming of the Civil War," we have used Stephen A. Douglas as our *Portrait* figure; Chapter 22 of Volume II, "Culture in the Age of the Dynamo," uses William James. But we have also portrayed some unfamiliar people. Chapter 10, on the Jackson era, for example, contains a *Portrait* of Sequoyah, the Cherokee Indian who helped make his people literate; Chapter 25 portrays Edna St. Vincent Millay, the quintessential poet and "flapper" of the Jazz Age.

Besides the *Portraits*, each chapter contains a short *Document* written by contemporary observers. These, we believe, catch the flavor of the life or the thought of the period. We hope the combination of *Portraits* and *Documents* will not only add an intimate personal element to the text, but will serve as useful teaching devices for the instructor.

Here, then, is the third edition of *These United States*. We believe that it is an improved version, and, to repeat a previous preface, "We hope that readers will be even more pleased with the new . . . than they were with the old."

ACKNOWLEDGMENTS

Like all authors, we have benefited from the help of many people and wish to express our gratitude for that help. First, we would like to thank the following individuals at Prentice-Hall who made it possible to complete this revision of *These United States* with such despatch: Stephen Dalphin, acquisitions editor; Edie de Coteau, his editorial assistant; Marjorie Borden, production editor; Judith Matz-Coniglio, designer; and Carole Freddo, copy editor. In the months we worked together we never ceased to feel that we were dealing with people who cared about the book. No author can expect more.

We are indebted to Robert Weiss of New York University for his concise essay, "Writing about History."

We have also relied on "the kindness of strangers." A group of nine scholars read the manuscript revisions and gave us the benefit of their knowledge and skills. These were: Alan Coombs of the University of Utah; Anthony O. Edmonds of Ball State University; Thomas L. Hartshorne of Cleveland State University; Joe Kudless of Somerset County College; Paul Lucas of Indiana University; Charles Roberts of California State University—Sacramento; Robert Sawrey of Marshall University; David H. Stratton of Washington State University; and Robert Trempy of Diablo Valley College. We did not invariably accept all of their suggested changes, but we always found them interesting.

1 The New World Encounters the Old

Why 1492?

very schoolchild knows that Columbus discovered America in 1492. It is a "fact" firmly established in our national consciousness. Yet Columbus was not the discoverer of America, if by that statement we mean the first person to encounter the "New World," the two great continents that lie between Europe and Asia. At least two other groups of people stumbled on the Americas before Columbus. Sometime between 40,000 B.C. and 12,000 B.C. people from northeast Asia reached the New World from across the Pacific and settled the two great continents. We call their descendants Indians. Then about A.D. 1000 Scandinavians from northern Europe called Norsemen encountered North America coming from the east.

Given these earlier discoveries, is there any special significance to that famous year 1492? Should we throw it off our list of crucial dates and substitute 40,000 B.C. or A.D. 1000? If we keep 1492, how do we justify it? Did Columbus's landing at San Salvador in the Caribbean have a greater impact on the world than the two earlier events? What did Columbus's discovery mean, both to those who lived in the Old World of Europe, Asia, and Africa and to those already living in the Americas? To answer these questions we begin by looking at the first discovery and its significance.

THE FIRST AMERICANS

The first Americans were migrants from eastern Siberia on the Asian mainland. Physically, they belonged to the same human stock as the modern Chinese, Japanese, and Koreans—a relationship suggested by the straight black hair, broad face, and high cheekbones of modern American Indians. The migrants were a hunting, fishing, and gathering people who depended on roots, berries, fish, and game for food. As decreasing rainfall reduced these resources in Siberia, anthropologists conjecture, the native peoples were gradually driven eastward. Today such people would be stopped by the Bering Sea, but in that distant era we know that a land bridge joined Alaska in North America with Siberia. On the eastern side of this bridge they found more abundant food supplies and a climate milder than in their homeland. Gradually they moved southward along various routes, and by the time Europeans arrived many thousands of years later, they had spread from just below the Arctic Ocean to Tierra del Fuego at the southern tip of South America and from the Atlantic to the Pacific Ocean. They had also grown enormously in numbers. From perhaps a few hundred or a few thousand migrants, by 1492 the Indian population had swelled to 75 million, a figure equal to that of Europe at the same time.

As their numbers grew over the centuries, the descendants of these Asian people diversified into many groups with distinct languages, cultures, and political and economic systems. By about 3000 B.C. some had begun to practice agriculture, with "maize" (corn), first developed from a grasslike native American plant, as their chief crop and the staple of their diet. They also grew tomatoes, squash, various kinds of beans, and, in South America, potatoes. Surpluses from agriculture transformed Indian life. Abundant food led to larger populations and also to more diverse societies. Now, not everyone was needed to produce commodities to sustain life, so classes of priests, warriors, artisans, and chiefs appeared. In the most fertile agricultural regions great civilizations arose whose command of technology, artistic sophistication, and political complexity were comparable to contemporary Asia and Europe.

The Great Indian Civilizations. One of these Indian civilizations, that of the Mayas, built great ceremonial and administrative cities in the dense rain forests of Yucatán and Central America. The Mayas had no single ruler. Instead each urban center was independent and governed by a group of priests. Mayan society was stratified, with sharp divisions of class and status among the people. It also possessed a culture of great sophistication: the Mayas alone among the Indian peoples had a written language and books, and their mathematicians developed the idea of zero as a number place long before the Europeans did. Mayan astronomers could calculate the cycles of the seasons and the times of eclipses as accurately as their Old World counterparts.

The Aztecs to the north, in central Mexico, borrowed much from their Mayan neighbors. But the Aztecs were a much more warlike people and around A.D. 1300 established the core of a great and powerful empire on the site of what is now Mexico City. From there they expanded through conquest over all of central Mexico, so that by the early 1500s the Aztec state ruled over 5 million inhabitants.

Aztec society, too, was stratified, but it was also centralized. At the head of the Aztec empire was a chief priest whose powerful authority enabled the Aztecs to conquer virtually all their enemies. In the course of many wars with their neighbors the Aztec rulers took thousands of prisoners and enormous quantities of feathered headdresses, jade jewelry, and beautiful gold and silver ornaments. The treasure went into the coffers of the chief priest and his nobles; the prisoners, by the thousands, were sacrificed by having their hearts cut out to appease the bloodthirsty Aztec war god.

By the early 1500s Aztec wealth and power equaled or surpassed anything in Europe. When the Spaniards first entered the Valley of Mexico in 1519 they were awestruck by the splendor that the Aztec conquests—and the Aztecs' own ingenuity and skill—had produced:

> . . . When we saw so many cities and villages built in the water and other great towns on dry land and that straight level causeway going towards Mexico, we were amazed and said that it was like the enchantments they tell of in the legend of Amadis, on account of the great towers and pyramids and buildings rising from the water and all built of masonry. And some of our soldiers even asked whether the things that we saw were not a dream?

> Gazing on such wonderful sights we did not know what to say or whether what appeared before us was real; for on one side on the land, there were great cities and in the lake ever so many more, and the lake itself was crowded with canoes, and in the causeway there were many bridges at intervals, and in front of us

stood the great City of Mexico, and we—we did not number four hundred soldiers.

The Incas of Peru, in the coastal mountains of South America, produced an empire even larger than that of the Aztecs—including within its borders 7 million people at its height. Strong rulers like the Aztec chiefs to the north, the Inca emperors built fortresses on the Andes mountainsides and a network of roads that held their far-flung domain together. The Inca people were among the most adept metallurgists of the time, making weapons, tools, and ornaments of gold, silver, copper, and bronze. The Inca privileged classes lived very comfortably, but the sick and handicapped were also provided for by the government. Inca society has sometimes been compared to a modern welfare state.

The Indians of North America. North of the great Indian civilizations were less complex tribal cultures and peoples. By 1492 there was a fairly substantial population in what is now the United States. In the past scholars estimated that the Indian population only numbered about a million, but it now seems there may have been as many as 9 million. This population, however large, was anything but uniform. There were, for instance,

This is a reconstruction of what Cortés and his men saw when they arrived at "the great city of Mexico." The structure at the center of the plaza is the altar where prisoners were sacrificed to appease the Aztec gods.

Courtesy of the American Museum of Natural History

twelve different language groups in present-day United States, each embracing numerous individual tribes. The tribes also had differing economies. Some consisted primarily of hunters and food gatherers, and others of people who skillfully cultivated maize, beans, squash, melons, and tobacco. The Indians of the Iroquois Confederacy, or Six Nations, were warlike; the Delaware, who called themselves Leni-Lenape ("real person"), were peaceful. Indian dwellings ranged from tepees of skin-covered poles, the typical homes of the Plains Indians, to the impressive lodges made of beams covered with bark that the Iroquois and other eastern tribes built. Among the Hurons and many southeastern groups these structures were often grouped into towns surrounded by stockades. Although some Indian groups were isolated and self-sufficient, there were among them traders who traveled long distances by canoe on the lakes and rivers to exchange goods with other tribes.

Many tribes were skilled in handicrafts, making beautiful pottery, light and swift birchbark canoes, and implements of copper. Some wove a kind of cloth from the inner bark of trees. Other tribes, however, lived very simply, with few artifacts. The numerous tribes of California, for example, blessed with a mild climate and abundant food, made do with simple clothing and crude houses. Only their beautiful basketwork revealed their skills.

The first Indians the English encountered in North America were the tribes of the Atlantic coast and the Mississippi Valley. Politically, these varied greatly. The Iroquois Confederacy, originally comprising five tribes, was a powerful league, the terror of its Indian neighbors and the later scourge of the European communities. On the other hand, the Chippewas lived in many small bands that had little in common besides language. Among the tribes government varied considerably. The Natchez of the lower Mississippi River Valley were ruled by an absolute despot called the Great Sun, who was chosen by the Female Suns when his predecessor died. The Iroquois had a kind of representative system. Female clan heads elected both the male delegates to the Confederacy council and the sachems, or chiefs, who governed the Six Nations.

Religion was important among virtually all Indians. Most believed in some sort of creator of

Indian tribes of North America

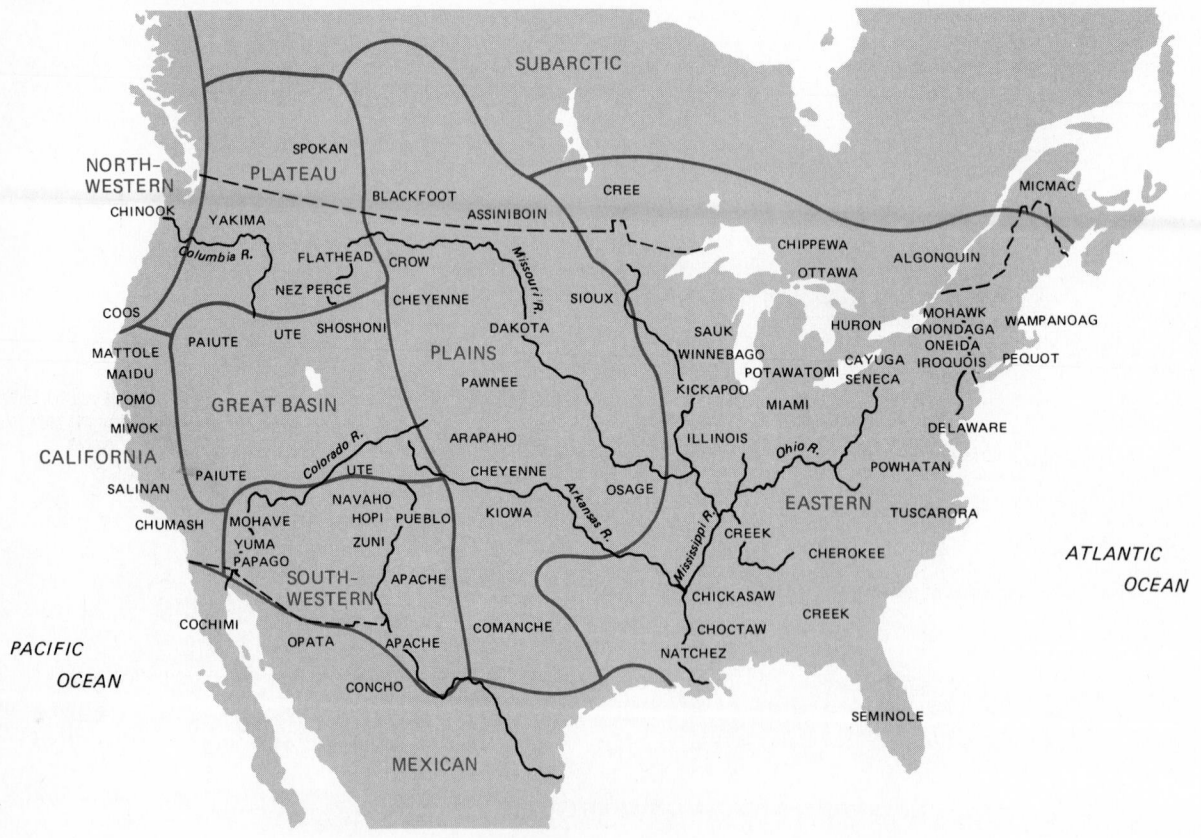

nature, humankind, and all the good things of life. These Indians were pantheists—that is, they believed that spiritual forces resided in natural things, both alive and inanimate. Like other religious peoples, they frequently expressed their feelings about the change of seasons, hunting, death, and war in elaborate ceremonies that included dancing, songs, feasting, and the wearing of vivid costumes and masks.

The Indians of North America held attitudes toward nature, property, and the land very different from those of the Europeans. Most whites saw nature as an obstacle to be overcome, a force to be subdued. They also found it natural to seek exclusive, individual possesion of land and other natural resources, and to measure wealth and power by how much a person possessed of these resources. In contrast, the Indians believed themselves a part of nature; they wished only to use it and preserve it so that it would yield its benefits for all time. They were natural conservationists and ecologists long before the terms had been invented. They also did not understand the European concept of ownership of the land. In Indian cultures one used the land for hunting and farming, but did not have the right to exclude others from using resources that one did not use oneself. Moreover, the community, not the individual, was the significant unit of Indian society. Insofar as the Indians recognized ownership, property was owned collectively by the tribe, not by individuals. Nor did Indians prize the accumulation of riches enough to be willing to sacrifice present satisfactions for remote future ones. These differing attitudes would have immense consequences for Indian-European relations.

THE FIRST EUROPEAN "DISCOVERY"

Europeans first made contact with the Americas long before Columbus. According to early Scandinavian sagas, in A.D. 986 a ship commanded by Bjarni Herjulfsson, a Norwegian merchant, was driven off course by a storm and narrowly escaped destruction on an unfamiliar coast. The land Herjulfsson and his crew encountered—probably Newfoundland or Labrador—was covered with "forests and low hills." They were on their way to the Norse colony of Greenland when the mishap took place. They were not interested in this new land and so did not disembark. But when they finally reached Greenland, they reported their discovery. They were probably the first Europeans to sight the mainland of North America.

Ever on the lookout for new lands to settle, other Scandinavians soon followed up on Herjulfsson's lead. In the year 1000 Leif Ericsson, one of the founders of the Greenland colony, sailed westward to investigate the report of the new country. He and his party found it relatively warm, densely forested, with steams overflowing with salmon. It seemed a far fairer place than icy Greenland, and the explorers settled down to spend the winter there. Finding what they later described as grapes, they dubbed the new country Vinland (Wineland) the Good.

Other Norsemen followed Leif Ericsson in an effort to colonize Vinland. In 1010 or thereabouts three boatloads of Greenlanders set out to establish permanent settlements in North America. Attacks by the Indian inhabitants drove the would-be settlers back home, but the Norse apparently made other efforts to colonize the new country. In 1960 archeologists discovered the remains of a small Norse village at L'Anse aux Meadows in northern Newfoundland. The find confirmed for the first time the sagas of medieval Scandinavian exploration. But the simple structures and the primitive tools uncovered also suggest how feeble the Norse colonizing effort was. Whether because of insufficient resources or Indian attack, the little settlement lasted for only a brief time.

Some knowledge of the Norse discoveries spread to other parts of Europe. Yet little happened. The first European contact with the Americas did not "take." Europe almost completely forgot the eleventh-century Norse voyages to North America. It was as if they had never taken place.

THE RISE OF MODERN EUROPE

Of course the isolation of the Americas did not last. The Old World eventually intruded into the New, and within a few generations the collision of these two different worlds completely transformed both societies. To the people of Europe this contact with the Americas seemed a "discovery"; actually, it was a meeting. As one scholar has written: "Columbus did not discover a new world; he established contact between two worlds already old."

Medieval Europe. Why did Europe fail to follow up on the Norse voyages? And why did it respond differently in 1492? What had happened during the centuries separating Leif Ericsson from Columbus to change the way Europeans reacted to the momentous meeting of the two worlds?

If we glance back to the years around A.D. 1000, when the Norse encountered America, we find Europe poor, politically divided, beset by local wars and civil disorder, its people largely illiterate and unfree. These weaknesses resulted from the breakdown of the unity that had characterized the ancient world. In ancient times a complex political system, the Roman Empire, had joined all parts of the Western European world into a peaceful, prosperous, civilized whole. Then came the Germanic invasions, the Muslim conquest of the Mediterranean, and devastating attacks on Europe by the Scandinavian Vikings. To impose order on this chaos there appeared a group of warlords, noblemen whose "keeps" and castles sheltered the common folk against raiders and brigands. Before long, however, the warlords became themselves the source of disorder as they battled one another for land and power. By the eighth or ninth century all long-range travel and trade had become unsafe. Goods, except for a few luxury items, ceased to move over the decaying European roads, and Europe ceased to be an economic whole.

Not surprisingly, Europe's economic and social integration declined. With trade and travel sharply reduced, each small region of the continent was forced to become self-sufficient. By the year 1000 an atomized, localized economic system had replaced the large-scale complex organization of the Roman Empire. Each nobleman's estate or manor—with its castle, peasants' village, and surrounding fields—had to provide all the food and implements it needed. Since each manor supplied its own needs, there was little reason to produce a surplus or find new ways to increase the output of crops or other goods. Meanwhile, cities that had been great centers of commerce and industry languished; outside Italy, many ancient cities disappeared entirely.

Most Europeans during this era were unfree peasants or serfs. Though not totally without rights, they could not leave the manor they were born on. Like farm animals, they went with the land when it was passed on from one nobleman to another through inheritance or conquest. In return for the right to till the soil, the peasant family gave the lord part of its crop plus various other payments in the form of work. Money seldom changed hands. Instead, payments and obligations were discharged through crops, animals, or services. Illiterate, superstitious, and often malnourished, as well as exploited, the serfs of Europe were a brake on economic change.

Even during the years 700 to 1000—the darkest of the "Dark Ages"—Europe had a small merchant class. But traders did not count for much in the eighth, ninth, and tenth centuries. Doing business on a very small scale, they wielded little economic power. Moreover, their social status was low. Neither serfs nor priests nor feudal lords, they did not fit into the medieval scheme of things, which presupposed a rural society composed of tilling peasants, praying clergymen, and fighting noblemen.

Nor did the Catholic Church, the ultimate repository of medieval values, find commerce congenial. The Church held that all economic relations must be subject to moral guidelines. Prices, for example, had to be "just," and were not to be determined by supply and demand or by what the traffic would bear. Charging interest was immoral; people borrowed money only when they were in desperate need, and to exploit them would be un-Christian. Capitalists—those who risked their capital in trade or moneylending—disregarded these principles. They looked only to profits, the Church thinkers said, and as a result their occupations were morally suspect. These attitudes toward merchants and their activities reinforced the economic backwardness of Europe.

By the year 1000 Europe had disintegrated politically as well as economically. Kings reigned in France, England, Portugal, and other realms, but they were not like later monarchs. They did not have armies, navies, or corps of civil servants. Instead, they relied on their vassals—the feudal nobility—to supply them with men and arms in emergencies and to administer the customary law in their districts. Nor did the monarchs of this era have large financial resources. Nowhere in Europe were there national taxes. Although theoretically supreme, kings were often inferior in wealth and power to one or more of the feudal lords who supposedly owed allegiance to them.

The one institution that held Europe together during the Middle Ages was the Roman Catholic Church. Retaining many features of the Roman imperial government—the Latin language, a corps of literate officials, and a supreme head, the pope, residing in Rome—the Church preserved many of the values and much of the culture and organizational skill of the ancient world. Possessing a virtual monopoly on literacy, clerics provided essential services to kings and other political leaders as scribes and officials. But the medieval church was no substitute for a powerful secular ruler. In fact, many people disputed its right to exercise political power at all.

Nor was the Church's learning as useful for practical affairs as it might have been. Indeed, its attention to the salvation of the individual's soul focused Europeans' minds on the afterlife rather than on worldly matters. Thus the Church probably discouraged the curiosity about the physical world that men and women of the ancient world had felt.

In the year 1000, in short, Europe could not rise to the challenge of the newfound world to the west. It did not have the economic or technical resources, the political and social cohesion, or even the interest to do so. The disorganized, politically feeble, otherwordly, largely illiterate Europe of Leif Ericcson's time was incapable of responding to the Norse discoveries.

EUROPEAN REVIVAL

The Lure of the East. Five hundred years later Europe reacted overwhelmingly when Columbus returned from the Caribbean to report the discovery of "the Indies." Crucial to this change in Europe's response was the remarkable revival of trade and commerce in the half millennium between Leif Ericsson and Columbus. This revival, and the growth of capitalism, would eventually undermine feudalism and the self-sufficient manor-based economy on which it rested. But for trade and traders to flourish, Europeans had to change their attitudes and awaken to the opportunities of commercial relations with distant lands and cultures. Ironically, it was violent confronta-

tion with an alien society that triggered the process of change.

From their first contact with the Islamic civilization that rimmed the eastern, southern, and western shores of the Mediterranean, Europeans had recognized the superior wealth and luxury of Christendom's major competitor. Compared with the rude commodities of France, England, and Germany, the silks, cotton, spices, cabinetwork, pottery, and swords of the Muslims were marvels of delicacy and sophistication. Until the violent clashes with Islam that we call the Crusades, Western Christians were content with what they had. But then, at the very end of Leif Ericsson's eleventh century, thousands of Europeans set out for Palestine to recover the Holy Sepulcher, Jesus' tomb, from the Muslim "infidels." After the Crusaders captured Jerusalem in 1099, Europeans settled in the newly conquered Levant on the eastern edge of the Mediterranean. Though they generally despised their Muslim foes as unbelievers, many Europeans came to appreciate the skills and artistry of Muslim craftsmen and developed a taste for sugar, silks, fine leatherwork, and other luxury goods of the Muslim world.

Even more intriguing, however, were the riches of the farthest Orient. By the fourteenth century an extremely valuable trade had sprung up among Europe, China, and India. Italian textiles, arms, and armor, along with north European

Germanisches Nationalmuseum Nurnberg

The spices displayed like jewels in this ornate box commanded high prices in Europe because merchants shipped them overland from the distant Orient. Emboldened by the profits a shorter, cheaper trade route would bring them, Europeans ventured beyond the limits of the world they knew.

copper, lead, and tin, moved eastward; silk, jewels, and spices moved the other way. The eastern end of the trade was in the hands of Asian traders—Chinese, East Indians, and Arabs. The western end was carried on largely by Italian middlemen from Venice and Genoa, whose immense profits soon made them the envy of other Europeans.

Most important in this East-West exchange was the spice trade. In the Middle Ages spices were more precious, relative to existing wealth, than oil or wheat are today. They seemed indispensable to comfortable living. Spices retarded decay, relieved the boredom of daily fare, and disguised the poor quality of meat. Of course, Europeans also used many locally grown herbs to flavor their food; but none of these could compare to pepper, cloves, nutmeg, and cinnamon, which were available only from India, Ceylon, and the "Spice Islands" of present-day Indonesia.

Contact with Islam and the revival of long-distance trade were accompanied by a change in attitude toward money and money getting. Rich capitalists could no longer be reviled and mistreated by noblemen and monarchs: their great wealth might be needed in an emergency to pay debts or procure arms. Rather than abusing them, rulers now began to grant merchants privileges and to provide them with protection. Before long the Church relaxed its rules against charging interest for lending money. Banking soon became a respectable and highly profitable enterprise.

The exposure to the East also helped to break down the self-sufficient manorial system. Before long the nobility had acquired a passion for the wondrous luxuries of Islam and the East. To buy them they needed cash. But almost all economic relations in the feudal world were based on long-established mutual obligations, payment in locally produced commodities, or services. The need to acquire cash soon changed these relations. Instead of payment in work or in crops, now serfs might be allowed to pay money for the right to work the lord's land. If peasants wanted to leave their manors, they might be permitted to buy their freedom. Lords might even allow serfs with a little silver or gold to buy some land and become peasant freeholders. Meanwhile, the up-to-date noblemen tried to improve their own cultivation methods to guarantee a surplus that they could sell for coin in the growing towns. By the thirteenth or fourteenth century the revival of trade had led to the breakdown of the manorial system in the many parts of Western Europe.

Still another result of the revival of trade was the rapid growth of cities and the flowering of urban life. As trade returned, new cities sprang up and old ones expanded. Former serfs flocked to the trading centers with their markets, warehouses, docks, and workshops to work for wages; to become laborers, artisans, and craftsmen; and to enjoy the greater freedom and variety of city life. Increasingly, educated men made the growing urban centers their home. Besides the older cities of the Italian peninsula, newer towns rose along the Baltic and North seas to distribute the goods of the East and to serve the growing commerce of northern Europe. In southern Germany merchants and bankers prospered by financing the shipping and distribution of eastern wares to central Europe.

The Nation-State. The merchant class of the growing cities was a powerful force for change in early modern Europe. The burghers, or bourgeoisie (from *burgh* or *bourg,* meaning "town"), were natural foes of the feudal political system, which produced constant disorder and interfered with trade. What the merchants needed was peace and order—goods and people moving safely and freely over long distances, protected and encouraged by a friendly and powerful central authority.

Inevitably the interests of the merchants made them the allies of feudal kings and helped revolutionize European political life. By borrowing money from the burghers, rulers could finance military forces to impose internal order and put down disobedient barons. They could free themselves from reliance on priests and bishops as administrators by turning instead to the new literate bourgeoisie. The revival of trade also created a money economy to replace the barter and exchange of services that had characterized the manorial economy, thus making it possible to impose national taxes. Before long, the modern nation-state, with its dedicated civil servants, its powerful armies and navies, and its capacity to mobilize resources to achieve national goals, had emerged in place of the chaotic, disjointed feudal system in Western Europe.

These political changes had immense implications for European expansion. Tax money would buy the ships, supplies, and merchandise needed for exploration and conquest. Royal officials would go out to the colonies to govern in the interests of Portugal, Spain, England, and France, using administrative methods employed at home. Profits from expanding overseas trade would further strengthen and enrich the national monarchies, which could then afford still bolder and more expensive enterprises. Once set in motion by the vast social and economic changes of the late Middle Ages, the process of exploration and overseas conquest would come to feed on itself.

Revolutions in Thought and Communication. Intellectual and cultural shifts were other factors that made 1492 different from A.D. 1000. People in the Middle Ages had little sense of historical change. To medieval Christians history was humanity's progress toward its final salvation. All that had preceded the birth of Jesus was a prelude to that great event; all that followed was a long epilogue that would culminate in his return and the "end of days." Medieval people gave ancient times little credit for uniqueness. Nor did they see the distinctive qualities of their own era.

Then, in fourteenth-century Italy, scholars began to perceive that ancient times were different from their own. How and why this new realization occurred is not entirely clear. It was probably sparked by the interchange with Greek-speaking Constantinople and the Muslim Mediterranean world, which had preserved and translated many ancient authors. Once under way, the new attitude toward the past was reinforced by the discovery of hundreds of Greek and Latin manuscripts hidden in monasteries, churches, and libraries for almost a thousand years.

The new contact with classical antiquity was a wonderfully stimulating experience. It was like encountering a new civilization, and it made European culture richer and more complex. Yet at the same time it gave Europeans a new confidence in their own society and in themselves. The ancients were great and creative people, surely, but their achievements were not beyond reach of the moderns. The new interest in history and literature—the new "humanism"—that this contact inspired also secularized the way people thought; that is, it directed their attention away from religion and salvation and toward the things of this world. The humanism of the era we call the Renaissance was not the irregligious, materialistic, and pleasure-obsessed set of attitudes people used to believe it was. But humanism did create new interest in the laws of physical nature and in the beauties of form, color, and shape.

The new interests were immeasurably helped by the invention of printing. In ancient and medieval times books were rare and expensive because they had to be copied laboriously by hand. By the end of the Middle Ages the revival of trade had created a new class of literate men and women, but the high cost of recording people's thoughts inevitably checked the spread of ideas and knowledge. In the ninth century the Chinese had begun to print whole pages of text from single carved wooden blocks. Then in the fifteenth century German craftsmen developed a way to print pages from movable type—individual, ready-made letters that could be assembled to form words and later disassembled for reuse again and again. The system, probably perfected by Johann Gutenberg of Mainz, soon spread throughout Europe.

By 1500 about 1,000 printers were working in the trade, and they had published 30,000 separate book titles in some 6 million copies. Many of these books were religious, but there were also scientific works, works on navigation and numerous accounts of discoveries in the Far East and West. Columbus's description of his first voyage to the "Indies" was quickly printed, widely circulated, and read. The new printed book marked another difference between the years 1000 and 1492. Cheap books encouraged literacy, and helped create a communications revolution that guaranteed that Europeans would not forget America a second time.

New Technology. Advances in navigation and naval architecture also explain why Europe was better able to exploit its knowledge of the Americas after 1492. Between the times of Leif Ericsson and Columbus marine engineering and the art of navigation had bounded ahead. In the year 1000 the Norse captains had been in the vanguard of navigation; half a millenium later their methods of locating their position by sighting the sun with the naked eye and guessing speed seemed primitive.

By this time Europeans had adopted the compass, a simple instrument consisting of a magnetized needle attached to a card marked with directions. The needle was attracted to the north magnetic pole. Now, even when the pole star was obscured by clouds, a ship captain could calculate his direction. By the fifteenth century, as expanding trade made the need for establishing position on the featureless open ocean more pressing, European seamen were also beginning to calculate latitude with the quadrant and astrolabe.

Improvements in navigation were accompanied by advances in ship design. The typical merchant ship of medieval Europe was a high-sided tubby vessel with a rudder at the side and a single large square sail, useful only if the wind blew directly from behind. Gradually these ships were modified to carry adjustable sails and rudders at the stern. Now vessels, by "tacking," could sail even against the wind. Faster, more maneuverable, and more stable ships expanded Europe's reach. As incorporated first into the Portuguese caravel and carrack during the fifteenth century,

Rare Book Division, New York Public Library, Astor, Lenox, and Tilden Foundation

A Portuguese galleon, of the sort that enabled Europeans to conquer the oceans and helped to create the Portuguese empire in the sixteenth century. The gun ports on the sides and stern are realistic in this contemporary engraving, but the men on deck and the fish are exaggerated in size.

and then a little later in the Portuguese, Spanish, French, and English galleons, these changes gave Europeans the equipment needed to undertake long ocean voyages with relative confidence.

One more innovation was needed before Europeans were equipped to conquer the world: gunpowder. Discovered after A.D. 1000, probably by the Arabs, it was first used to propel missiles from cannons early in the fourteenth century. Artillery gradually became miniaturized so that by 1360 primitive small arms were being used. Within a century the arquebus, a hand-held weapon that looked like a modern rifle and was fired by a trigger, had become a common infantry weapon. These weapons were heavy and inaccurate; but when combined with the horse, pike, metal armor, and steel sword of the Europeans, they would prove devastating against the native peoples of the Americas.

EUROPEAN EXPANSION

The invention of an easier way to produce books; the development of gunpowder, better ships, and navigational instruments; the rise of the strong nation-state; the growth of trade; the appearance of a sizable merchant class; the passing of feudalism and the self-sufficient economy of the manor—

these are some events that made Europe in 1492 different from Europe in 1000. Even before Columbus they had produced their effects: by the 1400s Europeans were launched on a campaign to explore the world and make contact with other lands and peoples.

The quest began with the effort of Prince Henry of Portugal, later known as Henry the Navigator, to seek out new lands to the south and west. Henry was not indifferent to gold, nor was he uninterested in filling the gaps in Europe's geographical knowledge. But he was not a fully modern man impelled primarily by curiosity or hope of profits. Rather, he was moved as much by medieval mystical and religious purposes as by modern practical ones. His chief concern, it seems, was to find the kingdom of Prester John (legendary ruler of a Christian land located in eastern Africa or central Asia) and reunite him and his people with the main body of Christendom.

To achieve these purposes Henry sponsored expeditions along the west coast of Africa. Each year ships left Portugal to venture ever farther south, their captains spurred on by Henry's rewards for progress. By 1445 Dinis Dias had rounded Cape Verde and reached the humid, fertile part of the African coast below the Sahara. Ten years later Alvise da Cadamosto reached the Senegal and Gambia rivers and discovered the Cape

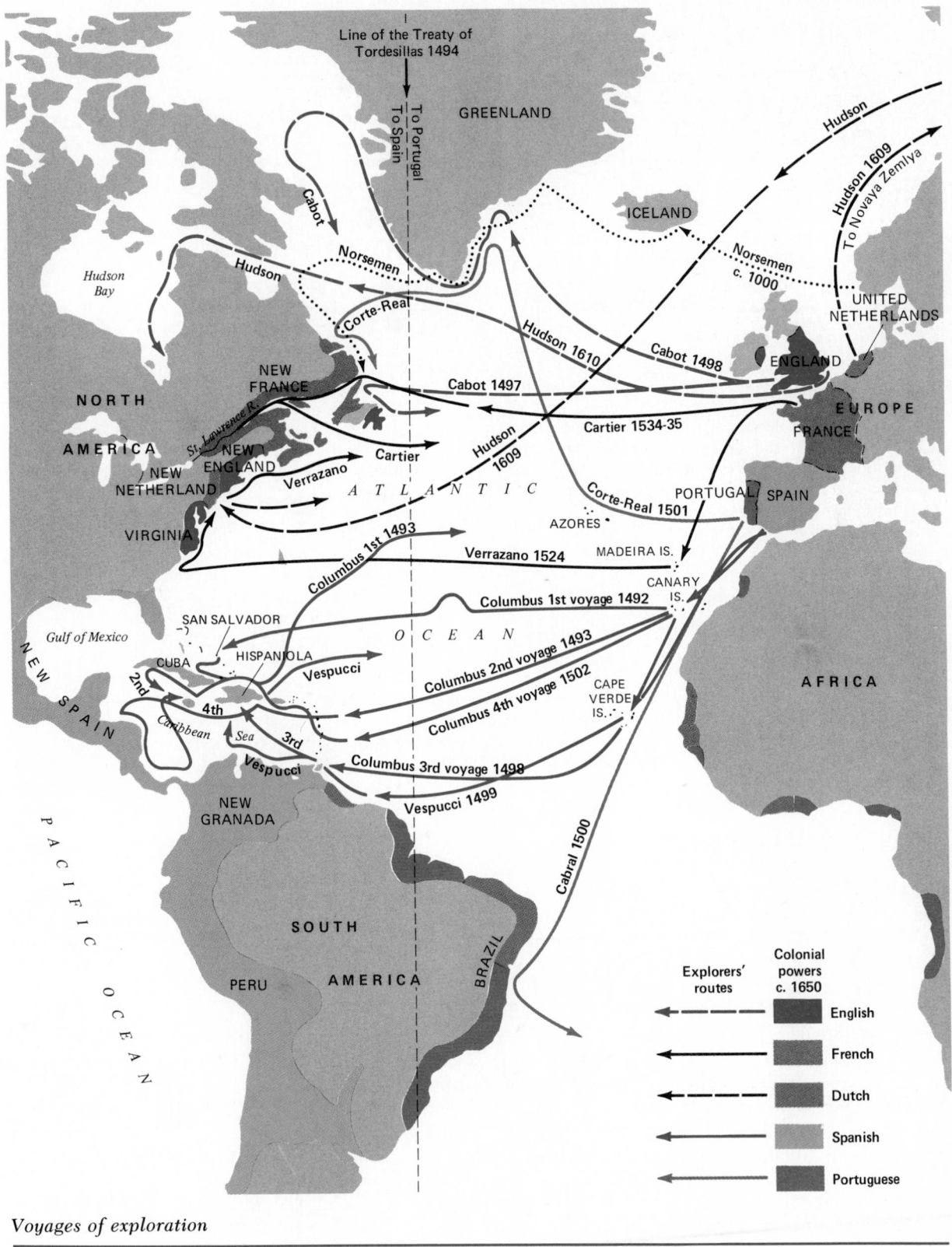

Voyages of exploration

Columbus Tells His Story

While still aboard the *Niña,* Columbus composed a brief letter to his sovereigns describing his first voyage. This letter was transmitted to Ferdinand and Isabella from Lisbon and reached them at Barcelona sometime in March 1493. Called by different names, it is the first account in a European language of the New World, if we except the Norse sagas of 500 years earlier. The letter was quickly printed in Latin and other languages and widely circulated in Europe.

Columbus's account gave Europeans their first glimpse of the New World. Unfortunately it played on their greed in a way that would have tragic consequences for the native peoples of the Americas. Note the simultaneous appeal to Ferdinand and Isabella's piety and cupidity.

"SIR. Since I know you will take great pleasure at the great victory with which Our Lord has crowned my voyage, I write this to you, from which you will learn how in . . . [thirty-three] days I reached the Indies with the fleet which the most illustrious King and Queen, our lords, gave to me. And there I found very many islands filled with people without number, and of them all I have taken possession of for their Highnesses, by proclamation and with the royal standard displayed, and nobody objected.

"When I reached Juana [Cuba], I followed the coast westward, and I found it to be so long that I thought it must be the mainland, the province of Catayo [a part of China]. And since there were neither towns nor cities on the coast, but only small villages, with the people of which I could not have speech because they all fled forthwith, I went forward on the same course, thinking that I should not fail to find great cities and towns. . . . [Later] I sent two men upcountry to learn if there were a king or great cities. They traveled for three days and found an infinite number of small villages and people without number, but nothing of importance; hence they returned. . . .

". . . I saw toward the east another island . . . to which I at once gave the name *La Spanola* [Hispaniola, or Haiti]. And I went there and followed its northern part . . . to the eastward for 178 great leagues. . . . As Juana, so all the others are very fertile to an excessive degree, and this one especially. In it there are many harbors on the coast of the sea, incomparable to others I know in Christendom, and numerous rivers, good and large, which is marvelous. Its lands are lofty and in it are very many sierras and very high mountains. . . . All are most beautiful, of a thousand shapes, . . . and filled with trees of a thousand kinds and tall, and they seem to touch the sky; and I am told they never lose their foliage, which I can believe, for I saw them as green and beautiful as they are in Spain in May, and some of them were flowering, some with fruit. . . . And there were singing the nightingale and other little birds of a thousand kinds in the month of November. . . . Upcountry there are many mines of metals, and the population is inumerable. *La Spanola* is marvelous, . . . and the lands are so beautiful and fat for planting and sowing, and for livestock of every sort, and for building towns and cities. . . .

"The people of this island and of all other islands which I have found and seen . . . all go naked, men and women, as their mothers bore them, except that some women cover one place only with the leaf of a plant or with a net of cotton which they make for that. They have no iron or steel or weapons, nor are they capable of using them, although they are well-built people of handsome stature, because they are wonderfully timorous. They have no other arms than arms of canes . . . to the ends of which they fix a sharp little

Verde Islands. Meanwhile, the Portuguese had stumbled on the Atlantic islands of Madeira and the Azores, conquered their inhabitants, and settled them with Europeans.

After Henry's death his work was taken over by the kings of Portugal, and the goals changed. Now there was little thought of Prester John; the sole purpose was to find the end of the African continent, round it, and sail northeast for India, Cathay (China), and Xipangu (Japan). For many years the spice trade had been in the hands of Genoese and Venetian merchants, and traders from the Levant. If the Portuguese could bypass the Italian and Muslim middlemen, all the profits of the Eastern trade would be theirs.

In 1488 Bartolomeu Dias finally rounded the southern tip of Africa. Unfortunately Dias's timid crew forced him to turn back before he could penetrate very far into the Indian Ocean. Yet his achievement was enormously important. Encouraged by Dias's report, Vasco da Gama boldly set sail for India in July 1497. The following May his little fleet of four ships arrived at Calicut on the west coast of India. Da Gama collected a cargo of pepper, ginger, cloves, and cinnamon and returned home safely in 1499, the first man to sail directly from Europe to India and back.

Once opened, the route around Africa became a busy thoroughfare. To expedite the trade in spices, silks, drugs, and precious goods, the Portuguese established "factories" (trading posts) along the Malabar coast of India, in Ceylon, and on the islands of the East Indies. In 1509 a Portuguese fleet of fast caravels armed with cannon defeated a Muslim fleet at Diu and established Portugal as the dominant power in India. Soon the Portuguese commercial empire expanded from the Persian Gulf to the western Pacific. By 1550

stick. . . . [O]ftentimes . . . I have sent ashore two or three men to some town to have speech, . . . and as soon as they saw them coming, they fled. . . . It is true that after they have been reassured and have lost this fear, they are so artless and so free with all they possess, that no one would believe it without having seen it. Of anything they have, if you ask them for it, they never say no; rather then invite the person to share it; . . . and whether the thing be of value or of small price, at once they are content with whatever little thing of whatever kind may be given to them. I forbade that they should be given things so worthless as pieces of broken crockery and broken glass, and ends of straps, although when they were able to get them, they thought they had the best jewel in the world; thus it was ascertained that a sailor for a strap received gold to the weight of two and a half *castellanos* [worth today about $500], and others much more for other things which were worth much less. . . . I gave them a thousand good and pleasing things which I had brought, in order that they might be fond of us, and furthermore might be made Christians and be inclined to the love and service of their Highnesses and of the whole Castilian nation, and try to help us and to give us of the things which they have in abundance and which are necessary to us. And they know neither sect nor idolatry, with the exception that all believe that the source of all power and goodness is in the sky, and they believe very firmly that I, with these ships and people, come from the sky, and in this belief they everywhere received me, after they had overcome their fear. . . .

"In these islands I have so far found no human monstrosities, as many expected; on the contrary, among all these people good looks are esteemed; nor are they Negroes, as in Guinea, but with flowing hair. . . . Thus I have neither found monsters nor had report of any, except in an island . . . which is inhabited by a people who are regarded in all the islands as very ferocious and who eat human flesh [the Carib Indians, that is]; they have many canoes with which they range all the islands of India and pillage and take as much as they can. . . . In another island, which they assure me is larger than *Espanola,* the people have no hair. In this there is countless gold, and from it and the other islands I bring with me Indios [that is, Indians] as evidence.

"In conclusion, to speak only of that which has been accomplished on this voyage, which was so hurried, their Highnesses can see that I shall give them as much gold as they want if their Highnesses will render me a little help, besides spice and cotton, as much as their Highnesses shall command; and gum mastic, as much as they shall order shipped; . . . and aloe wood, as much as they shall order shipped; and slaves, as many as they shall order, who will be idolators. And I believe that I have found rhubarb and cinnamon, and I shall find a thousand other things of value. . . .

"So, since our Redeemer has given this victory to our most illustrious King and Queen, and to their famous realms in so great a matter, for this all Christendom ought to feel joyful and make great celebrations and give solemn thanks to the Holy Trinity with many solemn prayers for the great exaltation which it will have in the turning of so many people to our holy faith, and afterwards for material benefits, since not only Spain but all Christendom will hence have refreshment and profit. . . .

"At your service.

THE ADMIRAL"

---

the small Atlantic nation had established a virtual monopoly on the world spice trade.

Columbus and the Spanish Explorations. The success of the Portuguese aroused the envy of the rulers of Europe's other nations. Eventually the Dutch, the French, and the English would challenge Portugal's stranglehold on the eastern spice trade around Africa. But meanwhile, a Genoese adventurer and visionary named Cristoforo Colombo (Christopher Columbus) had arrived at an alternative that both promised a shorter route and seemed likely to avoid a direct confrontation with the Portuguese.

Columbus's scheme was simple, and based on false premises. He believed that the globe was far smaller than it actually is and that Asia was immensely wide, extending much farther east than it does. Only water—and a rather small stretch at that—he thought, lay between Europe and the Indies. The conclusion was clear: a ship sailing west, after only a few weeks, would reach Asia and its riches.

After peddling his idea to every monarch of western Europe, Columbus finally interested the rulers of Spain. Pledging her jewels as security, Queen Isabella borrowed some of the money Columbus needed from a Spanish religious order. The rest of the capital came from the small city of Palos, whose burghers were ordered to supply "the Admiral" with three small vessels. The total cost of the expedition was probably about 2 million maravedis (today about $14,000), a great fortune that could not have been marshalled for such a purpose a few centuries earlier. With this sum Columbus fitted out three small vessels, manned them with Spanish seamen, and stocked them with supplies. On August 3, 1492, he and his crew of ninety left Palos. They arrived at the Caribbean island of San Salvador ten weeks later, almost exactly five hundred years after the first European had sighted North America.

Columbus's first voyage was followed by three others, each better equipped than the first. The "Admiral of the Ocean Sea" explored the Caribbean, discovered its major islands, and touched the mainland of the Americas at several points. He also brought many settlers, and on the islands of Hispaniola, Puerto Rico, Jamaica, and Cuba established the first permanent European communities in the New World. From these settlements Spanish commanders launched expeditions to the mainland. One of these under Vasco Nuñez de Balboa crossed the Isthmus of Panama in 1513 to become the first group of Europeans to see the eastern shore of the Pacific Ocean.

But Spain's ambitions went beyond the

Columbus's first voyage to the New World aroused intense interest all over Europe. This 1493 illustration accompanied an edition of Columbus's letter to his royal patrons printed in Switzerland. The landscape, with its European-style castles and houses, is imaginary, but the large ship does resemble the Admiral's flagship, the Santa Maria.

Rare Book Division, New York Public Library, Astor, Lenox, and Tilden Foundation

Americas. In 1519 the Spanish crown sent the Portuguese navigator Ferdinand Magellan to finally do what Columbus had attempted—find an ocean route to the Far East by sailing west. In November 1520 Magellan discovered the strait at the tip of South America that bears his name, sailed through it, and launched his small fleet into the vast Pacific. After harrowing experiences with hunger, scurvy, and thirst, he arrived in the Philippines. There he was killed in a skirmish with the natives, but one of his vessels reached Spain by sailing westward around Africa. Though the route was far too long to be practical for the Europe-Asia trade—others would try again and again to improve on it—Magellan's voyage proved that the Americas were not part of the Indies and was the first circumnavigation of the globe, a milestone for humankind.

Spain Encounters the Indian Civilizations. Spain's Far Eastern empire never expanded much beyond the Philippines. Meanwhile, in the Americas its conquests soon made it master of two continents. In 1519 the Spaniard Hernando Cortés set out from Cuba with 600 men, 17 horses, and 10 cannons, landed at Veracruz, and marched to the Aztec capital of Tenochtitlán. The Aztec ruler, Moctezuma II, was a determined and aggressive man, but his resolve was undermined by his belief that the Europeans were the white gods that Aztec myths said would one day return to the world of men. His warriors, moreover, were startled and demoralized by the Spaniards' strange horses and firearms. Taking advantage of this combination of trust and fear, the Spaniards seized Moctezuma and plundered the overflowing Aztec treasury. Soon after, Cortés left the capital briefly to deal with an expedition sent from Cuba to punish him for departing on his adventure without permission. During his absence the Aztecs at the capital turned on the remaining Spaniards, and Moctezuma was killed in the fighting. Cortés returned to the city with a larger force of Spaniards, as well as many Indian allies who deeply resented the harsh Aztec rule. In the battle that followed, the Spaniards fought to kill, unlike the Aztec warriors, who were used to fighting to take captives only. The Spaniards' ferocity, guns, and horses produced an astonishing European victory. In the next few months Moctezuma's successors sought to rally the Indians of Mexico against the invaders, but few tribes would cooperate. By 1521 resistance was over. The mighty Aztec empire had fallen to a few hundred Europeans.

The conquest of Mexico was soon followed by that of the Inca empire in Peru. The *conquista-*

dor this time was Francisco Pizarro, a young man of lowly birth and overweening ambition, who had heard of a great native empire full of wealth along the Pacific coast of South America. Wasting no time, Pizarro joined two other eager adventurers and set off to find the fabled land. For a while it eluded him, but in 1532, after a forty-five-day climb up the high wall of the Andes from the Pacific coast, Pizarro and his 102 men and 62 horses finally reached the frontier of Peru.

Through emissaries Pizarro assured the Inca ruler, Atahualpa, that he and his men intended to stay in the Inca realms for only a short time. Confident of his own strength, Atahualpa allowed them to advance. When he finally confronted the Europeans, they attacked, cut down 5,000 Indian soldiers, and took the Inca emperor prisoner. The royal captive offered the Spaniards a roomful of silver and gold to buy his freedom. Pizarro accepted. Then, when the treasure was safely in his hands, he had Atahualpa bound to a stake and strangled.

In the next few months the Spaniards found various puppets among the Inca royal family to aid them in their conquest; in addition, they had the advantage of guns and horses. Eventually the Indians cornered the Europeans in Cuzco, the Inca capital, and sought to starve them out. But the Spaniards held out long enough to force the Indian army to abandon the siege. This was the end of effective Inca resistance. Over the next few years the Europeans extended their control over the whole of the vast Inca domain, from modern Colombia to what is now central Chile.

The conquest of the Mayas was slower and less dramatic because there was no single Maya state to confront the invaders. In 1527 Spanish forces first entered Yucatán and encountered guerilla resistance. Over the next twenty years the Spaniards advanced and retreated; not until about 1550 were the Mayas of Central America subjugated and placed firmly under the control of the Spanish king. The last great native civilization was gone.

Spain's Rivals. By the end of the sixteenth century Spain had conquered virtually all of Central and South America except for Brazil, which was awarded to Portugal by the Treaty of Tordesillas in 1494. In 1580 Spain absorbed Portugal, adding

---

Spanish explorations in the Gulf of Mexico and Central America

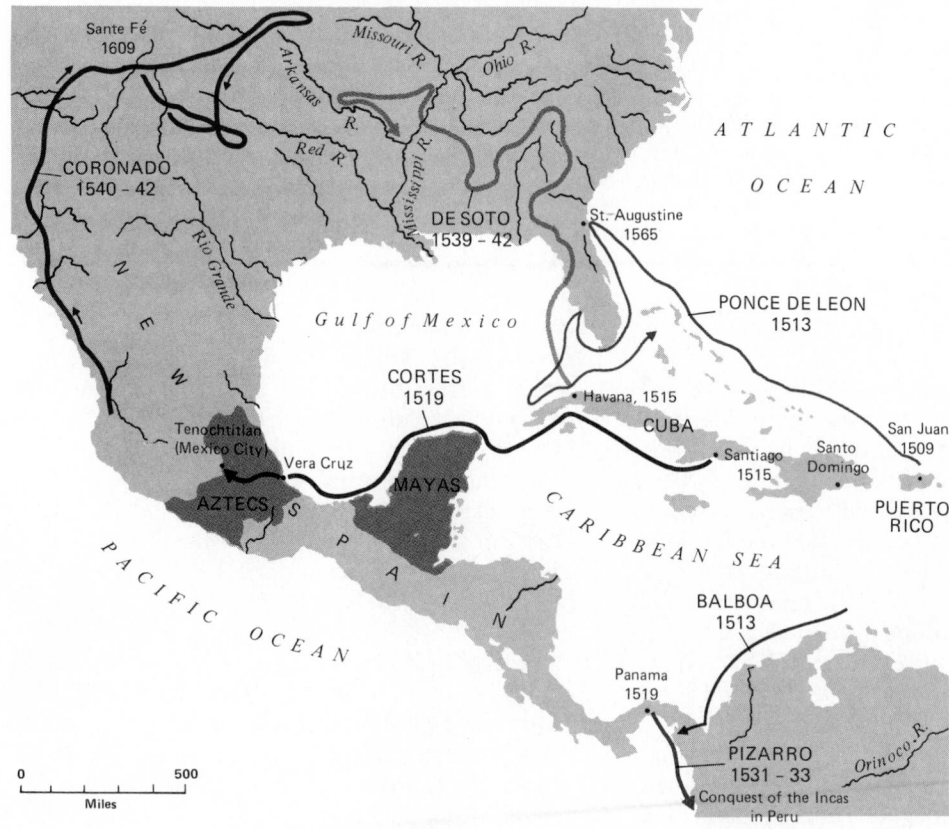

An Historical Portrait   Isabella of Castile

Isabella, queen of Castile, was called "the Catholic" by her subjects to honor her piety and her deep devotion to her faith. Though married to Ferdinand, king of Aragon, she was not merely a royal consort, for in her own realm, Castile, she was sovereign. Like that other reigning early modern queen, Elizabeth I of England, Isabella was not "womanly" in the traditional sense. She was one of the most powerful and vigorous rulers of early modern times and she helped transform Spain into a strong, modern nation.

Isabella was already married to Ferdinand, the young heir apparent of neighboring Aragon, when she came to the throne of Castile in 1474. When Ferdinand became king of Aragon several years later, their alliance united the two realms that occupied the largest portion of the Iberian peninsula and ultimately formed the core of the modern Spanish state.

But Spain was anything but united religiously, culturally, or politically when the two young monarchs took up their joint reign. For centuries the Iberian peninsula had been a meeting ground—and a battlefield—of diverse peoples. Conquered in the eighth century by "the Moors" (Muslims), it had been reclaimed through fierce struggle by the Christians. The process had been a slow one, however, and

until the end of the fifteenth century the Moors continued to rule Grenada in the southeast. In addition, the peninsula was home to thousands of Jews, who formed a class of artisans, merchants, and professionals who contributed much-needed skills to Spanish society.

This diversity seemed deplorable to Spanish Christians, few of whom believed religious or cultural tolerance a virtue. They considered the non-Christians infidels whose beliefs were wicked and dangerous. Though over the centuries there had been periods of relative harmony among the different Iberian communities, there had also been periods of fierce religious strife. Such conflict had helped mold the passionate, valorous, and often ferocious temperament of the Spanish aristocracy. Isabella's accession to the throne of Castile ushered in the last stage of the Christian reconquest. By 1481 the Catholic monarchs were engaged in a final drive to conquer Grenada and thereby eliminate the last Muslim outpost in Western Europe.

Earlier Christian successes had not led to Christian order. Until Ferdinand and Isabella, Spain was a land wracked by turmoil and lawlessness, most of it inspired by the proud, warlike Spanish nobility. These men preyed on city folk and peasants alike, and their undisci-

plined retainers ravaged the towns and the countryside, stealing, murdering, and raping. The previous rulers of Castile had been too weak to stop these unruly grandees, whose defiance effectively reduced the central government to an empty shell. Spain at the time of Isabella's accession exhibited the worst aspects of the feudalism that had characterized the Middle Ages and kept Europe too feeble to exploit the growing geographic knowledge of distant lands.

Isabella determined to smash the unruly aristocrats, reassert the authority of the crown, and put an end to lawlessness in the realm. Her methods were not gentle. In the province of Galicia her agent, Don Fernand de Acuna, razed forty-seven castles of the unruly nobility and hanged some of the worst offenders. Hordes of brigands and assassins fled the province.

The monarchs' chief instrument for imposing order was the Hermandad, or brotherhood, a league of city people disgusted with the lawless aristocrats. Under the crown's sponsorship, the Hermandad contributed men and money for an internal police force to suppress brigandage and violence in the towns and along the highways. Its militia exacted terrible penalties of the culprits they caught. "The executioners," in the words of one later historian, "cut off feet and hands,

that small country's rich empire for a time to her own.

The wealth of the New World proved immense. Gold and silver confiscated from the Indians poured into Spain. Additional floods of precious metals soon flowed from new mines in Peru and Mexico. From 1500 to 1650 Spain extracted almost 20,000 tons of silver and 200 tons of gold from its American colonies. In addition, cocoa, tobacco, dyes, and other American products found ready markets in Europe, providing another source of Spanish income. All this New World bounty helped make Spain the richest and most powerful nation in Europe.

At first Spain's rights in America were unchallenged. But the Spanish monopoly could not last. To the monarchs of France and England and,

somewhat later, the leading merchants and gentlemen of the Dutch Republic, Spain's example seemed irresistible. True, Spain and Portugal between them claimed sole rights to the entire New World. But this assertion seemed outrageous to most other Europeans. As the French king Francis I remarked to the Spanish ambassador in 1540, "the sun shone for him as for others," and he wondered where in "Adam's will" the Americas had been divided between Spain and its Iberian neighbor.

England was the first northern European country to join the scramble for a share in the New World. In 1496 Henry VII authorized John Cabot to sail west under the king's "banners and ensignes . . . to seeke out, discouer, and finde whatsoeuer isles, countryes, regions, or prouinces of

shoulders and heads, neither sparing nor veiling the rigor of justice."

In their drive to consolidate Spain under royal authority, Isabella and Ferdinand waged implacable war against all those elements within the Iberian peninsula who marred the kingdom's religious unity. These included many nominal converts from Judaism and Islam who had changed their faith to Christianity out of expediency. In 1478 the royal monarchs established, under papal authority, a tribunal called the Inquisition to root out secret backsliders among the "New Christians" and punish them, by burning at the stake if necessary. But this was not all: The practicing Jews and Muslims remained, and these groups, too, had to be dealt with. They were.

In that momentous year of 1492, the Jews of Spain were ordered expelled from the kingdom. At the very same time, after a decade of war, the Moorish kingdom of Grenada fell to the Christian knights and soldiers. Faced with the alternative of exile, most of Grenada's Muslim inhabitants accepted baptism into the Catholic faith.

Columbus was a major beneficiary of Isabella's determination and strength of will. The success of Spain's joint rulers in suppressing the aristocracy and establishing their authority gave the crown the resources needed to support such speculative ventures as voyaging west to reach India and the Far East. If the plan succeeded, the newly united Spain would steal the lead on Portugal's attempt to bypass the Italian middlemen in the fabulous spice trade with the Orient. Columbus also enjoyed a special rapport with the queen. He and Isabella, physically, were as alike as brother and sister: both were blue-eyed and auburn-haired, rarities in southern Europe. More important, they had similar personalities. Isabella, like the Genoese mariner, was a visionary who responded to Columbus's bold schemes. Columbus would later write of his patroness: "In all men there was disbelief, but to the Queen, my lady, God gave the spirit of understanding and great courage and made her heiress of all. . . ."

But the queen was no instant convert to the "Enterprise of the Indies." Columbus visited the Spanish court several times over a span of seven years before Isabella agreed to sponsor and finance his expedition. Finally, early in 1492 the monarchs authorized the expedition and furnished "the Admiral" with the necessary documents to set his enterprise in motion.

They joyously greeted Columbus in Barcelona when he returned from his first voyage in 1493, confirmed all the titles and privileges they had promised, and provided him with the means to return to "the Indies" as soon as possible. During the following years, while the discoverer collected enemies in Spain and in the new colonies, the queen remained his champion. But by the time he returned from his fourth voyage in 1504, she was old, sickly, and bowed with cares. A devoted mother, she had seen three of her children die while still young. Another child, Joanna, surviving heir to the Spanish throne, was insane, and the queen trembled at the prospect of the kingdom under her rule.

During the last months of her life Isabella, always pious, turned more and more to her devotions. On November 26, 1504, she died. Her will made no provision for Columbus, and when he passed away scarcely eighteen months later, he was a near pauper.

Invigorated by the treasure of the New World, Spain would become the most powerful nation in Europe. But having driven from the realm some of its most creative people and confirmed a tradition of intolerance, it ultimately failed to benefit from its good fortune. In the following centuries Spain became an economic backwater and surrendered leadership in science and the arts to other nations. In the end Isabella had bequeathed to her beloved nation an ambiguous legacy.

---

the heathens and infidels whatsoeuer they be. . . ." Cabot, a Venetian, made two voyages to North America. On the first he sighted either Nova Scotia or Newfoundland, and on the second he sailed down the east coast as far as Delaware Bay or Chesapeake Bay. The English government did not follow up on these voyages, but Cabot's report of codfish in Newfoundland waters did attract many fishermen from France and England to the area. More important, his voyages became the basis for English claims to North American territory.

France joined the quest for overseas wealth in 1523, when Francis I dispatched the Florentine mariner Giovanni da Verrazano to seek out the Far East by the still-elusive western route. Verrazano reached the Americas, probably somewhere along the Carolina coast, and sailed north, touching New York and Narragansett bays and Nova Scotia. Later Francis sent better-financed expeditions under Jacques Cartier to the region farther north. Cartier explored the coasts of Newfoundland, Prince Edward Island, and the Gaspé Peninsula, and later the St. Lawrence River to the site of Montreal. Like Cabot's voyages, Cartier's did not lead immediately to colonizing efforts, but they did give France a claim to part of North America.

The Dutch began exploring relatively late. By the beginning of the seventeenth century most of modern Holland had achieved autonomy from Spain and was developing into a prosperous country dominated by aggressive merchants and bankers. In 1609 a group of these capitalists joined as partners in the Dutch East India Company and hired Henry Hudson, an English sea captain, to

This illustration from a 1615 Spanish chronicle of life in the New World depicts a cultural difference between Europeans and Indians present from the beginning. The Inca asks: "Do you eat this gold?" The Spaniard replies, "Yes, we eat this gold."

find a water route to the far East through North America. Hudson was no more successful than the other explorers who had sought this Northwest Passage, but he added to Europe's geographical knowledge and Holland's claim to part of North America by sailing down the Atlantic coast from Newfoundland to Virginia. During this trip Hudson explored Cape Cod and Delaware Bay and sailed partway up the broad river that now bears his name.

These expeditions were only a small part of the sixteenth- and early-seventeenth-century exploration of the Americas. There were scores of other expeditions along every coast and into every accessible bay, inlet, and navigable river of the two western continents. At the same time Spanish captains like Hernando de Soto and Francisco Vásquez de Coronado, and the Frenchman Samuel de Champlain, pushed deep into the heartland of North America. By about 1650 Europeans knew the essential outlines of the New World continents and had even learned something of their remote interiors.

THE "COLUMBIAN EXCHANGE"

In 1552 the Spanish historian Francisco López de Gómara declared "the greatest event since the creation of the world (excluding the incarnation of the death of Him who created it) is the discovery

New York Public Library Picture Collection

Europeans saw America as a land of savagery, but at times they also saw it as a paradise. In this seventeenth-century picture it is a land of milk and honey. Note the chief in the center, smoking tobacco in an outsize pipe. Note also the hammocks, left background, an Indian invention that Europeans came to appreciate.

Library of Congress

A French engraving of the 1590s, illustrating Las Casas' account of Spanish atrocities against the Indian population of the Caribbean.

of the Indies." If we discount the exaggeration and the misuse of the word *discovery,* López was correct: few if any events have so changed the history of the world as the encounter of Europeans and American Indians at the end of the fifteenth century.

In Central and South America, except in the most remote interior regions, Europeans quickly swept away all traces of Indian self-rule. North of Mexico the process of conquest was slower but no less thorough. Vicious warfare against the Indians was part of the history of every European colony and every European colonial power—not just Spain.

Some Europeans defended the native Americans. At times the kings of Spain, France, and England sought to protect their Indian subjects. Friars, priests, and ministers often denounced the cruel treatment of the Indians. Yet these efforts seldom did much good. Even when Europeans refrained from outright murder, they treated the native Americans harshly. In the Spanish colonies Indians were enslaved and sometimes worked to death. Where not enslaved in a strict legal sense, they were forced to work for European masters. Well into the nineteenth century Indians in Spanish-held lands remained "peons" whose lot resembled that of medieval serfs. In the English col-

onies the Indians escaped forced labor generally, but less because of human considerations than because the North American tribes were less settled than their southern counterparts and could slip away from their oppressors into the forest.

Contact with the Europeans injured the native American peoples even when the Europeans intended no harm. Because of their long separation, the peoples of the Old and the New Worlds had developed immunities to different diseases; as a result, neither people could fend off the infections of the other. Europeans encountered a virulent form of syphilis in America, and it quickly spread over all of Europe. Thousands broke out in horrible sores and died before Europeans learned how to deal with the malady. The Indians suffered far more. Even European childhood diseases like measles became killing scourges among populations without immunities. Smallpox, too, along with tuberculosis and cholera, hit the native populations hard. In Mexico disease reduced the 25 million Indians of 1519 to 2.5 million by 1600. Along the Atlantic coast of North America a similar grim process took place. In 1656 Adriaen Van der Donck reported that the Indians of New Netherland claimed "that before the arrival of the Christians, and before the small pox broke out amongst theme, they were ten times as numerous as they

New York Public Library Picture Collection

Syphilis fell like a scourge on Europe shortly after Columbus returned from the New World. It was the real "Moctezuma's Revenge." This picture of a victim was drawn by the German artist Albrecht Dürer in 1496.

introduced by the conquerors. European manufacturers swamped native crafts and undermined native skills. Even efforts to export the Christian faith often did serious harm. The European missionaries hoped to benefit the Indians by bringing them the blessings of Christianity. At times they won converts by their example of humility, kindness, and courage. At other times, however, they sought conversions by fierce assaults on the Indians' religion, including their temples and religious artifacts. Bishop Diego de Landa of Yucatán destroyed thousands of Mayan books in his effort to stop idolatry, impoverishing both the Mayas and our knowledge of their civilization and history.

Europe Benefits. The transatlantic encounter after 1492 was no less momentous for Europeans. But the effects were almost diametrically opposite. With few exceptions (such as the scourge of syphilis), the contact between the Americas and Europe benefited Europe dramatically. Its fabulous American treasure catapulted Spain into the first rank of European powers. Simultaneously, the deluge of American gold and silver stimulated European trade, commerce, and industry, though Spain benefited less from these advances than Germany, France, and the Netherlands, which were better prepared to take advantage of rising commodity prices. These same rising prices helped further weaken the feudal system by accelerating the conversion of labor services into cash payments. The treasure also provided national rulers with enormous new incomes, giving them an additional edge over their unruly and disobedient vassals. Finally, the events following 1492 accelerated the rise to wealth and influence of the merchant-capitalists who entered the American trade. In short, the "discovery" of America speeded the modernization of Europe that was already well under way when Columbus sailed from Palos.

The transatlantic contact also provided Europeans with an enormously expanded and improved diet. Potatoes and Indian corn would eventually become staples consumed by millions of Europeans. Tomatoes, pumpkins, a wide assortment of beans, and many new fruits were also brought eastward to be widely grown in Europe. Rubber and chicle were other useful American borrowings. Not all the plant imports were blessings. Tobacco would prove almost as serious a scourge as syphilis, and there are those who have their doubts about chewing gum, made from chicle. Yet it is clear that America was a botanical as well as a mineral treasure trove.

now are. . . ." Indeed, the English and Dutch occupations of the East Coast were greatly eased because many Indians had been killed by white man's diseases that had spread to North America from the south even before the white men themselves appeared.

Disease was only part of the incidental damage that the Europeans inflicted on Indian societies. In many areas native agriculture was destroyed by the great herds of sheep and cattle

Rare Book Division, New York Public Library, Astor, Lenox, and Tilden Foundation

Maize, or Indian corn, was America's greatest contribution to the world's stock of grains. It was used extensively by European settlers in America from the outset. By contrast, the tomato was treated mostly as an ornament until rather recently. Both, however, were major New World contributions to human nutrition.

The Old World's encounter with the New also enriched Europe's intellectual life. In some ways it merely confirmed the European sense of superiority. After observing the Aztec sacrifices, the Spanish were certain that the native religions were bloodthirsty superstitions. The relative ease with which Europeans conquered the New World peoples also encouraged European arrogance—on the theory, apparently, that strength and ferocity equaled virtue. But not all Europeans found their prejudices reinforced. Some felt wonder at the variety of the world's cultures. Some saw native Americans as "noble savages" living in the same state of simplicity and grace Adam and Even had enjoyed in the Garden of Eden. It is not surprising that the first modern utopia was conceived by Sir Thomas More in 1516, soon after the Spanish discoveries. This contact with new cultures widened Europe's horizons and produced new social sciences, including the ancestors of anthropology and sociology.

CONCLUSIONS

We focus on 1492 as *the* date of America's discovery for several good reasons. One of these, no doubt, is that we tend to accept a Europe-centered view of the world. Still, from any cultural perspective, 1492 was a profound historical turning point. After Columbus's return from the New World, human history changed fundamentally. For the millions in the Americas, the change was a social disaster marked by disease, misery, bondage, and cultural disintegration. For Europe as a whole, 1492 marked the beginning of a new era of expansion—geographic, intellectual, and economic.

Columbus's landing at San Salvador in 1492 was an event that transformed two worlds. The encounter did not confer equal benefits on both populations, but that it was of transcendent importance for humanity cannot be doubted.

By 1500 Europeans were also about to embark on the greatest mass migration of all time, one that would eventually pull 100 million human beings across the Atlantic. We have seen something of the "forces" that led to this momentous occurrence. Let us now consider the personal motives that impelled countless ordinary, and not-so-ordinary, individuals to risk their lives and their fortunes creating new communities in the strange lands across the ocean.

FOR FURTHER READING

Alvin M. Josephy, Jr. *The Indian Heritage of America* (1968)

This is an overall survey of the Indian peoples of both American continents, region by region and era by era. Josephy recounts the story of each native American culture group and briefly describes Indian-white contacts and relations over the centuries. The book contains excellent picture portfolios.

Francis Jennings. *The Invasion of America: Indians, Colonialism, and the Cant of Conquest* (1975)

Jennings has written an angry book about Indian-European relations. An "ethnohistorian" who deals with the evolution of cultures, Jennings seeks to redress the traditional story that makes the Indians into "savages" and the Europeans into the civilized party to the Old World–New World encounter after 1492. He is especially hard on the Puritan settlers of New England, whom he considers hypocrites. Jennings pushes his useful reinterpretation too far.

Alfred W. Crosby. *The Columbian Exchange: Biological and Cultural Consequences of 1492* (1972)

Crosby sees the contacts between Europeans and the native peoples of America as a two-way street—both for good and ill. He notes the exchanges between Old World and New World of animals and plants. A particularly fascinating section of the book describes the exchange of lethal diseases: European smallpox for American syphilis.

J. H. Parry. *The Age of Reconaissance: Discovery, Exploration, and Settlement. 1450–1650* (1963)

An excellent review of the roots and course of late medieval–early modern European overseas expansion.

Samuel Eliot Morison. *The European Discovery of America: The Northern Voyages, 400–1600* (1971); and *The Southern Voyages, 1492–1616* (1974)

Both of these volumes are superb blends of lucid, meaty text, maps, and photographs by a sailor-historian who was a master of his craft. They deal with men, ships, and weather more than with "forces." You will learn how sailors spent the day at sea in the sixteenth and seventeenth centuries, what they ate, what songs they sang. You will also learn how a ship was navigated in this early age of sail.

Samuel Eliot Morison. *Christopher Columbus, Mariner* (1955)

This is the condensed paperback edition of one of the great biographies in American historical literature, *Admiral of the Ocean Sea*. Morison demolishes most of the legendary nonsense and phony mystery that has grown up around the figure of Columbus. The author's preparations for writing this book included following Columbus's routes in ships comparable in size and rig to those the great explorer himself sailed.

Charles Gibson. *Spain in America* (1966)

An informative and tightly written analysis and interpretation of Spanish-American history from the earliest explorations to the nineteenth century. Gibson discusses the power and influence of the Roman Catholic Church, relations between Spaniards and Indians, and the social, economic, and labor patterns that developed in Spain's American colonies. Valuable for the contrast it reveals between Spanish-American and British-American history.

2 The Old World Comes to America

What Brought Europeans and Africans to the New World?

1517–21   Martin Luther launches the Protestant Reformation

1527–39   Henry VIII of England defies the pope and declares himself head of a new Church of England

1577   Elizabeth I of England privately begins to promote exploration and colonization in America

1587–88   Sir Walter Raleigh founds England's first American settlement on Roanoke Island

1607   The London Company establishes the first permanent English settlement at Jamestown

1619   The first Africans in British North America arrive at Jamestown • The House of Burgesses is established as Virginia's legislature

1620   The Pilgrims settle at Plymouth on Cape Cod Bay

1624   The Dutch establish New Netherland in the Hudson Valley

1629   Puritans receive a charter for Massachusetts Bay Colony

1632   Lord Baltimore is granted a charter to found Maryland

1635   Roger Williams establishes Rhode Island at Providence

1636   Bostonian Thomas Hooker founds colony at Hartford, Connecticut • Dissenter Anne Hutchinson is banished from Massachusetts

1664   New Netherland becomes the English colony of New York

1681   William Penn receives a charter to found the Quaker colony of Pennsylvania

1701   East Jersey and West Jersey are united as a single province

1701–03   Delaware is separated from Pennsylvania and becomes a separate colony

1732   James Oglethorpe founds Georgia as refuge for English debtors

As we have seen, America was not an empty continent when Columbus first stumbled on San Salvador in October 1492. Yet today the Indian population of the United States represents less than 1 percent of the total. The rest are descendants of men and women who crossed the oceans from some part of the Old World after 1492.

The process of emigration from the Old World to the new would last for hundreds of years. Indeed it continues today. Immigration to America is one of the great sagas of world history and a central part of the American experience. We will have occasion to talk about it again, when it becomes important in later periods. Here, however, we will consider the first wave of Old World settlement, the one that began in the early seventeenth century and built the foundation of the modern American community.

Establishing a colony in the New World required both promoters and settlers. Someone had to conceive, organize, finance, and lead an expedition to the coast of North America and then guide it through its formative years. But besides promoters there had to be men and women who actually risked themselves, whose contribution to the new colony was their own lives.

The reasons some people promoted colonies, some people settled colonies—and a few did both—are not obvious. America may be a land of freedom, plenty, and stability compared to many other nations today, but it was surely not these things in the year 1600. Early explorers by sea claimed they had found an earthly paradise, a "fruitful and delightsome" land with "most sweet savours" wafting from its shores. But most Europeans took these descriptions with a large grain of salt. Europeans of the day were repelled by raw, untamed nature. To such people America, with its vast gloomy forests, its wild beasts, and its painted "savages," seemed full of "thorns and thistles." Besides, there was the ordeal of getting there. During the two to four months the average transatlantic passage took in the seventeenth and eighteenth centuries, crews and passengers were packed into tight quarters on tiny ships, confined below deck in bad weather, and fed on salt meat, worm-infested biscuit, and foul water. "Ship fever," a form of typhus, frequently raged through these vessels, carrying off weak and strong alike. Shipwreck was common. During the age of sail thousands of people went to watery graves without ever seeing their new homeland. Promoters, too, had reason to be skeptical of the new land. America might have great potential resources, but to find and develop them was certain to be risky. Why take a chance on the financial uncertainties of a distant, savage land when there were better alternatives at home?

Yet despite the fears, the discomforts, and

Rare Book Division, New York Public Library, Astor, Lenox, and Tilden Foundation

This vision of plenty supported reports of Virginia's abundance. Many aristocratic Englishmen believed the New World a potential feudal paradise, and eagerly sought great estates there.

the risks, promoters and settlers staked their lives and their money on the gamble of America. What moved these people? Was their goal wealth? Did they crave adventure? Were they seeking prestige? Were they in quest of religious or political freedom?

THE ARISTOCRATIC IMPULSE

Early colony promoters were often driven by the desire for glory, adventure, status, and power. England about the year 1600 was full of young gentlemen and aristocrats who found life at home uninteresting and galling. Under the English laws of primogeniture (the term is derived from Latin words meaning "the first born"), the eldest son alone inherited his father's land and—if a nobleman—the family title. Younger sons had to make their own way in the world. Many turned to the professions; others swallowed their lofty disdain for trade and entered business. Still others sought out rich wives. None of these alternatives fully compensated for the accident of being born in the wrong order, and by the early years of the seventeenth century many had begun to look expectantly at America. Not understanding the realities of the American environment, they envisioned a New World England where they might live as feudal noblemen amidst the trappings of chivalry and privilege—a life already largely past in England itself.

The English gentleman of this period was not lazy, but he did not enjoy soiling his hands with work. He disdained the bourgeois virtues of prudence, patience, and frugality, and valued and cultivated boldness, passion, and openhanded hospitality. Such men saw exploration and colonization of the New World as a bold adventure. As one gentleman explained in verse:

> Who seeks the way to win renown
>   Or flies with wings of high desire;
> Who seeks to wear the laurel crown,
>   Or hath the mind that would aspire;
> Tell him his native soil eschew,
> Tell him go range and seek anew.

The Roanoke Attempts. Such attitudes imbued the earliest serious British attempts to plant a settlement in the New World. The first of these, Sir Walter Raleigh's 1585 expedition, transported 100 men, most of them gentlemen determined to find glory and treasure, to Roanoke Island off the coast of North Carolina. Belligerence toward the Algon-quian tribes and disdain for fishing, farming, and hard physical labor made the colonists' lot precarious. In 1586, after only a year, the small band returned home.

Settlement in North America required more substantial virtues than aristocratic gallantry and courage. Yet the noble promoters of English colonization in America did not learn the lesson easily. In 1587 Raleigh sent a second expedition under the immediate command of John White. This time women and children went along, including White's daughter and son-in-law, whose child, Virginia Dare, was born soon thereafter. But again, there was also a sizable group of gentlemen with coats of arms to identify them and their descendants as members of the new feudal aristocracy they hoped to establish in America. The colonists arrived on Roanoke Island toward the end of July, too late to plant a crop, and had to rely on the Indians for food. In less than a year the colony had disappeared, apparently destroyed by the local tribes, who probably found the Europeans' dependence on them too great a burden.

Aristocratic Entrepreneurs. The aristocratic yearning for adventure and disdain for work continued to handicap English colonists long after Raleigh's failures. The first permanent English settlement in North America, established at Jamestown in 1607, would also suffer from the idleness of gentlemen more interested in finding gold, carving out personal estates, or despoiling the Indians than in clearing the land, raising crops, and founding self-sustaining communities. Still, we must not dismiss the contribution of aristocratic impulses to settlement of the New World.

The strength of the aristocrats' yearning for the feudal past as a colonizing force can be seen in the case of the "proprietary" colonies. In the region from Pennsylvania southward most royal charters for new colonies conferred on a noble "proprietor" the powers of great feudal lords. The 1632 royal charter for Maryland, for example, gave George Calvert (Lord Baltimore) the right to create special titles of nobility and confer them on his friends and associates. These vassals of the proprietor in turn would rule over a population of tenants, the American equivalent of serfs. Disputes among these tenants, as in feudal England of the past, would be brought before manor courts where the lord presided as chief magistrate. Calvert and his descendants were also allowed to levy "quit rents." These were taxes in place of medieval labor services to the lord of the manor. Maryland was not the only colony that sought to impose this kind of outlandish feudal scheme. The Carolina colony, established in the 1660s, was to have "landgraves," a new kind of titled nobleman, ruling over rent-paying commoners. Even the Dutch, though more democratic than the English, tried a feudal plan in their colony along the Hudson River. Any Dutch gentleman who brought fifty settlers to New Netherland could claim a sixteen-mile stretch of land along any navigable river where he might reign as "patroon," or lord of the manor.

All these attempts to establish a feudal system in America eventually failed. The English proprietors and the Dutch patroons did succeed in inducing some men and women to come to their domains by paying their passage or by granting them certain privileges. But in general the aristocratic scheme was not successful as a colonizing approach. There were simply too many applicants for the position of manor lord and too few for the job of serf. The proprietors and would-be patroons quickly found that they could not compete with colonies where land was cheap and distinctions of rank not so sharp. In the end the schemes to recreate a feudal world in America had to be abandoned.

This portrait of Sir Walter Raleigh, painted in 1602, shows the sort of proud aristocrat inspired to promote colonies by love of glory and fame.

Library of Congress

THE PROFIT MOTIVE

More important for colony promotion was the simple yen for wealth. Whether we consider the role of the state or that of private promoters, the desire for profit and riches overshadowed the desire for rank and titles in summoning forth colony-founding energies.

Mercantilism and the Nation-State. No group of Europeans was more eager to exploit the riches of the New World than kings and princes. Besides Spain's example, they were influenced by a group of thinkers called mercantilists whose goal was to glorify their nation and elevate it above all others. The key to supremacy among nations, they held, was wealth—especially gold and silver. These were the "sinews of war" that enabled a ruler to hire soldiers, buy weapons, build fleets, and conduct an ambitious and successful foreign policy. Such had been the experience of Spain, and would be the experience of any state wise and lucky enough to imitate her example.

The English mercantilists hoped, of course, that like Spain, their own nation would find fabulous mines of silver and gold in its overseas possessions. But even if England were not so lucky, colonies were still certain to bring it wealth. For one thing, an overseas empire would provide the mother country with vital consumer goods for its own citizens plus surpluses to sell. Northern Europe, they noted, could no longer do without tropical products such as sugar, tobacco, dyewoods, and citrus fruit. England also lacked furs and adequate timber. Buying these commodities from foreign countries drained gold and silver from the kingdom. If England had colonies of its own, these losses would cease. In fact, like Spain, England would be able to sell surpluses of colonial goods for hard cash and so draw coin from other nations.

And this was not all. The colonies themselves might even be markets for English goods. According to such mercantilists as Richard Hakluyt the Younger, the native peoples of America were certain to be eager consumers of English manufacturers. In his *Discourse Concerning Westerne Planting* (1584) Hakluyt pictured the North American Indians clothed in English woolens, sleeping in English beds, and using English tools. These new customers would greatly stimulate English industry and overseas trade. Eventually, he wrote, hundreds of ships would crisscross the ocean, carrying American products to Britain and British products to America. Employment in Brit-

Copyright Society of Antiquaries, London

The Virginia Company sometimes ran lotteries when investments and other means of raising funds proved inadequate. This broadside announces a lottery held in London in 1615, a year when news from Jamestown was bad.

ain would leap, turning the thousands of jobless "sturdy beggers" who roamed the English countryside into busy workers and seamen.

Hakluyt addressed his *Discourse* directly to Elizabeth, England's shrewd and ambitious queen. But Elizabeth felt that England was not yet strong enough to challenge directly Spain's claim to sole possession of North America. She did encourage Raleigh's two attempts at settlement, but on the whole she preferred to work behind the scenes, secretly investing her own money in exploratory missions and encouraging English sea captains such as the "sea dogs" John Hawkins and Francis Drake to attack and plunder Spanish ships and settlements in America. In 1577 she financed the half-exploratory, half-piratical around-the-world expedition of Drake, which established England's claim to present-day California and British Columbia and made Drake and the queen rich from the proceeds of a captured Spanish treasure galleon.

After Elizabeth's death in 1603, the English crown proved more willing to defy Spain. Yet none of the Stuart monarchs sponsored a colonization project directly out of public funds. The colonizing role of the English state was indirect, though vital. Under James I and his successors the crown provided exclusive charters and grants to proprietors and commercial companies, thereby encouraging them to risk their funds. It suspended laws that restricted emigration from England to help colony promoters people their grants. As we shall see, it conferred various economic privileges on producers of colonial products needed in Brit-

ain. Finally, it provided military and naval protection to new settlements. All in all, it is hard to see how British North America could have been created and successfully nurtured without the aid of the monarchs who ruled the English nation-state.

Merchants and Profits. Even more directly moved by potential profit than English rulers were English merchants, the bourgeois businessmen with capital to invest who had become such a great force in postfeudal European society. These men hoped to get rich by trading in the furs, timber, metals, and tropical products that Britain needed and the colonies could supply. They also anticipated making money transporting passengers to the new settlements. Some also looked forward to large windfalls from speculating in land.

Unfortunately, few individual merchants could afford the large sums needed in the early stages of exploration and settlement. Although almost no one foresaw how long it would take to make a colony a going concern and how uncertain the outcome, commercial investors did recognize that it would be wise to divide the risk with others by pooling their capital. Accordingly, merchants interested in colonial investment sold shares in joint-stock companies. These shares, like those of modern corporations, represented ownership in the company. They entitled investors to a part of the company's profits in proportion to their investment. Shareholders often had other privileges as well, such as a personal claim to a certain amount of land in the New World or the individual right to trade with the Indians. If all the company's ventures failed, all alike suffered moderately; no one lost everything.

Jamestown: A Commercial Enterprise. The first of the commercially inspired colonies—and the first successful English "plantation" in the New World—was Jamestown in Virginia. Behind this enterprise were two groups of merchants, one from London and the other from the smaller ports in the west of England, including Plymouth and Bristol. In 1606 these two groups combined their interests and secured a dual charter from the crown that established two Virginia companies. ("Virginia" was the name Sir Walter Raleigh had given to the entire eastern coast of what is now the United States in honor of Elizabeth, the unmarried "Virgin Queen.") One of these, the Plymouth Company, under the merchants from the western ports, had the right to plant settlements anywhere between the Potomac and what is now Bangor, Maine. The second, the London Company, controlled by London-based investors, was given the right to settle between Cape Fear in present-day North Carolina and close to the site of what is now New York City. Governing their combined areas would be a royal council; ostensibly an arm of the English government, it was made up largely of company officials.

Each group got off to a quick start. In the summer of 1607 the Plymouth Company deposited forty-four men on a rocky projection of the Maine coast as the preliminary to a larger effort the following year. After one cruel winter the Maine settlers had had enough; when spring came, the survivors returned home, leaving behind the rotting timbers of Fort St. George. Discouraged by this fiasco, the Plymouth group abandoned colonization.

The better-financed Londoners were more successful. In April 1607 three vessels under their sponsorship arrived off the Virginia coast with a complement of 105 passengers. After a month's search the colonists disembarked on a point of land jutting into the James River and set up tents and shacks. The promoters hoped that the new settlement—called Jamestown after James I— would be self-sustaining. When the vessels departed from home with a cargo of clapboards soon after, it seemed that all would go well.

It did not. Part of the problem was the colony's human material. Not a single one of the first settlers was a woman, a fatal flaw in what was meant to be a self-sustaining colony. Thirty-six, moreover, were gentlemen who could not be expected to dirty their hands with manual labor. Besides, the site of the town, which was chosen partly for defense against the Spaniards, was swampy and malarial. That first year, and for many years thereafter, the Jamestown settlers would suffer from dangerous fevers and "agues."

During the first summer the colonists planted orange trees, cotton, and exotic melons, not the grain they needed for food. Meanwhile, despite the efforts of John Smith, head of the seven-man governing council, to get them to cooperate, they squabbled and fought. The winter was still worse. In January a company ship arrived from England, bringing 120 new settlers to reinforce the surviving 38, which further strained the settlement's limited resources. Soon after, a fire destroyed all the houses and storehouses. The colonists were now virtually without food, but instead of foraging for supplies, they threw themselves into a frantic search for gold.

Fortunately Smith was able to keep the settlers alive. He stopped the gold hunt and put men to work building, planting, and producing pitch, tar, and wood ashes. To tide the settlers over until harvesttime, he negotiated with Powhatan, the local Indian chief, for food. The game, corn, fish, and other supplies Powhatan gave them cut the death toll to fewer than a dozen during the winter of 1608–09.

Smith's successor as president of the council was not as able, and could not maintain good relations with the Indians. Powhatan's warriors attacked settlers on the colony's outskirts and drove them back to Jamestown proper, where overcrowding and bad sanitation killed many. The winter of 1609–10 was Jamestown's tragic "starving time." Food was so scarce that some colonists resorted to cannibalism. In the spring, when another contingent of settlers arrived, the supply situation became even more critical; at one point the colony's leaders decided to abandon the settlement altogether.

The following year, 1611, was the turning point. Under Sir Thomas Dale strong leadership was restored. When, in 1612, colonist John Rolfe learned that the native tobacco could be made palatable to Europeans, the colonists discovered their true vocation: tobacco growing. In a few years English smokers were paying premium prices for "Virginia leaf."

Jamestown quickly became a boom town. Men gave up cultivating grain and other food crops to plant tobacco. Seamen reaching the colony abandoned ship and stayed to raise the "noxious weed." Before long, tobacco was growing in the very streets of the community. Small fortunes were quickly made and quickly lost; gambling, drunkenness, and crime became rampant. Yet to-

New York Public Library Picture Collection

In this sketch of Jamestown, made in 1622 by a Dutch visitor, the settlement resembles a factory town more than an ordinary residential community. This is no accident; the Virginia Company and its commercial goals still dominated the colony's life.

bacco provided a solid base for growth. When tobacco prices came down after 1630, the settlers turned once more to grain and livestock production; but they continued to raise tobacco for a steady world market. Thereafter the colony's economic survival was no longer in question.

The London Company's policies, as well as the tobacco bonanza, helped ensure the settlement's permanence. In 1619 the company began to grant some of its land to settlers as their private property. That same year it established an assembly consisting of a council to the governor and a group of elected "burgesses." The House of Burgesses was the first representative political body in English America. To cap the effort to build a permanent, self-sustaining colony, the company began to pay for the shipment of young women from England to become the wives of planters.

In the midst of these gains Virginia was plunged into a devastating Indian war. Until 1622 the relations between Indians and whites in Virginia had been held in balance by mutual exploitation. Powhatan had tried to use the Europeans as allies against his tribal enemies, and they in turn had counted on him for food during lean times. A few company officials believed in the possibility of an integrated community. They tried to establish a college where Indian youths might learn Christian ways and offered to settle Indian families in the white communities in houses donated by the company. Though this plan obviously reflected the European sense of superiority, it was at least benevolent. Unfortunately, whatever the colony's leaders felt, most settlers despised the Indians. As a Jamestown official noted, "There is

scarce a man amongst us that doth soe much as afforde them [the Indians] a good thought in his hart and most men with their mouthes given them nothinge but maledictions and bitter exercrations."

For a while Powhatan's successor, Opechancanough, ignored the insults. But when the expanding white population pushed out along the banks of the James River, ignoring Indian claims, he decided to strike. In March 1622 Opechancanough's warriors attacked the unsuspecting Virginia settlers, killing 347 men, women, and children.

After lulling the Indians into a false sense of security, the English struck back with a war of extermination. They wiped out whole communities and resorted to such dirty tactics as setting out casks of poisoned wine for unsuspecting Indians to drink. When the smoke of the campaign had cleared, the English had virtually destroyed the tribes of coastal Virginia and ended the "Indian menace."

Although the colonists had eliminated their human foes and established a firm economic base, profits eluded the London Company. Between 1607 and 1624 it declared not a single dividend, and indeed called for additional funds from its English stockholders to keep itself from bankruptcy. In 1624 the crown intervened, annulled the company's charter, and made Virginia a royal colony under a governor appointed by the king.

The Virginia experience was not unique. Few joint-stock colonizing ventures made money for their investors. The Plymouth Company effort along the Maine coast, as we saw, ended dismally.

The Old World Comes to America **29**

Dutch investors in the joint-stock Dutch West India Company established several settlements along the Hudson River from 1624 on, but the Dutch never considered their colony much of a commercial success. When the English captured New Netherland in 1664 (and renamed it New York), the Dutch did little to get it back. Few people made money, then, from these merchant-promoted settlements. Nevertheless, the joint-stock company proved to be an invaluable way to pool economic resources and harness the profit motive to the task of founding colonies in America.

"THE BEST POOR MAN'S COUNTRY"

However useful they were as promoters, aristocrats and rich merchants could scarcely populate the new settlements by themselves. Few chose to leave the wealth and comfort of England, and in any case, there were not many of them to begin with. Immigrants in large numbers had to be drawn from the "common" people of Britain; America had to be made attractive to laborers, artisans, servants, and farmers—both men and women—if the new settlements were to take firm root and prosper.

Mixed Motives. Most immigrants to America during the seventeenth and eighteenth centuries came willingly, though not always for wise reasons. Boredom sent some to America, as did flight from the law or from unpleasant jobs or family sit-

Population growth in the colonies, 1610–1780
Source: *Historical Statistics of the United States, Colonial Times to 1957.*

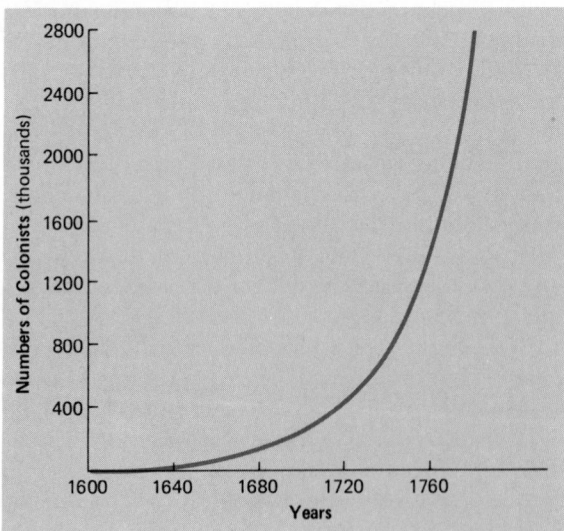

uations. In 1660 the mayor of Bristol, England, a favorite point of departure for the New World, described the motives of some of the emigrants collecting in his city to leave the kingdom:

> Among those who repair to Bristol from all parts to be transported to his majesty's plantations beyond the seas, some are husbands who have forsaken their wives, other wives who have abandoned their husbands, some are children and apprentices run away from their parents and masters, . . . and many that have been pursued by hue-and-cry for robberies, burglaries or breaking prison, do thereby escape the prosecution of law and justice.

In 1732 debtors, who were often jailed when they could not pay their creditors, joined the stream of people fleeing the heavy hand of English law. In that year a group of philanthropists led by James Oglethorpe founded Georgia as a haven for English debtors, a place where they could get a new start in life. Georgia was the last British colony to be established in North America, and would still be a sparsely settled community at the time of the Revolution.

Only a small minority of emigrants were runaways, lawbreakers, or debtors, however, and relatively few of them were women. According to surviving lists of seventeenth-century emigrants from London and Bristol, female emigrants were about a quarter of the total. Most of these women were in their early twenties, the usual age for marriage in England. There is reason to believe that many were seeking husbands in America, where women were especially scarce during the first generation or two of settlement.

Among the male majority on the Bristol and London lists, motives were probably mixed. Some were orphan boys sent to the colonies by the church in order to release British taxpayers from the burden of supporting them. The adult males emigrating from Bristol were mostly farmers; those departing from London were mostly artisans and tradesmen—carpenters, weavers, ship- and wheelwrights, barrel makers, and shoemakers. Propelling these people from their homeland were low wages, increasingly high rents, and severe depression in the woolen industry.

High Wages and Cheap Land. In addition to the forces pushing people from Europe, there were attractions pulling them toward America. During the seventeenth and early eighteenth centuries colonial promoters paid agents to travel throughout England and the European Continent recruiting colonists. Since these agents often received a fee for each prospective immigrant they signed up, they were not always scrupulously truthful about life in the New World. On the Continent "Newlanders," wearing jewels and fancy clothes, circulated among the peasants, spreading stories that America's mountains were full of precious metals and its springs gushed milk and honey.

It was not all humbug. Ordinary people could expect to make real gains by moving to America. The New World was not a paradise: no one could succeed there without hard work. But hard work paid richer dividends there than in Europe. The reason was simple. North America was a vast continent bursting with resources that could be turned into wealth. The missing ingredient was labor, and those who could supply it were certain to be in a fortunate economic situation.

For Europeans of the colonial era, then, America promised high wages. Still better, it promised cheap land. This fact was well understood by seventeenth-century colony promoters, who soon began to offer a free "headright" of fifty or a hundred acres to settlers who paid their own way to the New World, and even more to those who financed additional settlers. Where land was not actually given away, it was sold cheaply. Proprietor William Penn, for example, sold 15,000 acres in Pennsylvania to a group of Germans for £300, less than 5 cents an acre.

Indentured Servants. It is clear that the material advantages of America exerted a strong pull on the peasants and laborers of Europe. But how could they take advantage of it? The Atlantic passage for a single person in the seventeenth century cost the equivalent of $100—far more than any laborer or landless husbandman could afford. The solution for most was the indenture—a labor contract. In return for having the cost of the passage paid by a ship captain or prospective employer, immigrants agreed to work for a specified time at a certain wage or for a specified amount of food, clothing, and shelter.

There were several kinds of indenture and several sorts of indentured servant. The most fortunate was the bondsman or bondswoman who possessed a needed or uncommon skill and therefore could get favorable terms while still at home. The indenture for these servants was normally four years. Often their labor contract specified the trade the servant would work at and defined acceptable working conditions; sometimes it promised generous "freedom dues"—such as a small grant of land or a suit of clothes when their indenture expired.

More typical for the unskilled servant were indentures that relied on "the custom of the country" to define the length and terms of the contract. These indentures contained few specific provisions favorable to the servant. "Redemptioners" were even less fortunate. These were people who in the eighteenth century fled Germany and Switzerland in the wake of war and hard times. Unlike the typical single bondservant, redemptioners moved as families. They arranged for merchants to pay their fare and agreed to reimburse them when they arrived in America. If they could not find the passage money immediately, they had to allow the merchant or his agent to sell their services for a time sufficient to recover the debt. This arrangement sometimes led to the separation of families; children might be sold to one master and their parents to another.

Indentured servants often had a hard life. Masters had the right to whip them for disobedience or failure to work. Normally, they could not marry, vote, or engage in trade. Their indenture and their persons could be transferred from one master to another. If they ran away, their terms of service could be extended. Many failed to survive the difficult indenture period and were buried in unmarked graves.

Yet a substantial proportion did achieve success in America, working off their contracts and establishing themselves as free farmers or craftspeople. News of their achievements drifted back to Europe and inspired others to follow, thus ensuring the indenture system's survival despite its risks and uncertainities. Indentured servants were not spread evenly throughout the colonies. New England was peopled overwhemingly by free families who either paid their own way or were sponsored by the community. But by 1750 a large part of the white population from Pennsylvania southward was composed of indentured servants or their descendants.

INVOLUNTARY IMMIGRANTS

Thus far, in considering the reasons why people from the Old World came to America during the colonial era, we have assumed that men and women made a personal choice, that they came voluntarily. But there were many thousands who had no choice, who were brought across the Atlantic against their will. In describing their motives for coming to America we must say, in effect, they had none; or rather, that the motives that brought them were the motives of other people, not their own.

Involuntary immigration was a product of greed. The inducements colonial promoters offered to would-be settlers were often not enough to attract the laborers needed to clear the forests, plant the fields, and build the towns. In the southern colonies especially, following the introduction of commercial crops such as tobacco, rice, and indigo, labor shortages could be crippling. Unless they could find an abundant supply of labor, planters could not take advantage of cheap land and a ready market for their crops in Europe. Rather than forgo profits, they were willing to pay good prices for forced labor from whatever source they could find.

Involuntary European Immigrants. Many of the involuntary immigrants were Europeans. During the seventeenth and eighteenth centuries kidnappers operated in every English port, enticing the young, naive, or intemperate aboard ship and collecting a fee from the captain, who would then sell the victims as indentured servants in the colonies. More numerous were "His Majesty's Seven Year Guests"—convicts given the choice of going to America as seven-year indentured servants or facing a hangman's noose at home. Those who accepted "transportation" were pardoned and turned over to merchants, who bore the expense of the transatlantic trip in exchange for the right to sell the felon's labor to the colonists.

Every colonial legislature protested this dumping of England's "thieves and villians" on America. Parliament remained unmoved, however, and the planters of Maryland and Virginia, where most felons were sent, were generally happy to have their labor. Historians estimate that some 20,000 convicts were sent to America during the eighteenth century alone.

Black Slaves. Indentured servants, convicted felons, and kidnapped youths notwithstanding, labor remained in short supply in America, especially in the regions south of Pennsylvania. Europe, it seemed, simply could not produce enough workers to satisfy the needs of the New World's profit-making enterprises.

But Africa could. Well before the first voyage of Columbus, Portuguese explorers were bringing back Africans to work in Europe and on the Portuguese islands in the Atlantic. When the Portuguese settled Brazil and began raising sugar, the market for black labor in the New World expanded enormously. Meanwhile, in the Caribbean destruction of the Indian tribes created a labor vacuum that Spanish planters quickly filled with African workers.

These black workers were not free in any sense. Though slavery no longer existed in Christian Europe, it survived in Islamic lands and existed in Africa itself among the native peoples. The Portuguese, the Spanish, and later the French, Dutch, and English responded to the lure of profits and readily adopted the system for their labor-short American colonies. Many Europeans rationalized slavery by arguing that the African peoples were "heathens" who worshiped idols, or "naked savages" who might benefit from contact with Christian, "civilized" people.

In reality, the Africans brought to the Americas were anything but savages. Slaves were plucked from many tribes and nations along Africa's Atlantic coast, largely between present-day Guinea and Angola, including the Ashanti, Fon, Yoruba, Beni, Pawpaw, Ibo, and Coromantin. These West African peoples practiced an effective hoe agriculture that provided them with abundant food. West Africans had also brought to a high level the arts of weaving, metalworking, pottery making, and wood and ivory carving. The bronze sculptures of Benin, the silver and gold jewelry of the Yoruba, and the rugs and carpets of the Ashanti were outstanding artistic achievements. In the arts of government, too, West Africans revealed great talent. States such as Benin, the Congo, and Ghana brought order and prosperity to large areas of Africa, conducting foreign affairs in much the same way as contemporary European kingdoms did.

The slave trade that ripped these people from their homes was a well-organized system by the end of the seventeenth century. At first Europeans themselves captured slaves along the Guinea coast. But this proved dangerous, for whites could not withstand West Africa's tropical diseases. By 1700 the white slavers had come to rely on black African merchants and chiefs to supply them with captured prisoners of war or victims snatched by raiders from the interior of the continent. Chained together, these unfortunate people were brought overland to the coast by the merchants or by war parties. There they were sold to the Europeans for guns, powder, cloth, beads, and rum.

Once aboard ship, the next step in the African slave trade was the infamous "middle passage." The slavers that carried this human cargo across the Atlantic were about the same size as the ships used for indentured servants, but they were far more crowded. Vessels as small as ninety tons—scarcely bigger than a fishing boat—sometimes packed in 400 slaves besides the crew and supplies. The captives were chained together to prevent rebellion and kept below deck except for brief periods. Wise captains attempted to keep them healthy, but they seldom succeeded. Slaves

Historical Society of Pennsylvania

Many English convicts were sentenced to forced indentured servitude in the colonies. Elizabeth Canning, shown before a London court in this contemporary engraving, was convicted of perjury and sentenced to one month in jail and "Transportation for seven Years, to one of his Majesty's Colonies in America." On August 7, 1754, she was put on board the Myrtilda *and set sail for Philadelphia.*

lived in filth below decks where temperatures rose into the nineties and higher. Inevitably the death rate was appalling. Some slave vessels arrived in the Americas with well over half their passengers dead from dysentery, smallpox, or some European disease to which Africans had little resistance.

The first slaves reached the English mainland colonies in 1619 when a Dutch vessel unexpectedly put in at Jamestown with a cargo of twenty Africans. These people were treated as indentured servants. Over the next thirty or forty years a small trickle of blacks were brought to the Chesapeake region and most, it seems, were kept as bondservants for a limited time and then freed.

At first the market for slaves in the plantation colonies was limited despite the labor shortage. Since the mortality rates of all immigrants to the southern plantation colonies were extremely high during the early years of settlement, the lifetime service of a black slave offered little advantage over short-term white servitude. And since few children could be counted on to survive, the fact that a slave's offspring became the property of the

master meant little to the owner. By the 1660s or 1670s, however, life expectancies in the southern colonies rose as settlers learned how to deal with American diseases and as food supplies improved.

African origins of the slave trade

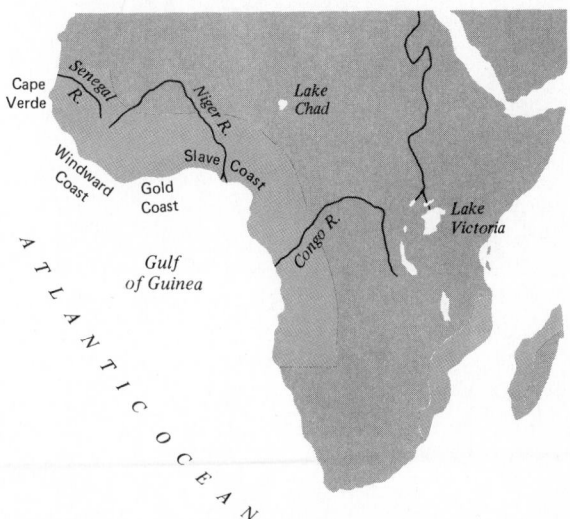

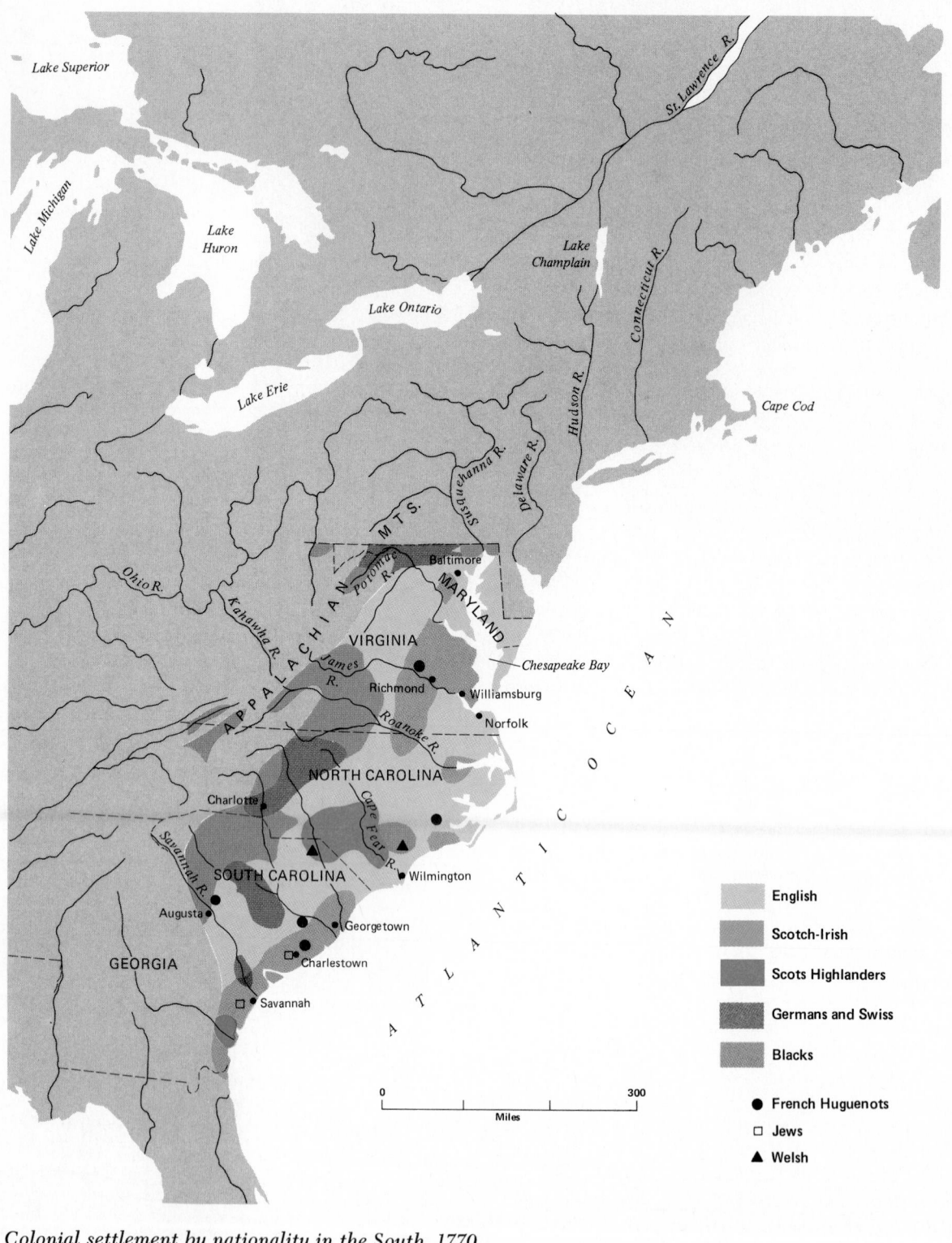

Colonial settlement by nationality in the South, 1770

At this point high-priced slaves for life began to promise an economic advantage over indentured servants for four years.

Racial attitudes as well as economics played a part in establishing slavery in North America. However harshly they were treated, white indentured servants were not without rights. As fellow Europeans, they could not be severely mistreated or abused with impunity. Women servants could not be exploited sexually. If the master of an indentured servant violated the custom of the country or the terms of the contract, he or she could be sued by the servant. Except in the earliest period, perhaps, Africans enjoyed no such rights. The English were prejudiced against the physical characteristics of Africans and viewed them as lesser beings. Brutally torn away from all that was familiar, brought among strangers, surrounded by other captives who did not speak their language, and confronted with an alien landscape and an unfamiliar climate, blacks were in no position to protect themselves.

As the value of African workers increased, they gradually ceased to be treated as indentured servants. First they became "servants for life," and then subject to ever more elaborate "slave codes" that defined their legal position in detailed ways and placed severe restrictions on their movements and conduct. Under these codes they became "chattel property," to be bought, sold, inherited, and bequeathed like houses, horses, or plows. By the end of the seventeenth century the distinction between black slaves and white servants had become sharply defined: servants were humans; slaves were things.

As slaves became more valuable as property, the planters sought to increase their number. Each year more and more were imported from Africa or from the Caribbean islands. Some 300,000 Africans were landed at the docks of the mainland colonies during the seventeenth and eighteenth centuries. More than ten times as many slaves were brought to the Caribbean and Latin America during this period. There the high profits on the sugar plantations permitted the owners to bring in few women, work the males to death, and then replace them by importing new male slaves. The Virginia planters, who made lower profits on tobacco, could not afford such an extravagant system, and from the beginning they imported female slaves as well. The relatively high proportion of women, plus the healthier conditions of the North American mainland, resulted in a rapid increase in the slave population through an excess of births over deaths. By 1759 more than a fifth of the inhabitants of mainland British America were black slaves, and many of these were native-born Americans.

AMERICA AS A RELIGIOUS HAVEN

Americans like to think of their country as a haven for the oppressed. Although we should be careful not to exaggerate this self-congratulatory view, the New World did serve as a refuge for thousands and ultimately millions of transatlantic migrants fleeing Old World oppression. In the seventeenth century most of these were refugees from religious intolerance, and they came primarily to the colonies north of the Chesapeake, especially to new England and Pennsylvania, imparting to these communities their values and characteristics as religious "dissenters."

Those moved by religion came from every class of European society. At the top, serving as

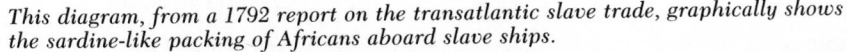

This diagram, from a 1792 report on the transatlantic slave trade, graphically shows the sardine-like packing of Africans aboard slave ships.

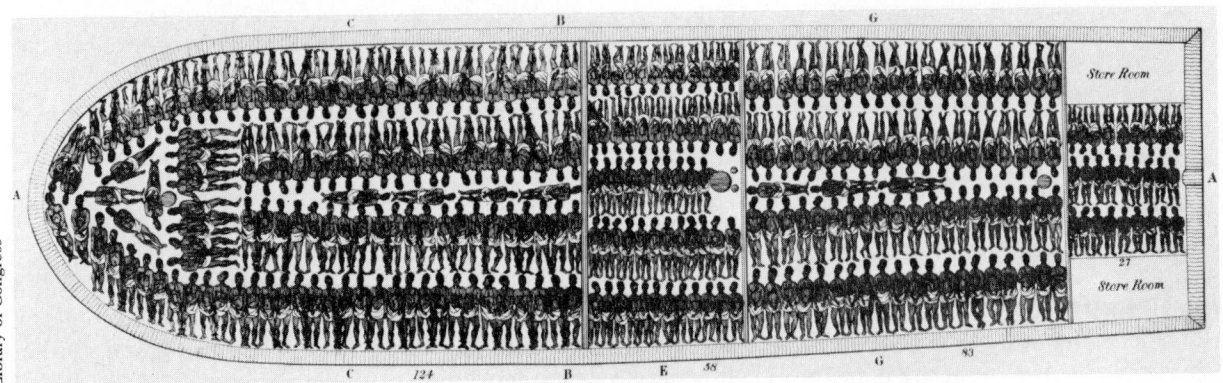

How Africans Came to America

The *Hannibal,* commanded by Captain Thomas Phillips, sailed to the west African coast in 1693–94 to take away a cargo of slaves for the West Indies market. In the Caribbean many of these unfortunate people would be "seasoned" for later transport to the mainland colonies. Phillips was a merchant under contract to supply slaves to the Royal African Company, which for many years possessed a monopoly on the slave trade to the English colonies.

Phillips was an unusual man. He kept a diary and also, despite his occupation, was capable of feeling some compassion for his victims. The portion of his account reproduced here tells of what followed the local king's sale of a slave parcel to the European slavers.

"The negroes are so willful and loth to leave their own country, that they have often leap'd out of the canoes, boat and ship into the sea, and kept under water till they were drowned, to avoid being taken up and saved by our boats, which pursued them, they having a more dreadful apprehension of Barbados than we can have of hell. . . . [W]e have likewise seen divers of them eaten by the sharks, of which a prodigious number kept about the ships in this place. . . . We had about twelve negroes did willfully drown themselves, and others starved to death, for 'tis their belief that when they die they return home to their own country and friends again. . . .

". . . When our slaves are aboard we shackle the men two and two while we lie in port, and in sight of their country, for 'tis then that they attempt to make their escape, and mutiny, to prevent which we always keep sentinels upon the hatchways, and have a chest full of small arms, ready loaded and prim'd constantly lying at hand upon the quarter deck. . . . The men are all fed upon the main deck and forecastle, in case of any disturbance; the women eat upon the quarterdeck with us. . . . When we come to sea we let them all out of irons, they never attempting to rebel, considering that should they kill or master us, they could not tell how to manage the ship. . . . I never heard that they mutiny'd in any ships of consequence, . . . but in small [vessels] where they had but few men . . . then they surpriz'd and butchered them, cut the cables, and let the vessel drive ashore. . . . We often at sea in the evenings would let the slaves come up into the sun to air themselves, and made them jump and dance for an hour or two to our bag-pipes, harp and fiddle, by which exercize to preserve them in health; but notwithstanding all our endeavour, 'twas my hard fortune to have great sickness and mortality among them. . . .

"We spent in our passage from St. Thomas to Barbados two months eleven days. . . . [A]mong my poor men and negroes, that of the first we buried 14, and of the last 320, which was a great detriment to our voyage, the royal African company losing ten pounds by every slave that died, and the owners of the ship ten pounds ten shillings. . . .

"I deliver'd alive at Barbados to the company's factors [agents] 372, which being sold, came to about nineteen pounds per head one with another. . . ."

---

colony promoters, were rich merchants and gentlemen who sought to find ways of aiding their poorer coreligionists. In the case of Massachusetts, many of the gentry actually joined the migration to America. Most of those who came to escape bigotry at home, however, were ordinary laborers, artisans, farmers, housewives, servants, and shopkeepers.

The Reformation. To understand what the emigrants were fleeing, we must look at the religious scene in sixteenth- and seventeenth-century Europe. Until the 1520s almost all of Western Europe was Catholic. The Roman Catholic Church held the keys to the kingdom of heaven because it administered the sacraments, prescribed penances, dispensed charity, and provided solace and hope for the multitude. Its spiritual control was reinforced by its guardianship of the Bible, which was available only in Latin, the language of the clergy and a small lay elite. The supreme head of the Roman Catholic Church, the pope, not only served as the final authority in matters of faith and morals but also sought at times to assert temporal power over the rulers of the European states.

By 1500 many Europeans had become critical of the Catholic Church. Some saw the richness of the Church's ceremonies as a reflection of a growing clerical taste for luxury and worldliness. They felt that popes, bishops, and even ordinary priests were far too interested in living well, that they had become obsessed with wealth and secular power. Even the monasteries and convents were no longer centers for the contemplative life, said the critics, but all too often were refuges for the idle and even the immoral. To the most skeptical it seemed that the Church had become hypocritical and corrupt and in need of fundamental reform.

In 1517 Martin Luther, an Augustinian friar, attacked the sale of indulgences—papal letters of remission of punishment due to sin that were being peddled in Germany to raise money to build St. Peter's basilica in Rome. From this assault on what he perceived as the Church's greed, Luther soon moved on to attack its claim to be the guardian of the gates of heaven. He asserted the "priest-hood of all believers"; that is, he said that salvation was a transaction between God and the individual, needing no priest as intermediary. He denounced the self-imposed isolation of monks and nuns and insisted that all Christians must participate in the world.

Luther's demands for change quickly spread through Europe. Before long the reform movement expanded into a thorough assault on Church ceremony, worldliness, papal power, and the belief that "good works"—pilgrimages, fasting, charity, frequent prayer, and participation in the ceremonies and sacraments of the Church—were essential to salvation. The attack begun by Luther against the established religious order eventually touched many other aspects of life, producing the Continent-wide upheaval known as the Protestant Reformation.

For a while the Reformation scarcely affected England. King Henry VIII had no quarrel with the Catholic Church's doctrines or forms or worship. But when the pope refused to annul Henry's marriage to Catherine of Aragon and excommunicated him for setting her aside in 1533 to marry Anne Boleyn, the king declared himself supreme head of the Church of England. He also authorized an English translation of the Bible so that it might be read by all literate people, not just priests and a tiny elite, and dissolved the monasteries, confiscating their vast property.

For the next century England became a battleground between the forces of Catholicism and Protstantism. Eventually, under Elizabeth I, a Protestant Church of England (the Anglican Church) emerged, controlled by the English crown but retaining many of the old religion's ceremonies and beliefs. This outcome did not please everyone. Some English people refused to accept Anglicanism and remained loyal Catholics. Others sought to go beyond Anglicanism and became followers of John Calvin, a French Protestant reformer, who had established his headquarters at Geneva. Calvinists denied the belief in salvation through works, an error, they felt, shared by both Anglicans and Catholics. They insisted that salvation came only through God's gift of faith, or "grace," as it was expressed at the time. It could not be bought through good works; God, in effect, could not be bribed. They demanded that the Church of England "purify" itself entirely of the Catholic ceremonies and church structure that it still retained. At first these "Puritans" were content to remain in the official Anglican Church as "Dissenters" or "Nonconformists," working to change it from within. Eventually, after being har-

assed and persecuted, many became "separatists" and left the church entirely.

In the half century following Elizabeth's death in 1603 England experienced a religious ferment that threatened to tear the country apart. New sects rose to prominence, each, it seemed, more extreme and unusual than the one preceding. There were various kinds of Antinomians (literally, opponents of the law) who believed that those on whom God had conferred his grace were incapable of sin and therefore exempt from moral restraint. Groups like the Baptists (originally called Anabaptists) and the Quakers insisted that individual conscience was the sole source of moral values. Some of these "sectaries" were intensely hostile to the existing social system, despising and denouncing political absolutism, class deference, intellectual authority, and even private property.

It is not surprising that the crown and its agents attacked the sectaries as subversives. But they also assailed the more moderate Nonconformists and the remaining Catholics. Merely by rejecting the Church of England, these people seemed to be undermining the authority of the crown and destroying the unity of the nation, besides endangering their own souls and the souls of all who came in contact with them.

Ironically, the victims of Anglican religious persecution generally did not advocate religious toleration. Only the Quakers insisted that all people be allowed to discover spiritual truth for themselves. Most of the others held that they alone were right and accepted the state's right to impose religious uniformity. Their only complaint was that Anglican uniformity was the wrong kind.

The Pilgrims of Plymouth. By the early 1600s several religious minorities had abandoned hope of change in England and had begun to consider emigration. The first to depart was a small body of radical Puritan Separatists, the Pilgrims. In 1608 this group moved to Leiden in the Netherlands, then a refuge for religious minorities from all over Europe. For a while they prospered, but as time passed the little congregation began to fear for its survival and its orthodoxy in the face of the easygoing religious ways of the Dutch. In 1617 the Pilgrim leaders decided to move the congregation to "Virginia," where they could maintain their preferred mode of life and form of worship without distraction.

Unfortunately the community was poor and could not provide itself with ships or supplies. It also had no royal charter that would guarantee English protection from Spain or ensure the Pilgrims' right to exclude undesirables. At this point the Pilgrims turned to the London Company: in exchange for liberty of conscience, the settlers agreed to develop some of the company's otherwise worthless land in America.

After selling their possessions in Holland and securing loans from the company and from Thomas Weston, a London merchant, about thirty of the Pilgrims departed for England. At Southampton they joined a larger group of nonseparatists hired to work in the colony by the profit-seeking Weston. On September 16, 1620, after many difficulties and much delay, the 180-ton *Mayflower*, with 149 passengers and crew, sailed from Plymouth harbor for America.

The Pilgrims' original destination was the region near the Hudson River. Severe storms drove them to the north, however, and they decided to stay where they touched land. This was at Cape Cod Bay, at a place they called Plymouth, after their port of departure. Fearful that the nonseparatists ("strangers") among them might dominate the community, and worried that their charter might not have legal force because the region was outside the London Company's grant, the Pilgrims adopted the Mayflower Compact before leaving ship. This short document established a civil government with powers "to enact, constitute, and frame such just and equal Laws, Ordinances, Acts, Constitutions, and Offices, from time to time, as shall be thought most meet and convenient for the general Good of the Colony."

During the first winter the colonists suffered grievously from disease. Fortunately the weather was relatively mild and they had few Indians to content with, for smallpox had swept the region shortly before the *Mayflower* arrived. The Indians who had survived, moreover, proved helpful. One, Squanto, had been seized by a European trader years before and taken to England, where he had learned the language. He and Massasoit, the grand sachem of the local Wampanoags, befriended the colonists, teaching them how to plant maize and other native plants and showing them the best fishing streams. In spite of this aid the Pilgrim community, like almost all early white settlements, went through a "starving time" that first winter. By spring nearly half the colonists were dead. During the summer the survivors put the Indians' teachings to good use; by fall their storehouses were well stocked. In November 1621 they celebrated their success with a harvest festival that has come down to us as Thanksgiving.

The Plymouth colony expanded gradually, reaching a population of about 1,000 to 1640 and 3,000 in 1660. Uncertainty over the charter persisted, however. There were financial problems, too. Successors to the London Company forced the Plymouth colonists to pay rent in addition to the sums they had borrowed to finance the settlement. To meet their debts the Pilgrims were forced to turn to fishing, trading with the Indians for furs, and commerce with the Dutch in New Amsterdam at the mouth of the Hudson. Although life was hard, William Bradford and the other Pilgrim leaders never forgot that their mission was to found a godly colony. Yet Plymouth orthodoxy was never intolerant or harsh. For seventy years the "Old Colony" modestly prospered. Then, in 1691, it was absorbed into the larger Massachusetts Bay community.

The Massachusetts Bay Puritans. The Puritans who settled the Masachusetts Bay Colony were also propelled by religion. The Puritan dissenters within the Church of England were more numerous, more prosperous, and socially more prominent than the Pilgrims and other Separatists. Until the 1620s they had hoped that they could reform the established church. By the middle of that decade, however, they, too, began to lose heart and to look to the New World as a promising refuge.

The Puritan concern was for the future of the godly in a nation ruled by Charles I and Anglican Archbishop William Laud. Considering Puritan doctrines wicked and erroneous, Laud, in cooperation with the king, suppressed Puritan books, forbade Puritans to preach, and attempted to impose Anglican practices and beliefs on all dissenters. Then in 1629 Charles dissolved parliament, where the Puritans had many friends, and assumed personal rule of England. Clearly, now was the time to leave.

A few Puritans had already departed. In 1625 forty had emigrated to the fishing colony of Salem, north of present-day Boston. Now a number of prominent Puritan gentlemen procured a royal charter for a new colony. This document established the Massachusetts Bay Company, a corporation authorized to own and govern all land between the Merrimack and the Charles rivers, from the Atlantic to the Pacific. The charter also prescribed a structure for the new Massachusetts Bay Company that omitted the provision, common to such grants, that the governor, assistants, and freemen of the company had to remain in England to do business.

In the summer of 1629 the promoters of emigration persuaded John Winthrop, a Cambridge-educated gentleman and attorney, to accept the governorship of the company. Winthrop agreed on condition that the settlers bring the company's charter to New England. There it would be out of easy reach of the English authorities, and the colonists would enjoy virtual autonomy in their political and religious affairs. Winthrop knew about the hard fate of the Virginia colonists and had terrible doubts about the new venture. He soon became its zealous promoter, however, and in a communication sent to leading Puritans argued that the tribulations of Jamestown should not deter others from going to America. The Virginia settlers had fallen into "great and fundamental errors," he stated, because, among other things, "their mayne end was Carnall and not religious." The new venture would avoid that mistake.

In addition to Winthrop's appeals and the desire to escape Laud's harassment, the depression in the English wool industry in the late 1620s helped push the Puritans to the New World. Men and women facing both persecution and hunger sold their property, paid their debts, and signed up for Massachusetts. In the early spring of 1630 four well-equipped, crowded vessels left for New England. They were soon followed by seven more, all of which arrived safely. In a few months 1,000 settlers were building cabins, clearing fields, and planting crops in the Shawmut (Boston) area. Despite some sickness and a few untimely deaths the first year, settlers continued to arrive and the population grew fast. By 1640 Massachusetts had about 9,000 inhabitants, almost as many as Jamestown, founded thirteen years before it.

Offshoots of the Massachusetts Bay Colony. Religious oppression would operate as a colonizing force in Massachusetts itself. Under John Winthrop and the other learned Puritan "magistrates," Massachusetts Bay functioned as a theocratic republic. All adult male family heads who were full-fledged members of the church were considered "freemen" and allowed to participate in political decisions. Women were denied all political rights, but so were many men who were not church members or who owned no property. Nor did the leaders of the colony welcome those who did not accept Puritan religious views. As John Cotton, a prominent Puritan minister later noted, "the design of our first planters was not toleration, but [they] were professed enemies of it. . . . Their business was to settle, and (as much as in them lay) secure Religion to Posterity according to that way which they believed was of God." Before long political and religious intolerance had begun to drive independent-minded people out of the Bay Colony itself.

One of the first to go was the Reverened Thomas Hooker. Though himself a minister,

New York Public Library Picture Collection

John Winthrop expected the Massachusetts Bay Colony to be an example of order, morality, and conformity for wayward humanity. "We shall be as a Citty upon a Hill, the eies of all people are uppon us."

Hooker demanded that Massachusetts church membership not be a requirement for voting. When the Massachusetts authorities refused to yield, Hooker joined with others who at this time were leaving the Bay Colony to find better land. In 1636 small groups of men and women seeking religious liberty trekked westward to the banks of the Connecticut River and settled in a region already claimed by both the Dutch and the Plymouth Pilgrims.

Hooker's group established a colony at Hartford and adopted the Fundamental Orders, a form of government that, though scarcely democratic, gave the magistrates less power than they had in the Bay Colony and imposed a more lenient religious test for full citizenship. Soon after, other former residents of Massachusetts established New Haven on the north shore of Long Island Sound. Still other communities, peopled from Plymouth, Massachusetts Bay, and the Connecticut River settlements themselves, sprang up on the north shore of Long Island Sound. In 1662 the river communities and those on the sound were merged as the self-governing colony of Connecticut.

An Historical Portrait   John Winthrop

At fifteen Master John Winthrop, son of Squire Adam Winthrop of Groton Manor in Suffolk, went off to Cambridge University to acquire the polish and classical learning expected of a seventeenth-century gentleman. He returned two years later and married Mary Forth, as had been arranged between his father and hers. Ten months later, while only seventeen, he became the father of a son.

Life was usually short in seventeenth-century Europe, so it was necessary to cram a lot into a brief period. Yet the young man's course marked him as precocious even for his time. But it was not surprising that John would act quickly to take on the responsibilities of adulthood, for he had become a Puritan, and like others of the breed, was imbued with a new seriousness of purpose and a sense that he must follow the Lord's commandments.

The Puritan view of the Christian life placed an enormous strain on believers. They must avoid sin while living with the world's temptations. Yet they could not count on earning salvation merely by virtuous behavior. Salvation was God's gift alone and preordained from the beginning of time. The young Winthrop enjoyed hunting; he relished good food. Like most Puritans, he was not a dour killjoy. But he also feared excess and closely examined his conscience and conduct to see if his recreations and pleasures had "ensnared" his "heart so farre in worldly delights" that he had "cooled the graces of the spirit by them."

Despite his prudence, Winthrop's life had its share of tragedy. Mary died in 1615 after bearing him six children. He married his second wife six months later, and within the year she, too, died. But he had his portion of joys as well; in 1618 he married for a third time. He would later describe Margaret Tyndal as "a very gracious woman," and the relationship would be a long and happy one. Meanwhile, John became an attorney and in the late 1620s spent much time in London on cases heard before the royal courts.

During these years England, under Charles I, was a deeply troubled land. The king believed that he ruled by divine right and need not heed Parliament, which spoke in some final sense for the people. He also despised the Puritans within the official Church of England and he and Archbishop Laud harassed and persecuted them. From his perch in London, Winthrop could see still another deplorable aspect of the existing regime: its extravagance and corruption.

For a time the Puritans hoped that their many friends in Parliament would help them, but in March 1629 the king disbanded parliament and began to govern directly. To many Puritans the time now seemed ripe to "separate" from England and seek refuge in America.

Winthrop had misgivings about the move, and when approached by a group of other prominent Puritan leaders, men associated with the newly chartered Massachusetts Bay Company, he dithered. Should the virtuous depart, leaving behind their fellow Puritans to face the wrath of Laud and the king alone? Would the new colony be able to achieve economic independence and attain some prosperity? Most of Winthrop's doubts were resolved by mid-1629, and that fall, while still in England, he was elected governor of the new enterprise.

The four small vessels that

The Connecticut settlements resulted from a mixture of economic, political, and religious motives. Rhode Island's origins were almost entirely religious. The father of Rhode Island was Roger Williams, another Puritan minister who came to Massachusetts in 1631 and promptly antagonized the Bay Colony's religious leaders. Williams quarrelled with the Massachusetts ministers and magistrates over whether the community had fully separated from the Church of England and whether its charter was legal. He further antagonized the Box Colony's leader's by denouncing the practice of requiring church attendance and the payment of taxes to support the Puritan clergy. In 1635 the Massachusetts authorities ordered his arrest, and Williams fled to Narragansett Bay, just east of Connecticut. There he bought land from the Indians and established the community of Providence Plantation. The new colony's key principles were the complete separation of religion and government (separation of church and state), toleration of all religious beliefs, and the sovereignty of the people.

Other dissenters soon flocked to the Narragansett area. One of the most remarkable was Anne Hutchinson, "a woman of ready wit and bold spirit," who like Williams had tangled with the leading clergymen of the Bay Colony over religious doctrine. Hutchinson espoused the idea that only those infused with the Holy Spirit could preach the word of God and that only a few, herself included, could determine to whom the Holy Spirit had been revealed. Besides threatening the leadership of the Bay Colony ministers, Hutchinson's outspokenness also defied the principle of female subordination. The church leaders summoned her to a hearing and demanded that she retract her views and cease to preach. She refused and in an unguarded moment warned her accusers that if they continued to persecute her, God would ruin them, their posterity, and "this whole State." When asked how she knew this would happen,

braved the rough north Atlantic in April and May 1630 carried 400 people, each of whom cost the community £50. Many paid their own way; others had their passage and outfitting paid for by richer Puritans like Winthrop or one of the other "gentlemen." Another 600 men, women, and children arrived in Massachusetts soon after.

The first months were hard, as in all the early settlements, even one so well planned and financed as the Puritan colony. During this difficult time Governor Winthrop was a rock of strength, though he had to cope with the personal tragedy of his son Henry's drowning shortly after arrival. He moved the settlers from their initial landing point near Salem to the east shore of Massachusetts Bay and eventually brought them to the site of what would be named Boston. Food was in short supply, and before the community became self-sustaining, he dispatched vessels to Cape Cod to collect corn for the winter and contacted the settlers' friends in England to raise money to buy provisions. Despite the sickness, hunger, hard work, discomfort, and danger, he did not lose heart. That

September he wrote Margaret, still in England: "I like so well to be heer, as I doe not repent my comminge. . . ." He had, he added, "never slept better, never had more content of minde."

Two hundred settlers died that first winter and an equal number returned to England in the spring. Yet the colony survived and eventually prospered. Margaret and the rest of Winthrop's family arrived in the fall of 1631, to be greeted by the whole colony and presented with gifts of "fat hogs, kids, venison, poultry, geese, partridges, etc., so as the like joy and manifestations of love had never been seen in New England."

During the next eighteen years Winthrop served his community well as governor, deputy governor, and assistant. At times he was accused of excessive leniency, though he was adamant in his prosecution of Anne Hutchinson and her followers. From our modern perspective, this was not admirable behavior, but few contemporaries anywhere believed that dangerous heretics and sowers of sedition like Hutchinson should be allowed to spread their poison. Winthrop was

not a democrat, but rather held the view that a good magistrate must act as he thought best without regard for the opinions of his constituents. That he was popular nonetheless is proved by the fact that he was reelected to office time and time again.

In 1647 Margaret died. In his journal John called her a "woman of singular virtue, prudence, modesty, and piety. . . ." He soon married a fourth time, but he was sixty and ailing, and in March 1649 he too went to his reward. Though he was not a perfect man, his strength of character, resolve, and good common sense stood the Puritan colony in good stead. His descendants would make distinguished contributions to Massachusetts, and the community he helped to found and sustain would bear the imprint of his own conscientious personality. Ultimately, in the shape of the "New England conscience," a part of John Winthrop of Groton Manor would be incorporated into the essential character of America itself.

she declared: "By an immediate revelation." Shocked by her boldness and presumption, the leaders expelled Hutchinson from the church and declared her a heretic. She and some of her followers soon moved to Aquidneck near Providence.

Other exiles and dissenters also came to the Narragansett region, enlarging the population of the little cluster of towns. In 1663 King Charles II granted Rhode Island and Providence Plantation a royal charter as a separate colony.

Penn's Woods. Pennsylvania, too, was the offspring of religious persecution—in this case of the Quakers, as outsiders called those belonging to the Society of Friends. Quakers believed that to understand God's will people needed only to examine their own consciences; an elaborate credo and a trained ministry were irrelevant. In the 1640s and 1650s, Quaker "enthusiasts" traveled around England passionately preaching their mes-

sage of the "inner light." They advised their listeners to throw off the vanities of the world and denounced war and excessive respect for authorities. Plain in their speech and dress, they refused to tip their hats to their social betters and were unusually respectful of the rights of women.

The Anglican clergy, and many orthodox English people, considered Quaker behavior and teachings even more offensive than those of the Puritans. One contemporary called them "a new fanatic sect, of dangerous principles, who show no respect to any man, magistrate, or other, and seem a melancholy, proud sort of people. . . ." The English government feared the Quakers' contempt for a "hireling ministry" and their refusal to take oaths or pay church tithes. In 1655 the government ordered the Quakers to desist from their disorderly practices and enforced the command with legal prosecutions.

During the 1650s Quaker missionaries fanned out from England, many going to the Brit-

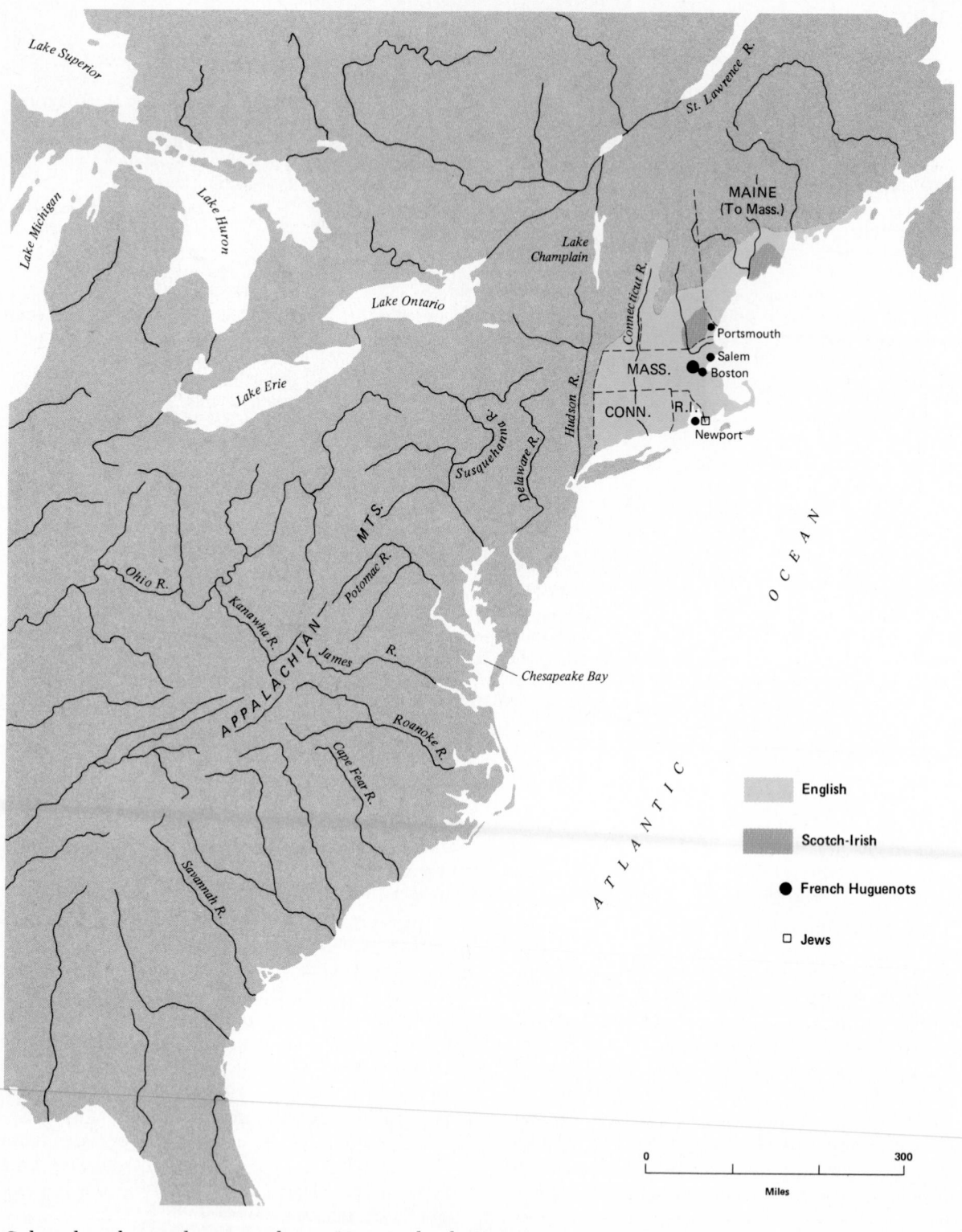

Colonial settlement by nationality in New England, 1770

ish colonies. Here, too, they were prosecuted. Except in Rhode Island, their emotional preaching and breaches of religious decorum resulted in savage punishment. For refusing to desist from preaching, several Quakers were whipped and imprisoned in Massachusetts. Between 1659 and 1661 four were hanged.

In the 1670s a few Quaker families from England began to settle along the Delaware River in an area that in 1701 joined with Puritan-settled East Jersey to form the royal province of New Jersey. Then, in the 1680s, the trickle of Quakers crossing to America became a flood. The organizer of this migration was William Penn, the son of an influential English gentleman, who had become a "Friend" against his father's wishes. When the elder Penn died, he left his son William a fortune that included a large financial claim against the king. In 1681 Charles II repaid this debt by granting the younger Penn a giant block of American territory. In addition, the king's brother gave Penn three counties along the lower Delaware River, which became the separate colony of Delaware in 1701.

Realizing his coreligionists had a dim future in England, in the 1670s Penn launched a scheme for a mass migration of Quakers to Pennsylvania (Penn's Woods). To prepare the way he constructed a "frame of government" for the colony and composed a set of laws. The result was one of the most enlightened political systems in the contemporary world. In Pennsylvania any male who owned or rented a small amount of land or who paid any taxes would be allowed to vote. No taxes would be imposed on anyone without the approval of the elected colonial legislature. All trials were to be before juries. In place of the long list of crimes punishable by death in England, in Pennsylvania there would be only two capital crimes: treason and murder. No atheists were to be admitted to the colony, but all who believed in God, regardless of their denomination, were welcome and would be allowed to worship in peace.

In 1682 Penn visited his new colony to observe the laying out of Philadelphia, one of the first modern planned cities. During this visit he also cemented cordial relations with the local Indians by paying generously for their land. Settlers soon began arriving in large numbers, drawn by Penn's policies of selling land at low prices and extending religious liberty to all Christians. Pennsylvania attracted not only thousands of British Quakers, but also French Protestants (Huguenots), who were in disfavor in Catholic France, and many German Pietists (radical Protestants), who were being persecuted by German Catholics and

Commonwealth of Massachusetts, Archives Division

Four Quakers were hanged in Massachusetts between 1659 and 1661. This statue of Mary Dyer, one of the four, was erected three centuries later. It stands on the grounds of the Massachusetts State House, across the street from Boston Common, the place of execution.

Lutherans alike. By 1689 the colony had 12,000 inhabitants. It was a success from the beginning.

The Limits of Religious Toleration. Seventeenth-century religious dissidents from Europe also settled in Maryland, the Carolinas, and New Netherland. Maryland was a particular refuge for George Calvert's Catholic coreligionists, though it also attracted Puritan and Anglican Protestants. In New Netherland the tolerant Dutch attracted religious minorities from almost every part of the Western world—Huguenots from France, Jews from the Portuguese colony of Brazil, and assorted religious refugees from Germany, England, Massachusetts, and elsewhere. By the end of Dutch

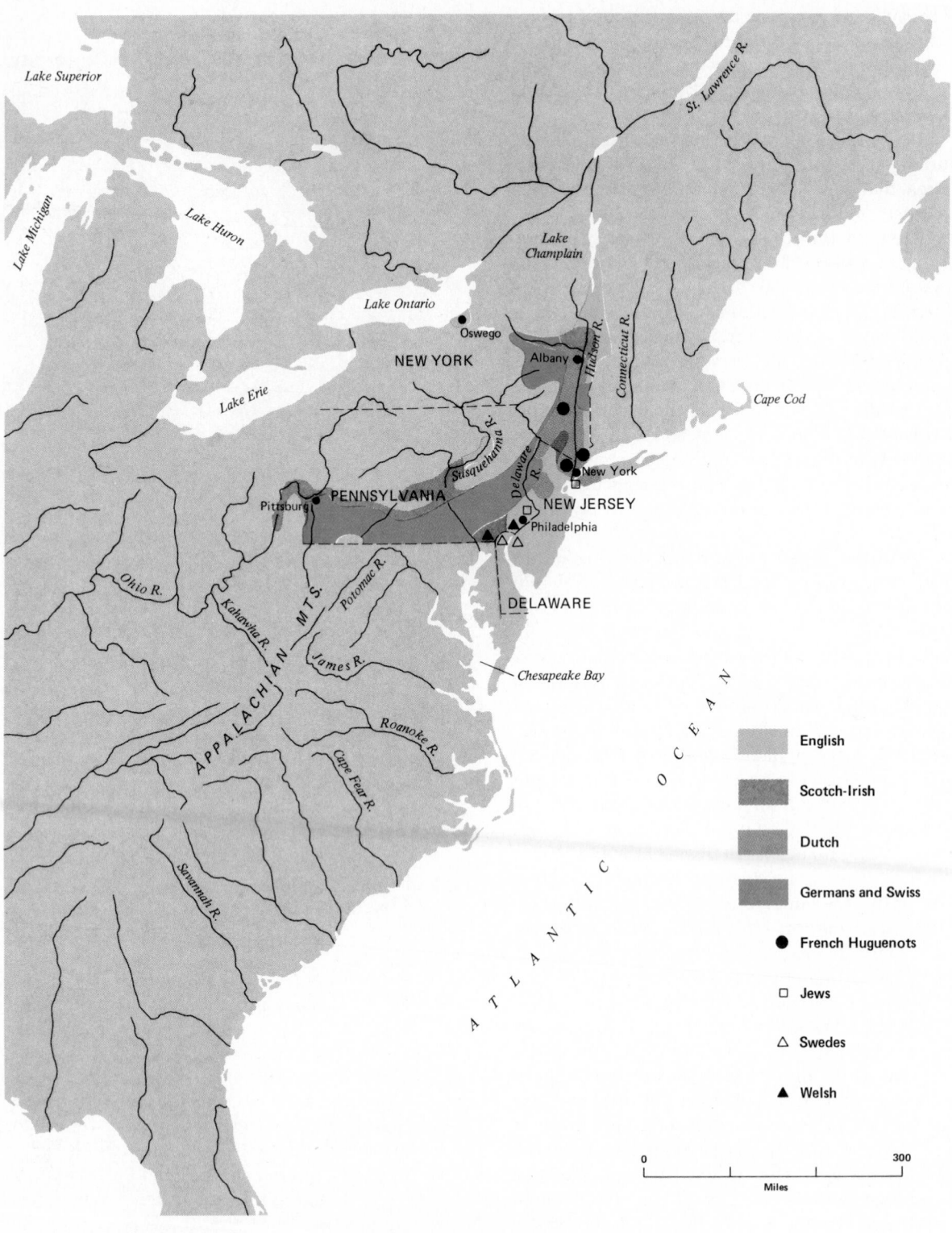

Colonial settlement by nationality in the middle colonies, 1770

rule in 1664, the small colony—and especially its chief town, New Amsterdam on Manhattan Island—had become a cosmopolitan community inhabited by many nationalities and a wide assortment of religious groups.

Thus America as a whole served as a refuge for religious dissenters from Europe. Pennsylvania, New Netherland, Rhode Island, and, for a while, Maryland accorded the right to worship to a wide array of faiths. But religious toleration was far from universal even in the mainland British colonies. In few places were Catholics or Jews allowed to practice their religion openly. Toleration, if accorded at all, generally meant toleration only for Protestants of various kinds.

In many colonies, as we have seen, even Protestants who differed from the founding group suffered disabilities. In most of New England only Puritans were welcome. In southern New York and most of the colonies south of Pennsylvania only Anglicans enjoyed full civil and religious rights. In both Calvinist and Anglican colonies ministers of the "established" churches received support from the provincial treasury through tithes—religious taxes—imposed on all residents of the colony regardless of their religious preferences. All other ministers had to rely on their parishioners to support their churches and pay their salaries.

Yet taken as a whole, religious toleration was more complete and general in the British mainland colonies than elsewhere in the Western world. Spain and France refused to allow religious dissenters to go to their American possessions, and this restriction seriously limited their colonies' growth. Much of the advantage in wealth and population eventually enjoyed by English America over New Spain and New France derived from the more liberal British approach, which preserved the energies and talents of religious dissidents for the advantage of the British Empire.

CONCLUSIONS

As we examine the motives of those who promoted and those who settled the American colonies, we perceive a mixed picture. Americans may prefer to see their country as founded primarily on freedom, a refuge for those fleeing oppression and bigotry, but at best this view is only a half-truth. New England, Pennsylvania, and, to a lesser extent, Maryland, New Jersey, and Delaware assuredly served as havens for religious dissenters. But they themselves exhibited religious tolerance

only for select groups. Nowhere, except perhaps in Rhode Island and New Netherland, were those of every persuasion welcome. Nor should we forget that for many men and women who crossed the Atlantic America was the opposite of a haven: it was a prison. For thousands of transported European felons and for an even larger number of Africans, America was a place of bondage.

For those who came voluntarily, moreover, the strongest lure was not freedom, it was material opportunity. Capitalists could make profits from trade, land speculation, and commercial agriculture; gentlemen could raise their status and restore their shattered fortunes; rulers could enrich their realms and make themselves more powerful. The expectations of Europeans who had only their lives to invest were more modest, perhaps, but they, too, were primarily economic. Most ordinary men and women crossed the Atlantic to acquire the economic independence and decent comfort that the social and economic systems of England and continental Europe denied them. Opportunity was America's basic premise in the beginning and would remain so throughout its history.

FOR FURTHER READING

Thomas J. Wertenbaker. *The First Americans, 1607–1690* (1927)
    Disregard the age of this book. It is still an excellent and well-written survey of the early settlement patterns of British America. Concentrates on Virginia and Massachusetts.

James Morton Smith, editor. *Seventeenth Century America: Essays in Colonial History* (1959)
    The work of many authors, this book includes several important essays on early colonization as well as good chapters on early Indian-white relations in North America.

Carl Bridenbaugh. *Vexed and Troubled Englishmen, 1590–1642* (1974)
    The author used manuscripts, printed plays, ballads, broadsides, letters, diaries, and court records to write this social history of ordinary English people during the early years of American colonization.

Edmund Morgan. *The Puritan Dilemma: The Story of John Winthrop* (1958)
    A fine biography of the early Puritan leader of Massachusetts who did so much to make that colony a success. Deals with Winthrop in England and America and tells us much of the Puritan motives for colonization. An impressive fusion of biography and history.

Alden T. Vaughan. *American Genesis: Captain John Smith and the Founding of Virginia* (1975)
    The early history of the Jamestown colony approached through the biography of the colorful

soldier John Smith. A lively way to learn the early history of Virginia.

Edmund S. Morgan. *American Slavery, American Freedom: The Ordeal of Colonial Virginia* (1975)
Not only is this brilliant book an excellent account of the early years of the Virginia colony, it also deals interestingly with the issues of race and labor relations between whites and Indians and between whites and black slaves in the first permanent British North American colony.

Abbot Emerson Smith. *Colonists in Bondage: White Servitude and Convict Labor in America, 1607–1776* (1947)
Tells how indentured servants and convicts were induced, seduced, kidnapped, and "spir-

ited" to America. Some discussion of their fate once here.

Daniel Mannix and Malcolm Cowley. *Black Cargoes: A History of the Atlantic Slave Trade* (1962)
The best brief survey of the subject. An eye-opener for readers who have accepted the conventional wisdom about early black Africa and the international slave trade.

John Barth. *The Sot-Weed Factor* (1964)
This long historical novel spoofs the heroic accounts of early American settlement. A bawdy and irreverent version of the John Smith–Pocahontas legend and the story of tobacco, transplanted from its original Virginia setting to Maryland.

3 Colonial Society
How Did Old World Culture Change in the Wilderness?

1636   Harvard, in Massachusetts, is the first college to be founded in the colonies

1642, 1647   Massachusetts Bay Colony enacts compulsory school laws

1662   The "Half-Way Covenant" allows the children of Massachusetts Bay church members to join the congregation without a conversion experience

1675–78   Indian-white tensions erupt into King Philip's War in New England

1675   Bacon's Rebellion in Virginia

1692   Twenty-one men and one woman are executed in the Salem, Massachusetts, witch trials

1705   Virginia's legislature establishes a Propositions and Grievances Committee to receive public petitions proposing new laws

1732   Publication of the first issue of Benjamin Franklin's *Poor Richard's Almanack*

1734–37   Congregationalist minister Jonathan Edwards sparks a religious revival in New England

1739   Stono Rebellion of South Carolina slaves

1740   George Whitefield's "Methodism" leads to a "Great Awakening" throughout the colonies

1746–52   Benjamin Franklin's experiments with electricity earn him international fame

In 1782, shortly before the end of the Revolutionary War, J. Hector St. John de Crèvecoeur, a French gentleman who had settled in the colonies, asked a question about America that would be posed again and again: "What, then, is the American, this new man?" Crèvecoeur's answer was that the American was a mixture of the old and the new. He was an individual

> who leaving behind all his ancient prejudices and manners, receives new ones from the mode of life he has embraced, the new government he obeys, and the new rank he holds. . . . Americans are the western pilgrims, who are carrying along with them that great mass of arts, sciences, vigour, and industry which began long since in the east; they will finish the great circle. . . .

Americans, then, were not simply transplanted Europeans, according to Crèvecoeur. They had carried with them to the new land many of the habits and much of the cultural heritage of the Old World. But they had also left behind a good deal, and much of what they had taken with them had been transformed in their new circumstances.

This 1674 painting of Boston merchant John Freake suggests another side of the Bay Colony's life. Freake's silver buttons, lace collar, muslin ruffs, and elegant brooch make it clear: a half-century after the founding of the "Citty Upon a Hill," the world and the flesh had intruded.

Worcester Art Museum

Were Crèvecoeur's conclusions correct? Had the human mixture of the colonies blended into a new type? Was there a distinctive American culture by the eve of the Revolution? Or were Americans merely transplanted Europeans with attitudes, values, and institutions directly traceable to the European continent? In what sense and in what ways were Americans "new," and if they were new, how had the change occurred?

A NEW MIXTURE IN A NEW LAND

It would have been very surprising if American values, ideas, artifacts, and institutions had not quickly diverged from those of Europe. Two powerful factors clearly worked in this direction: a different physical environment, and a different mixture of human beings.

A New Physical Environment. If Europe in the seventeenth and eighteenth centuries was a continent of ancient cities, well-tilled fields, vineyards, and orchards, as late as the Revolution America was still almost entirely a wilderness. Most of the population was confined to a narrow strip of coast between the Appalachian Mountains and the sea, stretching from present-day Nova Scotia to Spanish Florida. Beyond the coastal tidewater region tongues of settlement extended along the rivers that rose in the mountains, but much of the "West" was a vast expanse of forest dotted by a few clearings and threaded by Indian trails. And even the most densely settled coastal areas of the colonies differed from Europe. In 1775 only five American towns had more than 10,000 inhabitants. Four of these—Boston, Newport, New York, and Philadelphia—were in the North. South of Pennsylvania, only Charleston, South Carolina, could be considered a true city. Elsewhere in the southern plantation colonies, outside of one or two small provincial capitals, the rural county was the significant political and social unit. Nor did the countryside, even in the older regions, much resemble its European counterpart with its trim fields, neat fences and hedgerows, stone barns, and well-built farmhouses. Everywhere in colonial America there were more woods than cleared land.

Travel in this great wilderness was slow and uncomfortable for transplanted Europeans. When Sarah Knight, a Boston schoolmistress, journeyed from her New England home to New York City in 1704, she described her trip as an ordeal. Roads were dirt tracks through the forests; bridges, where they existed at all, were logs laid across stones. Knight found few inns and was forced to put up at farmhouses where the beds were infested with fleas and the food was skimpy and ill-cooked. Nor was her experience unique. So slow was colonial overland communication that the mounted riders of the continental postal service took three weeks to cover the ground from Boston to Philadelphia. It is not surprising that people and freight moved by water wherever possible.

The difficult physical environment helped to shape the settlers' daily lives and ultimately their attitudes and culture. To master it required enormous outlays of time and energy. As the astronomer John Winthrop, descendant of the Bay Colony founder, explained in 1768:

> Plantations in their beginnings have work enough and find difficulties sufficient to settle a comfortable way of subsistence, there being buildings, fencings, clearing, and breaking up of ground, lands to be settled, orchards to be planted, highways and fortifications to be made, and all things to do as in the beginning of the world.

Not only was America wild and untamed compared to Europe, it also had a different climate. The East Coast of North America was warmer in summer and colder in winter than Western Europe, where most white immigrants came from. This difference challenged Europeans to adapt their food, clothing, and shelter to suit the new environment. The adjustment was often slow. Until quite recent times, for example, American men continued to wear wool jackets and neck pieces (ties, cravats, etc.) even during the fierce summer heat, at least on formal occasions.

Diversity Among the Europeans. Crèvecoeur believed that in America "individuals of all nations are melted into a new race of men," but even white Europeans often refused to mingle, much less melt. True, Crèvecoeur's Protestant compatriots, the French Hugenots, had quietly merged with the majority when they reached America. In South Carolina, particularly, the Huguenot families of the seventeenth century joined the English elite and in a few years lost their original culture. Intermarriage among different groups did occur. Crèvecoeur told of one family in which each of four sons had married a woman of a different nationality. Yet such complete assimilation was not common. In the seventeenth century, as streams of Huguenots, Dutch, Swedes, and Germans joined the largely English population, the result was a lumpy demographic stew rather than a smooth blend. Most groups retained their charac-

teristics generation after generation, practicing their own religion, speaking their own language, pursuing their own customs, and marrying within their own fold.

New streams of European immigrants converged on America soon after the Treaty of Utrecht in 1713 ended the War of the Spanish Succession and brought peace to Europe. Between 1700 and 1775 about 100,000 Germans crossed the Atlantic to the mainland British colonies. Many went to Pennsylvania, which had provided a haven for Germans in the previous century; many others settled in western Maryland and western Virginia.

Unlike the Huguenots, the Germans tended to hold onto their own ways rather than adopt those of the English-speaking majority. As Philadelphia scientist Benjamin Rush wrote in 1789, even their farms seemed different from those carved out by English settlers:

> A German farm may be distinguished from the farms of . . . other citizens . . . by the size of their barns, the plain but compact form of their houses, the height of their enclosures, the extent of their meadows, and the general appearance of plenty and neatness in everything that belongs to them.

Because they were numerous and slow to assimilate, the Germans aroused the suspicion of English-speaking Pennsylvanians. In 1727 the Pennsylvania legislature required the newcomers to take oaths of fidelity to the king, the colonial proprietor, and the colony charter. Still, suspicions lingered. In the 1750s Benjamin Franklin, usually the most cosmopolitan of men, penned an outburst against the "Palatine boors" that expressed a widely held view of the dangers they posed:

> Advertisements intended to be general are now printed in Dutch [German] and English. The signs in our streets have inscriptions in both languages, in some places only German. They begin of late to make all their . . . legal instruments in their own language . . . which . . . are allowed in our courts, where the German business so increases that there is continued need of interpreters; and I suppose within a few years they will also be necessary in the Assembly, to tell one half of our legislators what the other half say. In short, unless the stream of importation can be turned from this to other colonies . . . they will so outnumber us that . . . we . . . will . . . not be able to preserve our language, and even our government will become precarious.

The Scotch-Irish were another group that poured into the North American colonies in the eighteenth century. These people were Presbyterians who had moved from the Scottish lowlands to the province of Ulster in northern Ireland in the early seventeenth century to settle on the lands of the dispossessed Irish Catholics. They prospered in their new homes by raising cattle and weaving wool and linen cloth until the British government imposed duties on imports from Ulster, severely damaging the Scotch-Irish economy. Masses of Ulster Presbyterians soon flocked to America.

Some tried New England, where their fellow Calvinists, the Puritans, seemed likely to provide a haven. But the New Englanders saw the newcomers as Irish rather than Calvinists and made them unwelcome. Thereafter most of the Scotch-Irish turned south, flooding into the Pennsylvania backcountry to the west of the older settled regions. Many also moved into western Virginia and then down through the Great Valley (the Shenandoah) and the frontier counties of the Carolinas into northern Georgia.

In Pennsylvania they disturbed the provincial government, which feared that they would not pay for land and that they would violate the rights of the Indians. Ever since the days of William Penn, the Pennsylvania authorities had maintained good relations with the colony's Indian tribes. They now feared that the Scotch-Irish might set off a major Indian war. These fears were not unfounded. The newcomers were the very image of the frontiersmen of legend: tall, red-haired, quick to anger, hospitable, fiercely independent. Such hot-blooded people did not get along well with their neighbors and were constantly embroiled in disputes and quarrels with the Indians. Yet they made valuable additions to the American population. Herdsmen and hunters rather than farmers, they filled in the colonial backcountry, where their qualities made them useful, if sometimes troublesome, pioneers.

Despite the separateness of the European groups, each contributed something to what was to become a distinctly American culture. Many Dutch words—including *stoop, boss, schooner, spook,* and *crib*—crept into American English. The Dutch St. Nicholas became the American Santa Claus. The log cabin, a Swedish introduction, was popularized by the Scotch-Irish and became the typical pioneer dwelling on the American frontier. The Germans set agricultural standards and contributed the long-barreled "Kentucky rifle" and the "prairie schooner," the Conestoga wagon, to the American heritage.

Native Americans. Europeans, as they spread across British North America, refused to treat the Indians as part of the emerging American community. They seldom married Indians; cultural mixing of white and Indian ways was also limited, although there were some exceptions.

The early settlers of New England had learned Indian farming techniques and borrowed many food plants and dishes whose Indian names, such as *squash, pecan, hominy,* and *succotash,* entered the English language. Some scholars hold that the powerful Iroquois Confederacy helped inspire colonial attempts at unity before 1776. For their part, the Indians acquired the colonists' muskets, powder, shot, cloth, iron implements, and other goods through trade in beaver pelts and deerskins. In later years several tribes in the Carolinas and Georgia absorbed the best of the white culture and produced an interesting new blend of native and European societies. Much of this exchange was superficial, however. The British colonists did not mix as readily with the Indians as did the Spanish in Mexico and the French in Canada.

Nowhere is the isolation of the English from Indian culture more apparent than in the realm of religion. In the Catholic colonies of France, Spain and Portugal thousands of natives' souls were "saved" by baptism. In British America only a few pious Christians felt uneasy about leaving the Indians without Christian solace. In the 1640s the Reverend John Eliot began to preach to the local Massachusetts tribes, and in the 1660s he translated the Bible "into the Indian tongue." Generously supported by English philanthropists and by the Bay Colony government, Eliot established several towns of "praying" Indians in the colony. But however sympathetic to the Indians' religious plight, he had little respect for their culture. In the towns the converts were expected to follow the white people's ways, abandon their customs and traditions, and become "civilized." And even Eliot's limited example had few imitators. All in all, Protestantism made little headway among the Indians of British North America during the colonial period.

Indeed, rather than Christian love, Indian-white relations were generally marked by hostility. Outside of Pennsylvania, where white officials respected Indian rights, Indian-white contacts produced constant warfare. In the 1620s Jamestown settlers had clashed with the tribes of the Virginia coastal region; in the 1630s the Pequot War destroyed the Indian population of eastern Connecticut. Most serious of all during the first century of settlement was King Philip's War of the mid-1670s.

The trouble had long been brewing. Until Massasoit's death, relations between the Wampa-

Library of Congress

Not all the English hated the Indians. Puritan minister John Eliot was one of those who felt that they too were God's children. Inevitably, however, their salvation seemed to require that they abandon their "heathen" ways and adopt the religion of the Europeans. Many did, but in the end the conversion did not save them from the wrath of the whites.

noag Indians and the Plymouth colonists had been cordial. Philip, Massasoit's son and successor, preserved the goodwill for a while, but when colony officials tried to impose tribute on him, he grew increasingly resentful. Meanwhile, other tribes in southern New England were also becoming restless in the face of steady encroachment by whites. Then, in 1675, Philip's warriors attacked the town of Swansea. Two tribes—the Narragansetts of Rhode Island and the Nipmucks of Connecticut—soon joined Philip's Wampanoags in the struggle.

The Indian method of fighting was too much for the New Englanders at first. Accustomed to moving in massed formations against an enemy that stood fast and fired back, they found the Indians' ambushes and surprise raids exasperating. The Indians, for their part, saw the European method of fighting as stupid. Armed for the first time with guns, the Indians devastated the white settlements with their hit-and-run tactics.

Before long the colonists adopted Indian methods of warfare: surprise raids, ambushes, and even scalping. Eventually the war against the "savages" made the colonists savage. Soon they were torturing prisoners and using large dogs to tear the Indians apart. In the end the Europeans' superior numbers and organization prevailed. By 1676 the southern tribes were defeated and subdued. By 1678 the Indians of Maine and New Hampshire, who had taken up arms in support of their southern brothers, were also pacified.

King Philip's War exacted an enormous toll on both sides. According to one estimate, one-sixteenth of the white male population of New England died in the fighting. The monetary cost to Plymouth, Massachusetts, and Connecticut was crushing. On the Indians' side, one casualty of the war was Eliot's praying Indians. Although they had remained loyal to the whites, they were interned for three years on Deer Island, where they were forced to live on shellfish. Many died. Philip himself was captured and shot, and many of his followers were sold into slavery in the Caribbean or indentured as servants to whites. Indian lands were awarded to the surviving white troops. After 1678 the New England Indians ceased to be a challenge to the white population except on the most remote frontiers bordering French Canada.

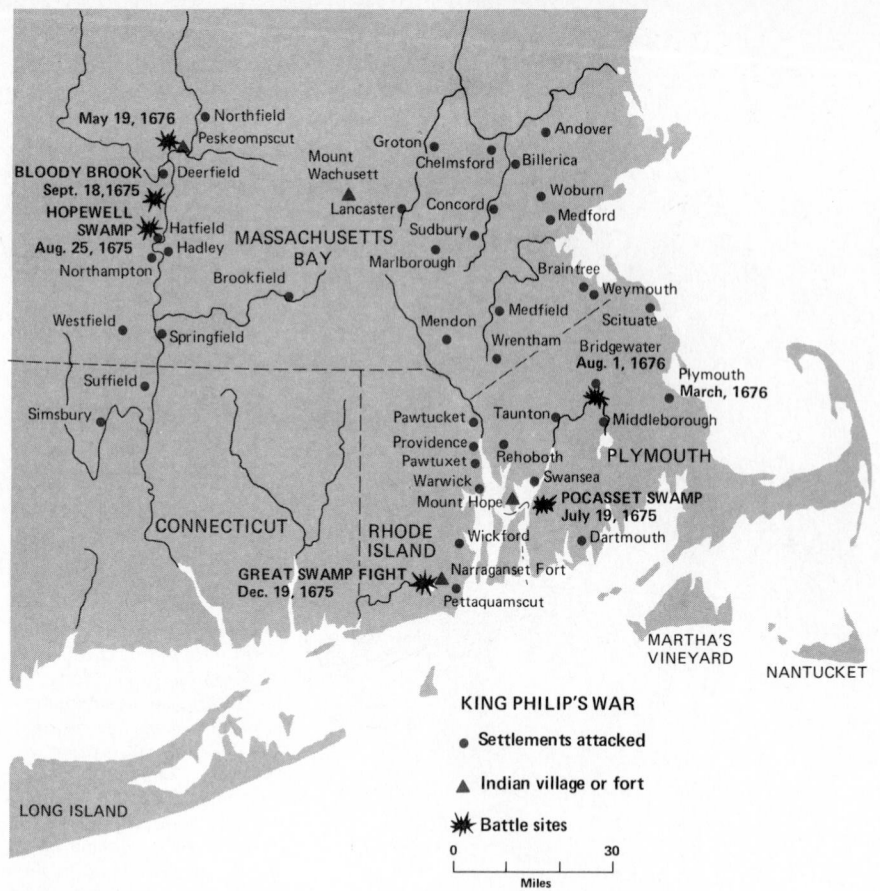

King Philip's War, 1675–1676

East-West Differences. Elsewhere in the English colonies the Indians remained a "problem" to whites for many years. The difficulties were especially acute along the western frontier, where the white population pushed against tribes unwilling to surrender additional lands or permit Europeans to settle among them. In the clashes that followed, the authorities in the older coastal areas, preferring to preserve the peace at all costs, sometimes sided with the Indians against the western frontiersmen. This response created deep resentment between East and West.

These East-West tensions first appeared in Virginia, where by the 1670s settlers had pushed beyond the tidewater, the coastal region where the slow-flowing streams rose and fell daily with the ocean tides, and moved into the piedmont, the plateau region immediately to the west. The piedmont settlers soon came to feel that the tidewater planters who controlled the government were unconcerned with their problems. They especially resented the tidewater leaders' indifference to Indian attacks on them.

In 1675 and 1676 Virginia's piedmont-tidewater tensions came to a head in Bacon's Rebellion. When Indian warfare broke out on the frontier, the Virginia governor, Sir William Berkeley, called for restraint; but the frontiersmen, under the leadership of piedmont planter Nathaniel Bacon, attacked and almost wiped the Indians out. Soon after, the governor declared Bacon a rebel. Eventually Bacon marched on Jamestown and forced the Virginia assembly to pass laws changing white-Indian relations and granting more power to the voters. He then burned Jamestown. When Bacon died, his rebellion collapsed. Berkeley regained authority and hanged thirteen of his followers.

Although Pennsylvania had long had an official tradition of fair dealings with the Indians, it too began to experience Indian-white and East-West tensions as the western frontier was settled. The Scotch-Irish settlers in the western part of the colony had complained for years that the Quaker-dominated government in Philadelphia did not support them adequately against the Indians. In

December 1763 a mob of frontiersmen from the towns of Paxton and Donegal, taking the law into their own hands, attacked a group of peaceful Conestoga Indians, killing six. When the horrified Pennsylvania assembly ordered the "Paxton Boys" arrested, the enraged westerners marched on Philadelphia, prepared to get "justice" at the point of a gun. For a while it looked as if the colony would be thrown into civil war. Fortunately, Benjamin Franklin intercepted the rebels and negotiated a solution. Though further violence was avoided, this near-rebellion left a legacy of sectional antagonisms within Pennsylvania that lasted almost to the end of the century.

Colonial Blacks. The cultural mix of the American colonies included not only diverse European and Indian groups but also Africans. In 1760 about 325,000 of the approximately 1.6 million people in British North American were black. Of these, 12,000 lived in New England, another 25,000 in the middle colonies (New York, New Jersey, and Pennsylvania), and the remainder in the southern colonies, with Virginia and South Carolina far in the lead. Most were slaves; only a few hundred were "free persons of color."

Black workers were an important part of the laboring class in colonial America. In New England and the middle colonies black slaves were employed largely as day laborers, seamen, house servants, or craftsmen's assistants in the towns and ports. In only a few places in the North—Rhode Island and here and there in the Hudson Valley—were black slaves field workers. In the Chesapeake region, the Carolinas, and eventually Georgia, slaves formed the backbone of the labor force on tobacco, rice, and indigo plantations. Even in these plantation colonies, however, blacks were employed as house servants and artisans as well.

This forced labor, on farms and plantations and in towns, transformed the culture of the enslaved Africans. Slaves had to learn occupations that were not part of their African culture. For example, in South Carolina, Virginia, and elsewhere they quickly acquired trades such as bricklaying, "plaistering," wig making, silversmithing, and gunsmithing. The cultural exchange was not all one way, however. Some slaves' tasks were based on skills and knowledge they brought from Africa. West Africans were familiar with boats and the sea; in South Carolina many of them worked as fishermen. They introduced the West African *periauger*—a kind of canoe—for transportation along the Sea Islands and through the many rivers and streams of the Carolina coastal lowlands. Slaves also introduced West African agricultural

products to South Carolina—including melons, gourds, and probably even rice, a crop that became one of the area's chief exports. Although black cooks learned the techniques of European cuisine, they contributed their own methods and ingredients; for example, sesame seeds and red pepper. Much of the South's distinctive cooking is derived from the merger of African and European elements.

The African family and kinship systems also survived in part. In most of the slaves' homelands each individual was tied to the community through elaborate kinship systems. These systems bound together parents, children, grandparents, cousins, uncles, aunts, nieces, and nephews, specifying the support and obligations they owed to one another. Through these elaborate networks of attachment, the slave family in America was able to endure severe external pressure. In their new homes husbands and wives, parents and children, were often separated against their will. But the inherited African kinship networks made it possible for slaves to remain in touch with distant relatives for many years, despite infrequent chances for contact.

Little is known about the religion of the first generation or two of American slaves. Most West Africans worshiped the spirits of the dead, who were believed to remain close by, protecting their descendants. Priests—usually the oldest member of each family line—conducted the group's ceremonies. It seems likely that the first slaves tried to practice their religion much as they had at home, though they were far from the graves of their venerated ancestors.

In most of the colonies few efforts were made at first to convert the Africans to Christianity, in part because Christians were not supposed to enslave their fellow Christians. Nonetheless, there is evidence that slaves absorbed the Europeans' faith to some degree in this early period, merely through contact. In the middle of the eighteenth century formal conversion of slaves became more common. By this time a new emotionalism had developed in Protestantism, and it made Christianity more attractive to many slaves.

The lot of the colonial American slave varied from place to place, time to time, and master to master. In New England slaves were relatively well treated because they often lived in close contact with whites in a family setting. In the South the slave system was harsher. By the standards of the day, slaves were usually well fed and given adequate medical care, but some masters abused their slaves cruelly. The Virginian Robert Carter, generally considered a decent man by his white

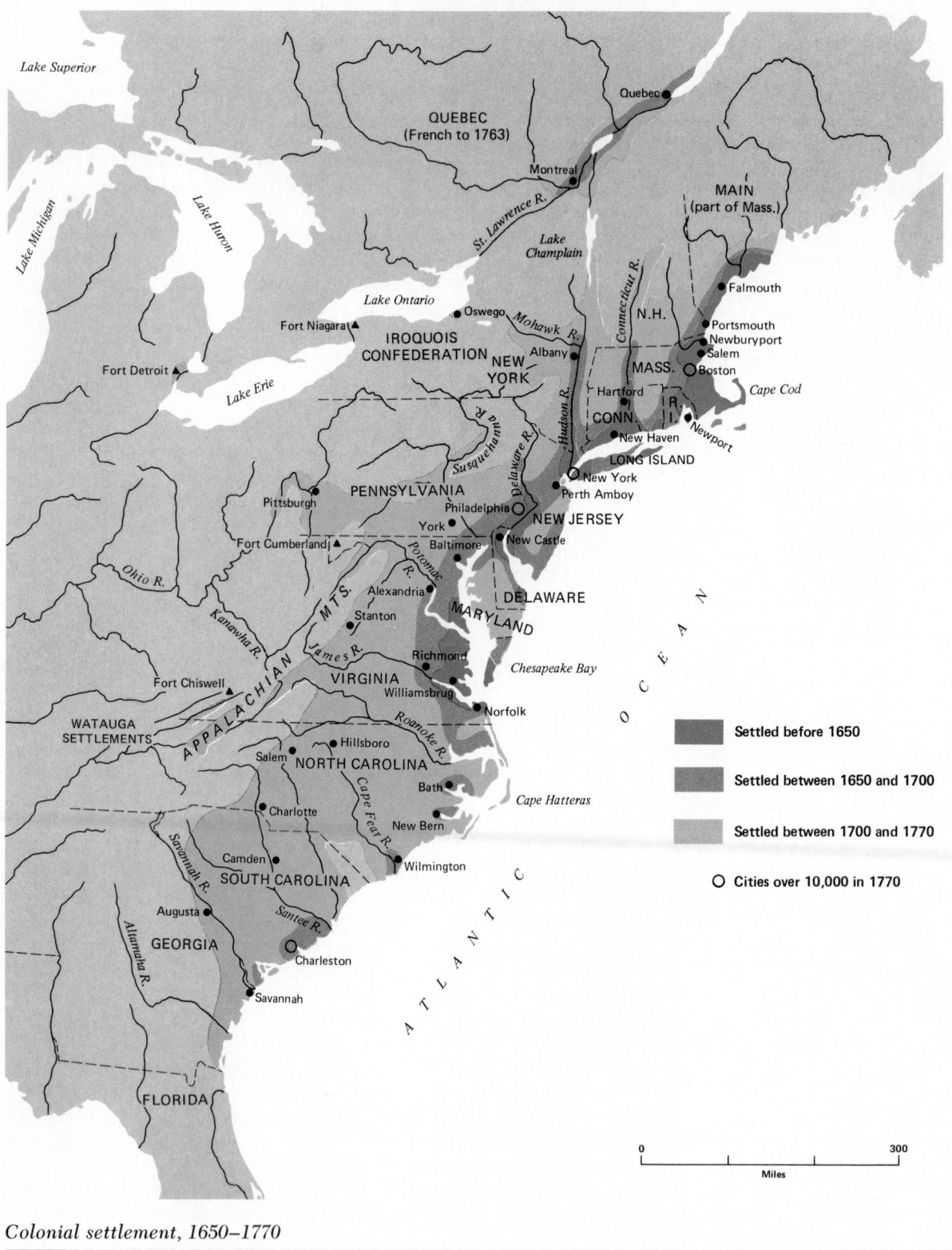

Colonial settlement, 1650–1770

Map legend:
- Settled before 1650
- Settled between 1650 and 1700
- Settled between 1700 and 1770
- ○ Cities over 10,000 in 1770

Scale: 0 — 300 Miles

neighbors, underfed his slaves and expected them to make up the deficiency by raising their own food in their spare time. The slaves' housing was often minimal. One eighteenth-century white Virginian, forced to take shelter one evening in a "Negro cabin" with six blacks, reported that the shack "was not lathed or plaistered, neither ceiled nor lofted above . . . one window, but no glass in it, not even a brick chimney, and as it stood on blocks about a foot above the ground, the hogs lay constantly under the floor, which made it swarm with flies."

Colonial slaves were tightly controlled. In seventeenth-century South Carolina slaves judged guilty of offenses such as murder, striking a white person, or plotting an insurrection could be castrated, branded, and burned alive. In the eighteenth century whipping replaced most of the earlier sentences, but whipping too was a brutal and terrifying experience.

Control consisted of more than punishment. In South Carolina slaves who left their plantations were required to carry "tickets" indicating their owners' permission to be away. In Charleston a professional company of constables was authorized to detain "suspicious" blacks and determine their business. In other parts of South Carolina mounted patrols stopped blacks on the roads, entered black homes for inspection, and confiscated black-owned firearms.

Despite all these controls, colonial blacks found ways to express their hatred of the slave system. They fought back by deliberately breaking their master's tools, injuring cattle and horses, destroying crops, and running away. From South Carolina slaves often escaped to the Spanish settlements in Florida. Some fled to the Indian frontier, though Indians and blacks were often enemies. Virginia slaves frequently destroyed property before they escaped. To discourage this behavior the colony "outlawed" runaways, allowing anyone who encountered such persons to kill them on sight without penalty.

The most serious slave protest was group rebellion. Nowhere in the mainland colonies did slaves mount a large-scale uprising or set up independent black communities, as slaves eventually did in Brazil and places in the Caribbean. But there were several organized rebellions during the colonial period. In New York City in 1712 twenty-five slaves armed with knives, axes, and guns set fire to a white man's outhouse. When whites rushed to save the burning building, the slaves attacked them, killing nine. The authorities called out the militia, who quickly rounded up the insurrectionists. Twenty-one were executed.

The Stono Rebellion in South Carolina, where slaves were far more numerous, was a much more serious threat to the white community. It began near Charleston in September 1739 when a group of slaves broke into a storehouse and seized arms and supplies. The rebels intended to flee to Florida; as they marched south gathering recruits, they attacked any white who got in their way. After a few days the militia caught up with the fugitives and destroyed them. In all, thirty whites and forty-four blacks lost their lives.

The Stono Rebellion sent a shock wave through South Carolina. The colony tightened its patrols, initiated a program to inculcate submission, and tried to limit slave importation. It also sought to improve the lot of slaves by limiting their hours of work to fifteen per day between March and September and thirteen the rest of the year. Once fears had quieted, the planters relaxed somewhat; but white South Carolinians would never feel entirely safe again.

FAMILIES

The mixture of peoples in British North America, then, did not produce a uniform new combination. The mixture remained full of undigested pieces. Far more than in our own era the diverse ethnic and cultural ingredients continued to be separate, leaving largely unchallenged the community's basic Anglo-Saxon heritage. But this does not mean that the New World environment did not change transplanted European institutions. On the contrary, the new setting modified the most basic institutions and, in the process, helped produce something characteristically American.

Birth Rates, Death Rates, and Family Size. Even the most fundamental institution of all, the family, was altered by the new American environment. Exposed to New World conditions, the English family became both larger and more egalitarian than it had been in the mother country.

Life generally was short in seventeenth-century Europe. Famines, plagues, and wars ravaged the land and cut down thousands of men, women, and children before their time. By itself this situation would have reduced family size. But there were also social reasons why families were relatively small. Scholars used to believe that English families of the early modern era were *extended* families consisting not just of parents and children, but also of grandparents, other relatives, and servants. We now know that except for the aristocracy, the *nuclear* family of parents and young children was typical; that once grown, children in England were expected to set out on their own. This custom, coupled with the high death rates in this period, made for relatively small families, not more than four or five people.

The new American environment created a different family pattern. In New England from the beginning, people were long-lived. Historian John Demos estimates that during the seventeenth century the average life expectancy for men in Plymouth Colony came close to that of our own day. In Dedham, in the Bay Colony, death rates were half those in contemporary Europe. In most of the New England towns birth rates were high, usually higher than in Europe. The net effect of these low death rates and high birth rates was to create larger families in America than on the other side of the Atlantic. The first American census in 1790 revealed that the average American household had almost six members, which made it a fifth larger than its European counterpart.

The long life and large families of seventeenth-century New Englanders were made possible by a distinctive social pattern. The settlers in the Puritan colonies lived in compact groups of families on lands allotted to them by the colonial authorities. These "towns" of 300 to 500 people often encompassed several thousand acres of woodland, pasture, and fields, much of which was held in reserve for future population growth. Houses in the New England town were clustered around a village green on lots assigned to each family head; each family also had fields for crops in the outlying area. With food abundant, neighbors nearby for help in emergencies, and little contact with Europe and its diseases, families in these self-sufficient New England villages were relatively healthy and grew large.

At first the family history of the southern colonies was quite different. Most early immigrants to Maryland and Virginia were single men who came either as planters or servants. The authorities tried to attract women by paying their passage, but until well into the eighteenth century many Virginians and Marylanders remained bachelors. In 1704, for example, only about 7,200 of the 30,000 white people in Maryland were women.

The generally unhealthy state of the Chesapeake region also held down family formation. Malaria and dysentery killed many people in early colonial Virginia and Maryland and hit pregnant women particularly hard. In addition, European diseases were carried to the Chesapeake region by the tobacco-collecting vessels that came directly to each planter's dock. In South Carolina the rice-growing lowlands with their "agues" continued to be unhealthy well into the 1800s.

Still, as time passed, an ever-larger proportion of the Chesapeake and Carolina population consisted of the native-born, a development that equalized the numbers of males and females. This return to a normal sex ratio made more marriages possible, so that by the eighteenth century the family became the normal household unit even in the South. Meanwhile, because of closer commercial contact with other parts of the world, smallpox, malaria, and other illnesses invaded New England, increasing mortality rates. By the later years of the colonial period the disparity in size between the southern and northern colonial family had virtually disappeared.

As the decades passed, the differences between European and American demographic characteristics also began to narrow. Yet they never entirely vanished during the colonial period. As we have noted, as late as 1790 American families were larger than their European counterparts. So was population growth. Since land was cheaper and more abundant in America than in Europe, young people could afford to marry early. In the absence of birth control they usually had many children. Even without heavy immigration this would have made for a rapid population increase. But the flood of European immigrants magnified the effects. All told, during the eighteenth century, with population doubling every twenty-five years, British North America was probably the fastest-growing part of the world.

Family Roles. In colonial America the family was the central social institution, one that served many functions. It was, for one thing, the center of education. Parents taught young children their first "letters" and their earliest religious precepts. Fathers taught their sons how to farm, repair tools, hunt, and fish. If the father was a skilled craftsman, he taught his son his trade. Girls learned from their mothers how to perform the many household tasks expected of colonial women.

The family was also a "little commonwealth" within which people's lives were prescribed and regulated, an agent through which acceptable social behavior was taught and enforced. Fathers were the rulers in these small political units; the law in the Puritan colonies even allowed them the power of life and death over their children, though none as far as we know ever chose to exercise it. This patriarchal system was deeply entrenched in Europe and was carried to America. It was reinforced by the father's control over the family land and property. In the southern colonies, with their looser settlement patterns and their more abundant fertile land, this arrangement was probably not a serious problem for children. In early New England, however, where towns were limited in size and where fathers lived long, the patriarchal system could be galling. Grown sons were often forced to live in their parents' household, subject to continued patriarchal control, or to become tenants on their father's land. Fortunately New England sons had an escape route. By the beginning of the eighteenth century an ever larger number were leaving the crowded Massachusetts and Connecticut towns to move to cheap land in the Berkshire Mountains, New Hampshire, and Maine.

Within the colonial family the roles of married women and men differed. Fathers typically carried on the family's public functions—such as casting its vote, serving in the militia, filling governmental positions—and its work outside the home. Mothers were responsible for private domestic matters and for acting as "helpmeets" to their husbands. Within this domain women had considerable power. Mothers were expected to supervise the children, particularly the youngest

ones; fathers generally did not involve themselves in everyday child-rearing matters. In addition to their household duties, many married women helped the family business, supplemented family income by running their own businesses or by selling surplus produce or handmade goods, and helped organize churches. Since women were considered subordinate to men, their tremendous behind-the-scenes contributions were sometimes credited to their husbands. A newspaper article praised a Newport man for the 300 skeins of yarn and 369 1/2 yards of cloth "spun in his own house." Of course, it was the women of his family who had done the work.

American women enjoyed a higher status and greater privileges than women in Europe. Colonial men recognized the value of women's work. In one Plymouth community a man was denied a license to run a tavern because he had no wife to help him in the business. Laws of the times granted American women higher legal status than their English sisters. Divorce was easier for wronged wives. Husbands who abused their spouses, especially in New England, were often reprimanded by the authorities. And colonial wid-

Fine Arts Museum of San Francisco

As the clothes of David, Joanna, and Abigail Mason suggest in this 1670 portrait, colonial Americans considered children merely smaller versions of adults.

ows were entitled to a larger fixed amount of their husbands' estates than was common in the mother country.

Yet when all this is acknowledged, it remains true that the colonial woman's role and status were inferior to man's. Her services as wife and mother, though important, conferred little prestige. Many women felt keenly their subordinate lot, although the response of most was resignation. As one South Carolina woman noted, her "self-denying duties" were "a part of the curse pronounced upon Eve" and nothing could be done about it.

Beneath father and mother were children, and perhaps servants and slaves. All helped in the family's work. As in England, servants were treated as part of the family because typically, unlike domestic workers today, they did not return to their homes after doing chores; they "lived in." Masters had the authority to discipline them and sometimes were obligated to provide them with an education. In the South slaves were in some ways members of the master's family, too. In law, slaves were treated as the children of their masters or mistresses, who, like parents, were expected to provide food, clothing, and shelter, and to mete out rewards and punishments.

Relationships between parents and those beneath them were sometimes despotic. But another family pattern, which historian Philip Greven has characterized as "genteel," also existed here and there in the colonies. This pattern was probably more common in the eighteenth century, after American society had become more complex, than in the seventeenth. Genteel families were prosperous, well educated, and generally less pious than others. They were bound together by affection rather than by authority and fear; they were more children-centered. These qualities, says Greven, had far-reaching effects. The children brought up in a genteel environment were self-confident and independent-minded. As adults they were apt to be leaders and doers. Their relatively egalitarian upbringing may have played an important part in shaping later American society.

GOVERNMENT

Political institutions, too, were modified by the new American environment. In England power had already begun to shift from the crown to the people; in British North America the process went even further. Yet *democracy*—rule by the people or their elected representatives—was not highly regarded as a political system by the best minds in the colonies. Indeed, democracy implied disorder and rule by the mob to contemporaries. Still, the most "enlightened" thinkers of the time did not wish to exclude democracy entirely, since the "popular voice" served as a useful check on tyranny. Accordingly most political thinkers prefered a system that mixed democracy with elements of monarchy (government by an absolute sovereign) and aristocracy (rule by a privileged class).

The English Model. At the opening of the seventeenth century England was not far removed from the rule by despotic kings and princes that prevailed in France, Germany, and elsewhere on the European continent. Then, between about 1630 and 1690, when many of the American colonies were being founded, the Stuart kings clashed with parliament over the powers of ruler and subject. Eventually the conflict produced civil war, the beheading of one king (Charles I), and the overthrow of another (James II).

By the end of the seventeenth century England had become a constitutional monarchy; that is, one in which the powers of the king were restricted by custom and law. Increasingly English sovereigns chose their ministers on the advice of parliament, and increasingly these ministers, not the crown, conducted the day-to-day affairs of the realm. Furthermore, parliament, not the crown, imposed taxes and passed laws.

But England's government was not democratic. The monarch remained powerful, and Parliament itself was not a very democratic body. Membership in the upper chamber—the House of Lords—was largely hereditary; its members were Anglican bishops and noble peers. Members of the lower chamber—the House of Commons— were elected, but the right to vote was strictly limited by property and religious requirements. In fact, only a small fraction of the adult males— about one in twenty-five—could vote. Even in the few districts that allowed a greater proportion of males to vote, the voters usually defered to their "betters" and sent only gentlemen and rich men to Parliament. The House of Commons, accordingly, was composed of nontitled gentry, merchants, and clients of the nobility, not the common people. Even local government was in the hands of the elite. Most officials were appointed, not elected, and most of those appointed were local gentlemen or squires.

Although the gentry dominated English political life, the system had liberal features. English subjects had rights that French, Spanish, and German subjects did not. Their homes were their castles, and the law could not invade them except

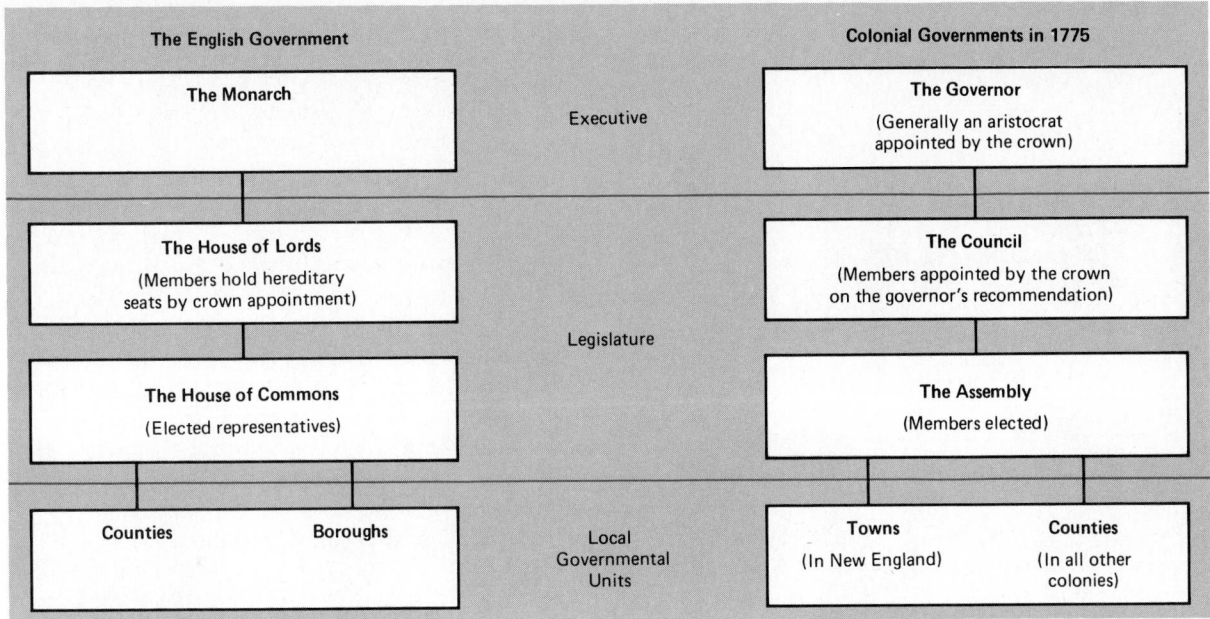

The English Government		Colonial Governments in 1775

The Monarch

Executive

The Governor
(Generally an aristocrat appointed by the crown)

The House of Lords
(Members hold hereditary seats by crown appointment)

Legislature

The Council
(Members appointed by the crown on the governor's recommendation)

The House of Commons
(Elected representatives)

The Assembly
(Members elected)

Counties   **Boroughs**

Local Governmental Units

Towns
(In New England)

Counties
(In all other colonies)

Note: The exceptions to this simple chart are many. In Connecticut and Rhode Island, for example, voters elected their governor. Pennsylvania's legislature was composed of only a single house.

Some similarities between colonial governments and their English model

with a warrant issued by a judge. English subjects could also count on a trial by jury if accused of a crime. Moreover, they were accorded equal protection under the law; there was one law for both lord and commoner. Nor was the average Englishman entirely without power in governing the realm. Even though few could vote, the English constitution recognized the representative principle that lawmakers derived their powers, if only indirectly, from those who were expected to obey the laws they imposed. To most English people, whether in Britain or America, this system seemed freer and more liberal than any other in Europe, and they took pride in their political heritage.

Colonial Political Structure. British immigrants to America brought with them the political ideas, customs, and practices of the mother country. On the local level, for example, both the town in new England and the church vestry in the South were political units transplanted from England. The colonial sheriff and justice of the peace were like the same officials in England, and there was an obvious parallel between Parliament and the colonial legislatures. Beginning with Virginia in 1619, settlers were empowered to set up legislatures in each of the British mainland colonies. These were given different names in different colonies (General Court, House of Burgesses, General Assembly), but they served the colonies much as Parliament served England. And like Parliament, most

colonial legislatures had a lower house and an upper house.

Each colony also had a chief executive, the equivalent of the crown. In royal colonies (in 1776, New Hampshire, Massachusetts, New York, New Jersey, Maryland, Virginia, North Carolina, South Carolina, and Georgia) the governor was appointed by the British sovereign. When the royal governor—or more likely his deputy, the lieutenant governor—came to America, he represented the royal power. In proprietary colonies (Pennsylvania and Delaware, and New York, Maryland, and the Carolinas before they became royal colonies) the governor represented the proprietor, the man who held the original charter. Only in Connecticut and Rhode Island was the governor elected by the local enfranchised citizens. No matter how he was chosen, the governor usually could veto acts by the legislature, much as, in theory at least, the English sovereign could veto acts of Parliament.

As time went by, the governors were forced to give up some of their power to the legislatures. At first British authorities refused to consider these bodies true legislatures. One British official described them as only "so many Corporations at a distance, invested with an Ability to make Temporary By Laws for themselves." But in time, encouraged by the growing colonial population, the distance from England, the official British policy of ignoring restrictions on the colonies to allow them

Colonial Williamsburg Foundation

This handsome Georgian structure is an exact reproduction of the Virginia colonial capital at Williamsburg.

to prosper and thus enrich England, and British inefficiency in administering colonial affairs, the colonial legislatures expanded their powers. Early in the eighteenth century the colonial lower houses forced the governors to allow them to debate freely without executive interference, to judge the qualifications of their own members, to exclude crown officials from their deliberations, and to meet when and for as long as they wished. Most important, they forced the governors to surrender to them "the power of the purse."

Gaining the right to control the purse strings required a long battle. When representative government was first established in the colonies, governors received an annual lump-sum appropriation from the legislature. The governors disbursed these funds as they saw fit. This system gave them the power to pursue policies without any check by the legislature. By the middle of the eighteenth

century, however, the assemblies had stopped the lump-sum grants; instead they earmarked appropriations for specific periods. They also began to pay the governors' salaries for a single year—and only at the end of it—to guarantee their good behavior. In several colonies these efforts to control the governors touched off furious battles. By the 1750s most of these struggles had been decided in favor of the legislatures.

By the end of the colonial era the provincial assemblies were miniature paraliaments exercising almost all the hard-won rights of their English model. These rights included control over taxation, expenditures, the salaries of officials, military and Indian affairs, and everything that affected religion, education, and what we today would call welfare. The legislatures' power was not unlimited, however. Governors continued to veto laws they opposed. And even if the governor approved a measure, it could be "disallowed" by the Privy Council in England. Especially during the early years of the eighteenth century, however, the English government did little to restrain the colonial assemblies, and during this period of "salutary neglect" much real political power slipped into the hands of the colonists.

Voters and Their Representatives. Although the framework of the colonial governments was similar to that of Great Britain, political power was more widely diffused in the colonies than in Britain. The upper houses of the colonial legislatures, the councils, were appointed and were composed of landed gentlemen, prosperous lawyers, and rich merchants. But membership was not hereditary, as it was in the English House of Lords.

More significant was the broad electorate that chose the colonial lower houses. By modern standards the colonial franchise was severely limited. Slaves, of course, could not vote, nor could indentured servants. At times some women exercised considerable public authority. For example, in the seventeenth century "Mistresse Margarett Brent, Spinster" ran her own plantation and, as executor of the estate of Leonard Calvert, proprietor of Maryland, virtually ruled that colony's affairs. But neither Margarett Brent nor any other colonial female had the right to vote. Even free white adult males had to own land or buildings, or lease them for a long period, to qualify as voters. This was only one side of the picture, however. Property was so easily acquired and so widely held in America that the laws disqualified relatively few free adult males from voting. Furthermore, traditional requirements linking church membership to voting privileges were undermined by the growing diversity of religions in America. The end result was a relatively broad franchise. In various Rhode Island towns in the mid-eighteenth century, for example, 60 percent or more of the total adult male population was eligible to vote. In some New York districts up to 80 percent of all adult males had the vote. In Massachusetts, according to Governor Thomas Hutchinson, "anything with the appearance of a man" was allowed to vote.

Though many ordinary people could vote, colonial officials were not carbon copies of the colonial population. Members of the colonial assemblies were richer, better educated, and of higher status than their constituents. Colonial voters generally preferred to send the local squire, a prosperous merchant, or a rising young lawyer to the House of Burgesses or House of Assembly rather than a farmer, craftsman, or shopkeeper. Local officials were also members of the elite. Southern vestries appointed their own successors and were dominated by the "squirearchy" of rich planters, who resembled the country gentry of England. Nor was the town, the basic governmental unit in New England, entirely democratic. Virtually all adult males participated in the town meeting, but town leaders were generally men of high status.

On the other hand, political deference—submission to social superiors—was decidedly weaker in America than in England. When the local squire ran for office, he had to campaign hard and promise to abide by the wishes of the voters. Candidates were expected to act democratically and avoid aloofness. During election campaigns they made it a point to mingle with the electors and offer them "refreshment," liquid or otherwise. When Colonel George Washington of Farifax County, Virginia, ran for the House of Burgesses in 1774, he provided the "Freeholders and Gentlemen" of Alexandria with a "Hogshead of Toddy." After the returns were in, he threw a victory party for the voters that was "conducted with great harmony."

Nor did representatives, once elected, forget their constituents. Colonial legislatures and governments were surprisingly responsive to the will of the citizens. By 1705, for example, the Virginia legislature had acquired a Propositions and Grievances Committee that regularly received public petitions proposing new laws. The committee would pass along the worthiest suggestions to the House of Burgesses, which then could act as it saw fit. Historians Robert and Katherine Brown have declared that "nothing in our legislative system today approximates the direct influence which the people of colonial Virginia could exert on their legislature."

We must conclude that colonial government was neither predominantly democratic nor predominantly aristocratic; it displayed both tendencies. Democracy as we know it did not exist anywhere in the seventeenth- and eighteenth-century world. But as political institutions were transferred from England to America, they were changed in ways that allowed greater popular freedom and self-determination.

RELIGION

Another institution that changed in the New World was organized religion. White settlers brought with them a great variety of faiths—Presbyterian, Quaker, Baptist, Anglican, Jewish, Lutheran, Mennonite, Catholic, and others. Before long, under the special conditions in America, the practices of many of these groups began to diverge from their European forms.

Guarding the Flame in New England. Religious change in southern New England is particularly well documented and instructive. The Puritans who immigrated to Massachusetts did not come to found a separate church. Rather, they came to escape the influence of a powerful state and the Anglican bishops. But once free of these restraints, they created the New England Way, a distinctive pattern that differed from both the Puritanism and the Anglicanism of Old England.

One of the differences involved church structure. In the Old World bishops or a council of church elders (presbyters) ruled the church. But in America the sparseness of the white population and the relative isolation of settlements encouraged church government by individual self-governing congregations. Each group of Christians, led by their ministers, developed, in the words of the Reverend John Cotton, "complete liberty to stand alone." This system was called Congregationalism.

The New England Way also changed Puritan doctrine. At the heart of the Puritan faith was the Calvinist notion that all people since Adam's fall were depraved and deserved damnation. Only a few—the "elect" or "saints"—would be saved from hell. European Puritans believed that this salvation was totally beyond the individual's control; the elect were chosen, or "predestined," long ago. But in New England the alternate idea of the "covenant" appeared: people could effect their salvation by entering into a kind of contract with God by which he would agree to guarantee them the faith needed for salvation. Thus saints were not predestined but "reborn," or converted.

These saints, the Puritans believed, would not only behave well outwardly, but would also avoid wicked thoughts. Their faith thus placed a tremendous moral and emotional burden on the New England Puritans. Some became tortured souls obsessed with a sense of their own sinfulness. Michael Wigglesworth, a minister at Malden, kept a diary between 1653 and 1670 in which he constantly lamented his depravity. A typical entry noted:

> Peevishness, vain thoughts, and especially pride still prevail in me. I cannot think one good thought; I cannot do any thing for God but presently pride gets hold of me. . . . I find my heart prone to take secret pleasure in thinking how much I do for others' good: but Lord how little is done for thee. I fear there is much sensuality and doting upon the creature in my pursuit of the good of others.

New England Puritans were concerned with their neighbors' salvation as well as their own. In order to shape people's lives in accordance with God's will, they closely linked the church with the colony's government. All were expected to attend services and pay taxes to support the Congregational ministry, regardless of their religious preference. But not all church attenders were church members: only those who had experienced conversion could belong to the church. And only converted males could vote or hold office, although everyone was expected to obey the laws. Massachusetts was, in a word, a little theocracy, a community where God was considered the ruler and his will was expressed through the church leaders. Some ministers held office; those who did not advised the secular rulers, and were consulted in all matters that pertained to public life and community policy. Questions that we today would consider matters of personal preference were treated as public issues subject to law. Sexual behavior in all its aspects fell under close public control; so did family concerns, such as children's disobedience. Blasphemy was a serious crime, as was breaking the Sabbath. Public education was intended not only to transmit skills and secular culture but also to imbue religious principles.

For a time it seemed possible to establish in Massachusetts a truly godly community—"a Citty upon a Hill"—where holiness might guide every aspect of life and people might be free of the corruptions of England. In the early days of settlement, when religious enthusiasm was high, young men and women could expect as a matter of course to have the required conversion experience, to demonstrate to the elders of the congregation "the worke of grace upon their soules," and to be admitted to the religious community as full equals. But as time passed, New Englanders increasingly turned to worldly affairs and shifted their attention from God to gain. By the middle of the seventeenth century the pious Puritan was already giving way to the get-ahead, enterprising Yankee. Before long many children of church members, to the chagrin of their parents, failed to experience conversion and so could not be admitted to church membership. This shrinking of the elect left many people without civil rights and threatened the churches with much-diminished membership.

In 1662 a group of ministers met in Boston to tackle the difficult problem. Their answer was the Half-Way Covenant, which provided that persons who had been baptized and who led virtuous lives could become church members. No conversion experience was necessary. These people could not participate in the Lord's Supper, one of the few sacraments remaining in Calvinism, but they were no longer disqualified from normal civil rights.

The new policy eased the crisis, but it did not check the erosion of orthodoxy in the Puritan colony. Some historians have connected the notorious Salem witchcraft trials of 1692, during which more than twenty persons were put to death, with this Puritan decline. Although belief in witches was widespread, this particular outbreak was almost a community hysteria. It may have been fanned by the earnest efforts of the Puritan clergy, including the Reverend Cotton Mather, to raise a new fear of sin and thus to return to the orthodox church.

The High Church in the Wilderness.

The American environment affected other denominations as well. In the Anglican communities on the Chesapeake local circumstances wore down traditional religion even more than in New England. With its elaborate ceremonies and complex organization, the Anglican Church was less suited to the wilderness than the Puritan Church. The distance between settlements and plantations in the Chesapeake area and the absence of cities and towns made it hard to practice Old World Anglicanism.

It was especially difficult to maintain the traditional governance of the church. In England bishops ruled the Anglican Church, but no bishop came to America during the colonial period. Low salaries, isolation from the amenities of civilization, and the absence of substantial towns made English Anglican ministers reluctant to accept duties in America. And with no bishop in the colonies, young Americans had to travel to England for ordination. Since few were willing to make the voyage, many parishes were forced to do without an ordained spiritual leader or to accept an inferior one. The net effect was that in Virginia, Maryland, and elsewhere the Church of England moved toward a congregational system, placing control of religious matters in the hands of the vestry, the ruling lay group of the parish.

The lack of long-accumulated wealth and the scattered settlement pattern also made it hard for Anglicanism to reproduce the rituals and ceremonies of the homeland. Increasingly, the American Anglican Church simplified its forms and dogmas. A Virginia planter expressed the religious preferences of many colonial Anglicans in 1720: "The high-flown up-top notions and the great stress that is laid upon ceremonies . . . are what I cannot come into the reason of. Practical godliness is the substance—these are but the shell."

Though Puritans and Anglicans tacked to the changing winds of America, they both suffered losses. Nor were they the only troubled religious bodies. By the beginning of the eighteenth century most of the transplanted European denominations were losing ground. On the frontiers of New York, New Jersey, and Pennsylvania the German Lutherans and Pietists and the Scotch-Irish Presbyterians were slow to form congregations. In eastern Pennsylvania, as the Quaker community grew richer, its members supplanted piety with worldliness.

The Great Awakening.

The general decline of orthodoxy created a vacuum in the lives of many people. Especially among farmers, craftspeople, and other ordinary men and women, religion seemed increasingly remote and unsatisfying. This attitude eventually triggered a religious resurgence that we call the Great Awakening.

The movement began in the 1720s as a series of revivals among the Presbyterians and Dutch Reformed groups in the middle colonies. During the next decade it was infused with new power by the Congregational minister Jonathan Edwards of Northampton, Massachusetts. Edwards, a Yale graduate, was appalled by the decline of orthodoxy that he observed all around him, and he resolved to do something about it. In 1729 he began to preach the old Calvinist doctrine of predestination, calling people back to God and threatening them with eternal damnation for their sins. Edwards's theology, was old-fashioned, but his emotional style was new, and his sermons shocked the traditionalists, who considered them unseemly. Ordinary people, however, flocked to hear him preach at his Northampton church. Before long preachers throughout New England were emulating Edwards's hellfire-and-damnation sermons.

In 1738 the English preacher George Whitefield visited America and turned the Great Awakening into a religious event of continental proportions. Unlike the Calvinist Edwards, Whitefield, borrowing from John Wesley, the English preacher who founded Methodism, believed that sinners might earn their salvation and that God did not confine his grace to a small elect. Whitefield was a spellbinder. Of one group of young women who came to hear him, Whitefield himself wrote: "A wonderful power was in the room, and with one accord they began to cry out and weep most bitterly for the space of half an hour. . . . Five of them seemed affected as those that are in

Library of Congress

This benign-looking man is Jonathan Edwards, the fire-and-brimstone preacher of the colonial Great Awakening.

tions. Within these churches congregations and clergy soon divided between those who followed the formal old way—the Old Lights—and those who followed the emotional new way—the New Lights. Many more people flocked to newer denominations such as the Baptists and later the Methodists. Thus, by producing new sects and dividing congregations and ministers, the Great Awakening further diversified religious expression in America.

The Enlightenment. The Great Awakening lured many ordinary people back into the traditional religious fold. But by the middle of the eighteenth century many educated people in America were turning not to religion but to a new set of beliefs known to us as the Enlightenment.

This major alteration in the way Western thinkers perceived the world was rooted in the scientific revelations of the day, especially in the ideas of Sir Isaac Newton. In the new view the world appeared a rational, orderly place, operating not according to the immediate will of God but by changeless natural laws. Several important

With religious centers across the sea and ministers in short supply, orthodox religion in America suffered. The Great Awakening—a spiritual revival led by George Whitefield—brought new fervor. Unstructured, emotional, and free from elaborate ceremony, revivalism fit America's simpler needs.

Library of Congress

fits. . . ." Benjamin Franklin, skeptical of organized religion in general and of Whitefield's appeals for money to found an American orphanage in particular, went to hear the preacher, but was resolved not to contribute to his cause. "I had in my pocket, a handful of copper money, three or four silver dollars, and five pistoles in gold," Franklin later wrote. "As he proceeded I began to soften, and concluded to give the copper; another stroke of his oratory determined me to give the silver; and he finished so admirably that I emptied my pocket wholly into the collector's dish, gold and all."

The doctrines of the revivalists varied, but most of their followers perceived their passionate appeal for surrender to Jesus and a commitment to live an exemplary Christian life rather than their theology. Whitefield, Edwards, and the other revivalists presented these views so simply and with such emotional effect that thousands were brought back to religion. Attacked by educated people as "shouters," "enthusiasts," and disturbers of the peace, the revivalists of the Great Awakening were immensely successful among common people. Many joined, or rejoined, the older denomina-

Sinners and an Angry God

Jonathan Edwards became his grandfather's assistant as minister at the Northampton Congregational Church in 1726. There he continued the Reverend Stoddard's vivid preaching and helped to launch the Great Awakening.

Edwards was a throwback to the early days of Calvinism when preachers proclaimed the infinite majesty of the Lord and the limitless sinfulness of humankind. Only by surrendering themselves to God's mercy and preparing to accept grace could men and women be saved, and even then few would attain the kingdom of heaven. Edwards's passion and vivid imagery, always impressive, were given a new intensity by his contact with the English preacher George Whitefield during his visit to America in the 1740s. Edwards's famous *Sinners in the Hands of an Angry God* (1741) is the classic expression of the "fire-and-brimstone" sermon, designed to put the fear of God into his congregation. It helped confirm his reputation as the most powerful revivalist in the English colonies.

"The God that holds you over the pit of hell, much as one holds a spider, or some loathsome insect, over the fire, abhors you and is dreadfully provoked; His wrath towards you burns like fire; He looks upon you as worthy of nothing else, but to be cast into the fire; He is of purer eyes than to bear to have you in His sight; you are ten thousand times more abominable in His eyes, as the most hateful and venomous serpent is in ours. You have offended him infinitely more than ever a stubborn rebel did his prince. And yet, it is nothing but His hand that holds you from falling into the fire every moment. . . .

"O sinner! consider the fearful danger you are in: it is a great furnace of wrath, a wide and bottomless pit, full of the fire of wrath, that you are held over in the hand of that God, whose wrath is provoked and incensed as much against you, as against many of the damned in hell. You hang by a slender thread, with the flames of divine wrath flashing about it, and ready every moment to singe it, and burn it asunder; and you have no . . . Mediator, and nothing to lay hold of to save yourself, nothing to keep off the flames of wrath, nothing of your own, nothing you have ever done, nothing that you can do, to induce God to spare you one moment. . . .

"Thus it will be with you that are in an unconverted state, if you continue in it; the infinite might and majesty, and terribleness, of the omnipotent God shall be magnified upon you. . . . You shall be tormented in the presence of the holy angels, and in the presence of the Lamb; and when you shall be in the state of suffering, the glorious inhabitants of heaven shall go forth and look on the awful spectacle, that they may see what the wrath and the fierceness of the Almighty is; and when they have seen it, they will fall down and adore that great power and majesty. . . ."

ideas followed from this view: first, that as members of this rational universe, human beings were good, not sinful; second, that by use of their reason, human beings could discover the natural laws of the universe; third, that knowledge of these laws would enable people to control their environment and society; and finally, that the inevitable result of this control would be progress over the course of human history. Science played a significant role in this world picture because it was by means of scientific method—observation and experiment—that natural laws could be discovered.

A few members of the "enlightened" generation rejected all religion and became agnostics or atheists. Most, however, chose deism. Deists continued to believe in God, but theirs was a god who operated through natural laws, not miracles. He revealed himself through nature, not Christian revelation. God's role in the world was much like that of a clockmaker—who makes a clock, winds it up, and then leaves it to work by its own mechanism.

Deism developed late in the colonial period, and it affected only a small group of Americans. They were, however, an influential group—including Benjamin Franklin, Thomas Jefferson, Ethan Allen, and Thomas Paine—who would have effects disproportionate to their numbers.

As Old Lights battled New Lights, Calvinists fought Methodists, and deists grappled with the orthodox, it became increasingly difficult to impose any sort of religious conformity on America. The multitude of colonists belonging to no church and the increasing variety of sects limited efforts to favor one religious group over the others. In the end the babel of conflicting religious voices undermined the established churches and led to greater toleration for a multitude of sects, though this development did not occur until the very end of the colonial period.

INTELLECTUAL AMERICA

The conditions of colonial America that led to the modification of the social, political, and religious institutions transplanted from Europe also molded science, education, and the professions that depended on them. For better or worse, intellectual

An Historical Portrait   Benjamin Franklin

Benjamin Franklin was the first self-made American. When Ben was born in 1706, his father, Josiah, was a candlemaker and soap manufacturer with premises on Milk Street in Boston. Like most of his forebears, Ben was destined for a leather apron, not a silk waistcoat; at the age of twelve he was apprenticed to his older brother, James, who ran a print shop in the New England capital. Though he became an intellectual celebrity, a major political leader, and a favorite of royalty, Franklin never forgot his origins in the sober, hard-working American lower middle class.

Ben and his brother did not get along, yet the lad profited by his work in the print shop. James was not only a job printer, he was also publisher of one of America's earliest newspapers, *The New England Courant.* This was a single-sheet weekly, like the handful of other colonial newspapers, but it afforded ample scope for young Ben's talents and energies. In the intervals between setting type, sweeping the floor, and running errands, he had time to make up for the deficiencies in his formal education. Ben read widely in the ancient classics in translation, as well as in the best of contemporary English prose. He also learned to write with skill, and at sixteen composed a series of humorous articles for the *Courant*

under a pseudonym. In later years he taught himself mathematics, Greek, Latin, and several modern languages, but he never lost the straightforward, unpretentious quality of the self-taught individual.

In 1723, following months of squabbling with James, Ben left Boston to seek his fortune as a printer elsewhere. He went first to New York, but when he could find no work there, he moved on to Philadelphia. The young man of seventeen arrived in a town of 10,000, a community smaller than Boston, but one that was growing faster and was more open to the talented go-getter. During the remainder of his long life Franklin would spend extended periods abroad, in London and then in Paris, but practical, tolerant Philadelphia left an indelible impression on him and provided the base for all his later success. Here he established his own newspaper, *The Pennsylvania Gazette,* and made his fortune as editor, pamphlet and almanac publisher, bookseller, and paper maker. Here he achieved international fame as "Poor Richard," a fictional old man whose lips spouted wise maxims and proverbs. Here he married Deborah Read Rogers, a young woman whose aid in the printshop-bookstore was an essential part of his financial success. Finally, the City

of Brotherly Love provided the setting for Franklin's extraordinary and wide-ranging intellectual activities.

Franklin was a philosopher, a scientist, and an inventor. In London, while on a visit to buy a press and type for his paper, he picked up the fashionable Deism of the day. He later wrote several pamphlets and articles defending the idea of a scientist-God who made "the glorious sun, with its attending worlds . . . and prescribed the wondrous laws, by which they move." But he gave him, characteristically, a practical twist. Franklin's God was not remote and aloof. He was a benevolent being who delighted in virtue and frowned on vice.

All knowledge interested Franklin. He was fascinated by the expanding world of contemporary science. He could not crack the mathematical complexities of Sir Isaac Newton's revolutionary work on gravity and planetary motion, but he was adept at empirical science. His famous kite experiments proved that lightning was a form of the mysterious "electrical fluid" and made Franklin a celebrity. Colleges and universities hastened to confer honorary degrees on the Philadelphian. Thereafter Franklin was universally addressed as "Doctor."

Franklin's intellectual labors

development in America lagged behind or diverged from the Old World experience.

Science. The seventeenth century was an era of immense progress in the natural sciences. It was the time when Galileo first used the telescope to observe the solar system, William Harvey detected the circulation of the blood, Johannes Kepler formulated the laws governing the orbits of the planets, and Isaac Newton discovered the basic laws of motion and the role of gravity. These scientists were all Europeans, however; the colonists made few contributions to basic scientific theory.

Neither the social nor the physical environment encouraged theoretical science in colonial America. Living in a near-wilderness, the colonists tended to be interested in practical, not theo-

retical, matters. Moreover, even at the very end of the colonial era the scaffolding necessary for a flourishing scientific enterprise was absent. Theoretical science requires laboratories, patronage, centers of learning, and stimulating discussion among many scientists and other thinkers. Colonial America—lacking large accumulations of wealth, inhabited by a sparse and scattered population, and far from the intellectual centers of the Western world—was not a likely birthplace for a Harvey, a Galileo, a Kepler, or a Newton. Twenty-five Americans were elected to the prestigious British scientific body known as the Royal Society of London before 1776, but they were honored for their acute observations of natural phenomena, not for grand theories or major intellectual breakthroughs.

Only one colonial scientist deserves compar-

were characteristically American. Even his most theoretical scientific work had a practical side. One important outcome of the kite experiment was the lightning rod to protect buildings in electrical storms. Besides this useful device, Dr. Franklin invented the fuel-efficient stove that bears his name and bifocal eyeglasses.

Franklin also carved out a distinguished career as a public servant. He served as a member of the Pennsylvania Assembly, as a delegate to the 1754 Albany Congress, as Pennsylvania's "agent" in London, and as joint deputy postmaster general in North America. As the strains between the American colonies and the British Empire grew during the 1760s and 1770s, he emerged as a leading "patriot" who supported increased autonomy for America and opposed Britain's drive to tighten imperial controls. Most of his work for his countrymen he performed abroad. Between 1766 and 1775 he served in effect as ambassador and chief lobbyist of the American colonies in London. Franklin returned to America in 1775 in time for the dramatic final crisis that led to independence and served on the committee of Congress that drafted the Declaration of Independence. In late 1776 he went to France as one of the three commissioners of the new United States

to negotiate a treaty of alliance that would offset powerful Britain in the fierce struggle now under way.

His work in France proved invaluable. He was more than the official United States envoy. Franklin fulfilled a fantasy about the "natural man" then in vogue among Europe's educated classes, and the French saw him as the very essence of the new American man, simple in dress and manner, practical yet learned, tolerant and industrious, and free of the Old World's corruptions. In all but possibly the last they were correct. Though there was a conscious element of guile and self-advertisement in Franklin, he was a blunt, pragmatic, unpretentious man. But he was also a man of strong appetites. His marriage to Deborah, with its long separations, did not meet his romantic needs. In France the American ambassador was especially popular among the ladies, and Abigail Adams, on a visit to the Franklin residence at Passy near Paris, was shocked by the free manners and the frankness of speech she encountered. Fortunately for Franklin and the United States, his gallantry only made him more popular with the French.

Franklin, of course, had more important things to do in France than please the ladies. While there he negotiated the Franco-American

Alliance of 1778 and the accompanying commercial treaty. In 1783 he, John Jay, and John Adams negotiated the peace treaty with Britain that ended the war and confirmed American independence.

In July 1785 Franklin left France for America, having been away from his native land for still another decade. He arrived in Philadelphia to be greeted by pealing bells and roaring cannon. Soon after, he was elected president of the Pennsylvania Executive Council under the state's novel new constitution.

The last important role of his career was as Pennsylvania delegate to the Constitutional Convention in Philadelphia. He had not been among those who deplored the country's state during the immediate postindependence period, but he approved the convention's results and wrote in favor of his state's ratification of the Constitution. His last public act, at the age of eighty-four, was to sign, as head of the Pennsylvania Society for Promoting the Abolition of Slavery, a petition to end human bondage in the United States. To the end Franklin remained enlisted in the party of humanity and enlightenment.

ison with the best of Europe: Benjamin Franklin. Franklin's experiments with electricity in the 1740s and 1750s greatly contributed to an early understanding of that phenomenon, and won him an honorary doctorate from a European university. Yet among the practical Americans "Doctor" Franklin was largely famous for his invention of the lightning rod to protect buildings and for the efficient parlor stove that bears his name.

Education. In America, education also took on a distinctive cast. At the lower levels American education was advanced for its day. Primary schools, staffed by both men and women, existed in every colony, but educational opportunities varied greatly. More boys than girls attended schools, a fact reflected in the higher literacy rate of colonial men. Slaves were excluded, though a few learned

to read and write. There were also strong regional inequalities in access to education. Because of the scattered settlement pattern in the southern colonies, it was hard to bring together a concentration of pupils sufficient to support a local school. Rich planters hired private tutors for their sons and daughters, and occasionally these tutors also instructed the sons and daughters of the planter's poorer neighbors. But educational opportunities in the southern colonies were generally limited, especially for the children of common farmers.

The more densely settled northern colonies, particularly New England, did better by their young people. The Dutch Calvinists in New Netherland were quick to establish schools supported by the colonial treasury. Still more conscientious were the Massachusetts Puritans, who believed that it was essential to salvation for individuals to

National Portrait Gallery, Smithsonian Institution

Benjamin Franklin in a characteristic—and carefully cultivated—informal pose.

be able to read and understand the Scriptures for themselves. In 1647 the Massachusetts General Court required each town in the province with fifty families to establish a "petty" school to teach children to read and write. Any town with at least a hundred households was also required to establish a "grammar" school to prepare students for the university and the learned professions. The purpose of the law, the legislators noted, was to defeat "ye ould deluder, Satan"; but its most important effect was to create in New England a body of literate people probably unique among contemporary Western communities.

Educated Americans kept in touch with European thought through books and journals, and some tried to nurture higher education even in the crude early settlements. In 1636, just six years after the Puritans settled Massachusetts, Bay Colony authorities established Harvard College in Cambridge, because the Puritans considered a literate, educated ministry vital to religion. At first the curriculum consisted primarily of humanistic studies and theology, but gradually it expanded to include "natural philosophy," or as we would say, science.

Massachusetts's example was soon followed by other colonies. By the time of the Revolution

eight other institutions of higher learning had been established: the College of William and Mary (1693); Yale (1701); the College of New Jersey, later called Princeton (1746); Queen's College, later called Rutgers (1766); King's College, later called Columbia (1754); the College of Philadelphia, later the University of Pennsylvania (1754); Rhode Island College, later called Brown University (1764); and Dartmouth (1769).

Like Harvard, these colleges were sponsored by religious denominations. They emphasized religion and the classics and turned out men with "liberal" educations who either became clergymen or, after further training, entered one of the other traditional learned professions—law or medicine. But at least one college took a different turn. Under the influence of Benjamin Franklin, Philadelphia's most prominent citizen, the College of Philadelphia devoted a third of its curriculum to mathematics and the natural sciences. Even this course of study differed greatly from the practical curriculum of a modern American university; but under Franklin's auspices, the first step toward higher education to advance the practical arts was taken.

Law and Medicine. Colonial conditions molded professional education, too. In England members of the legal profession endured a long and elaborate training process at the old and respected Inns of Court. English lawyers included barristers to plead cases, attorneys to start the legal machinery going, solicitors to offer legal advice, and notaries to prepare legal documents. The structure resembled England's class system: an elite at top with lesser folk beneath.

The struggling colonists could not support this elaborate and expensive system. At first there were no lawyers in the colonies except for a few who had been trained in England; when a legal profession did appear, its structure was much simpler than in England. There was only one all-purpose attorney, who drew up documents and briefs, advised clients, and pleaded cases before the courts. Instead of attending laws schools like the English Inns of Court, lawyers learned by working in law offices, reading standard law books, such as Sir William Blackstone's *Commentaries on the Laws of England* and Sir Edward Coke's *Reports,* attending court, and performing minor legal chores for senior attorneys.

Toward the end of the colonial period, however, the legal profession drew closer to its English model. Some Americans began to go to London for legal training. But despite America's growing exposure to English forms, the English

Library of Congress

Harvard College in the mid-eighteenth century, a century after its founding.

legal structure remained too cumbersome for America, with its weaker system of higher education and its more open class structure.

A similar simplification took place in the colonial medical profession. Despite scientific advances in medicine in seventeenth-century Europe, medical men still enthusiastically embraced theories of disease expounded by ancient or medieval authorities. These theories usually ascribed disease to some imbalance in the four "humors"—choler, blood, bile, and phlegm. The physician's task was to diagnose the nature of the imbalance and restore equilibrium—often, as it happened, with harsh and ineffective remedies. Fortunately for Americans, the European physicians' learned ignorance could not be transplanted easily to North America. In Europe doctors trained at the universities. Few cared to surrender the high fees and status they enjoyed in Europe to come to the American wilderness, nor did American colleges teach medicine until the eve of the Revolution. Moreover, the exotic drugs and preparations used by European doctors were hard to duplicate in America.

The dilution of European practices in the colonies probably improved medical care. Colonial medical practitioners, like colonial legal practitioners, learned by apprenticeship and from day-to-day contact with patients. Without mistaken theories to lead them astray, doctors relied on experience, observation, and common sense. Instead of purges, poultices, bleeding, and the foul potions prescribed in Europe, they turned to local herbs, often ones recommended by the Indians, for cures. Even when these did no good, they generally did no serious harm.

American medicine was also structured more democratically than European medicine. The shortage of trained personnel created opportunities for people who could not have practiced in England. Many medical practitioners in the colonies were women, and a number of slaves and free blacks were respected for their medical knowledge. Cotton Mather, who became a crusader for smallpox vaccination over the objections of European-trained physicians, first learned about the procedure from his slave Onesimus.

THE ARTS

In the fine arts Americans tended to copy European models. Educated Americans wrote essays in the style of the English authors Joseph Addison

Colonial farmers and businessmen craved practical information, and they made almanacs bestsellers. Wrote Nathaniel Low in 1786: "No book we read (except the Bible) is so much valued, and so serviceable to the community. Almanacs serve as clocks and watches for nine-tenths of mankind."

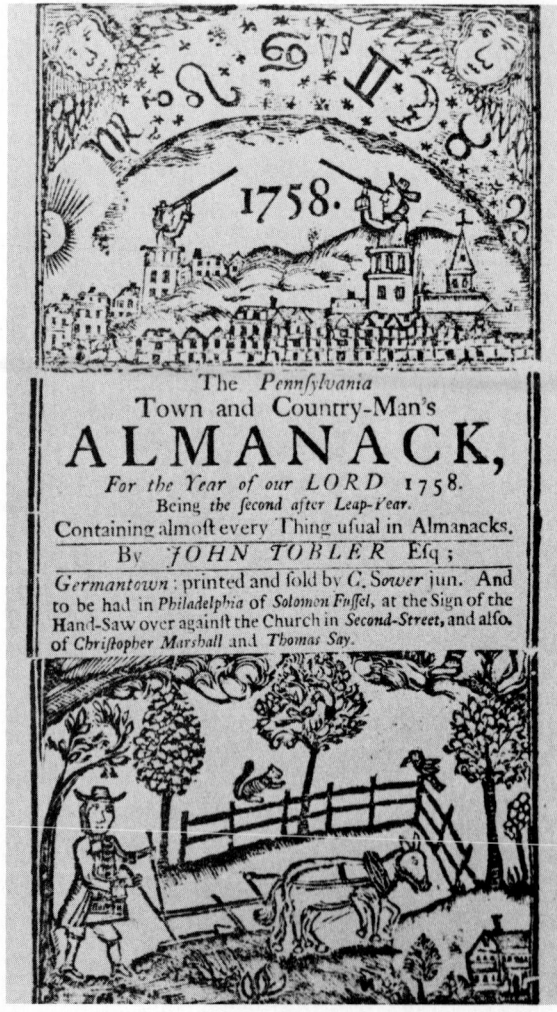

Library of Congress

and Sir Richard Steele and poetry in the manner of John Dryden and Alexander Pope. Their themes even resembled those of their English models, often dealing with genteel romance, gothic churches, ancient gods and goddesses.

But there were exceptions. One was Anne Bradstreet of Andover, Massachusetts, a talented and original poet—a "Tenth Muse lately sprung up in America," as her publisher called her. In 1630, at the age of eighteen, Bradstreet had come to the Bay Colony as a bride. Like many pioneer women, she had been dismayed by the frontier environment. But as was expected of colonial women, she accepted her fate. "I changed my condition and was marryed," she later wrote, "and came into this country, where I found a new world and new manners, at which my heart rose [that is, was stirred against it]. But after I was convinced it was the way of God, I submitted to it. . . ." During the next forty years, amid the cares and labors of raising eight children and attending to her busy husband, she wrote reams of verse. Her later work, with its unaffected language and faithful images of the American landscape, is the first authentic American poetry.

Although creative literature did not flourish in colonial America, newspapers, broadsides, pamphlets, instructional books, and almanacs were produced in abundance. The colonists read widely because they wanted practical information. Newspapers were read by proportionately more Americans than Europeans; they contained vital information about colonial affairs. Almanacs were useful to farmers and merchants, who had to know about prices and the weather. In the hands of Benjamin Franklin, the famous *Poor Richard's Almanack* came close to being a form of creative literature. Besides the usual data on planting times, seasonal changes, tides, eclipses, and the like, *Poor Richard's* contained entertaining little word sketches by "Richard Saunders" (Franklin's pseudonym) and pithy maxims that have become part of America's folk heritage. Americans also wrote and imported practical handbooks on medicine, navigation, agriculture, architecture, brick making, and other skills that could help them conquer a continent.

Music did not fare as well in colonial America. Colonial churchgoers, especially Puritan ones, enthusiastically sang the psalms. But as the European traditions receded, the colonists' music became so dreary and unmelodious that Cotton Mather, no great aesthete, labeled it "an odd noise." Folk songs that we still know, such as "Greensleeves" and "Barbara Allen," began as Elizabethan English folk music and were modified

New-York Historical Society

Americans made little distinction between artists and craftsmen until late in the colonial period, when the wealthy began to have their portraits painted. Before portraying the most distinguished of the Revolutionary War generation, Charles Wilson Peale, who painted his large family here, was a saddler and signpainter.

by American singers. But there were two important American composers before 1776: William Billings, a self-taught musician who composed "fuguing-tunes" for several voices singing different parts; and Francis Hopkinson, a talented Philadelphia composer of songs and instrumental pieces. (Hopkinson also painted, wrote poetry, and—contrary to the myth about Betsy Ross—designed the first American national flag.)

While Americans lagged behind Europeans in the fine arts, they poured their creative energies into the production of functional objects. Painting, for example, flourished in colonial America. Although we do not think of painting as a practical art, it had very practical ends in America before 1776. The only people wealthy enough to be art patrons were planters and merchants—self-made people who saw little value in art for art's sake. Portraits were the only paintings attractive to these patrons, for they were the equivalent of photographs. Rich men wanted to be remembered at the height of their prosperity and fame or wished to capture the likenesses of their wives and children.

The earliest American portrait painters were amateurish; but toward the very end of the colonial period, Boston and Philadelphia respectively produced John Singleton Copley and Benjamin West. Although Americans wanted and could afford talented portrait painters during the second century of settlement, the country was still too provincial to support and encourage the full range of such artists' talents. In 1760 West left for Rome and soon after settled in England. In 1775 Copley also went to England to expand his horizons.

At first American architecture was also primitive and limited. After a brief period when the settlers lived in lean-tos, dugouts, and tents, Americans began to imitate European building models. In New Amsterdam the Dutch settlers copied the urban structures of the Netherlands, buildings with high gabled ends and narrow sides to the street. Most seventeenth-century houses in Massachusetts resembled medieval English ones, replete with gables and small-paned leaded windows. Even the log cabin was a European borrowing, brought to the Delaware region in the seventeenth century by Swedes and Finns.

As time passed, American architecture became more original. The new style of the eighteenth century took its name—Queen Anne or Georgian—from the English monarchs in whose reigns it fully matured. With its regularly spaced rows of windows, white-trimmed brick, and fine detail at doors and openings, Georgian architecture was not strictly speaking a native genre at all. But it was adapted to American needs and circumstances in ways that frequently transcended mere imitation. The best of eighteenth-century colonial architecture blended admirably with the American environment; to this day Independence Hall in Philadelphia and domestic buildings like William Byrd's Virginia mansion, Westover, convey a sense of a vigorous provincial society that was evolving a distinctive cultural tradition.

A similar progression from imitation to innovation can be observed in the minor arts and the crafts. In the seventeenth century there were few skilled craftsmen in the colonies, and the settlers either used English artifacts or made their own crude ones. But by the eighteenth century many talented workers in brass, pewter, glass, silver, clay, and wood had immigrated to America from England and the Continent. Meanwhile, the skills of both white and black Americans had matured to a high level. Combining native inspiration with imported forms and designs in silver was the specialty of Paul Revere. At his glassworks at Mannheim, Pennsylvania, the German entrepreneur Henry William Stiegel produced glassware that is still eagerly collected. Skill and creativity marked the approach of colonial women to functional crafts, such as recycling bits of material into boldly designed quilts. Their work is now being recognized and appreciated as the expression of artistic sensitivities that transcended the drudgeries of primitive life in the New World.

CONCLUSIONS

Crèvecoeur was right. By the eve of the Revolution America was not a carbon copy of Europe, and Americans were not simply transplanted Europeans.

Several factors had contributed to the change. British North America included a mixture of racial and ethnic components unknown in Europe; even the European components of this mix were present in different proportions and existed in different relationships to each other than in the Old World. Americans were not Englishmen, though many were English immigrants or their descendants. In part, they were German, and exhibited a skill in agriculture still uncommon in Britain. They were also Scotch-Irish, and on the frontier revealed a sternness and militancy not typical of England. The Indian and African elements in the New World mixture were completely unknown to Europeans; yet they affected the military practice, technology, language, and customs of the new society.

In addition to the changes that accompanied the mingling of diverse cultures, there were those produced by the special physical and social environment of the New World. The abundance of land relative to the population made for better health, larger families, and ultimately a larger electorate and a more democratic political system. The relative scarcity of women allowed them some freedom to take on nontraditional roles and helped improve their legal status. A more scattered population and a less elitist social structure made it difficult to implant complex European institutions intact; as a result, the legal and medical professions were simplified and transformed. Meanwhile, the absence of a substantial leisure class, of great universities, and of private and government patronage altered the character of the arts and learning, pushing them toward greater practicality.

Nevertheless, we must qualify Crèvecoeur's announcement that a "new man" had arrived. Many of the distinct national and cultural groups existed side by side without blending. In the case of blacks and Indians, much of their potential contribution to the larger whole was deliberately excluded by the white European majority. It would take generations before a uniform new American mixture would emerge, and it is doubtful that the process has yet been—or ever will be— entirely completed. And finally, at the very end of the colonial era, there was a reversal in the process. As population grew and communication across the Atlantic improved, the initial accommodation to a primitive setting often gave way to a closer approximation to Western Europe. In religion, the professions, the arts, and political life American society had become a provincial offshoot of Britain's by the eve of the Revolution.

Yet the differences remained: America was not Europe; at most it was a close relative. And although American and English institutions had converged, the actual interests and values of Americans and Englishmen were beginning to draw apart. Before long, British-American differences would be out in the open. Eventually disagreement would become war.

FOR FURTHER READING

Daniel Boorstin. *The Americans: The Colonial Experience* (1958)

A bold attempt to demonstrate how the American environment altered transplanted Old World institutions and culture. Boorstin probably exaggerates the extent to which the transplants were changed by wilderness America, but along the way he makes many interesting points about colonial religion, language, the arts, and the professions.

John Demos. *A Little Commonwealth: Family Life in Plymouth Colony* (1970)

A fascinating study of family life in Plymouth Colony drawn from both the written records and the archeological evidence of surviving artifacts, houses, and utensils. Demos reconstructs the roles and relationships within the Pilgrim family and shows how the family influenced the individual development of its members.

Philip Greven. *Four Generations: Population, Land, and Family in Colonial Andover, Massachusetts* (1970); and *The Protestant Temperament* (1977)

The first of these two books is a demographic study of a seventeenth-century New England town that shows the remarkable longevity and prosperity of the early settlers and the gradual deterioration of both as population became excessive for the town's area. The second deals with child-rearing practices in America from 1600 to 1830. It makes the point that there were three types of families—pious, aristocratic, and in-between—largely associated with religious views. Difficult but interesting.

Kenneth Lockridge. *A New England Town, The First Hundred Years: Dedham, Massachusets, 1636–1736* (1970)

This is a brilliant study of one New England town during its first century. It deals with land, population, families, and social and political power. If you want to know how the early social unit of New England, the town, functioned, you must read this model study.

Carl Bridenbaugh. *Myths and Realities: Societies of the Colonial South* (1952)

Bridenbaugh maintains that the colonial South was not one but three distinct cultures: a Chesapeake society, a Carolina society, and the back settlements. A brief and readable treatment of the often neglected southern colonial heritage.

James T. Lemon. *The Best Poor Man's Country: A Geographical Study of Early Southwestern Pennsylvania* (1972)

Much broader than its title suggests, this is an interesting study of the interplay of the institutions and physical environment of early Pennsylvania. Written by a geographer, it is nonetheless an excellent social history. Makes the point about colonial Pennsylvania expressed in the title.

Peter Wood. *Black Majority* (1975)

This study of early South Carolina is by far the best treatment we have of colonial slavery. Wood believes that transplanted Africans contributed significantly to the culture and institutions of early southern society. In all likelihood, for example, it was they who introduced the cultivation of rice and the canoe.

Louis B. Wright, editor. *The Cultural Life of the American Colonies, 1607–1763* (1957)

This general survey of colonial cultural and intellectual history summarizes developments in religion, literature, education, science, architecture, theater, and music. Written with wit and admiration.

Henry F. May. *The Enlightenment in America* (1976)

Intellectual history at its best by a master of the field who left his usual period, the Gilded Age and Progressive era, to take a new look at the eighteenth and early nineteenth centuries. May sees the American Enlightenment as a complex three-part development, with the phase described in this chapter (the defense of balance and order) as the most characteristically American.

Charles Sydnor. *Gentlemen Freeholders: Political Practices in Washington's Virginia* (1952)

A brief reinterpretation of Virginia's colonial political life that emphasizes its "popular" features by contrast with the aristocratic ones given prominence by earlier authors.

Robert E. Brown and B. Katherine Brown. *Virginia 1705–1786: Democracy or Aristocracy?* (1964)

The Browns' answer to the question that they raise in their title is clear: Colonial Virginia was a remarkably democratic society in a political sense. Some scholars believe the Browns' position is overstated.

Robert E. Brown. *Middle-Class Democracy and the Revolution in Massachusetts, 1691–1780* (1955)

Massachusetts, Brown believes, was a middle-class democratic society by the eve of the Revolution and that it was the threat to the liberty of a people used to freedom that tripped off the anti-British defiance of the period 1763–75.

Jack P. Green. *The Quest for Power: The Lower Houses of Assembly in the Southern Royal Colonies, 1689–1763* (1963)

This scholarly study deals with the struggle of the southern provincial assemblies to become independent legislatures rather than rubber stamps of royal governors or Parliament. Green shows how much they had already achieved by the 1760s to make the American colonists a self-governing people.

Nathaniel Hawthorne. *The Scarlet Letter* (1850)

A classic of nineteenth-century American literature, *The Scarlet Letter* is an incomparable introduction to the gloomy, brooding, morbid side of Puritan New England. Hawthorne's great-grandfather, a judge at the Salem witch trials, was cursed by an old woman, one of those condemned to death.

4 Moving Toward Independence

Why Did the Colonists Revolt?

1651 England passes the first "navigation act" to prevent Dutch intrusion into the colonial trade

1688 The overthrow of James II begins the "Glorious Revolution" in England

1699 The Woolen Act • France establishes the settlement of "Louisiana" on the Gulf of Mexico

1721–48 The period of "salutary neglect"

1732 The Hat Act

1733 The Molasses Act

1750 The Iron Act

1754 Benjamin Franklin proposes the Albany Plan of Union to the colonies, but it is never adopted

1754–63 The French and Indian War: Colonists disobey England's ban on all trade with France and its colonies

War with France ends with the Treaty of Paris • Colonial settlement west of Appalachians prohibited by the Proclamation of **1763**

1764 The Sugar Act • The Currency Act

1765, 1766 The Quartering Acts

1765 The Stamp Act • The intercolonial Stamp Act Congress resolves that colonists should be taxed only by a representative legislature

1765–66 New York and other cities respond to the Stamp Act by adopting nonimportation agreements

1766 Parliament repeals the Stamp Act, but reaffirms with the Declaratory Act its right to legislate for the colonies

1767 The Townshend (or Revenue) Acts provoke another boycott of British goods

1770 Parliament repeals Townshend duties, except those on tea • The Boston Massacre

1773 The Tea Act threatens to undercut the colonial smuggling trade • East India Company tea is destroyed in the Boston Tea Party

1774 Boston harbor is closed by the Coercive (or Intolerable) Acts • The First Continental Congress attacks Britain's restrictions on colonial trade

1775 Armed confrontation at Lexington and Concord

Few events in American history are as fundamental as the great struggle that ended with independence in 1783. Yet the causes of this crucial upheaval have long been controversial. Thomas Jefferson believed that the British crown had fashioned "a deliberate, systematical plan of reducing us to slavery," and that this tyrannical scheme had spurred Americans to take the drastic step of declaring their freedom. Other participants in the events of 1763–76 blamed religion as much as politics for inciting the Revolution. John Adams recalled many years later that the British threat to establish Anglican bishops in America "spread a universal alarm against the authority of Parliament." Yet a third group of contemporaries, as well as later scholars, stressed economic oppression as the ultimate cause of strains in the imperial relationship. In 1766 two British customs officials in Rhode Island complained bitterly that the interests of "the Mother Country & this Colony" were "deemed by the People almost altogether incompatible, in a commercial View. . . ." Any official, they declared, who attempted to defend British trade policies would be "threatened as an Enemy to this Country . . . and Destruction must be inevitably his Doom. . . ." A hundred and seventy-five years later Louis Hacker declared that the "basic reason for the onset of crisis and the outbreak of revolutionary struggle" was the "economic vassalage" imposed on the colonies.

Which of these explanations is correct? Is each partly correct? Is one fundamental and the others secondary? Let us assess the third of these explanations, the economic one, first.

THE COLONIAL ECONOMY

What was the colonial economy like, and what were its strengths and weaknesses? Did British policy hinder or help it? Did Americans have valid economic grievances against the mother country?

Agriculture. Agriculture was the foundation of the colonial economy. It employed 90 percent of the working population and created most of the wealth produced. A majority of American farmers engaged in mixed agriculture—growing corn, rye, or wheat; raising cattle, sheep, and hogs; and planting fruit trees, potatoes, and vegetables. The farmer's family consumed most of these products; but except on the frontier, where distance and poor transportation isolated the farmer, there were usually some surpluses for sale in nearby towns and even to distant customers.

American farmers were not efficient by the best European standards. Except for the German settlers of Pennsylvania, the colonists impressed foreign visitors as slovenly and wasteful cultivators. They neglected both the fertility of the soil and their livestock, and seemed uninterested in new agricultural methods then being tried in Europe. The foreign observers were right, but there was a simple reason for this behavior: American farmers knew they could rely on the sheer abundance of fresh, fertile land to carry them through. Besides, better methods would require more labor, and labor, unlike land, was scarce and expensive. In later years many Americans would learn to regret this attitude, but it suited the circumstances of the day.

There were many regional differences in colonial agriculture. New England farmers faced such rocky soil almost everywhere except in the Connecticut Valley that it was said they planted corn by shooting seed into the ground with a gun. Few Yankee farmers could do more than provide for their own families and the small group of local townspeople who did not till the soil. Connecticut produced some livestock, grain, and dairy products for export, and Rhode Island raised horses for the Caribbean islands. But with these exceptions New England agriculture had only local importance.

In contrast, New York, New Jersey, and Pennsylvania were the "bread colonies," producing large surpluses of wheat from their fertile soils. This grain was converted to flour by grist-

A depiction of Martin van Bergen's eighteenth-century Hudson Valley farm. The Catskill Mountains are seen in the background.
New York State Historical Association, Cooperstown

mills run by water power, and then exported to the Caribbean or to southern Europe. In addition, the bread colonies exported potatoes, beef, pork, and other farm products.

The Chesapeake Bay region, which included the colonies of Virginia and Maryland, was the great tobacco-growing area. Since the seventeenth century tobacco cultivation had moved from the tidewater, where years of growing the soil-exhausting crop had reduced fertility, to the piedmont plateau, where the soils were fresher and more productive. The piedmont planters, however, had transportation problems. Located above the fall line, where the westward-flowing streams dropped sharply to the tidewater, they could not put their crop aboard ocean-going ships directly, as their tidewater counterparts could. Instead they sold their tobacco to local merchants, who packed the leaf into hogsheads and rolled them to towns like Richmond and Petersburg along the fall line. There they could be placed aboard vessels for shipment to foreign buyers.

Throughout the eighteenth century Chesapeake tobacco output increased at a fairly steady pace. By the 1770s Maryland and Virginia were shipping about 100 million pounds annually for the pipe smokers and snuff takers of England, Scotland, and continental Europe—tobacco worth £1 million, or perhaps $50 million in modern American terms.

Rice was the major crop of the South Carolina lowlands, though some was also grown in Georgia. A crop that required vast amounts of water as well as a long growing season, it was suited to the swampy coastal regions and proved highly profitable there. In 1700 South Carolina exported about 400,000 pounds. By 1770 the rice-growing colonies, with South Carolina far in the lead, exported almost 84 million pounds. England received a large part of the crop, but the sugar plantations of the Caribbean, the other mainland colonies, and southern Europe were also large buyers of American rice.

Along with rice, the lowland areas of South Carolina and Georgia produced indigo, a blue dye widely used for coloring woolen cloth. Indigo was introduced into South Carolina in the 1740s by Eliza Lucas, an enterprising young woman newly arrived from the Caribbean island of Antigua. Helped by a British government subsidy (bounty) of one shilling a pound, the production and export of indigo quickly leaped. Though never as important as rice, by 1770 almost 600,000 pounds of indigo valued at over £130,000 were being shipped from Charleston each year.

One other product of the southern mainland deserves mention: naval stores—that is, the pitch, tar, resin, and turpentine extracted from the pine trees of coastal North Carolina (and also New Hampshire). These items were essential for the shipping industry and Britain's dependence on the Baltic region for their supply made her vulnerable in time of war. To meet this danger British officials sought to encourage naval store production within the empire and in 1704 they began to offer a bounty for pitch, tar, and resin. The indus-

From the Rare Book Collection of the Perkins Library, Duke University

Black slaves producing blue dye from indigo, a cash crop in the coastal South. Roughly twenty percent of the population in 1775, slaves provided the basis for much of the prosperity enjoyed by the white population.

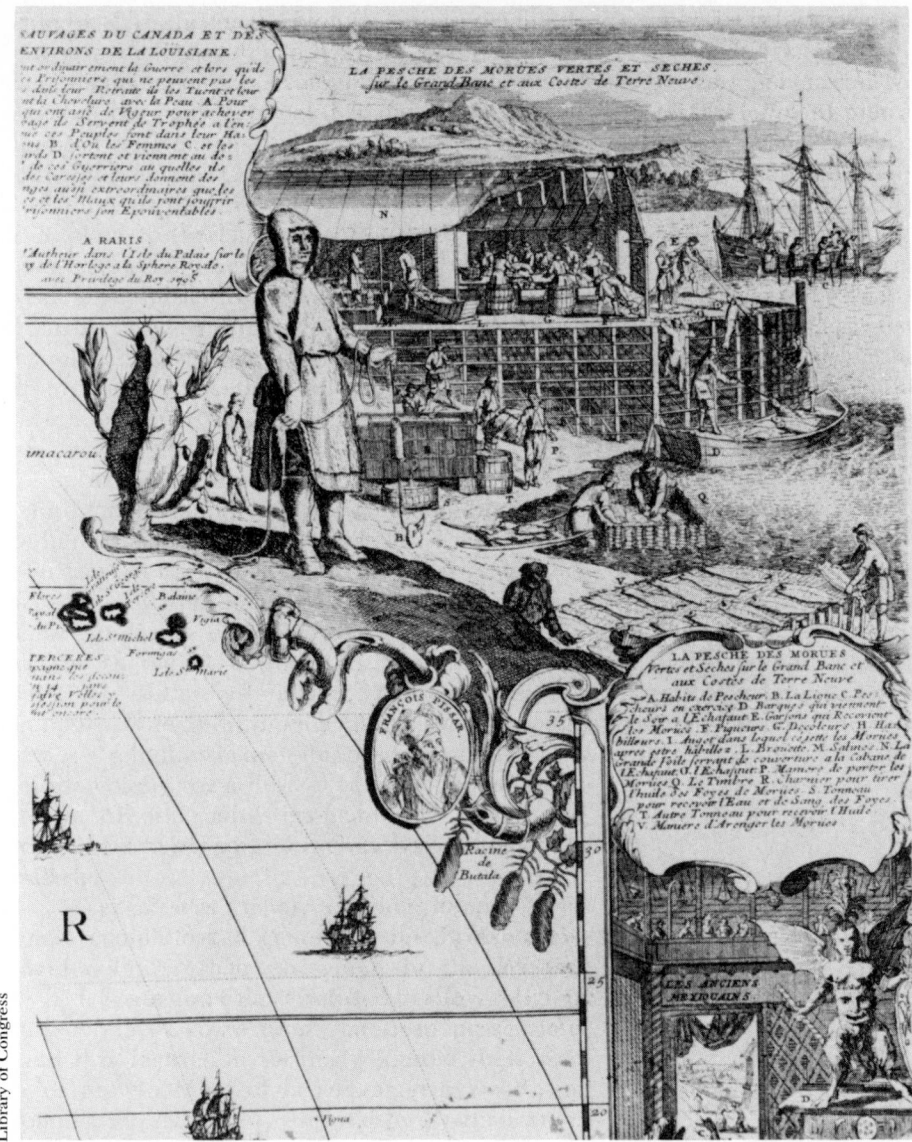

Library of Congress

A French illustration of the colonial Grand Banks cod fisherie. The racks in the background were used for drying the fish.

try soon took off. By 1770 North Carolina was exporting naval stores worth about £35,000, almost all of it to Britain.

Fishing and Whaling. The sea was one of the earliest sources of New England food and wealth. The first Massachusetts settlers caught local hake, haddock, halibut, and mackerel for their own tables. By about 1633 they were beginning to sell the preserved catch to distant customers.

When fully developed, the New England fishing industry was based on cod. Hundreds of vessels sailed from the towns of Gloucester, Marblehead, and Salem to fish for cod at the Grand Banks off Newfoundland. These craft were manned by crews who received between a sixth

and a tenth of the season's catch to share among themselves, the rest going to the boat owners.

The cod catch was an important item in the Massachusetts economy. Some of it was consumed at home, of course; but when salted and dried, the best grades were sent to southern Europe, while the worst went to the Caribbean to feed the sugar plantation slaves. The export trade in dried fish represented a large part of the Bay Colony's total exports.

Whaling was another profitable industry of the northern colonies. It had begun as a local activity in small New England and eastern Long Island ports. Then in the eighteenth century, as the local whale supply declined, capitalists began to employ larger vessels for longer trips well into the

Atlantic. The whalers from Nantucket, New Bedford, and Sag Harbor were not interested in the flesh of the great mammals. Their goal was whale oil, which supplied much of the lighting fuel for colonial homes, and spermaceti, a waxy substance from the heads of sperm whales used to make fine candles. One firm, headed by the Browns of Providence, Rhode Island, shipped fine spermacetic candles all over the Western Hemisphere.

Colonial Industry. Besides the 90 percent who tilled the soil, 5 percent or so of the colonial work force were craftsmen, tradesmen, or laborers in the cities, towns, and villages.

Almost all colonial manufactured goods were produced by hand, often in the home. There women, working part-time, were important contributors. Colonial farm women spun wool and linen fiber into thread and then wove it on hand looms into cloth. They manufactured candles from wax extracted from bayberries. They produced butter and cheese from milk from the family cow and made cider from apples and perry from pears. Men, too, used the home as a workshop. Farmers often devoted long winter evenings to carving axe handles, gunstocks, and other wooden products.

Homemade goods were produced for the family's immediate use, and perhaps for sale to neighbors for a little extra money. In addition, there were many full-time craftsmen who regularly produced items for customers out of their workshops. Every colonial town of any size, especially in the middle colonies and New England, had a long list of craftsmen. Coopers made the barrels that packaged colonial flour, sugar, tobacco, and other bulk goods. Wheelwrights turned out the wheels for carts, wagons, and coaches. Cordwainers produced shoes; blacksmiths made nails, horseshoes, and shovels and repaired metal tools. Every fast-growing community needed housing, and the demand was met by carpenters, masons, housewrights, bricklayers, and various laborers. As the community became richer and more populous, colonial craftspeople became increasingly skilled. By the eve of the Revolution they were producing beautiful silverware and cabinetry. In addition, the small cities were full of barbers, wig makers, tailors, milliners and other skilled providers of services and goods for the prosperous.

There were no factories in our sense in colonial America. The typical workshop was run by the owner, with perhaps a young apprentice and an older journeyman who had not yet set up for himself. The urban master craftsman generally lived above his shop, which in effect was both a little factory and a retail store. Much of his work was done on direct order from a customer, but he often made additional goods to have ready for people coming to the door. Often the craftsman's wife handled the selling in the front while he and his helpers turned out the product in back.

In only a few industries do we find anything resembling a modern factory. In every colony

Value of trade between England and the colonies, 1700–1776
Note: The pound of colonial times is roughly equal to fifty modern dollars.
Source: *Historical Statistics of the United States, Colonial Times to 1957.*

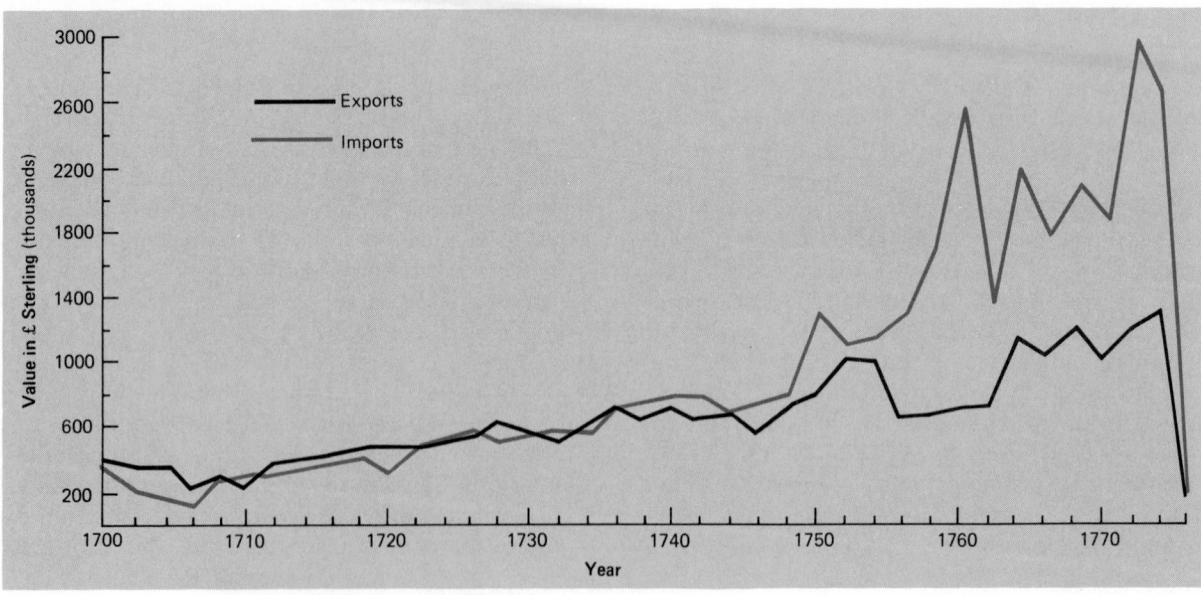

there were sawmills and gristmills that used water power and employed four or five workers per mill. In the ports of the middle colonies and in New England, shipbuilding, sail making, and rope making were conducted on a relatively large scale. The first colonial-built ship was a thirty-ton vessel, the *Blessing of the Bay,* launched in Boston in 1631. By 1670 Massachusetts had produced 730 vessels, and between 1696 and 1713 the colony built more than 1,000 ships of almost 70,000 tons total weight. Besides the shipyards along the Charles River, there were large shipbuilding establishments in Salem, Portsmouth, Newport, and Philadelphia, each employing scores of workers.

Another relatively large scale colonial enterprise was iron manufacturing. It, too, had its start in Massachusetts when, in 1644, Governor John Winthrop set up an iron foundry at Lynn. Before long the center of the industry had moved to Pennsylvania, though New Jersey, Maryland, and Virginia also had furnaces to produce pig iron. By 1700 the American colonies were producing about 2 percent of the world total, and by the 1770s they accounted for about 15 percent of world production. The two largest colonial iron foundries employed about a hundred men each, and represented capital investments of £100,000 and £250,000 respectively.

Commerce. Overseas commerce, or trade, was the final leg of the colonial economy and in some ways the most important. Commerce sustained the bread colonies, which relied on the Caribbean market as an outlet for their surplus grain and flour. Without markets in Britain and the European continent the tobacco, rice, indigo, and naval stores colonies would have been ruined. Overseas trade also supported the shipbuilding, sail-making, and rope-making industries, and encouraged flour milling, saw milling, and iron manufacture. Without foreign markets Americans would have been far poorer.

Exports also helped Americans pay for the sophisticated luxury goods they could not produce themselves. The better grades of paper, hardware, and woolens, silks, many books, fine furniture and housewares, wines, and scientific instruments could only come from Britain or the Continent. To pay for these, Americans needed coin or commercial credits from sales abroad. Unfortunately colonial trade relations were out of balance geographically. England needed the tobacco, rice, indigo, and naval stores of the Chesapeake and the Carolinas; these regions, accordingly, easily earned the income needed to pay for what they imported. The English also bought pig iron, some lumber, and ships from the northern colonies, but the major northern products—fish, grain, and cattle— were not wanted in Britain because they competed with English goods. Since each year the northern colonies bought more from the British than they sold to them, they were forced to find

Colonial trade routes

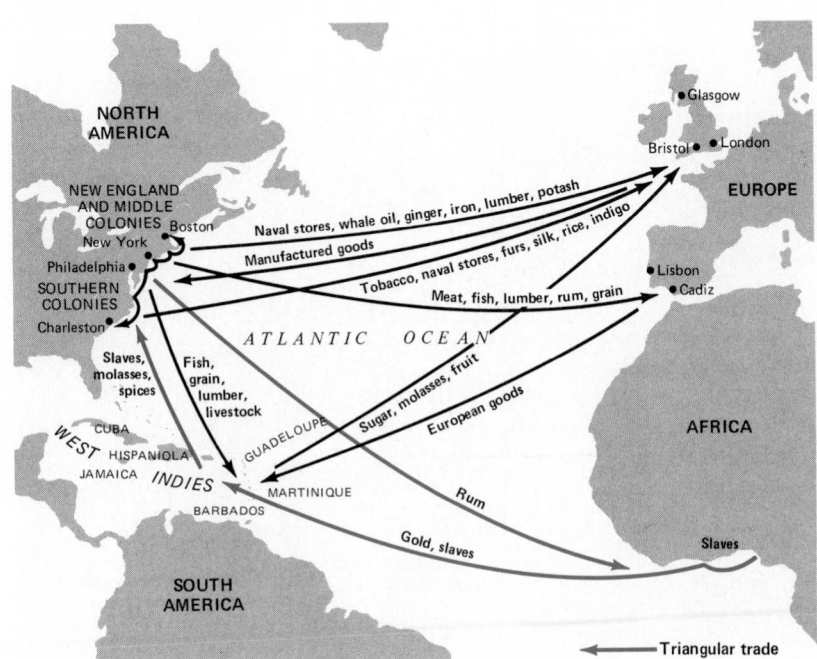

other customers who would buy their surpluses so that they could pay for British and European manufactures.

New England and the middle colonies found these largely in the Caribbean islands, where black slaves, working for a few hundred European planters, concentrated all their energies on growing sugarcane for the European market. The islanders' almost total neglect of everything but sugar made them excellent customers for cheap food, horses, timber, and other products from the northern colonies. By 1700 merchants were sending hundreds of vessels from northern ports each year with provisions, flour, and dried fish to feed the slaves and their masters, and lumber for construction and for making barrels.

Once he had found buyers for his mixed cargo, the Yankee or middle-colony trader accepted payment in several forms; coin, of course, was one, but molasses and sugar were also welcome. These products could be consumed directly at home; or the molasses could be converted into rum, which could be traded with the Indians or exported. The trader could also accept bills of exchange on England. These were certificates that served as cash to pay for English goods or to pay debts to English creditors. With their holds full of molasses and perhaps a little Caribbean cotton or citrus fruit, and the captain's strongbox stuffed with coin or bills of exchange, the ship from Boston, Providence, New York, or Philadelphia then sailed for home.

Slaves were also traded in this Caribbean exchange. Most of the slaves carried from Africa to the West Indies in the eighteenth century were transported by the French, the British, or the Dutch; but some were carried by slavers out of Boston and Newport. The typical New England slave trader sent a small vessel to the west coast of Africa with a cargo of rum distilled from Caribbean molasses. On the African coast the Yankee captain met a trader from London or Bristol and exchanged some rum for English goods, such as iron, cloth, gunpowder, cheap jewelry, and glass beads. With this cargo he bought slaves from African middlemen. The slaves were then transported to the Caribbean to be sold for coin, bills of exchange, or molasses, or were brought to the Carolinas or the Chesapeake on the mainland.

The Caribbean and African trading routes were the most important, but there were many others. Hundreds of sloops, schooners, brigs, and other small vessels piled the waters along the Atlantic coast, bringing Philadelphia flour to Charleston or Salem, or Yankee codfish to Annapolis or Savannah. Relatively few colonial ships traded directly with Britain; this route was dominated by larger English-owned vessels. But ships

Surinam was a Dutch sugar-growing colony on South America's Atlantic coast. It was an important trading partner for British North America, and especially for Rhode Island. In this 1758 John Greenwood painting we see a group of Rhode Island seacaptains—including a future governor of Rhode Island and a future commander in chief of the Continental Navy—rowdily enjoying their layover in Surinam before returning home with sugar, molasses, and rum.

City Art Museum of St. Louis

from the northern colonies did trade with France, Spain, Portugal, and Italy—handling most of the rice, fish, flour, and other commodities that went to these countries and the wine and salt that came back. In fact, colonial merchants often carried these goods for English merchants. They also insured vessels sent on long voyages, a business later taken over by marine insurance companies.

Wealth and Inequality. How did Americans fare under this emerging economic system? Did prosperity benefit every person equally? Historians believe the answers to these questions may help us understand why some groups supported the revolutionary cause after 1763 and others did not.

Among rural Americans—free ones, at least—the location and availability of land determined individual levels of prosperity. Yeoman farmers who owned a hundred or so acres near a market could grow surplus crops for sale. This income made them more prosperous than either the tenant farmer, who had to rent land, or the yeoman farmer growing only enough for his own family. Commercial agriculture made for prosperity, but it also created inequality. In towns close to the Boston market, such as Milton or Roxbury, for example, where farmers produced surpluses for urban consumers, the result was a sharp division between rich and poor: in 1771 about a quarter of the taxpayers in these two towns were landless, while the wealthiest 10 percent owned 46 percent of the real estate. In general, both less wealth and greater equality were to be found in the frontier regions of each colony, where land was abundant, landholding widespread, and markets too distant to support commercial agriculture. Thus Goshen, Connecticut, which was then just emerging from the frontier stage, had forty landowners in 1741 out of a population of fifty-seven adult males. In the South the picture was similar: regions of subsistence farming such as the Shenandoah Valley had many landowners and so relative equality. By contrast, the commercial rice- and indigo-growing Carolina coast and the tobacco-growing Chesapeake tidewater were the realms of the great slaveholding landed gentry. White yeoman farmers of the middle rank were rare in these regions of large estates. Poor folk living on infertile marginal land were more common.

Colonial cities had a different economic hierarchy. Here marketable skills counted as much as real estate in determining an individual's prosperity. Apprentices, laborers, and seamen, groups that had the fewest skills to sell, made up the urban lower class. Craftsmen and shopkeepers did better, and at the top of the pyramid were merchants. Those who peddled light goods in the nearby rural areas were poor by comparison with the great merchants who traded with Europe or the Caribbean. It was difficult to break into the ranks of the overseas traders, but the merchant class was not completely closed to the energetic, ambitious, or lucky.

Obviously economic inequalities existed in the American colonies. An important question for many historians has been whether those inequalities were growing or lessening in the years before the Revolution. Were the rich getting richer and the poor poorer? The most recent analyses seem to show that inequality was increasing in the larger cities and parts of the older settled regions. But this trend was being canceled out for America as a whole by the frontier settlers: where land was abundant, greater opportunity for economic equality existed, and those who had not succeeded in the older regions could try their luck again.

Whatever the trend, it is clear that Americans thought of themselves as a people blessed with equality beyond any other people. A British nobleman visiting America in 1764 noted: "The levelling principle here, everywhere operates strongly and takes the lead, and everybody has property here, and everybody knows it." Lord Adam Gordon certainly exaggerated, but his statement reflected what many Americans believed to be true of—and valued in—their society.

COSTS AND BENEFITS OF EMPIRE BEFORE 1763

Until at least the 1760s, then, the colonial economy fostered a fair amount of equality. But what about the overall performance of the economy, its capacity to produce wealth? Since colonial economic life developed within the framework of the British Empire, the colonists' perception of this performance was certain to affect how they felt about the political relationship with Great Britain.

The Economic Balance Sheet. As we look at the colonial economy it is clear that it both benefited and suffered from the colonial relationship. The colonists were not free to trade where they pleased, but from the 1650s on were forced to accept a multitude of restrictions. Though frequently violated or circumvented, these regulations limited their ability to work out their own economic destiny.

The system of commercial regulation was based on a theory of empire called mercantilism that harked back to Elizabethan times. As we saw in Chapter 2, colonies were supposed to enrich the mother country by supplying it with exotic commodities and raw materials and by consuming its surplus manufactures. Meanwhile, trade with the colonies would give needed jobs to a host of people in the mother country. It was these expectations that had led the mercantilists and the crown to support colonization at the outset.

With these potential benefits in mind, parliament began in the mid-seventeenth century to enact a series of measures collectively called the Navigation Acts. Some of these acts were designed to keep the profits of British colonial trade from falling into the hands of the Dutch; they restricted imperial trade to vessels owned, manned, and built by the British or the colonists. Other acts established lists of "enumerated" articles that had to be shipped to England first, whatever their ultimate destination; the lists included some of the most valuable colonial exports such as tobacco, rice, and indigo. In Britain these exports were taxed. Parliament further required that almost all non-English goods bound for the colonies be shipped first to England. These measures, besides excluding foreigners from the imperial trade, were supposed to make Britain the distribution center for most commodities entering and leaving the colonies. Thus British merchants would have a vital role in the colonial trade, and the government could collect taxes on goods passing through Great Britain. Still other legislation—the Hat Act (1732), the Iron Act (1750), and one clause in the Woolen Act (1699)—attempted to limit colonial competition with British manufacturers by either forbidding certain branches of these industries, limiting their size, or restricting the export of their product.

Americans undoubtedly were penalized by these trade regulations. Enumeration hurt Maryland and Virginia especially. The enumerated tobacco sent to the European Continent had to be unloaded and reloaded in England first. True, the tax paid in England was rebated; but the charges for this roundabout method of export were high, and the planters lost money because of it. Also on the debit side was the regulation that European goods be sent first to England before crossing the Atlantic. This rule forced Americans to pay higher prices for French, German, Dutch, and Spanish goods.

Was the penalty paid by the colonies severe? To answer this question fairly, we should consider the benefits of the empire as well as the costs. The foremost benefit was that Britain assumed the expense of the empire's defense. During the seventeenth and eighteenth centuries, as we shall see,

four great European wars jeopardized the safety of the colonies. The British army and navy often proved indispensable to colonial defense. Recognizing their stake in the outcome, the colonists contributed money and men themselves; but most of the cost by far was borne by the British. Without the mother country's contribution, the colonies would have been forced to lay out millions of pounds in extra taxes, a financial burden that would have retarded their economic growth.

And America received other benefits as part of the empire. The British paid bounties to encourage production of items that did not compete with English-made goods and for raw materials that were needed by English manufacturers; these brought thousands of pounds a year to American indigo growers, pig-iron manufacturers, and naval-stores producers. The merchants and shipwrights of New England and the middle colonies gained by having their shipping and their shipbuilding enjoy the same protected status as those of their counterparts in Great Britain. This was the credit side of the ledger.

The measures to restrict colonial manufacturers do not fall either in the debit or credit columns. The Iron Act, aimed at finished iron products, did little to restrain the colonial iron industry because it was not rigorously enforced. As for the Woolen and Hat acts, they did not, as we might suppose, kill off promising industries. Many years after independence, when these measures were no longer in force, Americans continued to buy hats and woolen cloth from Great Britain and other foreign nations. The intention of these measures was clear: they were designed to limit future growth that might injure British producers. Still, in their day they probably had little effect.

On the whole, the American experience within the mercantile system was positive. The colonial economy thrived. Seldom has an agricultural society advanced so fast or brought such benefits to its members. And Americans recognized, generally, how much they had gained economically from the imperial relationship. During the great controversy that led to the Revolution, the Navigation Acts as developed before 1763 were seldom mentioned by the colonists as a grievance. Only one economic measure caused serious friction. This was the Molasses Act of 1733, which imposed a tax on molasses and sugar brought into the colonies from the Dutch, French, and Spanish West Indies. Intended to protect the British Caribbean sugar planters from the competition of lower-cost foreign producers, the act threatened the profitable trade between New England and the foreign West Indies. Yankee merchants responded by turning the smuggling of foreign molasses into a fine art. The law, never strictly enforced, became a dead letter.

The Political Ledger. When we measure the political debits and credits of the British-American relationship, we encounter a similar even balance through the 1760s. British rule in America before 1763 was generally considered "mild" by most colonists, although there were periods of rather strict rule. During the reigns of Charles II (1660–85) and James II (1685–88), the British authorities had tried to tighten imperial control. In 1684 they revoked the Massachusetts Bay charter and soon after merged New England, New York, and New Jersey into the Dominion of New England. Especially under the firm rule of Governor Sir Edmund Andros, residents of the northern colonies were denied the right to tax themselves or to make laws regulating their day-to-day concerns. In the proprietary colonies farther south, the crown sought to impose direct royal control. This effort at tight imperial control, while arousing deep fears among many colonists, proved short-lived. In Britain itself Protestants grew anxious when the Catholic James II came to the throne in 1685. Drawing inspiration from a group of powerful political thinkers, including John Locke, a group of Whig leaders overthrew James, forced him into exile, and placed on the throne his Protestant daughter, Mary, and her Dutch husband, William of Orange.

This Glorious Revolution of 1688–89 produced a resounding echo in America. Led by the Puritan clergy, Massachusetts rebels arrested Governor Andros and his officials and shipped them all back to England. The Dominion of New England was ended and the individual colonies separated once more. In 1691 Massachusetts received a new charter that merged Massachusetts Bay with Plymouth. In New York the Glorious Revolution led to a more powerful General Assembly with enhanced power to meet and make laws. In Pennsylvania, too, more independent representative institutions soon appeared, granting the colonists greater control over their own affairs. Indeed, the main thrust of the Glorious Revolution was to strengthen the idea that Englishmen, on both sides of the Atlantic, were entitled to a large measure of self-government through legislatures and assemblies modeled on Parliament.

By the early eighteenth century, then, the colonists had achieved a large measure of political autonomy. The English Privy Council was permitted to "disallow" measures passed by the colonial legislatures and approved by the colonial governors; but of some 8,500 colonial laws submitted to the council, only 469 were declared null. Nor was the Board of Trade, which shared colonial administration with the governors and the Privy Council, any more coercive. Particularly from 1721 to 1748, when Sir Robert Walpole and the Duke of Newcastle were the crown's chief advisers, the English government gave colonial economic growth higher priority than tight and tidy English rule. This era of so-called salutary neglect helped create in the colonists an even greater sense than before that they were self-governing in all internal matters.

For several years during the 1750s this autonomy seemed threatened by the Earl of Halifax. Appointed head of the Board of Trade in 1748, he attempted to increase the board's power. At one point Halifax directly challenged the New York assembly for defying his instructions. But when Halifax left office in 1761, the Board of Trade once more lapsed into inactivity.

The Issue of Religion. Before 1763, then, Americans had little reason to complain of British political coercion. Nor did the issue of religion loom large in the relations of colonies and mother country. By the middle of the eighteenth century most colonists were Protestant Nonconformists of one kind or another. Some Nonconformists feared that if the Anglicans had their way, they would establish "a tyranny over the bodies and souls of men," destroy the religious liberties of Americans, and restrict public office to Anglicans. But most Americans apparently did not take the warnings of the alarmists very seriously.

In fact, the British government was not interested in establishing an Anglican episcopate in America. High British officials recognized that religious dissenters in the colonies were often firm supporters of the crown; accordingly, in the words of one British official, they "shou'd not be provoked or alienated" by imposing bishops on them. Occasionally London did force the colonies to extend religious toleration to some unpopular religious group, but that was as far as British control in religious matters would go. In religion, as in politics and economics, the conflicts between mother country and colonies remained muted before 1763.

THE CRISIS OF EMPIRE

After 1763 many thousands of the most influential and articulate people in the colonies would find the system of imperial administration galling and the actions of the British government intolerable. Before long they would demand that they be changed. An important cause of the dramatic change of heart was the end of the French threat to English America.

The English-French Confrontation. French Canada (New France) and English America had been planted at approximately the same time. Thereafter the two communities had evolved in different ways. The French did not permit their Protestant dissenters (the Huguenots) to emigrate to New France. French Catholics might have come in large numbers; but the government at Paris fa-

vored aristocratic *seigneurs* over small farmers in granting land, and few French peasants found the terms attractive. By the mid-eighteenth century Canada was a sparsely settled region with some 55,000 farmers cultivating the lands of the gentry, ruled autocratically by a royal governor. Pious and conservative, the French Canadians accepted the dominance of the *seigneurs*, the church, and the appointed royal officials without serious question.

Friction between English America and New France was almost inevitable. Both communities were political extensions of their respective mother countries and inevitably became enmeshed in the quarrels of the two European arch-

The French in North America

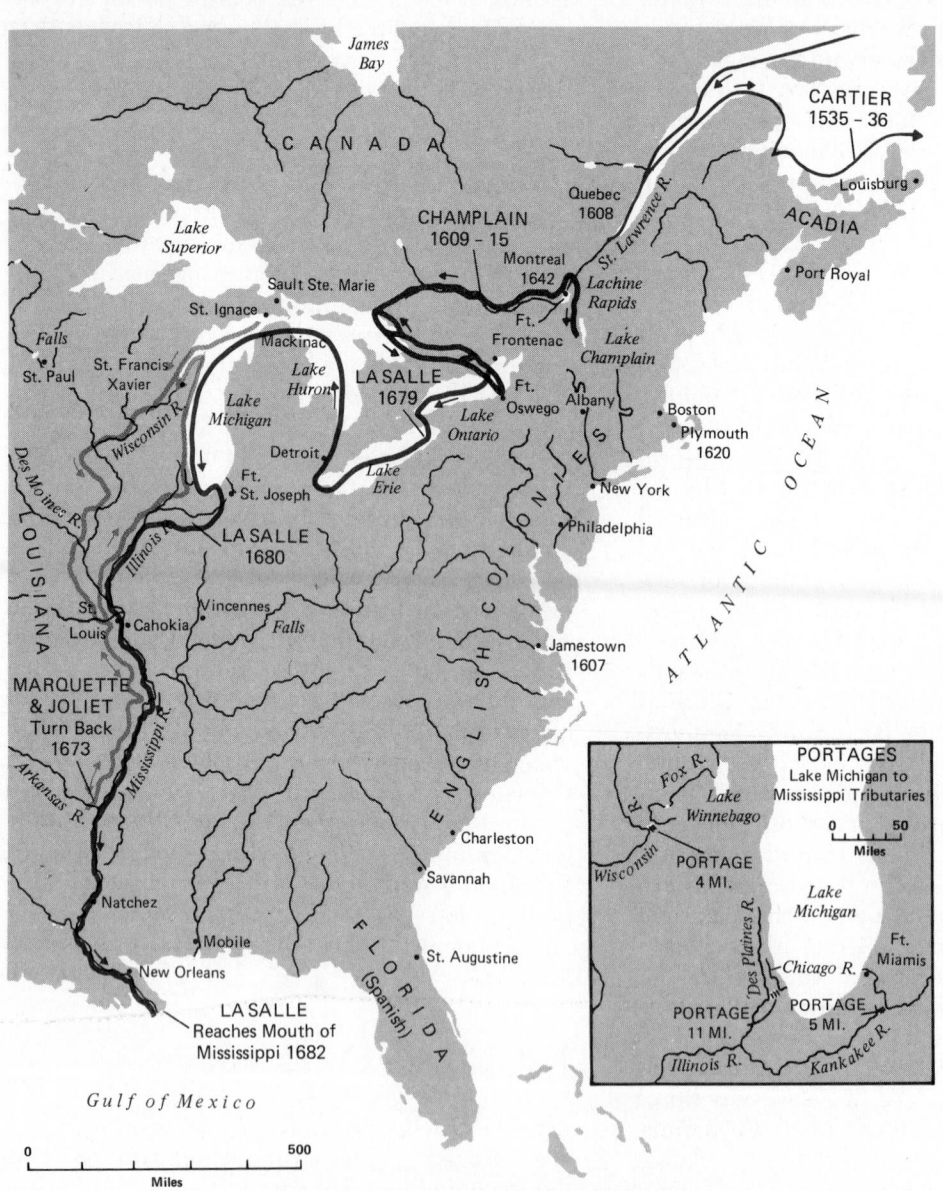

rivals. Both were also religious antagonists. Before long Catholic New France and Protestant English America resumed the fierce political and religious conflict that had beset the European world for two centuries.

Just as important as these transplanted European frictions were the tensions native to America itself. New France and "new England" vied over control of the fishing trade in Newfoundland and over competing claims in the Caribbean. Even closer to home was rivalry over the fur trade with the Indians. For many years English traders based in Albany and French traders based in Montreal had competed for the beaver pelts that the Indians supplied from the interior. The British had the advantage of cheaper and better trade goods; the French, on the other hand, were more effective in winning the allegiance of the Indians. Canadian traders went to the Indians for furs rather than waiting for the Indians to deliver them to the European settlements. They lived with the Indians and often married Indian women. Their half-European, half-Indian children in turn forged bonds that the English could not match. French religious institutions also gave them an advantage with the

Indians. Unlike the Protestants to the south, French Catholics were effective in winning Indians to Christianity.

Among the few native American groups that the French could not win to their side were the Iroquois, the powerful Indian confederation of western New York. The French incurred the hostility of the Five Nations early in the seventeenth century when they sided with the Iroquois' ancient enemy, the Hurons. Later, in the 1680s, egged on by Governor Thomas Dongan of New York (a royal official who hoped to seize the western fur trade for the English), the Iroquois attacked the French and drove them back to Montreal.

Soon afterward England and France clashed in the first of four major wars that would be fought all over the world. In the first (King William's War, 1689–97) colonial troops from Massachusetts captured the French base at Port Royal in modern Nova Scotia. In the end, however, little was achieved and the post was returned to the French by the Treaty of Ryswick (1697). Soon after, the French decided to settle the Mississippi Valley, a region jointly claimed by them and the American

An "on-the-spot" depiction of Amherst's seizure of the French fortress of Louisbourg in 1758, drawn by Captain Ince of the 35th Regiment.

Library of Congress

colonists, and established outposts through "Louisiana," at Cahokia (near present-day St. Louis), at Kaskaskia (on the Mississippi in southern Illinois), and on the Gulf Coast. When war broke out again in 1702 (Queen Anne's War, 1702–13), French troops with their Indian allies clashed with the Anglo-Americans in a vast arc from Maine to the outskirts of the new colony of Louisiana. By the Treaty of Utrecht (1713), which ended this conflict, England acquired Newfoundland, Acadia, and the Hudson Bay region.

Following the Treaty of Utrecht, the French sought to consolidate their hold on Louisiana by establishing new posts and communities in the disputed region. In 1718 they settled near the mouth of the Mississippi and called their new community New Orleans. The British countered by constructing Fort Oswego on Lake Ontario and fortifying the northern frontier against the pro-French Abenakis. When war broke out again (King George's War, 1740–48), both sides once more attacked one another in North America. New England troops captured the French strong point of Louisbourg in Nova Scotia, while in New York William Johnson, the province's commissary of Indian affairs, induced the Iroquois to attack the French. In retaliation the French and their Indian allies raided Albany and burned Saratoga.

The French and Indian War. Each of these three wars originated in disputes in Europe. The most destructive and momentous of all the colonial wars, however, started over an issue of immediate concern to many Americans.

French expansion into the Mississippi Valley seemed to threaten the colonists' very existence as a self-governing Protestant community. Besides, a string of interior French colonies promised to block westward expansion and confine the eastern colonists within their existing boundaries. Colonial farmers looking to the west for fresh, fertile lands for themselves and their sons would be walled off and confined to the dwindling acres east of the mountains. Would-be speculators in western lands, who were especially prominent and vocal in Pennsylvania and Virginia, would be

The French and Indian War

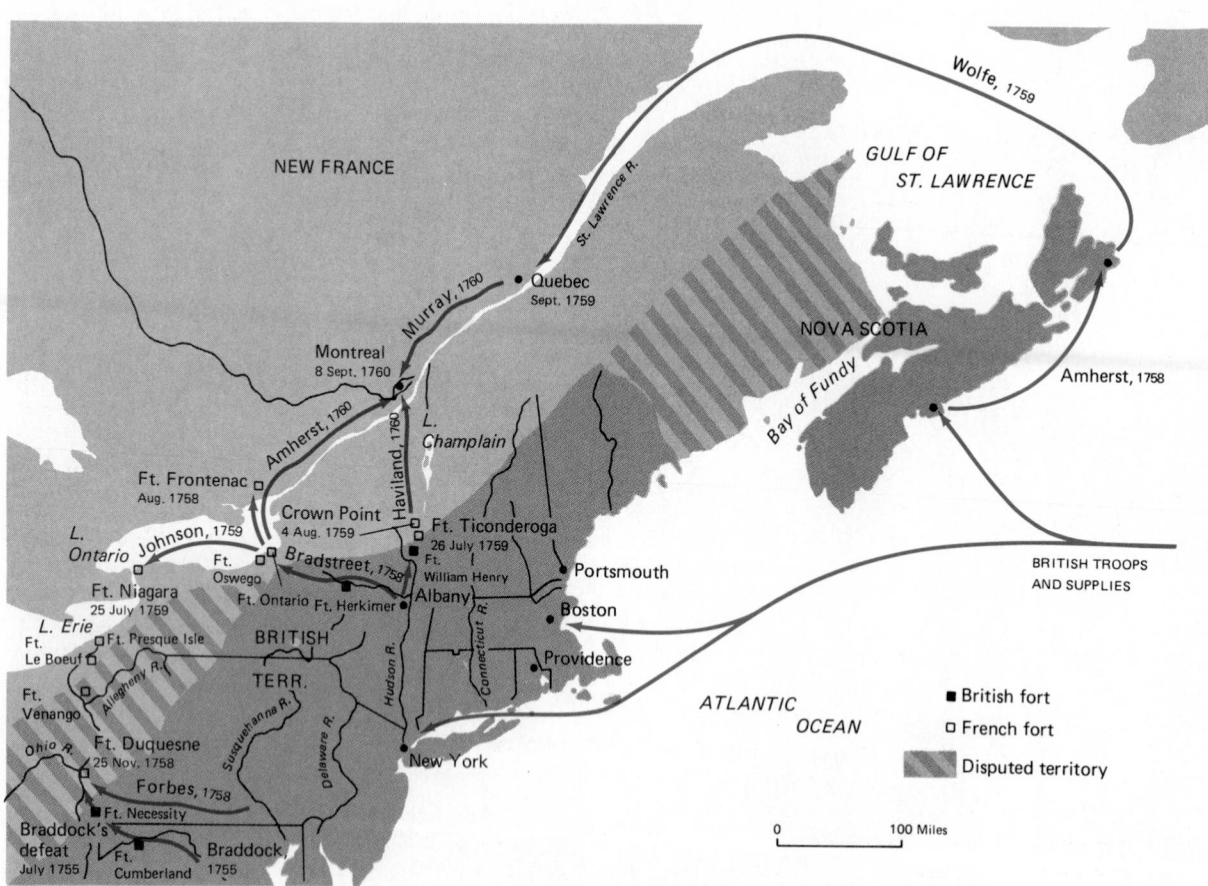

denied their expected windfall profits from land sales.

The crisis came in what is now western Pennsylvania and Ohio. Here, during and shortly following King George's War, Pennsylvania fur traders, led by George Croghan, had established a string of trading posts to collect pelts from the Indians. Hoping to head Croghan off, the French, under the Canadian Marquis Duquesne, decided to build a chain of forts from Lake Erie to the Forks of the Ohio at what is now Pittsburgh. In 1753 a construction party of several hundred Frenchmen and Indians established three stockades along Lake Erie and on French Creek. Still left to construct when winter came was the projected post at the strategic Forks, where the Allegheny and Monongahela join to form the Ohio River.

News of the French project alarmed Governor Robert Dinwiddie of Virginia, who not only feared Virginia's loss of the vast interior claimed under her early charter but also saw his own speculative profits evaporating. Dinwiddie responded by dispatching a young Virginia squire, George Washington, with a force of armed men to scout out the French incursion. The following year, after the French had completed Fort Duquesne at the Forks, Washington returned to oust them. Though outnumbered ten to one, the young Virginian foolishly allowed himself to be engaged by the French. At Fort Necessity, a hurriedly constructed American bastion, the French defeated the intruders and took them prisoner. When released from captivity, Washington and his little force returned to the Virginia capital, Williamsburg, carrying news that the French were on the verge of making good their claim to the great interior valley.

The confrontation of a few hundred men in western Pennsylvania triggered the French and Indian War, a struggle that lasted from 1754 to 1763. In 1756 the conflict spread to Europe itself when Britain and Prussia concluded an alliance against France, which in turn allied itself with Austria and then, in 1762, with Spain. Since Britain, France, and Spain were great imperial nations, the struggle quickly turned into a "world war." Before it was over, armies and fleets had grappled in the Mediterranean, the Caribbean, the Far East, India, and on the Continent, as well as in the dense forests of North America. At first the war went badly for the English. But then, in 1757, William Pitt the Elder took over the war's management and brought Britain a series of brilliant victories that changed the course of history.

In America, as elsewhere, the war started badly for the Anglo-Americans when the British general, Edward Braddock, suffered a severe defeat in his effort to capture Fort Duquesne. Braddock's small force of 1,400 British redcoats, 450 Virginia militiamen under Washington, and 50 Indian scouts marched on the French, hacking their way through the tangled woods. On July 9, 1755, they encountered 600 French and 200 Indians seven miles from the French post. With flags flying and bagpipes skirling, the British advanced in the best European fashion. But matters did not go according to plan, and the battle quickly degenerated into a wild melee with the French and Indians pouring deadly fire into the redcoats and Americans from concealed positions on either side. Wounded mortally, Braddock ordered a retreat. As the combined Anglo-American force limped back to their base, they were attacked by the enemy from behind every tree and rock. Only 500 of the 1,900 men who had set out arrived home safely.

Other British commanders were more successful. In the fall of 1758 General John Forbes, with a force of 6,000 men, cut his way through Pennsylvania toward the goal that had eluded Braddock. Seeing this powerful Anglo-American army approaching, the Indians of the Ohio country deserted the French. On November 24 the handful of French soldiers remaining at Fort Duquesne blew it up and fled, leaving it to the British, who reconstructed it as Fort Pitt. Impressed by this British victory, the Indians turned on their former French allies and virtually drove them out of the upper Mississippi Valley.

A still more brilliant British triumph came in the summer of 1759 when General James Wolfe and an army of 4,500 redcoats scaled the heights above the St. Lawrence River and debouched on the Plains of Abraham outside the walls of Quebec. The small city was the very soul of French Canada, seat of the governor and the bishop. Its commander was the able Marquis de Montcalm, but his force consisted only of ill-trained provincial troops. They bravely attacked the British; but in the face of the redcoats' deadly musket volleys, they quickly fell back to the town and soon surrendered. Both of the commanders died in the battle. With the fall of Quebec, followed later by the capture of Montreal, French power in Canada was broken.

The war lasted for many months following the fall of New France. In 1761 Pitt, despite his successes, resigned. The new king, George III, replaced him with Lord Bute and other "Tory" advisers who were more friendly to the idea of royal power than Pitt and his fellow Whigs. By this time the British people were weary of the war, which had cost them well over £100 million and raised taxes to record levels. Soon after Pitt's departure the British, French, and Spanish opened negotiations and in February 1763 concluded the Peace of Paris.

The treaty made sweeping changes in the political map of North America. By its terms France ceded Cape Breton Island and all of Canada to Great Britain and recognized the region from the Appalachians to the Mississippi and from the Great Lakes to Florida as British territory. Spain gave Florida, including much of the eastern Gulf Coast, to England. In return for this loss, Spain gained from the French what they had retained of Louisiana; that is, the portion west of the Mississippi. Other territory changed hands in India, Africa, and the Caribbean. To the Americans the crucial matter was that powerful France was now eliminated from the entire North American continent except for two tiny fishing islands off Newfoundland.

The end of the French danger abruptly altered American attitudes toward the British Empire. So long as the French were nearby, the Americans had to seek the protection of England. Now that the French menace was gone, the colonists could afford to consider the disadvantages of their subordinate relationship with England. Moreover, the French and Indian War had created serious tensions between the British government and its American subjects that would not easily be resolved.

British-American Relations During the War. From the British point of view, the Americans had not been the best of subjects during the war, or even the best of allies. When, for example, the British had prohibited trade between the colonies and France in 1756 (the Rule of 1756), the Americans had defied the regulations. American vessels had sailed to the French Caribbean islands and traded sugar for the supplies that these islands could not obtain because of the British naval blockade. American merchants had also exchanged American flour and fish for French wines and gold at Hispaniola, initially a neutral Spanish port, despite Pitt's charge that this trade enabled the enemy "to sustain and protect" the "long and expensive War."

A major British weapon against the illegal commerce with France was the writ of assistance. This was a general warrant allowing customs officials to search private property—ships, warehouses, even homes—to determine whether smuggled goods were present. Though such writs had been issued before, during the French and Indian War they aroused fierce opposition among colonial merchants, who saw them not only as a threat to their lucrative new trade but also as a dangerous violation of the rights of private citizens. In 1760 several Boston traders hired attorney James Otis to argue against the legality of the writs. In a fiery address that John Adams later called the "first scene of the first act of opposition" to British authority in America, Otis denounced the writs as "against the fundamental principles of law" and the British constitution, and hence void. In the end the writs were upheld by the Massachusetts court and confirmed by the Townshend Acts, but they were never effectively used in the Bay Colony.

Nor, in British eyes, was the flouting of trade regulations the only American offense during the war. The Americans had also resisted paying their share of the war's costs. To help meet these, Pitt had adopted a "requisition" system whereby each colonial assembly would share with the British treasury the expense of recruiting and supplying troops. In addition, the British would reimburse the colonial legislatures for part of their initial outlays in the following year. This was an extremely generous scheme, British officials said, since the Americans were fighting the French as much for themselves as for the British. Yet time and again, it seemed to British officials, the Americans had failed to do their part. They had delayed voting money or even refused outright. According to Lord Loudon, British commander in chief in America, it had been "the constant study of every province . . . to throw every expense on the Crown and bear no part of the expense of this war themselves."

The Americans had also refused to cooperate in a common policy toward the Indians. In 1754 the Board of Trade had issued a call for a colonial congress to deal with the tribes south of the Great Lakes and induce them to support the Anglo-Americans against the French. The congress, attended only by the New England colonies, New York, Maryland, and Pennsylvania, met in Albany and took up Iroquois grievances against American fur traders and land speculators as well as Indian charges that they had been left defenseless against the French. The congress recommended various measures to meet the Indians' complaints and also urged that a colonial supergovernment be established to deal with all the problems of the West.

The Albany Congress failed to achieve anything. None of the colonies wished to surrender control over western policy; Virginia particularly, with its large western interests, feared that such a supergovernment would thwart her plans for land development in the region. None of the congress's recommendations were adopted, and Indian-white relations remained chaotic.

Worse problems soon followed. In the wake of the British conquest of the West, hundreds of American traders crossed the Appalachian Mountains. Most were out for quick profits and did not care how they made them. They cheated the Indians and plied them with drink. At the same time scores of American, Scottish, and English speculators besieged parliament, demanding land grants in the West that could be sold to eager would-be settlers. Hundreds of small farmers were already pouring into the Pittsburgh region, displacing the local Indians. British officials in the West were no more sensitive to Indian feelings than the Americans. Lord Jeffrey Amherst despised the "savages" and advised spreading smallpox among the tribes. In 1762 Amherst abruptly cut off the food and ammunition traditionally supplied to the Indians during the winter.

To the northern tribes Amherst's act seemed the final straw. By this time a major Indian renewal movement was under way, inspired by a religious leader called "the Prophet," who urged his people to abandon white ways and reassert their independence. One of the prophet's disciples was the Ottawa chief Pontiac. In May 1763, shortly after the Treaty of Paris, Pontiac and his followers attacked Fort Detroit. The post held out, but the assault set off a fierce Indian uprising throughout the West that in two months drove virtually all the whites back over the mountains. The British struck back and by the summer of 1764 had put down Pontiac's rebellion. But the affair highlighted the chaos in Indian affairs and, more generally, Britain's problems in controlling its empire.

The Proclamation of 1763.

With the French war over, British as well as American attitudes toward the empire changed. In general, the Whig leaders who had governed England during the period of salutary neglect had accepted the validity of colonial claims to autonomy in managing local American affairs. Philosophically, they had opposed the assertion of royal power at home, and this attitude had carried over to their view of how to govern America. But the government of Lord Bute was dominated by men of a different temper. Bute and Chancellor of the Exchequer George Grenville were Tories who supported the crown against Parliament and had little use for colonial "preten-

sions" to self-rule. In addition, these men saw American behavior during the war and the problems with the Indians as proof of the dangers of lax imperial control. Tighter administration of the empire, they felt, was clearly needed.

The first move to tighten control of the colonies was the Proclamation of 1763. This measure prohibited colonists from settling west of the Appalachians and required all those already there "forthwith to remove themselves." East of the mountains, colonists were forbidden to purchase land directly from the Indians. The entire trans-Appalachian region was to be placed under the control of the British commander in chief and to remain an exclusive Indian preserve until further notice. Through the proclamation the British hoped to pacify the Indians and to give themselves time to contrive a rational policy for disposing of the crown's lands, especially in the West. Eventually colonists would be allowed to move across the mountains, but not before Indian claims had been satisfied and an orderly system of land transfer and settlement worked out.

Historians have argued that British western policy was very much like the one adopted by the American government itself after 1783, when it fell heir to the western lands. It was, they say, a rational attempt to avoid disorderly and expensive development of the public domain, and in any case it was temporary. Be that as it may, the proclamation disturbed many Americans. Those who had anticipated profits from land speculation, fur trading, and farming saw their hopes evaporate. Particularly in Virginia, which claimed much of the trans-Appalachian region, many influential men were infuriated by the new policy. The check on western settlement, they insisted, was designed to allow Englishmen to grab an unfair share of speculative profits in the American West. At the same time, the new western policy threatened to close an escape hatch for small farmers. Land was becoming scarce in the East, and delaying western settlement seemed sure to widen the gap between rich and poor.

Changes in British Tax Policy.

Even more disturbing to most Americans, however, was Parliament's effort to raise revenue in America. Never before had this been attempted. The British government had imposed duties on certain imports through laws like the Molasses Act, but its primary purpose had been to regulate commerce, not to extract money from the Americans. Even during the recent war the requisition system had allowed the colonial assemblies the right to actually raise the money needed. But now there were other con-

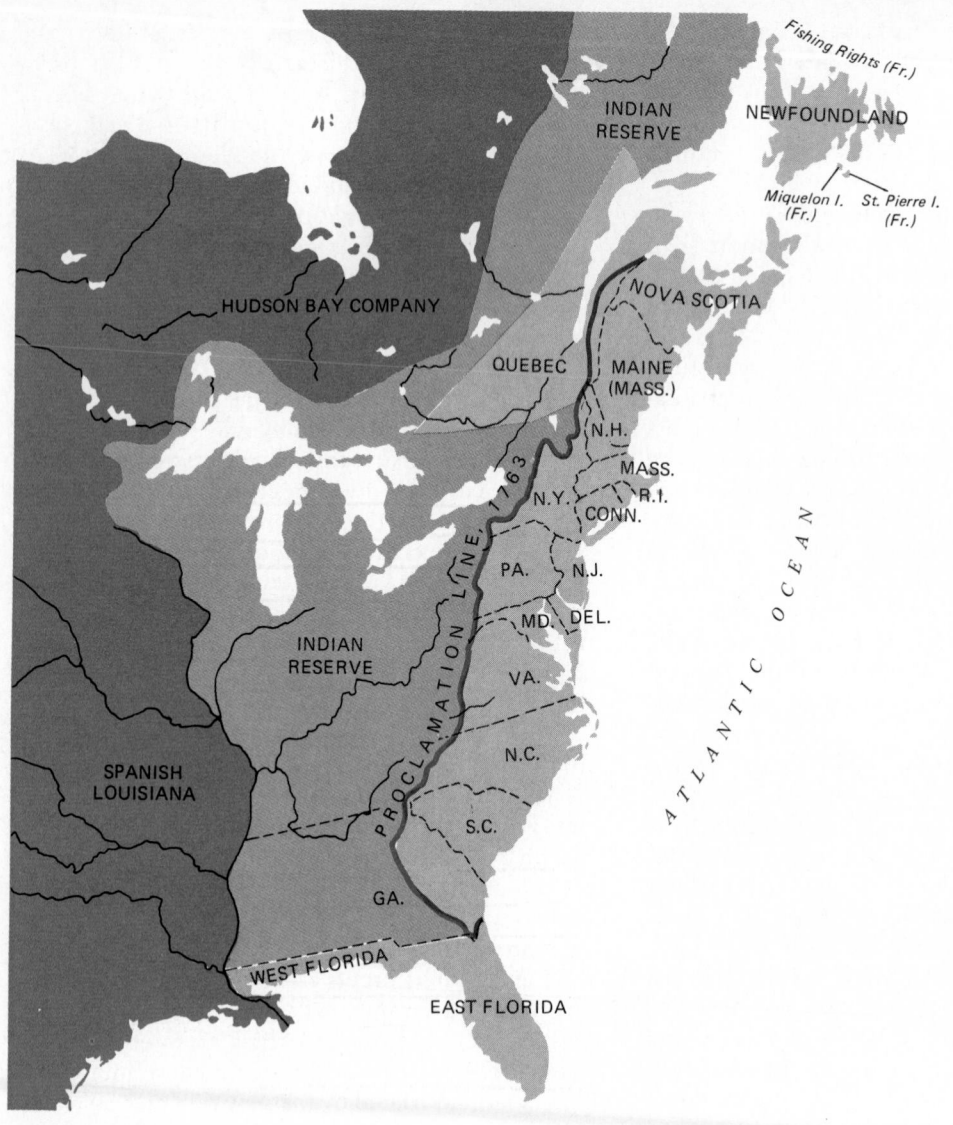

North America in 1763

siderations. Britain after 1763 labored under an immense debt that was costing it £4.5 million a year in interest alone. Military costs, too, were certain to continue. Though the French had been driven out of North America, Britain would have to maintain an expensive army to protect the colonists against the Indians. How could the British taxpayer be relieved of these costs? The conclusion was obvious: make the Americans themselves pay the bill.

The first revenue measure of the Grenville ministry was the Sugar Act (1764). This law imposed import duties on non-English cloth, indigo, coffee, wine, sugar, and molasses. The tax on molasses was especially offensive. Even though the new duty was actually lower than the Molasses Act rates, it remained too high to suit northern merchants. More important, the money was now really to be collected. To prevent the smuggling that had made the Molasses Act a sham, the new law forced American merchants to pass through a thicket of certificates, affidavits, oaths, and inspections. In addition, the law added a new vice-admiralty court to those established earlier to enforce the Navigation Acts. The new court could try suspected smugglers under rules that put more of the burden of proof than previously on the accused.

Most American merchants balked at this renewed effort to exclude them from the profitable foreign West Indies market. The Navigation Acts had pressed only lightly on the colonies thus far, largely because the Americans had offset their disadvantages through trade with the Caribbean. By cutting off trade with the foreign West Indies, the Sugar Act not only threatened profits but also endangered the northern colonists' elaborate adjustments to the requirements of the imperial economy.

The Stamp Act. The Proclamation of 1763 injured Virginians primarily; the Sugar Act promised to hurt New England and the middle colonies. The Grenville ministry next proposed a measure that angered powerful groups in every one of the colonies and threatened the political autonomy that Americans as a whole had gained over a century of effort.

During the summer of 1763 Grenville decided to impose a tax on legal documents and other items, to be paid with stamps purchased from the British treasury. The law required that a revenue stamp be affixed to all licenses to practice professions, to documents used in court, to papers concerning land transfers or exports or imports, to all private contracts, to newspapers, and even to college diplomas. These stamps were to be paid for in gold or silver, and the money collected was to be set aside for exclusive use in the colonies. Violations of the law would be tried in both the ordinary and the admiralty courts.

Before proceeding with the measure, Grenville had had the foresight to consult the colonial governors and confer with agents of the colonial legislatures in London who informally represented colonial interests at the seat of empire. The Americans were dubious about such a tax, but the colonial assemblies, Grenville learned, would not accept the alternative of taxing themselves. Under the circumstances, he decided to push his scheme. In early 1765, after a short debate, Parliament passed the momentous Stamp Act.

Two other measures formed part of Grenville's program of tightening imperial control. The Quartering Act (actually two separate measures of 1765 and 1766) required colonial authorities to provide barracks and supplies for British troops or, in lieu of barracks, to make provision for billeting troops in inns or unoccupied dwellings. The Currency Act (1764) forbade colonial legislatures to issue legal tender paper money. Previously applied only in New England, the prohibition was now extended to all the colonies.

The Quartering and Currency acts deeply offended Americans. The first seemed a dangerous extension of British military power in America. The second hampered the colonial legislatures'

Library of Congress

Although colonists could seldom cooperate in other ways, they did agree on their response to the direct taxes these innocent-looking stamps represented.

efforts to provide currency that American business could substitute for scarce coin. Neither law, however, produced the wave of outrage that greeted the Stamp Act.

The Stamp Act touched almost every aspect of colonial social and economic life—the professions, commerce, the press, and education. It penalized two of the most articulate and influential groups in the colonies—lawyers and newspaper publishers. It also threatened the hard-won authority of colonial assemblies, which had previously exercised the power to levy taxes. Furthermore, the Stamp Act raised profound and disturbing constitutional issues. First, were the colonies subordinate to Great Britain, or equal partners in the empire? Second, must American colonists pay taxes imposed by Parliament, where they were not formally represented? Few colonists expected their representatives to be seated in the English Parliament; rather, they wanted Parliament to recognize the authority of colonial assemblies, including their authority to tax. Unlike most British measures during the imperial crisis that followed the French and Indian War, the Stamp Act jeopardized all the colonies equally. Thus it did more to create a common bond of opposition to British policies than the other measures. It was probably the most foolish and inexpedient bill passed by the British Parliament in its long history.

News that Parliament had passed the Stamp Act reached the colonies in mid-April 1765. In May the Virginia House of Burgesses, goaded by the young firebrand Patrick Henry, boldly resolved that Americans had all the rights of Englishmen and that only their own legislatures could tax them. Virginia's action electrified Americans everywhere. Newspapers all over the colonies praised the resolutions and denounced British policy. Other colonial assemblies quickly joined the House of Burgesses in attacking the act, and the Massachusetts General Court called for a colonial congress to meet in October to consider united action in the crisis.

But outraged citizens did not wait until the congress met. In almost every colony news of the act stirred up violence. Mobs of artisans, shopkeepers, sailors, and merchants, some organized as "Sons of Liberty," hanged and burned effigies of Grenville and royal officials in America and physically attacked tax collectors and supporters of the new tax. In Boston they burned the house of Lieutenant Governor Thomas Hutchinson. So effective was this intimidation that almost all the stamp distributors resigned their commissions.

By the time the Stamp Act Congress convened in New York (October 7–25, 1765), the act was a dead letter in every colony except Georgia, where an unusually firm governor succeeded in making the citizens comply with it. The congress adopted petitions addressed to the king, the House of Lords, and the House of Commons. Although mild in tone, they insisted once again that Americans could be taxed only by bodies that represented them directly.

The petitions did little to move the British government, and mob violence only angered English conservatives: Grenville, for one, was prepared to use troops to enforce the law. A few English leaders, such as Edmund Burke, supported the Americans, but in the end it was economic pressure that killed the tax. The merchants of England, skeptical of the Stamp Act from the outset, grew increasingly hostile to the measure as time passed because the law proved disastrous for trade with America. In some places in the colonies the courts were disrupted and the legal processes for enforcing commercial contracts stalled. Still more dismaying were the nonimportation (boycott) agreements initiated by New Yorkers and widely adopted in the other colonies. Citizens pledged not to buy British goods, and merchants agreed not to import them. The resulting drop in transat-lantic trade soon brought many British manufacturers and exporters to the brink of bankruptcy.

Parliament could not resist the protests of the English merchants against the Stamp Act. On March 18, 1766, it repealed the detested measure but simultaneously adopted the Declaratory Act, affirming its right to legislate for the colonies "in all cases whatsoever." In effect, the English government was telling the Americans that it acknowledged the stamp tax as a mistake, but that it would not accept the principle of "no taxation without representation" that had been used to oppose it.

The Townshend Acts. The rejoicing that followed news of the repeal of the Stamp Act was short-lived. In January 1766 the New York assembly refused to contribute support for British troops as required by the Quartering Act. Over the summer hostile feelings arose between New York citizens and British soldiers, and several Americans were injured in violent clashes between redcoats and Sons of Liberty, the secret organization formed to protest the Stamp Act. At the urging of Charles Townshend, Grenville's successor, Parliament suspended the New York legislature's powers in mid-1767.

During the debate over taxation Townshend had noticed that some Americans had made a distinction between a tax for raising revenue and one intended to regulate commerce. The first, they had said, was a dangerous novelty; the second was traditional and acceptable. "Champagne Charlie"—a witty, charming, but shallow man—now seized on this distinction as a way around American resistance to revenue taxes. In May 1767 he proposed legislation that proved almost as foolish and inept as the Stamp Act: the Revenue Act of 1767.

Commonly referred to as the Townshend Acts, the law imposed new import duties on glass, red and white lead, painters' colors, paper, and tea. The imposts (taxes) were to be paid in coin and the money used to pay royal officials in the colonies, thereby ending their dependence on colonial legislatures for their salaries. The Townshend Acts also authorized the colonial higher courts to issue writs of assistance to help customs officers search private property for violations of the new law. A companion measure established a board of customs commissioners with headquarters in Boston and new vice-admiralty courts in Halifax, Philadelphia, and Charleston to enforce both old and new trade regulations.

Patriots again attacked British policy and demanded a boycott of British goods. This time the colonial merchants were determined to keep the violence under control, and for a while they succeeded. Before long, however, the public began to defy the customs commissioners openly. In a number of places mobs rescued ships and cargoes held for suspected smuggling. In Rhode Island the courts were intimidated into acquitting accused smugglers.

The disorder never became as widespread as it had during the Stamp Act crisis, but it seemed sufficiently alarming to the royal governor of Massachusetts, Sir Francis Bernard, to require drastic action. Responding to Bernard's reports, the British government ordered Commander in Chief Thomas Gage to move troops from New York to Boston. At the same time the British ministry sent the governor two more regiments of redcoats from Britain. The troops were greeted with hostility and deep suspicion by Bostonians, who were convinced that the soldiers were there to intimidate the colony and arrest Patriot leaders. Actually their purpose was merely to keep order, but the people of the city remained apprehensive and skeptical.

Meanwhile, in Britain pressure mounted to repeal the Townshend duties. They had brought relatively little revenue and by encouraging a second boycott had led to another drastic drop in American trade. Once more adopting an expedient course, Parliament canceled the duties in 1770, except for a three-penny tax on each pound of tea. By now, even such firm friends of America as William Pitt were beginning to fear that the colonists wanted to overturn the basic laws governing commercial relations between Britain and the colonies.

Fears for Colonial Religious Autonomy.

The tightening of imperial bonds was not confined to the political and economic spheres. In religion, too, the advent of the crown's Tory advisers tripped off efforts to limit colonial autonomy. In March 1763 the archbishop of Canterbury, head of the Church of England, wrote that he and his fellow bishops finally intended to "try our utmost for bishops" at the next session of Parliament. The colonies did not have an episcopal structure; this, the archbishop said, would have to be remedied.

The archbishop's scheme to attach the colonies more securely to Anglicanism eventually failed. Yet controversy over the religious issue continued to rage, constantly fed by rumors that the effort to establish Anglican bishops in America had not ended. Especially in New England where hostility to Anglicanism had always been intense, many colonists came to believe that there was a plot to impose upon them bishops, tithes for the Church of England, and even laws restricting public office to Anglicans. Inevitably the religious and political issues merged. The link between these issues seemed confirmed by the role of the Anglican clergy in America. Unlike the Dissenting ministers, who were often the most vehement enemies of the Grenville and Townshend programs, clergy of the Church of England opposed active resistance to the stamp tax and Townshend duties,

New York Public Library Picture Collection

This is an unusual contemporary view of Gage's troops being disembarked at Boston in 1768. Note the fact that the tallest buildings in this eighteenth-century American city were the churches.

urging their flocks to obey the law and show respect for royal officials.

Patriot Ideology. Before 1763 Americans had taken enormous pride in their British heritage and had willingly acknowledged their loyalty to British authority. After that year they developed a rationale for autonomy and then revolution that would carry them all the way to independence.

During the imperial crisis of 1763–76 some of the best minds of America were devoted to the task of justifying colonial "rights." At various stages of the British-American conflict such men as John Dickinson, Thomas Jefferson, John Adams, and Benjamin Franklin published letters, pamphlets, and editorials that indicted British policies in the name of fundamental political principles. At times their writing was important largely for its immediate political utility. Dickinson's *Letters from a Farmer in Pennsylvania to the Inhabitants of the British Colonies,* for example, was an attack on the Townshend duties that emphasized the illegality of collecting internal taxes in America as opposed to merely regulating commerce. *Letters from a Farmer* helped rally support against those measures in 1767 and 1768. But there were also searching and thorough defenses of American freedom and the right to resist authority that, taken together, announced a new attitude toward government and the individual's relations to it.

Few of the pamphleteers and writers were original thinkers. They borrowed widely from European, especially English, sources. Many of them turned to the radical Whig publicists of the late 1680s and 1690s, who had sought to justify the Glorious Revolution against James II and later had worked out arguments to limit the power of the crown. Locke's treatise *Of Civil Government* was an especially fertile source of ideas. Society, said Locke, was based on an agreement between ruler and ruled to preserve the natural rights of man inherent in the order of the universe. Although obedience to a just ruler was required by this "social contract," disobedience to tyranny was also an obligation.

Borrowing these and other ideas, Patriots almost always maintained that they were defending traditional rights guaranteed under the unwritten British constitution and endangered by either the king or his chief ministers. Far from demanding what was legitimate obedience from their subjects, they argued, the tyrants in Britain were attempting to subvert rights sanctioned both by history and by the laws of nature. Such arguments became vital weapons in the Patriot arsenal; as

incorporated in the Declaration of Independence, they would be handed down to later Americans as part of their political heritage.

The Whig thinkers also provided Americans with a moral rationale for independence. In England political dissenters during the early eighteenth century had come to regard English society as corrupt. Compared with the past, royal officials were mere "placemen" who served royal power with no other aim but to grow rich. England itself had grown wealthy, its people a prey to luxury and vice.

Americans seized on this bleak picture enthusiastically, using it to support the Patriot position. In contrast to corrupt Britain, American society was pure and unspoiled. The colonists still lived honestly and simply. But would all this not end if Bute, Grenville, and the rest had their way? If Americans did not resist, surely a horde of locusts in the shape of royal officials would descend on America and eat up the substance of American society, meanwhile exposing the colonists to the dissipations and moral laxity that the young society had till now been spared. If for no other reason than to preserve American innocence, British policies must be resisted at all costs.

Massacre in Boston. Meanwhile, as the journalists, pamphleteers, and lawyers learnedly or passionately argued the extent of natural rights, ordinary men and women grew ever more hostile to British policy and restless at the visible symbols of British authority. Some outburst of violence was probably inevitable in Boston. The city was a hotbed of anti-British feeling and townspeople and redcoats had been trading insults ever since the soldiers had arrived from New York. To make matters worse, many Boston artisans deeply resented the fact that British soldiers were taking part-time jobs and so depriving them of scarce work. Then, one evening in March 1770, a mob attacked a British sentry at his post. The soldier called for help, and when the men dispatched to rescue him arrived, they encountered a rapidly growing, angry crowd. At some point someone gave the command for the redcoats to fire. When the smoke of the muskets cleared, three Americans lay dead and several were wounded, two of whom later died.

The incident threatened to touch off a major uprising. The townspeople, Governor Hutchinson reported, were in a perfect frenzy and might attempt to drive out all 600 redcoats stationed in Boston. If they attacked, it would plunge the colony into full-scale rebellion against the crown, the consequences of which would be too horrible to contemplate. Although unsure of his authority,

American Antiquarian Society

Library of Congress

These two pictures illustrate the radical change in colonial attitudes toward King George III after 1763. The first—a 1762 American engraving—celebrates George's recent coronation. The second—a later English cartoon—shows America ridding itself of tyrrany, personified by the king carrying an odd whip to beat the American horse.

Hutchinson quickly ordered the arrest of the soldiers involved in the "massacre" and directed that the British garrison be removed from their barracks in town to Castle William in Boston harbor. From there they could continue to guard the city but would no longer be in direct contact with the irate citizens. Eventually seven of the redcoats were tried for the massacre. Ably defended by John Adams and Josiah Quincy, five were acquitted and two received light sentences.

The Gaspee Incident. Repeal of the Townshend duties in April 1770 cooled the argument between Britain and America. Yet the next two or three years were not without jarring incidents of American defiance and British reprisal. The most serious of these was the *Gaspee* incident.

The *Gaspee* was a British revenue cutter operating out of Narragansett Bay. On June 9, 1772, while pursuing a suspected smuggler, it ran aground on the Rhode Island coast near Providence, a hotbed of patriot sentiment. That evening a group of the city's prominent citizens boarded the vessel, wounded its commander, disarmed the crew, and burned the ship to the keel. This was not only a crime against the king's property but

The Sons of Liberty

Sons of Liberty organizations first sprang up in many American towns in 1765 to oppose the Stamp Act. Often led by prosperous merchants and lawyers, they were responsible for much of the violence against Stamp Tax agents and citizens who complied with the detested act. In Boston the Sons were responsible for burning the records of the vice-admiralty court and destroying the library and elegant home of Lieutenant Governor Thomas Hutchinson.

The Sons continued to be active through each confrontation with the English government over the next five years, but then, during the quieter years of the early 1770s, they became relatively quiescent. The 1773 Tea Act revived the Patriot cause and the Sons of Liberty as a militant expression of that cause. The following resolution was adopted by the New York Sons of Liberty in late November 1773 to protest Parliament's apparent attempt to thrust East India Company tea on the colonists through favored agents, thus bypassing other merchants and creating a potential monopoly for British interests. The argument used, however, resembles the earlier protests against "taxation without representation."

". . . To prevent a calamity which, of all others, is the most to be dreaded—slavery, and its terrible concomitants—we subscribers, being influenced from a regard to liberty and disposed to use all lawful endeavors in our power to defeat the pernicious project, and to transmit to our posterity those blessings of freedom which our ancestors have handed down to us; and to contribute to the support of the common liberties of America which are in danger to be subverted, *do,* for these important purposes, agree to associate together . . . and faithfully to observe and perform the following *resolutions, viz.*

1st. *Resolved,* That whoever shall aid, or abet, or in any manner assist in the introduction of tea . . . into this colony, while it is subject . . . to payment of a duty, for the purpose of raising a revenue in America, he shall be deemed an enemy to the liberties of America.

"2d. *Resolved.* That whoever shall be aiding, or assisting, in the landing, or carting of such tea, from any ship or vessel, or shall hire any house, store-house, or cellar . . . to deposit the tea . . . he shall be deemed an enemy to the liberties of America.

"3d. *Resolved.* That whoever shall sell or buy . . . tea, or shall aid . . . in transporting such tea . . . from this city, until the . . . revenue act shall be totally and clearly repealed, he shall be deemed an enemy to the liberties of America.

"4th. *Resolved.* That whether the duties on tea, imposed by this act, be paid in Great Britain, or in America, our liberties are equally affected.

"5th. *Resolved.* That whoever shall transgress any of these resolutions, we shall not deal with or employ, or have any connection with him."

---

also a blatant attack on a royal officer. Royal officials immediately posted a large reward for information leading to the conviction of the guilty parties and convened a commission of leading American Loyalists to investigate the affair. But no one chose, or dared, to come forward with information, and royal officials could only fume with frustration.

The Tea Act. The *Gaspee* affair notwithstanding, the period between 1771 and 1773 was one of relative calm. During these years the Patriot cause, without new outrages to feed on, went into eclipse. The militant Sons of Liberty were determined to compel the British government to rescind the remaining duty on tea and tried to force merchants to continue the nonimportation agreements. They were rebuffed. Instead, British-American trade revived—to the joy of the merchants, who no longer saw any purpose in boycotting English wares now that the other Townshend duties were dead. Meanwhile, Americans—then a tea-drinking people—evaded the duty by smuggling their favorite beverage in from Dutch sources.

Now the government in England blundered once more and set in motion the final phase of the British-American confrontation. The occasion for this misstep was the distress of the British East India Company. After decades of growing profit in trade with India and the Far East, the company had been brought to the edge of ruin by mismanagement and fraud. Its last remaining asset, 18 million pounds of tea, could not be sold because taxes in Britain and America made smuggled Dutch tea cheaper. To help the company the British government, under the Tea Act of 1773, agreed to allow it to sell its tea in the colonies through its own agents. By eliminating American middlemen, the company might pay the three-pence-a-pound tax and still undersell smuggled tea.

Once again, everyone involved in the plan miscalculated the effects British policy would have in America. The measure particularly riled the so-called free traders among American merchants—those who would not deal in taxed tea but sold only the smuggled variety. If Parliament could bypass them by selecting favored merchants to sell East India Company tea, could it not do the same thing with other goods? In the eyes of many colonial merchants the Tea Act suggested that Britain might abuse its power to regulate imperial commerce by giving monopoly privileges to cooperative colonial businessmen while denying them to unfriendly ones.

In each major port artisans, shopkeepers, and merchants gathered to condemn this latest threat to American liberty. Information was passed from cities to villages and from colony to colony through the Committees of Correspondence, building a broad and organized resistance. In New York radical leaders, inactive for three years, used the new outrage to reorganize the New York Sons of Liberty. In Philadelphia old Sons of Liberty resumed their defiant attacks on British policies and forced the merchants who had pledged to receive the tea to now refuse it. The radicals urged all Americans to abstain from drinking tea. Patriot women responded by turning to native concoctions that they loyally pronounced "vastly more agreeable" than anything out of India.

In Boston during the winter of 1773 the Tea Act produced an explosion that initiated the final step to independence. Leading the Boston radicals were the fiery Samuel Adams, who had organized the Sons of Liberty, and a prominent free trader, John Hancock. In late November the first tea-carrying vessels had arrived in Boston. On the evening of December 16 a group of Patriots dressed as Mohawk Indians boarded the ships and dumped the contents of 342 chests of tea—worth £10,000–into the harbor. Hundreds of people watched from the wharf as a thick layer of tea leaves spread over the water. They did not know it, but they were watching part of the British Empire sink beneath the waves.

Intolerable Coercion. Between March and May 1774, following other attacks on tea-carrying vessels, an angry Parliament passed the so-called Intolerable or Coercive Acts. The first of these measures was designed to punish Boston by closing the port to all commerce until the East India Company had been paid for its tea. The second, intended to prevent local juries from frustrating enforcement of imperial trade regulations, allowed royal officials accused of crimes while stopping a riot or collecting revenue to be sent to Britain for trial. The third modified the charter of unruly Massachusetts by giving the royal governor enlarged appointive powers and limiting the authority of the town meetings, which had served as forums for anti-British radicals. The fourth measure, intended to intimidate all the colonies alike, extended the provisions of the Quartering Act so that troops might be lodged in occupied private dwellings. A fifth law, the Quebec Act, established a highly centralized administration for the new province of Quebec. Stretching Quebec's boundaries into an area south of the Great Lakes previously claimed by Virginia. Connecticut, and Massachusetts, it also offered religious toleration and civil rights to the French Catholics of the province. Though not meant to punish the colonies, its generous recognition of Catholic rights offended many American Protestants, and Patriots lumped the Quebec Act together with the other coercive measures.

The First Continental Congress. It was now America's turn to be furious. In response to a widespread demand for a united colonial front against the Intolerable Acts, fifty-five delegates representing all the colonies except Georgia met at Philadelphia in September 1774. This First Continental Congress was composed of men with widely differing views. There were radicals, who claimed that American rights were founded on natural law and that, accordingly, Parliament could not abridge them in any way. As one of them, Roger Sherman, expressed it, there were "no other legislatures over the colonies but their respective assemblies." There were also moderates who argued that American rights came from the British constitution and that Parliament had the right to legislate at least on matters of imperial trade.

During the debate a copy of the Suffolk Resolves, recently drafted in Massachusetts, arrived in Philadelphia. These condemned the Intolerable Acts and urged the people of Massachusetts to establish an armed militia, boycott British goods, and withhold taxes from the royal government. Presented to the delegates, the Suffolk Resolves were endorsed as the congress's own resolutions. In its own name the congress proved equally radical. Its Declaration of Rights and Grievances sharply attacked virtually all British trade legislation since 1763 and established a Continental Association, which forbade the importation or consumption of British goods and urged that colonial goods not be exported. The congress resolved to meet the following May if American grievances had not been redressed by then.

The First Continental Congress was a milestone on the road to American solidarity. Until this time provincial legislatures had acted independently; there had been no body that could claim to speak for Americans as a whole. This disunity reflected the entire sweep of colonial history, which had begun with individual settlements and had continued for over a century as a series of parallel

An Historical Portrait Mercy Otis Warren

"History," complained John Adams, "is not the Province of the Ladies." He was referring to *History of the Rise, Progress and Termination of the American Revolution* by Mercy Otis Warren, historian, patriot, playwright, and poet. Adams felt that Warren had been unfair to him in this three-volume work when she alleged that "his passions and prejudices were sometimes too strong for his sagacity and judgment." He wrote her an angry letter and a furious exchange ensued. Ultimately Adams and Warren reconciled and exchanged locks of hair as peace offerings.

The woman who had so aroused Adams's fury was born in Barnstable, Massachusetts, in September 1728. The third of thirteen children and the oldest daughter of Mary Allyne and James Otis, Mercy could claim ancestors on both sides renowned for their lively intelligence and fiery tempers. Her maternal great-great-grandfather, Edward Dotey, had been an indentured servant on the *Mayflower* who had threatened mutiny aboard the ship and participated in the first duel in America. He emerged from the duel unharmed and finally settled down to become a productive citizen. Her father, a prosperous farmer and merchant, was descended from John Otis, an early-seventeenth-century settler in Higham, Massachusetts.

One of Mercy's earliest memories was of her father reading law books at the kitchen table, where her older brothers also studied. He became a lawyer when Mercy was still a young girl, eventually entering politics and becoming speaker of the General Court of Massachusetts. Reading was an important part of the Otis household and Mercy joined her brothers at their study table. Although a college education was unattainable for the Otis daughters, Mercy was allowed to go along with her brothers for instruction at their uncle's. Reverend James Russell supported his niece's desire for an education and encouraged her to read books from his well-stocked library. Here Mary found the *History of the World* by Sir Walter Raleigh, a book that influenced her own writings. Another source of inspiration was the political discussions among prominent Massachusetts personalities of the day held round the Warren dining table.

In 1754 Mercy, now twenty-six years old, married James Warren of Plymouth, a Harvard graduate, merchant, and farmer. Mercy and James, "first friend of my heart," had five sons. She managed the large household in Plymouth with great competence. She believed, she told her friends, that if women organized themselves efficiently, they could not only do their household chores but also have time for the pleasures of "the book and the pen." She continued her interest in politics through the activities of her husband, a member of the Massachusetts legislature, and her brother, James Otis, who, having resigned his post as king's advocate general, became the chief spokesman against writs of assistance—the general search warrants used by the British government to enforce the detested Sugar Act of 1764.

By the 1770s Mercy's house in Plymouth had become a gathering place for leading Massachusetts opponents of royal policies, including John and Samuel Adams. To serve the Revolutionary cause, Mercy decided to write political satire in the form of plays meant to be read rather than performed. In 1772 the *Massachusetts Spy* printed the *Adulateur,* set in the fictional country of Servia. Important Massachusetts political figures appeared in this play, camouflaged as Roman citizens. The hero was her brother, James, disguised as Cassius, leader of the Patriots. The villain was Rapatio, the ruler of Servia, in reality Thomas Hutchinson, the royal governor of Massachusetts, a man despised throughout the province by Patriots because of his unswerving loyalty to the British crown. In *The Adulateur* Rapatio, an ambitious, power-hungry tyrant, is determined to smash "the ardent love of liberty in Servia's free-born sons." In 1773 a Boston publisher brought out a pamphlet containing a series of letters written by Hutchinson and his relative and friends, which further inflamed Patriots by allegedly threatening "total destruction to the liberties of all *America.*" Mercy Warren may have been among the first to see these letters, which were reportedly taken confidentially to her house in Plymouth before they appeared publicly. After the letters were published, she wrote another

---

but separate provincial developments. During the colonial wars the colonies had cooperated with one another in a limited way. But, as we have seen, the one serious effort at forming a voluntary union for limited purposes—the Albany Congress in 1754—proved a failure. Now, in 1774, another and greater crisis had finally broken through the selfish localism that had so often marred colonial relations. Americans would continue to resist surrendering local political autonomy to a collective government. But they had taken the first step toward political union.

Lexington and Concord. In the next months the Patriot leaders prepared for the worst. In every colony men joined militia units, collected arms and powder, and began to engage in military drill. In Massachusetts these groups were called Minute Men because they were expected to "Stand at a minute's warning in Case of alarm." Many of the assemblies also took action to support the people of Massachusetts, who were suffering economically and politically under the Intolerable Acts. Meanwhile, General Gage, now installed as governor of Massachusetts, prepared his forces for a

play, *The Defeat,* again featuring Rapatio as the villain.

In 1774, after the Boston Tea Party, Hutchinson escaped to England. At John Adams's request, Warren wrote a poetic celebration of the event in which sea nymphs were enchanted by finding "a profusion of Delicious teas . . . Choice Sochong and the imperial Leaf" in Boston harbor. That fall she started a new play, *The Group,* which denounced the mandamus councillors, appointees of the crown under the Massachusetts Government Act, one of the "intolerable measures" of 1774. These men were disguised as Hum Humbug, Sir Spendall, Judge Meagre, and Brigadier Hateall. Since Hutchinson was in England, he did not actually appear in this work, but Warren had her "group" acknowledge him as their master. They also readily admitted to their sins of greed, hatred, and hunger for power. The "group" was surrounded by "a swarm of court sycophants, hungry harpies and unprincipled danglers . . . the whole supported by a mighty army and navy from Blunderland."

During the Revolution Mercy Warren frequently visited Watertown, where the Massachusetts legislature had rented a house for its council meetings. One of the bedrooms was reserved exclusively for the use of James Warren. Mercy presided there as hostess on many occasions, getting to know virtually all the Revolutionary leaders. "Everybody," said her husband,

"either eats, drinks or sleeps in this house." In addition, she carried on a correspondence with Thomas Jefferson, John Dickinson, Samuel Adams, James Winthrop, Elbridge Gerry, Abigail Adams, and Mrs. Catherine Macaulay Graham, the English historian. It was at Watertown that she conceived the idea of writing a history of the war with Britain, which as wife, sister, daughter, and friend of Patriots she could observe at first hand. In her bedroom above the chamber in which the council met, Mercy began to record her "introductory Observations."

After the Revolution the Warrens went into political decline. James Warren lost his legislative seat in 1780, and later in the decade he and his wife were condemned by political conservatives for their alleged endorsement of Shays' Rebellion. No public statement or private letters of theirs seem to support this accusation, and in the last volume of her *History* Mercy explicitly criticized the rebellion's participants. The charges were probably a Federalist response to Mrs. Warren's *Observations on the New Constitution,* which opposed ratification of the federal Constitution. These same Federalists were also angered by her defense of the French Revolution.

The remainder of Mercy Warren's life was devoted to writing her *History.* It took her twenty-five years to complete. In its 1,200 pages she covers the period between the Stamp Act and the close of the

century. Warren takes into account the importance of Canada, the Indian question, and the beginnings of American nationalism. Though the work strongly reflects the opinions of a Massachusetts Jeffersonian Republican, readers could point to few errors of fact. It was her anti-Federalist bias—as well as her personal criticisms—that angered John Adams and others.

In October 1814 Mercy Warren died at her house in Plymouth at the age of eighty-six. She had survived her husband, her brother, and three of her sons. She had also lived through two of her country's wars and succumbed, still alert mentally, in the midst of a third. Critics at a later date judged Warren's plays as "inferior fragments" and "literary fossils," but at the time her talents were highly respected by such folk as Alexander Hamilton, John Adams, and Elbridge Gerry, not to speak of ordinary citizens who read the excerpts of her writings available in the newpapers. In recent years critical opinion has reversed itself. Merle Curti, a modern scholar, has called Warren's major work a "realistic history of the struggle for independence." A vivid narrative of the Revolution by an author who personally observed its events and participants, it is also a remarkable testimony to one woman's ability, through her intelligence and skill, to triumph over the handicaps of her time and place.

Patriot attack. Gage particularly feared the Boston Committee of Safety, headed by John Hancock, which had been formed to coordinate patriot military actions and to call out the Minute Men upon further British provocation.

In mid-April Gage received orders to enforce the Intolerable Acts, by military action if necessary, and to stop Patriot preparations for armed defense. Immediately he dispatched a force of 700 men to Lexington to arrest Hancock and Samuel Adams. Learning of the redcoats' destination, the Boston Committee of Safety sent Paul Revere and

William Dawes to warn the two Patriot leaders and to alert the countryside. When the redcoats arrived at Lexington at dawn on April 19, 1775, they found seventy Minute Men ready for them. After repeated British commands to disperse, the outnumbered Americans complied. At this point someone fired a shot. The British then let off several volleys; the Americans replied but got the worst of the exchange. At the end of the skirmish the British occupied Lexington Common, where eight Americans lay dead.

The British now marched to Concord, where

The Connecticut Historical Society, Hartford

Amos Doolittle recorded the Battle of Lexington for posterity, but he fiddled with the facts. The British were surprised and unprepared to fight the colonists. Here they appear as orderly, methodical killers.

they destroyed some Patriot supplies. By this time the countryside had been thoroughly aroused, and as the British troops marched back to Boston, they were attacked on every side by colonial militia. The sixteen miles to Boston became a murderous gauntlet as Minute Men by the hundreds fired at the redcoats from behind walls, barns, and trees. By the time the British reached the safety of their base, 250 had been killed or wounded. Also dead were 100 Americans.

CONCLUSIONS

Lexington and Concord turned a disagreement into a war. For the next eight years North America would be the arena for struggling armies and dying men. At the end there would be an independent United States.

In one sense this momentous result was the climax of the long process we observed in Chapter 3 that had helped to create a distinctive society and culture in America and a sense among the colonists that they were not simply transplanted Europeans. It was also related to the growing economic and political maturity of British North America. Here, ironically, British policy was itself largely to blame. Unlike the other European colonial powers, Britain had done much to foster colonial political autonomy and economic prosperity. By 1763 British North America had the population, the technical resources, and the political self-confidence to defy one of Europe's most powerful nations.

But cultural, political, and economic maturity by themselves were not enough for revolution. The ties to Britain remained too strong. The actual imperial crisis was precipitated by the special circumstances after 1763. One crucial matter was the French and Indian War. By relieving the colonists of a long-standing danger, it weakened American dependence on Britain. At the same time it loaded the British taxpayer with debt and demonstrated to Pitt's Tory successors that the Americans could not be counted on to bear the burdens of empire in an acceptable way.

However justified from the British perspective, the policies adopted after 1763 were foolishly conceived and executed. A few in Britain saw that the American colonies had become a mature society fast approaching England in wealth and numbers; but most Englishmen and, most crucially, King George's Tory ministers could see them only as disobedient children. Charging ahead blindly, they imposed measures that threatened many occupational and economic groups, deeply disturbed the elite merchants and planters, and aroused fears among many thousands of ordinary people that they were to be enslaved and exploited by harpies in the shape of bishops and royal officials.

In short, we cannot separate the economic, religious, and political strands of causation. All together motivated the colonists who eventually sought independence; and in each of these areas we find a common anxiety: fear of oppression. It was a fierce colonial attachment to self-determination in all spheres that was the ultimate source of the Revolution.

FOR FURTHER READING

Gary M. Walton and James P. Shepherd. *The Economic Rise of Early America* (1979)
> The best brief, overall view of the colonial economy. Also contains an interesting chapter on the economic impact of British imperial policies after 1763. Though written by two economists, the book is not difficult for students of history since the authors are careful to define all their technical terms.

Arthur M. Schlesinger. *The Colonial Merchants and the American Revolution, 1763–1776* (1917)
> Examines the contribution of colonial traders to the origins of the Revolution. The author sees them largely as protective of their economic interests and opposed to the more radical revolutionaries, though at many points the interests of both overlapped. Very much in the tradition of Charles Beard and the "Progressive" historians.

James Henretta. *The Evolution of American Society, 1700–1815: An Interdisciplinary Analysis* (1973)
> An interesting attempt by a social historian to integrate the social, economic, and political history of early America. Henretta takes a dimmer view of the equality of wealth and power in colonial America than I do.

Jackson T. Main. *The Social Structure of Revolutionary America* (1965)
> Main studied the income, style, and cost of living, distribution of property, in rural and urban society in mid-eighteenth century America. He depicts the colonies—and colonists—as prosperous and socially mobile. Colonial America, he says, was indeed "the best poor man's country in the world."

Edmund S. Morgan and Helen M. Morgan. *The Stamp Act Crisis: Prologue to Revolution* (1953)
> The best short treatment of this crucial step along the road to independence. A balanced account of an unbalanced period in our history.

Bernard Bailyn. *The Ideological origins of the American Revolution* (1967)
> Bailyn takes ideas seriously as fundamental moving causes. In this examination of the pre-Revolutionary battle of words, Bailyn shows how the libertarian ideas forged in the seventeenth- and early-eighteenth-century English struggle with the crown helped mold the actions of American Patriots before 1776.

Robert A. Gross. *The Minutemen and Their World* (1976)
> This study of the town of Concord, Massachusetts, before 1776 captures the hopes, frustrations, and fears of a small American community caught in the vortex of great imperial changes. Gross has a talent for combining the social scientist's hard facts with the humanist's sensitivity to ordinary people's feelings and responses.

Pauline Maier. *From Resistance to Revolution: Colonial Radicals and the Development of American Opposition to Great Britain, 1765–1776* (1972)
> Professor Maier shows that the "radical" leaders of the American independence movement were really orderly and prudent men who opposed mob violence. Her book helps explain why the American Revolution seldom erupted into social excess.

Bernard Bailyn. *The Ordeal of Thomas Hutchinson* (1974)
> This biography of the American-born royal governor of Massachusetts on the eve of the Revolution is a fine study of the mind and views of a leading American Tory. Bailyn makes it clear how difficult it is to find simple villains—and heroes—in history.

Merrill Jensen. *The Founding of a Nation: A History of the American Revolution, 1763–1776* (1968)
> A long and well-written study of the whole sweep of events, from the French and Indian War onward, that culminated in the declaration of Independence. Jensen gives attention to forces as well as human actors and deals with society as well as politics. He is convinced that the "history of the period is . . . one of extraordinary intricacy" and so he avoids simple answers to the problem of "causes."

John C. Miller. *Sam Adams: Pioneer in Propaganda* (1936)
> A classic older study of a major Revolutionary radical. Still worth reading.

Dumas Malone. *Jefferson the Virginian* (1948)
> By far the best treatment of Jefferson during the years he was intimately involved in the colonial struggle with Great Britain. This is volume

I of a multivolume work, now completed, called *Jefferson and His Time*. Malone's monumental opus has been criticized as a eulogy of Jefferson.

Carl Van Doren. *Benjamin Franklin* (1941)
A classic of American biography by a brilliant stylist. Covers far more than Franklin's work as Patriot leader; deals also with his contributions to science and journalism. A work of literature as well as history.

Douglas Southall Freeman. *Washington: An Abridgment* (1968)
This is the one-volume condensation of Freeman's monumental seven-volume life of Washington. The abridgement has been skillfully done.

5 The Revolution
How Did It Change America?

1775 The Second Continental Congress meets in Philadelphia; it declares war on Britain, organizes the Continental Army under George Washington, authorizes a navy, and appoints a Committee of Secret Correspondence • Ethan Allen captures Fort Ticonderoga • The Battle of Breed's (Bunker) Hill in Boston

1776–79 Main theater of war is in middle colonies; Philadelphia and Yorktown occupied by the British

1776 Paper money—"continentals"—printed • Thomas Paine's *Common Sense* • in Congress Richard Lee of Virginia introduces a resolution of independence from Britain • Congress approves the Declaration of Independence • Congress appoints a committee to plan for a permanent constitution

1777 Congress recommends that states sell Loyalist property • Horatio Gates defeats General Burgoyne at Saratoga, the turning point of the war • Congress approves a draft of the Articles of Confederation

1778 France and the American colonies establish a military alliance

1779 Spain declares war on Great Britain

1779–81 Main theater of war shifts to the southern colonies

1781 Final victory at Yorktown • Articles of Confederation ratified • The colonial monetary system collapses; Congress appoints Robert Morris to organize Bank of North America to strengthen public credit

1782 Americans and British agree on a preliminary peace treaty dealing with the states' western boundaries, fishing rights off Newfoundland, British garrisons in the West, colonial debts, and payment for Loyalist property

1783 The Treaty of Paris brings full independence • Massachusetts court interpretation of the state constitution prohibits slavery; thereafter slavery is illegal in the Bay State

1786 Virginia legislature adopts the principle of separation of church and state in an act drafted by Jefferson

Writing in the summer of 1775, shortly after Lexington and Concord, John Adams described an encounter with a person he had defended as an attorney in the courts. The man—"a common Horse Jockey," Adams labeled him—greeted the Founding Father on the road. "Oh! Mr. Adams," he exclaimed, "what great Things have you and your Colleagues done for us! We can never be grateful enough to you. There are no Courts of Justice now in this Province, and I hope there will never be another!" Adams was appalled. Would the future of America be as the "common Horse Jockey" hoped? Would the colonies, in the course of changing governments, jettison all social controls and have their entire social structure torn apart and turned upside down? "If the Power of the Country should ever get into such hands," remarked Adams, "and there is great danger that it will, to what purpose have we sacrificed our Time, Health, and every Thing?"

Adams—and other conservative Americans—worried throughout the war about a take-over of power by the less respectable people of the colonies. Their concern was understandable. Eight years of bitter fighting followed the skirmishes at Lexington and Concord. During that time the American community expended vast amounts of energy and wealth and sacrificed thousands of lives. Surely a struggle of this magnitude—one, moreover, fought in the name of freedom from tyranny—had to alter values, transform relationships and institutions, and revise perspectives. The obvious and fundamental result of the American Revolution was independence. But how profoundly did the Revolution change American society? Did Adams's fears prove to be justified?

AMERICAN PROSPECTS

As Americans considered their prospects in the days following Lexington and Concord, they found it hard to discern what lay ahead. Ties of memory, habit, interest, and affection, and fears of the unknown, all acted as deterents to a complete break with England. Few as yet wanted independence. Even among the most ardent Patriots the common hope was that Britain would see the light, abandon its punitive policies as expressed in the Intolerable Acts, and reconsider its fundamental relations with America. This hope was reflected in the Olive Branch Petition adopted by the Second Continental Congress in July 1775. Written by John Dickinson, the petition declared that the colonists remained loyal to King George

and asked him to intervene to protect his American subjects against Parliament's tyranny. Loyalists, needless to say, were even less willing to break with the past. Whether loyalist or patriot, virtually all Americans in the spring of 1775 recoiled at the thought of complete independence.

But whatever their ultimate goals, Americans recognized that resistance to the mighty British Empire was a chancy policy. Clearly there were strengths and weaknesses on both sides. Though still not a populous land, Britain was probably the strongest nation on earth in 1775. Just twelve years earlier it had defeated France, its archrival in Europe, and now was dominant in North America, India, South Africa, and many other parts of the world. On the face of it, the British had an enormous advantage over the Americans in numbers, military experience, and political unity.

But the English also labored under great difficulties. British military and naval capacity had been formidable indeed at the end of the French and Indian War in 1763. Thereafter it had deteriorated. Meanwhile, France had rebuilt its military and naval forces and was in a position to challenge Britain again. More important, Britain's victories in the late war had won it enemies and left it isolated. France, Spain, Holland, and Russia all feared British power and had specific grievances against England that they hoped to redress. These nations, especially France, were potential American allies in 1775. Their hostility to Great Britain would prove indispensable to the American cause.

Britain also faced enormous strategic problems in fighting a war in America. The British Isles were three thousand miles from the military action, and troops and supplies sent to the battle-fields would take two or three months to arrive. When they did, the troops would have to fight on unfamiliar terrain, often surrounded by a hostile populace. Americans were on their home ground, close to supplies and manpower, and able to mobilize every bit of strength they had for the battle at hand.

Yet the "rebels," too, faced colossal difficulties. Several hundred thousand Americans were not only opposed to the Patriot cause but were willing to risk their lives and property to defeat it. The Loyalists would be a great source of strength to the British. Several regiments of Loyalists would be enlisted in the British army and would fight ferociously against their countrymen. Generally speaking, Loyalist troops were more enthusiastic than the British themselves and would be widely feared and detested by the Patriots for their zeal.

Military Forces. Few Americans had military experience, let alone the knowledge required for raising, equipping, and leading a large army. Some colonials had served as officers during the French and Indian War, but none, not even George Washington, had held a rank higher than colonel. And the professional foreign soldiers who flocked to America seeking military appointments were often incompetent. The Marquis de Lafayette, the Germans Johann Kalb (known as Baron de Kalb) and Baron Friedrich Wilhelm von Steuben, and the Pole Thaddeus Kosciusko were skilled soldiers. But there was no officer on the American side who had the experience of commanding large bodies of troops in the field or of planning military strategy for the whole continent.

The colonists were better off in ordinary military manpower. Americans believed then, and would continue to believe for most of their history, that a volunteer soldier was better than a hired mercenary. British redcoats, and still more the Hessians—German soldiers hired by the king to help put down the rebellion—were men who fought only for pay and lacked the spirit of those fighting for their homeland. On the other hand, Continental troops, most Patriots insisted, were dedicated young men with freedom in their hearts.

In reality the situation was more complicated than this simple estimate. Colonial troops lacked the rigorous training of the redcoats and at times this difference strongly favored the British. On the other hand, most Americans knew how to use a rifle or musket, and many had experience in Indian warfare. In fact, their lack of traditional European military experience helped as much as it hurt. At the outset of a battle, British soldiers were trained to fire unaimed volleys at their opponents and trust to the sheer volume of lead to shock and disrupt the enemy. Then the ranks would charge the foe with bayonets. These tactics worked well enough on the open fields of Europe, where opposing armies faced each other in full view. They sometimes worked in the better-settled portions of America, too. But in the forests that covered so much of the colonies, where men could hide behind every tree and bush, they were unsuitable. Far more effective in the terrain of the New World was the American approach, in which troops equipped with accurate Kentucky rifles were deployed from behind cover. The British tried to modify their tactics to suit American conditions. Loyalist troops, moreover, were familiar with guerrilla fighting and were valuable auxiliaries to the British army. But on the whole, American commanders and enlisted men remained better adapted to war in America than the British.

Superior tactics might have helped even the odds, but the Patriots could not count on a consistent and stable supply of manpower. It was one thing to turn out with your gun for a local skirmish, and many young men did so willingly. It was another to enlist for a long term as a regular in the Continental Army, fight battles against professional soldiers, subject yourself to military discipline, and spend months or possibly years away from home and family. Under the circumstances it proved hard for the Continental Congress and the individual states to raise troops. At first patriotism was enough to bring in recruits; later, cash boun-

Library of Congress

The variety of uniforms in Baron Von Closen's watercolors of colonial troops suggests the fragmentation of Patriot forces during the Revolution.

ties and promises of land were necessary to induce men to enlist. And once they were in the army, the new recruits were hard to keep on the front lines fighting the British. Many joined for just a few months and then—with or without authorization—returned to civilian life. Almost 400,000 men passed through the Continental armies during the war, but George Washington never had more than 20,000 troops under his command at one time.

Another American military problem was conflicting jurisdiction. In reality, there were fourteen Patriot armies: the Continental Army under Washington and thirteen state armies, called "lines." The men in each were paid differently and were enlisted for different periods. Often the armies acted at cross-purposes, and Continental and state officers frequently argued over who had the greater authority or higher status.

Supplying the army was also a problem for the Americans. There were many fine gunsmiths in the colonies, but they produced so many types of sizes of weapons that securing the proper ammunition was difficult. There was also a shortage of gunpowder and shot, and the shortage at times threatened to put the entire American army out of action. Artillery was in especially short supply, for the country was not yet capable of manufacturing big guns.

When it came to ships, the new nation was somewhat better off. American shipyards were not equipped to build large ships of the line, the battleships of the day. The Continental Navy, accordingly, could scarcely challenge the British fleet in direct battle. But Americans could and did produce excellent small craft that served effectively as privateers—armed private ships commissioned to attack the enemy. Privateers provided most of the American naval punch. Licensed by Congress with "letters of marque" to prey on British commerce, they attacked enemy merchant ships even within sight of the British coast. During the war privateers captured 3,200 British ships, at immense cost to Great Britain and its citizens. Privateering helped to balance the great losses suffered by northern shippers from the British blockade of American harbors and their seizure of hundreds of American merchant vessels on the high seas.

Creating a Government. At the beginning, the Second Continental Congress was the country's only central political authority. This was a serious weakness. Although it regularly passed resolutions and proposed emergency measures, the Continental Congress was not an effective government. Sovereignty continued to reside in the individual provincial governments; in fact, the assemblage in Philadelphia was more like a diplomatic conference of sovereign states than a government. In the end every proposal Congress made depended on the support of the thirteen state legislatures, and these could as easily ignore its wishes as accept them.

Despite its limitations, for many months the Second Continental Congress acted as the government for the American people. It created the Continental Army with George Washington as commander in chief. On May 29, 1775, it adopted an address to the people of Canada asking them to join in resisting British tyranny. In July it approved the Olive Branch Petition; and after that was rejected by the king, it disavowed American allegiance to Parliament. That same month Congress established a post office department and appointed commissioners to negotiate peace treaties with the Indians. In the fall of 1775 it authorized a navy for the "United Colonies," and soon after appointed a five-man Committee of Secret Correspondence to approach Britain's European enemies for aid.

Wartime Finance. These moves were promising, but they did not create a strong, effective central government. One of Congress's chief weaknesses was that it lacked the power to tax. The state governments could tax; but Americans were unused to heavy taxation, and the states found it hard to make their citizens bear the full burden of the war's cost. During the various colonial wars of the past the individual colonies had met this same problem by issuing paper money. Now, once more, Congress and the states resorted to the printing press to pay contractors, the army, and public officials. The paper money issued by Congress were called "continentals," and by 1780 notes with a face value of about $200 million had been circulated. The states issued almost as much during the same period.

The American folk expression "not worth a continental" suggests the fate of this paper money. At first the continentals and state notes kept their face value surprisingly well. But as the volume of issues grew, the purchasing power of the notes fell. By 1780, $40 in continentals were worth less than $1 in gold and silver coin. Paper money prices soared so high that a bushel of corn that had sold for $1 in Massachusetts in the spring of 1777 sold for $80 by the summer of 1779. The governor of New Jersey, whose nominal salary was $40,000 a year, estimated in 1780 that the prewar purchasing power of his salary was less than $1,000.

In a modern nation such hyperinflation is

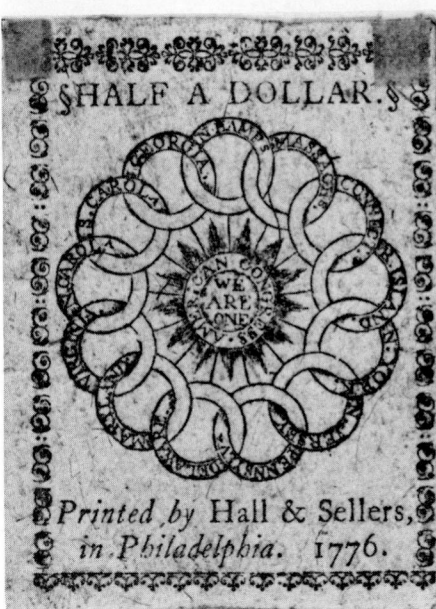

"We are one," proclaims this 1776 half-dollar certificate. Yet the conversion table for the swarm of currencies circulating during the Revolution suggests that colonial unity was less a fact than a dream.

§HALF A DOLLAR.§

WE ARE ONE

Printed by Hall & Sellers, in Philadelphia. 1776.

American Antiquarian Society

likely to produce social and economic disaster. Every creditor who is owed money, everyone with a fixed income, is seriously hurt. All business transactions are jeopardized, for no one can count on the future. But inflation had milder effects in eighteenth-century America. Few Americans in those years had investments in securities; bank accounts and life insurance policies were unknown. A few patriotic citizens did buy Congress's bonds ("loan office certificates"), and more took commissary or quartermaster certificates—IOUs, in effect—in payment for supplies and services furnished Congress. Both of these did fall in value, but the number of creditors hurt by the inflation was not large. Inflation also caused distress to the officers and men of the Continental Army, who found their wages declining rapidly in purchasing power. But relatively few people worked for money wages in these years or paid cash for the food they ate or the clothes they wore. The paper money system, then, generally worked rather well as a way of financing the war. In any event, neither Congress nor the states had any real alternative, given the financial traditions of the community and Congress's inability to tax.

THE ROAD TO INDEPENDENCE

Early Battles. While the Second Continental Congress struggled to establish an independent government and to raise men and money for the war, important military events were taking place in the field. Following the skirmishes at Lexington and Concord, General Gage found himself besieged in Boston by several thousand New England troops. In early June 1775 he prepared to dislodge the rebels from Dorchester Heights. The Americans countered by fortifying Breed's Hill (not Bunker Hill, as legend would have it) in Charlestown, across the harbor from Boston. On June 17 British naval vessels began firing on the Americans, and at noon 2,400 redcoats landed on the Charlestown peninsula. Twice the heavily laden "lobster-backs" trudged up Breed's Hill into the murderous fire of the Americans entrenched on top; twice they retreated. The third time General William Howe ordered them to drop their packs and charge with fixed bayonets. The redcoats swept the Americans off their perch and off nearby Bunker Hill as well. At the end of the day the British held the field, but at the enormous cost of over a thousand dead. Though technically an American defeat, the Battle of Bunker Hill was a moral victory that helped convince Americans they could stand up to British regulars.

Bunker Hill had been preceded by Ethan Allen's daring capture of the small British garrison at Fort Ticonderoga on Lake Champlain. It was soon followed by a double American thrust, led by Benedict Arnold and Richard Montgomery, against Montreal and Quebec, designed to deprive Britain of a base of operations against the Americans. The expedition was dogged by bad luck and nearly led to disaster for the Americans. Montgomery took Montreal, but Quebec, defended by British regulars and Canadians who had rejected Congress's invitation to join the struggle against England, held out. In the battle to capture Quebec Montgomery was killed, Arnold wounded, and several hundred Americans were killed or captured.

In the South the fighting went better for the Americans. There a force of Virginians and North Carolinians encountered the royal governor of Virginia, Lord Dunmore, and his army of white Loyalists and black slaves. The blacks had been prom-

A cartoon illustrating the British retreat from Concord and Lexington, obviously from a Patriot perspective.

National Archives

ised their freedom if they supported the king. Lord Dunmore's small force fought enthusiastically but was overwhelmed by the Patriots.

The year 1776 began well for the Patriot cause. In a series of actions in the Carolinas between February and June, the Americans beat off the attacks of generals Sir Henry Clinton and Charles Cornwallis. In March, after Continental troops had dragged the big guns captured at Ticonderoga down to within range of Boston, General Howe evacuated the city. The British never seriously threatened New England again.

Turning Points. As the months passed, many of the remaining emotional ties to Britain snapped. The use of Hessian mercenaries, the king's contemptuous rejection of the Olive Branch Petition, the British proclamation in December 1775 stating that the colonies were in open rebellion, and the closing off of all formal commerce with the rebellious Americans—these acts made it increas-

ingly clear to Patriots that reconciliation was impossible. A critical event in the South was Lord Dunmore's arming of the slaves. This move violated one of the South's strongest racial taboos, and Chesapeake planters who had previously held back now rushed to support the Patriot cause.

With each passing day, then, Patriots found it easier to consider independence as their ultimate goal. Their need for allies provided an additional push toward independence. France viewed the British troubles in America with glee. Resentful of their defeat in the French and Indian War, the French hoped to see Britain humbled and France restored to an important place in North America. Both France and Spain considered Britain a threat to their Caribbean possessions and expected a weak, independent America to be easier to deal with than the mighty British Empire. Early in 1776 the French foreign minister, the Count de Vergennes, sounded out Spain on aid to the Americans. Soon both countries began to funnel secret

Central campaigns, 1776–1778

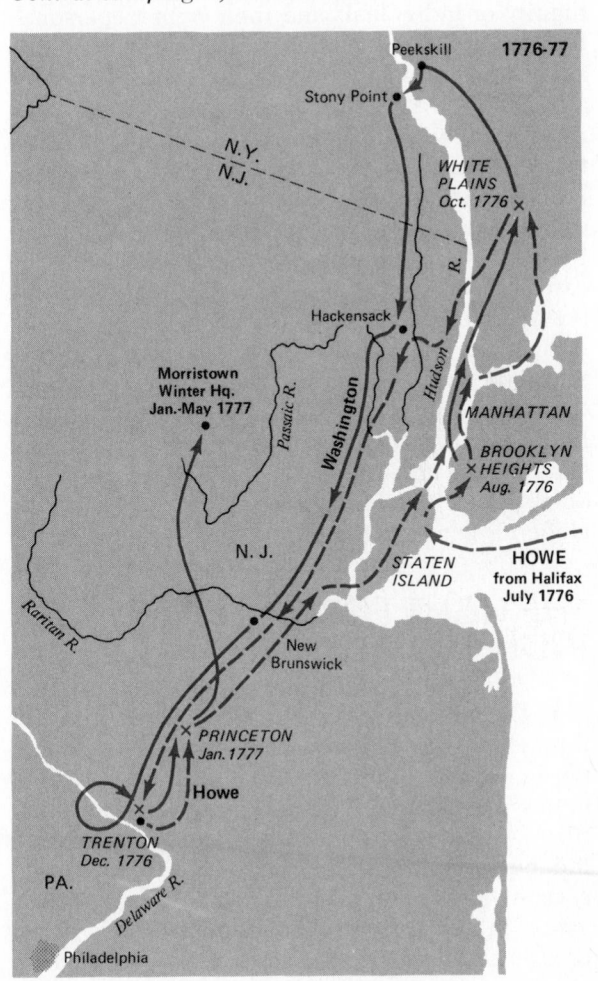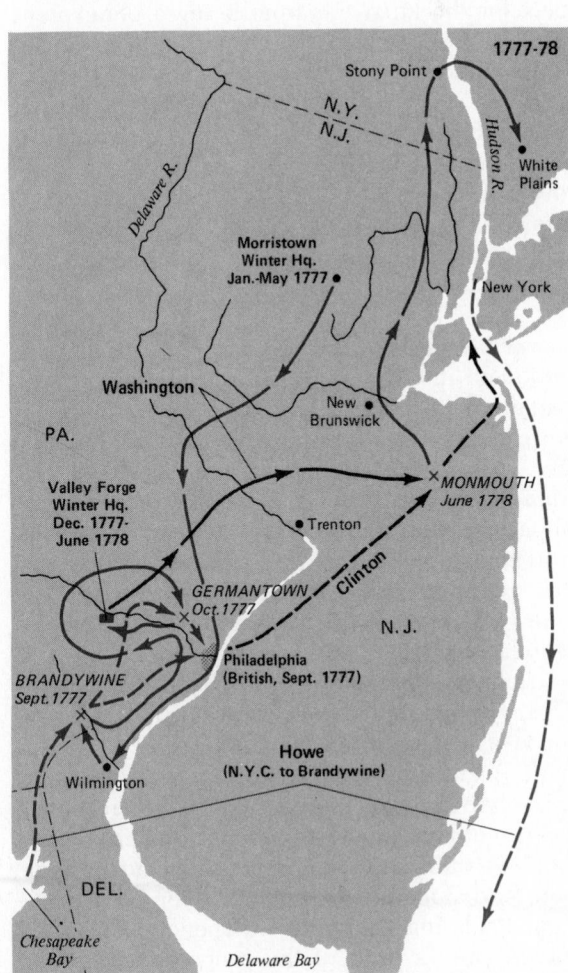

money and supplies to the colonists. Americans welcomed the aid but realized that all-out French and Spanish support depended on their own willingness to fight for independence, for only independence would accomplish what the two continental powers wanted: a crippled Britain.

Yet something more was needed to convince most Patriots that they should take the final step. Even though they had become disillusioned with Parliament and the king's ministers, they still had a touching faith in the king himself and hoped that he would see the light. Then in early 1776 a recent immigrant from England, Thomas Paine, published a fifty-page pamphlet called *Common Sense* that destroyed their last illusions. It is hard to estimate the political influence of words, but if we can ever ascribe a major political event to mere eloquence, we can in this case. *Common Sense* was eloquent to a rare degree. In bold and ringing phrases Paine denounced King George and the British government and insisted that the time had come to sever completely the ties with Britain. Calling George the "royal brute," Paine helped to destroy the colonists' awe of the crown and respect for the king. Far from being a benevolent father to his people, George had unleashed the wrath of redcoats, Hessians, Indians, and desperate slaves on them. He was not worthy of their esteem. Furthermore, he represented a tyrannical system. Monarchy, Paine declared, was a form of government condemned by God; kings were "crowned ruffians." Concluded Paine: "The blood of the slain, the weeping voice of nature cries, 'TIS TIME TO DEPART.'"

Independence Declared. Paine's moving polemic sold 120,000 copies in three months and was read throughout the colonies. Tories denounced it as treasonous and certain to encourage "republican" views—that is, ideas of representative government. *Common Sense* had an immense impact on patriots. Washington found it "working a powerful change in the minds of many men." In April a convention of North Carolinians authorized the colony's delegates in Congress to support independence. Virginia, the most populous colony, did the same the following month. Then, on June 7, 1776, Virginia delegate Richard Henry Lee introduced a resolution in the Continental Congress that the United Colonies "are, and of right ought to be, free and independent States." In response to this motion, Congress appointed Thomas Jefferson, Benjamin Franklin, John Adams, Roger Sherman, and Robert Livingston to prepare a document declaring American independence. At the end of June a draft of the proposed statement,

composed largely by Jefferson, was sent to Congress. On July 2 Congress voted for the principle of independence and on July 4 formally approved the revised Declaration of Independence.

The declaration had two aspects. One was a detailed indictment of King George for cruelties, crimes, and illegal political acts against humanity and America. George was made into a villain who personified British wrongdoing. The attack was unfair; the king was no worse than a host of parliamentary leaders. But it was an effective propaganda device. The second aspect was a statement of principles. The signers adopted Paine's radical antimonarchism to justify the drastic action they proposed to take. The people, not the divine right of kings, were the ultimate source of political authority, they declared. Governments were established to assure citizens of "certain unalienable rights," including the rights to "Life, Liberty and the pursuit of Happiness." These words were borrowed from Locke, but significantly changed. Locke had written "life, liberty, and property." Jefferson and his colleagues, though deeply respectful of property, shifted the emphasis to the dignity of individuals and their right to personal fulfillment. The declaration also asserted boldly and bluntly that "all men" were "created equal."

The words that followed these expressed the view, borrowed from the radical English Whigs, that the people had the right to overthrow a government not based on the "consent of the governed." Revolution should not be resorted to "for light and transient causes." But when, as in this case, "a long train of abuses and usurpations" had been committed, with the goal of an "absolute Despotism," then it was the people's right "to throw off such Government, and to provide new Guards for their future security." Though written in the heat of military and political crisis, the declaration was an eloquent defense of human freedom, and it would inspire millions around the globe for generations.

THE FIGHT FOR INDEPENDENCE

The Declaration of Independence was greeted throughout the nation with bonfires, toasts, fireworks, and bell ringing—the usual accompaniments of public celebration in those years. But there was still a long way to go before the reality of independence could be established. The British, certainly, did not take the declaration at face value: in September 1776 General Howe and his brother, Admiral Richard Howe, offered Congress a settlement that stopped well short of independence. Congress listened to their proposal that the declaration be rescinded but rejected it. The fighting went on.

The War in the East, 1776–77. But the war did not go well for the Americans. Foreseeing Sir William Howe's move to make New York the base for British operations in America, Washington moved his victorious troops south from Boston soon after the British evacuated that city. In July of 1776 Howe landed his forces on Staten Island opposite New York City. At the end of August, with 20,000 men under his command, Howe attacked Washington's troops on Long Island (Brooklyn Heights), defeated them, and forced them to flee to Manhattan. When the British crossed the East River in pursuit, Washington retreated again, first to White Plains and then to New Jersey. Howe had won New York, and the British kept it until the end of the war. At the very end of the year Washington partly redeemed his defeat in New York by attacking a force of Hessians at Trenton. The German troops were taken by surprise, and almost a thousand surrendered to the Americans.

The year 1777 held mixed fortunes for the rebels. Washington won an important victory at Princeton in January and cleared the British out of much of New Jersey. But in the summer Howe and Cornwallis routed the American general Anthony Wayne and occupied Philadelphia, forcing Congress to flee.

Still, 1777 brought the turning point of the war. During the summer, while Howe was moving on Philadelphia, British troops under General John Burgoyne were advancing south from Canada. The British plan was to split the colonies along the line of Lake Champlain and the Hudson River. As Burgoyne moved south, Howe was to advance up the Hudson after taking Philadelphia. Howe's campaign to capture Philadelphia took too long, however, and he never launched his northward attack. In late June Burgoyne's army of 8,000 British, Canadians, Indians, and Germans left Quebec and marched on Fort Ticonderoga. They captured the fort but were soon struggling through the dense forests of northern New York, using up their supplies and getting farther and farther from their Canadian base. Near Lake George, Burgoyne's troops encountered stiff resistance from the troops of Horatio Gates. Gates's army consisted of Continental regulars and New England militia who had flocked to his ranks to avenge the brutal killings of civilians by Burgoyne's Indian allies. Burgoyne suffered serious losses and sought to retreat northward, but the move to es-

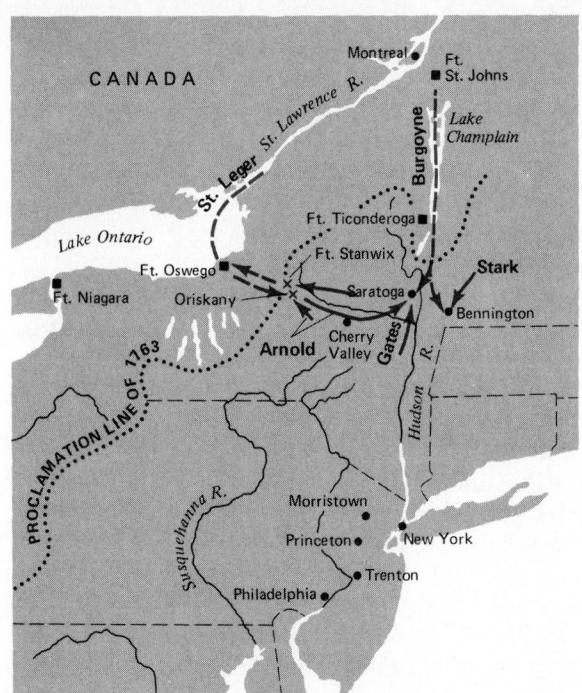

Northern campaigns, 1777

cape was futile. He got as far as Saratoga and there was surrounded. On October 17, 1777, "Gentleman Johnnie" surrendered his remaining 6,000 men.

The French Alliance. The victory at Saratoga convinced the French that the Americans might very well make good their claim to independence. In September 1776 Congress had dispatched Silas Deane, Benjamin Franklin, and Arthur Lee to Europe to negotiate treaties with Britain's enemies. In January 1778 the French minister of foreign affairs, Vergennes, convinced that the Americans had a chance to win independence but fearing that British peace feelers might thwart that goal, told the American envoys that France was prepared to ally itself with the United States. Soon after he and the American representatives negotiated two important treaties. The first, amounting to a commercial declaration of independence from Britain, guaranteed each nation free trading rights with the other. The second was an alliance for joint military effort against Britain, to last until the United States had won its freedom. Each party promised not to conclude a peace with England without the other's consent.

In early May Congress ratified the French treaties. France was now in the war. Spain, although less certain of her strength and concerned that the rebellious Americans would set a bad example to her own New World colonies, declared war on Britain the following year. The Dutch, too, having clashed with the British over their smuggling of munitions to the rebels through their Caribbean possessions, broke relations with Britain in early 1781, though they never formally declared war. Soon French, Spanish, and later Dutch money—both gifts and loans—began to pour in, enabling Congress to pay for much-needed arms, food, and equipment. Several other northern European nations, including Russia, Sweden, and Denmark, organized the League of Armed Neutrality to keep the British from stopping their vessels supplying the Americans. In all, by the end of the Revolution Britain had been effectively isolated and placed on the diplomatic defensive. The European aid proved invaluable to America.

War in the West. The war that engulfed the East also cast its lurid light across the West. On almost every colonial frontier Americans fought with the British for the friendship and aid of the Indians. In this struggle the British often had the advantage: they possessed the trade goods that the Indians wanted and, unlike the American settlers, posed no threat to the Indians' possession of ancestral lands.

During 1775 the settlers of western North Carolina fought off the Cherokees, who had proclaimed their allegiance to George III. More exposed to British-inspired Indian attack were the infant settlements in eastern Kentucky, just over the Appalachians, established by Richard Henderson and Daniel Boone only months before Lexington and Concord. In the summer of 1776 bands of Shawnee and Delaware, encouraged by the British, began to harass the Kentuckians and drove many in the outlying areas back to the settlement's three main villages. These managed to hold out and remained havens for many whites throughout the war, but away from the log walls of the stockades, hostile Indians pounced on isolated travelers, stole livestock, and prevented farmers from planting crops.

On the New York frontier the plight of the Americans was even worse. There the British had the support of the powerful Iroquois and their leader, the Mohawk chief Joseph Brant. They also were aided by many Loyalists, organized as the Tory Rangers. The first clash in the region ended in a tie. In August 1777 American militia at Fort Stanwix stopped a British advance designed to reinforce Burgoyne. Soon afterward a supporting party of Americans under General Nicholas Herkimer was caught in an ambush at Oriskany, losing

200 men to the Indians, Loyalists, and Germans under Colonel Barry St. Leger.

During 1778 Iroquois and Loyalists ravaged the New York and Pennsylvania frontiers. The Loyalists attacked the inhabitants of the Wyoming Valley in Pennsylvania and massacred hundreds. Meanwhile, the Iroquois spread panic throughout upper New York.

By this time it was clear that defensive policies in the West had not worked. In the summer of 1778 the Kentuckians, led by George Rogers Clark, determined on their own to go on the attack. On July 4 Clark and a small band of trained Indian fighters pounced on the British post at Kaskaskia and captured it. Clark and his men soon seized the other northwestern settlements established by the French a generation before. Clark's success inspired Congress to take the offensive, and in 1779 it dispatched several expeditions to nail down the West for the United States. Several forays led by Clark himself and by Colonel Daniel Brodhead and General John Sullivan succeeded, but others failed and threatened to undo much of their work.

Throughout the frontier area the tide flowed back and forth through the remaining years of the Revolution. Both sides resorted to ambush and guerilla war; and both at times spared neither women nor children. By the time the war ended, the Americans were in firm possession of the frontier in the South, but the British controlled the Northwest. The war in the West ended in a draw.

Eastern Battles, 1778–80. It was in the older settlements that the war would be won. After their defeat at Saratoga in 1777, the British, though far from beaten, were weary. At news of the defeat, Lord North, the prime minister, expressed his heartfelt desire to get out of the "damned war." By now British taxpayers were complaining of the war's high costs, and British merchants, badly hurt by the loss of American trade, were in desperate straits. Hoping to avert the impending alliance between France and America, Lord North dispatched a commission under the Earl of Carlisle to offer the Americans new terms for reconciliation. These included ending all efforts to impose revenue taxes on America and suspension of all parliamentary acts for America passed since 1763. When this effort failed, North offered to resign; but the king, who remained stubbornly and bitterly opposed to American independence, insisted that he remain. Out of loyalty he did.

The Americans, too, had their problems after Saratoga. In fact, the winter of 1777–78 is generally considered the low point for Washington's army. Worn down by sickness and losses, the Continental Army withdrew to winter quarters at Valley Forge, just twenty miles from Philadelphia, where the British were living in comfort. Valley Forge was a wretched place. Recent fighting had left the area barren of supplies. Food and clothing might have been brought in, but a breakdown of supply services left the men cold, hungry, and ill-clothed. To make matters worse, discontent was rife among the officers, whose salaries were small or—as was often the case—unpaid. For a time the aggrieved officers threatened to resign en masse. Eventually Congress improved the pay situation, and a new quartermaster general, Nathanael Greene, established a more efficient supply service. Even so, the Continental Army barely survived the awful winter.

For the next three years the fighting went on intermittently and inconclusively. In the winter of 1778–79 the British won control of Georgia by capturing Savannah and Augusta. In 1780 General Sir Henry Clinton advanced on Charleston and captured the port, along with 5,000 American troops and 300 guns. Clinton's victory heartened southern Loyalists. In the interior of South Carolina the suppressed Tories now rushed to take up arms against their countrymen. Horatio Gates, the hero of Saratoga, attempted to recapture the state but was badly beaten by Cornwallis at Camden.

Fighting continued in the north as well. In August 1778 a joint Franco-American operation to capture Newport failed when a storm drove off the French fleet under Admiral d'Estaing. In New Jersey, New York, and the West the Americans were more successful. In July 1779 Anthony Wayne's troops captured a British garrison of 700 at Stony Point on the Hudson at the cost of only 15 American lives. In August Major Henry Lee drove the last British troops out of New Jersey.

Victory at Yorktown. The years 1780 and 1781 were full of confused advances and retreats, and American morale sank almost as low as during the Valley Forge winter. In May 1780 Washington's

Southern campaigns, 1780–1781

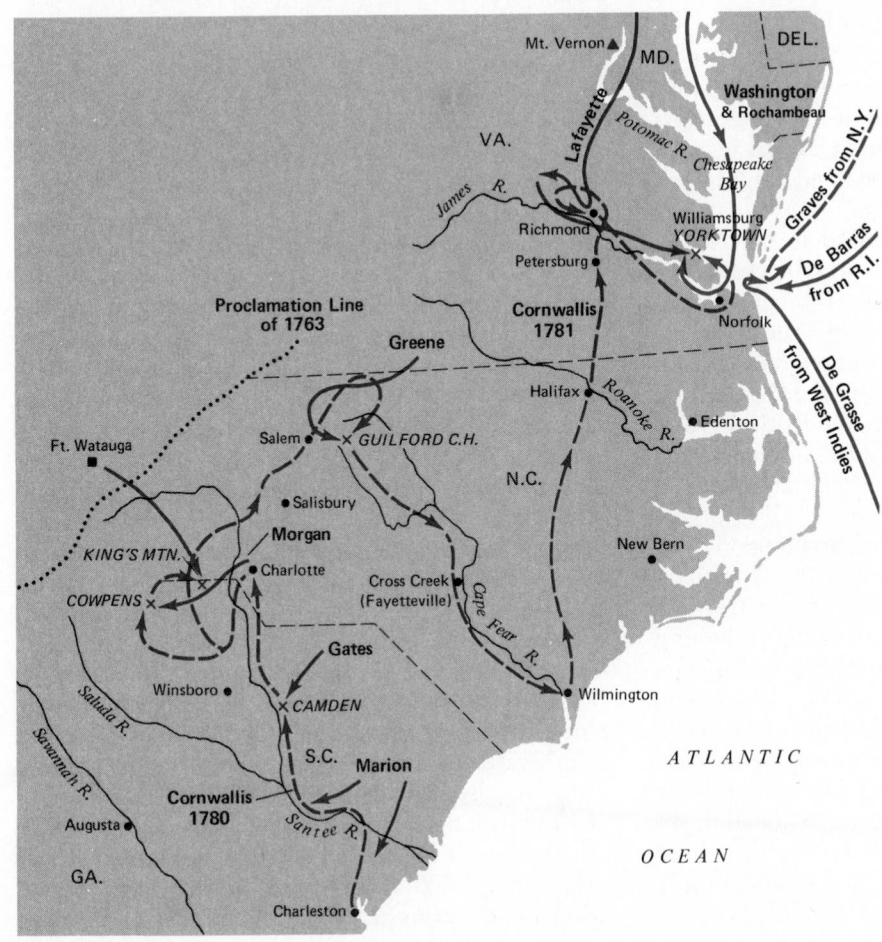

Library of Congress

A fanciful French view of the siege of Yorktown that ended the military phase of the Revolution. The ships offshore are the vessels of French admiral DeGrasse.

troops near Morristown, New Jersey, nearly mutinied. Restlessness among front-line regiments continued through the following year. In January 1781 troops on the Pennsylvania and New Jersey lines did rebel.

Disaffection was not limited to the lowest ranks of the army. In the fall of 1780 American militiamen captured Major John André of the British army near Tarrytown, New York. André carried papers that proved that General Benedict Arnold, now commanding American forces at West Point, planned to surrender his post to the British. When Arnold learned of André's capture, he fled to the British lines and eventually became an officer in the king's forces.

Although initially discouraging, 1781 brought final victory at Yorktown. The Yorktown campaign opened in April 1781, when General Cornwallis left his base in North Carolina, hoping to crush the American forces in Virginia. He soon encountered troops under the young Frenchman, the Marquis de Lafayette. For four months Cornwallis and Lafayette danced around one another without reaching a showdown. When Wayne came to Lafayette's aid, the British commander retreated to the coast, hoping to establish a base where the Royal Navy could protect and supply him.

Washington heard of Cornwallis's move while he was besieging the British at New York. He quickly abandoned his effort to recapture the city and moved south. The moment was especially favorable because the French fleet under Count de Grasse could now join the attack. De Grasse soon stationed his ships off the Virginia coast, where Lafayette had pushed Cornwallis onto the narrow Yorktown peninsula. On September 14 Washington's troops and 5,000 French soldiers led by the Count de Rochambeau arrived at Yorktown. Immediately they besieged the smaller British force. Bit by bit, remorseless French and American pressure reduced the area under British control. Cornwallis had counted on help from the sea, but the French fleet—twenty-eight ships of the line—was too much for the British navy. Under relentless attack, Cornwallis notified Clinton, his superior in New York: "If you cannot relieve me very soon, you must prepare to hear the worst."

Clinton set out on his rescue mission on october 19. But he was too late. Three days earlier Cornwallis had made a desperate attempt to escape across the York River and had been frustrated by a storm. Seeing all hope for his army gone, the British general resolved to surrender. On October 19, 1781, 7,000 British and Hessian troops laid down their arms. Legend has it that as the de-

Library of Congress

A view of the Battle of Charleston in June 1776. The British tried to subdue the American blockhouse (the log structure on the lower left), but failed.

feated army marched out of its camp, the British military bands played a tune called "The World Turned Upside Down." If the account is true, it marks one of those rare instances when contemporaries understand that they are witnessing a great historical event. Yorktown was not only the last important battle of the war; it was also the end of the old British Empire.

THE ARTICLES OF CONFEDERATION

Victory had come not a moment too soon. By the fall of 1781 the United States was in serious financial trouble, its monetary system collapsing and prices and wages soaring out of sight. In the last months of the war Congress turned for help with its money problems to Robert Morris, a shrewd Philadelphia businessman. Morris was a former member of Congress who had already performed valuable financial services for the government. In February 1781 Congress appointed him superin-

tendent of finance for the United States. He proceeded to reorganize the government's financial affairs, strengthened the public credit, and eliminated unnecessary items in the budget. Soon after taking office he also organized the Bank of North America, the first commercial bank in the United States.

The closing months of the war also saw the beginning of a new American government. It had taken the states almost five years to agree on a new political structure. In the meantime, as we have seen, the Continental Congress had acted as the American government. Little more than a convention of sovereign powers—the states—it had not been effective, and since the beginning of the war it had been clear to most American leaders that the country needed a more formal and permanent government. In June 1776 Congress had appointed a committee to establish a constitution for the United States that would end all doubt about congressional authority to conduct war and would provide the structure for a permanent union. The committee's proposal, composed largely by John

Dickinson, called for a legislature in which each state would have one vote. The new congress would have fairly broad powers, but not the power to tax—Americans were still tax-shy. Instead, it might ask the states for contributions proportional to their population.

The Dickinson scheme immediately came under attack. Delegates from large states complained that small states would be overrepresented since each, regardless of population, would have one vote in the proposed congress. At the same time, states with large slave populations thought that basing financial contributions on total population was unfair. Slaves, they pointed out, were only property, not citizens, and so should not be counted.

The major stumbling block to adoption of the Dickinson plan, however, was its provision for western lands. It gave to the proposed congress the power to set westward limits to the states, to grant lands to private parties in regions beyond those limits, and to create new states in the West. This scheme stepped on many toes. Seven states claimed that their charters gave them boundaries that extended well into the trans-Appalachian region. Virginia alone claimed the region known as Kentucky and the whole of what would later be the states of Ohio, Indiana, Illinois, Michigan, and Wisconsin. Seven states, on the other hand—New Hampshire, New Jersey, Rhode Island, Connecticut, Pennsylvania, Delaware, and Maryland—had no claims to western lands and generally favored congressional control over them. Why, they asked, should the common struggle to win independence lead to a few states grabbing the western domain that all had fought for? Marylanders and Pennsylvanians, many of whom were deeply involved in speculations over lands acquired from the Indians, had an additional reason for favoring congressional control: if most of the land went to Virginia, their purchases from the Indians would in effect be void.

The opponents of the Dickinson plan delayed its consideration until the fall of 1777. This time it passed, but with modifications. Each state would continue to have one vote in Congress. But Congress would not be allowed to set westward limits to the states, and state contributions to the central treasury would be based not on population but on the value of improved lands in each state.

This modified scheme won the support of twelve states by the end of 1778. Maryland, however, refused to go along with it because her big neighbor, Virginia, still had title to the lion's share of the upper Mississippi Valley. Months of jockeying followed until finally the Virginia delegates agreed to accept the right of Congress to control the western region. Soon afterward the Virginia legislature formally ceded its western lands to Congress. Finally, in March 1781, with Maryland's objections withdrawn, Congress announced the formal adoption of the articles of Confederation.

The Articles were a clear improvement over the old arrangements. Most important, they established a formal union of the American states, which had not existed before. In specific terms, they gave legal standing to several powers that the Continental Congress had exercised earlier. The Confederation Congress could conduct war and foreign affairs, make commercial treaties, and negotiate with the Indians. It could borrow and coin money and issue bills of credit. The Articles also gave Congress the new power to manage public lands in the West.

Yet many imperfections remained. The new government consisted of only a legislature; it had no separate executive or judicial branches. And not all of the new Congress's powers were exclusive. The states could continue to deal directly with foreign governments and engage in war with Congress's consent. And even without it, they could borrow, maintain mints, and issue bills of credit. The states also had the sole right to legislate in matters concerning debts, contracts, and family affairs. Most important of all, they alone could tax their citizens. And if experience showed that changes in the Articles were desirable, they would be hard to make, since amendments required the consent of every state.

Still, the Articles of Confederation were a substantial move toward American national unity. Until the middle of the eighteenth century the notion of a common national identity had been weak in America. Colonists often had closer contacts with residents of England or the West Indies than with their fellow "continentals." After 1763 their sense of common interests and needs had grown, and after 1775 the Revolution had reinforced continental ties and sentiments. Many young men serving in the Revolutionary forces saw more of America in a few years than their parents had in a lifetime. In Washington, Jefferson, Adams, and Franklin they found national heroes to praise and admire. The Continental Congress had not fully reflected these change in attitudes. It had been a makeshift, a purely voluntary association entered into to deal with the imperial crisis. Now, with the Articles of Confederation, for the first time there was a permanent American government, one that would speak for the citizens of the thirteen states.

The feeling of a common nationality remained incomplete, however, and in 1781 Americans continued to talk of Virginia, New York, or Massachusetts as "their country." The weaknesses of the Articles reflected Americans' still limited national allegiance. But the Articles were an important milestone in a steady development that would not be completed until 1865.

SOCIAL CHANGE

The growing sense of a common nationality was only one of many changes that the war initiated. As Americans looked around them between 1775 and 1783, many were certain that they were also witnessing a social revolution. American Loyalists, for example, believed that the Patriots were more intent on overthrowing the social order than in righting the wrongs of imperial government. The Reverend Samuel Peters of Connecticut called the Patriots "ungovernable, righteous and high-handed moberenes." Another Yankee Loyalist saw Patriot control of Massachusetts after 1775 as the triumph of the rabble:

> 'Everything I see is laughable, cursable, and damnable; my pew in the church is converted into a pork tub; my house into a den of rebels, thieves and lice, my farm in possession of the very worst of all God's creatures; my few debts all gone to the devil with my debtors.'

The suffering these Tories had endured at the hands of their rebel fellow Americans doubtless colored their comments. But even Patriots felt uneasy about the class resentment and the "levelling spirit" that disorder and change had brought to the surface. Langdon Carter of Virginia worriedly reported to Washington that some Patriots in his vicinity wanted "a form of government that, by being independent of rich men, every man would then be able to do as he pleased." John Adams, after recounting his meeting with the disrespectful "Horse Jockey," described earlier, exclaimed: "Surely we must guard against this Spirit and these Principles or We shall repent of all our Conduct. . . ."

Carter, Adams, and other moderates feared that what had begun as a dispute over the governing of the empire was turning into a social revolution. A number of modern historians, too, have seen the War of Independence as an internal revolution. As one, Carl Becker, expressed it, the war with Britain was as much over "who shall rule at home" as over "home-rule."

A Revolutionary Experience? The French Revolution of 1789 and the Russian Revolution of 1917

Library of Congress

Many Loyalists fled the colonies, but those who remained behind found the Revolution a trying time. Here a Virginia merchant signs a nonimportation agreement to escape being tarred and feathered.

are examples of what we mean by *social revolutions*. These are abrupt and often violent overthrows of an elite that has exercised most of a society's power and enjoyed most of its wealth and income. The new rulers, claiming to speak for the poor and the powerless, either expel or exterminate the old "oppressors," seize their property, and distribute it among "the people." Does this model fit the American case as events unfolded between 1775 and 1783? Was the American struggle for independence in fact a social revolution?

At first glance the term *revolution* does seem to fit some of what took place during these years. The fate of the American Loyalists, who formed about 20 percent of the population, resembles that of the French and Russian aristocracy. During and immediately after the war 100,000 Loyalists fled the United States to settle in Upper Canada (present-day Ontario), the Canadian Maritime Provinces (New Brunswick and Nova Scotia), England, and the Caribbean. Often they left hurriedly, completely abandoning their property—which the states promptly confiscated—or selling it in panic at low prices. This exile and confiscation, or forced sale, of property looks very much like social revolution. By removing an aristocracy

An Historical Portrait   Benedict Arnold

Arnold was a respected name in colonial New England. The first American Arnold had been associated with Roger Williams in the founding of Rhode Island. The first Benedict Arnold, his son, was a rich merchant of Newport. Thereafter, Arnolds continued to be prominent citizens of southern New England for generations, though the family's fortunes fluctuated. Benedict Arnold IV was born in 1741. His name would become a synonym for "traitor" to most Americans.

Benedict grew up in Norwich in southern Connecticut. As a child he was a leader, recognized by his neighbors as "bold, enterprising, ambitious, active as lightning." Though apprenticed to a merchant, his spirit of adventure led him to join the American forces during the French and Indian War and he served briefly during the French attack on Fort William on Lake George.

Despite his unauthorized flight to join the army, Arnold pleased his employers, the Lathrops, and in 1762, when he had completed his apprenticeship, they gave him £500 to establish an apothecary shop in New Haven. Arnold succeeded in New Haven. He not only sold drugs; he also invested in the West Indies trade and soon had a flourishing business selling horses and mules to the sugar planters of Antigua, St. Croix, and other Caribbean islands. In 1767 he married Peggy Mansfield, daughter of one of New Haven's respected merchants, and soon after entered into partnership with his father-in-law.

Like many New England merchants, Arnold was a violent opponent of British imperial measures after 1763. In 1764 he led a mob protesting the Sugar Act, which had cut into the New England trade with the foreign sugar islands. In 1774 he denounced the Boston Massacre as "the most cruel, wanton, and inhuman murders. . . ." When news of Lexington reached New Haven, Arnold left with sixty militiamen under his command to join George Washington's forces outside of Boston.

Arnold rose rapidly in the ranks of the Continental Army. He fought at Ticonderoga as a colonel and in December 1775 led a hopeless attack during a snowstorm against the British bastion of Quebec, garrisoned by a larger force than his own. The attack failed, and Arnold's co-commander, General Richard Montgomery, was killed. Arnold was forced to lift the siege, but despite this failure, Congress recognized his skill and gallantry by promoting him to brigadier general. The following year he further distinguished himself by helping to stop Guy Carleton's advance from Canada on New York City. In 1777 Arnold commanded American troops in the battles that led to the defeat of Burgoyne at Saratoga, the campaign often judged the turning point of the war.

At no time during these tumultuous months was there any outward sign that General Arnold was anything but a fiercely loyal Patriot. But his sense of grievance had begun to build. In February 1777 Congress

passed him over for promotion to major general. He eventually got the promotion, but the delay rankled. His real disaffection, however, dates from mid-1778, when he was appointed military commander at Philadelphia, then newly evacuated by the British.

The general's first wife had died three years before, and Arnold soon became enamored of Peggy Shippen, the beautiful eighteen-year-old daughter of Edward Shippen, a prominent Philadelphia lawyer and admiralty judge allied before the war with the colony's proprietors, the Penn family. Despite this connection and his role as an officer of the crown, Judge Shippen, a timid man, had tried to stay neutral in the evolving struggle between the Patriots and the British government. When the first Continental Congress met in Philadelphia, Shippen invited the delegates to dinner. Then, when the British occupied the town in September 1777, Judge Shippen was happy to welcome the young English officers to his house to pay court to his daughter. Among those who vied for a smile from the lovely Peggy was Lieutenant John André, the young aide-de-camp of the British general Charles Grey.

The British evacuated Philadelphia in June 1778. Arnold, as American military commander, moved into the mansion formerly owned by Penns and was soon emulating General Howe's grand style with housekeeper, coachman, groom, seven other servants, and a fine coach-and-four. Such an establishment could not be supported on

of rich landowners, prosperous lawyers, and successful merchants and dividing their land among the poorer Americans who remained, surely the nation was made more democratic and more egalitarian.

The facts do not support such an interpretation, however. Loyalists were not all from the upper classes. They came from every part of colonial society. Many of the leading Tories assuredly were "high-toned" folk. Rich merchants and landlords, successful lawyers, royal officials, and much of the Anglican clergy supported the British cause.

Yet many poor people, especially in rural areas, also chose to fight for the king. This was true in New York, where tenants of the Hudson Valley landlords were told they would receive the land of Patriot patroons if they remained loyal. It was also true in the backcountry of the Carolinas, where yeomen farmers bitterly resented the political domination of the states by the rich Patriot leaders on the coast and during the early 1770s as "Regulators" had fought the coastal elite. There were also black Tories. Lured by promises of freedom if they would desert their masters and fight the

the salary of a Continental officer, and he entered into several morally dubious deals with merchants in New York and other British-occupied towns to trade in illegal goods. These shady schemes got him into trouble with the Pennsylvania authorities and with Congress. To clear his name Arnold demanded a court-martial. Though declared innocent of most charges, he earned a public reprimand from Washington. During this time he also began to associate with Philadelphians who favored a negotiated peace without independence.

Inevitably the middle-aged general was drawn to the young and vivacious Peggy Shippen, who belonged to the circle of near-Tories. Ambitious for social distinction and wealth, Peggy was attracted to Arnold in turn. In April 1779 they were married in a simple ceremony appropriate to the now strained pocketbook of Edward Shippen, and went to live in Arnold's newly purchased mansion, Mount Pleasant, on the banks of the Schuylkill.

It was while in Philadelphia that Arnold began to correspond with British General Sir Henry Clinton, commander in chief of his majesty's forces in America. Arnold's motives for betraying his country were clearly mixed. First, probably, came money. The general found good living irresistible, and with a young, extravagant wife to please, he was desperate for cash. He was also angry at the mistreatment he felt he had received at the hands of Congress and the Pennsylvania authorities. He may also have had less

ignoble motives than lucre and resentment. As a good New England Protestant, Arnold despised the alliance with Catholic France and believed it tainted the American cause irretrievably. Better to abandon independence and return to the British fold than to accept association with the despised French.

From mid-1779 through 1780 Arnold sold information to André, now Clinton's aide, concerning American and French naval and troop movements, the disposition of supplies, and the identities of French spies in the British camp. Peggy conducted her own spying operation and at one point was paid £350 for her services. The couple's value to the British leaped when, in the summer of 1780, Washington appointed Arnold commander of the vital American post at West Point on the Hudson. Here was a real prize indeed, and Arnold demanded £20,000 for its surrender to the British. Clinton sent André to negotiate. On the way back from the meeting, André was intercepted by American militia while in civilian clothes. When Arnold learned of the capture, he fled to a nearby British ship. André was tried as a spy and executed in October 1780.

During the remainder of the war Arnold served as brigadier general of Tory forces in the British army. In late 1780 he conducted a series of ruthless Tory raids in Virginia. Governor Thomas Jefferson offered a £5,000 reward for his capture. The following year Arnold led Tory attacks against the Americans in Connecticut. Soon after, he and

Peggy sailed for England, where they remained permanently.

Like many Tory exiles, they found life away from their native land a grim trial. In their last years the Arnolds associated with the circle of Loyalist exiles in London. They found some comfort in these relationships, but it never consoled them for the self-inflicted wounds of betraying their native country. Arnold never received more than £5,000 or £6,000 for his treason, though he frequently petitioned the British government for a more generous reward. The best he could get was a land grant in Canada in 1797. He never visited his Canadian lands and never profited by them. Peggy's life in England was not happy. She kept in touch by letter with her family in Philadelphia, but missed her native city fiercely. In late 1789 she visited Philadelphia, hoping to find a spirit of forgiveness. She was disappointed. Many of her old friends cut her and she went back to England after a few months, never to return. Toward the end of her life Peggy became a semi-invalid.

Arnold tried to get a military command from the British government during the Napoleonic Wars, but failed, though his grown sons were more fortunate. He turned to business once again, and for a time was active in the West Indies trade. His ventures did not restore his fortunes, however, and when he died in 1801, Peggy was left to pay off his debts.

rebels, thousands of blacks joined the crown's forces. So alarming was this defection that Congress reversed Washington's policy of rejecting black enlistees in an effort to counter it. Thereafter, black soldiers, both slaves and freemen, fought in the Continental and state forces. Nevertheless, thousands of blacks preferred the king. At the war's end many of them refused to return to the land where they had been enslaved and decamped to Canada or the Caribbean.

Patriots, too, came from both the highest and lowest reaches of colonial society. Slaves, as we

have just noted, fought for the Patriot cause, as did seamen, apprentices, mechanics, and craftsmen of the port cities. But so did many of the colonial elite, from the planters of the South to the great merchants of New England and the middle states. As for the middle class of small farmers and shopkeepers, it was they, or at least their sons, who formed the backbone of the Continental Army. In short, the Patriots were anything but "a rabble." Like the Loyalists they were a cross section of the American people.

What this evidence points to is clear. Since

AP/Wide World

The reluctance of Americans to enlist slaves in the military did not extend to free blacks. This picture of a free black Continental sailor, painted in 1779, was discovered recently in Newport, Rhode Island.

the social profile of those who supported independence and stayed in America was about the same as those who resisted it and left, the Tory exodus could not have deprived the new country of an aristocratic ruling class as did the departure of exiles and *émigrés* from France in the 1780s and aristocrats from Russia in 1917. Accordingly, it does not support the view that America experienced a social revolution between 1775 and 1783.

And what of the redistribution of wealth, the second standard by which we may identify a social revolution? The property of many Loyalist landlords, planters, and merchants, especially those who fled to the British lines during the war, was indeed taken away by the state governments as soon as it could be seized. Pennsylvania took over the Penn family's lands, reported to have been worth £1 million, and gave the heirs only £130,000 in compensation. Maryland confiscated the property of Lord Baltimore's heir, and the rebel government of Virginia seized the giant Fairfax estate. Declaring 117 persons guilty of treason in 1778, Georgia confiscated their property. New York took over the valuable city property of the Delancey family in Manhattan.

Did these seizures revolutionize existing patterns of property holding? The answer seems to be no. Late-eighteenth-century America was not, after all, a society of a few large landlords and a vast landless peasantry. Many people owned land. Then, too, compared with the country's total acreage, the amount of land confiscated was not very large. Even if every acre seized had been handed over to the landless, that would not have done much to equalize landholding. Besides, when the states sold the confiscated land, the farm acres and town lots did not generally go to the poor or the middle class. Most of it was snapped up by neighboring Patriot landholders or by speculators. Existing inequalities were, if anything, confirmed by the resale of confiscated Tory real estate.

It seems clear, then, that the expulsion of the Loyalists and the takeover and sale of their lands did little to change the character of property holding in America or to alter the social makeup of the community. But this is not to say that the Revolution did not liberalize American life. Indeed, it helped in many ways to make America a more democratic community.

America's Unfortunates. Slavery, the most blatant social inequality in America, was seriously weakened by the Revolution. In the South thousands of slaves won their freedom by cooperating with the British. Unfortunately slavery did survive south of Pennsylvania, where slaves were numerous and the institution tightly woven into the social fabric. Though temporarily weakened, the institution eventually recovered its strength. In the

DISTRIBUTION OF ASSESSED TAXABLE WEALTH IN CHESTER COUNTY, PENNSYLVANIA, 1760–1802

Data on landholding and wealth before and after the Revolution are not available for all the colonies. Studies on a smaller scale suggest, however, that the resale of abandoned and confiscated Loyalist property did not redistribute wealth to the poorer classes. In Chester County, in fact, the rich as a class were better off after the Revolution than before it.

Taxpayers	Percentage of Total Wealth Held in		
	1760	1782	1800–02
Top 10%	29.9	33.6	38.3
Next 30%	43.3	44.5	44.2
Next 30%	20.5	17.3	13.7
Lowest 10%	6.3	4.7	3.9

James Lemon and Gary Nash, "The Distribution of Wealth in Eighteenth-Century America: A Century of Changes in Chester County, Pennsylvania, 1693–1802," *Journal of Social History,* vol. 2 (1968), pp. 1–24. Reprinted by permission.

Slavery Struck Down

Though it was not a deep-running social upheaval, the American Revolution wiped away vestiges of the past's privileged order. Yet none of the social changes it produced was more significant than the blow against slavery north of the Mason-Dixon line. In most of those northern states that took steps to end slavery during the Revolution and immediately thereafter, the process was accomplished by act of the legislature. In Massachusetts, however, slavery ended as the result of a judge's decision as to the meaning of a provision of the state constitution of 1781. The case before the Massachusetts court involved an assault by a white man on a black man. The white man was indicted, but pleaded not guilty on the grounds that the man he had struck was his slave. This plea induced the judge, Chief Justice William Cushing, to consider the question of whether slavery legally existed in the commonwealth. His decision, expressed briefly below, reflects the liberating spirit of the Revolutionary era.

"CUSHING, C. J. As to the doctrine of slavery and the right of Christians to hold Africans in perpetual servitude, and sell and treat them as we do our horses and cattle, [it is true that it] has been heretofore countenanced by the Province Laws . . . but nowhere is it expressly enacted or established. It has been a usage— a usage which took its origins from the practice of some of the European nations, and the regulations of British government respecting the then Colonies, for the benefit of trade and wealth. But whatever sentiments have formerly prevailed in this particular or slid in upon us by the example of others, a different idea has taken place with the people of America, more favorable to the natural rights of mankind, and to that natural, innate desire of Liberty, with which heaven (without regard to color, complexion, or shape of noses . . .) has inspired all the human race. And upon the ground our Constitution of Government, by which the people of this Commonwealth have solemnly bound themselves, sets out with declaring that all men are born free and equal—and that every subject is entitled to liberty and to have it guarded by the laws, as well as life and property—and in short is totally repugnant to the idea of being born slaves. This being the case, I think the idea of slavery is inconsistent with our own conduct and Constitution; and there can be no such thing as perpetual servitude of a rational creature, unless his liberty is forfeited by some criminal conduct or given up by personal consent or contract. . . . *Verdict Guilty.*"

North, however, it collapsed under the blows of war and revolution.

Although white Americans were mostly concerned with their own rights and freedoms, the dispute with Britain following 1763 forced them to ponder the issue of human liberty. Most Patriots were able to protest colonial bondage to Britain and at the same time excuse or forget the slaves' bondage. But some could not. How can we "reconcile the exercise of SLAVERY with our *professions of freedom*," Richard Wells, a Philadelphia Patriot, asked pointedly. John Allen, a Baptist minister in Massachusetts, accused his fellow Americans of hypocrisy in refusing to admit the evil of slavery. "Blush . . . ye trifling patriots! who are making a vain parade of being advocates for the liberties of mankind, [and] . . . are . . . thus making a mockery of your profession by trampling on the sacred and natural rights and privileges of Africans."

Happily, the attack on slavery went beyond words. In 1775 Philadelphia Quakers, who had always rejected human inequality, established the first antislavery society. Five years later Pennsylvania passed the first law providing for the gradual freeing of slaves. In 1783 the Massachusetts courts interpreted the state constitution as prohibiting slavery, and thereafter slavery was illegal in the Bay State. Other northern states soon followed these leaders. And even in the South slavery was affected by the ferment of egalitarianism. Prominent Patriots like Jefferson and Henry Laurens, imbued with the ideals of the Enlightenment, attacked the system. Several southern legislatures passed laws making it easier for masters to free their own slaves and restricted the slave trade in various ways. By the end of the century, in every state from Pennsylvania northward, slavery was on the way to extinction, and it seemed to many Americans that the South would not be far behind.

The attack on slavery and its gradual disappearance in the North were social changes initiated by the revolutionary zeal for freedom. Another sign of the increased concern for human rights was the effort to improve the treatment of lawbreakers. In those days men and women convicted of felonies were subject to savage punishment. Criminals were placed in stocks or branded, whipped, and mutilated. Shortly after 1776 New York, Pennsylvania, and several other states reduced the number of crimes punishable by death, and for lesser crimes replaced torture with imprisonment.

Women, too, eventually benefited from the liberal ideas unleashed by the Revolution. Colonial women had worked hard to make the boycotts

New-York Historical Society

"A New Touch on the Times," by an anonymous Daughter of Liberty. So great was the temporary improvement in women's status that a very few fought in colonial armies as fully paid regulars.

against British goods effective before 1775, and afterward they were equally enthusiastic supporters of the Patriot cause. In the absence of husbands and fathers many became the chief support of their families. A few women, moreover, contributed directly to the war effort. Esther Reed, for example, headed a women's association that raised $7,000 to provide the Continental Army with shirts. Mary Ludwig Hays McCauley, better known as Molly Pitcher, took her husband's place behind a cannon at the Battle of Monmouth when he was overcome by the heat.

Some women expected their sex to benefit as a group from the war. The spirited Abigail Adams wrote her husband John in 1776 that "in the new code of laws" then being considered by Congress—that is, the Articles of Confederation—it was important for the legislators to "remember the ladies and be more generous and favorable to them" than their ancestors had been. "Do not," she urged, "put such unlimited powers in the hands of the husbands."

Abigail Adams and those who thought like her would not fully realize their hopes. And yet the war and the forces it released did have some

effect on women's circumstances. In new England the rhetoric of freedom led to liberalized divorce laws that placed women on virtually the same plane as men when they sought separation from a brutal or unfaithful spouse. The years of debate over American rights also stimulated the first feminist questioning of existing female education. In the 1770s, for example, Judith Murray of Gloucester, Massachusetts, charged that traditional upbringing and education for girls trivialized their minds and forced them to rely excessively on their physical attractions. Most of the great battles for female "emancipation" lay in the future. Yet we must not dismiss the revolutionary impulse entirely as a force for female liberation.

New Politics. The political system also felt the liberalizing effects of the great upheaval. As they ceased to be provinces and became "states," the former colonies were freed to revise their constitutions. In some the changes were relatively modest—not much more than the replacement of the appointed governor by one elected either by the voters or by the state legislature, and the replacement of the appointed upper house of the colonial legislature by an elected one. In other states there were more sweeping changes. Virginia, Pennsylvania, North Carolina, and Massachusetts ended or reduced the gross underrepresentation of their frontier counties. Pennsylvania, Delaware, North Carolina, Georgia, and Virginia liberalized their franchises so that almost any male taxpayer, no matter how poor, could vote. Most states reduced the power of the executive branch, which was considered aristocratic, by taking away the governor's veto over laws passed by the assemblies. In Pennsylvania the shift of power to the legislature was carried the furthest. The Keystone State entirely eliminated the legislature's upper house, thereby concentrating all power in the lower one, and fragmented the executive branch by substituting for the governor an executive council of thirteen members. Virginia and several other states pioneered another important democratic advance: they adopted formal written bills of rights guaranteeing freedom of speech, conscience, assembly, petition, and privacy, as well as the right to a trial by jury and other legal safeguards for the individual.

A final democratic innovation, widely adopted in these years, was the constitutional convention, a meeting called for the specific purpose of altering the fundamental frame of government. Only such a convention, it was believed, could validly express the wishes of the people. Its decisions, especially when confirmed by a direct vote of the electors (referendum), took precedence over actions of a mere legislature. First put in practice by Massachusetts during the Revolutionary era, the concept that a convention best expressed the will of the people governed the call for the federal Constitutional Convention in 1787. It was a major contribution to democratic theory and practice.

The use of conventions to frame instruments of fundamental law reflected the new idea that in some ultimate sense "the people" alone were the source of power. Republicanism was a related concept. Republicans wished to reduce the role of birth, breeding, rank, and family influence in political life. These seemed relics of colonial days and royal government when, despite the widespread franchise, Americans had acknowledged hereditary authority and had shown deference to officials. Such attributes, said republicans, should no longer count; only talent, virtue, and devotion to the common good should qualify a person for political advancement and high office.

We must qualify the idea that political ideology was liberalized, however. The leaders of the Revolution were carried by the logic of their opposition to royal government to condemn hereditary privileges, but few of them ever got over their fear of pure democracy, in which numbers alone counted and everyone was equal. Though they acknowledged that "the people" were the source of power, they did not include women, blacks, Indians, and men without some property in the term. Moreover, except for a few "violent men"—or, as we would say, radicals—republicans did not believe that elected representatives should be completely under the sway of the voters. Instead, they favored a "mixed" government in which the popular voice representing "numbers" would be combined with the "talent" of unusual and superior leaders.

Privilege. In several areas of colonial life the law had upheld the privileged position of specific institutions and individuals; here, too, the Revolution had a liberalizing effect.

In those states with an established Anglican Church there was progress toward the complete religious toleration and separation of church and state that we have come to consider peculiarly American. It was inevitable that Anglicanism should lose standing after the Declaration of Independence. It was, after all, the denomination most closely associated with the English crown, and many Anglican clergymen were Loyalists. But the whole idea of an established church had become increasingly distasteful to Patriots. This dislike induced Jefferson—allied with Baptists, Methodists, and other Dissenters—to fight for disestablishing Anglicanism in Virginia during the war and to carry through passage of the Bill for Establishing Religious Freedom not long afterward (1786). Other states also disestablished the Anglican Church, and several of them removed restrictions on non-Protestant voting and office holding.

Despite efforts by the growing number of Baptists, however, little progress toward religious equality was made in New England, where Congregationalism was established. Unlike the Anglicans, the Congregationalists were not identified with England. In fact, the Congregational clergy were among the most ardent defenders of the Patriot cause. Because of this close association with the fight against Britain, Congregationalism enjoyed an extended period of privilege. Not until 1833, when Massachusetts disestablished the Congregational Church, did New England finally achieve the separation of church and state that came elsewhere during the era of the Revolution. Yet on the whole, in religion as in government the effects of the Revolution were liberating and created precedents that would be incorporated into the federal Constitution.

The Revolution also ended entailing and primogeniture, two practices that reinforced economic inequality and privilege. *Entailing* was a legal procedure that allowed a property holder to forbid his heirs to sell their inheritances. *Primogeniture* was the practice of favoring the first-born son in inheritances in the absence of a will providing for a more equal distribution. Together these two practices were designed to preserve large landholdings and buttress the power and wealth of aristocratic families.

Although both procedures had fallen into partial disuse in the colonies, to men like Jefferson they seemed decrepit survivals of feudalism and offensive to a free society. In 1776 Jefferson drafted a law that abolished entail in Virginia. Similar laws were soon adopted in other states. The last elements of primogeniture began to be swept away in 1777, when the Georgia legislature prohibited it, and by 1800 the practice was dead everywhere in America.

MAKING THE PEACE

Much of this liberating change had taken place against the background of war; peace would bring other challenges and other changes to the new nation. But first the terms of that peace had to be settled. After Cornwallis's surrender in 1781, Con-

Library of Congress

At Versailles a lady offers Benjamin Franklin a laurel wreath, perhaps to replace the fur cap he often wore to charm the French court. Franklin, a marvelous diplomat, secured formal recognition of the United States and a military and commercial alliance with France; later he helped negotiate the Treaty of Paris, which brought the war to a close.

gress wrestled with both thorny domestic problems and complicated negotiations in Paris.

France and the United States had agreed not to negotiate a separate peace with Britain, but the temptations for both countries to work out their own arrangements was irresistible. By 1781 the French were tired of the war and in financial difficulties themselves. They had achieved their goal of humbling Britain and wanted out. The Americans, too, saw no reason to fight on. Unfortunately there was Spain. The 1778 treaty with France that had brought Spain into the war provided that she be given Gibraltar as her reward—if she could capture it. Acting on this agreement, Franco-Spanish forces had besieged the great fortress without success. Month after month the British defenders held out, depriving the Spaniards of their goal. If Spain now made peace at the behest of the French

and Americans, she would never acquire Gibraltar. When approached by Vergennes to consider peace, the Spanish government balked. It looked as if peace for France and independence for America depended on the transfer of a pile of rocks.

And there were other difficulties. In early 1782 Lord North finally resigned, and his successor, the Marquis of Rockingham, prepared to concede independence to America. But what did independence mean? What geographical boundaries would the new nation have? What privileges would it enjoy beyond them? The British hoped to restrict American sovereignty to areas actually controlled by American arms. This seemed to exclude a large portion of the Northwest that the British and their Indian allies controlled. The French for their part saw nothing wrong with a United States limited to the coastal regions of North America or even to New England. Indeed, they loosely talked of settling the American question by dividing the former colonies between England and themselves.

Knowing that the United States had to look out for itself, John Jay, John Adams, and Benjamin Franklin, the American representatives in Paris, began informal and separate peace negotiations with the English. The American negotiators were strong-minded men who did not intend to allow French or Spanish interests to determine America's fate. While pretending to consult with French Foreign Minister Vergennes, they negotiated directly with England's Richard Oswald.

In November 1782 the Americans signed a preliminary treaty with the English. Under this agreement Britain recognized an independent United States with western boundaries at the Mississippi and southern boundaries at Spanish Florida, agreed to allow Americans to fish in British territorial waters off Canada and Newfoundland, and promised to evacuate American territory still under British control "with all convenient speed."

North America, 1783

In return, the United States promised to place "no lawful impediment" in the way of British creditors' collecting outstanding American debts and declared it would recommend that the states restore Loyalists' civil rights and property.

The French were not happy about the negotiations and complained that the Americans had violated the 1778 treaty. Franklin apologized, but hinted that if France attempted to block the agreement, the Americans might be forced to ally themselves with Great Britain. Vergennes had reason to be angry with the Americans. At the same time he realized he could put the treaty to good use. The Franco-Spanish effort to secure Gibraltar had bogged down badly. At the rate it was going, France might remain at war with Britain till doomsday to satisfy its Spanish ally. Rather than try to scuttle the Anglo-American agreement, Vergennes told the Spaniards that the Americans, regrettably, had forced his hand. Because of the American betrayal, France could no longer support Spain's claims to Gibraltar in spite of its best intentions to do so. Faced by Vergennes's withdrawal, the Spaniards relented. Soon after, the United States, France, Spain, and England formally concluded a joint peace. On September 3, 1783, the Treaty of Paris, incorporating the previous American agreement with Britain, was finally signed. The great struggle was over.

CONCLUSIONS

At news of the peace, a wave of elation and thanksgiving surged through the country. So intense was the joy in Philadelphia that prudent citizens urged the city fathers to restrain the celebration lest it get out of hand.

The jubilant mood could not last. The infant nation now confronted the problems of repairing the damage of seven long years of war and learning how to function as an independent state. The difficulties would be formidable. The war had caused extensive physical damage to both the cities and the countryside. In the South the British had carried off thousands of slaves and destroyed dikes and dams. New Jersey, "cockpit of the Revolution," where so many battles had been fought, had been ravaged by advancing and retreating armies. All this destruction would have to be repaired.

There would be social mending to do as well. Loyalists—at least those who had not fled for good—would have to be reconciled to the new regime. Several thousand free blacks in the North would have to be absorbed into the larger society.

But on the whole, these adjustments would be minor. American society had not undergone a true social revolution. The war had accelerated processes that had long been moving the American community toward greater democracy, legal equality, and religious toleration. Between 1776 and 1783 religious establishments had been severely undercut, slavery had been eroded, the treatment of women and prisoners had improved, and the few surviving vestiges of feudalism had been swept away. Yet compared with the fundamental upheaval that marked the great French Revolution of 1789 and the Russian and Chinese revolutions of our own century, these were relatively small changes.

But if America did not experience a major social revolution, it did undergo a political one. From a colony it became an independent nation. The Revolutionary War was primarily a colonial war of independence. If it resembles any upheaval of recent times, it is the decolonization struggles of African and Asian peoples after World War II. And the problems that the new nation would face belonged largely in the same realm: the political. Though the war had advanced the unity of English-speaking America and helped create a sense of shared nationality, it had not forged a cohesive nation. Previous republics had always been small, homogeneous city-states. Never had one been so large in extent. Could this unusual creation called the United States, with its 900,000 square miles and 3 million people, survive and prosper as an independent republic? In the next few years the issue would be put to the test.

FOR FURTHER READING

Howard H. Peckham. *The War for Independence: A Military History* (1958)
A brief narrative of the military aspects of the Revolution. Peckham takes note of the weaknesses of both sides.

Samuel Eliot Morison. *John Paul Jones: A Sailor's Biography* (1959)
This portrait of the Revolutionary sea captain also describes the growing pains of the tiny American navy. The fight between Jones's *Bonhomme Richard* and the superior *Serapis* is splendidly rendered—as are the inventory of Jones's ship and his adventures ashore with women.

Henry S. Commager and Richard B. Morris, editors. *The Spirit of '76: The Story of the American Revolution as Told by Participants* (1958)
This is history straight from the sources. It is a vast miscellany of letters, diaries, journals, diplomatic correspondence, parliamentary debates, and more. The editors provide a long introduction.

Alfred F. Young, editor. *The American Revolution* (1976)
A volume of essays emphasizing class conflict in several states during the Revolution. Several contributors detect a "popular" ideology, opposed to government by the rich, and see this as a potent source of Revolutionary zeal.

James Franklin Jameson. *The American Revolution Considered as a Social Movement* (1925)
The classic statement of the social dimensions of the American Revolution. Jameson sees the Revolution as a powerful engine of social as well as political change. In many ways the book is dated, but it is still the takeoff point for any discussion of the issue it deals with.

Richard B. Morris. *The American Revolution Reconsidered* (1967)
This work, originally a series of lectures, is an attempt to update Jameson. On the whole, it suggests that the Revolution was less revolutionary than Jameson claimed.

Mary Beth Norton. *Liberty's Daughters: The Revolutionary Experience of American Women, 1750–1800* (1980)
An important and interesting book that supports the view that the Revolution—like other wars—helped to improve the lot and increase the freedom of women. Professor Norton does not emphasize new laws so much as new attitudes.

Arthur Zilversmit. *The First Emancipation: The Abolition of Slavery in the North* (1967)
The best study of the process, extending well beyond the years of the Revolution, by which the northern states excluded slavery from their borders.

Jack Sosin. *The Revolutionary Frontier, 1763–1783* (1967)
Tells the important story of the West in both the origins and the course of the Revolution.

Gordon Wood. *The Creation of the American Republic, 1776–1787* (1968)
An important reinterpretation of the Revolutionary period as well as the Confederation era that emphasizes the rise of a republican ideology. Difficult, somewhat disorganized, but rewarding to the serious student.

Kenneth Roberts. *Arundel* (1930) and *Rabble in Arms* (1933)
Benedict Arnold is a principal character in these two entertaining historical novels. Most of *Arundel* deals with Arnold's heroic Canadian expedition to capture Quebec. *Rabble in Arms* ends with the Battle of Saratoga. The work is sympathetic to the Loyalists and Arnold, though he was to become the archtraitor of American history.

6 The Origins of the Constitution

By Popular Demand?

1781 Articles of Confederation ratified • Congress proposes a duty on imports to raise revenue, but it is defeated by Rhode Island

1783 Congress proposes another import duty; it is defeated by New York • Fearing attack by unpaid American troops, Congress flees Philadelphia • Robert Morris sends *Empress of China* to open trade with China

1784 Spain refuses to allow Americans to transship their goods from New Orleans

1785 Congress adopts the Land Ordinance of 1785, a model for future federal land policy • Maryland and Virginia sign an agreement about navigation rights on the Potomac and in the Chesapeake Bay

1785–87 Shays' Rebellion in Massachusetts

1787 The Ordinance of 1787 prohibits slavery in the Northwest Territory and establishes that new states coming from it will be fully equal to the original states • Constitutional Convention meets at Philadelphia; state delegations approve the completed draft of the Constitution

1788 Delaware, Pennsylvania, New Jersey, Georgia, and Connecticut ratify the Constitution • Massachusetts ratifies with a request for a Bill of Rights • Rhode Island rejects • Maryland, South Carolina, and New Hampshire ratify • Congress certifies adoption of the Constitution • Virginia ratifies with a request for a Bill of Rights • New York ratifies • Congress adopts the first ten amendments to the Constitution (the Bill of Rights) • Rhode Island and North Carolina ratify

1789 George Washington becomes president; John Adams, vice president

The great nineteenth-century English statesman William Gladstone once described the American federal Constitution as "the most remarkable work—in modern times—to have been produced by the human intellect at a single stroke in its application to political affairs." Clearly not every American has agreed with this estimate or we would not have fought the Civil War or amended the document twenty-six times. But few Americans today would deny that our unique frame of government has served the nation extraordinarily well over a span of 200 years.

From a modern vantage, then, it does not seem remarkable that Americans held a convention at Philadelphia in 1787 to compose the Constitution. Yet it required a tremendous act of faith and will to abandon the Articles of Confederation and replace them with a new political framework for the federal union. What forces lay behind the movement for a new political structure? Six years earlier the states had ratified the Articles. Although by no means perfect, they had established the sort of political union most Americans wanted—indeed, to the end of the Confederation period, the Articles would have loyal supporters. Obviously many Americans must have had a change of heart. Who were these people and what caused them to alter their views?

The origins of the federal Constitution have interested historians for many years. In the nineteenth century it was usually held that the failings and inadequacies of the Articles were so obvious that all could see them. John Fiske called the Confederation period—the time between the British surrender at Yorktown in 1781 and the establishment in 1788 of the new federal government under the Constitution—the "Critical Period." He believed that during these years the nation was "rapidly drifting toward anarchy." Since the Articles were unable to provide the political and social glue to hold the country together, the calling of the Constitutional Convention and the adoption of the document it produced were merely the logical and valid results of broad public concern. The Constitution, in effect, carried to its natural conclusion the nationalistic trend of the Revolution itself.

Fiske's view reflected the self-congratulation that was common among nineteenth-century Americans. In our own century this gave way to greater skepticism. Just before World War I Charles A. Beard attacked Fiske's interpretation. The Critical Period, he said, was not so critical. The country was "in many respects steadily recovering order and prosperity," and "the economic condition of the country seemed to be improving." Ultimately, he wrote, only one group had suffered under the Articles: those who held the wartime securities of the Continental and state governments. These men—few in number but powerful—wanted the public debts repaid fully. They feared that the state governments and the Confederation Congress would not be able to withstand pressure from taxpayers to scale the debts down. Taxpayers had the advantage of numbers over creditors, and a democratic system in which each man's vote counted would favor their cause. The only way for the creditors to protect their interests was to establish a strong central government that would limit the power of numbers and have sufficient taxing power to collect the public debts. The net effect of a new constitution would be to check what the merchant-creditor class considered an excess of democracy following the Revolution. The American federal Constitution of 1787, Beard and his disciples insisted, was a reactionary document intended to restore to a small elite the power they had lost during the Revolution. It was not called for by wide popular demand or justified by broad national need; instead, it was intended to protect the economic interests of the powerful.

Let us examine the state of the nation in the 1780s to see which of these interpretations is more convincing, to see how and why the Constitution replaced the Articles of Confederation and became the fundamental law under which Americans have lived for almost two centuries.

AMERICA IN THE 1780S

Agriculture. Peace brought economic troubles to American farmers. During the war years armies had swept across the countryside, destroying fences and barns, burning crops and farmhouses. On the frontier Indian raids had pushed back the line of settled farming. In the Carolinas the dikes that controlled the tidal streams in the rice country had been damaged by troops and neglect. In Virginia the flight of Loyalist slaves and the removal of others by the British had seriously depleted the labor force on the plantations.

In time the physical damage and the labor disruption were repaired, but political changes continued to cause difficulties for American agriculture. The severing of the imperial connection had unforeseen consequences for farmers. Once the war ended, the British government removed the bounty that it had paid indigo planters, and indigo virtually disappeared as a crop from the Carolina coast. Still more damaging was British commercial retaliation. Before independence American agricultural commodities had found a ready market in the British West Indies. But then Americans had been subjects of King George. Now that they were foreigners, they no longer could expect special rights in British-controlled markets. Shortly before the war ended, the English government clamped down on the export of many mainland commodities to their Caribbean possessions. Items such as horses, cattle, hogs, poultry, beans, potatoes, flour, rice, and oats could be sent from the mainland only in "British built ships owned by His Majesty's subjects"; cured meats, fish, and dairy products were excluded totally. Farmers of Massachusetts, the Connecticut and Hudson valleys, eastern Pennsylvania, and the grain-growing areas of the Chesapeake were thus deprived of markets for their surpluses. Unsold crops piled up; farm prices fell.

Frontier farmers beyond the Appalachians also found their lot difficult after the war. By the middle of the 1780s thousands of settlers lived across the mountains in what is now Kentucky and Tennessee. These people wanted salt, guns, powder, shot, farm implements, cloth, notions, and small luxuries. To pay for these they grew extra grain, raised extra livestock, or gathered furs and cut lumber. But how could they get these goods to market? As the crow flies, the farmers of eastern Kentucky and Tennessee were not very far from their customers on the seaboard. Unfortunately the trip by pack animals across the Allegheny and Blue Ridge mountains was hard, slow, and expensive.

The Mississippi River and its tributaries were the natural links between the western farmers and the outside world. They could load their products on rafts or flatboats, float them down the current, and land them at New Orleans to be shipped to the east coast or the Caribbean. But under the 1763 treaty ending the French and Indian War, Spain controlled the mouth of the Mississippi; and Spain was reluctant to allow Americans to land their wares at New Orleans for such a purpose. Although the Spanish had supported the Americans during the Revolution, they considered the revolt a dangerous example to their own discontented colonies and also feared that the Americans would one day seize the loosely held Spanish lands in the West. Why help them prosper? The potentially busy Mississippi waterway remained unused, while surplus crops went unsold and western farmers complained bitterly.

Commerce. Commerce, too, was depressed in these years. Admittedly, independence brought some gains. The imperial Navigation Acts had restricted direct American trade with many parts of the world. Americans, for example, could not export directly to northern Europe, and most European imports had to come by way of Britain. Though there had been no legal impediments to colonial trade with the distant East, English merchants had been so dominant in the trade with China, India, and the East Indies that Americans had, in effect, been excluded. With the Navigation Acts gone and newly independent Americans more confident of their prowess, enterprising men jumped at the chance to develop trade with new customers and to open new trading routes. For the first time American ships visited places like Co-

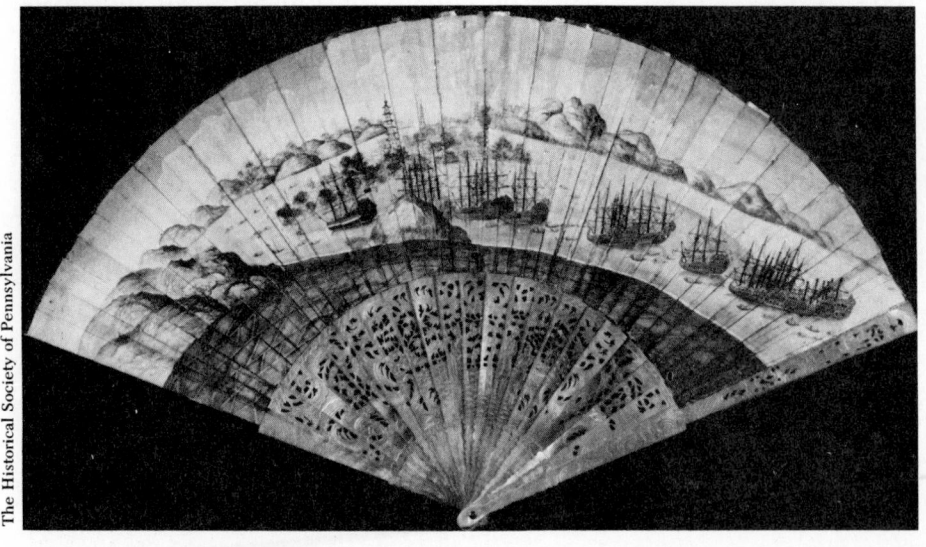

The Historical Society of Pennsylvania

This fan is reputed to have been manufactured in China in 1784 to the specifications of Captain John Greene of the Empress of China. *Note the picture of the vessel left of center.*

penhagen, Rotterdam, Stockholm, Bremen, and even ports in faraway Russian North America. In 1783 Robert Morris opened direct trade with China when he and his associates sent the *Empress of China* on a voyage to Canton that brought extraordinary returns to the promoters. Thereafter, American vessels from Boston, Salem, New York, Philadelphia, and other East Coast ports regularly rounded "the Horn" or "the Cape" on the way to the East Indies and China, the "Celestial Empire." Trade with France, much restricted before 1776, swelled under the treaty of 1778, which gave Americans special privileges in French dominions. American commerce with the French, Dutch, and Danish West Indies also grew remarkably.

Yet the new trade routes were not enough to compensate for the loss of British imperial markets. The new markets were limited by European import restrictions on American products like tobacco and by fierce competition among the Atlantic nations for world trade. By the end of the 1780s American foreign commerce had partly recovered from the disruptions of the war and the immediate postwar period, but all told, per capita American

Value of trade between England and the United States, 1776–1788
Note: The pound is roughly equal to fifty modern dollars.
Source: *Historical Statistics of the United States, Colonial Times to 1957.*

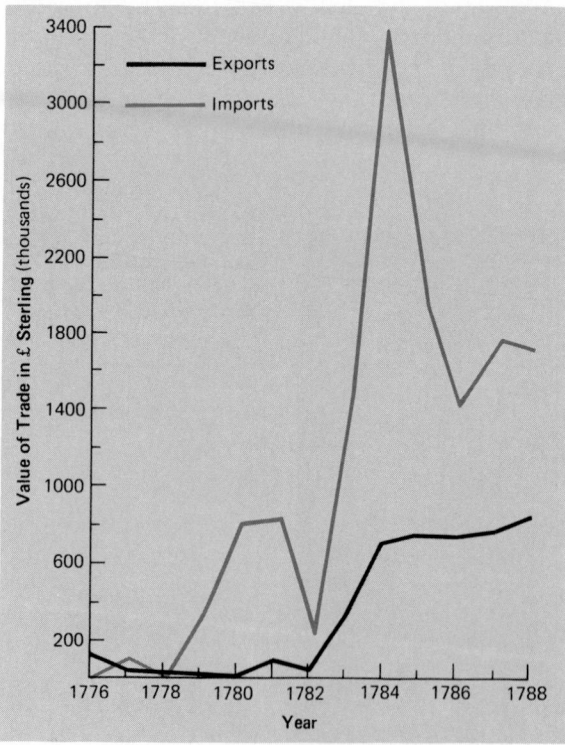

exports were considerably lower in 1790 than in 1775.

And other problems beset the country's commercial interests. After 1783 the agents of British firms set up offices and warehouses in every American port and began to push Americans out of the large transatlantic trade in British goods. Before long British vessels were even carrying British products from port to port along the Atlantic coast at the expense of American coastal traders. American merchants demanded that the United States favor imports carried by American ships and exclude foreigners from the coastal trade. Such laws—in effect, American "navigation acts"— would be no different from the British mercantile restrictions that Americans had been subjected to. Few Americans saw the irony; self-interest was enough to overcome foolish consistency.

Industry. The livelihoods of city artisans, mechanics, and craftspeople—the "manufacturers" of the day—were also uncertain in the immediate postwar era. During the war consumers in many areas had been forced to turn to domestic artisans and craftspeople for goods formerly imported from Great Britain. American manufacturers had flourished until, with the return of peace, consumers went on a spending spree for British wares. Suddenly the American cabinetmakers, weavers, hat makers, tailors, silversmiths, and cobblers found their shops empty of customers.

The "manufacturers" appealed to the state legislatures for help. One Massachusetts petition sought relief for "persons out of employ who have wives and children asking for bread." Several states came to the rescue. They exempted some industries from taxes, lent money to others, and offered premiums to investors and inventors. What the artisans really wanted, however, was tariff protection—high duties that would make foreign imports expensive and thus force American consumers to buy the home product. Massachusetts, Rhode Island, New Hampshire, Connecticut, Pennsylvania, New York, and several southern states did impose taxes on imports. Where importing merchants opposed these, they generally lost to the artisans.

Unfortunately for the new nation's industries and those who earned their livings by them, the system of duties was piecemeal and ineffective. The states tried to avoid conflicts with one another by exempting goods imported from other states. This practice simply nullified the duties. Importers in states without tariffs sent foreign goods into neighboring states disguised as American-made commodities. New York engaged in a preposterous trade war against New Jersey and Connecticut over this evasion. In 1787 the New York legislature decreed that foreign goods coming through the two nearby states must pay four times the duties of American goods. New Jersey retaliated by making New York pay £30 a month for the privilege of maintaining the Sandy Hook lighthouse on New Jersey property. Connecticut imposed duties on goods coming from New York.

The economic warfare among the states never went very far, but it could have led to a system of commercially insulated, competing states that would have thrown away the blessings of free trade throughout the continent. Before long, alert citizens were asking how the country could avoid such an outcome and still protect itself against the superior industry of Great Britain.

Creditors and Debtors.   Creditors, too, found the Confederation period a trying time. Unable to impose taxes, Congress ceased paying the interest and principal of the national debt. Thereafter, the value of government securities—Congress's promises to pay back money it had borrowed during the Revolution—dropped sharply. Speculators willing to take the chance that Congress might eventually pay its obligations bought up government IOUs at a fraction of their face value and soon held a large part of the national debt. The original holders of the securities thus got something for their money, but many felt cheated. Many state creditors felt the same way. After the war some states taxed themselves heavily and paid their debts. Others did not, and their depreciated securities, like Congress's, soon passed into the hands of speculators.

A 1790 view of Mississippi commerce in New Orleans. In the center of the picture is a keelboat; to the right a flatboat. The river's width is greatly reduced.

The Historic New Orleans Collection

Nor were private creditors much better off. The postwar years brought a sharp drop in general prices. Imports, as we have just seen, had boomed briefly after 1783 as American consumers, starved for British goods during the war, snapped up every cargo from Bristol, London, and Liverpool. To pay for this merchandise merchants and customers shipped overseas the gold and silver coin left behind by the French army or lent to Congress during the war by Dutch bankers. But there was a limit to the available cash, and the country soon reverted to its normal condition of currency famine.

When money is scarce, it becomes more valuable relative to the things it buys. Thus prices for domestic goods now fell sharply and painfully. This *deflation* hurt farmers and artisans, who produced goods for sale. It also hurt debtors, who found it hard to get money to pay their creditors. To relieve their distress, debtors demanded paper money, and in several states the legislatures passed measures to oblige them.

In most states the paper currency caused few

Rhode Island Historical Society

One of the last paper notes issued by Rhode Island. The state was known for its excesses in the battle over war debts that plagued the Confederation.

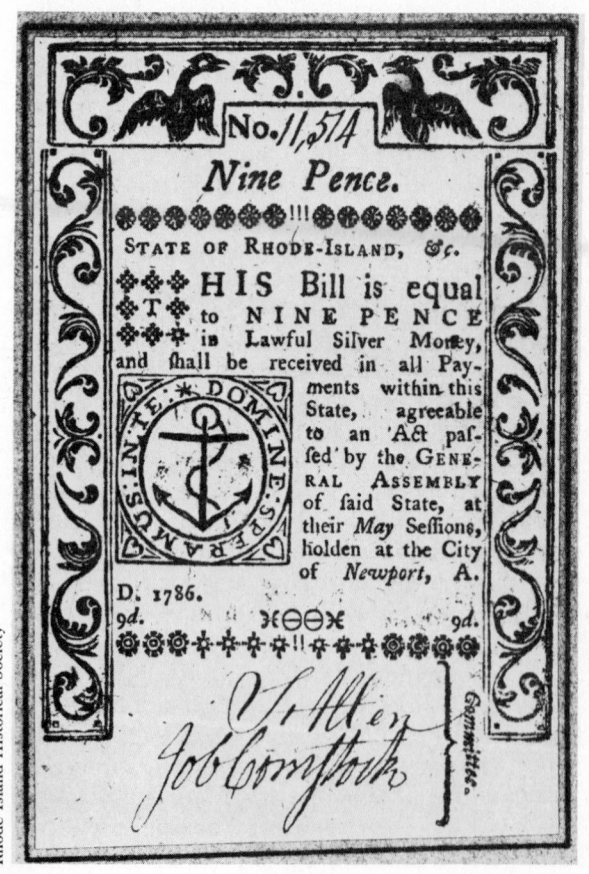

problems because they printed only moderate amounts and did not make it "legal tender" that creditors had to accept even if they did not want to. New York and Pennsylvania businessmen actually supported their state's paper money issues to help end the currency famine and make business easier to conduct.

The situation was very different in Rhode Island. In that turbulent state the debtors were in complete control and seemed determined to cheat their creditors. In 1786 the legislature, acting under debtor pressure, issued £100,000 of legal tender paper money and declared that everyone had to accept it at face value even if it lost purchasing power. A creditor who resisted was breaking the law, and the debt would be canceled. Soon debtors were pursuing their creditors and paying them without mercy. Creditors complained bitterly, but to no avail.

The evidence thus confirms the economic difficulties of the Confederation period. And it also shows that the distress was widespread, not confined just to creditors, as Beard argued. Merchants, farmers, and craftspeople, as well as creditors, had good reason to complain in these early postwar years.

The general distress had important political repercussions. Who was to blame for the problems? Why had prices dropped? Why had the British refused to make trade concessions to Americans? Why could Spain close the port of New Orleans? Why were American craftspeople not protected against cheap foreign goods? Why could Rhode Island debtors arbitrarily scale down their debts? Why must national creditors sell their government securities to speculators at a fraction of their face value? The fault, many Americans would soon come to believe, was the weak national government established by the Articles of Confederation. Something had to be done to strengthen it if the country was to prosper and fulfill its economic promise.

Confederation Finances. Congress had not paid Revolutionary soldiers, security holders, or any of its other creditors—and could not deal with many of its other pressing problems—because it lacked financial resources. Under the Articles of Confederation the central government had no power to tax and could do no more than assign revenue quotas to the states. Raising these funds then became the responsibility of the thirteen state legislatures. Under this scheme money came in very slowly because the states had their own expenses and were reluctant to fulfill their national obligations.

To meet its needs Congress offered large

blocks of western land for sale to speculators. Under one such arrangement, 1.5 million acres of land were sold for just $1 million to a group of Boston businessmen and promoters. Congress also resorted to borrowing money from abroad as well as from Americans. But these loans were a mere stopgap, since the government could not expect bankers to continue to lend to it when it had no means to repay them. Meanwhile, Washington's restless army remained unpaid and undischarged in its camp at Newburgh, New York.

Hoping to solve the government's revenue problems, in 1781 some members of Congress proposed an amendment to the Articles allowing Congress to levy a duty of 5 percent on all goods entering the country. The revenue from this "impost" would be used to pay the defaulted debt. Amending the Articles, however, required the unanimous consent of the states. Twelve states quickly ratified the amendment, but Rhode Island held out. In November 1782 it rejected the proposal. Another impost amendment, put forward in 1783, failed when New York ratified it with crippling conditions that the other states would not accept.

These failures had serious consequences. As we have seen, many people were forced to sell their government securities to speculators for whatever they would bring. Veterans were denied the cash bonuses Congress had promised them. Continental officers, who believed they were entitled to half-pay for life, were especially angry and were soon muttering of rebellion in the army's camp at Newburgh.

Nationalism. Besides economic distress, another important source of political change in this period was nationalism. This is the feeling that links individual happiness to the interests and welfare of the nation as a whole; it is the emotional bond that joins citizens of a country to one another. Nationalism is a powerful force that can overwhelm individual and group interest and inspire sacrifice of life itself.

The active nationalists of the period were mostly young men who had served in the Continental Army or in Congress. They had fought and worked for the United States. They had seen many parts of the country, had met men like themselves from every region, and had shared with them their hopes for a new national future. Their experiences had broadened their perspectives into a "continental" view and had made them aware of the inadequacies of localism.

The heightened continental consciousness could be seen in many realms in the immediate postwar period. Before 1776 Americans had looked to Britain and Europe for religious, cultural, and intellectual leadership. During the Confederation period they sought to end this inferiority. In these years Americans established religious autonomy from Europe. American Anglicans (who took the name Episcopalians), led hitherto by distant church superiors, now acquired their own bishops and a separate church government. In 1784 the Methodists left the British-controlled Methodist Conference and organized an independent American Methodist Episcopal Church. In 1789 the pope selected the first resident American Catholic bishop, a move that recognized American nationhood.

Americans also declared their cultural independence of the Old World. In 1780 a group of Bostonians formed the American Academy of Arts and Sciences to encourage "every art and science" that might add to "the interest, honor, dignity, and happiness of a free, independent, and virtuous people." Five years later a reinvigorated American Philosophical Society issued its first volume of scientific transactions. A leader of the new movement for cultural independence was Noah Webster, a Connecticut-born Yale graduate. Soon after Yorktown Webster set out to create a distinctive intellectual life for "the confederated republics of America." In 1783 he published his *Blue-Backed Speller,* a volume, he proclaimed, that would help make America "as independent in *literature* as she is in *politics*." In the next few years he also published a grammar and a reader that used stories and examples drawn from American life as exercises for children learning their letters. Another sign of the new cultural nationalism—a dubious one perhaps—was the publication in 1787 of the first American history textbook.

To the growing body of nationalists the Confederation's political feebleness seemed humiliating. Everywhere they looked they found distressing signs of their country's plight. In June 1783 Congress had made itself look ridiculous by fleeing Philadelphia in fear of attack by unpaid and mutinous Continental troops. During the next months it wandered from town to town trying to find a decent resting place. When the new Dutch minister to the United States arrived to present his credentials, Congress was ensconced in Princeton, a small college town without proper facilities for state occasions. The embarrassed president of Congress, Elias Boudinot, wrote the representative of the nation's former ally to apologize for the inadequacy: "We feel ourselves greatly mortified that our present circumstances in a small Country village prevent us giving you a reception more agreeable to our wishes. But I hope these unavoidable deficiencies will be compensated by the sincere Joy on this occasion." In the end the ceremony went off creditably, but few who observed Boudinot's plight were proud of their country's government.

Though alert when threatened by physical attack, Congress seemed indifferent to everything else. In the six weeks following ratification of the 1783 peace treaty so few members attended sessions that it was difficult to gather a quorum to do business. In mid-February 1784 James Tilton of Delaware wrote a fellow member that "the situation of Congress is truly alarming; the most important business pending and not states enough to take it up. . . ." Another member declared: "The Congress is abused, laughed at and cursed in every company." Is it any wonder that sincere patriots feared for their country's future?

FOREIGN AFFAIRS

Even more disturbing to patriotic nationalists than the domestic weakness of the Confederation was its feebleness in foreign affairs. Almost everywhere the United States was treated with contempt. France remained friendly and honored the trade privileges specified by the treaty of 1778; but Spain and Britain were antagonistic, and even minor powers felt they could disregard American interests. As Jefferson, serving as American minister in Paris, wrote in 1784: "All respect for our government is annihilated on this side of the water from an idea of its want of energy."

The British, in particular, took advantage of American weakness. Besides excluding Americans from the profitable West Indies trade, they refused to evacuate a flock of forts and trading posts on American soil. The British had good commercial reasons for thus violating the 1783 peace treaty. With British troops garrisoned at Michilimackinac, Detroit, Niagara, Oswego, and other posts, American fur traders were forced to surrender the Northwest to their Canadian rivals from Montreal. But the continued occupation was also a political response. The Americans had failed to live up to two provisions of the Treaty of Paris: they had not fully compensated Loyalists for their property losses, and they had not paid all prewar debts owed British merchants. Although Congress earnestly recommended that the states encourage both actions, the plea had been largely ignored. Loyalist groups and British creditors complained bitterly, but it did little good. The American government could not force its own citizens to comply.

The American minister to London, John Adams, pleaded with the British to adopt a more generous policy toward American trade and to evacuate the northwestern posts. Royal officials treated the American envoy with a "dry decency" and cold "civility," but refused to budge. Britain might have dealt more generously with the United States if Congress had been able to impose duties on British imports. As Jefferson noted, the United States "must show" the English that "we are capable of foregoing commerce with them, before they will be capable of consenting to equal commerce." But of course Congress lacked the power, and the British knew it. As Lord Sheffield, a defender of British shipping interests, remarked, it would "not be an easy matter to bring the American states to act as a nation. They are not to be feared as such by us."

American relations with Spain during the Confederation era also revealed Congress's weakness. Besides closing the Mississippi to American trade, Spain refused to allow American ships to trade with their colonies in Latin America, thus cutting off a profitable trading relationship that had developed during the war. These blows to American interests finally goaded even the sleepy Congress to act. In 1785 it authorized John Jay, the secretary for foreign affairs, to open negotiations with Spain over these issues.

Once more the American government proved incapable of achieving results. The Spanish minister, the gallant Don Diego de Gardoqui, was willing to make concessions on trade with Spanish-American ports, since these did not threaten his nation's control over territory. He refused, however, to yield on the right of deposit at New Orleans, that is, the right to unload Mississippi River cargo and place it aboard oceangoing ships. His position suited some influential easterners, who feared that a too-rapid growth of the West would draw off population from the older states and eventually lead to western secession from the United States. It also coincided with the interests of northeastern merchants, who stood to gain by enlarged trade opportunities with Spanish America but saw little advantage in the right of deposit. Yet it was just this right of deposit that was the crucial matter to westerners.

Despite this disunity in American goals, a stronger government might have forced each group to accept a compromise for the national good. As it was, the treaty finally negotiated with Spain outraged the West. In exchange for Latin-American trade concessions, the United States agreed to forgo the right of deposit for twenty-five years. Unrepresented as yet in Congress, the westerners received the support of southern congressmen, who saw little gain for their section in the trade provisions and so could afford to take a nationalist position. Voting solidly against adoption, the southern representatives defeated the treaty. No one got anything. Once again, American weakness had betrayed American interests.

In the Mediterranean, too, the feeble American government was humiliated. For centuries the Barbary states in North Africa—Morocco, Algiers, Tunis, and Tripoli—had lived by preying on the commerce of Europe. Swift Barbary corsairs would swoop down on merchant ships and seize their cargoes; the pirates would then remove passengers and crews and hold them for ransom. Most European powers either paid tribute to the Barbary beys and bashaws in return for safe passage or provided their citizens with naval protection. In the colonial period English men-of-war had protected American commerce against the corsairs. Now that Americans were independent, they could no longer rely on the Royal Navy, and their merchant ships soon became fair game for the Barbary corsairs in the Mediterranean and off the coasts of Spain and Portugal. In 1787 the United States signed a treaty in which Morocco agreed to respect American rights. But negotiations with the other Barbary states failed because they insisted on bribes, which Congress could not pay. Unable either to pay tribute or to provide naval protection for its shipping, the United States suffered continuing harassment from the North African pirates.

THE PUBLIC DOMAIN

In one important area of national concern—the administration of the public domain—the Confederation government can at least be given a mixed review. When Virginia finally surrendered its claims to the Northwest in 1784, Congress found itself with almost a quarter of a billion acres of some of the finest land on earth. What should be done with this princely realm? How should it be disposed of, and to whom? Should it be thought of primarily as a source of revenue, or as an opportunity to shape American society in some desirable way? And how should the communities carved out of this land be governed? If the problems were immense, so were the stakes, for the future of the country depended on the course taken.

The Land Ordinance of 1785. The first issue Congress tackled was how to transfer land from public to private hands. As yet no one seriously considered giving the land away, if for no other reason than Congress needed some source of revenue. But there remained many other, unanswered questions. Should the price be high or low? Should the land be sold in large blocks to speculators, or in small parcels to farmers? One crucial question was whether to adopt the New England system of first surveying the land and then selling it in compact blocks or the scheme more common in the South of selling a receipt for a particular number of acres and then allowing the buyer to choose his land more or less where he pleased. The New England plan had the advantages of encouraging orderly and compact settlement and of avoiding overlapping land claims. But it was likely to slow the pace of settlement by forcing people to buy bad land along with good and by requiring that each section opened be filled before others became available. The New England pattern also promised to avoid the sort of pell-mell rush to the West that was certain to disturb the Indians. On the whole, however, westerners favored the southern scheme, for all its potential for trouble, because it promised faster settlement.

The Land Ordinance of 1785 was Congress's attempt to choose a course among these conflicting alternatives. It provided that all government lands be surveyed and divided into square townships of six miles on an edge. Each township in turn would be cut into thirty-six sections, each of a square mile, or 640 acres. Half the townships would be sold as complete units of over 23,000 acres each. The other half would be sold in 640-acre sections. Some land was reserved for Revolutionary veterans after the land was surveyed; all the rest would be sold at auction at a minimum price of a dollar an acre.

The Land Ordinance more closely resembled the New England than the southern tradition. As in New England, orderly surveying and compact tracts were mandated. Southerners, however, preferred relatively small tracts, so they got part of what they wanted in the provision for sale of single sections. On the other hand, the measure also allowed for the large block sales that speculators preferred. All in all, the scheme favored the principles endorsed by northeasterners over those desired by the rest of the country. Westerners, in particular, would not find it satisfactory. Over the next century they would agitate to alter the public land laws to favor the small farmer and the family farm over the land speculator and the large estate.

Congress's Indian Policy. Congress was no more successful in dealing with the Indian tribes than

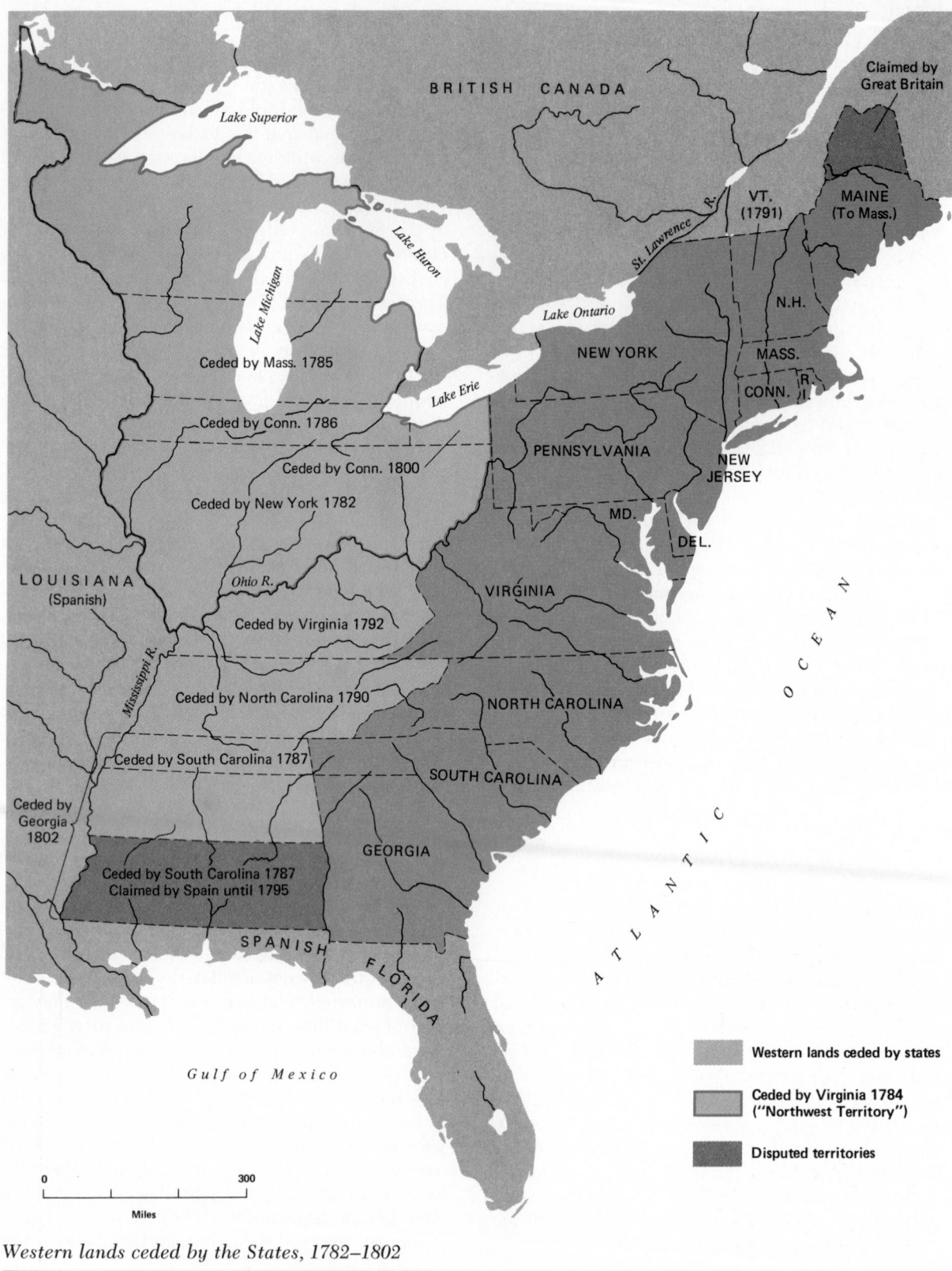

Western lands ceded by the States, 1782–1802

Map labels:
BRITISH CANADA
Claimed by Great Britain
Lake Superior
Lake Huron
Lake Michigan
Lake Ontario
Lake Erie
St. Lawrence R.
VT. (1791)
MAINE (To Mass.)
N.H.
MASS.
NEW YORK
CONN.
R.I.
Ceded by Mass. 1785
Ceded by Conn. 1786
Ceded by Conn. 1800
Ceded by New York 1782
PENNSYLVANIA
NEW JERSEY
MD.
DEL.
LOUISIANA (Spanish)
Ohio R.
Ceded by Virginia 1792
VIRGINIA
Mississippi R.
Ceded by North Carolina 1790
NORTH CAROLINA
Ceded by South Carolina 1787
SOUTH CAROLINA
Ceded by Georgia 1802
Ceded by South Carolina 1787 Claimed by Spain until 1795
GEORGIA
SPANISH FLORIDA
Gulf of Mexico
ATLANTIC OCEAN

Legend:
Western lands ceded by states
Ceded by Virginia 1784 ("Northwest Territory")
Disputed territories

0 — 300 Miles

These roads in present-day Michigan follow the actual survey lines established by the Northwest Ordinance. Congress voted to organize the territory rationally, preventing uncertainties about borders, but one historian has dubbed the ordinance "an exercise in metaphysics . . . and prophecy."

Grant Heilman

with foreign powers. In 1784 it dispatched a group of commissioners to the Northwest to get the local tribes to surrender a major portion of their lands to white settlers. At Fort Stanwix the commissioners induced the Iroquois to give up all claims to the region for a few presents. Soon after, at Fort McIntosh, they persuaded the Chippewa, Ottawa, Delaware, and Wyandot Indians to make a similar concession. But these two treaties did not accomplish their aim. The Indians of Ohio charged that the Iroquois had no right to dispose of their lands at all. And the Shawnee objected to the Fort McIntosh agreement and refused to join the other tribes in signing it. The two treaties also provided an excuse to bands of renegade whites from Kentucky, Virginia, and Pennsylvania to cross the Ohio River and stake out claims on Indian lands still in dispute. By the spring of 1786 it looked as if a major Indian war was about to erupt in the Northwest.

At this point the western settlers, in a pattern that would be repeated many times in later years, decided to take matters into their own hands. Their first step was to call on the Indian fighter George Rogers Clark to come to their aid. Though old and in ill health, Clark rose to the challenge and launched an offensive of white settlers against the Ohio Indians. It failed when the western volunteers mutinied. Much encouraged, the Indians now repudiated the two treaties and declared that white settlers would be excluded from the whole Northwest. The "line now cutting Pennsylvania,"

they announced, "shall bound them on the sun-rising, and the Ohio shall be the boundary between them and the Big Knives." Congress was dismayed by this Indian barrier, but in its usual feeble way could do nothing about it.

Clearly, then, many aspects of the postwar years suggest economic reasons for dissatisfaction with the Articles. But many more groups than the congressional and state creditors were dissatisfied with the Confederation government's performance. And the facts also support a nationalist interpretation. No matter how content groups of Americans may have been with the existing economic arrangements, the overall failure of the Confederation government in its relations with foreign powers and the Indian tribes humiliated many Americans and made them deeply dissatisfied. By 1785 it had become obvious to many citizens that Congress was little more than a shadow, unable to protect American interests abroad or solve major problems at home. Was it for this, patriots asked, that Americans had fought and died?

The Ordinance of 1787. Despite its weakness, the Confederation Congress could claim one major accomplishment: the Northwest Ordinance to organize and provide a government for the region north of the Ohio and west of Pennsylvania.

In 1784, following Thomas Jefferson's suggestion, Congress had adopted an ordinance providing for ten communities in the trans-Appalachian region. When the population of any of these

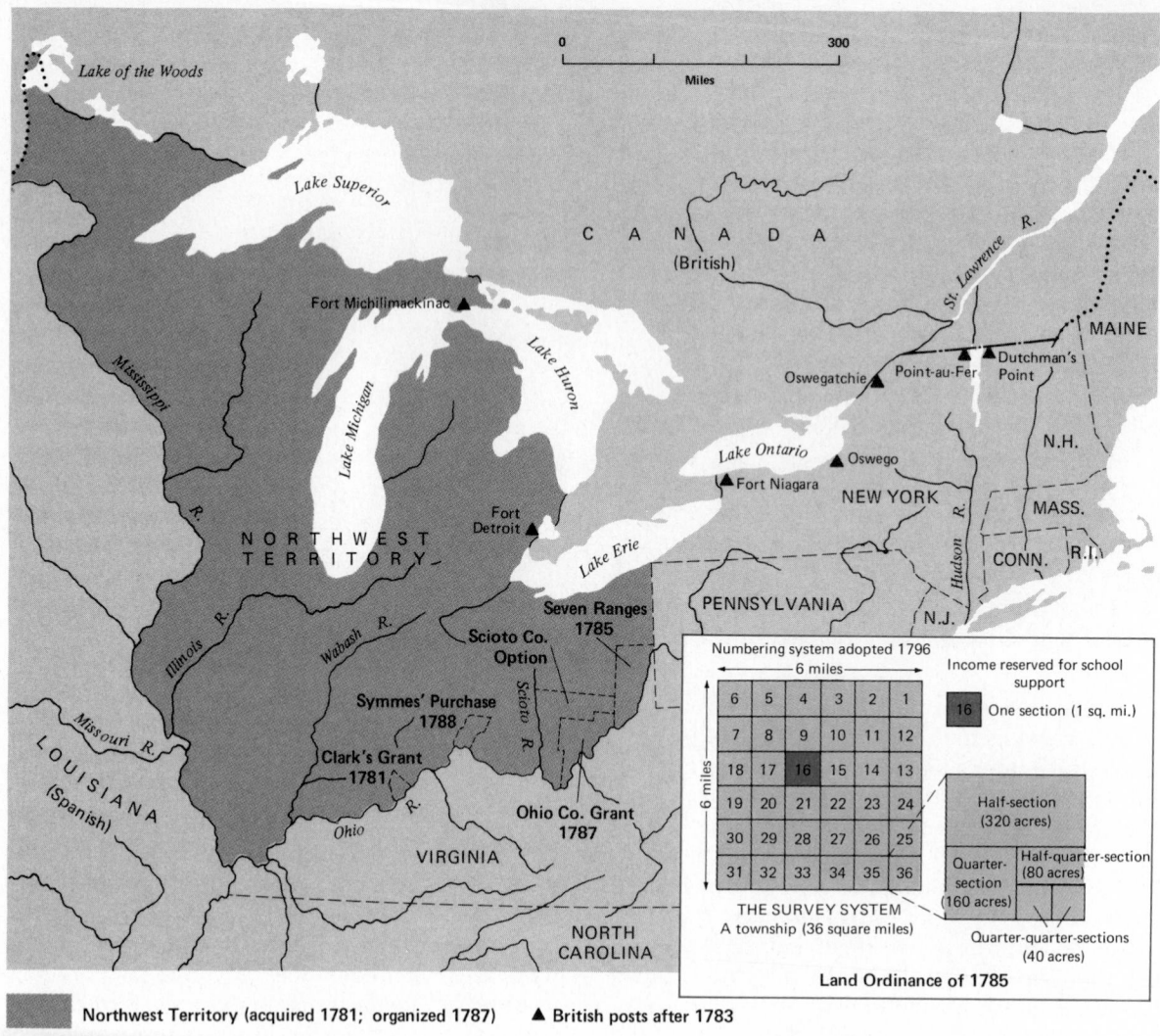

The Northwest Ordinance of 1787

Map labels:

Lake of the Woods • Lake Superior • Lake Michigan • Lake Huron • Lake Ontario • Lake Erie • Fort Michilimackinac ▲ • Mississippi R. • Illinois R. • Wabash R. • Missouri R. • Ohio R. • Scioto R.

CANADA (British) • St. Lawrence R. • MAINE • Oswegatchie ▲ • Point-au-Fer ▲ • Dutchman's Point ▲ • Oswego ▲ • Fort Niagara ▲ • Fort Detroit ▲ • NEW YORK • N.H. • MASS. • Hudson R. • CONN. • R.I. • N.J. • PENNSYLVANIA

NORTHWEST TERRITORY • Seven Ranges 1785 • Scioto Co. Option • Symmes' Purchase 1788 • Clark's Grant 1781 • Ohio Co. Grant 1787 • LOUISIANA (Spanish) • VIRGINIA • NORTH CAROLINA

0 — 300 Miles

Numbering system adopted 1796 — 6 miles

6	5	4	3	2	1
7	8	9	10	11	12
18	17	16	15	14	13
19	20	21	22	23	24
30	29	28	27	26	25
31	32	33	34	35	36

6 miles

THE SURVEY SYSTEM
A township (36 square miles)

Income reserved for school support
16 One section (1 sq. mi.)

Half-section (320 acres)
Quarter-section (160 acres)
Half-quarter-section (80 acres)
Quarter-quarter-sections (40 acres)

Land Ordinance of 1785

Northwest Territory (acquired 1781; organized 1787) ▲ British posts after 1783

---

reached 20,000, the inhabitants could adopt a constitution and apply for admission to the Union as a state equal to the states already composing the Confederation. Although it was never put into effect, this measure served as the model for the Northwest Ordinance adopted three years later.

The 1787 Northwest Ordinance mandated that no more than five or fewer than three states be formed out of the Northwest Territory and that slavery be forever prohibited throughout the area. In its political provisions the ordinance was less democratic than Jefferson's plan. Instead of allowing a new territory autonomy from the outset, it required that Congress appoint a governor, a secretary, and three judges to govern it. When the territory attained 5,000 free male inhabitants, it could elect a territorial assembly, but the governor would have absolute veto over its acts. Only after

its population had reached 60,000 free inhabitants and it had submitted an acceptable constitution to Congress would the territory become a self-governing equal state of the Union.

The Northwest Ordinance was a momentous piece of legislation. Its exclusion of slavery ensured that the entire North would be free territory. Equally important, the ordinance determined the future of the West and the Union by establishing the principle that new states would be equal to the original thirteen. If we consider the possible alternative of holding new territories in colonial thralldom, we can see how beneficial a precedent the ordinance was. Ray Billington, a historian of the American West, has declared:

> The Ordinance of 1787 did more to perpetuate the Union than any document save the Consti-

Annapolis Convention

Many steps intervened between first perceptions of the inadequacy of the Articles of Confederation and the actual meeting of the Constitutional Convention at Philadelphia during the summer of 1787. One of the more important was the Annapolis Convention, called originally by Virginia as a commercial meeting to discuss the chaotic trade relations among the states. Nine states accepted the invitation, but only five actually sent delegates. The poor turnout made it impossible for the twelve delegates present in the Maryland capital to proceed with their business. But they were not to be deterred from their nationalist purposes. Under the leadership of New York's Alexander Hamilton, they drafted a "call" for a new convention to meet in Philadelphia in May. This meeting would discuss not only trade disunity but all the weaknesses of the government under the Articles. The following is a shortened version of that call.

"To the Honorable, the legislatures of Virginia, Delaware, Pennsylvania, New Jersey, and New York—

"The Commissioners from the said States, respectively assembled in Annapolis, humbly beg leave to report . . .

"That the express terms of the powers of your Commissioners supposing a deputation from all the States, and having for object the Trade and Commerce of the United States, your Commissioners did not conceive it advisable to proceed on the business of their mission, under the Circumstances of so partial and defective a representation.

"Deeply impressed, however, with the magnitude and importance of the object confided in them on this occasion, your Commissioners cannot forbear to indulge an expression of their earnest and unanimous wish that speedy measures be taken, to effect a general meeting of the States, in a future Convention, for the same, and other purposes, as the situation of public affairs may be found to require. . . .

"That there are important defects in the system of the Federal Government is acknowledged by the Acts of all those States which have concurred in the present Meeting; that the defects, upon a closer examination,

may be found greater and more numerous, than even these acts imply, is at least so far probable, from the embarrassments which characterise the present state of our national affairs, foreign and domestic, as may reasonably be supposed to merit a deliberate and candid discussion, in some mode, which will unite the Sentiments and Councils of all the States. In the choice of the mode, your Commissioners are of the opinion that a Convention of Deputies from the different States, for the special and sole purpose of entering into this investigation, and digesting a plan for supplying such defects as may be discovered to exist, will be entitled to a preference from considerations which will occur without being particularised.

"Your Commissioners decline an enumeration of those national circumstances on which their opinion respecting the propriety of a future Convention, with more enlarged powers, is founded; as it would be a useless intrusion of facts and observations, most of which have been frequently the subject of public discussion, and none of which can have escaped the penetration of those to whom they would in this instance be addressed. They are, however, of a nature so serious, as, in the view of your Commissioners, to render the situation of the United States delicate and critical, calling for an exertion of the united virtue and wisdom of all the members of the Confederacy.

"Under this impression, your Commissioners . . . beg leave to suggest their unanimous conviction that it . . . may advance the interests of the union if the States . . . would themselves concur, and use their endeavours to procure the concurrence of the other States, in the appointment of Commissioners to meet at Philadelphia on the second Monday of May next, to take into consideration the situation of the United States, to devise such further provisions as shall appear to them necessary to render the constitution of the Federal Government adequate to the exigencies of the Union, and to report such an Act for that purpose to the United States in Congress assembled, as when agreed to by them, and afterwards confirmed by the Legislatures of every State, will effectively provide for the same."

tution. Men could now leave the older states assured that they were not surrendering their political privileges. [By enacting the Ordinance] Congress not only saved the Republic, but had removed one great obstacle to the westward movement.

THE CONSTITUTIONAL CONVENTION

The Confederation government, then, was not without accomplishments. But they were far outweighed by its failures. By 1785 it seemed clear to many Americans, not just a small elite, that the nation needed a more powerful and effective central government to serve its interests and express its patriotic yearnings.

The road to the Constitutional Convention was roundabout, however. The process of revising or replacing the Articles began in 1785 when Maryland and Virginia signed an agreement over navigation rights on the Potomac River and Chesapeake Bay. The success of this pact induced Maryland to call for a broader arrangement that would include Pennsylvania and Delaware and cover

An Historical Portrait   Daniel Shays

Like other states of the young Union, Massachusetts found the peace after Yorktown a dubious blessing. In the coastal regions of the state the end of hostilities brought nothing but difficulties. The Barbary pirates cut off trade with the Mediterranean. The English vengefully excluded American vessels from the West Indies. Hardship for the merchants also meant hardship for the sailors, the sailmakers, the ship carpenters, and all the other "mechanics" who worked in the port towns and earned their living from overseas commerce.

The difficulties soon spread to the farmers of the interior. The people of Massachusetts had gone on a buying spree when British goods became available soon after Yorktown. Unable to ship goods to the English West Indies colonies in exchange, they had to pay for these British goods in specie—gold and silver. The import deluge quickly drained the community of all hard money and compelled hard-pressed import merchants to demand quick repayment of all outstanding debts. Soon they were dunning their customers among the retail shopkeepers of the interior market towns. The retail merchants in turn had no alternative but to pressure *their* customers—the local farmers and mechanics—to immediately pay all outstanding debts, and in coin, not farm produce as in the

past. By this chain reaction, before many months the cash shortage of the coastal port towns had been transmitted to the entire state.

The cash dearth proved a bonanza to local lawyers, for when their farm customers refused to pay, the besieged storekeepers turned to the courts. Between August 1784 and August 1786 the Hampshire County Court of Common Pleas prosecuted almost 3,000 debt cases, a 260 percent increase over 1770–72. Matters were made worse by the state's tax system. Land bore two-thirds of the total tax burden, while the personal property of the business and professional classes escaped taxation. The result of this combination was that many farmers in the interior and western counties faced not only suits for debts but also the forced sale of their property for nonpayment of state taxes.

Into this picture of severe rural distress intruded the figure of Daniel Shays of Pelham in Hampshire County. Shays was seen as Robin Hood by his supporters; his foes considered him a dangerous social leveler. He was really neither. A former captain in Washington's army, Shays had fought gallantly at Bunker Hill, Saratoga, and Stony Point. But Captain Shays had none of the "nobler" qualities expected of a hero. In 1780 he sold for cash a sword that the Marquis de Lafayette had presented to him

as a mark of esteem. The act scandalized many of his fellow officers. Soon after this event Shays resigned his commission and returned to his native state.

Shays was not the chief mover of the events that have been given his name. The "rebellion" started as a wave of peaceful petitions to the state legislature for relief in the form of paper money and the closing of the courts where creditors had brought suit against the farmers. Patience soon wore thin, however, and during the late summer, fall, and winter of 1786 spontaneous bands of "regulators," attempting to stop the lawsuits and the forced sales, attacked the courts in western Massachusetts. Captain Daniel Shays played little part in the earliest of these attacks. But when in late September the rebels tried to stop the sitting of the court in Springfield, he was abruptly catapulted into leadership. Wearing his old buff-and-blue Continental officer's uniform, Shays rode up and took charge of the protesters in front of the courthouse. He talked General Shepard, commander of the militia, into allowing the regulators to parade around the town square without interference to express their grievances. He was now a marked man.

During the remainder of 1786 Shays was in the thick of the growing disorders. In late November,

---

disputes over import duties, currency, and other commercial matters. Nationalists in the Virginia legislature quickly proposed that *all* states meet in September 1786 at Annapolis to consider common commercial problems. Only five states attended the conference, but the nationalists—led by Alexander Hamilton of New York, James Madison of Virginia, and John Dickinson of Delaware—took advantage of the situation. Since a majority of states were not present, they convinced the delegates to petition Congress for a full-scale convention to meet at Philadelphia in May 1787 to discuss not only economic problems but fundamental political changes as well.

By this time, Congress's long decline had brought it close to paralysis. The Annapolis Con-

vention's resolution was referred to a committee of three, which proposed to submit it to another committee of thirteen, which the legislators never got around to appointing. Congress, it seemed, intended to let the proposal die.

Shays' Rebellion.   Then events in Massachusetts, a center of political turbulence since the 1760s, jolted the country and Congress into action. Massachusetts was one of those states that had obligated itself to pay its war debt. This commitment required substantial amounts of revenue, and the Bay State legislature had imposed on its citizens the heaviest taxes in New England. To farmers already suffering from low crop prices, the taxes were a disaster. Debts and bankruptcies soon

following the violent capture of two rebel leaders by the loyal militia, Shays signed a manifesto proclaiming that "the seeds of war are now sown. . . ." He was soon busy organizing an attack on the court due to meet in Worcester in early December.

A thousand insurgents assembled in Worcester to stop the meeting of the court, prepared if necessary to die for their cause. The sacrifice proved unnecessary. A winter storm descended on central Massachusetts the evening before the court session, completely blocking the roads and preventing the judges from getting to the town. The insurgents, cold, wet, and miserable, soon drifted off for home. Shays and a number of other disappointed leaders had to settle for another proclamation detailing the sufferings of the farmers and demanding the release of rebel prisoners and the suspension until spring of the courts in three western counties.

By this time the conservative citizens of the commonwealth were in a state of panic and demanding "condign punishment" of the rebels. The state legislature responded with a barrage of measures punishing rioting, suspending the writ of habeas corpus, and making "the spreading of false reports to the prejudice of government" an indictable crime. It also passed an Act of Indemnity pardoning all rebels who would take an oath of allegiance. Meanwhile, an alarmed Confederation Congress in New York, at the behest of the Massachusetts authorities, voted to raise a force of federal troops to put down the rebellion, the money to be supplied by a requisition on the states of $530,000.

As usual, nothing came of Congress's good intentions. The states refused to appropriate the money and the Massachusetts authorities were forced to suppress the rebellion by themselves. In January 1787 Governor James Bowdoin began to organize a small army of volunteers, financed by private contributions, to put down the rebels. Money and recruits poured in, and by the end of the month five companies of troops under General Benjamin Lincoln were on their way to the scene of the disorders. Before they arrived, Shays and his associates, in quest of arms and ammunition, attacked the federal arsenal at Springfield. The attack was met by the militia, who opened fire with big guns loaded with grapeshot. The third volley smashed into the charging rebels, killing three. Shays tried to rally the men, but most had never faced gunfire before. Crying "Murder!", they broke and ran for cover.

During the next few weeks Shays and his little army retreated before the approaching forces of General Lincoln. At Petersham Lincoln and his men caught up with the Shaysites and surprised them at breakfast. Fortunately there were few casualties. The rebels once again panicked and ran from the field. Most escaped and over the next few months continued a sort of guerrilla war against the authorities. But the Petersham defeat broke the back of the rebellion.

Shays himself fled to Vermont with a price on his head. In 1788, with order restored in the commonwealth, the Massachusetts legislature pardoned the rebel leaders. Shays returned home and for a while lived quietly in Pelham. Then he joined the trek of many rural Yankees to western New York, where he spent his remaining years as a Revolutionary War pensioner.

Occasional visitors came to see the notorious rebel. They were generally disappointed. The firebrand was just a genial old man, a little too fond of the bottle. Shays died in Sparta, New York, in 1825 at the age of 84. By this time few remembered the man who had inspired terror among the rich and mighty of the commonwealth of Massachusetts and, by giving a final push to the nationalists' demand for a stronger federal union, helped alter the course of American history.

---

mounted in the western counties, and many yeomen fell behind in their tax payments. As if this were not enough, Massachusetts law required that the pettiest commercial transactions be recorded by a court, necessitating the payment of high fees to lawyers and court officials. The large volume of legal business resulting from hard times thus added to the heavy tax load imposed on the state's citizens.

By the summer of 1786 discontent among farmers in the western counties had reached the flash point. In late August they convened in Worcester and condemned the taxes and heavy legal fees. Shortly afterward, an armed mob of 1,500 men, eager to end foreclosures for tax delinquency and debt default, stopped the convening of the Hampshire County Court. In early September three more county courts were kept from sitting by groups of angry men.

Although the Massachusetts legislature made some effort to ease the burden of debtors, disaffected westerners began to arm and drill as if they expected to take on King George's redcoats once more. Led by Daniel Shays, a former Continental Army officer, they formed a committee to resist what they considered intolerable conditions. Meanwhile, in the eastern part of the state, people had begun to panic. In Boston Governor James Bowdoin decided to raise a military force to suppress the disorders. Rather than impose new taxes to support this small army, Bowdoin appealed to the city's rich men, who, in their fright,

National Portrait Gallery, Smithsonian Institution

Crude but vigorous contemporary portraits of the rebels Daniel Shays and Jacob Shattucks. Both of these leaders of Shays' Rebellion had been officers during the Revolution.

promptly came up with $25,000. In January 1787 a rebel force of 1,200 met the smaller group of Bowdoin's militia at Springfield. The state troops fired a single artillery volley, and the rebels fled in panic. The uprising was over by spring.

Shays' Rebellion amounted to very little, yet it frightened many people. Some envisioned social revolution. One citizen insisted that if the rebels had won, there would have been "an abolition of all public and private debts" followed by "an equal distribution of property." The rebellion also dismayed the country's nationalists. Washington wrote that he was "mortified beyond expression" by the disorders. For the country "to be more exposed in the eyes of the world and more contemptible" than it already was seemed "hardly possible." Congress at last took heed of the restless mood of many citizens, and on February 21 it

voted to ask the states to send delegates to a proposed constitutional convention at Philadelphia. All except Rhode Island did.

The Challenge. The meeting at Independence Hall on May 14, 1787, was an assembly of giants. Leading the rest in prestige were George Washington, Benjamin Franklin, James Madison, Robert Morris, James Wilson, John Dickinson, and Alexander Hamilton. There was also a large contingent of less famous but immensely able men: George Mason, George Wythe, and Edmund Randolph, all of Virginia; John Rutledge and Charles Pinckney of South Carolina; William Paterson of New Jersey; Roger Sherman and Oliver Ellsworth of Connecticut; and Rufus King of Massachusetts. The rest of the fifty-five delegates made lesser contributions to the convention's work, though most enjoyed high standings in their states and had played important roles in national events.

Seldom has any group taken on so momentous a task. Civilized governments have invariably been the products of a gradual evolution of tradition, experience, and historical accident. The idea of a written frame of government, of a structure of fundamental law put down in precise words at one time, is an American invention. The practice began, as we saw in Chapter 5, with the making of state constitutions after 1775. Its finest expression is the federal Constitution of 1787.

The "Founding Fathers" did, of course, draw on the traditions of the colonies and Great Britain; the English experience is embedded in every legal and governmental institution of the United States. They also relied on their understanding of the ancient world, especially Rome, and on the views of the great political and legal

National Park Service, Independence Hall

The room in Independence Hall, Philadelphia, where the debates on the Constitution were held in 1787.

Library of Congress

This 1790 engraving of the Pennsylvania State House (later renamed Independence Hall) shows a rear view of the structure where, three years earlier, the "Founding Fathers" hammered out the Constitution.

thinkers of their own time. But in the end they were guided primarily by their own practical experience of government.

A number of the men at Philadelphia owned substantial amounts of unpaid Continental and state debt certificates. But although most were rich men, their wealth was largely in the form of land. A more important bond among the delegates than their status as creditors was the nationalism, or continentalism, that we noted earlier. The period from 1781 to 1787, they would have agreed, was indeed critical: America had been treated with contempt abroad while mob rule had threatened at home. There were some defenders of states' rights at Philadelphia—Robert Yates of New York, George Mason of Virginia, and Luther Martin of Maryland, for example—but most delegates believed that the Articles of Confederation had failed as an instrument of government and that Americans needed a stronger central authority.

Few of the delegates, however, wished to strengthen the government at the expense of freedom. The goal of the majority was balance, an end much harder to achieve. They wished to establish a "mixed" government, combining popular and elitist elements, that would protect private property, but also personal liberty. They intended to construct a strong central government, but one that would preserve local autonomy and local rights. In a nation of continental proportions the

diversity of interests, opinions, and philosophies made the task formidable. During the deliberations small states would clash with large states, slave states with free states, commercial interests with agrarian interests, democrats with aristocrats, champions of local rights with nationalists. In the end, compromise would be unavoidable.

*The Debate on Representation.** Following some preliminary skirmishing over procedural rules, the convention began its real work when Edmund Randolph, acting for James Madison, submitted a proposal that has come to be known as the Virginia Plan. Randolph advocated, not merely a revision of the Articles of Confederation, but a completely new government, with separate legislative, executive, and judicial departments. Congress would have two houses, and the states would be represented in each in proportion to their population. In each house the elected members would vote as individuals, not as part of a single state unit, as they did under the Articles. They would, in effect, represent their constituents, not their states. The legislature would choose the persons to fill positions in the executive and judicial branches of government.

The Madison-Randolph proposal emphasized the central government as opposed to the

* The text of the completed Constitution may be found in the Appendix.

states. Randolph hoped to establish a "strong *consolidated* union, in which the idea of states would be nearly annihilated." The Articles had created a league of virtually independent states; the new plan would confer broad powers on the central government, which would "legislate in all cases to which the separate States are incompetent"—that is, in every area where it chose to go. But Randolph's proposal did not spell out the new government's powers.

The Virginia Plan was countered by the New Jersey Plan, submitted by William Paterson. Paterson recommended that the Articles be revised, not replaced. His new government was to be a "federal," not a truly centralized one; that is, there would be a central government, but the states would retain independent authority in some spheres. The New Jerseyite, speaking for a smaller state than Randolph, endorsed the one-house legislature of the Articles, in which each state was represented equally, regardless of its wealth or population. States would continue to vote as units in Congress, so that the states, rather than the people, would be represented in the new government. But the New Jersey Plan did improve on the Articles by granting the national government the power to tax and regulate foreign and interstate commerce. It made federal laws and treaties superior to all state laws, and that, too, was an advance.

It is easy to see that the New Jersey Plan would benefit states with small populations more than the Virginia Plan. If Paterson's arrangement was adopted, the less populous states would have representation in Congress equal to that of the more populous ones. If, on the other hand, the Virginia Plan prevailed, the small states' voices would be drowned out by those of their larger neighbors. For this reason it is often said that the two plans represented a conflict between large and small states. But the disagreement was just as much between the strong centralists and their more locally oriented colleagues.

The two proposals became the basis for debate, and both were modified in the discussions. On the whole, the centralizers came out ahead. The new government would have greatly enlarged powers, but they would be specified and not left to Congress to decide. It would also be a true central government. Congress would represent the citizens of the United States, not the states as entities. Members of Congress would therefore vote as individuals, and not merely help cast a state vote. On the other issues of representation, a compromise was adopted. In one house, the Senate, each state would have equal representation regardless of population; in the other, the House of Representatives, population would determine the size of state delegations.

Now members raised the issue of what constituted "population." Were slaves only property, or were they people? If the former, they might, like other forms of property, be the basis for levying taxes but could not be considered in calculating a state's representation in the lower house of Congress. If they *were* people, they should be counted for determining representation. However, because slaves were not free and could not vote, treating them as people would give the southern states a voice in Congress disproportionate to the actual number of their voters. Each voter in the South, where slaves were numerous, in effect would have more power than each voter in the North, where they were few. Northerners naturally objected to such a scheme. Southerners, noting that their wealth in slaves would force them to pay a heavy tax bill, insisted on some political compensation for the burden they would bear.

The issue was very sensitive, for it touched on the continued existence and prosperity of slavery in the South. And slavery, the South's "peculiar"—that is, special or unique—institution, was entangled in every aspect of southern life. True, ever since the Revolution had proclaimed that "all men are created equal," the supporters of slavery had been on the defensive. But slaves still tilled the South's fields, built its fences, and performed its household chores. Though slavery was fast disappearing in the North, only a handful of enlightened southerners were willing to contemplate its abolition in their own section.

The men at Philadelphia would deal with slavery at several other points; this time they elected to compromise. Taxes and representation in the lower house of Congress would be based on "the whole number of free Persons," excluding Indians but including indentured servants and "three-fifths of all other Persons." Thus, with the "three-fifths compromise," America's Founding Fathers managed the neat trick of simultaneously treating a slave as property and as three-fifths of a human being.

Freedom or Order? Not only did the Founding Fathers compromise conflicting interests, they also compromised conflicting principles. As we have noted, the delegates desired both the representative principle on the one hand, and order and rule by the "best men," a kind of elitism, on the other. Some leaned strongly to one side, some to the other; most were in the middle.

The give-and-take among these approaches

resulted in several important features of the Constitution, particularly the principle of separation of powers. Borrowing from the French philosopher Montesquieu, the delegates adopted the idea that each branch of government—executive, legislative, and judicial—must exercise distinct powers and be selected in a distinct way. This separation would ensure the independence of each branch. In addition, the Founding Fathers adopted the idea that each branch must be able to "check and balance" the others. By such an arrangement the greatest freedom would be ensured, for if one branch grew too powerful and sought to dominate the others, it could be stopped.

Checks and balances were a defense of freedom in one way, but they could also be a brake on excessive freedom—say of a Daniel Shays. During the years when the states were writing their own constitutions, extreme democrats generally favored weak governors and strong legislatures. At Philadelphia the principle of checks and balances seemed like a fine way to accomplish both things at once: check "the mob" and also check the executive.

To this end, the chief executive was to have a veto over acts of Congress, the democratic part of government. But the president was not to be all-powerful. His veto could be overridden by a two-thirds vote of Congress. The chief executive could make treaties with foreign powers, but they would have to be confirmed by a two-thirds vote of the Senate. He was to be commander in chief of the army and navy, but only Congress could declare war. Finally, he could appoint a host of officials, but these appointments would have to be confirmed by the Senate. As a final check on the president—and his appointees—the House of Representatives could bring impeachment charges against federal officials. If impeached officials were then found guilty of "high crimes and misdemeanors" by the Senate, they would be removed from office.

Standing guard against the excesses and abuses of Congress and the president was to be the third branch, the federal judiciary, capped by a Supreme Court. Although it is nowhere stated in the Constitution, legal scholars believe that tne delegates at Philadelphia assumed the right of the federal courts to declare acts of Congress contrary to the Constitution and hence invalid. To free the judges of political influence, they gave them lifetime tenure and declared that during their terms of office Congress could not reduce their salaries.

Checks and balances offered one way to combine strong and stable government with a popular voice. The mixture of democratic and aristocratic methods of choosing the officers of each branch was another. The president would be selected not by the direct vote of the people but by an electoral college chosen by the states as they saw fit. The number of electors from each state would be equal to the number of representatives and senators it sent to Congress. State law would determine how they would be chosen, but it was assumed that they would not be elected directly by the people. Nor was the Senate, the upper house of Congress, conceived of as a stronghold of democracy. Senators would be selected by their state legislatures. To limit popular control of Congress further, senators were to have long terms of six years; only one-third would be seeking reelection in each congressional election held every two years. Finally, the federal judiciary, including the Supreme Court, was to be appointed, and thus far removed from the popular will. To temper these aristocratic features, the House of Representatives would be directly controlled by "the people." Representatives would be elected for two-year terms by the same liberal rules that governed the selection of members of the lower houses of the state legislatures.

Powers of the New Government. Besides establishing a new structure, the Constitution greatly enlarged the powers and scope of the national government. The new government, as we have seen, would impose its authority on the people directly, not through the states. It would also fuse the nation into a single legal whole. Under the new charter each state was required to give "full faith and credit" to all laws and court decisions of the others and to surrender to others all violators of the law who fled across state lines to avoid prosecution. The new government could also do many specific things its predecessor could not do. It could impose and collect taxes from citizens, though by the Constitution's original terms these taxes had to be proportionate to each state's population. It could control and regulate foreign and interstate commerce, although at the urging of the southern states that shipped large amounts of rice and tobacco abroad, it was forbidden to tax exports. The new government had sole control over the coinage of money and could establish a postal system, build post roads, and pass laws of naturalization. The power to establish a system of uniform weights and measures and a uniform bankruptcy law also belonged to the national government. Finally, the Constitution declared that the new government could "make all laws which shall be necessary and proper for carrying into Execution the foregoing Powers, and all other

Powers vested by this Constitution in the Government of the United States." This provision, which is known as the elastic clause, later became the justification for greatly expanded federal authority. In sum, a strengthened national government was to exercise broad authority over economic and political affairs, and over a single economic and legal unit.

Still, the Constitution created not a unitary but a federal government; that is, it left the states with independent authority in some spheres. Crime and breaches of the peace were in the states' jurisdiction, except when a state legislature or governor specifically requested federal help to put down local violence. Social relations, including marriage, divorce, and education, were also left to the states, as were laws regarding commercial relations and most business affairs.

Although slavery was considered a "domestic" institution much like the family, it could not be left solely to the states' jurisdiction. Conflict over representation had resulted in the three-fifths compromise, and the problems of slaves escaping to free states as well as the slave trade itself also had to be considered. After much debate the Philadelphia delegates agreed that Congress could not forbid the foreign slave trade until 1808, but thereafter it might do so if a majority wished. Congress could, however, pass laws to deal with runaway slaves who crossed state lines and guarantee slaveholders the right to recover such fugitives regardless of local antislavery laws.

All through the summer and into September the delegates debated every issue. The discussion, like the weather, was often heated. To quiet ruffled tempers and encourage greater goodwill among the delegates, Franklin at one point proposed that a chaplain be invited to open each morning session with a prayer. Washington, the presiding officer, also worked to maintain peace; and although he said little, his dignity and calm demeanor helped to keep the delegates' differences from getting out of hand.

Nothing could prevent disagreement. A number of the delegates considered the completed draft of the Constitution far too centralizing. New York's Robert Yates and John Lansing, George Mason of Virginia, Luther Martin and John Mercer of Maryland, and Elbridge Gerry of Massachusetts denounced the work of the convention. Lansing, Yates, and Mercer went so far as to quit Philadelphia in protest. On the other hand, the most extreme centralizers believed the proposed constitution did not go far enough. Alexander Hamilton wanted the states abolished in favor of a strong, unitary government. The views that ultimately prevailed were those of James Madison, Oliver Ellsworth, and Roger Sherman, who succeeded in mobilizing the majority around the compromise proposals.

On September 8 the convention sent the completed draft to the Committee of Style and Arrangement. This group of five polished the convention's paragraphs and rearranged them in logical order. One of its members, Gouverneur Morris of Pennsylvania, wrote a preamble that described the promotion of "the general welfare" as one of the purposes of the new framework of government. On September 17, 1787, each of the state delegations voted its approval, and the convention adjourned.

RATIFICATION

Now the Constitution's friends faced the problem of securing its adoption, and it seemed likely that the battle would prove difficult. The Confederation Congress had authorized the Philadelphia convention only to "revise" and "amend" the Articles of Confederation—not to propose a new form of government. Would Congress reject the convention's work? On September 29 the new Constitution was presented to Congress. That body was almost dead and had no heart for resistance. After some minor debate it recommended the plan to the separate states for adoption by convention. The more difficult task was winning ratification by the states. The opposition fought hard against it. Certain groups of debtors, aware that state-issued paper money would be illegal under the new government, were naturally opposed to it. So were taxpayers in states that had paid their debts and feared that through new federal taxes they would pay someone else's as well, and those who considered strengthened national government a retreat from "true republicanism." Finally, there were the temperamentally cautious people, inclined to stick to the ills they had than fly to others they knew not of.

At one time scholars emphasized the formidable opposition to the Constitution and described the battle to get it adopted as a fierce struggle. In part, this view projects back into the adoption period attitudes that gelled in the years immediately following. It also reflects the fact that in a few states the adoption issue was indeed hard-fought. Because it would have been difficult to achieve a successful Union without them, the debates that took place in these states *were* important. Still, it is clear that the "federalists"—those

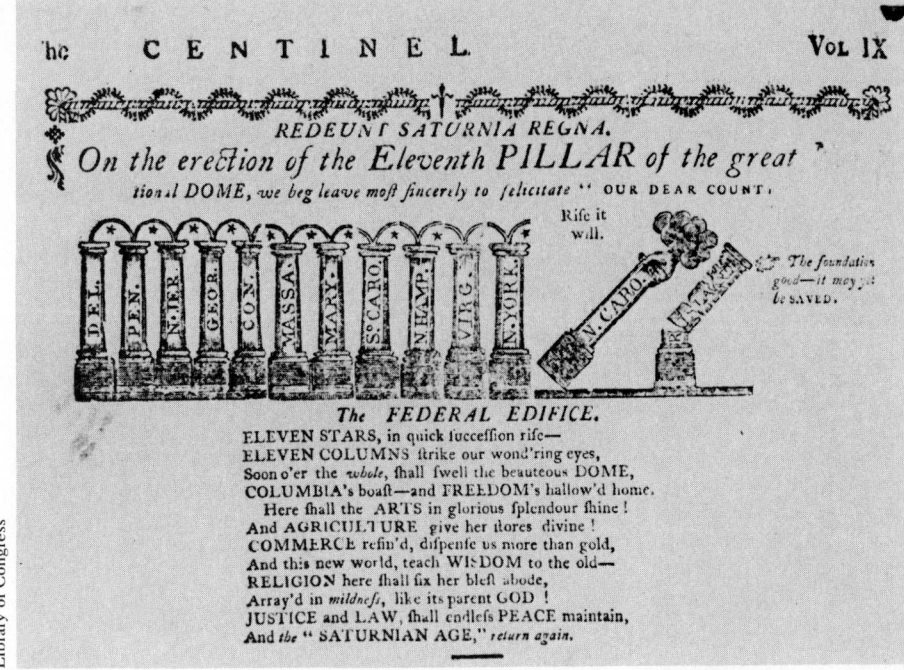

Library of Congress

Cartoon from the Massachusetts Centinel *of July 26, 1788, expressing hope that the two holdout states, North Carolina and Rhode Island, would ratify the Constitution and join the new Union.*

who favored the new federal government—won with relative ease.

The delegates at Philadelphia had decided that the new government would go into operation when nine states had ratified the Constitution. Delaware, Pennsylvania, and New Jersey were won over almost immediately, the first and third by unanimous votes. Early in 1788 Georgia's convention also ratified unanimously. Connecticut soon followed with a heavy federalist majority. In Massachusetts the friends of the Constitution encountered their first serious opposition. By early estimates the state convention had a solid antifederalist majority. Among the initial opponents were the influential Sam Adams and John Hancock, for years leaders of the state's popular party. If these men could be converted, enough delegates would follow them to carry ratification. Fortunately for the Constitution, Adams was induced to change his mind by a mass meeting of Constitution supporters staged by Paul Revere. Convinced that the rally expressed the views of the state's common folk, Adams agreed to support the Constitution. Hancock, now the state's governor, was coaxed and flattered by federalists into believing he was in line for high federal office under the new Constitution.

One of the federalists' problems in Massachusetts and a number of other states was that the Constitution lacked a bill of rights to protect citizens against federal tyranny and to guarantee civil liberties. Some who complained of this lack were interested merely in delaying or defeating adoption. But others, such as Hancock, were sincere in their concern. When Hancock agreed to endorse ratification, he proposed simultaneously that nine amendments be added to protect the citizen against federal tyranny. With this request tacked on to its motion, the Massachusetts convention voted 187 to 168 for adoption.

In March the federalists suffered their first actual setback when maverick Rhode Island overwhelmingly rejected the Constitution by a popular vote. The state, as we saw, had been the center of debtor-imposed paper money schemes and had not sent a delegation to Philadelphia. During the ratification battle the federalists did not stand a chance, so they boycotted the vote. The results were as expected: the Constitution received only 10 percent of the votes cast.

Rhode Island's rejection did not stop the federalists' forward momentum, however. In April and May Maryland and South Carolina joined the parade of adoptions, and by large majorities. Then, by a close vote on June 21, New Hampshire became the ninth state to ratify the Constitution. Under the rules that the convention had prescribed, the Constitution was now officially in force. But New York and Virginia had not acted. If these two large states voted no, it would be impossible to maintain a workable political system.

Federalist forces in Virginia were strong and well organized. Among them were some of the most prestigious men in the state, including James

Library of Congress

True to his revolutionary principles, nine-term Massachusetts Governor John Hancock refused to support the proposed Constitution without amendments guaranteeing the rights of citizens.

Madison, George Wythe, Edmund Randolph, and John Marshall. Also working in the federalists' favor was the general assumption that the first president under the Constitution would almost certainly be the state's greatest son, George Washington. Not yet the "father of his country," he was nevertheless a commanding figure in the new nation and seemed to embody the finest type of patriotism.

On the antifederalist side, however, there was an impressive array of talent, too, including Patrick Henry, Richard Henry Lee, James Monroe, and George Mason. Henry was the spearhead of the antifederalist attack. In an impassioned speech to the state convention he portrayed the new Constitution as dangerous to liberty. Under it the citizen would be abused, insulted, tyrannized. Henry also appealed to localism and the self-love of his listeners. "The Constitution reflects in the most degrading and mortifying manner on the virtue, integrity, and wisdom of the state legislatures," he declared. It assumed "that the chosen few who go to Congress will have more upright hearts, and more enlightened minds, than those who are members of individual legislatures."

Many in his audience believed it was the finest address of his distinguished career as an orator. In the end, though, Henry's eloquence was not enough. The convention voted to ratify with the proviso that a bill of rights be added to the new frame of government.

The battle now shifted to New York. Without New York the Union would be physically split in half; with it, the Union would be complete in all essentials. For weeks the federalists had been bombarding the state's newspaper readers with articles written by Hamilton, Madison, and Jay. These *Federalist Papers*, explaining, defending, and praising the new Constitution, were, of course, partisan expositions of the federalist position. But they were more than propaganda; they were also brilliant analyses by unsentimental men of the way politics was practiced in the real world. Ordinary men were not equipped to govern the country directly, they stated. They did not have the necessary knowledge or understanding. The country would be well ruled only by those who recognized that government was a "complicated science" requiring "abilities and knowledge of a variety of other subjects, to understand it." Every just and successful government must respect the wishes of ordinary people, but wisdom must temper the decisions of majorities. Majorities were often temporary and more often moved by passion than by mature judgment. In the future, moreover, when social inequalities had become greater than at present, they were certain to attack property rights. Government must be strong enough to guard against the natural but mistaken leveling tendencies of democracy.

The persuasiveness of the *Federalist Papers* and Hamilton's impassioned presentation of the federalist position at the state convention gave the adoption drive a great boost. But the pro-Constitution people had more than eloquence on their side. If New York State did not join the Union, New York City might choose to join anyway to avoid losing the lucrative commerce that flowed through it to New Jersey and southern New England. What would the state do then? The argument was convincing, and in the end the logic of circumstances prevailed. On July 26, 1788, the New York convention voted 30 to 27 to adopt the Constitution.

The new Union was now secure. Early in 1789 national elections were held for the first time under the Constitution, and federalist candidates won a majority in the new Congress. In January the electoral college voted unanimously for Washington as president and settled on John Adams as his vice president. Rhode Island and North Caro-

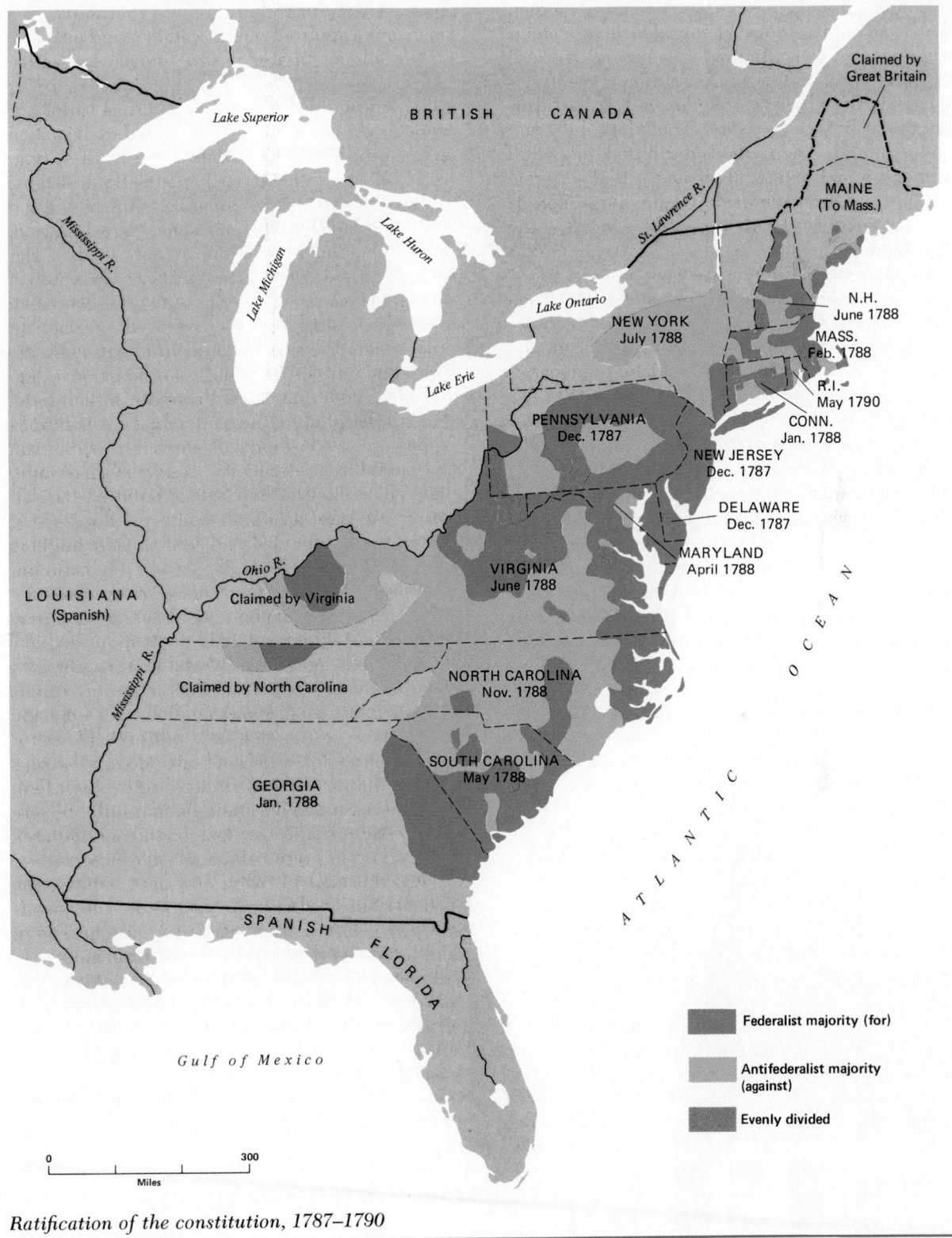

Federalist majority (for)

Antifederalist majority
(against)

Evenly divided

BRITISH   CANADA

Claimed by
Great Britain

MAINE
(To Mass.)

N.H.
June 1788

MASS.
Feb. 1788

R.I.
May 1790

CONN.
Jan. 1788

NEW YORK
July 1788

NEW JERSEY
Dec. 1787

DELAWARE
Dec. 1787

MARYLAND
April 1788

PENNSYLVANIA
Dec. 1787

VIRGINIA
June 1788

LOUISIANA
(Spanish)

Claimed by Virginia

Claimed by North Carolina

NORTH CAROLINA
Nov. 1788

SOUTH CAROLINA
May 1788

GEORGIA
Jan. 1788

SPANISH   FLORIDA

Gulf of Mexico

ATLANTIC   OCEAN

Lake Superior

Lake Michigan

Lake Huron

Lake Erie

Lake Ontario

St. Lawrence R.

Mississippi R.

Ohio R.

Mississippi R.

0   300
Miles

Ratification of the constitution, 1787–1790

lina were still outside the Union, and their citizens did not participate in the election.

Soon after the elections the new government, as promised, adopted the first ten amendments to the Constitution that are commonly called the Bill of Rights. The first nine guaranteed the rights of free speech, press, and assembly, and forbade the federal government to make any law "respecting the establishment of religion or prohibiting the free exercise thereof." They affirmed the right of the people "to bear and keep arms," protected citizens against "unreasonable searches and seizures," required jury trials in criminal and major civil cases, and forbade "excessive" bail or fines and "cruel and unusual punishments." The tenth amendment "reserved" to the states all powers not given the United States by the Constitution.

Note that these amendments placed limits on Congress and the federal government in the area of fundamental civil rights; they did not apply to the state governments. Since most states already had similar restraints in their own constitutions, it was considered unnecessary to guard the citizen against tyranny by state governments.

With their last objections gone, and fearful of being treated as foreign nations if they did not join the Union, North Carolina and Rhode Island reversed their earlier stands and ratified the Constitution in 1789 and 1790, respectively. The United States was now a nation; it had ceased to be a league of petty states.

CONCLUSIONS

Between Yorktown in 1781 and Washington's inauguration in 1789 the country underwent a constitutional transformation of startling dimensions. The end of fighting did not bring the blessings of peace and freedom to the American people. Instead, it ushered in a period of declining trade, falling prices, and unemployment. It also brought national humiliation. In foreign affairs the United States was treated with contempt; even minor powers felt free to disregard American rights.

Thousands of citizens found the period deeply disappointing. Farmers, planters, craftspeople, creditors, and merchants—easterners as well as westerners, northerners as well as southerners—looked on hopelessly as material conditions worsened; they longed for a way to protect their interests and improve their circumstances. Patriots, who saw their dreams of a glorious national future fading, felt despair, and demanded a more effective government to assert their country's position in the world community.

All of these groups turned to constitutional revision as their solution, and the great convention at Philadelphia was the result. Predictably, the Constitution that emerged from the deliberations reflected the feelings of the nationalists and all those who blamed weak central government for their plight. One can almost deduce the political and economic problems of the "Critical Period" from the specific grants of power to the new federal government. No doubt, that government was supported by the country's elite and the defenders of strong restraints on debtors and social levelers. But it was also endorsed by thoughtful and politically active citizens of every social persuasion. We will never be able to say for certain whether a majority of adult Americans in 1788 supported the Constitution. For more than a generation, however, scholars have been convinced that the federal Constitution was indeed written and adopted "by popular demand."

Here Washington takes the oath of office in New York's Federal Hall as first President of the United States.

Library of Congress

FOR FURTHER READING

Merrill Jensen. *The New Nation: A History of the United States During the Confederation, 1781–1787* (1948)

This work seeks to refute the notion that the Confederation era was a critical period. Jensen stresses the successes of the Articles of Confederation, which he understands as the true embodiment of the Declaration of Independence, and brands those who wanted them changed as antidemocratic.

Marion Starkey. *A Little Rebellion* (1955)

In this enjoyable account of Shays' Rebellion, Starkey captures the bitterness of western Massachusetts farmers and the fear and hatred they aroused in the seaboard merchants.

Jackson Turner Main. *The Anti-Federalists: Critics of the Constitution, 1781–1788* (1961)

Main sees the opponents of a stronger central government in the 1780s as largely isolated farmers who were not tied to the sale of commercial crops and so had little interest in foreign trade.

Irving Brant. *James Madison: The Nationalist, 1780–1787* (1948)

The second volume of a three-volume biography of Madison describes government under the Articles of Confederation and Madison's concern with reforming the courts of Virginia, establishing free public schools, and ensuring religious liberty for his native state. Most important, however, is the story of Madison's dismay at the weaknesses of his country during the 1780s and his efforts that culminated in the federal Constitution.

Charles A. Beard. *An Economic Interpretation of the Constitution of the United States* (1913)

The classic "Progressive" interpretation of the Constitution's origins that all later historians have had to reckon with. Beard's thesis is that the fathers of the Constitution—most of whom, he insists, were wealthy merchants and government creditors—constructed a frame of government that was designed to serve the economic needs of their class. In a sense, in Beard's view the Constitution was a counterrevolutionary retreat from the democratic and egalitarian spirit of the Declaration of Independence.

Robert E. Brown. *Charles Beard and the Constitution* (1956)

A reexamination of Beard's thesis that finds it seriously wanting. Brown reveals how even great scholars like Beard can commit errors and distort facts if they are too intent on making a point.

Forrest McDonald. *We the People: The Economic Origins of the Constitution* (1958); and *E Pluribus Unum: The Formation of the American Republic, 1776-1790* (1965)

The first of these two books challenges as oversimplified Beard's description of the economic factors and groups behind a stronger central government in the 1780s. The second is an interesting if sometimes highly personal discussion of the drive toward the Constitution and the formation of a new national government.

Benjamin F. Wright, editor. *The Federalist* (1961)

The *Federalist Papers*, written by Madison, Hamilton, and John Jay, are essential to understanding the thinking of the Constitution's supporters. Wright has converted the language of the essays into modern usage to make them easier to follow, and he introduces them with a helpful essay.

Robert A. Rutland. *The Ordeal of the Constitution: The Anti-Federalists and the Ratification Struggle of 1787–88* (1966)

Sympathetic to the antifederalists who opposed ratification of the Constitution, Rutland explains the strategy of the two opposing groups and the reasons for antifederalist defeat. He concentrates on the important Virginia debates.

Irving Brant. *The Bill of Rights: Its Origin and Meaning* (1965)

This full treatment (515 pages), by a leading biographer of Madison, of the first ten amendments to the Constitution deals with the Bill of Rights' origins in both English and American experience, its creation early in the new republic, and its application over the many years that have ensued. The book goes well beyond the period covered in this chapter, but this should not deter the serious student.

7 The First Party System

What Issues Divided the New Union?

1789   The French Revolution • Congress adopts the Tariff and Tonnage acts to raise the first federal revenues • Congress establishes the State, Treasury, and War departments, and prescribes the structure of the Supreme Court and the federal courts in the Federal Judiciary Act

1790–91   Hamilton presents his financial program to Congress

1790   Congress enacts Hamilton's plan for public credit in the Funding Act

1791   Congress charters the Bank of the United States

1793   War breaks out between France and Britain, Spain and Holland • France sends "Citizen" Genêt as minister to the United States • Jefferson resigns as secretary of state and is replaced by Federalist Edmund Randolph

1794   Britain authorizes the seizure of neutral ships trading between the French West Indies and Europe • The United States and Britain sign the Jay Treaty • General Anthony Wayne crushes the Indians at Fallen Timbers; rapid settlement of the Northwest Territory follows • The Whiskey Rebellion in Pennsylvania

1795   The Pinckney Treaty concluded between United States and Spain • With the Treaty of Greenville the Indians cede territory in what will later be Ohio

1796   Washington's Farewell Address; Adams elected president

1797   The French order American ships carrying British goods confiscated

1797–98   The "XYZ Affair"

1798   Congress votes to triple the size of the army and enlarge the navy • The Federalist Congress passes the Alien and Sedition Acts; Secretary of State Timothy Pickering prosecutes opposition leaders under the laws • Kentucky and Virginia declare their right to nullify acts of the national government

1800   The Convention of 1800 between France and the United States nullifies the Treaty of 1778 • Jefferson elected president

Americans had every reason to expect the government under the newly adopted Constitution to be stronger and more effective than its predecessor. The nation finally had the political machinery to deal with its public business. Or did it?

Today every representative government operates through a political party system. Parties are continuing organizations of people with roughly similar views on political issues who collectively select platforms, choose candidates for office, and formulate legislative programs. They are essential attributes of a modern democratic nation in which free elections are held.

The delegates at Philadelphia in the summer of 1787 did not see things this way. They had established offices for the new federal government with defined powers and modes of selection, but they had supposed that these positions would be filled by men whose only concern would be disinterested public service, not the furthering of a particular political group or viewpoint. Public officials, moreover, would be chosen by citizens who placed the common good above their own special needs. Each issue would be decided on its own merits, not on the basis of ideology or preconceived positions. When the Philadelphia delegates considered political parties, the word they commonly used was *factions,* by which they meant groupings around particular political chieftains for purely selfish reasons, such as the rewards of political office or the favor of the leader. Factions or parties, they believed, would divide citizens into hostile camps. They were not part of the legitimate machinery of government; they were cancers on it. Government by party, then, seemed a disruptive, selfish, and often dishonest way to conduct a nation's political affairs.

And yet within a decade after the adoption of the Constitution two great national parties had emerged in the United States. Many thoughtful citizens were horrified that the country should so quickly fall from political virtue. But this first party system, which lasted until about 1815, became an essential part of the young republic's political life. Without it, Americans learned, it was difficult to get anything accomplished; without it free government itself was endangered.

What produced this momentous change of heart? Were the new parties the result of differences over ideology? Did opposing views of the Constitution create the party divisions? Were the parties deliberately planned to meet administrative or political needs? Were they the outgrowth of personality clashes among magnetic individuals driven by opposing ambitions? Let us look at the circumstances under which the parties emerged, for events generally determine the shape of evolving institutions.

But first one confusing matter should be clarified. One of the two parties that appeared during the 1790s was called Federalist; the other was often referred to as Anti-Federalist, though it was also called Republican or Democratic-Republican, or sometimes Jeffersonian. These two groups must not be confused with the federalist and antifederalists of the period when the Constitution was being debated. It is true that many of the federalists who endorsed and fought for the Constitution later became members of the Federalist party. But Madison and Jefferson were both federalists in the first sense; yet they became the organizers of the Democratic-Republican party. And Patrick Henry was an antifederalist who opposed adoption of the Constitution, yet he later became a strong Federalist. There was, perhaps, an overlap between the positions of federalists and Federalists and between those of antifederalists and Anti-Federalists, but it was not great. The issues that divided the two political parties of the "first party system" went far beyond the disputes of 1787–89.

THE NEW GOVERNMENT LAUNCHED

National Finances. When Congress convened in New York early in 1789, the atmosphere reflected a common determination to solve the country's major problems. Clearly the new government needed revenue, and early in the first session the legislators adopted two important tax measures: the Tariff Act of 1789, which placed duties on a wide range of imported articles, and the Tonnage Act, which taxed foreign vessels entering American ports. Congress also established various executive departments—State, Treasury, and War— and in the Federal Judiciary Act prescribed the structure of the Supreme Court and the federal court system. The Tonnage Act debate revealed some important sectional seams. Northerners, who did the nation's shipping, favored American merchants. Southerners, who exported tobacco and rice, wanted cheap shipping, whether provided by Americans or foreigners. Representatives from the two sections squabbled a bit over the Tonnage Act, but generally debate was calm and disagreements were muted. It is the measure of the relative political peace of these early months that Washington could appoint Jefferson, soon to be the leading Republican, and Hamilton, soon to be the leading Federalist, as his first secretary of state and secretary of the treasury, respectively.

Yet even in this first session of the First Congress there were signs of trouble to come. One hint was the farcical dispute over how the president should be addressed. Was Washington to be called "His Elective Majesty," "His Highness the President," "His Excellency," or merely "Mr. President"? The first three titles had overtones of British monarchy; the last suggested American republicanism. The argument seems trivial, but it divided people into temperamental aristocrats and temperamental democrats, and foreshadowed later party differences.

Relative harmony became loud discord when, in its second session, the First Congress confronted the pressing issue of the unpaid war debts. Millions of dollars of state and national obligations were long overdue. Some money was owed abroad, and failure to pay it had hurt the prestige of the United States and made it impossible for the American government to borrow from foreign bankers. Most of the debt, however, was owed to American citizens, including war veterans, former army suppliers, and those who had lent money to Congress or the states. The public creditors also included many businessmen and speculators who had bought up securities and debt certificates in the hope that they would rise in value when the government was finally able to repay them. How were all these people to be paid? And were they to be paid fully and equally?

Hamilton's Plan for America. The man who had to answer these questions in practice was the new secretary of the treasury, Alexander Hamilton of New York. Hamilton was one of the most intriguing and controversial men who ever occupied high office in the United States. Born illegitimately in the West Indies, he lacked the advantages of "good birth" and family wealth so useful in getting ahead in eighteenth-century America. But he made up for this by exhibiting at an early age enormous charm, drive, and intelligence. The young man so impressed prominent men on the island of St. Croix that they sent him to be educated at Kings College (now Columbia) in New York.

At eighteen Hamilton arrived in New York in the midst of the imperial crisis and promptly joined the Patriots. In 1774 he enrolled in a New York militia unit and was soon in action against the British. Before long his skill as an artillery officer brought him to Washington's attention, and he was appointed aide-de-camp to the American commander in chief. After Yorktown he returned to his adopted city and set up as a lawyer. His rise might have been slow despite his war record and his legal brilliance; there were many bright and ambitious young veterans in the city anxious to make their mark. But in 1780 he married Elizabeth Schuyler, daughter of the rich and prominent Philip Schuyler. This connection gave him the social standing and influence that his foreign birth and dubious parentage would have denied him. His career was soon flourishing.

Hamilton was an excellent choice for Washington's cabinet. Skeptical of human nature and convinced that people must be firmly restrained, he believed in strong government and had been instrumental in getting New York to adopt the Constitution. He believed the new Union was still too weak, but at least, he reasoned, it was better than the old Confederation. When he was offered the job of secretary of the treasury, Hamilton leaped at the chance. In that office he could help forge a strong national government and transform the United States into a unified and prosperous nation.

Whatever we may think of his ambition and distrust of human nature, Hamilton was a political innovator with an expansive vision of America's future. The United States of 1790 was a nation of 4 million people, most of them farmers or farm laborers. The first national census recorded that only about 3 percent of the population lived in cities with more than 8,000 people. The country was more than self-sufficient in food, fiber, and raw materials; but it continued to import most manufactured goods just as it had in colonial days. Exported grain, rice, tobacco, lumber, beef and pork, and other "primary" products of its fields and forests paid for the imports.

Hamilton hoped to change this society. He recognized the importance of agriculture in America and understood that it would remain the country's economic mainstay for many years to come. Yet he believed that the United States must turn to manufacturing for its future prosperity. Industry would free the nation from foreign dependence. It would also transform it. Looking at England, then fast becoming the workshop of the world, Hamilton perceived the wealth and power that might lie in store for America.

In 1791 Hamilton had joined a group of friends in supporting the Society for Establishing Useful Manufactures. Now, as a public servant, he hoped to do more than just straighten out the country's tangled finances. In many ways the first secretary of the treasury was the first great national planner. Like more recent leaders of under-

Report on Manufactures

A critical issue separating the two political parties during the 1790s was whether the country's future lay with agriculture or with industry and commerce. The apostle of the second course, one that required major changes in America's economy and social system, was the first secretary of the treasury, Alexander Hamilton. In his *Report on Manufactures* of 1791 Hamilton argued for government policies that would transform America from a land of farms into one of workshops, mills, and busy cities as well. This document, the last of four major reports, did not lead to immediate congressional action, but like the others it helped define the coherent political philosophy that we associate with the Federalist party. By its challenge to those who wished to keep America as it was, it also helped to clarify the position of the Jeffersonian Anti-Federalists.

"There . . . are . . . respectable patrons of opinions unfriendly to the encouragement of manufactures. The following are . . . the arguments by which these opinions are defended.

"In every country (say those who entertain them) Agriculture is the most beneficial and *productive* object of human industry. This position . . . applies with peculiar emphasis to the United States on account of their immense tracts of fertile territory, uninhabited and unimproved. Nothing can afford so advantageous an employment for capital and labour, as the conversion of this extensive wilderness into cultivated farms. . . .

"To endeavor, by the extraordinary patronage of Government, to accelerate the growth of manufactures, is, in fact, to endeavor, by force and art, to transfer the natural current of industry from a more, to a less beneficial channel. Whatever has such tendency must necessarily be unwise. . . . To leave industry to itself, therefore, is . . . the soundest as well as the simplest policy.

"This policy is not only recommended to the United States by considerations which affect all nations . . . it is [also] dictated to them . . . by the smallness of their population compared with their territory. . . . [This fact] conspires to produce . . . a scarcity of hands for manufacturing occupations, and dearness of labor generally. . . .

"If contrary to the natural course of things, an unseasonable and premature spring can be given to certain fabrics, by heavy duties, prohibitions, bounties, or by other forced expedients, this will only be to sacrifice the interests of the community to those of particular classes. Besides the misdirection of labor, a virtual monopoly will be given to the persons employed on such fabrics; and an enhancement of price, the inevitable consequence of every monopoly, must be defrayed at the expense of the other part of society. . . .

"[In reply to these arguments] . . . it ought readily to be conceded that the cultivation of the earth . . . has *intrinsically a strong claim to pre-eminence over every other kind of industry*. . . . But, that it has a title to anything like an exclusive predilection in any country, ought to be admitted with great caution. . . .

". . . [M]anufacturing establishments not only occasion a positive augmentation of the Produce and Revenue of the Society, but . . . they contribute essentially to rendering them greater than they could possibly be, without such establishments. These circumstances are—

1. The division of labour.
2. An extension of the use of Machinery.
3. Additional employment to classes of the community not ordinarily engaged in the business.
4. The promoting of emigration from foreign Countries.
5. The furnishing of greater scope for the diversity of talents and dispositions which discriminate men from each other.
6. The affording a more ample and various field for enterprize.
7. The creating in some instances a new, and securing in all, a more certain and steady demand for the surplus produce of the soil.

"Each of these circumstances has a considerable influence upon the total mass of industrious effort in a community. Together, they add to it a degree of energy and effect, which are not easily conceived. . . ."

---

developed nations, he sought to encourage economic growth and social modernization. Although today we can see some of the drawbacks of unrestrained industrialization, for its time Hamilton's was a progressive vision.

Hamilton incorporated these goals into three major reports submitted to Congress between January 1790 and December 1791. The First Report on the Public Credit proposed a plan for putting national finances on a sound basis. Now that the government had a guaranteed revenue from tariffs, let is pay its own creditors. Let it also take over ("assume") the remaining state debts. Hamilton knew that even with its newly acquired taxing power the government could not simply pay off these debts in one lump sum. There was a way around this difficulty. The government would issue new securities that would bear an attractive interest rate, and holders of the old, defaulted debt could exchange it for the new "funded debt."

Hamilton's motives here were in part political. He hoped to strengthen the national government by attaching to it the interests of the rich and powerful, the country's chief creditors. But he also

Alexander Hamilton sought government protection for American industries. The new Congress did pass some measures favoring American shipping and protecting several industries, but years would pass before the federal government would embrace Hamilton's plans for industrialization.

debt—that is, government bonds—which would-be investors in the bank could use instead of specie to buy bank stock. These bonds would now be used as the backing for an issue of paper money—"bank notes"—that could then be lent out to investors and used as the normal cash of the country. By such means, Hamilton theorized, banks in general and the federal bank in particular could become "nurseries of national wealth."

In his final important state paper, the Report on Manufactures, Hamilton urged Congress to support industry with subsidies, a tariff, and a system of roads, canals, and other "internal improvements." Pointing out that America's high labor costs and its shortage of investment capital put it at a disadvantage against the better-developed European countries, he declared that these handicaps could be overcome only by government action. So long as certain industries were weak, the government should nurture them. When they grew strong, they could compete independently in the world marketplace and government aid would become unnecessary. The benefits of supporting "infant industries," Hamilton was sure, would be felt not only by promoters of industry and the laboring classes but also by farmers, who would find new markets for their products in the manufacturing cities and towns that the government's protective policies would spawn. Of Hamilton's three major reports, only this one on manufactures resulted in no immediate action by Congress. But as a glimpse of the future and an arsenal of arguments for government protection of American industry, it, too, was a landmark.

Enacting the Hamiltonian Program. The Funding Act of 1790 sought to enact the first part of Hamilton's program. The bill had two sections. Part one authorized all present holders of national securities to convert them into federal bonds at face value, though at differing rates of interest. Part two empowered the federal government to assume the outstanding state debts. State creditors, too, could convert their securities into the new funded debt.

had larger purposes. Defying conventional thinking, the secretary believed that a public debt was a blessing, not a curse. The new funded debt would be a form of property, and like any other property—land and houses, for example—it could be used as security for raising money. An abundance of money or credit—which amounted to the same thing—would in turn stimulate commerce and provide investment capital for a capital-poor nation. The new funded debt would be "an engine of business, an instrument of industry and commerce."

The secretary spelled out the way this process might operate in the second of his major reports, the Report on a National Bank. In this document he recommended that Congress charter a bank. Besides providing a convenient agency for handling federal tax collections and disbursements and for aiding private business transactions, a federally chartered bank would provide money for circulation and credit for investment. Only part of the bank's capital, he explained, needed to be silver and gold, commodities in short supply in America. The rest could consist of the funded

The measure aroused the ire of James Madison, now a leader in the House of Representatives, where the Hamiltonian program had to begin its legislative course. The Hamiltonians, Madison said, were showing excessive consideration for speculators and not enough for the "original holders," who had paid cash or provided valuable goods or services in exchange for Continental or state securities during the war. These people had expressed their faith in the patriot cause, but many had been forced to sell their securities at large

National Portrait Gallery, Smithsonian Institution

discounts to speculators. Why should these original holders not receive some part of the gain that would come when the debt was funded? Why should all the profit go to the gamblers?

Though he talked about the ethical aspects of the issue, Madison was also concerned about the interests of his section—the South—just as his opponents were about theirs. Assumption was offensive to many southerners. The southern states had already paid most of their debts. Now burdened southern taxpayers would be asked to pay federal taxes to redeem the debts of delinquent northern states.

Though it took a sectional form, the debate also reflected social differences. To Madison and his supporters the North represented trade and commerce; the South, agriculture. The Funding Act, accordingly, seemed designed to benefit the commercial interests at the expense of the agricultural interests. After all, they declared, most of the speculators who would gain from the act lived in the port towns of New England, New York, and Pennsylvania.

The first section of the Funding Act passed after a bitter battle. But the second, which authorized assumption, seemed certain to go down to defeat. Hamilton persisted, however, and appealed to Madison not to cripple his plan. With Jefferson's approval the two arranged a deal. In exchange for yielding on assumption, the South would get the new national capital. After first moving to Philadelphia, in the North, for ten years, the seat of the federal government would be established in 1800 at a site in the South, on the Potomac between Maryland and Virginia. Thus sugarcoated, the Funding Act, with both sections intact, passed. In the end principle had yielded to sectional pride.

Early in 1791 Congress received Hamilton's bank bill. Madison attacked this measure, too. His objections were probably based on an agrarian suspicion of banks and on a reluctance to advance commerce and industry at the expense of agriculture. But preferring to appeal to higher principles, he based his arguments on the Constitution. Though he had been a strong nationalist in the 1780s, Madison now expressed the fear that the central government might become too powerful. Where in the Constitution, the astute Virginian asked, was Congress authorized to incorporate such a bank? He refused to accept Hamilton's answer that certain powers were implied in the Constitution.

Despite Madison's resistance, Congress established the Bank of the United States with a twenty-year federal charter. The new institution would function in part as a privately owned commercial bank does today. It would accept deposits, make loans, and perform other familiar banking services. In addition, it would do several things

Library of Congress

The building that housed the first Bank of the United States helped set the fashion in Greco-Roman bank structures that has continued to our own day. The architect clearly intended to inspire confidence in the durability of the building and the institution.

normally done in the twentieth century by the Treasury Department or by the Federal Reserve System. It would, for example, handle the government's financial business, including its tax collections and outlays. More important, it would issue up to $10 million in paper money, backed partly by gold but largely by the funded debt. In this way, as Hamilton intended, the federal debt would become the basis for a money circulation and a source of credit for a capital-poor land. In structure the bank would combine public and private features. Five of the twenty-five directors of the bank were to be appointed by the government, the rest by private stockholders.

When the bank bill came before Washington for his signature, the president was frankly puzzled about what he should do. Washington would eventually become the Federalists' hero, but at this point he was not yet a strong political partisan. He understood his symbolic role as a wise, dispassionate, and just father who must rise above the fray. To take an obviously partisan stand without very good reason might destroy the image. In his dilemma he turned to his cabinet—Hamilton, Jefferson, and Attorney General Edmund Randolph—for advice. Two written statements resulted, presenting the classic arguments for "loose construction" and "strict construction" of the Constitution. Hamilton defended the bank with his doctrine of implied powers. Jefferson and Randolph argued that powers not explicitly granted Congress by the Constitution were beyond its authority. In a decision that foreshadowed his later shift to Federalism, Washington accepted Hamilton's views and approved the bill.

THE BEGINNINGS OF PARTIES

The Economic Division. The Hamiltonian program drove a wedge through the nation, dividing Americans into opposing political camps. On one side were the emerging Federalists. They included speculators in government securities, merchants, manufacturers, and would-be manufacturers. Those they employed—merchant seamen, artisans, clerks, bookkeepers, and all who worked in trade—also tended to support Hamilton's program. On the emerging Republican side were many small farmers and southern planters, especially those of middle rank.

The division along occupational lines transcended geography. The "commercial" classes were particularly numerous in New England and the Middle Atlantic states; southerners mostly belonged to the "cultivator" class. This situation largely accounts for the sectional split in Congress over the bank and funding. But in the South, wherever there were large pockets of people engaged in finance, trade, and industry, Federalists established secure footholds. In Charleston, Baltimore, Norfolk, and Savannah Federalism spoke in a southern drawl. On the other hand, there were many Republicans in the North. In places like the valleys of the Susquehanna, Delaware, Connecticut, and Hudson rivers, where surplus crops were produced for export, the farmers were Federalists. In more isolated farm areas cultivators expressed Republican sentiments in the "Dutch" accents of New York and Pennsylvania, the twang of New England, and the rough, direct speech of the frontier.

The Ideological Division. Economic interest, however, was not the only factor that separated Hamiltonians from Jeffersonians, Federalists from Republicans; there were deep ideological and philosophical differences as well—differences in their attitude toward freedom, their vision of the good society, and their commitment to majority rule.

To Republicans like Jefferson, Madison, and John Taylor, the Hamiltonian dream was a nightmare. These men feared tyranny more than they feared chaos. They believed that unless checked, government would grow overpowerful and end by destroying freedom. They saw their opponents as monarchists who were essentially latter-day equivalents of King George and his ministers. Government, they insisted, must be balanced so that the executive branch did not become too strong and overwhelm the liberties of the people.

Agrarianism, too, was a vital part of the Republican position. The Republicans cherished the ideal of an agricultural society of small freeholders led by landed gentlemen. According to Jefferson, the farmers of the nation were "the chosen people of God, if ever he had a chosen people." By contrast, the artisans, journeymen, and laborers who made up the "mobs" of the cities were "the panders of vice and the instruments by which the liberties of a country are generally overturned."

Agrarians were not merely defending property against those who lacked it. They were also defending the country against the city. They liked city property no more than they liked city people. Virtue inhered in fields and flocks, not in factories, shipyards, or hotels. Even more dubious than these were those shadowy forms of urban property, stocks and bonds. Sharing the folk tradition of rural America, the agrarians believed there was a moral stigma attached to commerce and money-lending in contrast to the honest, righteous quality of agriculture. Ironically, many of the sophisticated planters who provided much of the Republican leadership were deeply involved in land speculation. Yet they could not—or would not—see that there was little moral difference between gambling in land and gambling in stocks and bonds. To men like John Taylor the "divine intelligence" had "selected an agricultural state as a paradise"; Hamilton and his kind, on the other hand, were in league with the "stock jobbers," the "speculators," and the "moneyed aristocracy."

The views of Jefferson, Taylor, and the other Republican social thinkers were defenses of the status quo. In the original sense of the word, they were conservatives—that is, they wished to conserve what was. The Republicans wanted to keep America a nation of farms and forests. Their motto could have been "Keep America Green!" Yet despite this disdain for change, or "progress," their attitudes suited many Americans.

The agrarian appeal is easy to explain. Simplicity, self-sufficiency, and the natural life strike a resounding chord in most people. And for Americans agrarianism was particularly attractive. From the outset land ownership had been widely dispersed in America. The Virginia Republican leaders were themselves landed gentlemen whose livelihoods came from plantations. Throughout history country dwellers have disdained commerce and industry and distrusted cities and towns and their inhabitants. Contemporary political wisdom reinforced this rural prejudice. Had not Locke and the other thinkers who strongly influenced the Revolutionary generation established that those who owned land were the most honest and independent citizens? What would happen to free government when urban populations became divided into, on the one hand, mobs of paupers, apprentices, sailors, mechanics, and factory "operatives"—people without "a stake in society"—and, on the other, a handful of rich manufacturers, merchants, and bankers? How could free government survive? Even Hamilton had doubts. Today many Americans are still convinced that the big cities are ungovernable and that their inhabitants make poor citizens.

Federalists and Republicans disagreed, too, over the workability of majority rule. Federalists tended to be elitists. They distrusted human nature and feared the rule of numbers for its possible "excesses." To Hamilton the people were "a great beast." Other Federalists were equally blunt in expressing contempt for the people and their "rabble-rousing" leaders. Harrison Gray Otis of Boston

Maryland Historical Society

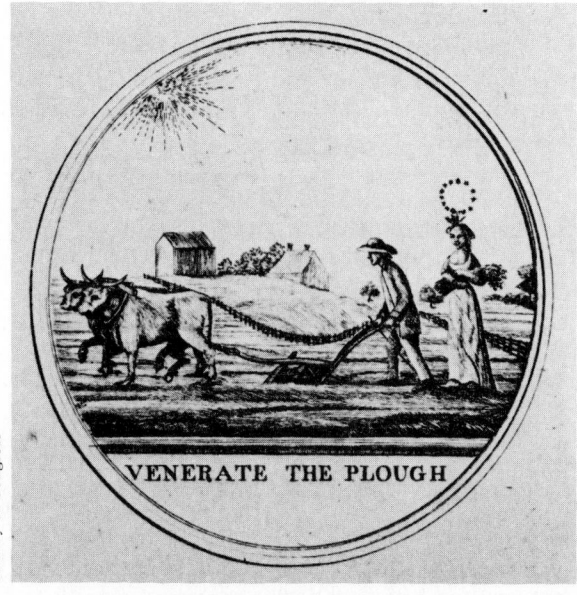

Library of Congress

VENERATE THE PLOUGH

He was not the best of farmers, but Thomas Jefferson did worship the plow. Unlike Hamilton, he placed his trust in the common people and dreamed of a nation of farmers. The class divisions that grew out of Hamilton's industrial economy threatened to destroy Jefferson's ideal of a virtuous agrarian republic.

called the voters a "duped and deluded mob." John Jay of New York, first chief justice of the United States, reflected that "the mass of men are neither wise nor good, and virtue . . . can only be drawn to a point and executed by . . . a strong government ably administered." Even John Adams, who was never one of the extreme or "High" Federalists, feared the end of all "decorum, discipline, and subordination" if popular government were not restrained.

Republicans, on the other hand, generally expressed strong faith in the people. Jefferson, their leader and high priest, regarded the people as thoroughly trustworthy and safe. "I am," he proclaimed, "not among those who fear the people; they, and not the rich, are our dependence for continued freedom." At times Jefferson even sounded like a radical. In letters to friends and associates he wrote that "the tree of Liberty must be watered periodically with the blood of tyrants" and "a little revolution every twenty years is an excellent thing." These statements show the Sage of Monticello playing with ideas—today he would be called an intellectual. In his public statements and acts he was far more reserved. We should also remember that he and his political allies tended to limit the "people" to the white tillers of the soil. Of the "mobs of great cities" they were far more suspicious. It is clear, nevertheless, that philosophically the Republicans were more democratic than their opponents.

We must not draw the distinctions between Federalist aristocracy and Republican democracy too sharply, however. Many southern Jeffersonians were slaveholders. Some—Jefferson included—deplored slavery in the abstract, but considered it unavoidable. Jefferson himself did not believe in absolute human equality but in "natural aristocracy." This was an elite based on talent and ability, rather than birth, but it was an elite nonetheless. Nor should we assume that Hamilton and his followers were unqualified aristocrats or "monocrats," as their enemies called them. Generally they accepted representative government as unavoidable in America and never seriously intended to establish a monarchy.

Yet when all these qualifications are noted, it remains true that Federalists had less faith in majority rule than their opponents. The Republicans, in turn, had less confidence in men of wealth and position than in "the people."

The Role of Religion. We have seen how the Federalists won their battle with the Republicans over Hamilton's financial program. Over the next decade they would win a fair share of both state and national elections and enact additional parts of their program. Their success is puzzling. Young America was largely a nation of farmers, and farmers as a whole admired Jefferson's principles and disliked Hamilton's. Why, then, were the elite Federalists, with their commercial biases and antidemocratic rhetoric, so successful in the nation's first decade under the Constitution?

Momentum from the Confederation period is part of the answer. In a sense, the Federalists had a mandate in the early 1790s to create a strong, sound government and economy. Before the mandate ran out, they had enacted much of their program. They were also helped by the prestige of George Washington. Although above the battle at first, he eventually drifted into the Federalist camp. As long as he was alive, his incomparable standing among Americans bolstered the Federalist position regardless of material or ideological factors. Another element of Federalist successes is that for reasons that we do not fully understand, not more than a quarter of the eligible voters went to the polls in the 1790s. A large proportion of the people who did vote were educated, and they were more inclined to support the "high-toned" Federalists than their "rabble-rousing" opponents.

But these factors are only part of the answer. Religion, too, helped determine party affiliation. In the 1790s the Federalists attracted Congregationalists in New England and Episcopalians in the Middle Atlantic states and the South. The Republicans won the support of a hodgepodge of Baptists, Methodists, Roman Catholics, nonbelievers, and deists. These groupings may not appear to make much sense—Roman Catholics and nonbelievers do not seem to have much in common. If we take a second look, however, we can see the pattern: members of established churches—those that received financial support from state governments and so had privileged positions—or formerly established churches voted Federalist, whereas the others tended to prefer the Jeffersonians.

The Republican appeal to nonbelievers is easy to understand. Jefferson himself was a deist whose religious creed was free from many orthodox Christian elements. Conversely, leading Federalists were often outspoken defenders of traditional Christian beliefs. The Republican appeal to Catholics and evangelical Protestants, such as Baptists and Methodists, requires a little more probing. These groups had long been victims of legal discrimination. By the 1790s they were still disqualified from holding office in some areas, and in parts of New England where Congregationalism was still the established church, they remained second-class citizens. The role of Jefferson and Madison in securing the Virginia Statute for Religious Freedom earned the Republican leaders the gratitude of all those outside the established religious pale everywhere. In Connecticut and Massachusetts the Republicans confirmed this attachment by leading the fight to end the preferred status conferred on Congregationalism. It is not surprising, then, that people who thought of themselves as religious outsiders should find Republicanism more congenial than Federalism.

Here, then, is an explanation for Federalist successes: although far more Americans belonged to occupational groups that benefited from Republican positions than to Federalist-leaning occupations, religion served to counteract occupation as a decisive factor. A Congregational farmer in Massachusetts, for example, might well vote Federalist, though the Republicans represented the agrarian interests. On the other hand, a Baptist merchant from Connecticut or a rich Catholic lawyer from New York—people we would normally expect to vote for the Federalists on the basis of occupation—might well support the Republicans for religious reasons.

RELATIONS WITH EUROPE

The first party system was only partly a response to domestic events and attitudes. It was also the offspring of America's complex relations with the rest of the Atlantic world.

America's foreign relations were in disarray in 1790. Many problems remained from the previous decade. Spain controlled the mouth of the Mississippi and still denied Americans the right of deposit at New Orleans. The British continued to restrict American trade with their empire and refused to abandon the military posts in the Northwest. And even France had begun to limit American trade with its colonies, despite the commercial treaty of 1778.

Revolution in France. The outbreak of the French Revolution of 1789 soon made these problems infinitely worse. The greatest political convulsion of modern times aroused strong passions in America. At first most Americans rejoiced at the overthrow of the corrupt, aristocratic, and worn-out Old Regime in Europe's most powerful nation. The fall of the Bastille, a hated symbol of tyranny, and the release of its prisoners seemed a triumph of the principles of freedom and equality that Americans had recently fought for. One enthusiastic Yankee orator saw the event as a "spark from the altar flame of liberty on this side of the Atlantic, which alighted in the pinnacle of despotism in France and reduced the immense fabric to ashes in the twinkling of an eye." In Boston streets were

renamed for revolutionary ideals—Royal Exchange Alley became Equality Lane. Some Americans replaced *mister* with the revolutionary *citizen*. At first even men of conservative temper welcomed the change. President Washington graciously received from Lafayette the key to the Bastille as a link between America's struggle against tyranny and France's.

But bipartisan support for the revolt quickly waned. The fall of the Bastille was followed by the overthrow of the French monarchy, the execution of King Louis XVI, the Reign of Terror against the Revolution's enemies, confiscation of the property of French nobles, and ever more violent attacks on the church and traditional religion. Public opinion quickly split. Federalists were shocked and frightened by the events in France. Fisher Ames, a Massachusetts Federalist, denounced revolutionary France as "an open hell, still ringing with agonies and blasphemies, still smoking with sufferings and crimes, in which we see . . . perhaps our future state." Other Federalists warned that the French "moral influenza" was to be more dreaded than a "thousand yellow fevers." If Americans were not careful, it might spread to their shores. Jefferson, Madison, and their allies, however, continued to admire the revolutionaries, cheering the end of "superstition" and applauding the "rule of reason." Many approved of the execution of Louis XVI and even saw virtue in the Reign of Terror.

The party split became wider when in 1793 war broke out between the new French Republic and England, Spain, and Holland. How should the United States respond? France was America's ally, and although it had not lately taken the friendship seriously, the French Republic needed American support now that it was locked in battle. The United States could be a source of food and supplies for France and the French colonies in the Western Hemisphere. It might even become a base of operations against British and Spanish possessions in North America.

Citizen Genêt. Hoping to gain American aid, the French government sent "Citizen" Edmond Genêt to the United States as its minister. Immediately Genêt became a magnet for controversy. Secretary Hamilton opposed receiving him for fear that it would involve the nation in the war. Secretary Jefferson claimed that if we refused, we would be repudiating our alliance with France. Neither man wished to see the United States enter the war, but they differed over how and when to assert neutrality. Hamilton believed that it was the president's task to proclaim neutrality and that he should do so at once. Jefferson held that Congress should make the announcement, but only after the United States had squeezed concessions out of both the British and the French.

Washington took his treasury secretary's advice and in April 1793 issued a proclamation of neutrality. The president asked Americans to be "impartial" toward the belligerents and forbade engaging in actions favorable to either side. Republicans found the proclamation offensive. It was too neutral. "The cause of France is the cause of man," declared one protesting Jeffersonian. Madison and Hamilton were soon engaged in a newspaper shouting match in which they loudly set forth their clashing positions on the momentous events in Europe.

Meanwhile, Genêt was making plans. Hoping to make the United States a base for operations against Britain and Spain, he hired George Rogers Clark, an Indian fighter and hero of the Revolution, to lead an expedition against the Spanish in Louisiana and Florida. At the same time he passed out commissions in the proposed army and authorized privateers to sail from American ports to attack British and Spanish shipping. Finally, in midsummer of 1793, Genêt demanded that Washington call Congress into special session to decide what the United States would do to aid the French Republic. If the president refused, Genêt arrogantly declared, he would take his case over Washington's head to the American people.

Genêt's activities further polarized American opinion. The Republicans at first befriended him, and Jefferson filled the Frenchman's ears with the misdeeds of his Federalist opponents. The Federalists despised him and used his activities as a stick with which to beat their opponents. The English-born Federalist journalist William Cobbett labeled the Republicans the "bastard offspring of Genêt, spawned in hell, to which they will presently return."

Before long Genêt's activities had so embarrassed the American government that even Jefferson agreed he must be sent home. France, however, was now in the hands of the radical Jacobins, who despised the moderates who had sent Genêt to America. Rather than send the amiable but foolish emissary to certain execution, Washington granted him asylum in the United States.

The Partisan Press. The controversy over Genêt propelled party conflict to new heights. By now Federalists were being sneered at as pro-British "Anglomen" by their enemies and were in turn calling their Republican opponents "Gallomen"—partisans of France. Differences over foreign policy, combined with the disagreements over the Hamiltonian program, had produced a combative party press that further aggravated the political rivalry. Americans today are used to partisan journalism. Most newspapers support one of the major parties and are not always generous to their political opponents. Compared with the party press of the 1790s, however, they are models of decorum, objectivity, and tolerance.

Federalist and Republican newspapers published scathing criticisms of their opponents. John

New-York Historical Society

A Federalist cartoon showing Washington leading American troops against French "cannibals" while Gallatin, Citizen Genêt, and Jefferson try to halt his chariot.

Fenno's *Gazette of the United States* made Hamilton into a demigod and spewed out insults against his enemies. These Jacobins—as the French revolutionary extremists were called—were working to corrupt the nation's youth and "make them imbibe, with their very milk . . . the poison of atheism and disaffection." The *General Advertiser*, edited by Franklin's grandson, Benjamin Franklin Bache, and Philip Freneau's *National Gazette* denounced the Federalists as outright monarchists and dupes of British policy. Bache even maligned Washington as the "scourge of all the misfortunes of our country," a man who had given currency "to political iniquity and to legalized corruption."

Within Washington's cabinet the relations between Jefferson and Hamilton became so bad that at the end of 1793 Jefferson resigned as secretary of state and was replaced by Edmund Randolph, a Virginia Federalist. But Jefferson's departure did not end his leadership of the Republicans. From Monticello, his hilltop home in Virginia, the former secretary continued to put out a flood of political advice, remaining in close touch with Madison, the party's chief tactician in Congress.

Relations with England. Just before Jefferson's retirement, European affairs once more reached a crisis. This time the nation found itself pitted against the world's greatest naval power, England. The difficulty concerned neutral rights on the high seas in time of war; it would not be settled for twenty years.

Basically the two nations disagreed over whether the United States could trade freely with France, England's enemy. The French, unable to protect their shipping against the British navy, had opened their imperial trade, normally restricted to French vessels, to neutral commerce. The British, rightly, saw this as a deception and invoked the Rule of 1756, which had been used against Americans trading with the French colonies during the French and Indian War. This rule declared that trade forbidden in time of peace could not be legally pursued in time of war. In effect, a weak naval power could not protect itself by hiding behind a neutral. Britain and the United States also argued over contraband. International law recognized the right of one nation to blockade its enemy's ports and prevent neutral nations from delivering certain war goods—contraband—through the blockade. But contraband was not clearly defined, nor was the legal status of neutral trade in other goods.

Soon after Anglo-French hostilities began, Britain proclaimed a blockade of France and its colonies and deployed its navy to destroy French shipping and commerce. The French immediately opened their ports to foreign ships and neutral America seized the opportunity to supply French shipping needs. For the next two decades, as Britain and France struggled to dominate Europe, French demand stimulated American trade beyond all previous measure. Hundreds of new vessels, manned by thousands of newly recruited seamen, scudded across the Atlantic and the Caribbean carrying cargoes to Europe and the West Indies. Salem, Boston, Providence, New York, and Philadelphia boomed as the value of foreign trade leaped from $46 million in 1790 to $140 million by 1796.

The British found this new American prosperity doubly offensive. The Americans were profiting from Britain's troubles and at the same time helping to make them worse by supplying its chief enemy. Even more annoying, England was unintentionally supplying many of the seamen for the bloated American merchant fleet. Some of these were deserters from the Royal Navy who preferred the lenient treatment and good pay of American merchant seamen to the harsh discipline, bad food, and dangers of the British navy. When a British man-of-war docked beside an American merchant ship in any harbor in the world, it was certain to lose part of its crew to the Yankees, who were always happy to get experienced mariners. British merchant seamen, too, jumped ship for the higher pay and better working conditions of the American merchant marine.

To deal with the loss of sailors, the British began to stop American vessels to inspect the crews for deserters, "impressing" both those deemed guilty and those who merely looked like apt recruits for the depleted Royal Navy. Americans were outraged by impressment, but their anger was tempered by fear that worsening relations with Britain would destroy the lucrative trade with France. To New Englanders and residents of the middle states' ports—the chief beneficiaries of this trade—it seemed wiser to submit to British practices, however arbitrary, than to defy Britain, provoke war, and see the new trade completely shut down. Expediency was reinforced by political sympathy. The port cities were also the centers of Federalism, and many of their inhabitants were unwilling to denounce Britain, the embattled bulwark against the Jacobins, no matter how ruthlessly it violated American rights.

The British and the Indians. In one area of Anglo-American relations, however, almost all Americans agreed that British policies were deplorable.

In the Northwest, a decade after the treaty ending the War for Independence, British garrisons still occupied American soil and British fur traders still monopolized business with the Indians. Besides these affronts to national pride and American commercial interests, Americans were also certain that the British were encouraging the Indians south of the Great Lakes in their policy of harassing American settlers. In 1790 General Josiah Harmar set out with a band of ill-trained militia to teach the Indians a lesson. At the Maumee River his men were ambushed and 183 killed. The following year Arthur St. Clair, governor of the Northwest Territory, walked into a similar trap. St. Clair and part of his force escaped, but they left behind 630 dead.

Jubilant over their successes during the winter of 1791–92, the Indians drove the Ohio settlers back to the region's two well-defended villages. Meanwhile, the British, seeing an opportunity to check the American westward advance, sent agents from Canada to urge the tribes to demand an Indian state north of the Ohio where no white man could settle. In the summer of 1792 Canadian officials and their Indian allies agreed to propose such a buffer state to the Americans at a meeting scheduled at Sandusky the following spring.

The Sandusky meeting never took place. Learning in advance of the Indian demands, the Americans called off the conference. President Washington now decided to settle the conflict by force and dispatched a new army under Anthony Wayne to the Ohio region. Wayne, an abler strategist than his predecessors, trained and seasoned his troops through the winter and spring of 1793–94. In August 1794 he encountered the Indians at Fallen Timbers and decisively defeated them.

The Jay Treaty. In the fall of 1793 the crisis between England and the United States came to a head when a British order in council—an executive proclamation—authorized English naval commanders to seize neutral vessels trading with the French Caribbean islands. In short order 250 American ships were boarded by British naval parties, escorted to British ports, and confiscated. The seizures infuriated Americans, and it soon seemed like 1775 all over again. Mobs roved the streets of seaport towns, denouncing Britain and insulting and threatening Englishmen, including the British minister to the United States. British tempers were equally hot. The commander of the British forces in the Northwest declared that he looked forward to meeting Washington "with adequate force and on a just occasion—face to face." War appeared imminent. To avoid a military show-

down, for which the United States was ill prepared, Washington decided to send a mission to England headed by Chief Justice John Jay.

Jay's instructions, drafted by Secretary of State Randolph, were conciliatory. But in late 1794 the British were flush with recent victories against the French and not inclined to be overly generous with the upstart Americans. In the end they drove a hard bargain. They agreed to surrender the western posts and pay for American ships recently confiscated. They also yielded slightly on the long-festering issue of trade with the British Empire. The United States would be allowed to trade with British India, and small American vessels would be permitted to enter British West Indies ports. But in most other matters they refused to budge. They refused to accept American demands for full commercial equality with British subjects. They denied liability for the slaves they had removed from the South during the Revolution. They rejected Jay's claim that American ships could legally carry a wide range of French goods. The final agreement contained a broad definition of contraband that made many American goods liable to seizure as well as a proviso that the United States must close its ports to French privateers. To satisfy long-standing English complaints, the United States also agreed to refer all unpaid American private debts owed English creditors to a joint commission for settlement. On western problems, too, the United States made concessions. In return for surrendering the Northwest posts, Britain would be allowed to send fur trappers south of the Canadian border as in the past.

The Jay Treaty brought down the wrath of the Republicans on Federalist heads. To France's friends and England's enemies the treaty seemed a sellout. Jay was denounced as an "archtraitor" and hanged in effigy all over the country. The agreement itself was referred to widely as "that damned treaty." For a while there was doubt that the Senate would confirm it or the president sign it. But the Senate's strong Federalist majority carried the treaty after striking out one of the more unfavorable trade provisions. Washington hesitated but approved the treaty when he realized that the alternative might well be war with England. Even after adoption the treaty continued to rankle, and Washington was reviled for endorsing it. Jefferson claimed that he had "undone the country," and a bitterly partisan Virginian ventured the toast: "A speedy death to General Washington."

Hostility to the Jay Treaty powerfully reinforced party formation. According to one historian of the Massachusetts Republicans, "More than any other act, the Jay Treaty influenced the development of party" in the Bay State. In the House of Representatives—the body that would have to appropriate money to carry out several provisions of the pact—Republicans organized the first congressional party caucus ever held to consider ways to defeat the treaty. In the end their attempt failed, but the close House vote revealed the new strength of the opposition and the extent to which foreign affairs had polarized Congress along party lines.

The Whiskey Rebellion; the Pinckney Treaty.
The major disputes with Great Britain now settled, however badly, the Washington administration turned to differences with Spain. In the Northwest Britain's surrender of the posts meant the abandonment of their Indian allies. Chastened by their defeat at Fallen Timbers, the Indians signed the Treaty of Greenville in 1795, by which they agreed to give up all of Ohio except for a small strip along Lake Erie. Before many months a mass movement of white pioneer farmers into the Northwest was under way. In the Southwest, where Indian resistance to the whites was weaker,

by 1796 there were already two new states—Kentucky and Tennessee—carved out of a region that had had no permanent white inhabitants twenty years earlier.

The westerners were a restless and unruly lot. For years frontier farmers had been angry over federal tax policy. Unable to sell their grain to distant urban customers because of high transportation costs, they had found an ingenious alternative. To make their grain portable, they had made it potable by distilling it into whiskey, which could be easily carried to market in barrels. When the government imposed a tax on distilled liquors in 1791 to raise money for Hamilton's funding plan, westerners defied the authorities and threatened tax collectors with physical harm.

In 1794 the farmers of western Pennsylvania carried defiance to the point of open rebellion. The "Whiskey Rebels" closed down federal courts and robbed the mails. They attacked federal troops guarding the tax collector for the Pittsburgh district. Seven years before, when Daniel Shays's men had defied the tax collectors in the same way, the central government had been helpless to act. Now Washington quickly ordered out the militia, which, with the militant Hamilton

Pinckney's Treaty, 1795

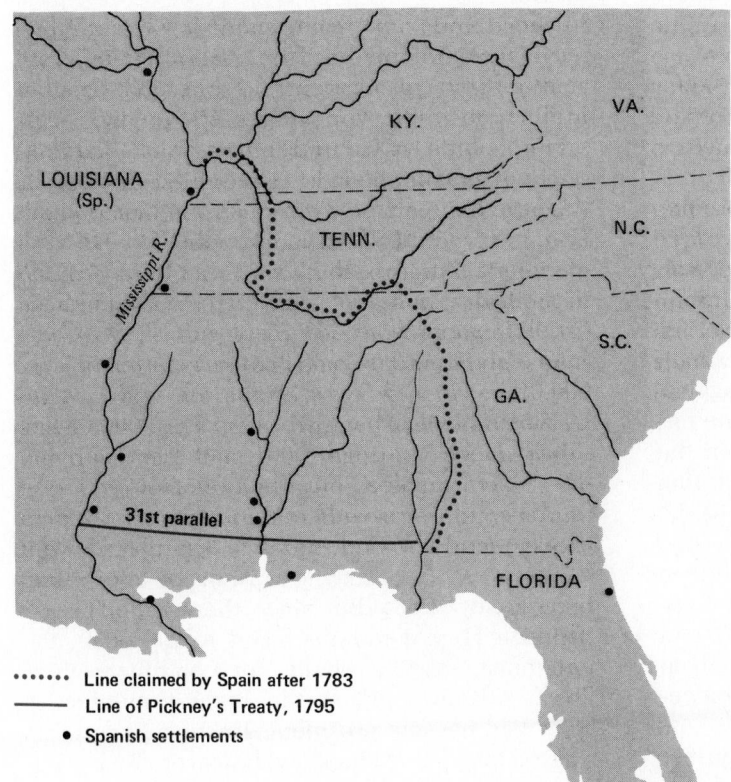

••••••• Line claimed by Spain after 1783
——— Line of Pickney's Treaty, 1795
• Spanish settlements

as second in command, marched on the rebels. To Hamilton's dismay the rebels surrendered without a shot. The government proved lenient. Some twenty woebegone prisoners were paraded down Market Street in Philadelphia; two were convicted of high treason and then pardoned.

No lives were lost in the incident, but it confirmed western disgust at the trigger-happy Federalists. At the same time it showed the government that westerners were not to be trifled with. Now they were demanding that the federal government do something about Spain's refusal to allow the right of deposit at New Orleans. If the United States government did not give them what they wanted, they threatened to take matters into their own hands and negotiate directly with Spain.

To prevent such an outcome, Washington ordered Thomas Pinckney to Spain to arbitrate the differences between the two nations. Fortunately for the United States, Spain was ready to negotiate. In short order Pinckney and the Spanish foreign minister concluded a treaty granting the United States free navigation of the Mississippi and the right of deposit at New Orleans for three years, subject to renewal. The treaty also set the boundary between the United States and Florida at the thirty-first parallel, where the Americans wanted it. The Jay Treaty had left many issues unresolved. The Pinckney Treaty, for the moment at least, settled the nagging problem of Mississippi navigation at virtually no cost to the United States, and was immensely popular.

Washington's Farewell.

In 1796 Washington decided that two terms were quite enough; he would retire to his gracious plantation home at Mount Vernon on the Potomac. Before leaving, however, he delivered a formal farewell to his fellow Americans in the form of a letter that was published in the newspapers. This "Farewell Address" has always been considered a foreign policy statement, but it was concerned largely with domestic matters. The departing president cautioned against "permanent alliances with any portion of the foreign world." But most of his message, even the part dealing with foreign relations, was a warning against the "spirit of party" and a tribute to the virtues of "fraternal affection" and national unity. Toward the end of his administration Washington had been drawn into the ranks of the Federalists. Still, he did not believe in the party system, and he told the American people that factionalism served to "distract the public councils and enfeeble the public administration."

Despite the president's warning, the spirit of party marked his very departure. To the Federal-

ists, who had borrowed his prestige to bolster their policies, his retirement was a blow. To the Republicans, it was a blessing. Benjamin Franklin Bache's paper rejoiced that a new era was dawning. With Washington gone, public measures would have to stand on their own merits. "The name of WASHINGTON from this day," it crowed, "ceases to give currency to political iniquity." Bache was right: the Federalists were now deprived of an immense political asset. In the election of 1796 they would not have the nation's greatest popular hero at the head of their ticket. This time there would be a real contest for the presidency.

The Election of 1796.

No one was quite sure how the candidates would be selected in 1796 and how, once chosen, they would be elected. Washington had faced no opposition as nominee or candidate and had not campaigned. Now things were different. How could matters be arranged? In a few states, notably Pennsylvania, there were permanent party organizations and a formal nominating procedure. In others, and at the national level, party machinery was primitive. The Republicans had an informal party chairman in the clerk of the House of Representatives, John Beckley, but the Federalists had no equivalent; and in any case, an informal party chairman did not wield much power.

In the end the leaders of each party met and announced their party's candidates. The Republicans' choice was never in doubt: Jefferson was their most impressive figure, and there was no one to challenge his candidacy. Among the Federalists, however, the leaders disagreed. The High, or extreme, Federalists supported Thomas Pinckney, the treaty negotiator. Moderates preferred Vice President John Adams. Because the Federalists were unable to settle on a single nominee, there were three candidates, two of them Federalists.

The contest was fought over the unpopular Jay Treaty and general foreign policy, though the Republicans tried to make the supposed monarchism of their opponents a major issue. Official electors were chosen by popular vote in only half the states; in the others the state legislatures made the choice. The Federalists won a majority in the electoral college, carrying most of the states from New Jersey north. But since they were divided between High Federalists and Adams men, the Federalist electors could not coordinate their votes. Adams received the highest number of votes and became president. Enough Federalists refused to support Pinckney, however, to give Jefferson the second-highest number of votes,

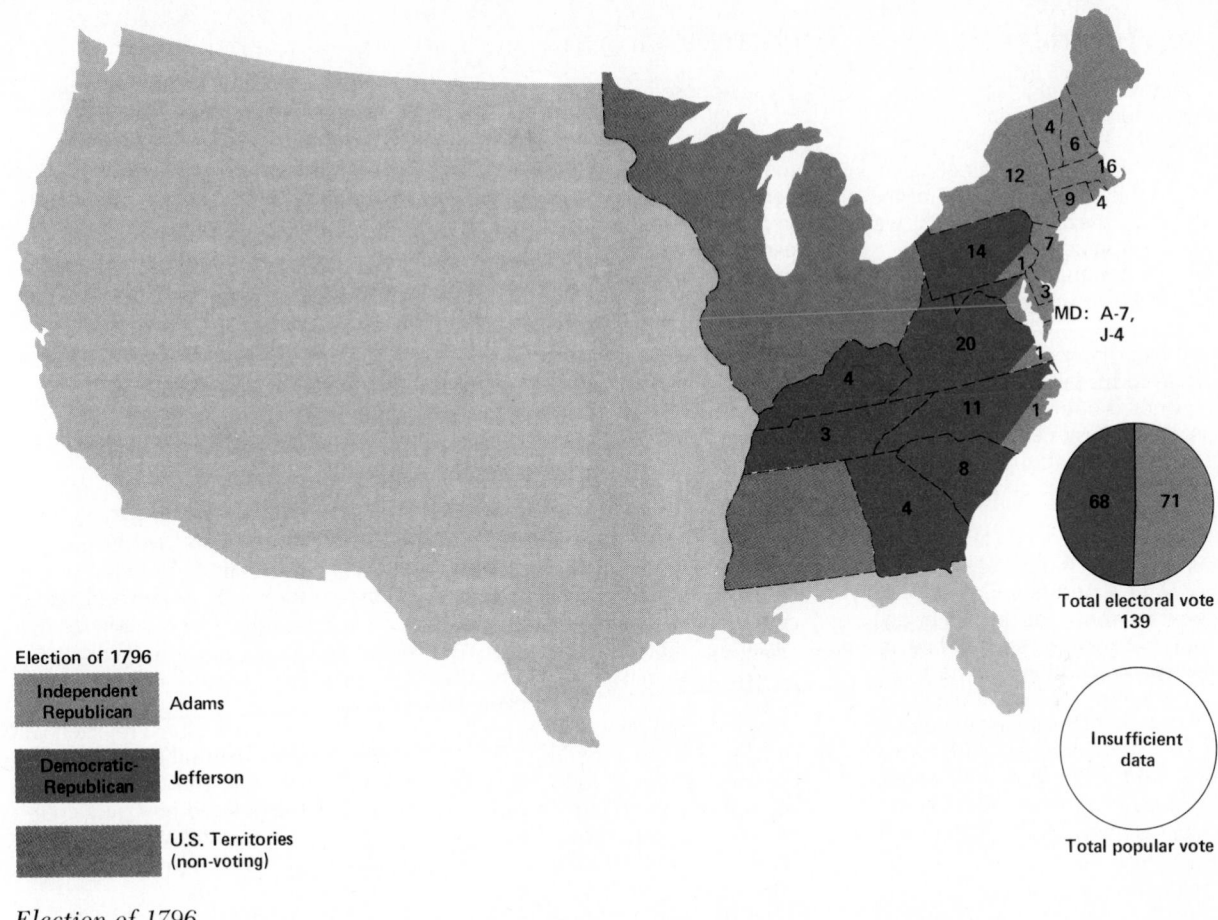

Election of 1796

- Independent Republican — Adams
- Democratic-Republican — Jefferson
- U.S. Territories (non-voting)

MD: A-7, J-4

4, 6, 12, 16, 9, 4, 14, 7, 1, 3, 20, 1, 4, 11, 1, 3, 8, 4

68 | 71

Total electoral vote 139

Insufficient data

Total popular vote

Election of 1796

thereby making him vice president under the existing terms of the Constitution. To us today it seems curious to have a president and vice president of opposing parties but of course the Founding Fathers had not anticipated a party system.

The XYZ Affair. John Adams no sooner took office than the United States found itself in an undeclared war with its recent ally, France. The French government, now in the hands of a new ruling group, considered the Jay Treaty a virtual Anglo-American alliance. The election of Adams, the candidate of the pro-British Federalists, seemed to confirm American sympathies for England, and French policy toward America quickly became more hostile. In 1797 the French authorities ordered that impressed American sailors captured from the British be hanged and that any intercepted American ship carrying British goods be confiscated. They also refused to receive the American minister, Charles Cotesworth Pinckney.

Adams might have used these insults to break relations with France. But unlike the High Federalists, who were more inflexible and more strongly prejudiced against the French, he chose to negotiate. As commissioners to settle with the French, he appointed the rejected Charles C. Pinckney; John Marshall, a Virginia Federalist; and Elbridge Gerry, a Massachusetts man with Republican leanings. At the same time the administration asked Congress to provide funds to expand the army and navy as a precaution.

When the American commissioners arrived in France, they were received by Charles Talleyrand, the French foreign minister. A wily and corrupt man, Talleyrand put them through numerous delays and then turned them over to three of his agents. These men—mentioned in the dispatches as X, Y, and Z—promised to speed up negotiations. But first the Americans were to pay Talleyrand and the directors of the French Republic $250,000, lend France $12 million, and apologize publicly for some harsh words President Adams had recently hurled their way. The commissioners refused to accept the French proposals. They had not been instructed to pay a bribe, they said, and such a large loan to France would seriously damage relations with England. Besides, how could

An Historical Portrait   Timothy Pickering

Timothy Pickering came by his reputation for self-righteousness honestly. His father, a prosperous farmer and businessman of Salem, Massachusetts, and deacon of the Third Congregational Church, was the town scold, constantly embroiled in public battles with those whose views on political and religious issues he considered wicked. The elder Pickering's appearance betrayed his personality. John Adams noted of the man that "he has an hypocritical demure on his face . . . ; his mouth makes a semicircle when he puts on that devout face."

Timothy attended Harvard, graduating in 1763 at the age of eighteen with almost nothing good to say about his four years in Cambridge. Back in Salem, he studied law and became an attorney, but he was never interested in legal practice. By this time the American colonies were embroiled in the struggle with Britain for autonomy, and Pickering, like his father before him, found public controversy more compelling than the humdrum pursuit of a legal career.

Salem, though more conservative than Boston, was a Whiggish town, and Pickering joined the ranks of those opposed to the British attempt to tighten control over their American empire. During the War for Independence he served as adjutant general and quartermaster general in the army. In these posts he became a close associate of Washington and many of the leading politicians of the new republic. During the months following Yorktown Pickering was one of those army officers who despaired at the feebleness of Congress, especially its inability to meet its back-pay obligations to the Continental soldiers. During the Critical Period he moved his family to Philadelphia and established himself as a commission merchant. But the postwar deluge of British imports soon drained the country of cash and hurt the firm of Pickering and Hodgdon.

Unable to make the private fortune he craved, in 1790 Pickering accepted appointment as federal agent to treat with the Iroquois Indians. He proved to be remarkably generous and fair and was rewarded for his success by appointment as postmaster general in Washington's cabinet.

Pickering at first stayed clear of the factional disputes that divided Washington's cabinet and molded the first political parties. Not until he became secretary of state in 1795 did he become an ardent Federalist, and it was through his attitudes toward France rather than over domestic issues. Retained in Adams's cabinet, the secretary became a member of the "war party," who held that nothing would "satisfy the ambitious and rapacious" French Directory except "universal dominion." England, he told the British minister, was "the last bulwark against the usurper of civilization." Following the revelations of French contempt for the United States in the XYZ Affair, Pickering urged an actual military alliance with Britain. His fear of France led him to support the Alien and Sedition Acts, which were designed to purge the nation of all "Gallomen" who might subvert the government. President Adams, though shocked by the XYZ revelations, rejected war and eventually resumed talks with the French. The president's conciliatory attitude placed him on a collision course with his warlike secretary of state, and in May 1800 he dismissed Pickering.

After a brief detour while he tried pioneer farming and land development in western Pennsylva-

---

they know whether, after paying, the United States would gain a favorable treaty?

When news of the negotiations reached the United States, it produced a tremendous uproar. Americans considered the French demands an unforgivable insult to their nation. The Federalists attacked the French and their Republican friends with renewed fury and made Pinckney and Marshall, the two Federalist commissioners, into heroes. One Federalist journalist proudly boasted that when the French had asked to be bribed, Pinckney had retorted: "Millions for defense, but not one cent for tribute!" What he actually said was far less eloquent: "No, no, not a six-pence!" Pinckney tried to set the record straight, but the story would not die. The phrase was engraved on his tombstone.

The bad feeling following the XYZ Affair tripped off a naval war between the former allies. French raiders from the Caribbean began attacking American vessels in United States coastal waters. Congress responded by voting money, over the opposition of the Republicans, to triple the size of the army and build forty new ships for the navy. In May 1798 it created the Navy Department with a secretary of cabinet rank to head it. Washington was recalled to public service and placed in command of the army, with Hamilton (yearning, as always, for military glory) second in command. In July Congress nullified the French alliance of 1778, ending the pretense of special friendship for that country. For the next few years American and French ships attacked one another in the Caribbean. The Americans also helped the British and their ally, the black patriot Toussaint L'Ouverture, overthrow the French regime on the island of Hispaniola and establish Haiti as the first black nation in the New World.

The pressure on Adams formally to declare war on France was immense; but the president,

nia, Pickering and his family returned to Salem. Here he resumed his political career as a High Federalist, and in 1803 the Massachusetts legislature elected him to the United States Senate. Pickering arrived in Washington when that raw capital was in the hands of the Jeffersonians. He might have assumed leadership of the Federalist opposition, but many of his party colleagues considered him an extremist so they consigned him to the obscure party backbench. Out of touch with the give-and-take of everyday politics, Pickering indulged his imagination and constructed a conspiracy theory that depicted his Republican opponents as subverters of the nation's institutions. Jefferson, he convinced himself, was conspiring to make himself president for life. The Republicans would not let the Constitution get in their way. Their sponsorship of the Louisiana Purchase, an act not authorized by the Constitution, made that clear. Pickering's penchant for controversy and extremist statements made him a favorite target of the Jeffersonians, who cited his intemperate remarks as a way of stigmatizing the entire Federalist party.

During the crisis with Britain that culminated in the War of 1812, Pickering predictably opposed the Republican administration's foreign policy. In 1813, after he had been rejected for a second Senate term, he returned to Washington as Representative from the Essex County district of eastern Massachusetts. As early as 1803 Pickering had conceived the idea of an independent confederacy of New England and other northeastern states opposed to the policies of the Jeffersonians. Now, in the midst of war, he once again entertained the scheme of New England secession from the Union and heartily endorsed the Hartford Convention called in late 1814 to consider regional grievances against the Madison government. When the convention adjourned without proposing secession, Pickering was bitterly disappointed.

During most of his political career Pickering's views had coincided with those of his eastern Massachusetts constituents, though he often expressed them in exaggerated ways. After the war, however, a gap opened between him and the Essex County voters. Eastern Massachusetts by 1815 had begun to turn

away from the sea and foreign trade and to take up manufacturing. Pickering's constituents supported the tariff bill of 1816, and when he opposed it, they were angry enough to repudiate him at the polls.

At the age of 72 Pickering left Washington to spend his remaining twelve years in Salem battling with everyone in sight. Fittingly for this son of the old deacon, he would embroil himself in religious controversy—but not as a defender of the old order. Pickering was a rationalist in religion and took the side of the Unitarians when they challenged the old Congregational establishment. The final irony of his career was his support of Andrew Jackson in 1824 over John Quincy Adams. But perhaps it was not so surprising after all. Resentment had always been a prime motivating force in his life, and he could never forget that the younger Adams's father had dismissed him from office a quarter century before. He died in January 1829, still defending his actions and denouncing his enemies.

---

aware of American unpreparedness, refused. In 1799 the French government, fearful that the United States might be a formidable adversary, began to show a more conciliatory attitude. Late in the year Adams sent three new emissaries to Paris to reopen negotiations. The president wanted the French to compensate Americans for their recent "spoliations" of American commerce, and he insisted that France formally accept nullification of the 1778 treaty. Now led by Napoleon, the French refused the first condition but accepted the second. On that basis the two countries signed the Convention of 1800. The United States had again avoided war.

REPUBLICAN TRIUMPH

The crisis with France stirred up American military ardor, improved Anglo-American relations,

and made the Federalists more popular. It also set in motion a train of events that ultimately led to the emergence of the Republicans as the majority party.

As yet, few Americans understood the role of a "loyal opposition." Equating active political opposition with disloyalty, if not treason, they could not see the value of a second party in keeping the first honest. Neither side pulled its punches and partisan hostility often went beyond the bounds of decency. In the *General Advertiser* Bache called the president the "old, querulous, bald, blind, crippled, toothless Adams." Vermont Congressman Matthew Lyon was almost expelled from Congress for spitting in a Federalist member's eye and wrestling with him on the floor of the House. Ideological passions inflamed partisan differences. To many Republicans the French Revolution, with its promise of "Liberty, Equality, and Fraternity," seemed the greatest event since the

Library of Congress

After the XYZ Affair it looked as if the United States would go to war with France. This appeal to "all brave, healthy, able bodied, and well disposed young men" was designed to meet the expected French threat.

birth of Jesus. To the Federalists the French Republic represented chaos, class war, and atheism, and those who defended it seemed little better than Jacobins themselves.

The Alien and Sedition Acts. Bitter partisanship, deep ideological differences, a sense that they were the custodians of the nation's virtue and its bulwark against foreign evil, and finally the surge of patriotism in the face of French danger—all these things explain (though they do not excuse) the extreme actions that the Federalists took against their enemies. In 1789 the Federalist Congress, claiming national security as justification, passed four laws that are known collectively as the Alien and Sedition Acts. The Naturalization Act extended the residence requirement for naturalization as a citizen from five to fourteen years. In effect, it kept the vote from recent Irish and French immigrants, many of whom were pro-French Republicans. The Alien Act gave the president power to expel from the country any alien considered dangerous or suspected of treasonable acts. He was also authorized, under the Alien Enemies Act, to arrest, imprison, or expel enemy aliens in the event of war. The Sedition Act affected the rights of citizens as well as aliens by making it illegal to (1) impede the execution of federal laws;

(2) bring the federal government, Congress, or the president into disrepute; (3) instigate or abet any riot, insurrection, or unlawful assembly; or (4) prevent a federal officer from performing his duties.

Under the Sedition Act Secretary of State Timothy Pickering prosecuted four leading Republican newspapers and several individuals, including Bache, Congressman Lyon, and Dr. Thomas Cooper, a prominent Republican scientist and pamphleteer. Ten of the indictments resulted in convictions, and a flock of foreign political activists left the country rather than face almost certain prosecution. Despite these "successes," the Alien and Sedition Acts were a tremendous political blunder. The Federalists had their opponents on the run until the passage of these laws. Unable to support the France of the XYZ Affair and the undeclared naval war, many moderate Republicans had defected to the side of the administration. Now the government's vindictiveness and total disregard of free speech rallied the waverers back to the Republican side.

Jefferson and Madison considered the Federalist measures a threat to civil liberties, including free speech, and a dangerous expansion of federal power relative to the states. To meet this challenge the two Republican leaders convinced the legislatures of Kentucky and Virginia to adopt

Library of Congress

Timothy Pickering as Secretary of State.

resolutions attacking the recent Federalist measures on constitutional grounds. These resolutions relied on the "compact theory" of the Constitution. That is, they held that the Constitution was a compact, or agreement, among the states to confer limited powers on the national government. Whenever it exceeded these powers—as it had outrageously with the Alien and Sedition Acts— the states had the right to take action against it. To clarify how this was to be done, the Kentucky legislature later asserted the right of states to resort to "nullification . . . of all unauthorized acts" by the national government.

Both states called on their fellow commonwealths to join them in protest. Few did. Where the Federalists were in control, the legislatures rejected the idea that the states were the proper judges of constitutionality. Even Republican legislatures were reluctant to approve the nullification doctrine. Nevertheless, the Virginia and Kentucky resolutions gave effective voice to widespread rank-and-file Republican outrage at the administration's disregard of civil liberties. They were also significant precedents for the later southern position on states' rights.

The Transfer of Power. By the time Congress ratified the Convention of 1800, Adams was out of office and Thomas Jefferson had become the third president of the United States. The 1800 presidential contest that ended in Republican victory was one of the most critical elections of American political history. It was the first time that one modern political party peacefully surrendered power to another. As such it is a milestone in the development of modern democratic party government. The magnitude of this achievement becomes all the clearer when we recall how bitter the political and ideological passions of the day were and how few Americans had confidence in party government during these years.

The Federalists seemed to be ahead when the 1800 campaign opened. Adams's peace policy was popular with the moderate public, and Federalists, despite the Alien and Sedition Acts, had made gains in the state elections of 1799. But actually the party was in trouble. Washington's death at the end of the year deprived his party of a powerful unifying force. Soon the personal rivalry and temperamental differences between Adams and Hamilton became an open scandal. Moreover, Republican efforts to woo northern businessmen and town laborers had begun to produce results. Few contemporaries as yet saw these weak spots.

In May 1800 a caucus of Federalist congressmen chose Adams and Charles Cotesworth Pinckney of the XYZ Affair as their candidates. The Republicans nominated Jefferson and Aaron Burr of New York by the same process. Both caucuses pledged to support each candidate equally, even though this commitment created the risk that the House of Representatives would have to choose between them for president and vice president if there should be a tie in the electoral college. This in fact was what happened.

The campaign was another step toward modern political parties. Federalists and Republicans employed, either for the first time or to a much greater extent than previously, such modern tactics as printed party tickets, appeals to party loyalty, and public speechmaking. When it was over, Adams had only 65 electoral votes, and Jefferson and Burr were tied with 73 votes each.

Who would be president and who second in command? No one doubted that the Republicans had intended Jefferson to be their presidential candidate; but as things stood, the House of Representatives would have to decide the question, with each state casting one vote, and the Federalists were in a position to check whichever candidate they wished. Here was irony indeed. The party that had savagely attacked the Sage of Monticello as an atheist, a two-faced intriguer, and the libertine father of several mulatto children now had the power to deny him his fondest goal.

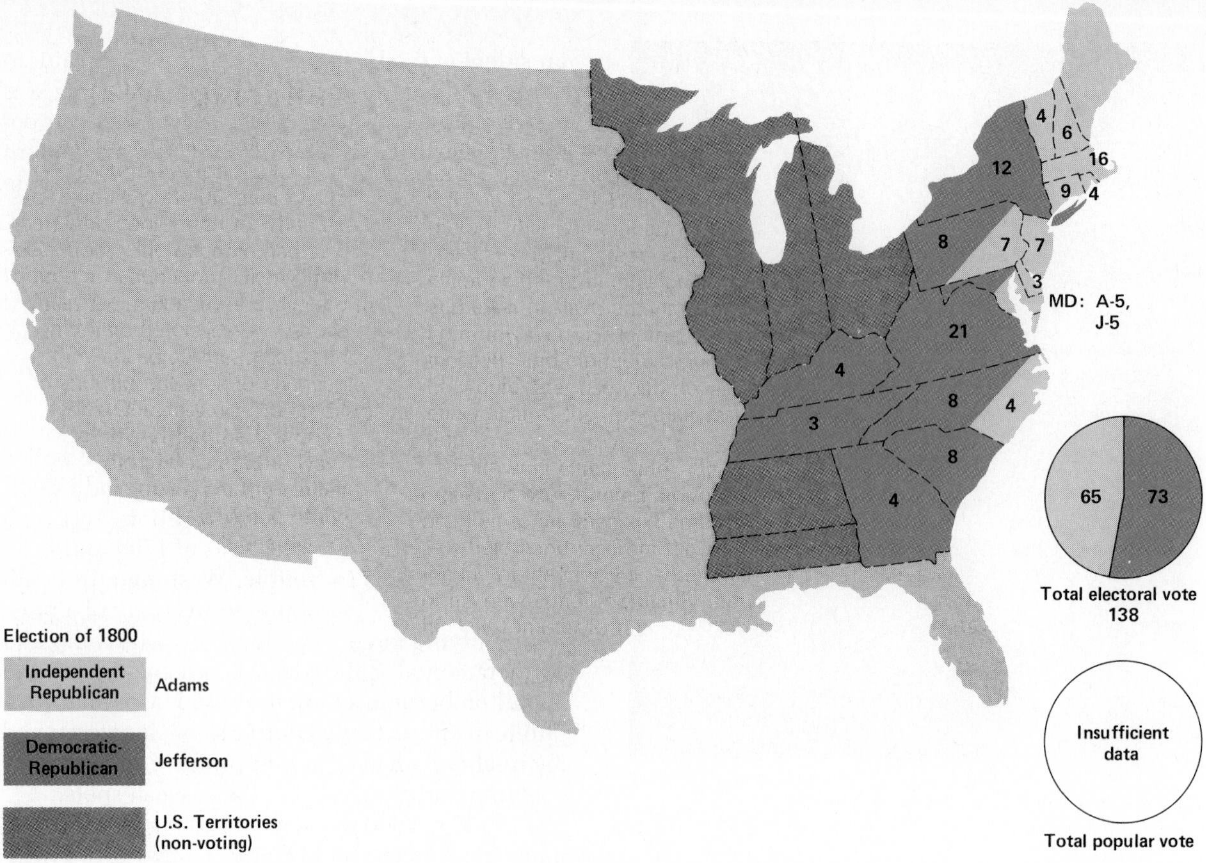

Election of 1800

Independent Republican	Adams
Democratic-Republican	Jefferson
	U.S. Territories (non-voting)

4
6
16
12
9 4
8 7
7
3
MD: A-5, J-5
21
4
8 4
3
8
4

65 73

Total electoral vote
138

Insufficient data

Total popular vote

Election of 1800

The nation's newspapers reflected and fostered the development of partisan politics. By 1804 Jeffersonian-Republicans were calling on their fellow citizens to save the country from Thomas C. Pinckney, and the Federalists were maintaining that Jefferson was a vile wretch compared to Washington.

New-York Historical Society

172

But would it? To some Federalists it seemed that if Jefferson was bad, Burr was even worse. Hamilton admitted that Jefferson "had some pretentions to character," but Burr was a complete rogue, a man "bankrupt beyond redemption." When Jefferson's friends gave the Federalist congressman from Delaware, James Bayard, assurances that the Virginian would leave Hamilton's financial system intact, maintain the armed forces at full strength, allow most Federalist civil servants to keep their jobs, and continue to steer the nation on a neutral course in foreign affairs, Bayard threw his state's vote to the Virginian. This shift of one state decided the election. The transfer of power was now complete. Jefferson, the arch-Republican, would be the third president of the United States.

CONCLUSIONS

In a little more than a decade Americans had laid the foundation of a modern party system. They had discovered that the machinery of government that the Constitution provided had to be supplemented by voluntary political institutions called parties. But Americans had not made a deliberate, considered decision; parties had been forced on them by the circumstances of the day. The need to put America's economic house in order and deal with its unsettled finances had created passionate disagreements between people with commitments to agriculture and those engaged in trade, banking, and manufacture. Differences over the French Revolution had divided the country between those who felt the exhilaration of a freer, more democratic, and more secular Europe, and those who saw revolutionary France as a dangerous enemy of religion and social order and Britain as a bastion of stability.

Constitutional biases also divided Americans. During the years of Washington's and Adams's administrations, the Federalists had, understandably, favored a broad interpretation of national powers; and they had stretched these to the limit to achieve their legislative ends. The Jeffersonians, by contrast, had fought centralized, concentrated national power and favored protection of the states' authority. Time would show that much of this difference depended on which party was "in" at the nation's capital and which was "out." After 1800, with Jefferson and his successors in office, the Republicans would talk far less about states' rights than before; the Federalists would reverse the process. And yet we must not be too cynical about the parties' professions of constitutional principles. What started as rationalization often ended as sincere conviction. In the end the Jeffersonians and their successors would express a persistent bias toward local power and against central power, while the Federalists and their successors would tend to reverse this order.

However it came about, by 1800 the country had acquired two great national parties. Neither had a monopoly of virtue or wisdom. The Republicans had shown greater sensitivity to personal rights and freedom; ideologically, they would point the way to a more open and democratic society. But their vision of the nation's social and economic future was naive. The Federalists had seen that America's greatness could not be limited by the past. They had recognized that the United States was fated to become a land of busy workshops as well as fertile farms and pastures. Yet they had failed to understand the average person's yearning for equality and the immense value of personal liberty in a progressive society. It remained to be seen now if the party of Jefferson could avoid the excesses of its opponents and find a workable balance for the nation.

FOR FURTHER READING

John C. Miller. *The Federalist Era, 1789–1801* (1960)
One of the best short political histories of the administrations of Washington and Adams. Miller carefully distinguishes between Adams Federalists and Hamiltonian Federalists.

Lance Banning. *The Jeffersonian Persuasion: Evolution of a Party Ideology* (1978)
Banning sees the Jeffersonian Republicans as men whose view of the political world was largely a product of "real Whig" ideology—as was the thought of those who led the Revolution. He takes ideology too seriously, probably, in explaining the rise of the first party system. Nevertheless, the book well repays reading.

Richard Hofstadter. *The Idea of a Party System, 1780–1840* (1969)
Like everything else Hofstadter wrote, this book is illuminating and graceful. It deals with the emergence of parties in the United States as a part of our intellectual history.

Joseph E. Charles. *The Origins of the American Party System* (1956)
The first modern interpretation of the first party system by a promising scholar who died young.

John C. Miller. *Alexander Hamilton: Portrait in Paradox* (1959)
Miller considers Hamilton's preoccupation with the creation and maintenance of a strong Union the key to all his ideas and policies. The

paradox is that his efforts to cement the Union contributed to a distinct cleavage between the North and the South.

Paul A. Varg. *Foreign Policies of the Founding Fathers* (1963)

An analysis of the economic and ideological factors in early foreign policy, the conflict between moralism and realism in policymaking, and the contribution of foreign policy disagreements to the early formation of national political parties.

Harry Ammon. *The Genêt Mission* (1973)

A brief, pro-Jefferson account of Edmond Genêt's mission to enlist American support for republican France against England.

Leland Baldwin. *The Whiskey Rebels: The Story of a Frontier Uprising* (1939)

The Whiskey Rebellion and its background treated with special attention to the feelings of those involved.

Manning J. Dauer. *The Adams Federalists* (1953); and Stephen G. Kurtz. *The Presidency of John Adams: The Collapse of Federalism, 1795–1800* (1957)

These are two essential monographs on the Federalist party after the departure of Washington from the political scene. Important, though somewhat dry, accounts.

Paul Goodman. *The Democratic Republicans of Massachusetts: Politics in a Young Republic* (1964)

This is a superior state study of the Jeffersonians in a commonwealth where it was an uphill fight for the followers of the Sage of Monticello.

James T. Flexner. *George Washington and the New Nation, 1783–1793* (1969); and *George Washington: Anguish and Farewell, 1793–1799* (1972)

These two volumes cover Washington's presidency and last years as completely as the student could wish. Despite their length, they make interesting reading.

Reginald Horsman. *The Frontier in the Formative Years, 1783–1815* (1970)

Tells the important story of the West during the early years of the republic, when Britons, Spaniards, and Americans all fished in troubled waters and all took advantage of the Indians.

James M. Smith. *Freedom's Fetters: The Alien and Sedition Laws and American Civil Liberties* (1956)

Jefferson termed the period 1798–1800 a "reign of witches." Externally threatened by France, the Adams administration encouraged national chauvinism and fear of internal subversion. Take note of when Smith wrote this book.

8 The Jeffersonians in Office

How Did Power Affect Republican Ideology?

1800 Jefferson elected president • Washington, D.C., becomes the national capital

1801 President Adams appoints "midnight judges" to tighten Federalist control of the courts

1802 The federal government sells its shares in the Bank of the United States • The Republican Congress repeals the Judiciary Act of 1801

1803–06 Lewis and Clark explore the West

1803 *Marbury* v. *Madison* • The Louisiana Purchase

1805 The *Essex* decision: Congress retaliates with the Nonimportation Act

1805–06 The Wilkinson-Burr conspiracy

1806–07 England and France issue decrees limiting neutral trade in Europe

1807 The *Chesapeake-Leopard* affair • Jefferson activates the Nonimportation Act of 1806 • The Embargo Act

1808 James Madison elected president

1809 The Nonintercourse Act

1810 Macon's Bill Number Two

1811 Southern and western "War Hawks" dominate the House of Representatives • American naval ship *President* attacks English navy's *Little Belt* • Congress defeats an attempt to recharter the Bank of the United States • Battle of Tippecanoe

1812 Congress provides for a 35,000-man regular army, gives Madison the power to call up state militias, and declares war on England

1814 Napoleon defeated in Europe; British troops are transferred to America and move on Washington • The Hartford Convention • The Peace of Ghent provides settlement of minor disputes between United States and Britain, leaves major issues of war untouched

1815 Andrew Jackson's victory over the British at New Orleans

1817 Rush-Bagot Agreement provides for demilitarizing United States–Canada border

n December 1815 James Madison sent his seventh annual message to Congress. The president reported Captain Stephen Decatur's defeat of the dey of Algiers, a victory that finally ended the generation-long struggle to free American shipping from Barbary pirate attacks. He also reported progress in concluding peace with the Indian tribes in the West and described the still-disturbed state of the country's finances. But the most arresting portion of the message was its last paragraphs. In these Madison recommended a protective tariff to encourage domestic industry, a program for building roads and canals, and "a national seminary of learning" within the District of Columbia, to be financed by the federal government. This national university would serve as "a central resort of youth and genius from every part of the country, diffusing on their return [to their homes] those national feelings, those liberal sentiments, and those congenial manners which contribute cement to our Union and strength to the great political fabric of which it is the foundation."

These proposals were startling indeed. Madison was the man who had fought Hamilton's scheme to fund the debt and establish a national bank. He had drafted the Virginia Resolution of 1798, which proclaimed the limited power of the federal government under the Constitution. His party was the party of states' rights and strict construction. Jefferson, the Republican sage, had warned Madison in 1796 against federal support of post roads, "a source," he declared, "of boundless patronage to the executive, jobbing [graft] to members of Congress and their friends, and a bottomless abyss of public money."

Now the leader of the Republican party was asking Congress for some of these very things. What had produced this about-face? Only fourteen years had elapsed between the disputed election of 1800, which made Thomas Jefferson president, and Madison's seventh annual message. What had taken place in this decade and a half to cause such a drastic change of direction among Republicans?

PRESIDENT JEFFERSON

Part of the answer is Republican adaptability. Once in office, Jefferson proved to be less strongly partisan and consistent than many of his opponents had feared. Instead of delivering a fighting, partisan inaugural speech or a crow of triumph, Jefferson sought to quiet fears and disarm his enemies. The recent political campaign had been bitter, he noted in his inaugural address. Now that it

was over, the country must unite. His party would respect the funded debt established by the Federalists. It would also respect the rights of political minorities. Though the two parties called themselves by different names, their members were "brethren of the same principle," Jefferson declared. "We are all Republicans, we are all Federalists." Nor would the victorious Republicans return the country to its feeble state before the Constitution. It was important, he said, to support "the State governments in all their rights"; but it was also necessary to preserve "the General Government in its whole constitutional vigor, as the sheet anchor of our peace at home and safety abroad."

A New, Republican Spirit. Despite Jefferson's conciliatory spirit, he worked to introduce "republican" principles into the conduct of the government. The new president reduced the formalities that had surrounded Washington and Adams. In place of his predecessors' regal ceremonial visits to Congress to express their wishes on new legislation or policy, Jefferson sent written messages. Instead of "levees," stiff, formal occasions at which members of the government and resplendent diplomats paid court to the president in strict order of rank, Jefferson gave state dinners at which guests took whatever seat they could find. Many affairs at the executive mansion, moreover, were open to the public; and ordinary people took advantage of the opportunity to rub shoulders with the great, much to the chagrin of the less democratic worthies. Still more characteristic of Jefferson were his small dinners, with guests seated at a round table where no one could claim precedence over anyone else. For these informal gatherings the president dressed in carpet slippers and a threadbare scarlet vest, his shirt not always perfectly clean. The guests discussed philosophy, the arts, literature, and science while eating food prepared by an excellent French chef, though often served by the president himself. Besides their use in conveying a new spirit of simplicity, these dinners had political value. Political guests, including congressmen and foreign envoys, were flattered and dazzled by the chief executive and found themselves unable to deny him the favors he asked. Some of Jefferson's legislative and diplomatic successes can be attributed to his talents as a host.

Federalist Legislation Repealed. Jefferson tried to break with the Federalist past in more fundamental ways as well. At first he labored to reduce the role of the national government, and he was

Jefferson in Office

Once elected, Jefferson, like most other victorious presidential candidates, sought to make peace with his opponents. His inaugural address of March 1801 was intended as an overture to the more moderate Federalists. The new president hoped to cool the heated feelings aroused by the election campaign. His goal was to make governing the nation a less difficult task. But the address also expressed some of Jefferson's most characteristic ideas: the rights of minorities, frugal and limited government, assured civil and religious liberties, the dangers of militarism, and the primacy of agriculture. Unfortunately he was not always as good as his words, but the inaugural address is an eloquent statement of traditional liberal principles.

"During the contest of opinion through which we have passed the animation of discussions and of exertions has sometimes worn an aspect which might impose on strangers unused to think freely and to speak and to write what they think; but this being now decided by the voice of the nation, . . . all will, of course, arrange themselves under the will of the law, and unite in common efforts for the common good. All, too, will bear in mind this sacred principle, that though the will of the majority is in all cases to prevail, that will to be rightful must be reasonable; that the minority possess their equal rights, which equal law must protect, and to violate would be oppression. Let us, then, fellow citizens, unite with one heart and one mind. Let us restore to social intercourse that harmony and affection without which liberty and even life itself are but dreary things. . . .

". . . [E]very difference of opinion is not a difference of principle. We have called by different names brethren of the same principle. We are all Republicans, we are all Federalists. If there be any among us who would wish to dissolve this Union or to change its republican form, let them stand undisturbed as monuments of the safety with which error of opinion may be tolerated where reason is left free to combat it. I know, indeed, that some honest men fear that a Republican government can not be strong, that this Government is not strong enough; but would the honest patriot . . . abandon a government which has so far kept us free and firm on the theoretic and visionary fear that this Government, the world's best hope, may by possibility want energy to preserve itself? I believe this, on the contrary, the strongest Government on earth. I believe it is the only one where every man, at the call of the law, would fly to the standard of the law, and would meet invasions of the public order as his own personal concern. Sometimes it is said that man can not be trusted with the government of himself. Can he then, be trusted with the government of others? Or have we found angels in the forms of kings to govern him? Let history answer this question.

"Let us, then, with courage and confidence pursue our own Republican and Federal principles, our attachment to union and representative government. Kindly separated by nature and a wide ocean from the exterminating havoc of one quarter of the globe; too high-minded to endure the degradation of the others; possessing a chosen country, with room for our descendents to the hundredth and thousandth generation; entertaining a due sense of our equal right to the use of our own faculties, to the acquisitions of our own industry, to honor and confidence from our own fellow-citizens, resulting not from birth, but from our own actions and their sense of them; enlightened by a benign religion, professed, indeed, and practiced in various forms, yet all of them inculcating honesty, truth, temperance, gratitude, and the love of man; acknowledging and adoring an overriding Providence, which by all its dispensations proves that it delights in the happiness of man here and his greater happiness hereafter— with all these blessings, what more is necessary to make us a happy and prosperous people? Still one more thing, fellow-citizens—a wise and frugal Government, which shall restrain men from injuring one another, shall leave them otherwise free to regulate their own pursuits of industry and improvement, and shall not take from the mouth of labor the bread it has earned. This is the sum of good government, and this is necessary to close the circle of our felicities.

"About to enter, fellow-citizens, on the exercize of duties which comprehend every thing dear and valuable to you, it is proper you should understand what I deem the essential principles of our Government, and consequently those which ought to shape its Administration. I will compress them within the narrowest compass they will bear. . . . Equal and exact justice to all men of whatever state or persuasion, religious or political; peace, commerce, and honest friendship with all nations, entangling alliances with none; the support of the State governments in all their rights, as the most competent administrations for our domestic concerns and the surest bulwarks against antirepublican tendencies; the preservation of the General Government in its whole constitutional vigor, as the sheet anchor of our peace at home and safety abroad; a jealous care of the right of election by the people—a mild and safe corrective of abuses which are lopped by the sword of revolution where peaceable remedies are unprovided; absolute acquiescence in the decisions of the majority, the vital principles of republics, from which is no appeal but to force, the vital principle and immediate parent of despotism; a well-disciplined militia, our best reliance in peace and for the first moments of war, till regulars may relieve them; the supremacy of the civil over the military authority; economy in the public expense, that labor may be lightly burthened; the honest payments of our debts and sacred preservation of the public faith; encouragement of agriculture, and of commerce as its handmaid; the diffusion of information and arraignment of all abuses at the bar of the public reason; freedom of religion; freedom of the press, and freedom of person under the protection of the habeas corpus, and trial by juries impartially selected. . . .

"Relying, then, on the patronage of your good will, I advance with obedience to the work, ready to retire from it whenever you become sensible how much better choice it is in your power to make. And may that Infinite Power which rules the destinies of the universe lead our councils to what is best, and give them a favorable issue for your peace and prosperity."

partially successful. The Seventh and Eighth Congresses, which spanned his first administration, passed only 173 bills, most of them unimportant. Meanwhile, the Swiss-born secretary of the treasury, Albert Gallatin of Pennsylvania, reduced the national debt by cutting down appropriations for the army and the navy, which the Republicans neither liked nor considered essential. At the same time the new administration was able to do away with several unpopular internal taxes imposed by the Federalists. This feat of simultaneously cutting taxes and reducing the debt was made possible by the large revenues from import duties during the great foreign trade expansion that lasted through 1809.

The Republicans attacked or eliminated other Federalist policies or programs. They repealed some of the Alien and Sedition Acts, allowed others to expire, and pardoned all those the Federalists had imprisoned for sedition. They also whittled away at the Bank of the United States and eventually disposed of it. Since it had a twenty-year charter, the bank could not be dismantled until 1811, but in 1802 the federal government sold its shares of bank stock at a profit and got out of the banking business.

A Strong Executive. The initial Republican attack on "big government" soon gave way to a more pragmatic approach. The third president, whatever his theoretical position, was by temperament a vigorous leader who did whatever was needed to advance the national interest as he saw it. He was also able to learn from experience. Although he had earlier condemned a powerful central government, after 1801, when he passed from opposition to control, he shifted ground. As president he decided that he could not be burdened with constitutional scruples if he was to get things done. His critics charged him with hypocrisy, but we can see the inconsistencies in Jefferson's behavior as growth. Jefferson learned that power was not necessarily bad if used for good ends, and he developed great skill in using the authority of his office.

Though willing to reassure his opponents, Jefferson had no intention of allowing them to dominate the national government or tie his hands. As yet, the politicians had not raised to a lofty, democratic principle the "spoils system" of replacing government personnel of the defeated party with members of the victorious one. Jefferson himself believed that the measure of fitness to hold appointive office should be merit. But he had to reckon with a number of realities. First, not all the Federalist officeholders could be counted on to administer fairly the laws passed by a Republican Congress and approved by a Republican president. Second, some of them were corrupt or incompetent. Finally, he could not disregard the fact that many Republicans lusted after the jobs of Federalists and could see no reason why they should not get them as rewards for loyal service to the president and the party. Jefferson would have preferred to allow positions to become available by retirement or death. Unfortunately, he noted, the vacancies "by death are few; by resignation none."

In any case, Jefferson did not have the opportunity for the wide-ranging appointments that later presidents had. In 1801, in the new, raw "Federal City" on the banks of the Potomac, there were fewer than 300 federal employees. In the rest of the country there were an additional 2,500. These 2,800 clerks, postmasters, marshals, and lighthouse keepers equaled about one-thousandth of the federal labor force in 1980. During Jefferson's first two years in office he replaced almost 200 Federalists with members of his own party.

Our Country by Benson J. Lossing, 1877

Thomas Jefferson first broke with tradition by walking to the Capitol on Inauguration Day. Although Jefferson disregarded etiquette in dress, a French chef cooked White House dinners, and one year's wine bill was $2,800.

Library of Congress

In 1800, Washington, D.C., was a city of "magnificent distances," as this picture attests. In the background you can see the President's House; it was not called the White House until after the War of 1812, when it was whitewashed to cover scorch marks left by fires the invading British had set.

Federalist leaders, who believed that the new president had promised to leave all positions below cabinet rank alone, protested, but to no avail.

The Attack on the Judiciary. A particularly thorny problem for the incoming president was the national judiciary. United States judges were virtually all Federalists, and these men were not impartial or disinterested. Supreme Court Justice Samuel Chase, for instance, the presiding judge at several sedition trials, had actively supported the prosecution and had insulted the defendants and their lawyers. Since United States judges were appointed for life, the president could not remove Chase or others like him. Matters were made particularly acute, from the Republican point of view, by the Judiciary Act of 1801, passed during the final days of the Adams administration. The act relieved Supreme Court justices of the burden of having to travel from place to place to hear lower court cases; it gave that job to sixteen new circuit judges. As a whole, the law improved national legal enforcement. It also gave the Federalist party even tighter control over the United States court system. On the evening of March 3, 1801, the day before Jefferson's inauguration, Adams signed the commissions of the new circuit judges along with those of a flock of new federal marshals, attorneys, and justices of the peace. All the "midnight appointees" were Federalist party members, and it now looked as if the opposition party had locked up control of at least one branch of the government for decades to come, despite the Republican victory of 1800.

The Republicans were enraged by Adams's action. Jefferson charged that the Federalists had "retired to the judiciary . . . and from that battery all the works of Republicanism are to be beaten down and destroyed." To keep the new appointees from assuming office, Secretary of State James Madison refused to deliver their commissions. As far as the new administration was concerned, the appointments were void. Soon after, the Republican Congress repealed the 1801 Judiciary Act and replaced it with one of its own, the Judiciary Act of 1802.

At this point the commanding figure of John Marshall, chief justice of the Supreme Court, enters the picture. A dignified Virginian of strong Federalist views, Marshall insisted that the Supreme Court had the right to check the fickle and headstrong representatives of the people by declaring acts of Congress unconstitutional. Judicial review, as this process is called, had been talked about earlier, but it had never been conclusively established. Republicans considered it unrepublican and claimed that the power to judge constitutionality belonged to either the executive or the legislative branch or both. In any event, they noted, judicial review at this point would just further strengthen the Federalist party.

Early in 1803 Marshall saw his chance. He

New York Public Library Picture Collection

Chief Justice John Marshall's ruling in Marbury v. Madison *helped entrench Federalist principles in American law. Marshall had fought at Valley Forge; his experience there, he wrote later, had confirmed him "in the habit of considering America as my country and Congress as my government."*

would assert his precious principle, but do so in a way the Republicans would find difficult to oppose. His opportunity came in the case of *Marbury* v. *Madison* in which William Marbury, who had been nominated federal justice of the peace by Adams and refused his commission by Madison, sued to have the commission delivered by the secretary of state. In 1803 Marshall, speaking for the Court, denied Marbury's claim by declaring the federal law under which he had sued to be unconstitutional. In effect, Madison and the government had won on the question of Marbury's appointment, but their victory depended on accepting the right of the Supreme Court to decide whether a law passed by Congress was in conflict with the Constitution and therefore void. An important claim held by many Federalists had been established: the Supreme Court, whose members were beyond easy reach of popular opinion, was to be the final judge of constitutionality.

Marbury v. *Madison* did not end Jefferson's attack on the existing court system. In 1803 the administration turned to impeachment to remove the most ardent Federalist partisans from the fed-

eral bench and replace them with Republicans. To launch their attack, they selected two targets: John Pickering, a federal district judge in New Hampshire, and the notorious Judge Chase of the Supreme Court. Both men were outrageously partisan Federalists; Pickering, besides being an alcoholic, was clearly insane. He was impeached by the House of Representatives and removed by the Senate with little difficulty. But Chase—however ill-tempered and unfair—convinced enough senators that he had not committed the "high crimes and misdemeanors" that were the specified constitutional grounds for removal from office. The government's case, pleaded by the unpredictable and eccentric John Randolph of Roanoke, was based on the claim that only unbecoming and unfair conduct need be proved for a federal official's dismissal. Randolph bungled the prosecution and failed to convince the Senate. Chase's acquittal virtually ended the Republican assault on the Federalist judiciary.

INTERNATIONAL POLITICS AND REPUBLICAN POLICY

It was the need to deal effectively with foreign powers more than any other single factor that pushed Jefferson and his successor toward Federalist principles of strong central government. Jefferson had always recognized the need for executive leadership in foreign affairs. He might delegate authority to his secretary of state, James Madison; but ultimately, he knew, the responsibility for foreign relations rested with him.

Jefferson Buys Louisiana. In 1801 the United States was still entangled in the complicated issues that had grown out of the French Revolution. Britain and France were briefly at peace following the Treaty of Amiens in 1802. But then in May 1803 hostilities between Napoleon and his enemies erupted once more and darkened the Atlantic world for another dozen years.

Once again America was sucked into the conflict. The first warning came in 1800 when Spain and France signed the secret Treaty of San Ildefonso. This agreement allowed France to resume control of Louisiana, which it had lost to Spain in 1763 as a result of the French and Indian War. News of the deal caused great alarm in the United States. Jefferson, skeptical of French policy and motives ever since the rise of Napoleon, feared France's effort to reestablish an empire in North America. It was not that the president had ceased to dislike the British, but for the moment his suspicions of the French were stronger. It was one thing for a weak Spain to occupy New Orleans. It was far worse for a powerful and arrogant France to control the mouth of the Mississippi, and be able to close off American commerce from the great river and its tributaries.

Even more than in the previous decade the United States had vital interests in the Mississippi Valley. Hundreds of thousands of Americans now lived beyond the Appalachians. Ohio alone in 1800 had over 45,000 people, Tennessee had 105,000 settlers, and Kentucky 220,000 more. Over 150 vessels regularly plied the great central river, carrying over 20,000 tons of freight annually. As Jefferson was painfully aware, whoever controlled the Mississippi wielded enormous power over the United States

> There is on the globe one single spot [he declared] the possessor of which is our natural and habitual enemy. It is New Orleans, through which the produce of three-eighths of our territory must pass to market, and from its fertility it will ere long yield more than half of our whole produce, and contain more than half our habitants.

If France gained control of the region, "from that moment we must marry ourselves to the British fleet and nation."

When rumors of the French agreement with Spain reached the United States, Jefferson dispatched Robert R. Livingston to Paris. Not knowing that West Florida was unaffected by the French-Spanish deal, Jefferson directed the American emissary to buy both that province and New Orleans from Napoleon. From the outset Livingston encountered difficulties. Talleyrand, the French foreign minister, would not let him see Napoleon. The devious Frenchman was waiting to see what would happen in Santo Domingo, where a French army was struggling to put down the slave revolt led by Toussaint L'Ouverture. If Toussaint was destroyed, France could protect Louisiana and once more establish itself as a North American power. The scheme did not work. The black liberator was eventually captured by trickery, but the Haitians refused to surrender. Black guerrillas slipped out of the mountains and mercilessly attacked the French troops. Even more dangerous was the yellow fever mosquito. Before many months had passed, the French commanding general was dead along with two-thirds of his army.

News of the growing French disaster trickled back to Paris slowly. Meanwhile, American anxiety increased when the Spaniards, who had not yet officially turned over Louisiana to the French, suspended the precious right of deposit at New Orleans allowed by the Pinckney Treaty of 1795. Spain's unfriendly act, Livingston's lack of progress, and the westerners' growing outcry against Spain goaded Jefferson to new action. In January 1803 he named James Monroe as joint negotiator with Livingston and arranged with Congress for an appropriation of $2 million for the purchase of New Orleans and part of West Florida.

By this time the mood in Paris had changed. It was now clear that the Santo Domingo campaign was a costly failure and that France must forgo all thought of a new North American empire. Besides, it looked as if hostilities were about to break out again in Europe. War, Napoleon realized, would expose Louisiana to British attack from Canada or conquest by the Americans. Louisiana, then, was virtually worthless to France—unless the great, rich province could be converted into cash, in which case it could contribute handsomely to French ambitions in Europe. On April 11, 1803, the first consul told his minister of finance, François de Barbé-Marbois: "I renounce Louisiana. It is not only New Orleans that I will cede, it is the whole colony without reservation. . . ."

Napoleon's new attitude completely altered the picture. No sooner had Monroe arrived in Paris than he and Livingston were confronted with a remarkable and totally unexpected proposition. Instead of only New Orleans, Barbé-Marbois asked, why not take all of the immense territory? Another 20 million francs would pay for outstanding claims of American citizens against France dating back to the naval war of the 1790s. This offer exceeded the expectations and instructions of the American emissaries, but they eagerly accepted it. On May 2, 1803, they signed the treaty transferring Louisiana to the United States for $15 million.

The treaty was a wonderful piece of good luck. But it left many questions unanswered and many problems unsolved. Spain had never formally surrendered the province to France and was chagrined at getting little or nothing of what Napoleon was due to receive. She could be expected to cause trouble. There was also great uncertainty about the territory's precise boundaries. When Livingston questioned Talleyrand on the colony's limits, the Frenchman had remarked cynically that the Americans had "made a noble bargain" for themselves and would no doubt "make the most of it." They would indeed; but in the meantime the uncertainty was sure to rile Spain and Great Britain, whose colonies of Mexico and Canada bordered Louisiana.

Chicago Historical Society

This 1805 painting shows the city of New Orleans shortly after the United States acquired it from France. Its harbor was already crowded with American seagoing vessels prepared to lead river freight for shipment to Europe and the Atlantic coast.

Most difficult of all, however, were the constitutional problems raised by the purchase. Fifty thousand French and Spanish Creoles—descendants of the original European settlers—inhabited the colony. Under the treaty they were to become American citizens. Did the United States have the constitutional right to incorporate these people without their consent? And what about the process of acquiring new territory by treaty? Nowhere did the Constitution confer authority on anyone to buy new territory for the nation. Federalists, who objected to almost anything the administration did, denounced these assumptions of powers. Each side called the other hypocritical for reversing its usual position on implied powers under the Constitution.

Jefferson himself was troubled by constitutional scruples, and for a while hesitated. But not for long. It seemed certain that the Louisiana Territory would support millions of small landholding farmers, and that prospect was dear to the president's heart. Trying to get a bargain and preserve his principles at the same time, Jefferson proposed that Congress should simultaneously con-

firm the treaty and adopt a constitutional amendment expressly authorizing such territorial acquisitions. But Napoleon would not wait for the president to overcome his philosophical misgivings. Warned that the first consul was becoming restless, Jefferson abandoned the idea of a constitutional amendment and pushed the treaty through the Senate. On December 20, 1803, in a simple ceremony at New Orleans, the French flag was lowered and the Stars and Stripes raised in its place. Louisiana, a region almost equal in extent to the whole United States after the 1783 peace treaty with Britain, was now American.

The Lewis and Clark Expedition. Even before Napoleon had made his startling offer to sell the Louisiana Territory, Jefferson had recruited his private secretary, Meriwether Lewis, and a former soldier, William Clark, to lead an expedition to explore the vast region. Jefferson's motives were a mixture of the political and the commercial. Initially, he hoped to establish an American claim to the region through exploration. More important, he saw Louisiana as vital to his Indian policy. The

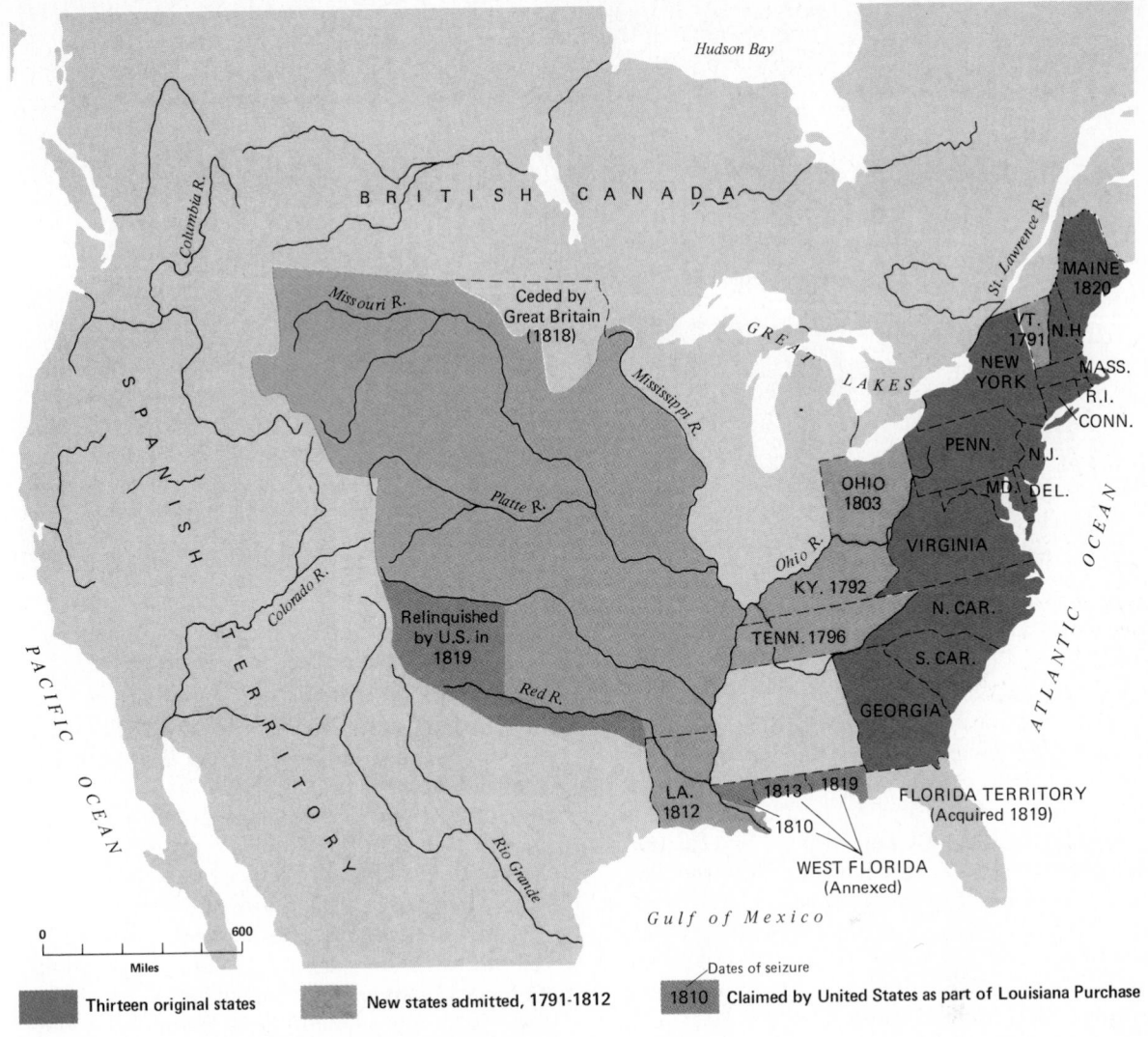

The Louisiana Purchase and new states, 1791–1812

Map labels: Hudson Bay; BRITISH CANADA; Columbia R.; Missouri R.; Ceded by Great Britain (1818); GREAT LAKES; St. Lawrence R.; MAINE 1820; VT. 1791; N.H.; NEW YORK; MASS.; R.I.; CONN.; Mississippi R.; SPANISH TERRITORY; Platte R.; PENN.; N.J.; OHIO 1803; MD.; DEL.; Ohio R.; VIRGINIA; ATLANTIC OCEAN; Colorado R.; KY. 1792; Relinquished by U.S. in 1819; N. CAR.; TENN. 1796; Red R.; S. CAR.; PACIFIC OCEAN; GEORGIA; Rio Grande; LA. 1812; 1813; 1819; 1810; FLORIDA TERRITORY (Acquired 1819); WEST FLORIDA (Annexed); Gulf of Mexico; 0 — 600 Miles; Dates of seizure

Legend: ■ Thirteen original states ■ New states admitted, 1791-1812 [1810] Claimed by United States as part of Louisiana Purchase

president hoped to gather the eastern Indian tribes into reservations where they could be induced to abandon their "savage" ways and settle down as "civilized" farmers. Jefferson conceived of this change as advantageous to the Indians themselves, and it was certainly far better than the extermination policies advocated by some American officials. But it also had the advantage of freeing vast tracts of land for white settlers. To carry out this policy, the president believed, the Indian traders who encouraged the Indians' roaming ways must be attracted to regions farther west. Lewis and Clark, accordingly, were asked to investigate the fur resources of the new region and also to attempt to establish commercial relations with the western tribes. News of the Louisiana Purchase added to these goals an intense curiosity

about what exactly the United States had bought for $15 million.

Lewis and Clark's small party of fifty spent the winter of 1803–04 in the St. Louis area; in the spring they set off up the Missouri River. By fall they had reached the villages of the Mandan Indians in what is now the Dakotas and settled down in a winter camp. The group that set out for the Pacific the following April consisted of thirty-seven men and a woman, Sacajawea. A Shoshone captive of the Dakota tribes, she was given her freedom in exchange for guiding the expedition across the Rockies. Sacajawea took them as far as the Lemhi Pass on the Continental Divide, where they were met by the Shoshones. Grateful for the return of their kinswoman, the Indians provided the expedition with horses and guides for the next

Montana Historical Society

A reconstructed scene of the Lewis and Clark expedition. York, Clark's slave, is at left shouldering the rifle. To his right is Lewis; then Clark; then Sacajawea, their Indian guide.

stage of the journey, over the remaining ranges of the Rockies to the valley of the Clearwater River. There they were given food and shelter by the friendly Flathead Indians, who also supplied a new flotilla of canoes. By mid-November, after traversing the rapids of the Clearwater and the Columbia, the weary explorers arrived at the shores of the Pacific.

On their return to St. Louis in September 1806, the explorers were received with wild enthusiasm. At the cost of only a single man and some $50,000, they had established relations with several important Indian nations; discovered usable passes through the Rockies; and provided important botanical, zoological, and anthropological data. Their expedition helped to open the trans-Mississippi region, and was soon followed by others that laid the groundwork for the wave of settlement that would carry millions of Americans across the continent.

The Wilkinson-Burr Conspiracy.

Acquisition of Louisiana had finally ended one source of western troubles: it was no longer a problem for western farmers to send their goods to market through New Orleans. But the Louisiana Purchase had not laid to rest all the westerners' complaints by any means. The West was still not sure that it could entrust its future to the government in Washington. Many easterners, the people of the trans-Appalachian region knew, were suspicious of growing western power and numbers. In

Massachusetts, for example, extreme Federalists, members of the so-called Essex Junto, were talking of detaching New England, New York, and New Jersey from the Union and forming a new confederation of states. This new nation would insulate the commercial Northeast from the attacks of the allied agricultural South and West.

Western resentments and suspicions offered opportunities for ambitious and unscrupulous men to carve careers for themselves as champions of the trans-Appalachian region. Two of the most dangerous of these adventurers were General James Wilkinson, commander of United States troops in the West and governor of the Louisiana Territory, and Vice President Aaron Burr of New York. Wilkinson was one of the most disreputable characters in American history. Though a trusted lieutenant of every American president from Washington through Madison, the handsome, hard-drinking officer was in the pay of the Spanish as Agent Number 13.

Burr was a far more talented man. Intelligent and cultivated, he exerted a strong fascination on men and women alike. Though descended from a long line of Puritan ministers, Burr was a compulsive womanizer, a reckless pleasureseeker, and a cynic, driven by ambition and the desire to win fame and glory. Despite these serious flaws, he still might have attained the presidency if he had not made a fatal misstep. In 1804, angered by Hamilton's role in defeating him when he ran for governor of New York, Burr challenged the former treasury secretary to a duel. The two men met on the New Jersey Palisades opposite New York. Hamilton deliberately held his fire; Burr shot to kill and succeeded. People called Burr's action murder. From that point on, a conventional course to power was closed to Burr, and he turned to intrigue and conspiracy to achieve his ends.

Burr looked to the West for a way to restore his shattered fortunes. He contacted Wilkinson, and the two men sought foreign support for a scheme to detach the West from the United States, combine it with parts of Spanish Mexico, and then set up an independent nation with themselves as rulers. To raise money Burr connived with the British minister in Washington, who seemed interested in any plan that promised to diminish American strength.

For a time Wilkinson was prepared to sell out his Spanish employers in order to further the scheme. But eventually the general decided to continue his profitable relationship with the Spanish authorities. Posing as an American patriot anxious to defend his country's interests, he betrayed Burr to Jefferson. Tried before Chief Justice Marshall, Burr was acquitted of treason but indicted for espionage. When he was released on bail, the archintriguer decided not to risk another trial and fled to Europe.

Neutral Rights Once More. The acquisition and exploration of Louisiana reveal Jefferson at his most energetic. Clearly the third president was capable of vigorous action in pursuing the national interest. But besides creating opportunities, European antagonisms caused serious difficulties for the United States that Jefferson found harder to handle.

After 1803 almost all the disputes between the United States and the major European belligerents, England and France, repeated those of the 1790s. Impressment, blockades, neutral rights, contraband, and Indian incitements continued to disturb America's relations with the two leading European powers. The country's foreign involvements during 1803–12 seem like a replay of 1793–1800 with the volume turned up.

Soon after the outbreak of hostilities between France and England in 1803, the British resumed their impressment policy. Before long, British ships were hovering off East Coast ports, ready to swoop down on American ships and seize seamen, British or American, for the Royal Navy. In July 1805, in the *Essex* decision, a British admiralty court declared illegal the American practice of carrying French West Indian produce to American ports and then shipping it to France. The

Americans, the court declared, could not make a convincing case that these commodities were neutral goods. They were really French and, under the Rule of 1756, could be confiscated like other French goods if intercepted by the British navy.

The American government protested this ruling, which threatened to destroy the immensely profitable reexport trade. But to little effect, and Congress retaliated in April 1806 by passing the first Nonimportation Act. This measure forbade the importation of many goods that Americans normally bought from Britain. The law was only a threat, however; its operation was suspended until the president chose to invoke it, and for the moment Jefferson preferred to keep it in reserve.

Tensions soon developed into a war of restrictions and counterrestrictions. In May 1806 Britain announced a blockade of the European continent from the Elbe River in Germany to the port of Brest in France. Napoleon responded with the Berlin Decree, placing Britain under blockade and forbidding all British commerce with France. The British then issued two orders in council threatening to confiscate all ships engaged in French coastal trade or entering those European continental ports still not off limits. Only if they first stopped in Britain, paid duties, and secured British clearance would neutrals be allowed to trade with any part of Europe. Napoleon replied with the Milan Decree, which declared that all vessels that obeyed the orders in council would be subject to French seizure.

The British-French war of regulations seemed designed to produce maximum irritation in America. If American merchants bowed to the British, they would offend the French, and vice versa. To make matters worse, the regulations contained large loopholes in both their provisions and their enforcement. These continued to entice Americans into the lucrative trade with Europe and the West Indies, but made it hazardous and uncertain. Americans might have been less aggrieved if they had known from the outset that they could trade with Europe only by engaging in outright smuggling.

The Chesapeake-Leopard Affair. While the barrage of decrees and orders in council flew through the air, the impressment issue became acute. Vice-admiral Sir George Berkeley, commander in chief of his majesty's naval forces at Halifax, Nova Scotia, was particularly irked by the supposed connivance of American officials in the desertion of British seamen. The situation was especially bad in the Chesapeake Bay region, where many

An Historical Portrait   Albert Gallatin

One of the most prominent leaders of the party established by Thomas Jefferson was not even American-born. Not until 1780, when he was nineteen, did Albert Gallatin come to the United States, the country where he was to achieve such great political distinction.

Gallatin was born in Geneva, an independent city republic in what is now Switzerland, of a distinguished French-speaking Protestant family. Given a classical education in the local schools, he reached his teens discontented with the limited economic opportunity and conservatism of his community. In school he had become acquainted with the writings of the Enlightenment philosopher Jean-Jacques Rousseau, himself a native of Geneva, and belonged to a circle of young men who yearned for a better political and social order than existed in Europe under the Old Regime. By now all of "enlightened" Europe knew of the brave cause of the Americans fighting against British tyranny, and in 1780 Gallatin and a friend left Geneva to cast their lot in with America.

Gallatin spent his first few years in the United States in a quest of a vocation. By the time he arrived, the war was virtually over, so a military career was precluded. For a while he taught French at Harvard, but he was drawn to the West and western opportunities. For a number of years he tried to make money as a speculator in western lands. Though these schemes did not work out, through them he became associated with western Pennsylvania and, in 1785, established his permanent home there.

Fayette County in the 1780s was frontier, with all the frontier openness to newcomers. Even a young man like Gallatin who was foreign and spoke heavily accented English could make his mark. In 1788 his fellow citizens sent the young man to represent them at a convention in Harrisburg called to change the recently adopted federal Constitution. There Gallatin met other men like himself who feared the centralizing tendencies of the new frame of government. This concern would remain an important part of Gallatin's political ideology and a major bond with the Jeffersonians.

Gallatin's career following this debut was meteoric. In 1790 he was elected to the Pennsylvania state legislature and served there for three terms. As a legislator he sponsored bills for a statewide system of public education, the abolition of slavery, and reform of the penal code. His program closely echoed the work that the great Jefferson had accomplished in Virginia as governor during the war. Yet at the same time, Gallatin was no enemy of banks or "fiscal responsibility." He helped rid Pennsylvania of its depreciated paper money, got the state to pay its public debt in specie, and sponsored a state-controlled bank. In many ways this program resembled Hamilton's almost simultaneous efforts at the federal level. But there was one crucial difference: Hamilton believed a permanent federal debt was a useful political device; Gallatin,

like all Republicans, believed public debt undesirable. The state must always follow the principle of pay-as-you-go for all its expenses.

In 1793 the legislature elected Gallatin to the United States Senate and he went to Philadelphia to take his seat. In the nation's temporary capital he met and married Hannah Nicholson, member of a New York family with close ties to the emerging Republican or Anti-Federalist party. Soon after, Gallatin was disqualified for his Senate seat on the grounds that he had not met the constitutional requirement of citizenship for nine years. He returned to his farm on the Monongahela with his new bride and a total fortune of £600 in cash.

He arrived in Fayette County just in time to become embroiled in the uprising against the federal authorities over the 1793 excise tax that we call the Whiskey Rebellion. Though a Republican and man of the West, Gallatin played a moderating role and succeeded in preventing a civil war. By the time the federalized militia appeared, the rebellion was over and nothing remained to be done but arrest a few holdouts and drag them to Philadelphia to be tried.

In 1794 Gallatin was elected to the federal House of Representatives. Here, during the three terms he served, he became a major Republican leader, second only to Madison, and a prime target for Federalists, who derided his accent and foreign birth and accused him of being a ring leader of the Whiskey Rebels. He quickly became known as an expert in finance who

---

deserters from the Royal Navy had taken refuge and a number had enlisted in the American navy. One of these deserters, Jenkin Ratford, now a sailor on the U.S.S. *Chesapeake*, was reported to be swaggering through the town insulting British officers on leave.

This was the last straw. On June 1, 1807, Berkeley directed his subordinates to stop the *Chesapeake* if they should encounter it beyond American territorial waters and search it for deserters. Not long afterward H.M.S. *Leopard* over-

took the American frigate as it left Norfolk bound for the Mediterranean on a shakedown cruise. The American captain, Commodore James Barron, suspecting nothing—for the British had never attempted to impress from an American *naval* vessel before—allowed a British officer to come aboard. Barron was presented with Berkeley's order and a note from the British captain demanding that the deserters be surrendered. Barron refused. The *Leopard*'s response was to fire into the American ship, killing three Americans and wounding eight-

could argue with the Federalists on their own ground and show where their much-vaunted financial measures had been costly and unnecessary to the economic health of the nation. He also succeeded in establishing the House Ways and Means Committee as Congress's permanent watchdog over treasury affairs.

Since he was one of the few Republicans who understood the intricacies of national finance, it was inevitable that Gallatin would become Jefferson's secretary of the treasury. He would serve in that office for almost thirteen years, until well into Madison's second term.

As secretary, Gallatin's first priority was debt reduction. His second, related to the first, was reduction of taxes. This in turn required cutting the budget drastically, especially the outlays for the army and the navy. Finally, he believed that Congress must be more careful in overseeing the finances of the country than it had been under the Federalists. All told, it was a good Jeffersonian program of frugality, simplicity, and limits on the operations and ambitions of government.

Yet Gallatin was also a man of vision. He did not oppose the Louisiana Purchase, though paying Napoleon's price required going many millions of dollars further into debt. Unlike his chief, Gallatin was not an inveterate enemy of the Bank of the United States. When the president demanded that the treasury transfer a large part of its deposits to various state banks, Gallatin resisted. Also at odds with the president was his support of "inter-

nal improvements" legislation to tie the country together with a network of roads and canals. In 1808 he issued a report laying out a grand design, estimated to cost $10 million, that would rectify all the deficiencies of nature's own plan for connecting the various parts of the Union. Congress, dominated by more conventional Jeffersonians, refused to fund this proposal. Not until the War of 1812 had demonstrated the dangers of a fragmented nation did party leaders reconsider their position.

Gallatin was skeptical of the War Hawks' zeal for war in 1811 and 1812, especially after the votes of many of these same men helped defeat a bill to recharter the Bank of the United States. Without the bank to help, the treasury would have trouble raising money for the government during the war. Fortunately for the secretary, he would not have to face all the difficulties of financing the war, for in May 1813 he left the treasury and went to Europe as American peace envoy. Eventually he helped negotiate the Treaty of Ghent, bringing peace between Britain and America.

Gallatin was never again active in American domestic politics. From 1816 to 1823 he served as American envoy to France. When he returned to the United States, he was disappointed at the low level of its politics. He soon went off to England as American envoy, but returned again after a single year.

In 1830 Gallatin moved his family to New York, where he accepted the offer of tycoon John

Jacob Astor to become president of a bank. The move to the country's commercial metropolis enabled Gallatin to help his two sons establish themselves financially and allowed him to be close to his married daughter, Frances, and his seven grandchildren. Gallatin continued to be active in public affairs, however. In 1830 he was approached by a group of New York business and civic leaders to lend his name and influence to establishing a modern university in the city. Gallatin joined the enterprise as a strong advocate of a new, more commercially and scientifically oriented institution of higher education. His help proved vital to the formation of what would later become New York University.

During his last years the alert old gentleman took an active interest in the city's intellectual life. He served as president of the New York Historical Society and helped found the discipline of "ethnology," the forerunner of modern anthropology. He also continued to pronounce on financial and political questions. When sectional issues came to the fore during the 1840s, he endorsed excluding slavery from the newly acquired regions in the West. In May 1849 Gallatin's wife of fifty-five years died. Six months later, at the age of eighty-eight, Gallatin himself died quietly at his daughter's summer house on Long Island.

Though a creator of one of the two great "persuasions" that have dominated American political life, Albert Gallatin was a voice for moderation and reason, a man who could see the best in the other side.

---

een. Not yet fully outfitted for combat, the *Chesapeake* was able to fire back only a token shot before it surrendered. A British search crew then boarded the vessel, lined up its crew, and removed Ratford and three other deserters.

The attack on the *Chesapeake* outraged Americans. Never before had the British so blatantly violated American sovereignty. Indignation swept the country, and protesters organized mass meetings in dozens of cities to condemn British highhandedness. In Virginia the governor called

out the militia to keep supplies from reaching the royal naval squadron cruising off the coast. The British consul in New York had to be given police protection, and a mob attacked and almost demolished a British vessel at its pier in the harbor. Many Americans expected war or hoped for it. The Washington *Federalist* declared:

> We have never . . . witnessed the spirit of the people excited to so great a degree of indignation, or such a thirst for revenge, as on hearing of the late unexampled outrage on the *Chesa-*

peake. All parties, ranks, and professions were unanimous in their detestation of the dastardly deed, and all cried aloud for vengeance. . . . The Administration may implicitly rely on the cordial support of every American citizen, in whatever manly and dignified steps that they may take, to . . . obtain reparation for the injury.

The Embargo. Jefferson could easily have brought a united nation into war at this point, but he chose instead to dampen the public outcry. The president issued a proclamation closing American waters to the Royal Navy and then, rather than initiate hostile actions, sent an emissary to negotiate with the British. Unfortunately the American representative accomplished little. Not until 1811 did the British make acceptable reparation for the *Chesapeake-Leopard* affair. Meanwhile, the clamor abated and war enthusiasm cooled.

Jefferson had mixed motives for taking a moderate course in the *Chesapeake* affair. War, he thought, was not necessary to solve the impressment problem. The president also realized American military weakness. Jefferson and the Republicans were themselves responsible for this impotence. Ever since the undeclared naval war with France in 1798–1800—which many Republicans believed a pro-British, Federalist scheme—they had considered standing armies and a strong navy "dangerous to liberty" and conducive to "the spirit which leads to war." Militarism was Federalist, not Republican, for it went along with Feder-

alist faith in centralized political power. Jefferson was not indifferent to American defense, but he thought it could be provided largely by the citizen militia and by small, lightly armed coastal vessels using oars and sails. Under this system the country would be spared a large and expensive military establishment.

Jefferson was also moved by other considerations. The United States had a better weapon against British and French highhandedness than an army and navy: the power to withhold its goods from the warring nations and close American markets to their exports. Americans had practiced such economic warfare effectively against Britain during the great imperial crisis before independence. Now, in December 1807, the president activated the first Nonimportation Act and soon asked Congress to place an embargo on all exports from the United States. Congress responded with the 1807 Embargo Act, which forbade American vessels to sail to foreign ports without special permission and forbade foreign vessels to carry off American goods. American ships could continue to engage in the coastal trade between domestic ports, but the owners of such vessels had to post bonds twice the value of the ships and their cargoes to guarantee that they would not violate the embargo. The law did not explicitly prohibit imports in foreign ships; but if foreign ship owners could not carry American cargo on their return trips, they had little incentive to trade with the United States. In effect, Congress had sealed off

Courtesy Thomas Jefferson Memorial Foundation

This Federalist cartoon shows public discontent with Jefferson's Embargo of 1807. Not only were farmers and merchants angered by the closing of America's ports, but Jefferson's fellow Republicans worried about the act's legality and feared the federal government's growing power.

the country from foreign trade on the theory that Europe needed America more than America needed Europe.

Theory was one thing; reality was another. The law was impossible to enforce. Some governors took advantage of its loopholes to peddle exemptions to merchants for cash or political support. Merchants, too, found ways to get around the law. Many risked the loss of their bond by directing their ships to sail for Europe or the Caribbean after they were out of sight of land. Others conducted illegal commerce with British Canada across the Great Lakes. Defiance was greatest in New England, where Jefferson was denounced as a tyrant executing an unconstitutional law. The embargo was also unpopular in the middle states, where the merchants of New York and Philadelphia suffered under it as much as their New England counterparts.

For a while, wholesale evasion made the law tolerable. But the Giles Enforcement Act of 1809 closed the loopholes, and trade virtually ceased. Farmers—especially those who sold grain, cotton, and tobacco for European markets—saw the prices of their crops plunge dramatically. Even more seriously hurt were the traders of the port towns and all who depended on them. New York in 1809, one contemporary reported, "looked like a town ravaged by pestilence." The city's waterfront streets were deserted, its ships dismantled, and its countinghouses closed and boarded up. Boston and seaboard New England were hardest hit of all, with thousands of seamen, dock laborers, sail makers, and rope makers idle. One Yankee expressed the region's suffering in verse:

> *Our ships all in motion once whitened the ocean,*
> *They sailed and returned with a cargo;*
> *Now doomed to decay, they have fallen a prey*
> *To Jefferson—worms—and embargo.*

And to top it all, the law failed to achieve its ends. It hurt some British manufacturers, but it was English wage earners and Caribbean planters and slaves who suffered the most, and none of these groups carried much political weight in Parliament. Even when the embargo finally began to pinch important commercial interests in Britain, sheer stubbornness kept the British government from yielding to American pressure.

For a year and a half the administration sought to enforce its policy, using militia and regulars to halt the overland trade with Canada and the navy to stop violations by sea. Driven by frustration, the president, a great defender of liberty while in the opposition, proposed to declare whole communities in rebellion and subject to prosecution for treason. At one point he told a Republican congressman that in times of emergency "the universal recourse is a dictator."

Popular opposition to the infamous embargo soon reached a crescendo. Town meetings throughout New England condemned the administration, and the Massachusetts and Connecticut legislatures proposed what amounted to nullification of the Embargo Act. Even Republicans in the shipping states pleaded that the policy be abandoned. In Congress the Federalists and a group of rebellious Republicans called the Quids, led by John Randolph, fought to have the embargo policy changed. Faced by this overwhelming pressure and the obvious failure of its policy to change British and French behavior, the administration finally yielded. In March 1809, as one of his last official acts, Jefferson signed the Nonintercourse Act, repealing the embargo and reopening foreign trade except with Britain and France, but allowing the president to restore trade with either country, or both, if they ceased violating American rights.

Madison Takes the Helm. Soon after, Jefferson left Washington for Monticello. Never again would he serve in high political office. The remainder of his long life was devoted to creating a university in his home state, completing his mansion near Charlottesville, playing his violin, and generally cultivating the arts and sciences.

Jefferson was not proud of his presidency, but he underestimated it. True, he had not solved the nation's major international problems; nor had he brought the country the prosperity he had sought. Nevertheless, he had successfully guided the United States through a major transition from the rule of one party to the rule of another; had doubled the size of the country; and had brought a new, more democratic tone to the nation's political culture. These were accomplishments that few presidents would match.

His successor, James Madison, was a man in the Jeffersonian mold. Cofounder of the Republican party, Jefferson's secretary of state, and one of the chief architects of the Constitution, Madison had earned the right to be his party's choice. His nomination was contested by the Quids, but Madison was the clear choice of the Republican congressional caucus and went on to defeat Federalist Charles Cotesworth Pinckney in the 1808 election.

Historians have generally considered Madison's presidency a failure. Although a profound student of government, an effective legislative leader, and a charming conversationalist, Madison

Library of Congress

Library of Congress

"A withered little applejohn" is what Washington Irving called James Madison. He looked even less like a head of state than his loose-jointed, informal predecessor. However, both he and his wife Dolley were highly cultivated and intelligent; Dolley was one of the liveliest and most charming first ladies in the nation's history.

lacked executive ability. In peace and war he would prove irresolute; and when he did bring himself to act, he would often do the wrong thing.

Madison's first blunder came in the second month of his presidency, when he arranged with David M. Erskine, the British minister in Washington, to suspend the Nonintercourse Act in exchange for British withdrawal of the 1807 orders in council. Erskine, however, had exceeded his instructions, and the British foreign secretary in London repudiated the agreement when he heard of it. Madison, now believed by many to be the dupe of the British, felt compelled to restore the prohibition on British-American trade.

The Nonintercourse Act having put too great an economic strain on the country, Congress in 1810 replaced it with Macon's Bill Number Two. This was a curious measure. The United States, the bill stated, would immediately reopen commerce with both Britain and France. If either country, however, should cease to violate American commercial rights, the president could then reimpose trade prohibitions on the other, after a three-month wait to give the slower-acting power a chance to rescind its trade restrictions. In effect, as an inducement to cease attacks on American trade, the United States promised to support against its enemy the first nation to act.

This tricky law was too clever by half. The wily Bonaparte saw that he might trap America into becoming his unwitting ally against England. The Duc de Cadore, the French foreign minister, quickly informed the American minister in Paris that the Berlin and Milan decrees had been revoked. Napoleon, however, did not intend to alter his policy toward American traders; in fact, on the

very day Cadore told the American ambassador of the supposed French change of heart, Napoleon signed the Decree of Trianon, which ordered the confiscation and sale of all American vessels that had called at French ports after May 20, 1809. Friends warned Madison that Napoleon was probably shamming, but the optimistic president swallowed the bait. On November 2 he announced that trade restrictions against Great Britain would be reimposed early in 1811. Without surrendering a thing, Napoleon had gotten the United States to punish France's archenemy.

Further Western Troubles. The British were understandably irked by Madison's actions, and Anglo-American tensions were further aggravated by events in the West. Though the British had finally removed their troops from the Northwest, western settlers and their spokesmen remained convinced that England was stirring up troubles with the Indians. In fact, the British were innocent of wrongdoing. They wanted to keep the western tribes friendly and, if possible, detach them from allegiance to the Americans, but they had not incited them to attack American settlers. Yet Americans were certain that British agents were behind the disorders. The continued presence of British-Canadian fur traders in the Northwest, as allowed under the Jay Treaty, created further antagonisms and suspicion of British intrigue.

Actually, Americans themselves were responsible for the Indian troubles. At the behest of land speculators, frontier officials, many of them Jefferson's appointees, had for years extracted vast tracts of land from the native Americans, giving them little in return. In 1802 Governor William

Henry Harrison of the Indiana Territory had called the Kickapoo, Wea, and Delaware tribes together and demanded that they cede to the United States several million acres in what is now southern Indiana. When the chiefs refused, he threatened to use force. The Indian leaders backed down. The resulting Treaty of Vincennes became the evil precedent for a rash of coerced agreements that compelled the northwestern and southwestern tribes to surrender millions of acres of choice lands for a few thousand dollars and a few baubles.

Harrison's provocative actions notwithstanding, by 1810–11 settlers throughout the West were certain that "British gold" was being used to encourage Indian militancy. Many of the fears and complaints centered on the activities of the Shawnee chief Tecumseh and his brother, "the Prophet." These two remarkable men recognized that Harrison's success at land grabbing depended to a large extent on the disunity of the Indian tribes. To defeat Harrison and his kind, they proposed establishment of a tribal confederation that would present a united front to white officials. But their ultimate goals were far more ambitious. Tecumseh proposed nothing less than the old dream of Pontiac: to expel the whites and free the Mississippi Valley for the Indians. The white men, the Shawnee chief told his people, must be driven "back whence they came, upon a trail of blood, they must be driven." Despite such threats, Tecumseh urged his followers to exercise restraint as long as Harrison did not try to take possession of the Indian lands that the Americans had inveigled.

The Shawnee chief had not counted on Harrison goading some of the younger Indian hotheads into an attack that would be used as an excuse to destroy their forces. In August 1811 the general marched to Prophetstown on the Wabash with a force of seasoned troops. As he hoped, the Indians led by the Prophet attacked, and they almost overwhelmed the Americans. Harrison's troops held, however; and when the American cavalry charged, the Indians broke and fled.

Though the Battle of Tippecanoe was hailed as a white victory and would help make Harrison's reputation as an Indian fighter, actually it could be regarded as a defeat. The vanquished Indian warriors abandoned their capital and scattered throughout the West. Wherever they went, they carried their hatred of the whites and their pan-Indian vision. Before long the whole West, north as well as south, was in flames.

Westerners had other grievances against the British. They were responsible for the hard times

Courtesy Field Museum of Natural History, Chicago

This determined man is Tecumseh, the great Shawnee leader. He tried to stop white encroachment on Indian land by welding all Indians into a defensive confederation. When this union failed, he joined the British and died fighting the Americans.

that followed the orders in council. British policies, it was said, had cut off the European market for western grain and created an unsold surplus. Prices had dropped, causing distress to many western farmers. Though the American embargo had only made matters worse, westerners hoped it would eventually force Britain to back down, and western representatives in Congress were among the law's staunchest supporters.

Western attitudes would have been an important element in the decision to go to war in any case. But western views were given added weight by the skillful maneuvering of the War Hawks— some forty western and southern representatives elected to the Twelfth Congress that met in 1811. Led by Henry Clay, they included such notable men as John C. Calhoun, William Lowndes, and Langdon Cheves of South Carolina; Felix Grundy of Tennessee; Richard M. Johnson of Kentucky; and Peter Porter of western New York. Marked off from other members of the Twelfth Congress by their aggressive nationalism and their resolve to shake the nation loose from subservience to Great Britain come what may, the War Hawks succeeded in electing Clay speaker of the House and packing the important foreign relations and naval committees with their members. Thereafter every move to condemn Britain or to appropriate money for the army and navy received their enthusiastic support.

Congress Votes for War. No single dramatic event pushed the country finally into war. All through 1811 relations with Britain deteriorated. The British government did not take kindly to Madison's proclamation reimposing the embargo on Anglo-American trade. British cruisers were soon gathering in increasing numbers off the Atlantic coast, stopping more American vessels than ever and removing suspected British deserters in droves. Once more, impressment set off a major naval incident. In May Commodore John Rodgers, commanding the frigate *President,* stumbled on the British corvette *Little Belt* off Virginia. Rodgers chased the British vessel, overtook it, and attacked, inflicting severe damage. The *President* did not sink the smaller British ship, but most Americans felt satisfied that the disgrace of the *Chesapeake* defeat had finally been avenged.

Matters swiftly came to a head. In April 1812 Congress gave President Madison power to call up the state militias for six months service. On the same day British Foreign Secretary Lord Castlereagh rejected the American demand that the 1807 orders in council be withdrawn. But the British economy was now beginning to feel the pinch of the embargo, and continued pressure would probably have forced the British to back down if fate had not unexpectedly intervened. On May 11, 1812, a madman shot Prime Minister Spencer Perceval, throwing the British government into turmoil. By the time it began to function again, Castlereagh was ready to suspend the orders in council. But his announcement, like other European news, took weeks to reach America and arrived too late to affect events. Two days after Castlereagh's concession to the United States, Congress declared war on England.

Who Wanted War. The declaration of war against Britain on June 18 was not unanimous. Of 128 representatives voting, 49 voted no. In the Senate 13 out of 32 members refused to support the war declaration. Historians have tried to determine the motives for war by analyzing the war declaration vote, but the picture remains murky. Representatives of coastal New England clearly opposed war, but those from interior New England favored it. New York, too, opposed the war, but Pennsylvania, including the port of Philadelphia, voted to fight. The South, especially the Carolinas and Georgia, was almost solidly in support of the war, as was the West beyond the Appalachians.

More important perhaps than whether a congressman lived in the North, the South, or the West was whether his constituents exported farm products—in which case he tended to support the war—or engaged in ocean commerce—in which case he was likely to vote against it. In other words, pocketbook considerations seem to have been more crucial than geography in determining the way individual representatives voted. Sectional factors in this view seem significant mostly because many westerners and southerners were certain that their prosperity depended on teaching the British that they must not interfere with American export trade, whereas many New Englanders feared that war with Great Britain would lead to the complete destruction of American commerce by the British navy.

Perhaps the most workable analysis, however, connects the war vote to politics and party. Generally speaking, John Randolph's dissenting Quid Republicans and the Federalists voted against the war; and administration Republicans, including, of course, the War Hawks, favored it. Professor Bradford Perkins estimates that fully 90 percent "of the real, available Republican membership [of the House of Representatives] backed the bill" to declare war. It is true that some administration Republicans had misgivings. Indeed, the president himself was not eager to fight. But the strong anti-British stand of the party ever since the 1790s, and particularly since Jefferson's embargo, committed them to taking this step.

If we look behind the war vote in Congress, we can identify something more fundamental than economic interest and party, however. The War of 1812 was the result of an upsurge of nationalism among Americans. By 1812 many citizens were determined to avenge the humiliation the United States had suffered at British hands for almost a generation. Though their country had won its formal independence in 1783, it still seemed to be under Britain's thumb. Impressment, orders in council, incitement of Indians, confiscation of American ships—all contributed to the anger and hurt pride that these Americans felt. Many Federalists and New Englanders might have preferred to ignore the incidents, believing it better to suffer these ills for the sake of profit and safety. Some westerners, as John Randolph charged, might have supported the war out of lust for the conquest of Canada to add to western wealth. But for a majority of the American people, the prospect of continued submission to haughty Britain seemed ample reason for military resistance.

THE WAR OF 1812

The eminent amateur historian Harry Truman would call the War of 1812 "the silliest damn war we ever had." On the whole he was right; the war was badly bungled. Yet we must remember that Commander in Chief Madison had a difficult task before him. Owing at least in part to Republican hostility to peacetime armies, American military and naval forces were puny at the outbreak of hostilities. Congress had provided for a 35,000-man regular army in January 1812, but at the beginning of June it consisted of only 6,700 officers and men. Worse, the troops were not stationed close to Canada, the most accessible part of the British Empire, but were scattered all over the country. Although he was authorized to recruit 100,000 militia into federal service, the president was effectively deprived of the best-trained state troops by New England's virtual neutrality during the war. Facing the motley American army would be an uncertain number of equally nondescript Canadian militia plus 7,000 British and Canadian regulars. Many of the British regular troops had fought the French in Europe, and behind them—once Napoleon was defeated—was potential reinforcement by many thousands of tough veterans of the Duke of Wellington's Spanish campaign.

The Americans were even worse off on the high seas. In June 1812 the American navy consisted of sixteen regular vessels, only seven of which were substantial seaworthy frigates, and over a hundred almost worthless gunboats. By contrast, Britain had over two hundred frigates and ships of the line—most with twice the firepower of the largest American vessels. Americans could and would add to their navy, and they would send out scores of privateers against British ocean commerce. The American naval effort during the war, nevertheless, would resemble a scrappy minnow nipping at the tail of a shark.

In financial matters, too, the United States was handicapped. In 1811 Congress had defeated by a close vote an attempt to recharter the Bank of the United States. The bank, as Hamilton had predicted, had helped the government manage its financial operations and had provided businessmen with much-needed credit and capital. Although hostile at first, Gallatin and other Republicans eventually came to favor it. But the bank had not converted all its opponents, and it had made new enemies among some business groups. These forces had defeated it. Now, without a central bank to make loans to meet the government's extraordinary wartime needs, the treasury found itself in difficulties. The situation was made worse by New England's reluctance to lend to the treasury from its large reserves of available capital.

Still another problem the president faced was poor communications. Although transportation up and down the Atlantic coast by ship was relatively swift and easy, communication with the interior, especially across the mountains, was slow and difficult. Roads were few throughout the na-

Northern campaigns, 1812–1814

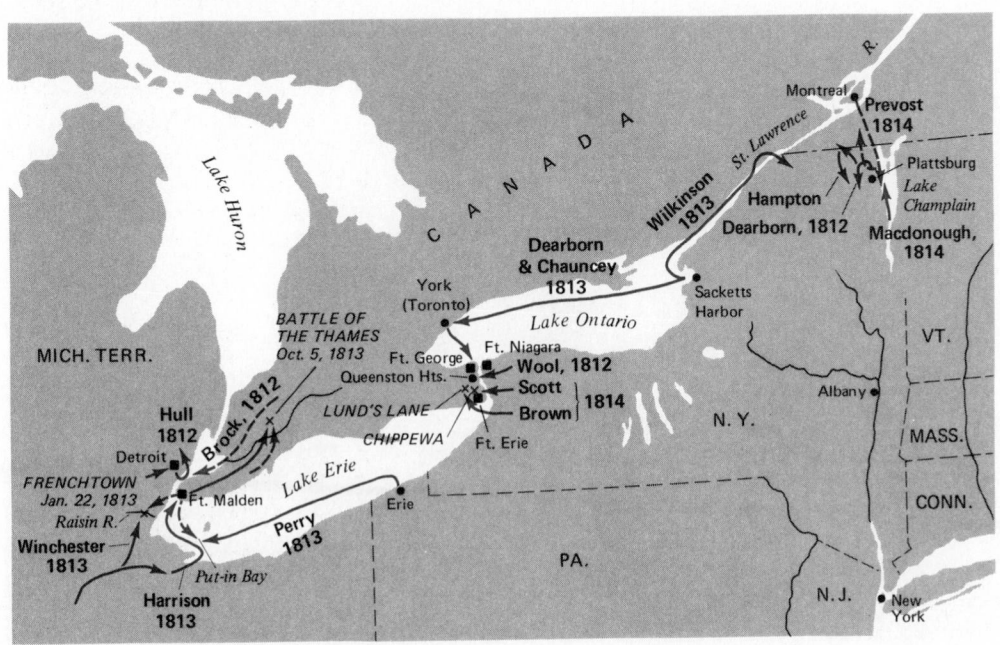

tion; those crossing the Appalachians were no more than Indian trails. The Great Lakes were potentially useful, but nowhere on American territory were they connected by water to the country's major population centers. Bad communications imposed serious handicaps on military commanders, who were forced to move supplies and men along crude trails hacked out of the forest.

The Hartford Convention. New England's financial tight-fistedness suggests some of the political difficulties in Madison's way. Almost the whole area north and east of the Hudson sat out the war. Many Yankees regarded Great Britain, not as America's enemy, but as the world's last hope against the tyrant Napoleon, and they condemned Madison for having made the United States Bonaparte's ally. Antiwar sentiment was especially strong in the Connecticut River Valley. In 1814, after seeing their commerce virtually swept off the seas by the British navy, antiwar Yankees forced the calling of a convention at Hartford, Connecti-

cut. There they intended to discuss how to deal with the war and to consider whether the discontented states should secede from the Union. Fortunately the extremists at Hartford were outmaneuvered by the moderates, and the convention took no action beyond endorsing state nullification of federal acts and proposing constitutional amendments limiting the power of the president and Congress over foreign relations. New England disaffection stopped short of outright disloyalty, yet the hostility to the war in the Northeast would be a dead weight around Madison's neck.

The Early Years of the War. After we acknowledge all of these difficulties, however, Madison still must bear much of the blame for the failures of the American war effort. As commander in chief, he appointed the generals, and his first choices were abysmal. Major General William Hull was sent to attack the British in Upper Canada (Ontario), but was forced to surrender to the British commander, Isaac Brock, near Detroit.

The battle of the U.S.S. Constitution *and H.M.S.* Guerrière *as depicted in a contemporary painting. Single encounters like this one were among the few naval victories the United States could claim in the War of 1812. They scarcely affected the outcome of the war, but they did help to keep American spirits high.*

New Haven Colony Historical Society

William Henry Harrison, ordered to retake Detroit, gave up much of the Northwest to the British and their Indian allies. An American invasion of the Niagara peninsula under Generals Stephen Van Rensselaer and Alexander Smyth was turned into a tragic farce by the incompetence and cowardice of the New York militia. When ordered to cross into Canada to fight the enemy, they refused on the grounds that they had no obligation to fight outside their state, and stood idly by watching the regulars across the Niagara River being slaughtered by Brock's troops. Only the famous victories of the frigates *Constitution* and *United States* in single-ship combat with the *Guerrière* and *Macedonian* kept up American spirits in the first year of war.

Despite the disasters in the field, Madison was reelected for a second term in 1812 over De Witt Clinton of New York, the Federalist candidate. During the election a group of younger Federalists tried to make their party and candidates more popular by adopting such Republican tactics as canvassing from door to door, treating the voters to food and drink, and putting on spectacular political rallies. They increased their party's vote in some areas; but despite Madison's spotty war record, they could not push their candidate to victory. The president's 128 electoral votes represented the prowar sections, largely in the South and West; Clinton's 89 represented the antiwar regions of New England, with New York, New Jersey, and part of Maryland thrown in.

The second year of the war went only a little better than the first. Under Harrison's overall command American troops continued to battle in the Northwest. In January Harrison's subordinates were defeated in a series of battles south of the Great Lakes. Since the British seemed likely to be successful so long as they could move freely on Lake Erie, the government ordered Captain Oliver Hazard Perry to build a small navy on the south shore of the lake. On September 1 Perry's fleet met a somewhat smaller flotilla under Captain Robert Barclay. In a fierce exchange Perry sank or captured the entire British force. "We have met the enemy and they are ours," read Perry's succinct dispatch to Harrison.

With Lake Erie under American control, Harrison moved against the British in Upper Canada. In the Battle of the Thames in early October he and his Kentucky militia encountered a small force of British regulars, Canadian militia, and some 1,500 Indians, these last led by Tecumseh. The shock of the first volley scattered the British and Canadians. The Indians held out longer, but they, too, soon turned and ran. Tecumseh was pre-

sumed dead, though his body was never found. This defeat led to the collapse of the Shawnee chief's confederation and the desertion of many tribes from the British cause.

The year 1813 also saw the outbreak of Indian troubles in the Southwest. The Creek War brought on the grim ambushes, scalpings, and indiscriminate murder of women and children invariably perpetrated by both sides in Indian-white wars. In August a Creek force of 1,000 killed 250 white settlers jammed for safety into Fort Mims in southern Alabama. Later that year the Tennessee militia avenged the deed by slaughtering 186 Indians near Jacksonville, Alabama.

The fighting during the Indian war marked the rise to prominence of Andrew Jackson, a Tennessee planter-politician who commanded the government's forces as major general of the state militia. Early in 1814 Jackson marched on the Creeks in what is now Alabama. At Horseshoe Bend he attacked and overran the Indians, massacring 800. This blow smashed the power of the southwestern tribes. The surviving Creeks were forced to sign a peace treaty at Fort Jackson surrendering a giant slice of territory in southern Georgia and central Alabama. For his services Jackson was made a major general in the regular army.

The Last Campaigns. Meanwhile, in Europe Napoleon had finally been defeated by a coalition of

Southwest campaigns, 1813–1815

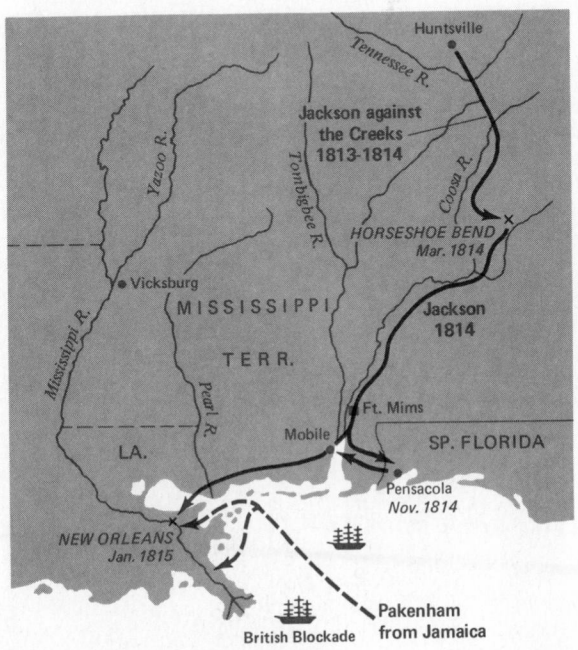

Gulf of Mexico

British, Austrians, Russians, and Prussians at the Battle of Leipzig, and in April 1814 he was sent into exile on the Mediterranean island of Elba. Bonaparte's surrender ended all hope of securing Lake Champlain. With the Americans in control of the lake, Prevost hurriedly retreated, leaving behind mountains of supplies and hundreds of deserters.

The second prong of the British knockout campaign, aimed at Chesapeake Bay, proved more successful. In June the British navy transported 4,000 troops directly from France to the Patuxent River. From there they advanced on the national capital. At Bladensburg, Maryland, a hastily gathered force of militia, sailors, and a few regulars tried to stop them. The British veterans routed the motley American army and then marched into Washington unopposed. Shortly before, Congress and the president had fled the city, leaving behind the spirited first lady, Dolley Madison, to save Gilbert Stuart's portrait of Washington. Mrs. Madison rescued the portrait, but other national treasures did not escape destruction. The British burned the Capitol, the presidential mansion, and all the city's public buildings except the Patent Office.

The redcoats now turned north to Baltimore, the country's third-largest city. Here they were checked. Fort McHenry and the fortifications quickly thrown up around the city were manned by thousands of militia, sailors, and some regulars. The British fleet bombarded the fort for two days, but it held out. To commemorate the heroic defense, Francis Scott Key wrote the "Star-Spangled Banner" to the tune of an old British drinking song. It is appropriate that the only serious literary work evoked by this mismanaged war is associated with befuddlement.

The third prong of the British campaign was an attack on New Orleans. In late November a British army of 7,500 under Sir Edward Pakenham left the island of Jamaica and landed at Lake Borgne, forty miles from New Orleans. Andrew Jackson sped south from Baton Rouge and engaged the enemy in skirmishes east of the city that slowed the British advance. On New Year's Day Jackson's skilled artillerymen severely punished the British troops, compelling Pakenham to wait for reinforcements.

On January 8, 1815, the British resumed their advance against Jackson's force of U.S. regulars, Kentucky and Tennessee riflemen, and New Orleans and Louisiana militiamen composed of Bayou pirates, free blacks, and young bluebloods from New Orleans. In a dense morning fog the British regulars moved forward against the Americans, who were lined up behind a low wall. Before the red-clad troops had gone very far, the fog began to lift, and at 500 yards the American artillery opened fire with devastating effect. Still the disciplined redcoats trudged on. When the British came within rifle range, Jackson ordered some of the big guns to cease their fire so that their smoke would not obscure the riflemen's targets. He then ordered the troops to blaze away.

New York Public Library Picture Collection

An unusually high American command allowed the British to capture Bladensburg and march on the capital unopposed. In retaliation for the destruction of Toronto, the British burned Washington's government buildings, including the "Yankee Palace."

The combination of rifle and artillery fire was too much for even experienced troops to bear. In less than an hour one-third of the British force was cut down, and three of the highest-ranking British officers, including Pakenham, were dead. Another third of Pakenham's original force was in complete disarray. Faced with the reality of defeat, General John Lambert ordered retreat. On January 27 the surviving British troops sailed for home.

The Peace of Ghent. The Battle of New Orleans, which cost the British over 2,000 lives, would never have taken place if transatlantic communications had been swifter in these years. On December 24 British and American negotiators had concluded a peace at Ghent in what is now Belgium. The peace treaty signed before Jackson's stunning victory was an ambiguous and tentative document that brought the United States few gains. It said nothing about impressment, ignored the neutral rights and Indian issues that had bedeviled British-American relations for years, and left the Canadian-American boundary where it had been before the war. Thus none of the goals that had prompted Americans to action were realized by the treaty.

The treaty did not satisfy the British either. For them the war had begun as a defensive one, but their early military successes had led Englishmen to hope for territorial concessions from the Americans and perhaps an Indian buffer state between the United States and Canada. War weariness and fear that fighting might shortly resume in Europe led the British to abandon these goals at Ghent.

Little was accomplished by the treaty, except for the restoration of peace. It provided for a commission to settle the disputed boundary with Canada in the far northeast and mentioned future settlement of differences over navigation of the Great Lakes and the Newfoundland fisheries. In 1817, to implement the agreement at Ghent, Britain and the United States signed the Rush-Bagot Agreement by which both nations accepted almost total disarmament along the Canadian-American border. Applied at first solely to the Great Lakes region, it eventually converted the whole of the Canadian-American boundary into the longest unarmed frontier in the world.

Yet the fact remains that the document ending the war was less significant than the victory at New Orleans. Weeks after the Ghent negotiations had ended, the British government ordered reinforcements to Pakenham—a move that suggests that if their army had defeated Jackson, they would have refused to confirm the treaty. Great Britain had never recognized the legality of the Louisiana Purchase, and it is likely that if Pakenham had taken new Orleans, Britain would have carved out a sphere of influence along the lower Mississippi. Jackson's triumph ended the possibility of a new British Empire at the expense of the United States.

More important, however, were the profound psychological results of Jackson's victory. New Orleans left Americans with a sense that they had defeated British tyranny a second time. It created a new national hero in the person of testy, rough-hewn Andy Jackson, and a proud new national mythology. Unspoiled, sturdy, and independent American frontiersmen, so the myth went, had taken on Europe's best and defeated them decisively. Jackson's triumph produced a surge of patriotism that all but obliterated the disunity that had afflicted the country at the beginning of the war. However it had begun, by its glorious ending the war reaffirmed American self-respect and pride. "The war," Gallatin would write a colleague, "has renewed and reinstated the national feelings and character which the Revolution had given, and which were daily lessened. The people have now more general objects of attachment. . . . They are more American; they feel and act more as a nation."

Gallatin's view is amply confirmed by the facts. President Madison's 1815 message to Congress expressed the new spirit that had captured the nation: even the party of states' rights must now devote its energies to forging closer national bonds and stronger national institutions. Republicans had learned their lesson. The country had been severely handicapped by poor communications and the absence of a central bank. Perhaps Hamilton and his friends had been right after all. Why not give their ideas a try at least?

Ironically, although the war made the Republicans into nationalists, it destroyed the party that formerly had had a virtual copyright on the nationalist label. If the war had ended on a sour note, the Federalists might have come out of it with enhanced prestige. As it was, New Orleans made the party of Washington and Hamilton seem unpatriotic and treasonous. After 1815 the Federalists would never again be a serious threat to the Republicans on the national level.

CONCLUSIONS

Between the 1800 presidential campaign and Madison's seventh annual message to Congress,

American attitudes had taken a 180-degree turn. Jefferson's election had been a repudiation of Federalist excesses and a mandate for the party that represented local as opposed to national power. The public had exaggerated Jefferson's differences from his opponents. Nevertheless, the Republican victory of 1800 represented an endorsement of a less activist national government and a repudiation of the strong centralizing bent of the Federalists.

The American people could not have foreseen that they and their leaders would do an about-face. Events would overtake everyone's theories. In the decade and a half that followed Jefferson's inauguration, the growing confrontation with France and England required an ever more active and effective central authority. The clash also created a new sense of national priorities, especially among southerners and westerners, whose agricultural interests, as opposed to the commercial interests of New Englanders, did not conflict with a strong stand against the country's foreign enemies. The war itself made clear to many former opponents of Federalist "follies" that to function, the country must accept much that Hamilton and his allies had proposed. Finally, with the splendid climax at New Orleans, the country experienced a new sense of unity and a self-confidence that would last until new issues once again reactivated the divisive forces of localism.

New Orleans and the Treaty of Ghent closed one chapter of American history. For fifty years the United States had been embroiled in Europe's remote affairs. Now, with Napoleon gone, Europe settled down to a long period of relative international calm. For almost a century the United States would be spared the clash of empires that had unsettled it for so long. And with peace, Americans could go about the business of exploiting their bounteous human and natural resources and converting them into tangible wealth.

FOR FURTHER READING

Merrill Peterson. *Thomas Jefferson and the New Nation: A Biography* (1970)
    Peterson relates Jefferson's private life and his thought to his public role, and is lucid on the political issues of the day. A fine fusion of biography and history.

Fawn Brodie. *Thomas Jefferson: An Intimate History* (1973)
    Here is a fascinating portrait of Jefferson the man—husband, father, slaveowner, and friend—as well as the political leader and so-

cial philosopher. Though criticized by some scholars for suggesting an intimate relationship between Jefferson and his female slave, Sally Hemmings, this work is a superior psychobiography of our third president.

Forrest McDonald. *The Presidency of Thomas Jefferson* (1976)
    This brief, well-written volume is like several other works by McDonald: it has a strong point of view that not every scholar can accept. Well worth reading, however.

Bernard De Voto, editor. *Journals of Lewis and Clark* (1953)
    The chronicle of a great adventure: the twenty-eight-month-long search for an overland route to the Pacific. De Voto's long introduction establishes the historical context of the explorers' expedition.

Leonard Levy. *Thomas Jefferson and Civil Liberties: The Darker Side* (1963)
    This is a revisionist study of the Jefferson presidency that depicts the third president as a man who often violated his own precepts in matters of civil liberties. A necessary antidote to the many Jefferson eulogies, yet Levy probably goes too far in seeking to redress the balance.

Bernard Sheehan. *Seeds of Extinction: Jeffersonian Philanthropy and the American Indian* (1973)
    Sheehan describes how the Indian reformers of Jefferson's day, hoping to lead the tribes from "savagery" to "civilization," only managed to drive them brutally into the interior, thereby making way for white speculators and settlers.

Bernard Mayo. *Henry Clay: Spokesman of the New West* (1937)
    Mayo tells the story of Clay's life to 1812, when he was the thirty-five-year-old speaker of the House of Representatives and leader of the War Hawks. He writes well about Clay's social background and political career.

Bradford Perkins. *Prologue to War: England and the United States, 1805–1812* (1961)
    Perkins ascribes the drift of Britain and America toward war to the unyielding and condescending attitude of the English on the one hand and to American insistence on neutral trade in a world beset by war on the other. He emphasizes the maritime factors behind the war more than the others that have been suggested in this chapter.

Julius Pratt. *Expansionists of 1812* (1925)
    Emphasizes how American interest in acquiring Canada, Florida, and possibly Mexico influenced the decision for war in 1812. Not all scholars agree.

Gore Vidal. *Burr* (1973)
    A historical novel about Aaron Burr in the form of a memoir. Vidal is very much biased toward Burr, and Washington, Jefferson, and Hamilton all emerge as narrow-minded, comical wheeler-dealers with much weaker characters than Burr himself. Good fun, if not too reliable.

9 The American Economic Miracle

What Made It Possible?

1793   Eli Whitney invents the cotton gin

1794   The Philadelphia-Lancaster Turnpike opens

1802   West Point established

1803   The Louisiana Purchase

1807   Robert Fulton's steamboat *Clermont* makes a round trip between Albany and New York

1811   The federal government begins work on the National Road at Cumberland, Maryland • Fulton-Livingston interests awarded an exclusive charter from the Louisiana territorial legislature to operate steamboats on the Mississippi

1815   Entrepreneur Francis Cabot Lowell's Boston Manufacturing Company produces cotton cloth on a new power loom

1816   The Second Bank of the United States chartered

1817   New York's legislature approves funds for the Erie Canal

1818   The National Road reaches the Ohio River

1819   Financial panic and economic depression

1825   Completion of the Erie Canal: shipping rates between Buffalo and New York fall more than 75 percent • Rensselaer Polytechnic Institute founded

1827   Mechanics Union of Trade Associates founded in Philadelphia

1828   The Baltimore and Ohio Railroad chartered

1830   Congress passes Pre-emption Act for the public domain

1837   Financial panic and economic depression

1844   Samuel F. B. Morse transmits the first intercity telegraph message

1847   Lawrence Scientific School established at Harvard

1853   The Gadsden Purchase secures an important southwestern railroad pass for the United States

1857   Financial panic and economic depression

1859   Edwin Drake drills the first successful oil well at Titusville, Pennsylvania

n 1833 Michel Chevalier, a French mining engineer, crossed the Atlantic to study the young American republic's canals and railroads. A keen student of the industrialization process then well under way in such European centers as Birmingham, Manchester, and Lille, Chevalier was amazed at what the Americans had accomplished. One of the most arresting sights in the United States was the city of Pittsburgh, where eighty years earlier the French had established Fort Duquesne amid the solitude of the unbroken forest. Now, he wrote, Pittsburgh was

> a manufacturing town which will one day become the Birmingham of America. . . . It is surrounded . . . with a dense black smoke which, bursting forth in volume from the foundries, forges, glasshouses, and the chimneys of all the factories and houses, falls in flakes of soot upon the dwellings and persons of the inhabitants. It is, therefore, the dirtiest town in the United States. . . . Nowhere in the world is everybody so regularly and continually busy as in Pittsburgh. I do not believe there is on the face of the earth a single town in which the idea of amusement so seldom enters the heads of the inhabitants.

The rest of the country, Chevalier found, had not changed as much from its eighteenth-century condition. Great expanses remained forested. Most cities were small. The majority of Americans were still farmers, and almost all the rest were employed in commerce. But as Pittsburgh demonstrated, immense changes were taking place. By 1860 the United States would have a dozen Pittsburghs, beehives of industry belching smoke into the air. It would also have clusters of cleaner factories humming with the sound of looms and spindles. Meanwhile, crisscrossing the fields and woods, chugging "iron horses" would carry the products of the new mills and factories, along with great quantities of grain, livestock, cotton, and other commodities created by a surging agriculture. On the eve of the Civil War the United States would be one of the world's economic giants, ahead of all but Britain, its people enjoying one of the highest standards of living in the world.

How did this "economic miracle" come to pass?

FACTORS OF PRODUCTION

Historians disagree over the causes of economic growth. Some emphasize the "supply" side of the process. They focus, that is, on the various factors of production—the labor, resources, skills, capital, and technology that have to be added to the economic mix to increase output. Other historians give special weight to the "demand" side of growth. They assume that the dynamic element in economic expansion is the swelling demand for goods and services, and they seek to discover why demand grew and how it called forth the needed resources, technology, capital, and labor. In reality, to understand how the United States increased its output enough to provide its people with abundance, we must look at both the supply and demand sides of the equation.

Resources. From the outset the United States was richly endowed by nature. The nation in 1815 consisted of over a billion acres. Its agricultural resources were enormous: no other country possessed so much level, well-watered, fertile land in the earth's temperate zone, where the growing season is long.

Few countries had timber reserves to equal America's. The forests, although they impeded farming, were a unique resource, for virtually everything in the nineteenth century was made of wood—houses, fences, wagons, even clocks and machinery. Wood, moreover, was a major source of fuel, used by steamboats, locomotives, factory steam engines, and most householders, even in the cities.

America was also rich in minerals. The ores of the Appalachian region from central Vermont to the Carolinas formed an "iron belt" that as early as 1800 was dotted with forges, smelters, and mines. Copper and lead deposits were found in Michigan and Missouri. Pennsylvania and Ohio had excellent coal and—though as yet unused—vast petroleum reserves.

In waterpower, too, the United States was blessed. The Appalachian chain, extending from Maine to Georgia, hindered westward movement, but it was also the source of many rivers that emptied into the Atlantic. Along the fall line, where the piedmont plateau drops abruptly to the Atlantic coast plain, scores of swift, cascading streams offered a vast reserve of power to turn mill wheels.

In 1815 relatively little of the country's land was being farmed. In the West dense settlement by white farmers was found only in the regions adjacent to the Ohio Valley and a few pockets elsewhere. Everything else remained Indian land or, although officially transferred to the government in Washington, was still unsettled by whites. Almost all of it was forest except tracts of present-day Indiana, Illinois, and Iowa, which were covered with tall prairie grass. Even in the Atlantic

Courtesy Carnegie Library of Pittsburgh

Courtesy Carnegie Library of Pittsburgh

Pittsburgh in 1796 and 1857. Located at the junction of three navigable rivers, the village thrived before 1800. In 1799 businessmen set up a nail factory there, and by the 1850s Pittsburgh's population worked in coal mines, steel mills, and glass factories under an ever-present cloud of industrial soot.

coast states forests and unused farm woodlots covered the landscape, especially in northern New England, New York, western Pennsylvania, and the mountain regions of the southern states.

Nor were the power resources much used. Aside from some gristmills for grinding wheat into flour and corn into meal, and sawmills for slicing logs into boards, the waterpower of the fall line went largely to waste. Also neglected was the coal of eastern Pennsylvania; as long as wood was cheap, people had no incentive to exploit the unfamiliar black stone for fuel. As for petroleum, though people knew it would burn, they did not know how to guarantee a steady supply, so it remained a curiosity sold by quacks and hucksters as medicine.

In the forty-five years following the War of 1812 the accessible and usable resources within the country's 1803 boundaries were greatly expanded. Growing population and easier access to consumers stirred farmers to cut the woodlots and expand their cultivated acreage. Increasingly, similar incentives moved businessmen to build water-powered mills and exploit coal deposits. In 1859 Edwin L. Drake, backed by New Haven capitalists, found that by drilling into the ground, an abundant supply of "rock oil" could be assured. Drake's well at Titusville, Pennsylvania, set off a "rush" to the oil regions that resembled the earlier gold rush to California.

But besides learning to exploit its existing resources, the country added to them by enlarging its boundaries. Between the Louisiana Purchase in 1803 and the Gadsden Purchase fifty years later, the United States grew by 830 million acres. A large part of the new territory was arid, but it also

Population density, 1820

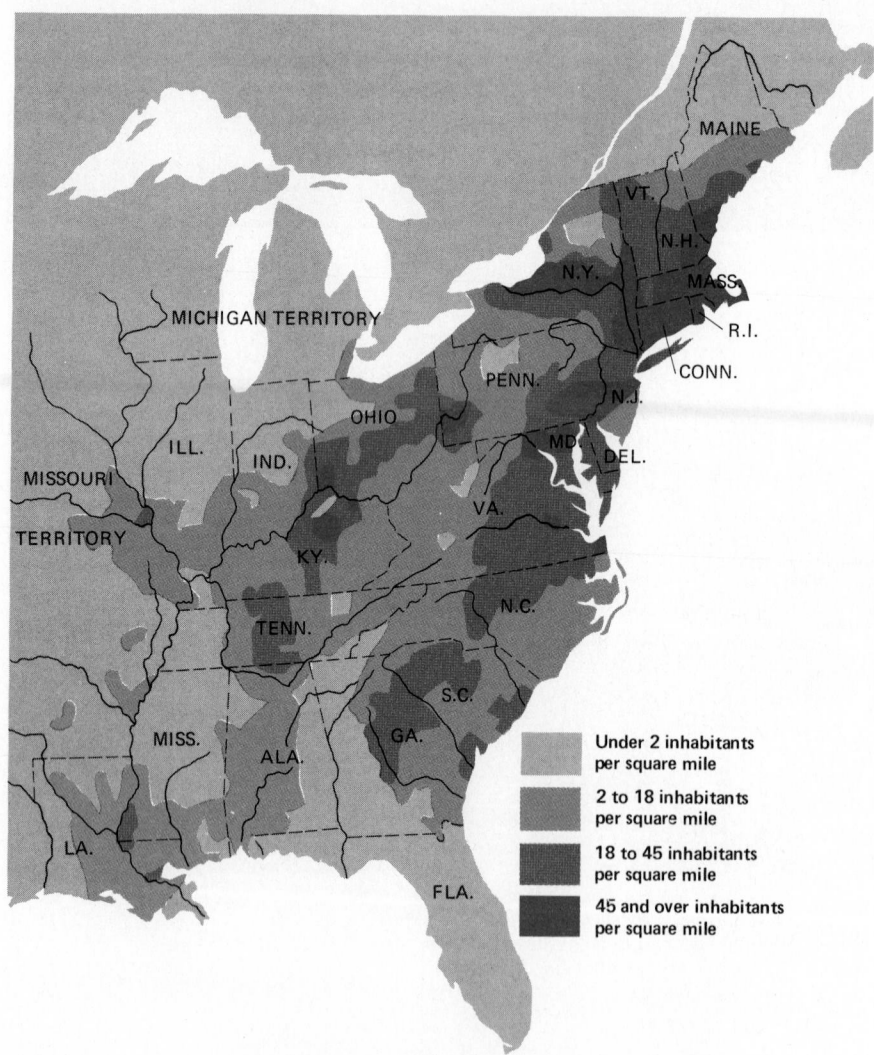

Under 2 inhabitants per square mile

2 to 18 inhabitants per square mile

18 to 45 inhabitants per square mile

45 and over inhabitants per square mile

included great stretches of fertile land in the Central Valley of California, in east Texas, and in Gulf Coast Florida; vast deposits of copper, silver, gold, lead, and zinc in the Rocky Mountain area; and unique timber resources along the coasts of California and Oregon.

Labor. The increasing availability of the nation's natural resources was one reason for America's extraordinary economic growth, but without men and women to utilize these resources, they would have remained merely "potential" forever. The United States was a sparsely populated country in 1815. With 8.5 million people spread over 1.7 million square miles, it had under 5 inhabitants for every square mile (640 acres) of land, compared with about 60 per square mile today. In 1820 the population reached 9.6 million, including some 1.8 million blacks. Though legal importation of slaves had ceased in 1808 (when Congress implemented the constitutional provision allowing it to end the Atlantic slave trade), blacks remained about 19 percent of the country's population.

With so few people spread over so much land, the United States had a labor shortage. Before 1815 the shortage was alleviated somewhat by the unusually high birthrate. The country's population was youthful: in 1817 the median age was 17. In an era when people began to work at 13 or 14, such a young population was a distinct economic asset. Offsetting this advantage, however, was the problem of disease and ill health. There were major cholera epidemics in 1832 and again in 1849–50 that killed thousands and disrupted economic life. In low-lying, swampy areas many people suffered each summer from "fevers" or "agues," mosquito-borne malaria. William Dean Howells, the writer, recalled that during his boyhood in southwestern Ohio during the 1840s "there were few houses where [malaria] was not a familiar guest. . . . If the family was large, there was usually a chill every day; one had it one day and another the next. . . ." In addition, typhus, typhoid, whooping cough, and tuberculosis killed or disabled vast numbers of working people every year. After 1815 the labor force was further depleted by a concerted attempt to limit family size. The American birthrate soon dropped sharply, so that by 1850 it was below that of many countries in Europe.

Immigration helped to offset the labor shortage. Between independence and 1815 no more than about 10,000 Europeans entered the United States annually, along with a smaller, though unknown, number of illegally imported Africans. Between 1815 and 1840 the average rose to over 30,000 a year. Then came the deluge of the 1840s. Economic dislocations in Germany and Scandinavia and the potato blight in Ireland made life hard, and in many cases intolerable, for vast numbers of

Steamships began crossing the Atlantic in the 1830s, but most immigrants—such as these arriving in New York in 1855—traveled in sailing packets. Of that year's 200,000 immigrants, almost half were destitute Irish peasants.

Museum of the City of New York

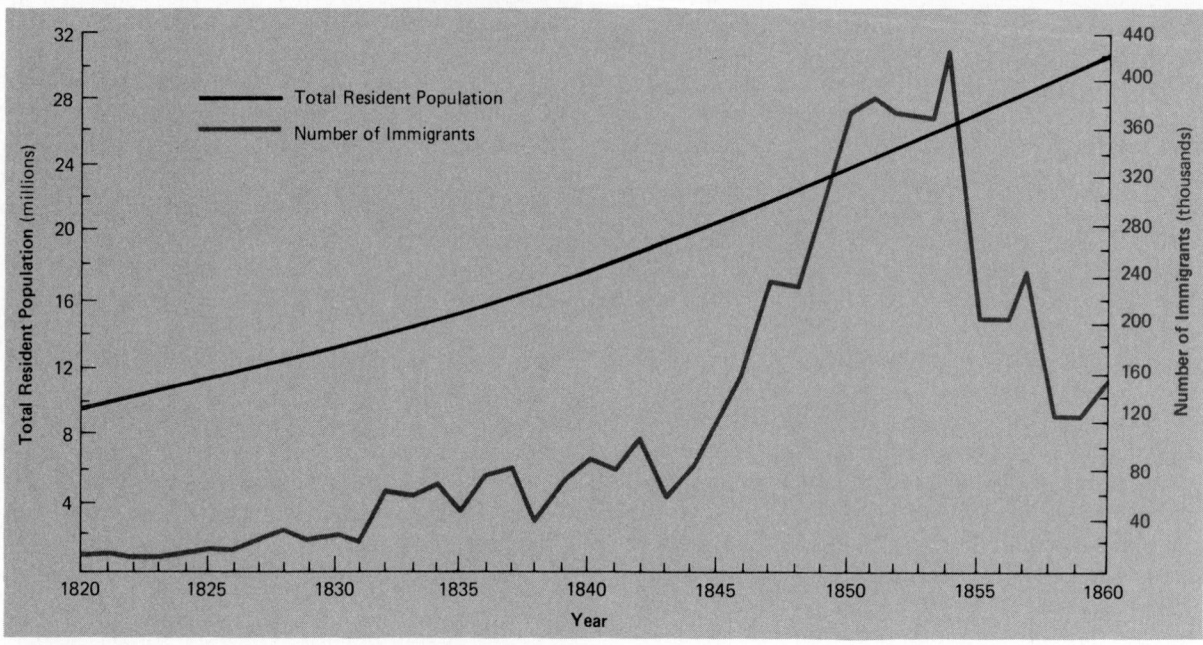

Population and immigration to the United States, 1820–1860
Source: *Historical Statistics of the United States, Colonial Times to 1957.*

Europeans. Combined with quicker and cheaper transatlantic passage and the growing knowledge of America's opportunities, these disruptions brought on a flood of people. During the 1840s and 1850s a staggering 200,000 arrived each year at Atlantic and Gulf Coast ports. Most of these immigrants were in their most productive years, and they added their brawn and skill to the American labor pool at scarcely any cost to their adopted nation. By 1860 the nation's labor force, as a result of natural increase and immigration, had grown to well over 11 million people.

Public Schools and Economic Growth. Modern economic development has depended as much on the creation of a literate, disciplined, and trained labor force—"human capital," economists call it—as on sheer numbers of workers. In America such a labor force was created by the public education system.

Educational standards had been relatively high in colonial America, especially in New England, but they had declined during the half century following the Revolution. In 1835 Professor Francis Bowen of Harvard complained that New England's celebrated school system "had degenerated into routine . . . [and] was starved by parsimony. Any hovel would answer for a school house, any primer would do for a textbook, any farmer's apprentice was competent to 'keep school.' " In the West, if we can believe the stu-

dents of one small rural school, the teaching level was still lower. At the end of the academic year these pupils inscribed this verse on the wall of their schoolhouse:

> *Lord of love, look from above*
> *And pity the poor scholars.*
> *They hired a fool to teach this school*
> *And paid him fifty dollars.*

But even as Bowen—and the "scholars"—wrote, labor leaders, philanthropists, businessmen, and concerned citizens were struggling to upgrade the country's educational system. The most effective worker for improved schools after 1835 was Horace Mann, a self-made man of remarkable charm and great persuasive powers. A lawyer who gave up a successful legal practice to become secretary of the Massachusetts Board of Education in 1837, Mann believed that an educated body of citizens was essential for a healthy democratic society, but he and his disciples also linked education to economic growth. As one of Mann's successors on the Massachusetts Board of Education noted: "The prosperity of the mills and shops is based quite as much upon the intellectual vigor as the physical power of the laborers." During Mann's twelve years as secretary of the board, Massachusetts doubled teachers' salaries, built and repaired scores of school buildings, opened fifty high schools, and established a minimum school year of six months. Other states, especially in the North, soon followed the lead of the Bay State.

The new school systems taught useful values as well as useful skills. Not only did children achieve literacy, they also learned punctuality, good hygiene, industriousness, sobriety, and honesty—all valuable qualities for an emerging industrial society. Lucy Larcom remembered in later years her experiences in New England schools during the 1830s. "I was," she wrote, "penetrated through every fiber of thought with the idea that idleness is a disgrace. It was taught with the alphabet and the spelling-book; it was enforced by precept and example." Other boys and girls remembered how the schoolmaster or schoolmistress told stories of success achieved through hard work and a willingness to sacrifice present pleasures for future gains. Even before the Civil War the rags-to-riches myth had become a powerful reinforcement for the industrial virtues. It would be a mistake to see this indoctrination as the central goal of pre–Civil War educational reformers, but there can be no question that the new public schools encouraged the qualities the nation needed in its labor force.

Many large gaps remained in the country's educational system even after the advent of the state-supported primary school. Secondary education, except in Massachusetts, remained the privilege of the rich who could afford private "academies" for their children. One of the most serious lacks was in the education of girls and young women.

At the elementary level young girls were not treated differently from boys. Beyond the first few grades, however, women's education was often inferior. American women did not attend colleges until Oberlin admitted its first female student in 1833. The typical female secondary school or academy about 1815 was a "finishing school" where the daughters of businessmen, professionals, and wealthy farmers or planters were taught French, music, drawing, dancing, and a little "polite" literature. Then, in the period 1820–40, educational reformers, both men and women, began to conceive of a new sort of secondary schooling for women.

These reformers attacked the idea that women should be mere playthings and ornaments. In a bustling progressive society, the reformers said, women had a vital role to play as mothers and teachers, educating the leaders of the nation in all areas of life. This "cult of domesticity" propagated by Catharine Beecher and Sarah Josepha Hale, editor of the widely circulated magazine *Godey's Lady's Book*, did not assert women's equality with

The Metropolitan Museum of Art

This unusual photograph of one of the new female academies—The Emerson School for Young Ladies in Boston—dates from the early 1850s. The poses seem stiff, especially that of the schoolmaster; but that may be as much the result of slow lenses and photographic emulsions that required long exposures, as of the social rigidity of the antebellum classroom.

men. But it did insist that in their own "spheres" women were an immense but seriously neglected resource and that this waste must not continue.

The new idea of the importance of the female role transformed women's education, especially in the Northeast. Under the leadership of Emma Willard, Mary Lyon, Joseph Emerson, and Catharine Beecher, female "seminaries" were established throughout the region. Schools such as Willard's Troy Female Seminary (1821) and Lyon's Mount Holyoke Female Seminary (1836), unlike the earlier finishing schools, taught algebra, geometry, history, geography, and several of the sciences. These more "muscular" subjects were thought appropriate for the mothers-to-be of statesmen, soldiers, and captains of industry. The most important role of these schools, however, was to provide a flood of trained women to fill the ranks of the burgeoning teaching profession. Without the female seminaries it is hard to see how the new public school movement could have succeeded.

Though the educational system had its failings, by 1860 the United States had a highly skilled and literate labor force. It was ahead of every nation in the world except Denmark in the ratio of students to total population, and New England was even ahead of the advanced Danes. Literacy made it possible for workers to read plans and make reports and gave them access to new ideas and new ways of doing things. It is no accident that the Yankee tinkerer became a legendary figure of ingenuity or that New England became a beehive of shops, mills, and factories, producing cloth, clocks, hardware, and machinery for the rest of the nation.

Technology. Americans have long had the reputation of being an inventive people. They had to be, for through most of their history they were pioneers, forced by their isolation to be self-reliant. During the colonial era the improvements in kitchen equipment and metal- and wood-working tools that emerged from ordinary household practices were supplemented by larger advances such as Benjamin Franklin's heat-conserving stove and his lightning rod to protect homes during electrical storms. After the Revolution the new patent laws of the federal government, along with labor scarcity, added to the incentives for mechanical improvements.

One man who rose to the challenge was Oliver Evans of Philadelphia. In the 1780s Evans developed an ingenious system of milling flour that eventually revolutionized the industry. In Evans's new mill the grain was carried in buckets attached to a water-powered moving belt to the top of the structure and allowed to descend to the bottom while being automatically cleaned, ground, cooled, sifted, and barreled. In his mill along the Brandywine in Delaware six men could convert 100,000 bushels of wheat into flour a year, a 60 percent saving on labor. Nor was Evans an isolated case. Eli Whitney of Connecticut invented a machine to make nails to offset the shortage during the Revolution. In the 1790s, as we shall see, he went on to perfect the "gin" that revolutionized cotton growing in the South. He also did important work on the use of interchangeable parts to speed the manufacture, and lower the cost, of rifles for the government.

The nation's vast size and poor roads also encouraged inventiveness in transportation and communication. Evans was interested in linking the steam engine to transport and designed a steam-powered vehicle that could be used on both roads and waterways. In 1787 John Fitch launched a steamboat using powered oars. This vessel proved impractical, but twenty years later Robert Fulton, a New Yorker, assembled the first commercially feasible steamboat, using paddle wheels. In August 1807 his vessel, the *Clermont,* made the trip up the Hudson from New York to Albany in thirty-two hours, proving the practicality of steam navigation and setting off a national steamboat craze. Some years later another Con-

necticut Yankee, Samuel F. B. Morse, invented the dot-and-dash code used in telegraphy and made many improvements in the primitive telegraph instruments then being developed. In 1844 Morse transmitted the first intercity telegraph message—between Baltimore and Washington.

All these men, and the many others who advanced technology in these years, were self-educated or had acquired their training on the job. Whitney learned about machinery at his father's farm in rural Massachusetts. Evans started as an apprentice to a wagon maker. Morse was a talented portrait painter who took up electrical experiments out of curiosity. Fulton was an artist and draftsman who taught himself the rudiments of marine engineering. Most of the country's first civil engineers learned their trade by working on the early turnpikes and canals.

Gradually, however, more formal means to train technicians and scientists were developed. West Point (founded in 1802), Norwich University (1820), Rensselaer Polytechnic Institute (1825), and the Lawrence Scientific School at Harvard (1847) eventually trained people to plan the canals, design the bridges, and survey the railroads that would knit the country together.

Growing Markets. We can treat the growing and ever more skillful population of the country as an addition to the supply side of the economic growth equation. It was also a factor on the demand side. As population increased, so did the market for everything, from babies' cribs to old folks' canes. Young families and new immigrants needed housing, and their needs stimulated construction in the towns and the countryside. Americans were already well supplied with food, clothing, and shelter; increases in their family wages produced large amounts of discretionary income—money for luxuries. This made them excellent customers for manufactured goods. Before the Civil War luxuries were commonly obtained from France and Great Britain; but with each passing decade American industry expanded to meet the growing market for jewelry, furniture, carriages, carpets, writing paper, clocks, fine cloth, and a thousand other manufactured articles.

Capital. The growing labor force of the United States was matched by a growing supply of capital. *Capital,* as economists use the term, is not just money but money invested in machines, barns, factories, railroads, mines—that is, money invested in "tools" that produce other commodities. (Today the term *capital* is also applied to the skills people acquire that improve their ability to pro-

Museum of the City of New York

"Buy American" was the cry of American manufacturers after the War of 1812. By the 1840s they were making goods previously imported and inventing all sorts of baubles to tempt domestic consumers. Here, in 1845, they exhibited their products at an all-American trade fair.

duce.) When invested, money becomes the basis for continuing economic growth.

Where did the capital come from that helped produce America's "economic miracle"? During the colonial period much of it came from abroad in the form of implements, credits, and coin brought by immigrants or lent to Americans by European promoters and merchants. After independence the United States continued to rely on foreign sources of capital. As the number of immigrants increased, so did the amount of money they brought to America. After 1840 this amounted to millions of dollars annually. Larger than this source of foreign capital were the loans extended by British, French, Dutch, and German businessmen and bankers. The total amount of the nation's outstanding foreign loans rose from under $100 million in 1815 to $400 million by the eve of the Civil War.

Foreign trade was yet another source of capital. The United States in this period exported vast quantities of raw materials to foreign nations. Cotton from the South represented almost half the value of the country's total annual exports in the mid-1850s. Profits from these sales enabled the country to buy not only European consumer goods like French wines and British woolens but also machinery, iron rails, locomotives, and other capital goods. At the same time the American merchant marine, whose swift clipper ships were the nation's pride, earned income carrying European goods to Australia, South America, and the Far East. Finally, after 1849, gold from California helped pay for capital goods imported from the advanced industrial nations of Europe. In personal terms, foreign trade created fortunes for merchants, particularly in the middle states and New England—fortunes often reinvested in home industry.

Personal savings, whether of nationals or foreigners, are always the source of funds for additions to a society's plant and equipment, but a person who has surplus money may not know what to do with it. Financial intermediaries—such as savings and commercial banks, mortgage and insurance companies—provide an outlet for personal savings. These institutions offer the depositor of personal savings a profit in the form of interest or dividends, while in turn lending that money to businesspeople and promoters who convert it into capital. A particularly effective device for attracting savings is the corporation. Like the seventeenth-century joint-stock company, corporations enable many individuals to pool their funds in a single firm, but they have the additional advantage of limited liability. That is, investors in a corporation buy as much stock as they wish or can afford; this is their total financial commitment. If the firm they have invested in goes bankrupt, the stockholders' liabilities are limited to the extent of their investment. No matter how large the debt of the corporation, the investors' other property or wealth is not endangered. Such an arrangement

An Historical Portrait   Samuel F. B. Morse

The career of Samuel Finley Breese Morse refutes the conventional view that artists are quixotic dreamers. One of America's foremost pre–Civil War painters, Morse was also the inventor of a practical system of transmitting messages by electricity and the creator of the telegraph industry, precursor of the vast tele-communications enterprise of today.

Born in Massachusetts in 1791, Morse came of distinguished New England forebears who included famous preachers, scholars, judges, and a colonel in the Continental Army. His father, Jedidiah, was a prominent Congregational minister, Federalist leader, and one of America's first geographers. Samuel (called Finley by his family after one of his middle names) grew up near Boston, in a household where people prized learning and knowledge.

Despite his family's cultivation, he was sent away to school at Phillips Academy in Andover when he was just eight. The young Finley disliked boarding school and did not do well, but he found consolation in drawing. Though his father preferred books to pictures, he did not at first discourage the lad and in fact proudly sent a specimen of his work to Finley's grandfather with the comment: "[H]e is self taught—has had no instructions."

In 1805, at the age of 14, Morse entered Yale. The college was not an intellectual feast in the early nineteenth century. It had only three professors and its curriculum was almost exclusively devoted to the classical languages. Yet at Yale he first learned about electricity. Equally important, to earn pocket money, he began to paint miniature portraits on ivory, a genre much admired in that day. The acclaim of his peers convinced him that his future lay in art and on graduation he told his father that he wished to study with Washington Allston, an American painter then passing through Boston. The Reverend Morse put his foot down. His oldest child, he said, would become a bookstore clerk in Boston while considering a proper career.

Though bitterly disappointed, Morse obeyed his father. But while working at Mallory's bookstore he continued to paint. The work he did in his spare time so impressed influential people that his father relented and agreed to send him to England in the company of Allston to perfect his talents and learn from the masters of Europe.

Morse spent the next four years in London, studying with Allston and painting a number of important pictures. He returned to Boston in 1815 and opened his own studio, full of hope that he could make a living from his painting and at the same time launch an artistic renais-sance in America. He was disap-pointed. People admired his pic-tures and liked the young man personally, but they did not give him commissions. No one wanted the landscapes and historical paint-ings that Morse preferred to paint. He did manage to make a little money doing portraits, but this required him to move from place to place to accommodate patrons. In the next eight years Morse wan-dered from Concord, New Hamp-shire, to Charleston, South Carolina, finally settling in New York in 1823.

During this period his talent matured, but it did not lead to the fame and recognition he craved. These were not good years for Morse. His wife, Lucretia, died in 1825, leaving him with four young children. His father and mother died soon after. In 1829 he returned for a while to Europe, where he believed that art and artists were better appreciated. When he came home in 1832, he was appointed professor of painting and sculpture at New York University, but the position was purely honorific, with-out salary. During these disappoint-ing years his frustrations led him into nativist, anti-Catholic politics, a position he later came to regret.

During the 1830s Morse also drifted away from painting. On a return voyage from Europe he had

---

can encourage timid investors to risk their pre-cious savings on a chancy new enterprise.

Changes in law were necessary to popularize the corporation. At the beginning of the nine-teenth century many people were suspicious of limited liability, which seemed a way by which bankrupts could escape paying their creditors. But gradually state legislatures, beginning with Mas-sachusetts in 1830, permitted limited liability pro-visions in corporate charters. After 1837 they also passed general incorporation laws that allowed businessmen and investors to get charters by ap-plying to a state official rather than by a special act of the lawmakers as before.

These early corporations seldom sold stock to the public at large as their counterparts do to-day. That development would not come until the end of the century. Rather, in most cases the stock-holders consisted of a few score or a few hundred friends, associates, or family members. Still, the corporation form allowed the investment net to be spread much wider than the old-fashioned firm consisting of one owner or a few partners. By 1860 the corporation was used more widely by Ameri-cans than by Europeans as a way to pool the sav-ings of many people, although the form had origi-nated in the Old World.

Banks and Banking. The country's banking sys-tem also made an important contribution to the growth of private capital between 1815 and 1860. Banks and other financial intermediaries encour-aged capital growth in two ways. They induced people to save and funneled their savings into the

first conceived the idea that electricity could be used to transmit messages over a wire. By 1832 he had set down in his notebook the plan for a device that would send signals by the opening and closing of a circuit, a receiving apparatus that would record the signals as dots and spaces on a paper strip moved by clockwork, and a code to translate the dots and spaces into the letters of the alphabet. Over the next few years Morse perfected his device, relying heavily on the scientific knowledge of Joseph Henry, a science professor at Princeton, and the financial backing of Alfred Vail, a rich young man whom he had taught at the university.

Morse filed his "electric telegraph" patent in 1837, but for the next seven years he could not secure enough financial support to demonstrate his invention's practical value. During this period, rather than go into debt, Morse actually went hungry at times. Finally, in 1843, Congress appropriated $30,000 to build an experimental telegraph line between Washington and Baltimore. On May 24, 1844, surrounded by friends and associates in the Supreme Court chamber of the Capitol, Morse tapped out the biblical phrase: "What hath God wrought!" In Baltimore Vail received the message and responded. The effect of this demonstration was strongly reinforced when the telegraph was used immediately after to transmit news of the Democratic national convention meeting in Baltimore. Vail sent news from the scene of the convention; Morse tacked up the messages on a board in the Capitol rotunda. It was the beginning of the new "information age" that is still evolving in our day.

Despite these successes, neither Morse nor the telegraph experienced clear sailing thereafter. Morse would have been happy to accept a government award and return to his art. But Congress refused his request for $100,000, and he was forced to seek commercial support for his invention. He was not a businessman, but fortunately he had Vail and a former postmaster general, Amos Kendall, to handle his business affairs. Morse and his partners beat off numerous lawsuits by other claimants to the invention and competed energetically with other companies offering telegraph services to newspapers and private users. Together the Morse associates and their competitors helped to wire the nation into a network of instantaneous communication. In 1858 Morse and his friends formed the Magnetic Telegraph Company in a deal that finally made the inventor a rich man after twenty years of struggle.

Morse lived until 1872, long enough to see a functioning Atlantic cable tie Europe to America. His last years were marked by contentment. He lived with his second wife and second family at an estate on the Hudson, while enjoying a townhouse in New York City. Colleges showered him with honorary degrees and governments awarded him medals and decorations. In 1871 the telegraph operators of America commissioned a bronze statute of the man who had created their industry, to be mounted in New York's Central Park. Morse did suffer one major disappointment in this period of his life, otherwise marked by comfort and acclaim. In 1864, when he tried to resume painting, he discovered that his talent had ebbed and gave up the attempt.

Morse's death was marked by memorial services all over the nation. It was the inventor whom the country honored; little was noted of the artist. Posterity has been kinder to the artistic side of his career, however. He is now regarded as one of the nation's greatest painters. Morse now seems, in the words of his chief biographer, the "American Leonardo"—like the great da Vinci, a man as talented in the realm of art as in the realm of technology.

hands of investors who borrowed from them. And they *created* money, or credit—which amounts to the same thing—and lent it to business borrowers.

The first function is easy to understand, but the role of commercial banks in creating money and credit is more mysterious. The key to this creation process is the fact that taken as a whole, the commercial banking system keeps only a small reserve against the loans it makes. This reserve is all it normally needs to pay its expenses, meet depositors' requests for withdrawals, cash checks, and the like. In this way a relatively small amount of cash can be used to float a large volume of loans to borrowers. In effect, the bank has created money that can be used for investment.

The system depends on trust. If bankers abused their trust, as they often did, by lending to unreliable borrowers or by lending far beyond what a reasonable reserve policy required, they were in danger of encouraging bankruptcy. Depositors or other creditors, fearful of the safety of their savings, might demand that a bank repay them immediately. If enough of the bank's creditors simultaneously demanded their money back, a "run" on the bank might develop, and the bank would have to "suspend"—that is, close its doors. Runs or panics were particularly common when businessmen were worried about the economy as a whole. Panics occurred in 1819, 1837, and 1857, and each ushered in a major long-lasting economic depression by destroying business and consumer confidence.

One important service that banks performed in the pre–Civil War period was to provide the

National Numismatic Collections, Smithsonian

This five-dollar note of the Second Bank of the United States dates back from 1819, when William Jones, the bank's incompetent first president, was still in charge. BUS notes such as these were redeemable in gold on demand and provided a sound and secure currency for the country until 1836.

paper money that people used in their daily buying and selling. A person who borrowed from a bank usually took a loan in the form of a packet of the bank's notes. The treasury also issued a coinage of gold, silver, and copper, but this was not enough to do the people's business. Instead, in all but minor transactions the "bank note," issued by some banking corporation, served the public as money. These notes were legally backed by a reserve of gold or silver that the banks kept on hand, but the enforcement of the requirement that banks pay out gold for each note presented for redemption was often lax. The Second Bank of the United States, chartered in 1816, had little trouble keeping its circulation of paper notes "as good as gold." Many of the state-chartered banks, however, issued excessive amounts, given their reserves, because each paper dollar lent to a borrower earned interest and made a profit. When a bank could not redeem its notes, it was forced to suspend operations in the same fashion as when it could not repay depositors. When this happened, those who held the bank's notes found themselves with worthless paper, much as depositors in defaulted banks found themselves with worthless bank accounts.

Growth of the Banking System. Despite these failings, the country's banking system aided the investment plans of aggressive businesspeople and promoters, accelerating the growth of the nation's pool of capital. In the years before the Civil War the American banking system expanded exuberantly. The first modern American commercial bank was the Bank of North America, chartered by Congress in 1781 and located in Philadelphia. In 1784 New York and Massachusetts chartered two additional banks. Another was added by New York in 1799 under the name the Manhattan Company.

Meanwhile, as we have seen, Congress, acting on Hamilton's financial program, chartered the

first Bank of the United States (or BUS). Like any other commercial bank, the BUS lent money, but it also served as the government's financial agent, holding the treasury's deposits, transferring government money from one part of the country to another, and even collecting United States customs duties. It also issued much of the country's paper money. Finally, before its demise in 1811, it took on some of the functions of a central bank. That is, it tried to control and stabilize the entire economy by providing extra funds to state bank lenders when credit was scarce and by seeking to limit the loans of the state banks when the BUS directors believed they were excessive.

The Second Bank of the United States, chartered in 1816, was even larger than its predecessor; it had $35 million in capital compared with the first BUS's $10 million. It, too, sought to provide a balance wheel for the economy. At times, however, it blundered badly. Under its first president, the Second BUS initially followed an easy-credit policy, lending freely to businessmen and speculators and failing to curb similar practices by the state banks. It was this policy that helped fuel a western land boom after 1815. When the second president came to office in 1819, he tightened credit by reducing the BUS's own loans and demanding that the state banks reduce theirs. This contraction was necessary and perhaps overdue, but it was too abrupt and helped set off the Panic of 1819.

Meanwhile, the state banking system was growing up alongside the federally chartered institutions. In 1820 there were 300 state banks; in 1834, 500; and in 1860, almost 1,600. At first most state banks were established by charters granted individually by state legislatures. By the 1840s, however, banks could use the same general incorporation system used by other businesses: securing charters by applying to designated state officials and meeting general requirements. In some states these requirements were strict. New York, for example, required that each state bank contribute a certain sum annually to a "safety fund" to be used to pay the bank's creditors in the event it failed. The provision helped ensure public confidence and financial stability and contributed to New York's growing preeminence as the nation's financial center.

Strict banking laws were most common in the Northeast, the region where savings were most abundant. In the newer parts of the country there were fewer people with money to invest; yet it was precisely there that the need for capital to clear land, build barns, construct railroads, and lay out towns was most acute. Interest rates—the price of money—accordingly were higher in the West than in the East. Under the circumstances, it is not surprising that many western states were lax in their banking laws and still laxer in enforcing them. Western banks often ignored requirements that each dollar issued and lent to borrowers have a partial gold reserve to back it. This led to large issues of "wildcats," paper money backed by hope and faith rather than "specie," that is, gold. Local western banks also often lent on such security as land, which they could not easily convert into cash in case of need. As a result, they encouraged a boom-and-bust pattern in the western economy, but their free-and-easy practices also helped meet a vital need for rapid increases in capital in the emerging parts of the country. All told, economic historians conclude, the banking system of this period, for all its faults, met the expansive needs of the economy well, providing for rapid capital growth without inflation.

Government Actions. Not all Americans believed the government should have a strong role in the area of economic growth. Old-line Jeffersonians continued to fear federal and state intrusion into the economy as a danger to freedom. Other citizens, influenced by the laissez-faire ideas of Adam Smith and David Ricardo, believed that government intervention would only hamper economic progress. The nation must rely solely on private enterprise, they said; the profit motive alone would lead to growth and prosperity.

These opponents of government intervention won some battles, but government in fact played a vital role in the country's growth. Through laws favorable to the easy chartering of banks and corporations, it encouraged private capitalists to pool their savings for investment purposes. The federal tariff system, proposed by Hamilton and implemented by the Republicans in 1816, by making imports more expensive, protected American manufacturers against foreign competition and so encouraged capitalists to risk their money in factories and mills. Finally, there was the tax system. Everywhere in pre–Civil War America taxes were low. No matter how much profit a businessman made, he kept almost all of it. The effect of this profit retention was to make large accumulations of private capital available for investment.

The government contributed to capital formation more directly too. Many investments, such as canals, required so much money and posed so many risks that private investors would not undertake them. Some projects did not promise sufficient returns to the individual investor, though they might eventually confer economic benefits on many people or whole regions. Railroads through wilderness areas, for example, might take years before they produced returns, though they promised to stimulate settlement enormously. To encourage growth in these instances, state and local governments in the years before 1860 joined with private promoters to build roads, canals, and railroads. The state of Pennsylvania invested in manufacturing concerns. Sometimes the states lent money to private capitalists; in the case of the canals, they often financed projects directly. New York put up the money for the Erie Canal after efforts to secure federal funds failed. The states' funds came either from taxes imposed on the public or, more often, from borrowed money raised by selling bonds to investors in the United States or Europe. The federal government, too, contributed, especially to transportation. Federal funds built the National Road, begun in 1811 and completed in 1850, from Cumberland, Maryland, to Vandalia, Illinois, a distance of 700 miles. The federal government also financed the St. Mary's Falls ship canal linking Lake Huron and Lake Superior, built coastal lighthouses, dredged rivers and harbors, and, in the 1850s, contributed millions of acres of land to promoters of the Illinois Central Railroad connecting the Great Lakes with the Gulf of Mexico.

States and localities also funded projects that encouraged growth by improving the health of the community or its educational level. All told, the government contribution to pre–Civil War investment was enormous. One scholar has estimated that by 1860 states, counties, and municipalities had spent about $400 million toward building the country's transportation network alone. If we add to this sum the federal government's contribution and the millions spent for schools, hospitals, and other vital public facilities, we can see that laissez-faire was more myth than reality in pre–Civil War America.

Unequal Sacrifice. However brought about, capital growth and the economic expansion it brings require that people forgo an immediate advantage for the sake of some expected future gain. They must lower their present level of consumption in order to enjoy a better one at a later time. Some of this sacrifice was made voluntarily by investors themselves, as when businesspeople used profits to expand their firms rather than to improve their personal living standards. But some was imposed on people without their consent. Large amounts of capital were squeezed out of slaves in the South by giving them only bare subsistence for their labor. Women also were exploited. In the few jobs where they competed directly with men, they received lower wages for similar work. When women teachers flocked to the new public schools, for example, teachers' wages fell. For traditional "women's work" the situation was similar: wages for household servants were low; in the case of the housewife, they were nonexistent. Manufacturers of straw hats, ready-made clothes, and shoes relied on a large pool of poorly paid female workers, many employed part-time at home and paid by the "piece." Nor were adult white male workers, the best-compensated labor group, able to avoid paying for capital growth. In the North and West agricultural workers and factory hands earned lower wages than they could have if businesspeople had not skimmed off profits for reinvestment.

To some degree, then, all groups sacrificed present for future gains under the forced-draft growth of the pre–Civil War American economy. But there can be no denying that the sacrifices exacted for the sake of high investment were unequal. In pre–Civil War America the richest segment of the population was increasing its wealth faster than the poorer parts. In 1850 Boston alone had eighteen millionaires, most of them merchants and manufacturers. When he died in 1831, Philadelphia merchant Stephen Girard was worth $8 million. John Jacob Astor, who made his money in real estate and the fur trade, was worth $20 million in 1848. Similar fortunes existed in the South, where cotton and slaves created a class of rich planters. The United States was becoming economically more unequal than it had been during the colonial period. It can be argued that this was an unavoidable cost of rapid expansion. Alternately, we can view this sacrifice as the price earlier generations paid so later ones would benefit.

THE COURSE OF AMERICAN ECONOMIC GROWTH

America, then, was endowed with stupendous resources, a skilled and growing population, and values and institutions conducive to hard work, saving, and capital growth. How did these elements combine to produce an economic miracle?

The Birth of King Cotton. Most people associate nineteenth-century economic growth with factories, forges, and mills. But agricultural advance was another vital part of the process. The nation's fields also became more productive in these years, and their food and fiber supplied the growing armies of labor in the towns and cities. They also provided surpluses of grain and cotton for export abroad to pay for the capital equipment imported from Europe.

The major economic advance in agriculture before the Civil War was the opening of the "cotton kingdom." Cotton cloth had been known for centuries as a light, easily washed fabric. East Indian calicoes, made from cotton yarn, were much prized in Europe, but hand-woven cloth from Asia was expensive. Toward the end of the eighteenth century several ingenious Englishmen developed machines to spin cotton yarn and to weave it into fabric. By the 1790s the mills of Lancashire in northwest England were producing cheap cotton cloth for an enthusiastic and ever-expanding market.

But where was the raw cotton to come from for the hungry mills? India could not produce enough. A small amount of cotton was grown on the Sea Islands off South Carolina and Georgia and on the immediately adjacent mainland. Sea island cotton is silky and has long fibers; laborers could easily remove its entangled seeds by hand. But the region where it flourished was limited, so the output remained small. Cotton with a shorter fiber would grow throughout the South's vast upland interior, but upland cotton had burrlike green seeds that clung tightly to the fibers and required much hand labor and time to remove. If the United States had had the teeming millions of India to draw on for labor, this quality of upland cotton might have been unimportant. But even in the slave South labor was relatively expensive. So long as short-staple cotton had to be "cleaned" by hand, it was not economical to grow. American cotton growing remained confined to the narrow Carolina-Georgia coast.

Yet the South badly needed a new crop. Its three major staples from colonial times—tobacco, rice, and indigo—had all suffered declining mar-

Library of Congress

By mid-century, Americans made the world's best farm machinery. Eli Whitney's gin cleaned cotton fifty times faster than a hand laborer, and incidentally increased the demand for slaves.

kets after independence. Wheat and corn remained, but neither could produce the cash income of the major colonial crops. What could be done to make short-fiber cotton a practical replacement for rice, tobacco, and indigo?

The answer was provided by the Yankee Eli Whitney. In 1793, while visiting the Georgia plantation of Mrs. Nathanael Greene (widow of the Revolutionary War general), Whitney learned about the problem confronting southern planters. As a gesture of gratitude to his gracious hostess, he put together a simple machine that would efficiently remove the sticky seeds from the upland cotton boll. Now a single laborer using Whitney's new "gin" (from *engine*) could do the work of fifty hand cleaners.

The gin, and cotton culture, quickly spread throughout the lower South. Thousands of planters, white farmers, and slaves migrated into western Georgia, Florida, Alabama, Mississippi, Louisiana, Arkansas, and east Texas to clear fields and plant cotton. From about 2 million pounds in 1793, short-fiber cotton output shot up to 80 million pounds by 1811. In 1859 the United States produced 5 million bales of 400 pounds each and had become the world's major supplier of raw cotton. On the eve of the Civil War cotton was "king," and its realm spanned the region from North Carolina on the Atlantic coast 1,300 miles westward to central Texas and from the Gulf of Mexico to Tennessee.

The North and West. If cotton was king in the South, wheat was king in the agricultural North, although its reign was not so absolute. Like cotton, wheat was a major cash crop, produced in vast amounts for sale. Some American wheat went abroad, but before the Civil War most was consumed at home. In the form of bread, it provided the chief item in the diet of the growing army of urban people.

Grown since colonial times in almost every part of North America except New England and the Deep South, wheat continued to be important in the Middle Atlantic states and the upper South after 1815. As late as 1839 Pennsylvania, New York, and Virginia each produced between 12 and 16 percent of the total American wheat crop. Thereafter, as canals and railroads made the prairie accessible, wheat growing moved westward. By 1859 Illinois, Indiana, Ohio, and Wisconsin had become the chief wheat-producing states.

The soils of the new wheat region were especially fertile. Besides, the prairies that covered large parts of several northwestern states were practically treeless, so farmers did not have to clear forest, an occupation that consumed so much of their time in the middle states. The shift of wheat growing to the Midwest accordingly increased the output of American agriculture and helped to supply expanding national markets at ever-lower costs.

Farm labor still remained a problem. There

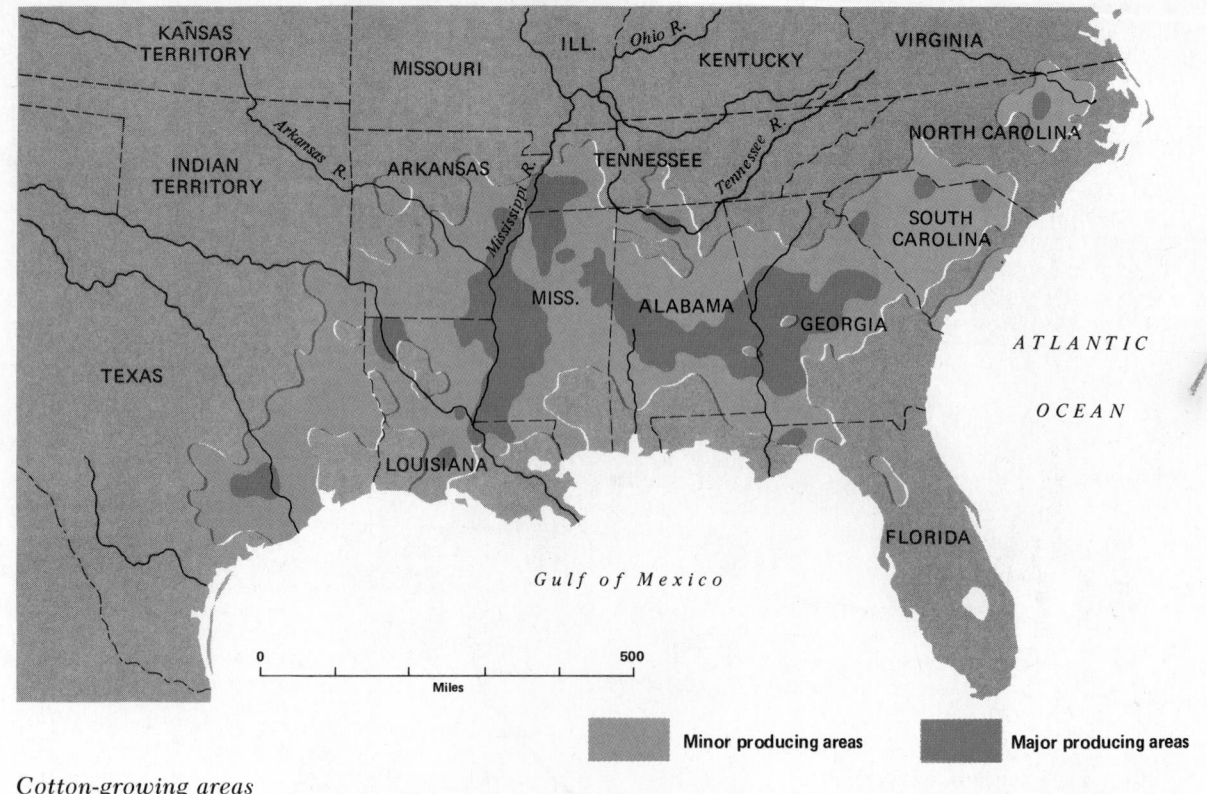

Cotton-growing areas

Minor producing areas | Major producing areas

was generally enough for plowing, planting, and cultivating. But at harvesttime, when the crop had to be gathered quickly, there was not enough help to go around. In the 1830s Obed Hussey and Cyrus McCormick invented machines to speed the harvesting. Both the McCormick and Hussey horse-drawn reapers had long metal blades mounted on a horizontal cylinder that turned as the horse pulled it along. The new machines added immensely to the productivity of harvest

Shrewd Cyrus McCormick, whose reaper sped the harvest of midwestern wheat, was one of the first businessmen to guarantee his products.

State Historical Society of Wisconsin

labor. A man with a hand-operated "cradle" could cut from three to four acres of ripe wheat a day; with the new reaper he could harvest more than four times as much. This lowered the cost of harvesting wheat by 50 cents an acre, a considerable saving.

The labor shortage was not all that encouraged farm mechanization in America. The size of the American farm also played a part. In 1850 the average American farmer owned about 200 acres of land. Fortunately the 200-acre family grain farm was large enough to employ reapers efficiently and their use quickly spread. By 1860 there were some 80,000 harvesting machines at work on the fields of the North and West—more than in the rest of the world. By that date the implements and machinery found on American farms were worth $246 million.

Land Policy. The size of the American farm was not accidental. It was a product of deliberate government policies pursued after 1800. Congress was under constant pressure to accelerate the conversion of public lands to family-size farms. In the West, particularly, the public demanded land policies that would provide the ever-growing population with family farms at low cost. In 1800 Congress allowed settlers to buy land at a minimum of $2 an acre in tracts of 320 acres, or half the smallest purchase previously permitted. The same law also gave the buyer four years to pay and provided a discount of 8 percent for cash. The Land Act of 1804 lowered the minimum price to $1.64 an acre and reduced the smallest amount purchasable to 160 acres.

Federal land policies, however, were not consistent. The states and the federal government occasionally sold public land in large blocks, some a 100,000 acres or more. But these large tracts were not worked as great estates. Rather, they were bought by speculators, often on credit, and sold in small parcels to settlers. The system allowed free-wheeling businesspeople to make large profits; yet in the end it did not prevent widespread ownership of land by people of small and middling means.

Low land prices and easy credit combined to set off periodic waves of speculation in the West. Buyers with little capital placed claims to much larger amounts of land than they could ever expect to farm themselves in the hope of selling most of it for profit later. Meanwhile, they met their payments to the government by borrowing funds from the banks. To prevent widespread default Congress passed relief acts that delayed collection of overdue payments. Such measures seldom

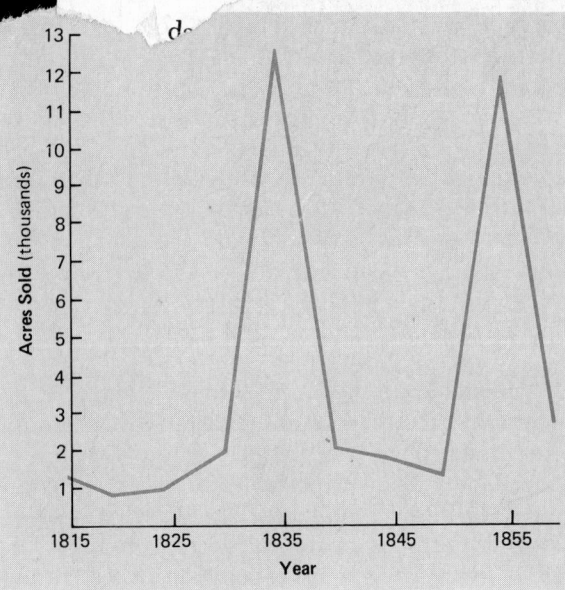

Public land sales, 1815–1860
Source: *Historical Statistics of the United States, Colonial Times to 1957.*

helped, however. When speculation got out of hand in 1819, the country experienced a major depression set off by panicky speculators trying to unload their land at a time when no one wanted to buy. After the panic, in 1820, Congress rescinded the easy-credit feature of the 1800 land law, but to offset this it reduced the minimum price to $1.25 an acre and lowered the minimum purchase to 80 acres. The Panic of 1837 also stemmed in part from western land speculation.

Not every would-be farmer waited for land to be surveyed and put up for sale. Many jumped the gun and went out to unsurveyed lands, cleared some acres, erected a log cabin, and in effect farmed illegally. Such "squatters" stood to lose everything—fences, barns, houses, and the land itself—when the tract they had settled and "improved" was finally offered for sale by the government. In 1830 champions of the squatters, like Senator Thomas Hart Benton of Missouri, convinced Congress to pass the Pre-emption Act to allow those who had occupied portions of the public domain on or before 1829 to buy up to 160 acres of land at the minimum price of $1.25 an acre before others were allowed to bid. In 1841 the time restrictions on the Pre-emption Act were removed.

The 1820 land law and the measures benefiting squatters remained the basis for land policy until the Civil War. Benton and his colleagues, joined at times by labor leaders, continued to fight for a "homestead act" that would give land free to all bona fide settlers. But many easterners feared that free western lands would drain off eastern labor; southerners feared it would give the government an excuse to raise the tariff to offset the loss of land-sale revenues and also that it would encourage the growth of free states. In 1854 an emerging alliance of the Northwest and Northeast permitted passage of the Graduation Act, which allowed land that had remained unsold for a given number of years to be sold at sharply reduced prices. But the continued opposition of the South blocked a homestead law until 1862.

Steamboats and Roads. In some ways American geography favored efficient, cheap transportation. The Mississippi River system combined with the Great Lakes made it possible for ships to penetrate deep into the vital interior of North America. But neither the rivers nor the lakes were ideal for navigation. At two points—between Lakes Huron and Superior, and between Ontario and Erie—the Great Lakes were connected only by unnavigable rapids. They also lacked lighthouses and port facilities. The drawbacks of the Mississippi system were still greater. Flatboats and rafts carrying mountains of heavy freight could easily be floated down to New Orleans, propelled by the current. But the trip upstream by poled keelboats required backbreaking labor and took far longer.

For some time capitalists and inventors had been working on schemes to apply steam power to river navigation, but as we have seen, not until Robert Fulton took up the quest, backed by the powerful Livingston family, did it become economically feasible. Soon steamboats were operating on schedule up and down the Hudson. In 1811 the Fulton-Livingston interests, having already secured a legal monopoly of steamboat traffic in New York State waters, received an exclusive charter from the Louisiana territorial legislature to operate steamboats on the lower Mississippi. If unchecked, the Fulton group might have monopolized steamboat navigation on all the inland waters. However, the Supreme Court struck down these monopoly privileges in the case of *Gibbons* v. *Ogden* and opened up steamboat navigation to all investors. Entrepreneurs were not long in seizing the opportunity. By 1855 there were 727 steamboats on the western rivers with a combined capacity of 170,000 tons; many more plied the Great Lakes as well as the streams and coastal waters of the Gulf and the Atlantic.

The steamboat revolutionized the schedules and costs of inland travel and transport. Where once it had taken four months to pole a keelboat upstream from New Orleans to Louisville, by 1819 the steamboat had cut the travel time to seventeen

ys; by 1853 it was under four and a half days. Freight rates on the same route fell from an average of $5 a hundred pounds to under 15 cents.

Despite this drop in price, promoters' profits remained high, attracting millions of dollars of private capital. Yet even where the incentives to private investment were adequate, the government made an important contribution. Although there was little government investment in steamboats themselves, the state and federal governments laid out large amounts to deepen river channels, remove snags, and construct canals around river obstructions, and to improve navigation on the Great Lakes.

Impressive as the advances in inland navigation were, there still remained the problem of transportation where there were no natural waterways. The obvious solution was to replace the muddy or dusty trails in use since the colonial period with all-weather, surfaced roads for horses, carriages, and freight wagons. To pay for these turnpikes, tolls would be charged to users. The first major turnpike in the country was the Philadelphia-Lancaster Road in Pennsylvania, built with private capital and opened in 1794. Soon the entire country caught the road-building fever. In the Northeast private capital built most of the turnpikes; in the South and West state governments built the roads directly or bought stock in private companies. By 1861 Virginia had contributed almost $5 million for roads and turnpikes, and other states had contributed lesser, but still substantial, amounts. The federal government also joined in the rush, investing $7 million in the construction of the National Road.

Canals. Turnpikes considerably lowered the cost and time of transporting people and goods, but land transportation remained more expensive than water. Where there were no navigable streams or lakes, the solution was canals. A few miles of artificial waterway were constructed in the Northeast just before the War of 1812. The real boom got under way after the war, in 1817, when the New York State legislature, on the urging of Mayor DeWitt Clinton of New York City, appropriated funds for constructing an enormously long waterway between the Hudson River and Lake Erie. This bold venture would connect the Great Lakes with the Atlantic Ocean, bypassing the Appalachian barrier by a more direct route than down the Mississippi to New Orleans and around to the Atlantic coast by sea.

The New York engineers were favored by geography: the north-south Appalachian highlands dipped to only a few hundred feet in the

Canals and roads, 1820–1850

central part of the state. Still, the project was an impressive achievement. The state authorities sent an observer to England to see how the British had built canals, but not even the English had ever tried to construct a project of such dimensions. The New York engineers learned on the job and improvised a score of new tools and techniques. In the end they moved millions of cubic yards of earth, constructed 83 locks, scores of stone aqueducts, and 363 miles of "ditch" 4 feet deep and 40 feet wide.

The completed canal, opened by a colorful ceremony in 1825, was an engineering marvel that astounded the world. Power for the canal boats was provided by horses and mules that treaded towpaths on either side of the waterway. Leading the animals was a man or boy; another man at the tiller kept the boat in midchannel and signaled passengers sitting on top of the cabin to duck by blowing a horn when the vessel approached a low bridge.

The canal was also an immense economic success. In 1817, before it was completed, the cost of shipping freight between New York City and Buffalo on Lake Erie was 19.2 cents a ton. By 1830 it was down to 3.4 cents. Freight rates to and from the upper Mississippi Valley also plummeted. By 1832 the canal was earning the state well over a million dollars yearly in tolls and was providing enough revenue to pay the bondholders for the

money the state had borrowed and leave a large surplus to construct new canals. Best of all, from the perspective of New York City merchants, the canal drew off much of the trade that had gone down the Mississippi and its tributaries and redirected it to the Atlantic metropolis, confirming its growing economic advantage over all the nation's other ports and business centers.

New York's experience inevitably aroused the envy of merchants in the other Atlantic ports. Baltimore, Boston, Philadelphia, and Charleston businessmen now demanded that their respective states follow New York's lead. At the same time, promoters, speculators, farmers, and merchants in the Northwest saw that their region's prosperity depended on constructing canals to link up with the waterways built or proposed. The pressure on state governments soon got results. By the 1830s the dirt was flying all over the Northeast and Northwest as construction crews raced to create a great network of canals. In 1816 there were about 100 miles of canals in the United States; by 1840

Locks such as these on the Erie Canal near Albany made it possible for canal boats to ascend and descend from one level to another. The motive force for the boats was provided by mules walking down a towpath, as seen at right.

New-York Historical Society

over 3,300 miles of man-made waterways crisscrossed the Middle Atlantic states, southern New England, and the Old Northwest.

Few canals built after 1825 were as successful as the Erie. Some such as Pennsylvania's "mainline" never overcame difficult engineering problems; others never attracted sufficient business to collect enough tolls to repay investors. Still others were built too late and were overtaken by the railroads, which provided quicker and less easily interrupted service.

Nevertheless, canals and steamboats conferred immense benefits on the United States. The sharp decline in freight and passenger rates was a great boon to interregional trade. Farmers in the West, whose surplus crops often sold for a song or piled up for want of buyers, now found new outlets in the East for their wheat, corn, pork, beef, and other commodities. With transportation costs lower, the price of manufactured goods in the West fell, enabling eastern manufacturers to sell more to western customers. By the 1850s manufactured goods were cheaper in the West and raw materials and foodstuffs cheaper in the East than ever before.

The Railroads Come. The railroads also helped knit the country together. First developed in England to haul coal from mines to riverside, the railroad was quickly seized on by Americans. Especially interested were the merchants of such cities as Boston, Baltimore, and Charleston, which lacked the geographical advantages of New York. These people feared the city on the Hudson would monopolize the continent's inland trade.

The early railroads were plagued by technical problems. Steam engines frequently broke down or even exploded. Passengers emerged from the cars nearly suffocated by engine smoke or with holes burned in their clothes from flying sparks. Rails were at first flatiron straps nailed to wooden beams. When these came loose, they sometimes curled up through passenger cars, maiming or killing the occupants. Cattle that got in the way of trains caused derailments. Some of these problems were inevitable in so new a system, but accidents were also the result of makeshift construction imposed by the shortage of capital and the desire to build quickly. Trains moving rapidly over lightly ballasted rails and around sharp curves did not always stay on the track.

Gradually railroad technology improved. The strip rail was abandoned for the all-iron rail. Passenger cars became more substantial. The cow catcher was added to the front of the locomotive to push aside all but the most immovable obstruc-

tions. Boilers were improved and made more dependable, smokestacks were enlarged to contain the hot sparks. Finally, to deal with the hairpin curves characteristic of American railroads, inventors developed loose-jointed engines and cars with wheels that swiveled to guide trains around turns.

The first major American railroad was the Baltimore and Ohio, chartered in 1828. In 1830 the first 13 miles of B and O track were in operation. Three years later the Charleston and Hamburg in South Carolina reached its terminus 136 miles from its starting point, making it the longest railroad in the world. By 1860 the country boasted some 30,000 miles of track, and passengers and freight could travel by rail from the Atlantic coast as far west as St. Joseph, Missouri, and from Portland, Maine, to New Orleans. The system was far from complete, and many communities remained without rail connections. The Great Plains and the Pacific coast had few if any railroads. Even in the East and Midwest track gauges (distances between the rails) varied from line to line, making frequent changes necessary for "through" passengers. Nevertheless, the accomplishment was impressive.

Surprisingly, the economic impact of the railroads was not as great as we might assume. Economic historians now conclude that the sharpest drop in pre–Civil War freight costs occurred before the railroads were built and was the result of canals and steamboats. Still, we must not dismiss the "iron horse" as a negligible contributor to American economic growth. The railroads, unlike the waterways, provided all-weather routes. When the canals, rivers, and lakes froze over, the railroads continued to run. They could also serve arid or mountainous regions, where canals could not penetrate, and areas where streams were nonexistent or too swift for navigation. Moreover, for fast freight like mail, parcels, or perishables, and for impatient freight like people, the speed of the train was a distinct advantage.

The Factory System. Growing cotton and wheat production and the expanding transportation network speeded the pace of the American economic miracle. Yet none of these would be so significant for the nation's future economic course as the rise of the New England textile factories. Much of the textile capital came from merchants who had made their money in foreign trade. The firm of Almy and Brown of Providence began as a commercial enterprise engaged in overseas trade; in 1790 it hired the English mechanic and inventor Samuel Slater to build the earliest successful cotton-spin-

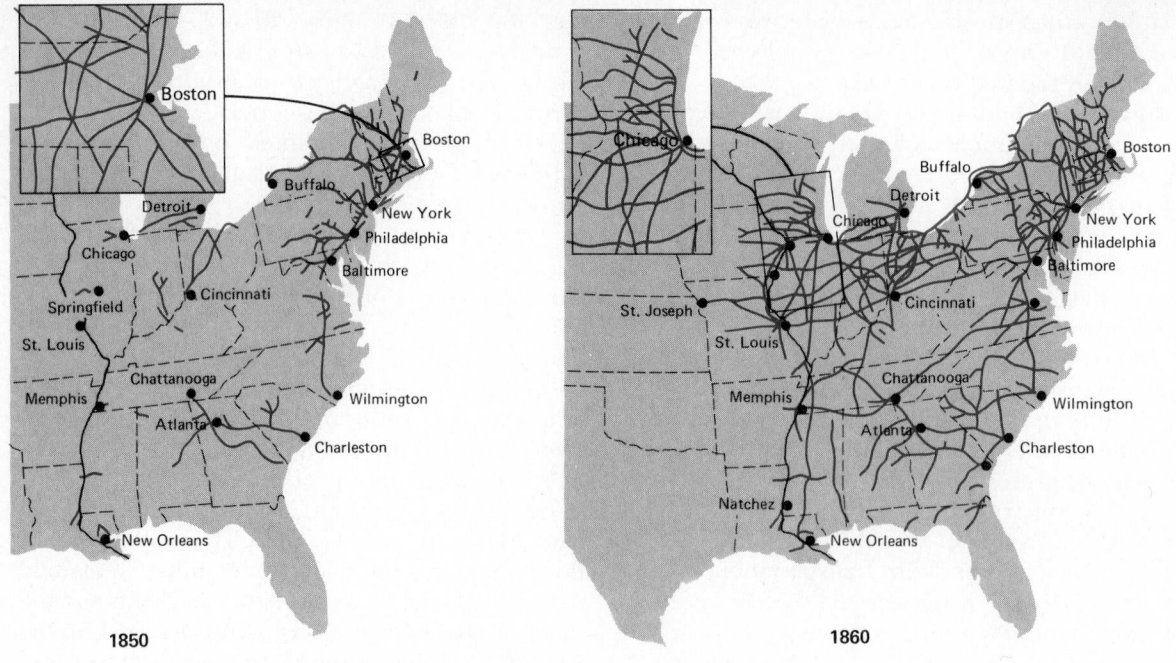

1850

1860

The railroad network, 1850–1860

ning mill. By 1800 there were seven mills in Rhode Island. Much of the entrepreneurial leadership of the Massachusetts cotton mills came from Francis Cabot Lowell, a Boston merchant hit hard by Jefferson's embargo. In 1810, while his ships remained idle, Lowell visited Lancashire, the British cotton center, and made careful note of the new power machinery that wove yarn into finished cloth. The market for cotton cloth was booming, and American planters were turning out 200,000 bales of green-seed cotton a year. Why not, Lowell asked, take advantage of the easy access to raw materials and the growing home market and beat the English at their own game?

Lowell was soon joined by other merchants, who together secured a corporate charter for the Boston Manufacturing Company. In short order the promoters established a mill at a waterpower site in Waltham on the Charles River. They used a new power loom designed by Lowell, whose technical ability matched his business skill. The first cloth came from the looms in 1815 and brought excellent prices.

Before long the promoters found that they could not produce enough cloth at the limited Waltham site to satisfy the demand, and they made plans for a complete textile community to be established along the swift-flowing Merrimack. For this purpose they raised $600,000 by selling

corporation shares to a select group of Boston investors.

The new mills at Lowell, Massachusetts were much larger than earlier spinning mills in Rhode Island. Attracting enough labor for the new mills and keeping it housed in good physical and moral health were major problems. The promoters solved their labor difficulties by hiring Yankee farm girls, a resource hitherto untapped. These young women could earn money to provide themselves with dowries or to pay off a family debt. They were attracted to Lowell by promises of good wages and cheap, attractive dormitory housing built at company expense. The company also provided a lyceum, where the literate and pious young women who worked in the mills could hear edifying lectures, and paid for a church and a minister. By the mid-1830s Lowell was a town of 18,000 with schools, libraries, paved streets, churches, and health facilities. The mills themselves numbered some half dozen, each separately incorporated, arranged in quadrangles surrounded by the semidetached houses of the townsfolk and the dormitories of the female workers.

So attractive did the Lowell scheme seem to contemporaries that its fame spread even across the Atlantic. Distinguished foreign visitors to the United States commonly made pilgrimages to

The Lowell Girls

Not all the workers at the Lowell Mills were content with their lot. As early as 1834 angry factory girls at Lowell "turned out" to protest wage cuts and other acts of the corporation "agents" that they considered arbitrary and unjust. Yet life at Lowell was a mixture of good and bad, and many of the farm girls found it a welcome relief for a few years from the boredom and narrowness of life in the declining New England countryside.

Harriet Hanson Robinson, whose account of her Lowell experience in the mid-1830s is excerpted below, was not entirely typical of the Lowell "operatives." She was born in Boston and moved to Lowell with her mother shortly after her father's death. There Mrs. Robinson ran a boardinghouse for girls who worked in the Tremount mill. Harriet herself, along with her three siblings, entered the mill at the age of ten and remained there until her mid-teens. She later married a newspaper editor and became an active women's suffrage leader. Below, from the perspective of over half a century, she tells what it was like to be a "doffer" in the mill.

"I had been to school constantly until I was about ten years of age, when my mother, feeling obliged to have help in her work besides what I could give, and also needing the money which I could earn, allowed me, at my urgent request (for I wanted to earn *money* like the other little girls), to go to work in the mills. I worked first in the spinning-room as a 'doffer.' The doffers were the very youngest girls, whose work was to doff, or take off, the full bobbins, and replace them with the empty ones.

"I can see myself now, racing down the alley, between the spinning frames, carrying in front of me a bobbin-box bigger than I was. These mites had to be very swift in their movements, so as not to keep the spinning-frames stopped long, and they worked only about fifteen minutes in every hour. The rest of the time was their own, and when the overseer was kind they were allowed to read, knit, or even to go outside the mill-yard to play.

"Some of us learned to embroider in crewels, and I still have a lamb worked on cloth, a relic of those early days, when I was first taught to improve my time in the good old New England fashion. When not doffing, we were often allowed to go home, for a time, and thus were able to help our mothers in their housework. We were paid two dollars a week; and proud I was when my turn came to stand up on the bobbin-box, and write my name in the paymaster's book, and how indignant I was when he asked me if I could 'write.' 'Of course I can,' said I and he smiled as he looked down on me.

"The working hours of all the girls extended from five o'clock in the morning until seven in the evening, with one-half hour for breakfast and for dinner. Even the doffers were forced to be on duty nearly fourteen hours a day, and this was the greatest hardship in the lives of these children. For it was not until 1842 that the hours of labor for children under twelve years of age were limited to ten per day; but the 'ten-hour law' itself was not passed until long after some of these little doffers were old enough to appear before the legislative committee on the subject, and plead, by their presence, for a reduction of the hours of labor.

"I do not recall any particular hardship connected with this life, except getting up so early in the morning, and to this habit I never was, and never shall be, reconciled, for it has taken nearly a lifetime for me to make up the sleep lost at that early age. But in every other respect it was a pleasant life. We were not hurried any more than was for our good, and no more work was required of us than we were able easily to do."

Lowell and were invariably impressed by what they saw. The British novelist Charles Dickens, who had encountered at home the worst evils of industrialism, noted that the girls at Lowell wore "serviceable bonnets, good warm cloaks and shawls . . . , [were] healthy in appearance, many of them remarkably so . . . , [and had] the manners and deportment of young women, not of degraded brutes."

During the "hungry forties," when the nation's business pace slowed, conditions in the mills worsened. The girls' wages were cut, and when they protested, they were replaced with newly arrived Irish immigrants who would accept lower wages. But for a time the Lowell system served as a showcase for the benefits of industrialization.

INDUSTRIAL WORKERS

In 1815, well before Lowell, the Erie Canal, and the Baltimore and Ohio Railroad, Americans were already a rich people by the standards of the day. Few European travelers failed to note the prosperity they encountered in the United States. One visitor to the Ohio Valley in 1818 wrote:

I believe I saw more peaches and apples rotting on the ground than would sink the British fleet. I was at plantations in Ohio where they no more knew the number of their hogs than myself. . . . And they have such flocks of turkies, geese, ducks, and hens, as would surprise you. . . . The poorest family has a cow or two and some sheep . . . and adorns the table three times a day like a wedding dinner—tea,

New York Public Library Picture Collection

This view of Lowell, Massachusetts, dates from the 1840s. It catches the campuslike quality of the town. The long building with many chimneys and the building with the cupola are the Merrimack mills. The two smaller buildings, left foreground, are boardinghouses for the mill girls.

coffee, beef, fowls, pigs, eggs, pickles, good bread; and their favorite beverage is whiskey, or peach brandy.

The economic changes following 1815 enormously increased the wealth and income of the American people. One scholar believes that between the mid-1830s and the Civil War total annual GNP (gross national product, a dollar measure of all goods and services produced) more than doubled. Yet it is clear that all Americans did not gain equally from the momentous changes taking place.

The urban middle class certainly benefited from the economic surge. In the early 1800s this group had consisted of shopkeepers, schoolteachers, lawyers, doctors, and ministers. As the mills, railroads, and mines expanded across the nation, they created jobs not only for laborers and factory operatives but also for engineers, clerks, bookkeepers, and managers. Most of these were native-born Americans, whose familiarity with the English language and American ways gave them an advantage over the foreign-born. The new salaried "white-collar" class enjoyed less prestige

than those who made up the older middle class, but they had higher incomes and status than the wage-earning "blue-collar" workers in the mills, mines, and railroads.

Wages and Working Conditions. But how did more ordinary working people fare? Unskilled labor was not well paid before the Civil War. The Lowell girls received $2.50 or $3.00 a week. Women needle workers who labored in their homes at piecework often could not earn more than 25 cents a day. Domestic servants, also largely women, received on the average a little over a dollar a week plus their room and board in 1850. Common laborers, who dug ditches and foundations, carted, stevedored, and the like, were paid 61 cents a day with board in 1850, or 87 cents without board.

Skilled labor was in short supply and so was generally better rewarded. Blacksmiths earned on the average about $1.10 a day in 1852. In 1847 a skilled iron founder in Pennsylvania could make as much as $30 per week. The Boston Manufacturing Company paid department superintendents $12 a week and machinists up to $11.

What did these wages mean? Today such money incomes would scarcely support a single individual, much less whole families. But money went much further in those times; there were many fewer consumer goods to buy, and those that were available cost much less. The *New York Tribune* estimated in 1851 that a minimum budget of about $10 a week was needed to support a family of five in expensive New York City. This meant that an unskilled worker could not support a family adequately without some help from other family members. On the other hand, wage earners were clearly better off in the United States than in Europe. Michel Chevalier told of an encounter with an Irish construction laborer working on the railroad during his American visit. The man was paid 75 cents a day and board, which included meat three times a day. When he wrote home to his family in Ireland, however, he told them he ate meat three times a week. Why, Chevalier asked, did he not tell them the truth? Because, the man replied, "if I told them that, they'd never believe me."

But there was more to the wage earners' lot than their wages. Working people's lives were not easy. Working hours were long. The Lowell girls worked a twelve-hour day, six days a week. Outdoor workers averaged eleven hours a day, fewer in winter, more in summer. True, the pace of factory labor was probably more leisurely than today, but it was difficult for people used to the slow rhythms of the nineteenth-century farm to adjust to the remorseless pace of the factory machines.

Pre–Civil War workers and their families also experienced great insecurity. Work accidents were common, and when workers were injured, they lost their income and often their job. When men were killed in the mines or factories, there was often no one to take care of their families. Besides industrial disaster, there was the uncertainty of employment. People's economic fortunes were at the mercy of the weather. A bad harvest or a particularly hard winter often left agricultural workers destitute. They were also victims of the business cycle. Severe periodic depressions produced acute hardship among laborers and factory workers. During the hard times that began in 1819, an English traveler through the East and Northwest noted that he had "seen upwards of 1,500 men in quest of work within 11 months past." Again following the 1837 and 1857 panics, unemployment forced many wage earners to turn to public officials for relief for themselves and their families. In 1857 there were food riots among the unemployed in several northern cities.

City and county authorities and various private charities provided some help for the unemployed, but not very much. Soup kitchens, emergency free bread, and the "poorhouse" or the county "poor farm"—gloomy institutions like asylums where paupers went to keep from starving—were about all the jobless and their dependents could expect. In what was still a largely agricultural society unemployment was treated as a freak event or an act of God. No clear distinction was made between the chronically poor and those impoverished because they were thrown out of work during a depression. Poverty, social opinion leaders said, was the result of improvidence or sloth. The community could not let people starve, of

Library of Congress

Young women formed the bulk of the labor force in the early textile mills. There were male workers, too—usually foremen or skilled mechanics who, needless to say, earned more than the women. Power for the looms came from overhead shafts and belts that were driven by waterwheels.

course, but it had little responsibility for finding jobs for them.

The limited concern of public authorities for the unemployed can be explained in part by the common belief that all who wished to work could find jobs in the West. But the West was a refuge for the out-of-work in only a limited way. Western cities, all growing very rapidly, were chronically short of mechanics and laborers, and even during business downturns they probably offered more job opportunities than the older communities of the East. But few unemployed eastern wage earners had the means to move west and reestablish themselves in their accustomed trades, much less take up farming.

Still another source of distress was the downgrading of skills and the loss of independence that sometimes accompanied mechanization and the factory system. The well-documented case of the

Massachusetts shoemakers shows that in the opening years of the nineteenth century they had been skilled, semi-independent craftsmen. Merchants brought them cut leather and paid them a given sum for each pair of shoes they sewed and finished in their "tenfooters," the ten-by-ten sheds they worked in behind their homes. These skilled craftsmen owned their own tools and often employed their wives and grown children to help with the work. Not only were they well paid; they also enjoyed a sense of independence that came from their relation to the merchant as a kind of subcontractor and from the fact that they were the heads of their households, not only in a social and legal sense, but also in a direct economic way.

Gradually, as the market for ready-made shoes, especially for southern slaves, expanded, the shoemakers' independence and incomes declined. Merchants broke up shoemaking into

THE AMERICAN ECONOMIC MIRACLE, 1815–1860

	1815		1860	
Total land area, in square miles	1,716,003		3,022,387	
Total population	8,419,000		31,513,000	
Rural	93%	(1820)	80%	
Urban	7%	(1820)	20%	
Population by region				
Northeast	50.4%	(1820)	36.5%	
South	30.4%	(1820)	25.6%	
West	19.2%	(1820)	37.8%	
Immigrants arriving annually	8,385	(1820)	153,640	
Labor force, ten years and older				
Free	2,185,000	(1820)	8,770,000	
Slave	950,000	(1820)	2,340,000	
Per capita GNP (1840 = 100)	67.6	(1820)	137.0	
Average monthly earnings with board for farm labor	$9.45	(1818)	$13.86	
Government investment in canals (cumulative)	under $50,000		$1,200,000,000	
Miles of railroad in operation	23	(1830)	30,626	
State-chartered banks	208		1,562	
Currency in circulation	$67,100,000		$435,407,000	
Patents issued	173		4,589	
Value of exports	$52,557,753		$333,576,000	
Value of imports	$85,356,680		$367,760,000	
Cotton exports	$17,529,000		$191,806,555	
Gross farm output, in current dollars	$338,000,000		$1,579,000,000	
Value of produce received in New Orleans from interior	$9,749,253	(1815–16)	$155,863,564	
Cotton production, in bales	209,000		3,841,000	
Lumber production, in board feet	600,000,000	(1819)	8,000,000,000	(1859)
Coal production				
Soft, in tons	253,000		9,057,000	
Pennsylvania anthracite, in short tons	2,000		10,984,000	
Pig-iron shipments, in long tons	20,000	(1820)	821,000	

Sources: Historical Statistics of the United States, Colonial Times to 1957; D. C. North, The Economic Growth of the United States, 1790–1860; and Paul A. David, "The Growth of Real Product in the United States before 1840," Journal of Economic History XXVII (1967).

smaller and simpler processes and "put out" the work to unmarried young women in New England country villages. Eventually power-driven machines that sewed heavy leather were invented, enabling the merchants to establish factories where wage workers could use the expensive, capitalist-owned machines. By the eve of the Civil War the independent master craftsman working in his tenfooter had been replaced with semiskilled labor working for weekly wages in large factories.

The Labor Movement. Clearly many wage earners were unhappy with the new aggressive capitalism and the new factory system. In 1836 the young women at Lowell went on strike to protest a wage cut. Three thousand gathered on one of the city's open places to hear one of their leaders give a passionate speech, one of the first labor addresses ever delivered by a woman. In the end the factory owners won and the wage cut stuck. In 1860 the shoemakers of Lynn, Massachusetts, "turned out" to protest declining wages; before the strike ended, some 20,000 Massachusetts shoemakers had left their places at the machines.

All through the antebellum period workers struck for higher wages or better working conditions. Most of the strikes were unplanned uprisings in response to some abrupt blow such as a wage cut. But some grew out of long-standing grievances such as the sheer drudgery of factory life or the loss of worker independence. These grievances created a labor movement of considerable dimensions. The small community craft societies organized in the early 1800s expanded over the next thirty years into city-wide labor unions, each representing a whole trade. Later local unions joined together into national organizations to improve working conditions and wages. Their strikes achieved some gains; but after the Panic of 1837, when the depression forced many workers out of their jobs, employers usually defeated the strikers by threatening to hire the many unemployed. Strikes failed and trade unions declined. In the next two decades labor discontent generally was diverted from labor unions to political action and various reform movements.

We must not exaggerate the extent of labor discontent during these years, however. The school system, as well as the churches, worked hard to instill the "work ethic" into the labor force, and on the whole, they were successful. By and large the American work force cooperated with economic growth. As one pre-1860 observer noted, in New England "every workman seems to be continually devising some new thing to assist him in his work, and there [is] a strong desire both

with masters and workman . . . to be 'posted up' [that is, kept informed] in every improvement." Skilled English workingmen who came to American machine shops in the 1830s and 1840s were often startled to find that their American counterparts, rather than fighting the shop owners, were "fire eaters" whose "ravenous appetites for labor" made their own performances look bad. Several eminent students of American economic development are convinced that this enthusiastic cooperation was one of the most important elements in creating the pre–Civil War economic miracle.

CONCLUSIONS

Many things contributed to the nation's impressive economic performance during the antebellum period. Nature had endowed the United States with uniquely rich resources. History had given it a vigorous, frugal, hard-working people. After 1815 Americans vastly improved on what they had inherited from nature and their own colonial past. During the succeeding decades European immigrants added their brains and brawn to the working population and its accumulated skills. Foreign investors, seeing the United States as a land of opportunity, sent their capital across the Atlantic. Government encouraged enterprise by passing general incorporation laws and tariffs, constructing schools, and investing directly in canals and roads. Skillful entrepreneurs, benefiting from low wages and low taxes, threw themselves into the task of making their communities—and themselves—rich. The country's values and ideals also contributed to material progress by creating a work ethic that made wage earners feel they had a share in the nation's economic progress.

Whatever the causes, economic growth was not an unrelieved blessing. Though most Americans benefited, the contrast between rich and poor became more pronounced. A by-product of America's spectacular economic surge, these inequalities would assume greater importance in the generations ahead.

FOR FURTHER READING

George R. Taylor, *The Transportation Revolution, 1815–1860* (1951)
> The best single-volume treatment of economic growth during the period covered by this chapter. As the title suggests, Taylor believes that improved transportation is the crucial item in pre–Civil War American growth.

Stuart Bruchey. *The Roots of American Economic Growth, 1607–1861: An Essay in Social Causation* (1965)

> This book takes a much longer running start than Taylor's. It is also more up-to-date in its reliance on modern economists' growth theory, though Bruchey also stresses the importance of national values and political, scientific, and technological developments.

Alan Dawley. *Class and Community: The Industrial Revolution of Lynn* (1976)

> Professor Dawley's book disagrees with one important part of the industrialization process as described in *These United States*. His interesting study of the mid-nineteenth-century Lynn, Massachusetts, shoemakers describes them as strongly opposed to the emerging industrial values and practices of the age and—borrowing from the English socialist scholar E. P. Thompson—he depicts them as determined to preserve a preindustrial working-class ethic even if that meant resisting "progress."

H. J. Habakkuk. *American and British Technology in the Nineteenth Century* (1962)

> Habakkuk, an English economic historian, compares English and American technology during the early industrial revolution. He finds American technology superior, in large part because American skilled workers were better educated and more willing to cooperate with their employers in furthering change than their English counterparts.

Ronald Shaw. *Erie Water West: A History of the Erie Canal, 1792–1854* (1966)

> The social and political history of the great canal. Includes the story of its sponsors and opponents, its construction and operation, and its social and cultural consequences.

Mark Twain. *Life on the Mississippi* (1883)

> Not a novel, but a beautifully written narrative of Twain's experiences as apprentice to a Mississippi River steamboat pilot before the Civil War. "Mark Twain," the pen name Samuel Clemens adopted, was the chant steamboaters sang out to the pilot to tell him that the river was two fathoms (twelve feet) deep and so safe for the boat to proceed.

Norman Ware. *The Industrial Worker, 1840–1860: The Reaction of American Industrial Society to the Advance of the Industrial Revolution* (1924)

> An older work that examines the roots of the American labor movement and sees it as a reaction to the loss of skill and autonomy ushered in by the factory system.

Hannah Josephson. *Golden Threads: New England Mill Girls and Magnates* (1949)

> A well-written social and economic history of the early New England textile industry. Deals with the mill workers as well as their bosses.

Anthony Wallace. *Rockdale: The Growth of an American Village in the Early Industrial Revolution* (1978)

> A fascinating study of an early textile community near Philadelphia. Written by an anthropologist, it is full of interesting details concerning how early textile mills worked and how those connected with them—both workers and owners—lived and thought.

Paul E. Johnson. *A Shopkeeper's Millennium: Society and Revivals in Rochester, New York, 1815–1837* (1979)

> This book describes the religious roots of the pre–Civil War work ethic. An interesting marriage of intellectual and social history.

10 Jacksonian Democracy

What Was It and How Did It Change Political Life?

1810 Americans in Spanish West Florida "revolt"; the United States claims the region as part of the Louisiana Purchase • *Fletcher v. Peck*

1812 James Madison reelected president

1816 Congress incorporates the Second Bank of the United States (BUS) • Tariff Act for the first time protects American industry from foreign competition • James Monroe elected president

1818 Andrew Jackson's raid on Spanish Florida

1819 *Dartmouth College* v. *Woodward* • *McCulloch* v. *Maryland* • The Adams-Onís Treaty with Spain

1821 *Cohens* v. *Virginia*

1823 The Monroe Doctrine announced

1824 Henry Clay's "American System" becomes the Whig platform • John Quincy Adams is elected president by the House and Jackson's supporters suspect a "corrupt bargain"

1828 Congress passes "Tariff of Abominations"; John Calhoun writes *Exposition and Protest* • Andrew Jackson elected president

1830 Indian Removal Act

1832 Tariff Act lowers 1828 duties only slightly; South Carolina declares the new tariff null and void • *Worcester* v. *Georgia* upholds Cherokee land claims • Jackson vetoes the bill renewing the BUS charter • Jackson removes government deposits from the BUS

1832–34 Biddle reduces the calls in BUS loans

1833 Congress passes the Force Bill; South Carolina agrees to a compromise tariff, but nullifies the Force Bill

1835–42 Florida Seminoles forcibly resist removal west

1836 Jackson issues Specie Circular • Martin Van Buren elected president

1838 Cherokees leave Georgia for Oklahoma on the "Trail of Tears"

1840 Whig William H. Harrison elected president

M arch 4, 1829, was moving day in Washington. Andrew Jackson was to be inaugurated seventh president of the United States, and for weeks many of the city's oldest inhabitants had been packing their possessions and preparing to leave for new residences. To Margaret Bayard Smith, the elegant hostess who had presided over Washington society for twenty-five years, the change was a tragedy. "Never before did the city seem . . . so gloomy," she wrote. "Drawing rooms in which I have so often mixed with gay crowds, distinguished by rank, fashion, beauty, talent, . . . now empty, silent, dank, dismantled. Oh! 'tis melancholy!"

While some were fleeing the still-raw capital on the Potomac, others were moving in. The city had filled with visitors, and the hotels overflowed. Washington endured a flood of new people every four years, of course, but this time there were more of them and they were different. Besides the usual frock-coated dignitaries and bureaucrats, rough-looking men in leather shirts and coonskin caps and equally unfamiliar types with Irish lilts to their voices strolled the capital's streets. The crowd was playful and good-humored, but also fiercely determined. Every face, according to Mrs. Smith, bore "defiance on its brow." "I never saw anything like it before," wrote the new senator from Massachusetts, Daniel Webster. "They really seem to think the country is rescued from some dreadful danger."

The determined mood of the newcomers was understandable. For fourteen years—ever since his great victory at New Orleans—Andy Jackson's admirers had worked hard to make their hero president. The general was the most charismatic political leader since Washington; to many his personal qualities of bluntness, courtliness, and charm, combined with his stature as a military leader, would always be his chief political assets. But was hero worship the only reason for the excitement? Or was there more than personal loyalty behind the defiant brows? Was something important taking place? Would Old Hickory's election make a difference in the way the country was run? Would it bring new groups to power with new ideas and new programs? Obviously Webster and Mrs. Smith believed they were witnessing some sort of revolution. So did the rough-hewn men who wandered the streets of the capital that week in March 1829. Were they right? Was a major political change in the air? And if so, what was it? To answer these questions we must look first at the era before Jackson's election.

THE ERA OF GOOD FEELINGS

By 1817, when James Monroe was inaugurated as fifth president, the "first party system" had run its course. The bad judgment that had led the Federalists to bet on the wrong horse in the War of 1812, along with the limited appeal of their aristocratic ideology, virtually destroyed them as a significant political force. Though the Federalists continued to be important in New England, Delaware, and a few other places, the party of Washington, Hamilton, and John Adams never recovered to challenge the Republicans in a national election again.

Federalist principles lived on, however. In the War of 1812, as we saw in Chapter 8, the Republicans learned the value of banks, roads, and national self-sufficiency; in 1815 President Madison had asked for a new national bank, a protective tariff, and a system of internal improvements. In Congress Henry Clay, John C. Calhoun of South Carolina, and other "new Republicans" who had learned their lessons from Hamilton supported the president. Madison got most of what he had asked for without serious opposition. In April 1816 Congress passed a measure to incorporate a second Bank of the United States with a larger capitalization than its predecessor. A few weeks later it approved the Tariff Act of 1816, which for the first time protected American manufacturers against the lower costs and greater efficiency of European industry. Early the following year Congress approved the president's third recommendation by enacting a major internal improvements bill.

With the Federalists gone, ideological tensions declined. For a while it looked as if Jefferson had spoken prophetically when he said in 1801: "We are all Republicans, we are all Federalists." Certainly the Republicans' adoption of Hamiltonian principles ended the bitter political disagreements of the 1790–1815 period.

Historians have labeled the decade following the War of 1812 the Era of Good Feelings. This is a useful tag if we consider only the placid presidential elections, contests without clashes of parties with distinct ideologies. It is a misnomer if it is intended to mean that political rivalry had ceased. Political disagreements continued during these years, but they took the form of intraparty squabbling and personal rivalry, as in colonial times. Within the states there were frequent battles between one Jeffersonian Republican faction and another. In New York the followers of De Witt Clinton, sponsor of the Erie Canal, and Martin

Jacksonian Democracy

Mrs. Margaret Bayard Smith, wife of a Washington banker, editor, and Jeffersonian politician, witnessed the transition from the Virginia dynasty to the age of Jackson. A keen observer of politics as it was played out in the nation's capital early in the nineteenth century, she recorded her impressions in letters to friends and family, later collected as *The First Forty Years of Washington Society*. The following excerpt from that work describes Inauguration Day, 1829, when the "people's" hero, Andy Jackson, became president of the United States, ushering in a new, more democratic age. It was an age that clearly did not fully please Mrs. Smith, who was unused to the unruly exuberance of the masses come to celebrate their day in the sun.

"A national salute was fired early in the morning, and ushered in the 4th of March. By ten o'clock the Avenue was crowded with carriages of every description, from the splendid Barronet and coach, down to waggons and carts, filled with women and children, some in finery and some in rags, for it was the people's President, and all would see him. . . . Some one came and informed us [that] the crowd before the President's house, was so far lessen'd, that they thought that we might enter. This time we effected our purpose. But what a scene did we witness! *The Majesty of the People* had disappeared and a rabble, a mob, of boys, negros, women, children, scrambling, fighting, romping. What a pity, what a pity! No arrangements had been made; no police officers placed on duty, and the whole house had been inundated by the rabble mob. We came too late. The President, after having been *literally* nearly pressed to death and almost suffocated, and torn to pieces by the people in their eagerness to shake hands with Old Hickory, had retreated through the back way or south front and had escaped to his lodgings at Gadsby's. Cut glass and china to the amount of several thousand dollars had been broken in the struggle to get the refreshments. . . . [P]unch and other articles had been carried out in tubs and buckets, but had it been in hogsheads it would have been insufficient. . . . [They supplied] ice-creams, and cake, and lemonade, for 20,000 people, for it is said that [that] number were there tho' I think the estimate exaggerated. Ladies fainted, men were seen with bloody noses and such a scene of confusion took place as is impossible to describe,—those who got in could not get out by the door again, but had to scramble out of windows. At one time, the President, who had retreated and retreated until he was pressed against the wall, could only be secured by a number of gentlemen forming around him and making a kind of barrier of their own bodies, and the pressure was so great that Col Bomford who was one said that at one time he was afraid they should have been pushed down, or on the President. It was then the windows were thrown open, and the torrent found an outlet, which otherwise might have proved fatal.

"This concourse had not been anticipated and therefor not provided against. Ladies and gentlemen only had been expected at this Levee, not the people en masse. But it was the People's day, and the People's President and the People would rule. God grant that one day or other, the People do not put down all rule and rulers. . . .'"

Van Buren, leader of the so-called Albany Regency, fought constantly over who should run the state government. In Ohio competing groups, both calling themselves Republican, organized around James Gazlay and General William Henry Harrison. Nationally, the differing political factions looked to Calhoun, Clay, John Quincy Adams, or Senator William H. Crawford of Georgia for leadership. But none of these men was as yet capable of evoking great enthusiasm among the voters. Moreover, the issues debated were obscure—if there were issues at all. Public indifference was widespread and the voter turnouts in elections everywhere were small.

National elections continued, of course, but they merely confirmed the choices of Republican leaders. At the highest level "King Caucus" decided who should be president. Every four years the Republican leaders in Congress "caucused"— got together and nominated the party's candidate—and in the fall their choices were duly ratified by the voters. Making matters even more cut and dried, the caucus leaders invariably chose either the incumbent or, if he had served two full terms, his secretary of state. Thus Secretary of State Madison succeeded Jefferson, Secretary of State Monroe succeeded Madison, and Secretary of State John Quincy Adams would succeed Monroe. To top off the whole cozy arrangement—and turn off the voters—four of the first six presidents were Virginians, and the other two were from Massachusetts. With so little real choice, it was no wonder that voter participation in elections declined so sharply.

The Virginia Dynasty. The presidents from Jefferson to Monroe (1800–25) were part of what is known as the Virginia dynasty. (John Quincy Adams, who followed Monroe in office, belonged to this group in spite of his Massachusetts origins.)

John Quincy Adams, shown in this early portrait, was typical of the presidents during the "Era of Good Feelings." Aloof and aristocratic, he lacked the personal warmth needed to attract voters. Still, he was a man of rigorous character who swam daily in the Potomac, even in the coldest weather, wearing only a skullcap and goggles.

Library of Congress

Jefferson excepted, none of these men was a dynamic leader. They were cultivated gentlemen, but they were also colorless and withdrawn. And they proved surprisingly timid in domestic affairs. Although Madison had recommended a major internal improvements program to Congress, he vetoed the measure that did pass, the so-called Bonus Bill establishing a fund to be used for roads and canals. Five years later President Monroe vetoed a measure to repair the lagging Cumberland Road and provide it with toll-collecting facilities.

John Quincy Adams was the boldest thinker of all these men, again excepting Jefferson. The sixth president was a man of exceptional intelligence and learning who sought to make the federal government a patron of science and the arts as well as a supporter of economic progress. His first annual message to Congress recommended federal support for a national university and a national observatory, a system of uniform weights and measures, a new Department of the Interior, reformed patent laws, and a massive program of internal improvements. But Adams, too, lacked

leadership ability. However intelligent and able, he was also aloof and humorless. One associate said of him: "It is a question whether he ever laughed in his life." It is not surprising that he found the normal roughhouse of national politics distasteful. Congress, controlled by his political enemies, ignored his recommendations, and the president, too fastidious to use his influence or the power of patronage to gain its support, accomplished little.

John Marshall's Court. The record of domestic political achievements might have remained nearly blank during the Era of Good Feelings if it had not been for the efforts of Chief Justice John Marshall. Marshall was a throwback to the earlier, confident Federalism of Hamilton. Unlike the new Republicans, he did not waver in the cause of strengthening national power and encouraging a climate attractive to business. In 1810, in *Fletcher* v. *Peck*, he had struck down a state law as unconstitutional—the first time the Court had done so—on the grounds that it violated a private contract. Nine years later, in the Dartmouth College case, he again upheld the sanctity of a contract when he forbade the state of New Hampshire to amend the royal charter of Dartmouth College. Clearly, so long as John Marshall had his say, contractual agreements entered into by governments would be off limits to politicians.

Marshall also fought to preserve the authority of the federal government over the states. In the same year as the Dartmouth College case, the state of Maryland attacked the Second Bank of the United States by taxing its paper money issues. Marshall, in a classic statement of the "loose construction" view of the federal Constitution, declared Maryland's tax law void. The issue, he announced in *McCulloch* v. *Maryland,* was twofold: Did Congress have the power to charter a federal bank, and could the states tax federal property? His decision was yes on the first question and no on the second. The right of Congress to charter a bank, he declared, could be readily deduced from the Constitution's "necessary and proper" clause and was implied by the federal government's powers to tax, borrow money, regulate commerce, and conduct war. As for state taxation of federal agencies, the "power to tax" was "the power to destroy." No state could destroy a legal creation of Congress, and hence the Maryland law was unconstitutional. In *Cohens* v. *Virginia* (1821) Marshall asserted that state court decisions were subject to Supreme Court review in cases involving federal laws.

Foreign Affairs. The Virginia dynasty presidents may have been indifferent leaders in domestic affairs, but they were vigorous and successful champions of American international and diplomatic interests. The years following the final defeat of Napoleon at Waterloo (1815) presented the United States with thorny problems and challenges. Spain had been seriously weakened by the international turmoil between 1793 and Waterloo. In 1810, while both Spain and England were preoccupied with Napoleon, the United States took possession of the western spur of Spanish West Florida to the Perdido River on the dubious grounds that this strip of territory had been included in the Louisiana Purchase. Spain protested vigorously, but could do little.

This serving of West Florida did not satisfy the American appetite, however. A sizable strip of the Florida Gulf Coast panhandle still remained in Spanish hands, but still more enticing was the great southern loop of the peninsula itself. Acquiring this would not only round out the southeastern corner of the nation; it would settle the problem of escaped slaves, hostile Indians, and white renegades who periodically staged raids from Florida into Georgia and then fled back across the border into Spanish jurisdiction, where the American authorities could not touch them.

Secretary of State John Quincy Adams urged Spain to transfer Florida to the United States for a price and at the same time settle the uncertain boundary between the Louisiana Purchase territory and the Spanish provinces in Mexico. Spain was not interested. In 1818 Andrew Jackson's impetuous behavior brought the situation to an unexpected head. As commander of American forces patrolling the Florida-Georgia border, Jackson was authorized to cross into Spanish territory to attack the raiders, but told to avoid attacking Spanish posts and settlements in the colony. The general had little patience with such a namby-pamby policy. Claiming that he had received instructions from the government to conquer Florida, Jackson made his move. He crossed the border, captured the Spanish fort of St. Marks, executed two British subjects—Alexander Arbuthnot and Robert Ambrister—he considered troublemakers, and went on to occupy Pensacola, deposing the Spanish governor in the process.

Americans cheered Jackson's bold acts; in Washington, London, and Madrid there was consternation. The only cool head was that of Secretary of State Adams, who saw that the general's rash behavior could be turned to America's advantage. Rather than apologize to Spain, Adams took the offensive. He dismissed Spain's loud protest, charged the Spaniards with failure to protect their own possessions, and enlarged United States claims to Spanish territory in the Far West under the Louisiana Purchase treaty.

Adams's tough tactics worked. The Spanish minister in Washington, Luis de Onís y Gonzales, blustered and complained, but his government recognized that it could no longer hold Florida and came to terms with the United States. In February 1819, in the Adams-Onís Treaty, Spain ceded Florida to the United States and surrendered its claim to Oregon. In return, the United States assumed the payment of $5 million in debts owed by Spain to American citizens and agreed to fix the southwestern boundary of Louisiana to exclude the Mexican province of Texas.

Spain's weakness created hazards as well as opportunities for the United States. By 1820 all of Spanish America, except the Caribbean islands, had won independence. But Spain still hoped to regain control of its former possessions. These hopes were encouraged by France, Prussia, Austria, and Russia, whose monarchs in 1815 had established the Holy Alliance to resist the forces of democracy and liberalism wherever they appeared. Among the European powers, only Great Britain opposed the Alliance. If the Alliance came to Spain's help in America, the British feared, France would regain her lost influence in the Western Hemisphere. A revived Spanish-American empire would also probably exclude Great Britain and other nations from the profitable trade that had developed with Latin America since its independence. Concerned with both these possibilities, the British foreign secretary, George Canning, proposed that his nation and the United States work together to prevent Spain from regaining control of her former colonies.

The Americans, like the British, were dismayed at the prospect of Spanish restoration and the intervention of the great European powers in the Americas. They were also disturbed by Russia's recent expansion from its Alaskan settlements down the west coast of North America. But Secretary Adams was skeptical of any joint arrangement. For the United States to cooperate with Great Britain would put it in the position of "a cockboat in the wake of the British man-of-war." Far better for America to go it alone without relying on Britain's uncertain backing.

On Adams's recommendation President Monroe included in his December 1823 message to Congress a statement regarding Latin America that has become known as the Monroe Doctrine.

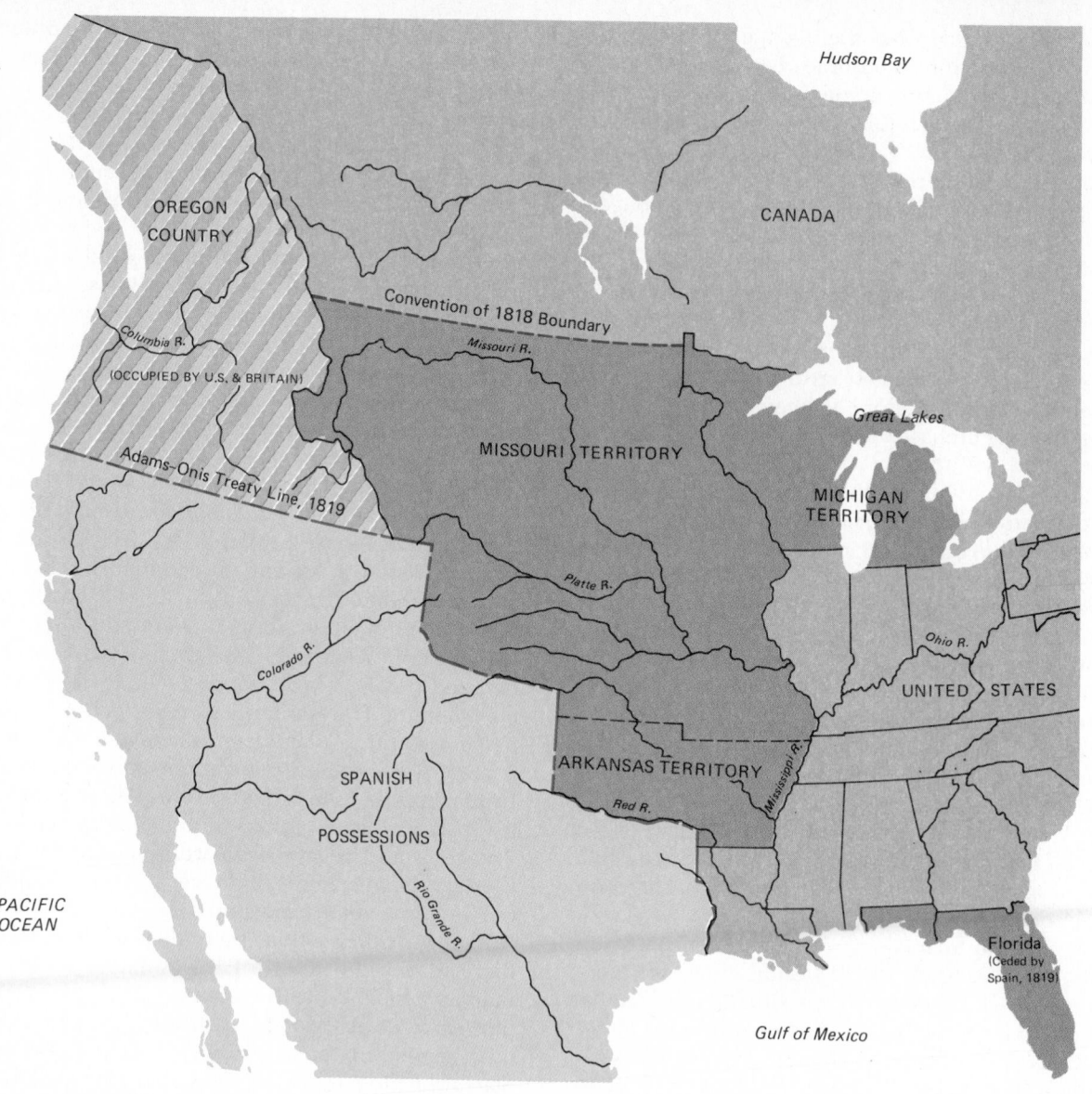

The United States territories, 1819

The president proclaimed four principles that would guide the United States in its relations with Europe and the rest of the Western Hemisphere. To counter the Russian advance, Monroe first declared that no part of the American continents were "to be considered as subjects for future colonization by any European powers." Second, the independent American nations must remain republics. "We owe it . . . to candor and to the amicable relations existing between the United States and those powers [that is, the monarchies of the Holy Alliance]," he noted, "to declare that we should consider any attempt on their part to extend their system to any portion of this hemisphere as dangerous to our peace and safety." The

third principle pledged the United States to respect existing European colonies in America and to stay out of purely European concerns. The fourth element in the Monroe Doctrine, actually announced in a separate diplomatic note to the Russian minister in Washington, asserted that the United States would oppose any transfer of existing colonies in the Americas from one European country to another.

Monroe's principles appeared to the nations of continental Europe to be "blustering," "arrogant," and "monstrous." They were. The United States was asserting rights unrecognized by international law or treaty—rights it also could not defend. The pretensions of the puny American nation seemed ludicrous. "Mr. Monroe, who is not a sovereign," scoffed the French foreign minister, "has assumed in his message the tone of a powerful monarch whose armies and fleets are ready to march at the first signal. . . . Mr. Monroe is the temporary President of a Republic situated on the east coast of North America. . . . Its independence was only recognized forty years ago; by what right then would the two Americas today be under its immediate sway from Hudson's Bay to Cape Horn?"

The United States was counting on Great Britain. Without her support the new policy would have been an empty gesture. Nevertheless, it took some courage for a nation of scarcely 10 million to defy the powers of Europe. It also took idealism. No matter how the United States might later twist the Monroe Doctrine to its own uses, it was originally a generous statement in defense of international freedom and republican institutions.

JACKSON RISES TO POWER

By this time the politicians were hard at work considering Monroe's successor. If precedent had remained a guide, there would have been little fuss. As secretary of state, John Quincy Adams was the obvious choice in 1824. But the precedents followed during the Era of Good Feelings were ceasing to exert much influence on American politics. The voters were tired of being King Caucus's rubber stamp. A people on the move across a continent, growing in self-confidence and national pride, Americans were less willing than in the past to have decisions made for them by gentlemen, however liberal, learned, and decent they might be.

Democratic Reforms in the States. The new attitude created a quiet political revolution. For some time a trend toward eliminating the last vestiges of state property qualifications for voting had been gaining strength. In some older seaboard states the impetus came from Republicans as they displaced their aristocratic Federalist opponents. In New York the arrival of great numbers of New England Yankees with liberal views was the crucial element. In a number of the more laggard eastern states, the suffrage reformers used the argument that the older states must emulate the newer western states or lose population to them. Whatever the reason, an already broad electorate became still broader.

Other changes also advanced the trend toward a more democratic political process. Several states in this period ended "stand-up" voting, which required citizens to acknowledge their candidate publicly on election day and face the possible wrath of influential men; they substituted printed ballots to protect the privacy and independence of the voter. Most states eliminated the remaining property qualifications for officeholding and reapportioned their legislatures to give underrepresented areas the political weight they deserved. By 1832 every state except South Carolina had also taken away the legislatures' power to choose presidential electors and given it to the voters. Many states changed appointive offices into elective ones. The convention system, in which the party rank and file had a voice, soon replaced the caucus as a method of nominating candidates for office. First adopted on the state level in New Jersey and Delaware early in the century, it spread to other Middle Atlantic states during the 1820s and to New England at the end of the decade. In 1831 the small Anti-Masonic party first used it to choose a presidential candidate, and the system soon became the norm in national as well as local politics.

It used to be said that these changes originated in the West and only later spread to the East. The evidence shows that it was often the other way around. In political affairs, at least, the East was the pioneer and eastern practices were carried west by emigrants. It was also at one time commonly held that Jackson and his supporters were responsible for many of the changes. In fact, most of the changes preceded rather than followed the Jackson movement.

The Election of 1824. Although he was not responsible for these new trends, Jackson was clearly their beneficiary. The general alone among the contenders in 1824 was a genuine popular hero. Adams was a man of great ability, but his aloofness and close association with the old Virginia dynasty hurt him with the voters. William Crawford of Georgia had supporters in the lower South but failed to strike sparks elsewhere. Even the formal endorsement of the dying congressional caucus would do him little good. Clay and Calhoun were endorsed by local groups in Kentucky and South Carolina, respectively; but despite their prominent roles as national leaders during and immediately following the War of 1812, neither had national support. Calhoun soon dropped out of the race. There was no opposition party in 1824. Except for the small group of Anti-Masons, everyone called himself a Republican, and in the end the campaign turned out to be primarily a popularity contest.

Politics became more democratic as states eliminated property requirements and "stand up" voting. With greater public involvement, candidates wooed the masses with parades, barbecues, and rallies, as shown here. Voters enjoyed this attention and appreciated the privacy of casting paper ballots in boxes.

The Historical Society of Pennsylvania

If the election was uneventful, its aftermath was not. No candidate won a majority of the electoral college vote. Jackson was first in both electoral and popular vote; Adams was second; and Crawford and Clay trailed well behind both. The Constitution provided that in the event no candidate received an electoral vote majority, the selection of a president would rest with the House of Representatives, where each state would cast a single vote for one of the top three candidates. The Constitution did not require that individual representatives vote for the man with the largest electoral or popular vote; if it had, there would have been no point to the procedure. Still, Jackson's supporters believed that the House had a moral obligation to endorse their candidate as the most popular man. When thirteen state delegations—more than half—gave Adams a majority, they denounced the result as a denial of the people's will. Clay, they charged, had used his influence in the House to throw the election to Adams. Ignoring the general ideological agreement be-

tween Clay and Adams, Jackson's supporters charged that the two had struck a "corrupt bargain" when the new president appointed Clay as his secretary of state.

Adams's administration was dogged by that charge and by the rancor of Jackson's supporters. The country had seen nothing like this for ten years, and the effects were unfortunate. As we have noted, almost nothing in Adams's domestic program passed Congress. Even in foreign affairs, where his great experience should have been an advantage, he accomplished little. Typical of his experience in diplomacy was the farce of the Panama Conference of 1826. When he and Secretary Clay recommended two men as delegates to this meeting of Western Hemisphere nations in Panama, their political foes in Congress tied up the appointments by months of angry debate. When Congress finally approved delegates, it was too late. One of them died on the way and the other set out so late that the conference had adjourned before he reached Panama.

The Tariff of Abominations. All through his administration Adams fought Jackson and his supporters. A major focus of their battle was the tariff.

By 1828 the last important tariff revision was already twelve years old. Now the modest protectionist provisions of the tariff of 1816 no longer suited many groups. The increasing number of wool growers, textile manufacturers, and ironmasters—and even many farmers—demanded higher duties on imports to protect them against foreign competition. The "protectionists" were concentrated in the Northeast and to a lesser extent in the Old Northwest. Southerners of virtually all economic classes opposed any increase in duties because they had little industry to protect. Indeed, they were happy to rely on Great Britain, the cheapest producer of manufactured goods, for their imports. In 1816, when the South's economic future was still in doubt, many southerners had endorsed the tariff. In 1828, after it had become clear that the region's fate was to be supplier of raw materials for a world market, its leading spokesmen saw the protective tariff as an instrument for increasing northern profits at the South's expense.

The issue was highly charged, and most politicians would have preferred to avoid it. But Martin Van Buren of New York's Albany Regency believed that a major tariff revision would help get his friend Jackson elected president by winning him support in the North and West. The tariff bill he sponsored, when it finally emerged from the pro-Jackson Congress, injured the manufacturers of New England by raising the rates on raw materials that they needed to produce their goods. At the same time, southerners faced the prospect of higher prices for many English imports. Only Middle Atlantic industrialists and the producers of hemp, raw wool, and a few other farm products got anything positive out of the bill. So objectionable was the measure that puzzled contemporaries assumed that the foxy Van Buren had intended to raise the political stock of the Jackson men by giving them a universally unpopular bill that they could then loudly denounce.

Most scholars now agree that Van Buren honestly favored the tariff of 1828 because his New York constituents wanted it and because he believed a higher tariff would win support for Jackson in the North and West, where its major benefits would be felt. Since the South would not vote for Adams in any case, this northern and western support would ensure the general's election. Van Buren did not intend the bill to offend northerners; that was the doing of Congress,

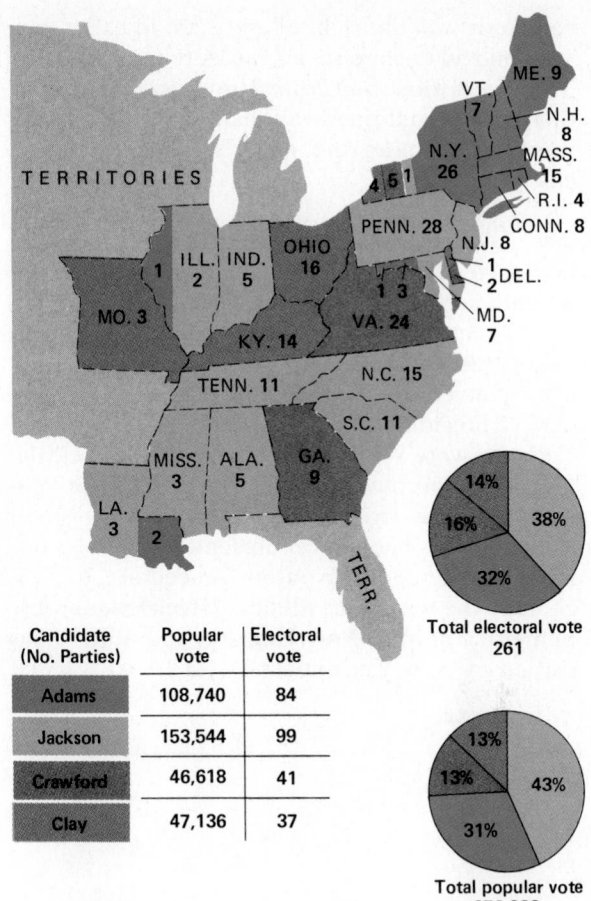

Candidate (No. Parties)	Popular vote	Electoral vote
Adams	108,740	84
Jackson	153,544	99
Crawford	46,618	41
Clay	47,136	37

Election of 1824

which in the give-and-take of tariff making had twisted the measure out of its original shape.

Whatever its purpose, this "Tariff of Abominations" particularly outraged the South. Everything southerners now bought would cost more, and this at a time when world cotton prices had taken a sharp drop. The southern outcry was general and emphatic, but it was John C. Calhoun who took it upon himself to make a constitutional case for his section's interests. Published anonymously by the South Carolina legislature, Calhoun's *Exposition and Protest* denied that Congress had the right to levy a tariff so high that it would exclude imports. The Founding Fathers had intended to impose only moderate duties on imported goods as a means to raise revenue. The 1828 law, he stated, was obviously discriminatory, favoring the manufacturing states and hurting those sections that relied on imports and had little industry to protect. Calhoun went beyond thse familiar low-tariff arguments to insist that if Congress persisted in taking such an unconstitutional course, it was the right of any state to call a convention and declare such a measure null and void. The *Exposition and Protest* revealed that its author, once a confirmed nationalist, was well on his way to becoming the great southern sectional champion.

The Election of 1828. Despite Van Buren's hopes, the 1828 presidential election revolved around personalities rather than issues. Adams, with Richard Rush of Pennsylvania as his running mate, was nominated by the "National Republican" convention at Harrisburg, the first major-party presidential convention. Jackson and Calhoun were selected by the Tennessee legislature and then placed on the ballot by their supporters in the various states. Although President Adams alone had the endorsement of the new, more democratic convention procedure, he was actually the weaker candidate. His partisans were numerous only in New England and other areas settled by New Englanders.

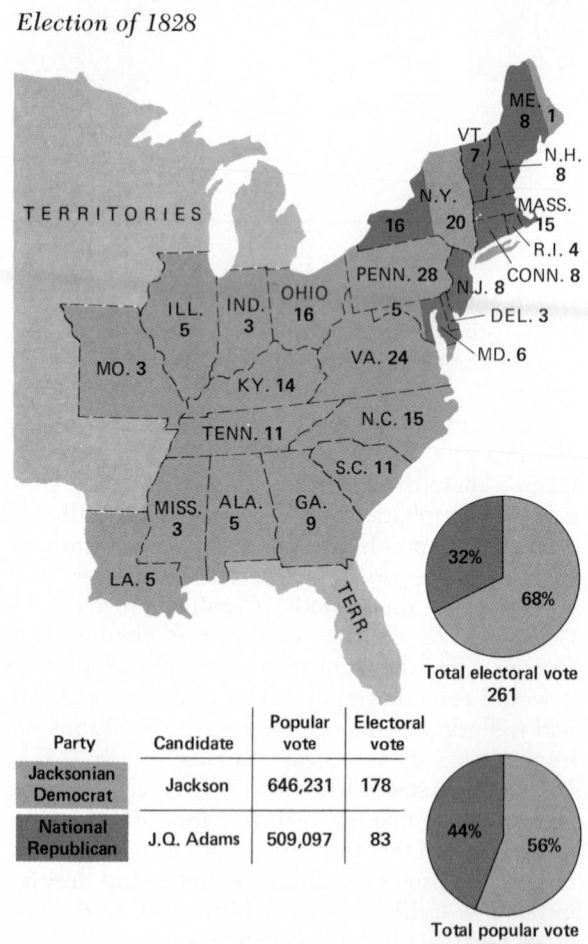

Election of 1828

Party	Candidate	Popular vote	Electoral vote
Jacksonian Democrat	Jackson	646,231	178
National Republican	J.Q. Adams	509,097	83

Total electoral vote 261

Total popular vote 1,156,328

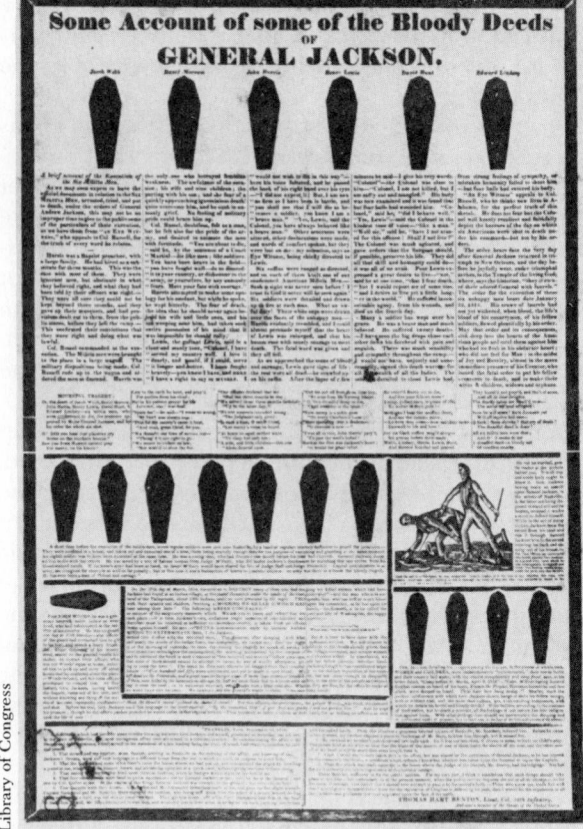

Library of Congress

The election of 1828 was an especially dirty campaign. The candidates' personalities became campaign issues. In this broadside, the so-called Coffin Handbill, Adams's supporters portray Jackson as a hot-tempered frontier brawler with a penchant for dueling and a harsh disciplinarian who had six militiamen court-martialed and shot.

The contest was one of the dirtiest on record. The Jackson men, who had long been brooding over their defeat in 1824, revived the corrupt bargain charge to discredit Adams and resorted to scandalmongering. In Pennsylvania the Jackson press claimed that Adams's wife, Louisa, had been born out of wedlock. A pro-Jackson Missouri editor charged that Adams had lived in sin with his wife before they were married. Equally scandalous stories were spread by the other side. Rachel Jackson, the Adams people said, had not been divorced from her first husband when she married the general. As for Jackson himself, he was a brutal man who had ordered the execution of six innocent militiamen during the campaign against the Creek Indians a decade before.

There was almost no discussion of issues. Though we conventionally date the rise of the second party system from this era, few principles seemed to separate the candidates. One contemporary noted that no one in the New York State convention that confirmed Jackson's nomination for president knew the candidate's views on public matters. A Pennsylvanian observed that "the great mystery of the case" was that "the South should support General Jackson avowedly for the purpose of preventing tariffs and internal improvements and that we should support him for a directly opposite purpose." Adams's positions were a little easier to discern. He stood for an active and paternalistic national government, if he stood for anything, and in New England the surviving Federalists clearly found him the more congenial candidate. Yet he also received the support of many Yankee Republicans, who saw him as the spiritual descendant of Jefferson.

Only the Anti-Masons seemed to have a clear program. This curious group had appeared in New York following the mysterious disappearance of William Morgan, a former Mason who in 1826 had written a book exposing the Masonic order's rituals and other "secrets." Morgan was presumed murdered by the Masons, and the public indignation that followed led to the formation of a political organization dedicated to reducing the power of secret groups in national affairs. In 1828 the new party generally supported Adams, but in later years the Anti-Masons would nominate their own candidates and mount an attack on privilege in government and the economy that would be far more wide-ranging than anything undertaken by the reputedly radical Jackson party.

The 1828 contest, if we ignore the Anti-Masons, did not contribute very much to establishing—or reestablishing—well-defined and competing party ideologies. On the other hand, in several states, especially in the Middle Atlantic region, the Jackson-Adams contest aroused political instincts dormant for over a decade. A two-sided contest, particularly one that included the colorful Jackson, was more gripping than either the rubber stamps of 1816 and 1820 or the four-sided competition of 1824. In much larger numbers than four years before, voters came out to cast their ballots. Jackson won decisively, receiving 178 electoral and 647,000 popular votes to Adams's 83 and 509,000.

KING ANDREW

The Spoils System. Jackson's first order of business was distributing the political loaves and fishes. The new president did not eject his political opponents from office wholesale, as scholars used to believe. In his first year and a half he re-

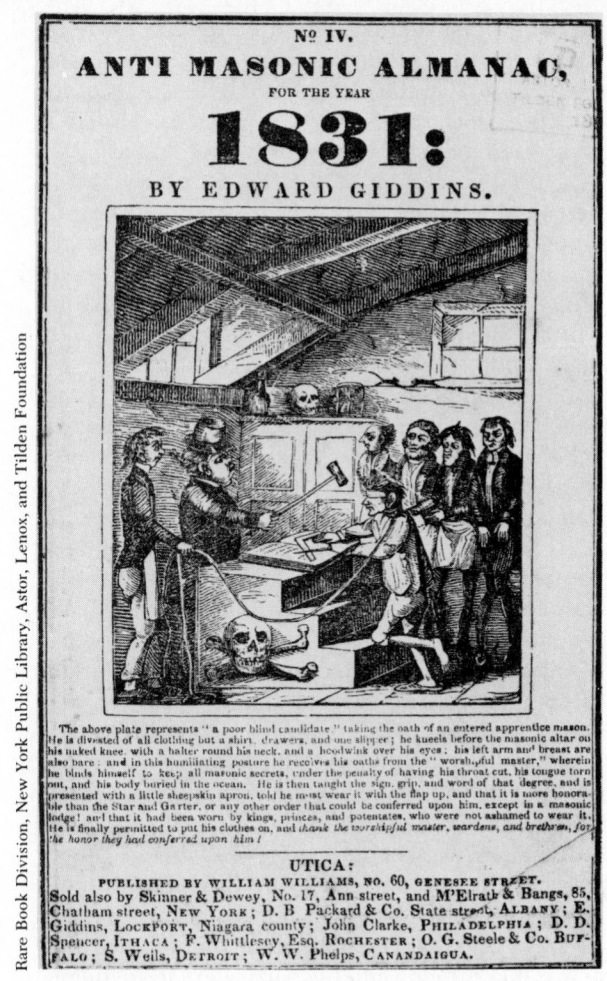

Rare Book Division, New York Public Library, Astor, Lenox, and Tilden Foundation

The Anti-Masons were certain that the order they opposed was a dangerous conspiracy against the liberties of a free people. As this cartoon from the Anti-Masonic Almanac *of 1831 shows, they also believed that the Masons were determined to humiliate any person so foolish as to join their ranks.*

moved 900 of over 10,000 federal employees, only about 9 percent of the total. Yet Jackson's policy was something new on the political stage. The Virginia dynasty presidents had favored members of their own party in filling vacancies, but they had seldom fired officeholders who opposed their policies primarily to create new openings. Jackson and his friends were fierce partisans and took no such moderate view of the federal civil service. Loyalty to the president, they quickly made clear, would be the prime consideration in retaining office. If the number of those actually dismissed was small, it was only because so many bureaucrats were already Jackson supporters or quickly became supporters to avoid losing their jobs.

Nor did Jackson's predecessors elevate the "spoils system" into a noble principle. At times the Jacksonians frankly admitted the narrow political reasons for removing long-time civil servants from office. "To the victor belong the spoils of the enemy," declared Senator William L. Marcy in 1832. Generally, however, they tried to pass it off as a political reform. "Rotation in office" was a democratic policy, they said, that ended the previous monopoly of officeholding by gentlemen and provided many more citizens with the opportunity to exercise power. Since, in Jackson's words, "the duties of all public officers are . . . so plain and simple that men of intelligence may readily qualify for their performance," no group need be excluded from serving the nation. Scholars, accepting the Jacksonians at their own word, have often treated the spoils system as a democratization of the political process.

In fact, rotation in office was not particularly democratic. It did not replace gentlemen with common folk; the Jackson appointees' social backgrounds differed little from those of their predecessors. Nor were the Jacksonians primarily interested in spreading power. Their chief purpose was to provide political muscle to the party system. The lure of office would be a powerful incentive to ambitious men to work for party causes, while officeholders could be assessed for contributions out of their government salaries to party coffers. The spoils system would be a useful and important component of the emerging second party system, but it should not be taken as evidence that Jackson and his party were more democratic than their predecessors.

The new policy damaged civil service morale, and at times the effects of job uncertainty were tragic. "A clerk in the War Office, named Henshaw," ex-President Adams recorded in his diary, "three days since cut his throat from ear to ear, from the mere terror of being dismissed. Linneus Smith, of the Department of State, has gone raving distracted and others are said to be threatened with the same calamity." Besides reducing efficiency, the spoils system encouraged corruption. In the New York customhouse, where dishonesty reached a nadir, the collector, Samuel Swartwout, embezzled over a million dollars and escaped to England.

Jackson's penchant for favoring friends and acquaintances over disinterested public servants is apparent in his choice of close advisers. Generally he ignored the official cabinet and instead, relied on his so-called Kitchen Cabinet, drawn from early supporters of his presidential bid. These men were given undemanding posts to support them while they devoted their time to politics and political service to Jackson.

Whatever the deficiencies of the Virginia dynasty presidents, they had maintained a high level of honesty and efficiency in the public service. The Jackson men—and their successors—undoubtedly lowered the moral and intellectual tone of American political life. At the same time, however, they did make it possible for the ordinary man to feel a sense of participation. This new mood was not at first reflected in the voting statistics, except in the 1828 presidential election. Larger election turnouts would have to wait until real two-party contests had appeared in all the states and the voters had been caught up in the rivalries of close elections. But the Jackson party did infuse a new, more open spirit into political life—a spirit essential to the success of the second party system.

Jackson's Style.   The spoils system was one Jacksonian contribution to be political revival of these years, though obviously one with mixed results. Another was a strong president. Jackson was a military man, used to command and unwilling to brook defiance by Congress, state legislatures, or the chief justice of the Supreme Court. A vivid personality who inspired intense feelings of either hatred or affection among the voters, he was not a learned man or even a clear and consistent thinker. The general acted on the prejudices he had acquired as a young man and never abandoned. A southerner and slaveholder, he had few objections to slavery and despised abolitionists. A man from the frontier state of Tennessee and a leader in the Indian wars, he had little love for the Indians. Having been almost ruined in 1819 by the tight credit policies of the Bank of the United States, he hated banks in general and the Bank of the United States in particular. Jackson personalized almost all his political attitudes, turning political opponents into enemies who had to be destroyed lest they destroy him. Many Americans thought Old Hickory principled and spirited, but his opponents condemned his irascibility and high-handedness and called him King Andrew. Their adoption of the name *Whigs* was intended to identify them as opponents of arbitrary power, just as the English Whigs had opposed royal absolutism in the late seventeenth century.

The Nullification Crisis.   Jackson's intolerance of opposition surfaced during the tariff controversy that marked his first term. Though he had criticized the Tariff of Abominations during the election campaign, Jackson disappointed the South by refusing to sponsor a substantial reduction in import duties. When, in 1832, Congress passed its own measure reducing the 1828 rates only slightly, South Carolinians, led by Vice President Calhoun, thrust the nation into a political crisis by calling a convention and declaring the tariff void in the Palmetto State.

The South Carolina Ordinance of Nullification reflected more than southern economic discontent. By 1832, as we shall see in Chapter 12, slavery had become a major social and political issue in the nation. Just two years before, a Massachusetts editor and reformer, William Lloyd Garrison, had begun to demand "immediate and complete emancipation" of southern slaves and had used angry language to denounce slaveholding and slaveholders. Garrison's attack had ushered in a new, more aggressive phase of the antislavery movement and had frightened and offended the South Carolina planter elite. These men now saw in the antislavery attack a serious threat to the stability and profitability of their slave-linked society. Nullification, they believed, was an appropriate weapon by which to defend the South's interests against a militant North that, for all they knew, had begun to rally around the new antisouthern movement.

South Carolina's action was a direct threat to the Union. Jackson, however, characteristically took it as a personal affront as well. The president declared that the state's action was "without parallel in the history of the world," and called Calhoun a madman. Yet this time, at least, he sought to avoid a direct confrontation. In his December 1832 message to Congress he pointed to imminent changes in the tariff duties and told South Carolinians that their reaction was exaggerated. Soon after, he issued a proclamation warning the people of the state that nullification endangered the nation's political integrity. At the same time, Jackson asked Congress for additional powers to enforce the customs laws—a request that Congress granted in the Force Bill. Some weeks later, with Clay's help, Jackson was able to get the tariff lowered.

Finding no support in other states, the South Carolina planter elite backed down. The state legislature rescinded the Ordinance of Nullification against the 1832 Tariff Act, but at the same time, as a gesture of defiance, it nullified the Force Bill. In the relief at getting past the crisis, few complained about the state's refusal to abandon the principle of nullification.

Indian Policy.   Jackson's position on nullification seems to confirm his strong nationalism. But he was perfectly willing to see the federal government's power disregarded when it suited his pur-

Library of Congress

Jackson's use of the veto, his tightening of executive control, and his personal approach to the presidency led Republicans to dub him "King Andrew." As proper for the enemies of kings, they called themselves "Whigs."

poses or accorded with one of his fundamental prejudices. A blatant instance of this was his defiance of John Marshall over Indian policy.

The peace treaty with England in 1815 had pulled the plug blocking western settlement. Settlers poured into the Great Lakes Plain, the Ohio Valley, and the Gulf Plain by the thousands to establish farms, plantations, and towns. The remaining Indian tribes, both north and south of the Ohio River, threatened to stop the rush of white civilization, and increasingly the government decided that the best way to deal with them was to remove them beyond the Mississippi. In 1817 Jackson, as agent for the War Department, had coerced a treaty out of the Cherokees of Georgia, by which they agreed to exchange their tribal lands for an equal amount of land in the West. Those Indians who did not want to go might remain and settle down as farmers. Though the Georgia lands would have to be surrendered as tribal holdings, each Indian family might have 640 acres as an individual holding. To Jackson's disgust, virtually every Cherokee chose to remain in Georgia; indeed, many bought slaves and began to raise cotton on their new 640-acre plantations.

This failure at Indian removal in the South was offset by successes in the North. In 1818 and 1819 the Wyandot, Chippewa, and Delaware tribes were removed by treaties from enormous areas in Indiana and Illinois. But such piecemeal progress seemed too slow, so in 1825 President Monroe announced that henceforth all the tribes of the eastern portion of the nation would be removed beyond the ninety-fifth meridian to a "permanent Indian frontier." There they could live in peace, the president declared, unmolested by whites and able to preserve their ancestral ways. No longer would the government attempt to turn the Indians into copper-skinned Europeans.

Under the direction of Secretary of War Calhoun, Congress set about removing the remaining tribes of the Northwest and South. Given Indian resistance, the new policy could only be carried out by unsavory tactics. Government agents bribed chiefs to sign treaties that committed their whole tribes to move, then claimed that the move was the will of the Indian people. Unwilling tribes were "persuaded" by military threats and force. In 1825 the Osage and Kansas tribes surrendered to the government all of Kansas and northern Oklahoma except for two reservations. Over the next fifteen years all the Northwest Indians were similarly moved—the Shawnee, Kickapoo, Sauk, Fox, Potawatomi, Ottawa, Iowa, Miami, and Peoria tribes. But the tribes of the Southeast proved more stubborn.

In Georgia, the Carolinas, Alabama, and Mississippi the Five Civilized Nations—the Cherokees, Creeks, Choctaws, Chickasaws, and Seminoles—owned some 33 million acres of valuable land. These Indians had become a settled agricultural people with a sophisticated political and social system and a high level of literacy. They had conformed to the white man's ways, and by all the professed principles of contemporary white Amer-

The Trail of Tears, the forced relocation of 15,000 Cherokees. Although Jackson apparently supported a strong federal government, he so hated Indians that he disregarded the Supreme Court's ruling that they had a right to their land. Such inconsistencies made Jackson's personality one of the divisive issues of his presidency.

Courtesy Woolaroc Museum, Bartlesville, Oklahoma

icans, they should have been left alone to enjoy their unusual blend of European and Indian cultures. But their holdings aroused the greed and envy of their white neighbors. When the Georgia legislature pressured the Cherokees to sell their lands and move west, the tribal leaders sued in the federal courts and were upheld by Chief Justice Marshall in *Worcester* v. *Georgia* (1832). Jackson refused to enforce the chief justice's decision, supposedly retorting: "John Marshall has made his decision, now let him enforce it!"

The confrontation with Marshall was only one manifestation of Jackson's Indian policy. The general shared the western contempt for Indians and lust for their rich lands, and he and his successor, Martin Van Buren, wholeheartedly supported the policy of removing them to an "Indian Territory" beyond the Mississippi. In 1830 Jackson signed the Indian Removal Act authorizing the government to evict the eastern tribes by force if need be. The measure was cruel and unfair. Even if the new lands had been as useful and fertile as the old, the removal would have unsettled thousands of people. In fact, they were inferior lands, and in any case unfamiliar.

Some of the southern tribes—the Creeks, the Choctaws, and the Chickasaws—were successfully cajoled and bribed into leaving. But other Indians resisted. The Seminoles of Florida took up arms and were subdued only after the Second Seminole War, which began in 1835 and dragged on to 1842, costing the government between $40 million and $60 million. The Cherokees at first resorted to the federal courts, claiming they were a separate nation not subject to Georgia law, and got a favorable decision in *Worcester* v. *Georgia*. In 1835 the government tried to bribe them with a $5.6 million grant to pay for their barns, houses, and cleared fields, and offered to provide free transportation to their new homes in the West. But most of the Indians repudiated this arrangement and, in 1838, the government used United States troops to oust them by bayonet. When the Cherokees finally set out on the "Trail of Tears" for what is now Oklahoma, their property was snapped up by corrupt state officials and white settlers eager for bargains. Some 4,000 Cherokees out of a population of 15,000 died of sickness and starvation on the sad trek west. Humane Americans, including Ralph Waldo Emerson, protested the removal policy, and the New England press denounced it as an "abhorrent business." But it continued unabated. Few instances of white-Indian relations in North America exhibit the total callousness of the removal of the civilized tribes by the Jacksonians.

The Attack on the Bank. Jackson hated banks—especially "The Bank"—even more than he hated Indians. After its inauspicious start when it helped trip off the Panic of 1819, the Second Bank of the United States had settled down to a useful existence under its third president, Nicholas Biddle. The bank lent money to merchants, helped expedite foreign trade, handled checking accounts, issued paper money backed by gold, held the deposits of the federal government, and transferred government funds from one part of the country to the other. Most important of all, it served as an informal central bank and the economy's balance wheel. As the nation's largest commercial bank, it could force the state banks to limit their credit when it felt the economy was too active or encourage them to lend readily when the economy was in the doldrums.

These operations made many friends for the bank. Many state bankers, especially in the capital-poor South and West, supported it, as did nationalist politicians and businessmen who often borrowed from it or used its foreign trade services. This support was not always disinterested, however. Newspaper editors and some of the most prominent men in government—including Daniel Webster, Henry Clay, and some Jacksonians—were in the bank's pay. The "God-like Daniel," who was frequently in debt, was a particularly shameless dependent of the bank, constantly asking that his "retainer" be "renewed or refreshed."

The bank also made many fierce enemies. Some aggressive and speculative businessmen found its generally conservative credit policies a hindrance. Its most important opponents, however, were agrarians like Senator Thomas Hart Benton of Missouri, who deplored all banks. Mostly southerners and westerners, these men favored "hard money" and believed that the paper money that banks issued was unwise and immoral. It provided a select few with profits based not on gold and silver—God's own money—but on doubtful promises to pay. An Alabama legislator noted: "Banking and paper money [are] in conflict with justice, morality and religion." Agrarians also held that banks in general, and the Bank of the United States in particular, endangered free government. With its $35 million in capital, Biddle's "monster bank" was the largest corporation in the country by far. Such size gave it a potential power over the economy that was frightening. Add to this the role of overseeing the economy that Biddle had given it and its influence on politicians, and it seemed obvious to many that the bank had to be destroyed or it would destroy the country.

An Historical Portrait   Sequoyah

The Indian genius called Sequoyah was born about 1770 in a village near the sacred Cherokee capital of Echota in Tennessee. We know little of his early life, except that following a crippling hunting accident he became a skilled silversmith and mechanic. During the War of 1812, when he was about forty, Sequoyah served in a company of Cherokees organized as part of the American forces to fight against the pro-British Creek Indians. He was present at the Battle of Horseshoe Bend, where Andrew Jackson decisively defeated the Creeks and forced them to cede a large part of the Mississippi Territory to white settlers. Clearly Sequoyah was not a man who saw all Indians as his friends and all whites as his enemy.

Soon after the battle Sequoyah was mustered out of service. The following year, using the English name George Guess, he married Sally, a cheerful and industrious young woman who long survived him. By this time he had become a leader among his people, respected for his skills and intelligence and his knowledge of the powerful white man's ways. In 1819 he joined a large party of fellow Cherokees moving to Arkansas to escape the pressure of the whites, which was making it difficult for the Indians to live in peace east of the Mississippi.

Even before the war Sequoyah had begun to ponder the possibility of developing a system of writing for the Cherokee language. At first he met with ridicule and doubt. According to a parable told by his detractors, the Creator had once given the Indians the book as well as the bow and arrow, but the white man had stolen it from them. Now Indians were destined to be warriors, not book writers and readers like the white man. Sequoyah laughed at the tale and refused to be deterred.

Sequoyah was still working on the problem of a system of writing for the Cherokee language in 1820. Part of the difficulty was that he could not read himself. He understood the principle of making signs serve as words, but in effect he had to virtually reinvent the idea of the alphabet. The system he eventually designed was actually a "syllabary" of eighty-six signs that included all the sounds and syllables of the difficult Cherokee tongue. For the first time since the days of the ancient Mayas one of the native New World languages could be inscribed on paper, and news and information could be quickly and widely disseminated to its speakers.

It was not easy for Sequoyah to get his new invention accepted. Many of his own people remained unconvinced of his achievement. He broke down their skepticism by demonstrating that he could communicate with his star pupil, his daughter, without any other contact than a written message. This success led the Cherokee elders to agree to let him educate several Indian youths as he had his daughter and prove that they, too, could communicate in writing. When this test was also successful, all doubts disappeared. A few years later Sequoyah invented a set of signs for the numbers and for indicating arithmetical operations.

Sequoyah's invention soon spread among his tribesmen, both those who had gone west and those who had remained on the ancestral lands in Georgia, Alabama, and the Carolinas. In the late 1820s, aided by the American Board of Missions, the Cherokees authorized a Boston firm to cast the syllabary in typemetal, and soon afterward they began to publish their own newspaper, the *Cherokee Phoenix*. This paper became a forum for discussing the critical issues that soon confronted the whole Cherokee nation.

During his remaining years Sequoyah, as a revered member of the Cherokee community, was at the forefront of the controversies that swirled around the forced resettlement of his people in Indian Territory. He was a member of the delegation that negotiated the removal of the Arkansas-based western Cherokees to Oklahoma. Though he did not oppose the move, he deplored the way the American government broke its word to the Indians, including its promise of $500 to him as a reward for his invention. In 1839, after 13,000 eastern Cherokee survivors of the Trail of Tears arrived in Oklahoma, he represented the earlier settlers from Arkansas, who felt overwhelmed by the flood of refugees and feared they would have to surrender power to the more numerous newcomers. Sequoyah helped negotiate the agreement that declared that the two parties were "one body politic under the style and title of 'The Cherokee Nation.'" Soon after, representatives of all factions adopted a constitution. This document continued to govern the Cherokee nation for many years.

Sequoyah left Indian Territory in 1842 with a dozen or so companions on a mission to Mexico to establish contact with various Cherokee communities detached from the main body. Well over seventy, he succumbed to the rigors of the journey. The year after his death the National Council of the Cherokee Nation granted his widow a pension for life. In the 1930s the Oklahoma Historical Society, with the aid of the federal government, acquired the house where Sequoyah had lived and, along with the surrounding land, made it into a monument to his memory. But Sequoyah's real memorial was the Cherokee people. Far more than other Indian peoples, they succeeded in taking the best from the white man's culture and using it to their advantage. No Indian people are more respected by their neighbors than the descendants of Sequoyah and his fellow tribespeople.

The bank's twenty-year charter was due to expire in 1836. Fearful of the opposition beginning to form among Jacksonians and wishing to ensure the bank's continuity, Biddle applied for renewal in 1832. The measure passed Congress, but Jackson vetoed it. In a stinging attack the president explained his motives in terms that appealed to old Jeffersonian values. He ignored the hard-money argument, but denounced the bank as a privileged monopoly controlled by foreign investors. Jackson warned that it would wield its great powers to punish its enemies if it became entrenched. The president undoubtedly believed that the Bank of the United States was a dangerous institution in a nation composed of many small economic units, but he also had a strong personal motive. "The Bank is trying to kill me," he told Van Buren, "but I will kill it."

The bank veto unleashed a storm of protest. Biddle called Jackson's veto message a "manifesto of anarchy." Webster, of course, also denounced it, as did two-thirds of the nation's press, much of the business community, and many state bankers. The veto immediately became the chief party issue during the 1832 presidential election, with Jackson's supporters treating it as an attack on monopoly and privilege and his foes condemning it as an example of King Andrew's tyrannical temperament.

Whigs and Democrats. By this time the second party system was rapidly taking shape. The Jack-

National Portrait Gallery, Smithsonian Institution

Nicholas Biddle, the powerful head of the Second Bank of the United States. Under his direction, the bank loaned businessmen money prudently and helped smaller banks survive temporary setbacks.

Sequoyah demonstrating his syllabary.

Library of Congress

son party, now beginning to be called the Democrats, was a heterogeneous group that differed in its programs and principles from one part of the country to another. Most Democrats tended to favor low tariffs, hard money, antimonopoly, and a government hands-off policy toward the economy. Jackson himself in 1830 had vetoed a federal appropriation for the Maysville Road in Kentucky on the grounds that the Constitution did not confer on the national government the power to finance internal improvements located entirely within a single state. But in some places—New York, New England, and Pennsylvania, for example—the Jackson men favored banks, protective tariffs, and government aid for internal improvements. On this last matter, Jackson was inconsistent. Though he vetoed the Maysville Road bill—some said mostly because it benefited Henry Clay's home state—he approved other federal outlays for roads.

The Whigs were less divided in their economic principles. Their "American System" called for protective tariffs, federal aid for internal improvements, and a strong national bank. First announced by Clay in 1824, the American System projected a paternalistic national government that would nurture business, protect industrial workers from cheap foreign competition, and provide a secure market for farmers in America's growing cities.

The Whigs and the Democrats also differed somewhat in their political ideologies. The Democrats claimed to be the party of the "common man," and there was some truth to their claim. James Silk Buckingham, an aristocratic English visitor, constantly heard the Democrats attacked as "agrarians, incendiaries, men who . . . desire to . . . seize the property of the rich and divide it among the poor." The Jackson men, wrote William Seward, a New York anti-Jackson leader, considered the parties distinctly different in their class orientation: "It's with them the poor against the rich."

Yet the differences between the parties must not be exaggerated. In New York the regular Democratic party often attacked the "Locofocos," a radical "equal rights" wing of their own party, as "infidels," "agrarians," and the "scum of politics." Moreover, the Jackson Democrats, as well as the Whigs, were led in these years by successful and prosperous lawyers, businessmen, and gentlemen, though the Jacksonians were probably somewhat less aristocratic than the Whigs. It is true that the Whigs had a "silk-stocking" element that had no real equivalent among the Democrats. These high and mighty folk often expressed contempt for the "rabble" that supposedly made up the political opposition. But they generally did so in private. The leading Whigs—Clay, Webster, and Seward—were popular figures who cultivated the voters and flattered them as effectively as Jackson, Van Buren, Marcy, and the other leading Democrats. And the Whigs' disdain for the ordinary voter did not color the party so intensely that a young ambitious Illinois politician like Abe Lincoln found any difficulty reconciling his obscure origins and sympathies for the common man with his affection for Henry Clay and his Whig political beliefs.

The differences between the parties' ideologies and class orientations, then, were not sharp, and each attracted voters from various classes, sections, and occupations. Clearly, if all farmers and wage earners had voted for Jackson and his Democratic successors—the supposed party of the common man—the opposition could never have won; farmers and wage earners, after all, were the great majority in the nation. But Jackson's opponents were not invariably defeated. Many husbandmen and workers withheld their votes from the Democrats. In the cities many "mechanics" voted for the Whigs or for various "workingmen's parties," which advocated "radical" measures such as laws

limiting the workday to ten hours and abolishing the inconvenient militia service required of male voters. Farmers, too, were split, with many rural voters, especially in New England and the Yankee-settled areas of the Old Northwest, voting for the Democrats' opponents. The Whigs were strongest in New England and those places where New Englanders had settled, but they had supporters in every part of the country. In the South small farmers voted Democratic; but large planters—despite their hostility to the tariff favored by Whigs—voted Whig largely because they needed cheap bank credit to market their cotton. Farmers in the West, eager for internal improvements, were also attracted to the Whigs. And in the cities the Whigs' American System attracted manufacturers and many industrial wage earners.

According to some scholars, however, what truly set Whigs and Democrats apart were distinctive cultural and religious emphases. Evidence is accumulating that in some states, such as Michigan and New York, the Democrats were the party of laissez-faire in religion and morals as well as in economic affairs, whereas the Whigs were determined to police the public's personal habits and behavior. Thus the Whigs often endorsed Sunday closing laws for businesses and insisted that the government not deliver the mail on the Christian Sabbath. They also favored laws outlawing alcohol or encouraging temperance. By contrast, Democrats generally believed that drinking and doing business on Sundays were private, not public, matters. These divergent attitudes also made the Whigs in the North more hostile to slavery than northern Democrats. Northern Whig voters often saw slavery as sinful and, like other sinful practices, within reach of government control; most northern Democrats believed that however deplorable slavery was, it was none of the government's business what southerners did with their local institutions.

These outlooks in turn appealed to different cultural and religious groups. Whig policies attracted evangelical Protestants, who considered politics a valid arena for moral reform. Democratic laissez-faire appealed to Catholics, Episcopalians, and freethinkers—all groups that preferred government to pursue a hands-off policy toward personal behavior and rejected politics based on morality. Since many New Englanders belonged to evangelical denominations, areas with a New England stamp voted Whig. Many of the recent immigrants were Catholics, and they generally joined the party of Jackson.

But as the election of 1832 approached, many of these distinctions were only beginning to emerge. Jackson's opponents, meeting in convention at Baltimore, nominated Clay. The Jackson supporters in turn renominated their hero, but selected Martin Van Buren as his running mate in place of Calhoun. The vice president by now was in Jackson's bad graces. His wife, the snobbish Floride, had snubbed Peggy Eaton, wife of Secretary of War John Eaton, who she believed was a loose woman. The president liked Peggy, and besides, remembering his own beloved Rachel's suffering under the false gossip of his enemies, he sympathized with her plight. He was also angry at the vice president for defending South Carolina's nullification position. Besides the two major parties, the Anti-Masons were in the field with William Wirt of Maryland as their candidate.

The chief issue in the campaign was ostensibly the Bank of the United States and the Jackson veto of the recharter bill. Actually, personalities were still vital to the voters. They were either utterly charmed by Clay—"Old Coon," "Harry of the West," "The Mill Boy of the Slashes"—or repelled by his easygoing ways, his drinking, and his card playing. Jackson was to some voters a great national hero; to others, the imperious and impetuous King Andrew. In the end the president won a decisive victory, with Clay second and Wirt a poor third.

Economic Ups and Downs. The outstanding event of Jackson's second term was the slow, agonizing death of the Bank of the United States. The president interpreted his election victory as a mandate to proceed immediately against the bank, even though its charter left it four more years of life. Disregarding the advice of two successive secretaries of the treasury, he ordered the removal of government deposits from the bank. These funds he then placed in twenty-three state-chartered banks especially favored by the Democrats, which the Whigs promptly labeled "pet banks."

Biddle considered the adminsitration's actions vindictive and determined to fight back no matter what the cost. "My own course is decided," he wrote a friend. "All the other Banks and all the merchants may break, but the bank of the United States shall not break." In the next months the BUS reduced its loans and called in those already outstanding, creating a credit squeeze that caused businessmen severe hardship. Actually, Biddle had few alternatives. With the treasury's $10 million removed from its reserves, the bank had to contract. But Biddle's determination to demonstrate the bank's importance to the country's prosperity made him forget his former principles of responsible and public-spirited financial manage-

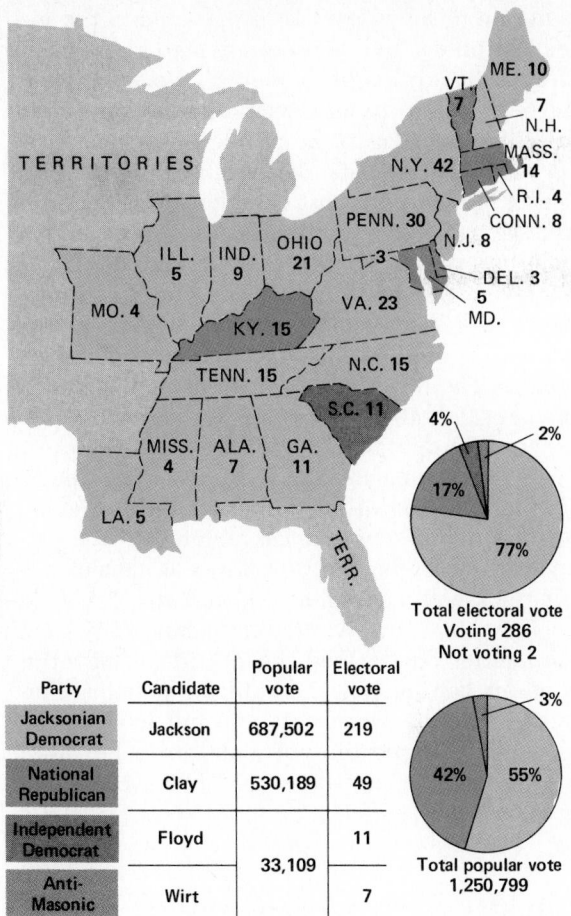

Party	Candidate	Popular vote	Electoral vote
Jacksonian Democrat	Jackson	687,502	219
National Republican	Clay	530,189	49
Independent Democrat	Floyd	33,109	11
Anti-Masonic	Wirt		7

Election of 1832

ment, and he contracted faster and further than strictly necessary.

Worse was soon to come. The Biddle contraction did not last long enough to set off a major financial crisis. But with the Bank of the United States no longer regulating the country's credit and money supply, a major source of financial restraint was gone. The pet banks, with millions in government money in their reserves, began to lend freely. Businessmen and speculators promptly invested their borrowed money in western lands, while states initiated ambitious canal-building schemes. The nation experienced a runaway boom that drove all prices, especially those of land, to record heights.

Jackson was dismayed. He had not struck down Biddle's "monster" only to see it replaced by a state bank system that was even more irresponsible and dangerous. Nor did Jackson wish to see the notes of the Bank of the United States, which were backed by gold, replaced by "wild-cats" of a hundred banks that were little more than vague promises to pay. To put an end to the unhealthy boom, the president issued the Specie Circular in July 1836. Henceforth, he announced, the federal government would accept only gold and silver in payment for public lands.

The Specie Circular pricked the bubble. The public abruptly lost confidence in the notes issued by the state banks and fought to convert them into specie. Hoping to hold on to their gold and silver, the banks in turn tried to call in their loans. Other creditors, fearful of the future, refused to lend further and clamped down on debtors. The result was a severe panic that halted business and brought down prices with a resounding crash. A decade of hard times followed.

Recent scholarship has absolved the Specie Circular of some of the blame for the panic and ensuing depression and has pointed to the collapse of international cotton prices as a major culprit. Jackson's supporters blamed the panic on "overbanking and overtrading." But many contemporaries condemned the president and criticized his hard-money and antibank policies. Fortunately for the Democrats, the full force of the economic collapse did not make itself felt until 1837, and so did not affect the 1836 presidential election.

POLITICS AFTER JACKSON

The Van Buren Administration. This 1836 contest was a confused affair. The Whigs, not yet a solid party, selected several regional candidates, including Webster of Massachusetts and Hugh Lawson White of Tennessee. Their strategy, masterminded by Biddle, was to run local candidates strong in a particular area, with the hope that (as in 1824) the election would be thrown into the House of Representatives. William Henry Harrison, the former governor of the Indiana Territory, received the Anti-Mason endorsement. The better-organized Democrats, required by the two-term tradition to pass over their leader, nominated Vice President Van Buren. Their convention did not adopt a formal platform, but Van Buren pledged to follow in Jackson's footsteps. On this basis he won a comfortable victory in the fall.

Scarcely was the new president installed in office when the full force of the economic storm broke. Van Buren called Congress into special session to deal with the emergency, but proposed little beyond a scheme to end all government connection with banks, central and pet alike. In a classic statement of the laissez-faire, let-alone position, he noted that government was "not intended to confer special favors on individuals or on any classes of them to create systems of agriculture, manufactures, or trade, or to engage in them. . . . The less government interferes with private pursuits the better for the general prosperity."

The timid response of the new Democratic president lends support to the label "laissez-fairist" that had been attached to the Jacksonians. But as if to refute this neat conclusion, Jacksonians in the states ignored Van Buren's philosophy. In Massachusetts and Pennsylvania Democratic administrations stepped in to rescue the local econ-

Voters in presidential elections, 1824–1840

Note: The graph on the left reflects the widening franchise. The graph on the right suggests increased voter interest: of those who had the right to vote, a larger portion actually exercised it.

Source: *Historical Statistics of the United States, Colonial Times to 1957.*

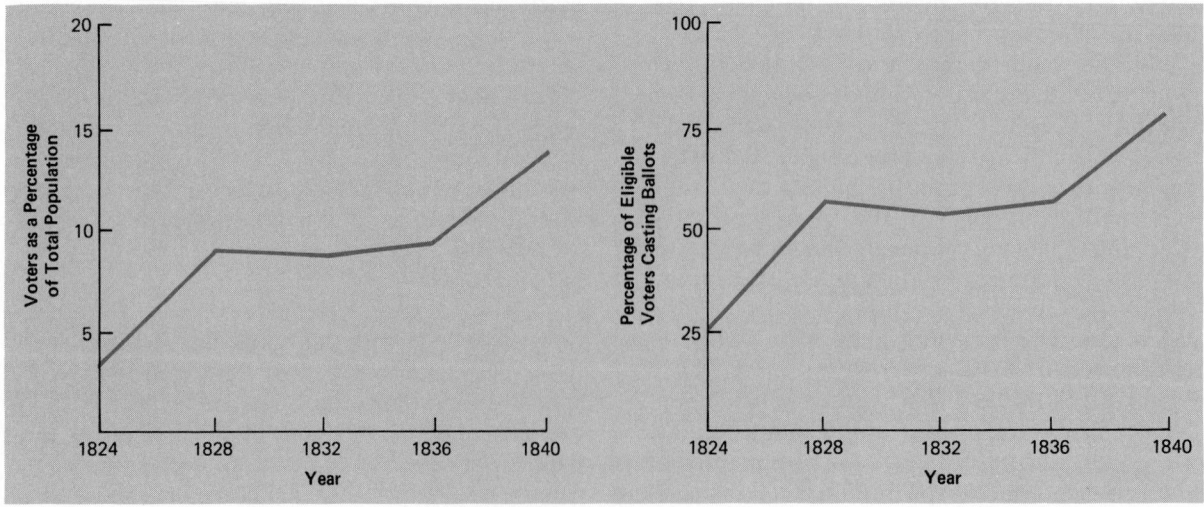

Cincinnati Historical Society

The mass political rally, such as this one held in Cincinnati shortly before election day, was a central part of Whig strategy in the 1840 campaign. An arch was erected across Main Street for the event, and Harrison flags and banners were widely evident.

omy by extending state aid to canal and railroad projects and by handing out many new corporation charters. Most western and southern states did not initiate such policies; but it was not solely for philosophical reasons that they failed to aid distressed business groups. As one witty scholar has said, in many parts of the country Jackson men had "feet of Clay" and had few scruples against supporting business enterprise. The deterrents were practical. Already deep in debt for the canal and road projects they had sponsored during the boom, western and southern states were finding it hard to pay the interest. By the end of 1842 nine states had defaulted on their bonds.

For the rest of Van Buren's ill-starred term the politicians remained preoccupied with the economy and economic legislation. To aid the treasury during the crisis, Congress ended the government's recently adopted policy of distributing to the states federal surpluses derived from excise taxes, the tariff, and land sales. In 1837 Van Buren proposed a scheme for a separate federal financial depository not dependent on banks. The proposal expressed Jacksonian suspicion of banks and paper money, and it seemed to the Whigs a primitive system that would leave the country without a financial balance wheel or an effective means to regulate the state banks. Whigs and Democrats fought over the issue until 1840, when the Democrats in Congress managed to establish the Independent Treasury System. Under this measure the treasury was required to collect and keep federal revenues and disburse them at need

from its own vaults without relying on private banks. Moreover, government transactions with the public—salaries, taxes, bounties, and so forth—would now be confined to gold and silver.

The Whigs Take Power. As the 1840 presidential election approached, the usual maneuvering for position began. Van Buren, despite his spotty record and the bad times, had few opponents among the Democrats. On the Whig side the logical choice was Clay, but the Whigs were wary of selecting a man too closely identified with the political battles of the past and with well-defined views. At the Whigs' first convention, in December 1839, the delegates passed over Clay. Instead, as has frequently been the case with the weaker party, they turned to a nonpolitician without strong political commitments: William Henry Harrison.

Harrison, though now sixty-seven, had a number of distinct advantages. He was the first "most available" man. A southerner by birth, he was sure to win many votes in the South that might otherwise go to the Democrats. He was also a military hero—having defeated Tecumseh's forces at Tippecanoe in 1811—and after Jackson, the Whigs had good reason to recognize the advantages of military renown. Most important of all, Harrison had no known political principles. For a party that had lost once by running its most representative figure, the obscurity of his views was a distinct asset.

The campaign revealed how well the Whigs had adapted to the sharp political partisanship that had appeared since 1828. The candidate, the party leaders concluded, would be kept from expressing his ideas on any controversial issue. Let Harrison "say not one single word about his principles or his creed," advised Nicholas Biddle. "Let no committee, no convention, no town meeting ever extract from him a single word about what he thinks or will do hereafter." The Whigs' major problem, besides their candidate, was their aristocratic image. Fortunately, a careless remark by a prominent Democrat—that if Harrison were given a pension, a barrel of hard cider, and a log cabin to live in, he would never run for president—bailed them out. The Whigs immediately seized on the snobbery implied by the characterization. Picturing the wealthy Harrison as a simple man and a true democrat, they painted Van Buren as an aristocrat who lived in lordly style on his estate in Kinderhook, New York. According to a Whig campaign song:

> *Tippecanoe has no chariot to ride in,*
> *No palace of marble has he to reside in,*
> *No bags of gold eagles, no lots of fine clothes—*
> *But he has a wealth far better than those;*

> *The love of a nation, free, happy, and true,*
> *Are the riches and portion of Tippecanoe.*

On the other hand:

> *Proud Martin rides forth in his splendor and*
>   *pride,*
> *And broad are his lands upon Kinderhook side,*
> *The roof of a palace is over his head,*
> *And his table with plate and with dainties is*
>   *spread;*
> *But a log cabin shelters a patriot true,*
> *'Tis the home of our hero, bold Tippecanoe!*

The "Log Cabin and Hard Cider" campaign was the first time a political party successfully marshaled the powerful forces of ballyhoo and propaganda to sell a candidate to the American people. The Whigs dressed up supporters as Indians to advertise Harrison's victory over Tecumseh. They distributed vast quantities of cider to thirsty voters. Whig party workers organized enormous parades with bands, giant banners, flaming torches, and flags.

The vote was huge—almost 60 percent greater than in 1836—and it was strongly Whig.

Election of 1840

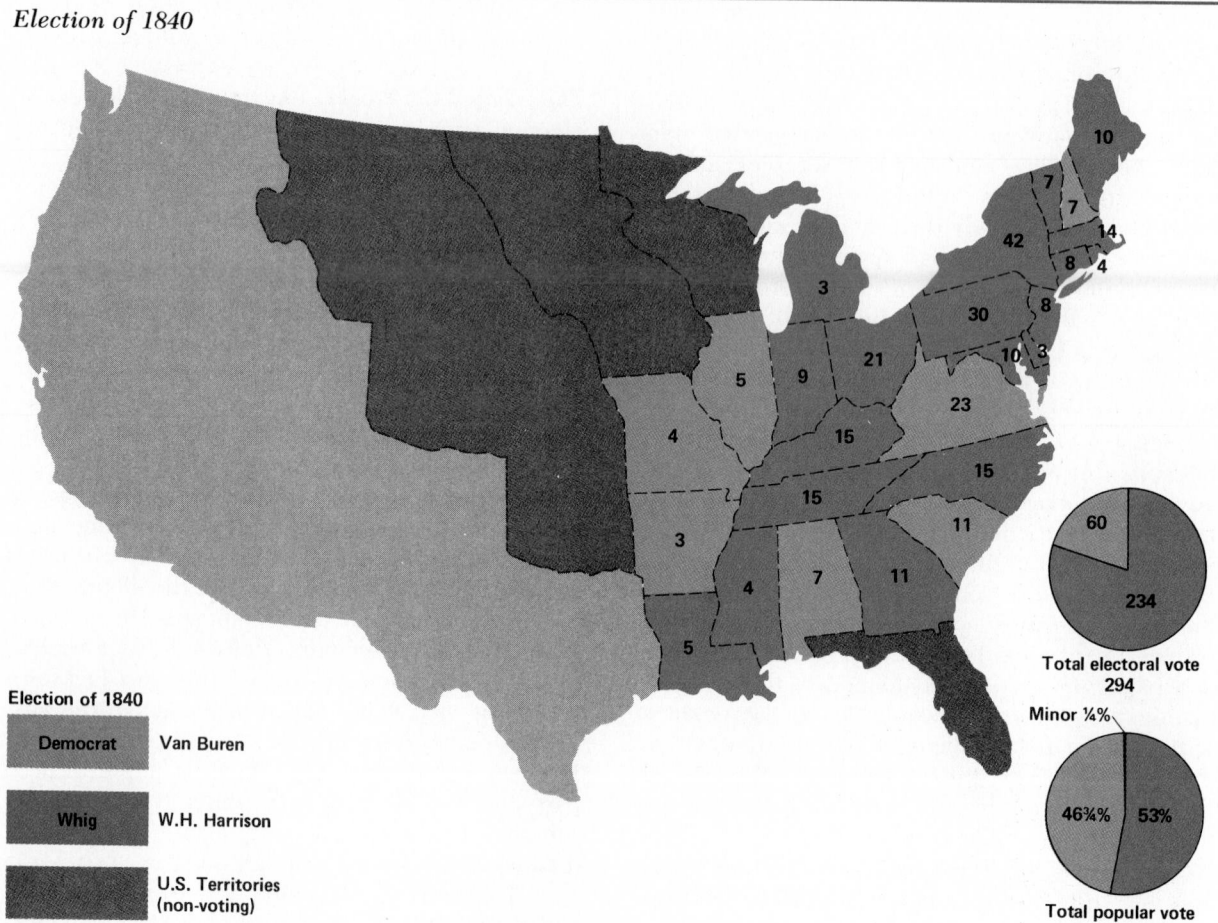

Election of 1840

Democrat	Van Buren
Whig	W.H. Harrison
	U.S. Territories (non-voting)

Total electoral vote 294

Total popular vote

Harrison and his running mate, John Tyler of Virginia, carried nineteen of the twenty-six states and received 53 percent of the popular vote, an unusually high proportion for this period. The opposition had succeeded in the difficult task of turning an incumbent president out of office and had demonstrated the vitality of the newly revived party system.

CONCLUSION

By 1840 two new political parties had come into being. After a long gap that saw government become the preserve of public-spirited gentlemen, the people once more insisted on being heard. The change was not Jackson's doing: it had begun years before, in the states. Jackson was its beneficiary, not its author.

The two new parties seemed to parallel those of Hamilton's and Jefferson's time. Whigs and Democrats superficially resembled Federalists and Jeffersonian Republicans, respectively—without the powdered hair and velvet knee breeches. But on closer examination we see that the reality was different. Neither party was as closely associated with a single class as their predecessors. There was a difference in the parties' social focus: Democrats probably won the support of more small farmers than the Whigs, and since small farmers were a majority of Americans, this made them in some sense the party of the common people. But we should not make too much of this tendency. In an age that professed to be democratic, both parties had to accept—or appear to accept—the voice of the "sovereign people."

The two new party organizations were not as clearly different in ideology as the old parties were, either. They differed on banks, tariffs, and internal improvements; but their leaders were apt to be more practical and accommodating than the Federalists and Jeffersonians. The emergence of the second party system marked the development of a pragmatic political consensus: both parties would avoid extreme ideological positions and try to stand close to the political center. This tendency continues in the politics of our own day.

The arrivals and departures in Washington on March 4, 1829, indeed betokened something momentous, but not what Mrs. Smith and Senator Webster believed: Jackson's victory did not set off a revolution in the social and political order. But it did loosen the rigid political framework of the day. By refusing to accept the gentlemanly procedures of the Virginia dynasty, the Jacksonians revitalized American political life. After 1828 the country would once more have a lively and effective two-party system, and the change would make the nation's government more responsive to public needs and public wants. What Mrs. Smith and Senator Webster were seeing was the return of parties to American political life.

FOR FURTHER READING

George Dangerfield. *The Era of Good Feelings* (1952)
>An elegantly written narrative history of the years between the War of 1812 and the rise of Jackson as a major political figure. The foreign affairs of this crucial period are also given attention.

Robert Remini. *Andrew Jackson* (1966)
>Andrew Jackson was an ardent officeseeker from his early twenties onward. This biography concentrates on his role in strengthening the presidency, his deft handling of the Calhounites, the nullification crisis, and his battle with the BUS.

Thomas Govan. *Nicholas Biddle, Nationalist and Public Banker* (1959)
>The public life of the BUS president during the years when the "Monster Bank" was locked in combat with "King" Andrew. Govan is pro-Bank and anti-Jackson, depicting Biddle as a public-spirited citizen and Jackson as a demagogue.

John William Ward. *Andrew Jackson: Symbol for an Age* (1955)
>Ward's book deals with Jackson's popular image as a folk hero. By describing Fourth of July orations, popular songs, campaign speeches, and political cartoons, Ward shows us how Jackson and Jacksonianism became an important cultural myth.

Arthur M. Schlesinger, Jr. *The Age of Jackson* (1945)
>This is now the classic defense of Jacksonian democracy by a master of historical prose. It concludes that Jacksonianism was genuinely democratic and forward-looking, and that its source was the industrial East rather than the frontier West.

Marvin Meyers. *The Jacksonian Persuasion: Politics and Belief* (1957)
>After considering the views of a host of representative Jacksonians, Meyers, in this subtle study, concludes that they were moralistic rather than materialistic, a conservative set of men who pined for an America long past.

Richard P. McCormick. *The Second American Party System: Party Formation in the Jacksonian Era* (1966)
>It has often been said that the Jackson era saw an upsurge of voter participation in elections. McCormick uses actual election data to prove

this assumption. He describes how the second party system actually came together during the 1820s and 1830s.

Lee Benson. *The Concept of Jacksonian Democracy: New York as a Test Case* (1961)

Written by one of the fathers of the ethnocultural school of political history. Benson claims that religion, culture, and ethnicity were more important determinants of party affiliation in New York during the second party system than class or occupation.

Ronald Formisano. *The Birth of Mass Political Parties: Michigan, 1827–1861* (1971)

A study of the second party system in a state where the ethnocultural interpretation of party choice works exceptionally well. By a student of Benson.

William W. Freehling. *Prelude to Civil War: The Nullification Controversy in South Carolina, 1816–1836* (1966)

Blending biography with economic, social, and political history, Freehling treats nullification primarily as a frightened reaction of the South Carolina planter class to abolitionism, which threatened to overthrow slave society.

Richard N. Current. *John C. Calhoun* (1963)

A short, well-written biography of the 1812 "War Hawk" who eventually became secretary of war, vice president, and ardent defender of southern minority "rights." Current devotes most of his book to Calhoun's political thought and its influence on his time.

Grant Foreman. *Indian Removal: The Emigration of the Five Civilized Tribes of Indians* (1932)

Foreman tells the story of the forced migration of the Choctaws, Creeks, Chickasaws, Cherokees, and Seminoles from their homes in the southeast to Oklahoma. His sympathies lie with the Indians, who were terrorized and defrauded by state governments and white settlers. Includes maps and illustrations.

Marvin E. Gettleman. *The Dorr Rebellion: A Study in American Radicalism, 1833–1849* (1973)

In Jacksonian Rhode Island democratic political change came in a violent way. This is a study of a group of political reformers far more radical than the Jacksonians as a whole—in Gettleman's view. A sympathetic attempt to find native American radical roots, but not uncritical of the Dorr rebels.

11 The Mexican War and Expansionism

Greed, Manifest Destiny, or Inevitability?

1803–06 Lewis and Clark Expedition to Pacific

1812 Astor establishes fur-trading post on Pacific in Oregon

1818 A treaty between Great Britain and the United States provides for joint occupation of Oregon Territory

1819 Adams-Onís Treaty establishes the western boundaries of the Louisiana Purchase

1823 Mexico grants Stephen Austin the right to settle in Texas with 300 American families

1836 Texas declares its independence from Mexico • Texans force captured Mexican leader Santa Anna to recognize the Texas Republic

1841 President Harrison dies and John Tyler becomes president

1842 Webster-Ashburton Treaty signed by Great Britain and the United States

1844 James K. Polk elected president

1845 Congress admits Texas into the Union • Anticipating war, Polk sends General Zachary Taylor and 4,000 troops to occupy Mexican territory on north bank of Rio Grande • Polk secretly authorizes American consul Thomas Larkin to encourage the secessionist movement in California • The Slidell Mission discusses Texas's southern boundary and offers to buy New Mexico and California for $30 million

1846 Mexico declares defensive war on the United States; Congress votes for war • The Oregon dispute with Great Britain is settled by treaty

1847 Polk authorizes General Winfield Scott to attack Vera Cruz and Mexico City

1848 The Mexican-American War ends with the Treaty of Guadalupe Hidalgo • Mexican Cession adds 339 million acres to U.S.

1850 Congress admits California into the Union

On May 11, 1846, the clerk of the House of Representatives read the war message of President James K. Polk to a solemn joint session of Congress. The message was expected. Rumors had been circulating for weeks that a break with Mexico was imminent. Just two days before, people in Washington had learned that Mexican troops had crossed the Rio Grande del Norte and attacked American army units on its northern side. Several Americans had been killed, and others injured.

"The cup of forebearance had been exhausted before the recent information from the frontier of the Del Norte," the president declared. "But now, after reiterated menaces, Mexico has passed the boundary of the United States, has invaded our territory and shed American blood upon American soil. She has proclaimed that hostilities have commenced, and that the two nations are now at war." "By every consideration of duty and patriotism," the president concluded, Americans must "vindicate with decision the honor, the rights, and the interests of their country."

Congress voted for war by an overwhelming majority, yet many representatives and senators were uneasy with the decision. During the next weeks and months, United States forces would go from triumph to triumph in a crescent of territory that stretched 2,000 miles from the Gulf of Mexico to the Oregon boundary; but Americans in and out of Congress would denounce the war. Senator Thomas Corwin of Ohio would describe it as blatant aggression, unjustified by anything except greed. "If I were a Mexican I would tell you," he trumpeted to his Senate colleagues, " 'Have you not room in your own country to bury your dead men? If you come into mine we will greet you with bloody hands, and welcome you to hospitable graves.' " In the House a young Illinois Whig, Abraham Lincoln, would call the president "a bewildered, confounded, and miserably perplexed man" with a "painful" conscience. Lincoln would spend much of his single term demanding that Polk prove his allegations that the Mexicans had provoked the war by attacking Americans on their own soil.

Outside Congress other critics were quite as fierce and determined. New Englander James Russell Lowell's fictional spokesman, Hosea Biglow, called the attack on Mexico "a national crime committed on behoof of slavery." An ardent enemy of slavery, Lowell was certain that the "slave power" was determined to seize Mexican territory "so's to lug new slave states in." Henry Thoreau, who valued Mexico as a refuge for escaped slaves, considered the American invasion justification for "honest men to rebel and revolutionize."

Different theories of the war's origins are implied by these charges. In Lincoln and Corwin's view the conflict is an instance of naked United States aggression against a weaker neighbor. Thoreau and Lowell's Hosea Biglow see the war as the result of a southern slaveholders' plot. Modern scholars, too, have advanced competing theories of causation. One recent supporter of the slave-power position is Eugene Genovese, who perceives the cotton South as forced to expand territorially or suffer from declining profits as soils lost their fertility and cotton ceased to produce abundant wealth. Another modern economic interpretation of the Mexican War emphasizes American interest in acquiring Pacific ports in order to establish commercial connections with the Far East. In this view it is the business classes of the North that provided much of the impetus to expansion.

Other historians are more inclined to see Americans as inspired in 1846 by the ideological attitude of continentalism or Manifest Destiny, which justified United States dominion over the continent—indeed, made it seem inevitable—on grounds of supposed American cultural, political, or even racial superiority. Mexican scholars agree in ascribing the war to America's sense of superiority, though they also blame it on Yankee greed. In either case, they insist, the United States was a blatant aggressor.

A final school of interpretation seeks to avoid simple praise or blame. In this view the pre–Civil War expansionist impulse was the expression of what was almost a physical law. To the west of the growing, vibrant United States, it says, lay a sparsely populated and loosely governed expanse of territory. It was almost an empty region in a political and social sense, and American expansion into it resembled the rush of air to fill a vacuum. The war, in this view, was an inevitable event arising out of the circumstances of history and geography.

The Mexican War marked the last phase of continental expansion that carried the American people to the Pacific. The war itself added 530,000 square miles of territory to the United States, and the related settlement of the Oregon boundary dispute with Great Britain added another 258,000. The total addition was truly imperial in extent, but was it also imperialist in origin? Was it greed—for ports or more cotton lands—that led Polk to send his war message to Congress that day in early May? Was it misperceived idealism? Or was it the working out of some sort of geopolitical law?

THE OREGON COUNTRY

In 1830 the line marking the western edge of dense agricultural settlement in the United States did not extend much beyond the bottomlands of the Mississippi River. Farmers had already moved out along the banks of the Missouri, Arkansas, and Red rivers well into the states of Missouri, Arkansas, and Louisiana. But with the exception of these projections, almost all of the trans-Mississippi West remained the domain of the Indian tribes. Beyond the western boundary of the Louisiana Purchase was a vast region of mountain, desert, plateau, and rocky coast still barely touched by European culture and institutions.

Political title to much of this region was uncertain. In 1819 the Adams-Onís Treaty had settled the boundary between American and Spanish possessions and surrendered Spanish claims in the Oregon country to the United States. But title to Oregon—a vast expanse including present-day Oregon, Washington, Idaho, British Columbia, and parts of Montana and Wyoming—remained in dispute between Great Britain and the United States. British claims rested on the voyages of Captains James Cook in the 1770s and George Vancouver in the 1790s, and on the activities of Canadian and British fur companies. American claims had a similar basis. For years before Vancouver's voyage, American merchant vessels had periodically visited the northern Pacific coast. In April 1792 Captain Robert Gray had discovered the Columbia River, which was named after his vessel. Then, in 1805–06 Lewis and Clark had wintered at the mouth of the Columbia.

Until the 1840s, however, the region called Oregon had no more than a handful of white inhabitants. A vast territory extending from the northern boundary of California to the southern boundary of Russian America (Alaska) at 54° 40′ north latitude, it was the home of many Indian tribes belonging to many diverse cultures. Along the coast were the salmon-fishing, woodworking tribes, the Tlingits, Haida, Kwakiutl, and Salish. In the interior plateau Indian tribes (among them the Flatheads and Nez Perces) fished along the streams and gathered roots and berries. Some of these tribes would cooperate with the whites; others would resist. In the end, as on so many other frontiers, all would be pushed aside.

Despite the presence of no more than a few hundred Americans, the United States guarded its claim to the Oregon region jealously. In 1818 Secretary of State John Quincy Adams negotiated a convention with the British providing for joint occupation of Oregon for ten years. In 1827 the Anglo-American occupation was extended for an indefinite period, subject to termination by either party on a year's notice.

The Far Western Fur Trade. Ultimately the dispute over Oregon was resolved not by diplomacy but by actual white settlement. But as on so many other frontiers, before the settlers—and preparing the way for them—came the fur traders. Ever since the beginnings of English North American

American Antiquarian Society

Lieutenant Henry Warre came to Oregon in 1845 with an expedition of the Hudson's Bay company intended to protect British claims and bolster British defenses. Sketches made by Warre on his journey—like this view of the settlement at Oregon City—give a fascinating glimpse of frontier life.

colonization in the seventeenth century, the quest for pelts had spurred geographical expansion. As early as the 1780s the fur trade had reached the Pacific Northwest after leaping over much rugged intervening terrain. For the next thirty years the beautiful skins of the Pacific sea otter attracted American merchants, who made the Oregon coast a stopping place on their way to China, where the skins were highly prized.

Several groups of businessmen were involved in the far northwestern fur trade. In Oregon the impresario was John Jacob Astor, a German-born entrepreneur who had come to the United States in 1783. Starting as a clerk in a New York City store, he soon became a successful fur merchant and entered the Oregon trade shortly after the United States acquired the Louisiana Territory. In 1811 he established a trading post at the mouth of the Columbia, which he named—in his characteristically modest way—Astoria. The post flourished briefly until the threat of British attack during the War of 1812 forced its sale to a Canadian firm. Thereafter Astor confined his fur-trading operations to the Great Lakes region.

After the war two fur-trading companies, the British-owned Hudson's Bay Company and the American-owned North West Company, entered the Oregon country. The English company built European-type forts where white employees lived apart and refused to accommodate to the Indian way of life. The North Westers accepted the necessity of providing the Indians with gifts, of feasting with them, and of avoiding any hint of force or coercion. After competing bitterly for a while, the two companies merged in 1821 into Hudson's Bay Company. Soon afterward the company established Fort Vancouver on the north bank of the Columbia River in what is now Washington State. Placed in charge of the new settlement was Dr. John McLoughlin, a man of great strength of mind and personality. McLoughlin soon set about the task of nailing down Britain's claim to the Oregon region and excluding the Americans.

Meanwhile, farther east in the Rocky Mountain region, another group of Americans under Missourian William Ashley was uncovering new fur-bearing regions in what is now southwestern Wyoming. Ashley saw that to make a profit he needed not only a new source of furs but also a new method of collecting them. In the past Indians had been the trappers, trading the furs to white agents. But beginning in the spring of 1825, Ashley sent his own employees to roam the newly opened region for furs. Under Ashley's successors in the Rocky Mountain Fur Company, as many as 600 "mountain men" of American, French, Mexi-

can, black, and mixed Indian-European backgrounds spent the year in the mountain wilds, many of them with their Indian wives and children. In the spring the trappers hunted the beaver along streams. In July they gathered at a "rendezvous," where they exchanged their "hairy bank notes" for cloth, rifles and shot, trinkets, food, liquor, and other commodities brought west by the company. Cut off from others for months at a time by the fiercely cold winters, the mountain men turned the July meetings into wild debauches. After a week or two of heavy drinking, gambling, fighting, and general hell-raising, the trappers and their families staggered off to rest for the coming hard year. The company agents returned east with furs worth twenty times their cost.

The Way West. The western fur trade helped open the trans-Missouri region for white settlement. Agents and officials of the fur companies—Kit Carson, Jim Bridger, Milton and William Sublette, and others—traveled widely through the Great Plains, Rocky Mountain, and Great Basin regions, marking convenient routes, exploring rivers, and discovering new passes through the mountains. In 1823 one of Ashley's agents, Jedediah Smith, found South Pass, a major break in the towering mountains that blocked the overland route west. The following year Peter Ogden, of the Hudson's Bay Company, was the first white man to view the Great Salt Lake. The fur traders opened the country in still another way. By bringing to the Indians the whites' ways, their superior technology, their vices, and their diseases, they helped erode the Indians' customs and institutions, and reduced their ability to resist the invaders.

Not all the explorations of the trans-Missouri region facilitated settlement. In 1806 Zebulon Pike returned from a government-authorized expedition through the High Plains and called the region too dry for cultivation. After a trip to the same region in 1820, Stephen Long, of the United States Topographical Engineers, named it the Great American Desert. The land was "wholly unfit for cultivation, and . . . uninhabitable by a people depending upon agriculture for their subsistence," Long wrote. This account of a Great American Desert just to the east of the mountains helped delay settlement for decades and turned people's eyes to the well-watered, forested lands of Oregon farther west.

The first Americans to make permanent homes in the Oregon country were Methodist missionaries who came in the 1830s to the Willamette Valley, south of the Columbia, to bring the Chris-

Denver Public Library

THE SUMMER RENDEZVOUS.

The yearly rendezvous between mountain men and fur company agents quickly turned into debauchery, since the trappers received whiskey as payment for their furs. Although wild and solitary, these men helped open the Oregon country to traders, missionaries, and settlers.

tian God and European notions of morality to the Indians. During the hard times of the 1840s, when farm prices were low, reports of cheap Oregon land and of insatiable markets for agricultural produce in Asia created an "Oregon fever" throughout the agricultural West. By 1845 there were over 5,000 Americans living in Oregon.

The journey of these Oregon pioneers was a rugged overland trek across hundreds of miles of dangerous, inhospitable country. Typically, the trip was made by families. One estimate has it that half the emigrants on the Oregon Trail were women and children. Each spring, beginning in 1841, eager Oregon-bound families assembled in Independence, Missouri, the jump-off point for the trip west. The travelers came with lumbering Conestoga wagons, which had served Americans as sturdy vehicles since colonial days. Into these they crammed supplies and as much equipment as they could carry. Oxen in teams of six drew the wagons, while women and older children—at least in good weather—walked. The men either drove or rode saddle horses to scout for game and potential danger.

Each party moving in a broad train several wagons wide was commanded by a captain elected by the men. Some of these men were skilled guides who had made the trip before or were natural leaders. Others, however, were incompetents who had to be replaced in midjourney. The going at first was easy. The lush green lands of the eastern portion of the Oregon Trail were level and pleasant to cross. Three hundred miles from Independence, however, the pioneers reached the Platte River, a shallow stream "too

thick to drink and too thin to plow." Full of quicksand, it was dangerous to ford. Five hundred miles farther on, the travelers encountered the Rocky Mountains. Here the real difficulties began. At times the wagons bounced over terrain so rocky that the trail was covered with blood from the oxen's bruised hooves. At many spots the men were forced to put their own shoulders to the wagons and push them along by brute strength. At this point, over the side would go all heavy gear—plows, stoves, tables, sofas, even pianos—that optimistic emigrants had stowed in hopes of making their new lives more comfortable. Finally, at the Dalles in what is now central Oregon, the travelers reached the Columbia River. After caulking the wagons' seams to make them watertight, they floated down the great river to their destination, the fertile and well-watered valley of the Willamette River.

Women found the trip particularly hard. To many the most difficult part was leaving behind familiar places and loved ones. "Nothing can atone for the loss of society of friends," wrote Anne Booth in her trail journal. Women tried to recreate the familiar by arranging their family wagons as small mobile homes. Nonetheless, the long trip was a trial for eastern women, who normally led sheltered lives. But it did have its compensations. The trail community was a foretaste of the new pioneer society that the emigrants were about to create, and like that society it lacked many of the rigid gender distinctions of the East. Women on the trail were essential for survival on a day-to-day basis. They often had to take on what were normally male responsibilities, such as hunting or

Denver Public Library

Severe hardships awaited those who took the way west. Many emigrants lost their possessions in turbulent rivers or quicksand. Others succumbed to the harsh weather and fierce terrain of the Rocky Mountains.

scouting or using a rifle to protect the wagon train. Such roles were especially unavoidable when, as all too frequently happened, husbands or fathers died of disease or accident along the way.

The British in Oregon watched this American influx uneasily at first. The settlers were clearly reinforcing the American claim to the Oregon country. The British were virtually all employees of the Hudson's Bay Company; nowhere could they match the Americans in numbers. It soon became clear that the British had lost the competition south of the Columbia, where in any case the beaver had been trapped out. At this point the company's John McLoughlin generously helped the settlers in the Willamette region by providing jobs and other aid. Thus the company surrendered what is now Oregon to the Americans, though it continued for a while to oppose American entry into what is now Washington State.

Before long, excluding Americans from that area began to seem hopeless, too. In 1845 the Hudson's Bay director, fearing for the safety of his valuable stores across the river from the American settlements, moved the firm's chief base many miles north to Vancouver Island in what is now British Columbia. The British had virtually conceded that the Americans would control the whole block of territory between Puget Sound and the California boundary.

THE MEXICAN BORDERLAND

For a generation preceding the migration to Oregon a few Americans had been drawn to the Southwest, where Mexico, formerly a Spanish colony, loosely held a million square miles of territory. Hundreds of miles distant from the capital city in the south, the Mexican borderland from Texas to California was a generally arid region. But within its limits there were tracts, such as east Texas and the great Central Valley of California, where the land was well-watered and enterprising farmers could raise fine crops.

The Native Peoples. At the time it began to arouse American interest most of the borderland was a sparsely populated area. About half the population was Indian. In Texas the Comanche, Apache, Kiowa, and other tribes were nomadic peoples who for centuries had hunted buffalo on foot with bow and arrow. During the late seventeenth century they had acquired horses from Spanish Mexico, and then rifles. These new possessions improved their prowess as hunters; they also made them formidable foes of their Indian neighbors and the Spaniards who began to push up from Mexico after about 1700.

Farther to the west, in what is now New Mexico and Arizona, were the Zuñis, Acomas, Hopis, and several other tribes grouped under the

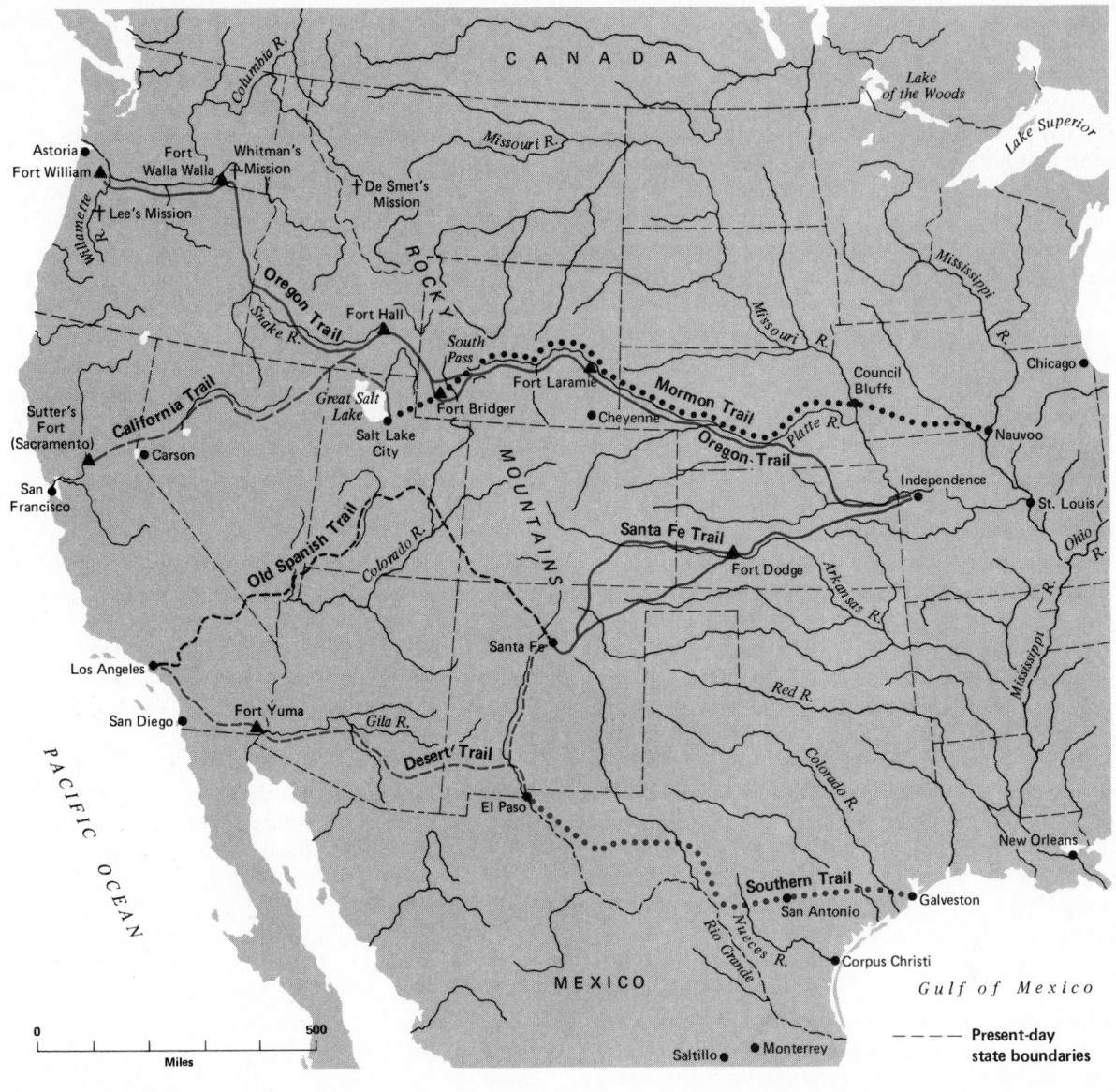

Trails to the West

name *Pueblos*. Dependent on agriculture, they lived in densely populated, settled communities (pueblos) with mud-brick (adobe) structures that resembled modern apartment houses. These dwellings sometimes rose to four stories and were often grouped around central plazas used for ceremonies and communal events. The Pueblo tribes were generally peaceful people; they seldom waged offensive war against their neighbors, though they were capable of fighting fiercely for their homes and rights.

Still farther west, along the Pacific in what is now California, was an Indian population composed of many tribal groups. When the whites ar-

rived in the eighteenth century, as many as 350,000 California Indians were spread through the narrow Pacific coastal plain, in the interior valleys, and along the lower reaches of the region's rivers. The California tribes had a simple economy and technology. The abundant acorns, from which nutritious flour could be prepared, and the warm climate simplified living and made agriculture and elaborate clothing and shelter unnecessary. Though their material possessions were meager, the California Indians had developed a rich and complex religious and ceremonial life, and an oral literature of songs, stories, and myths passed on from generation to generation.

Spanish Penetration. The remainder of the region's population consisted of people of Spanish background or mixed Spanish-Indian ancestry. The earliest Spanish settlers had come to the interior of the Southwest around 1600, when parties of soldiers from Mexico established Santa Fe in what is now central New Mexico. Soon afterward, a different kind of Spanish penetration took over. On every previous Spanish frontier soldiers had led the way and missionaries had followed. Now missionaries preceded the military, pushing into every corner of the present-day American Southwest.

The pattern soon became standardized. A Spanish friar of the Dominican, Franciscan, or Jesuit order would set off with a few Indian dependents for an unsettled region. When he had located a favorable spot, he went back to "civilization" and gathered a few soldiers, several families of Christianized Indians, and some fellow friars. He then returned with them to the new frontier, where he gathered local Indian labor and constructed a community consisting of an adobe church, gardens, blacksmith shop, gristmill, and other workshops. If all went well, in a decade or so the friars had established a mission with vineyards, cultivated fields of grain, herds of cattle, and clusters of Indian huts, all dominated by a mission church, elaborately decorated to beautify Christian worship and hold the attention of the Indian converts. Before long this new pocket of Spanish colonial civilization would send out other shoots to repeat the process and contribute to the steady advance of the European cultural frontier.

California. In California the missionary process began in 1769 when Franciscan friar Junípero Serra and fourteen brown-robed brothers led a party of 126 Indians and soldiers from present-day Arizona to San Diego Bay. Dispatched by the Spanish authorities to forestall Russian designs on the California coast claimed by Spain, the move combined imperial self-interest with the desire to gather souls for the Lord. Over the next half century another twenty missions, along with two garrisoned towns *(presidios)*, were established in what is now the state of California.

In many ways these missions were immensely successful enterprises. By 1800 they housed some 13,000 Indians and had taken on the charming physical form that tourists see today: whitewashed churches with red-tiled roofs, courtyards with arched colonnades and fountains, and ingenious workshops containing the artifacts of skilled Indians. It is also easy to imagine the vineyards, grain fields, fruit and olive orchards, and vast grazing herds that no longer exist.

But there was another, grimmer side. Infant mortality in the crowded missions was appalling. In 1820, 86 percent of all children born at the California missions died before adulthood. Mortality as a whole was high. During the entire mission period—1769–1833—a total of 82,000 Indians lived in the missions. A normal death rate for such a population in this period would have been around 40,000. Instead, there were 62,000 deaths among the mission Indians. Nor was this the full extent of the demographic disaster visited on the California Indians. The whites as usual brought their diseases and their almost equally lethal culture. The former killed directly; the latter killed by undermining Indian morale and family life. All told, between 1769 and 1846 the Indian population of California dropped to about 100,000—one-third of what it had been when the friars first came.

San Francisco at the time of the Gold Rush. No cable cars, no Fisherman's Wharf—but the magnificent Bay is the same.

Library of Congress

New-York Historical Society

Three hundred years before the Spanish arrived in New Mexico, the Zuñi Indians lived in adobe apartment houses, some four stories high with as many as 500 rooms. Their culture had a distinct identity and resisted the influence of Catholic missionaries. Tradition seems to live on in this 1873 photograph.

The mission era ended in the 1830s when the Mexican government, at the behest of would-be landowners, deprived the missions of thousands of acres and threw their lands open to private ownership. At the same time it ended the friars' paternal but stern control over the Indians. In the next few years aggressive entrepreneurs established some 700 ranchos, each covering thousands of acres. Devoted largely to cattle raising, each giant estate was controlled by a ranchero, usually of Spanish descent, who supervised groups of *vaqueros* (cowboys) who did the common labor of herding, fence mending, branding, and slaughtering.

Life in California in the years immediately preceding American occupation was colorful and, for the rancheros, almost idyllic. Little news came from the outside world to disturb the few thousand Spanish-Mexicans in their pursuit of pleasure amid the abundance provided by their lands and the delights of the region's climate. Government in Mexico City was remote, and its hand rested lightly on the inhabitants. If we can believe the accounts of visitors, the life of the small Spanish elite was a round of fiestas, races, dancing, and courtship.

Americans in small numbers began to drift into California in the 1830s, attracted by the climate and the carefree life. Some, such as Thomas Larkin and the part-black William Leidesdorf,

came by sea and established themselves as merchants in Monterey, San Diego, and other towns. Others came overland by way of the California Trail and became successful ranchers. Europeans came, too. The Swiss John Augustus Sutter arrived in Monterey in 1839 and talked the Spanish governor into granting him a giant domain near present-day Sacramento, which he named New Helvetia in honor of his homeland. Many of the newcomers converted to Catholicism and married into prosperous Spanish families.

The prosperity of the rancheros, whether Spanish or American, was not matched by that of the majority of Californians. For the former mission Indians, life was scarcely better than before. Freed from bondage to the friars, they were recruited by the rancheros as laborers and spent long days purifying tallow, tanning hides, and loading skins onto ships for markets in the United States and Europe. They were paid nothing for their labor beyond their food, clothing, and shelter. If they left the ranch, they were hunted down like slaves. It is not surprising that the California Indian population continued to fall at an appalling rate.

New Mexico. California's political and cultural isolation was matched by that of another Mexican borderland, New Mexico. This region—bounded by the Louisiana Purchase on the north, the Mojave Desert on the west, and Texas on the east—was separated from the nearest settlements of northern Mexico by 600 miles of barren plains and rugged mountains. Like California, though a century and a half earlier, the region had been settled by friars who planted missions as centers of Christian civilization and incidentally as outposts to protect New Spain against the French in Louisiana.

Unlike the indigenous peoples of California, the Indians of the New Mexico region were not easy to dominate. The mission system put down only shallow roots. The Pueblo Indians had no need of the friars. Though they acquired sheep and goats from the Spaniards, they kept their tight-knit agricultural communities intact, and to this day preserve a distinctive and strongly defined culture. Several Hopi pueblos are the oldest continuously occupied settlements in what is now the United States.

Whereas the Pueblo peoples managed to fend off the Spaniards by their cohesion, the nomadic Apache, Navaho, and Comanche tribes in the New Mexico–Arizona–west Texas region repelled the Europeans by their warlike qualities. Before the Spaniards came, these tribes had attacked the Pueblo Indians, stealing slaves and booty. When the Spaniards arrived about 1700, they attacked them. Enmity between the Europeans and these fierce warriors was perpetuated by the Spaniards, who enslaved captured Indians and offered bounties for their scalps. When these hostilities first began, the Indians fought on foot; once they acquired horses from their enemies, they became formidable mounted warriors whose swift raids and quick retreats made them difficult to subdue. Indeed, not until the advent of the repeating revolver in the mid-nineteenth century would the European become the military equal of the Apache or Comanche horseman.

Despite these difficulties, the Spaniards succeeded in establishing several permanent communities in the New Mexico–Arizona region. By the 1820s New Mexico had about 40,000 settled inhabitants, many of them clustered around the provincial capital, Santa Fe. Like the Californians, these people (mixed Indian-Mexican-Spanish) were self-sufficient in food, but they were starved for manufactured goods that distant and economically undeveloped Mexico could not supply. American traders were happy to fill these needs in exchange for the gold, silver, and furs of the region. In the early 1820s a Missouri merchant, William Becknell, launched a lucrative trade in textiles, rifles, tools, and other goods between St. Louis and New Mexico by way of the Santa Fe Trail. By 1824 parties of as many as eighty men with a score of wagons and over a hundred pack animals were using the trail blazed by Becknell.

Texas. The growing American influence in New Mexico and California was minor compared with the American impact in Texas, then an ill-defined region between Louisiana and the northern desert of Mexico. Like the other outlying Mexican provinces, Texas was sprinkled with a few missions and garrisons. Early in the nineteenth century Americans in small numbers began to cross the Sabine River into Spanish-held territory. In 1823 the Mexican Republic, newly independent from Spain, granted Stephen F. Austin the right to bring in 300 American families as permanent settlers to help develop the region. The newcomers were required to be of high moral character and were to adopt the Catholic faith. In return, the Mexicans promised each family a free square league (about 4,000 acres) for farming and raising cattle. Austin's settlement was followed by others. Fearful of the flood of Americans, in 1830 the Mexican government prohibited further United States immigration. The law was not enforced, however, and by 1835 there were almost 30,000 transplanted Americans living in Texas.

THE ANNEXATION OF TEXAS

Texas might have remained a contented province of Mexico but for difficulties that were not solely of the Texans' making. Religious and cultural differences between the American settlers and the Mexican officials played a part. The Americans were Protestant and resented efforts to make them turn Catholic and to prevent Protestant worship. Most were southerners who wanted to grow cotton using slave labor, and they disliked Mexico's laws forbidding slavery. Moreover, most transplanted Americans disdained Mexicans as culturally or racially inferior. Yet despite these points of friction, the American settlers proved remarkably loyal to their adopted country. When, in 1826, a small band of dissident Americans led by Haden Edwards revolted against the central government, the main body of settlers under Austin helped the Mexican authorities put down the insurrection.

The Texas Revolution. Unfortunately, neither the citizens of the United States nor the Mexican government could let the Texan-Americans alone. In the United States many people regretted the surrender of Texas to Spain in the Adams-Onís

Treaty of 1819. Six years later, as president, John Quincy Adams tried to undo his own work by offering Mexico $1 million for Texas. His successor, Andrew Jackson, raised the price to $5 million and sent Anthony Butler to Mexico City to pressure the Mexican government into accepting it. Butler tried to bribe Mexican officials; failing to do so, he urged Jackson to take Texas by force.

The Mexican government, too, could not let the Texans be. Its policies, including those regarding immigration, were markedly inconsistent. Mexican officials, holding two competing philosophies of government, continually battled among themselves. "Federalists" advocated local autonomy for the individual Mexican states and weak control from Mexico City. This circle of politicians favored policies to encourage immigration. "Centralists," on the other hand, demanded tight, centralized government to hold the unwieldy country together. Centralists were generally unfriendly to immigration. When they held power, they revoked the provincial autonomy that made immigration attractive and feasible to Americans. These two groups—and innumerable other factions organized on ideological lines or around particular leaders—constantly squabbled. The country was frequently plunged into civil war; almost never was there a peaceful succession of administrations, and the government was seldom able to maintain any policy for very long.

The bewildering shifts of factions and leaders within the Mexican government had serious effects on the relations between Mexico and her newest citizens, the Texans. In 1834 Antonio Lopez de Santa Anna, who had first won and then lost power in the 1820s, became the nation's leader for the second time. Possessing an exceptional talent for detecting the latest political currents and riding them to power, Santa Anna would be the leading figure in Mexican political life during the 1830s and 1840s. His return was bad for the Texans. A Centralist, he rescinded the powers the Federalists had allowed the states and set himself up in Mexico City as dictator.

Santa Anna's dictatorship worsened an already uncomfortable situation. For some time the Texans had been unhappy with their limited self-rule. Governed from Saltillo, the capital of Coahuila, 700 miles to the south, they hoped to establish a separate state within the Mexican federal republic. Santa Anna's arbitrary actions dashed these hopes and convinced them not only that their existing grievances would not be corrected but also that the Mexican government might try to expel all Americans from the republic. When Santa Anna sent troops to garrison several points within Texas, these fears seemed to be confirmed. Soon sporadic fighting broke out between Texans and Mexican troops.

In 1835 Santa Anna dispatched an army to the north to chastise the rebellious Texans; the Texans responded by assaulting Mexican military posts at Gonzales and San Antonio. These were serious deeds that the Mexican authorities could not overlook; for the Texans there was now no turning back. Meeting at the little village of Washington in the spring of 1836, fifty-nine Texan delegates adopted a declaration of independence, established a provisional government, and selected Sam Houston, formerly a United States army officer and governor of Tennessee, as commander in chief of the Texas armed forces.

Meanwhile, Santa Anna's army arrived in San Antonio, where a small force of Texans occupied an abandoned mission called the Alamo. The 187 Texans bravely defended themselves against the Mexican army of 4,000, but on March 6 they were overwhelmed. In the final assault every defender, including the frontier heroes William B. Travis, Jim Bowie, and Davy Crockett, died. Soon after this victory the Mexicans attacked a Texan force of 300 at Goliad. Greatly outnumbered again, the Americans surrendered this time—only to be shot down in cold blood on Santa Anna's orders.

The events at the Alamo and at Goliad enraged the Texans, who vowed to win their freedom at all costs. In the next few weeks, however, Houston was forced to retreat before Santa Anna's superior numbers. Matters looked hopeless, but Houston was playing a canny game. As he moved eastward he toughened his little army and picked up reinforcements, many of them volunteers from across the American border. At San Jacinto, Houston finally turned to face the enemy. At noon on April 21, 1836, his small band of 800 seasoned campaigners, shouting "Remember the Alamo," attacked the Mexicans and defeated them. Six hundred Mexicans were killed in the fighting and 730, including Santa Anna himself, were captured.

San Jacinto brought Texas its independence. Houston forced the Mexican leader to sign treaties ending the war and accepting the independence of Texas. The new republic would have as its southern boundary the Rio Grande River.

When news of Santa Anna's defeat and capture reached Mexico City, the Mexican Congress promptly repudiated the agreements on the firm ground that they had been coerced. Little attention was given to the question of the boundaries of Texas, since from the Mexican standpoint Texas was still part of Mexico and the whole issue was irrelevant. Despite its renunciation of the treaties,

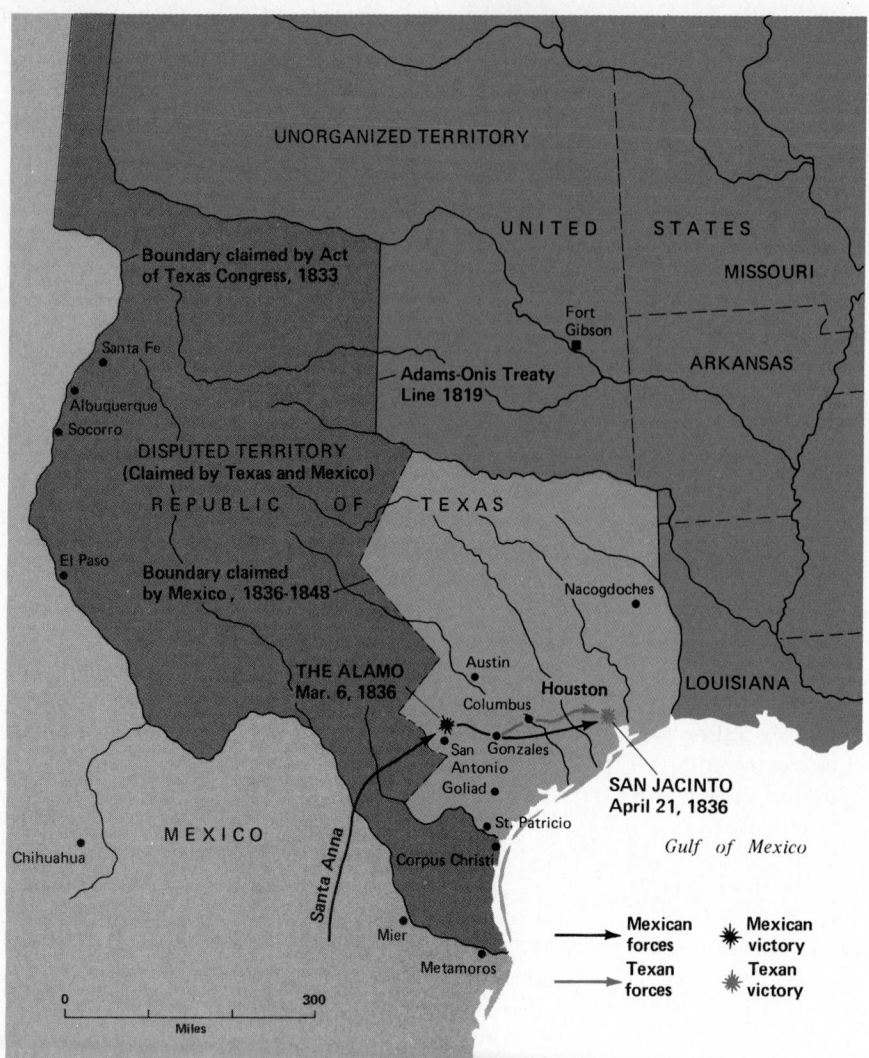

The Texas Revolution

---

however, Mexico was in no position to resume the war, and Texas settled down uneasily to a brief existence as an independent nation.

EXPANSIONISM: ADVOCATES AND OPPONENTS

The problems of Oregon, of the Mexican borderland, and indeed of virtually all the boundaries of the United States fell into the lap of President John Tyler when he assumed office in April 1841. A dour and rigid Virginian and a former Democrat who had broken with Jackson over King Andrew's dictatorial ways, Tyler became president when William Henry Harrison contracted pneumonia and died a month after his inauguration. This was the first time a president had died in office, and it was not clear whether "His Accidency," as his opponents called Tyler, could exercise the full powers of a duly elected chief executive. Aware that Tyler had been a Democrat until he was placed on the 1840 ticket with Harrison to win southern and Democratic votes, many Whigs were reluctant to accord him the respect a president deserved. Tyler refused to accept an inferior status and stubbornly and successfully asserted his full prerogatives.

In domestic matters Tyler's doggedness and vigor accomplished little. With Harrison in office, the Whigs had looked forward to rechartering a national bank, raising the tariff, and carrying out other nationalistic measures. Congress, under Whig control, did pass a new bank bill; but Tyler,

Manifest Destiny

Every nation with expansionist designs has found a rationale for its goals. The United States was no exception. Its justification was called Manifest Destiny, and it was the creation largely of a New York lawyer-journalist named John Louis O'Sullivan, who probably first used the phrase in 1845.

In the July-August 1845 issue of his paper, *The United States Magazine and Democratic Review,* O'Sullivan argued in favor of Texas annexation against those who attacked it as either a "slave power" scheme or an act of pure greed against a weaker neighbor. The excerpt of this editorial included here carries the argument beyond Texas to justify all of American continental expansion. Note O'Sullivan's emphasis on demography and his prediction of America's population a century ahead.

". . . Texas has been absorbed into the Union in the inevitable fulfillment of the general law which is rolling our population westward; the connexion of which with that ratio of growth in population which is destined within a hundred years to swell our numbers to the enormous population of *two hundred and fifty millions* (if not more), is too evident to leave us in doubt of the manifest design of Providence in regard to the occupation of this continent. It was disintegrated from Mexico in the natural course of events, by a process perfectly legitimate on its own part, blameless on ours; and in which all the censures due to wrong, perfidy, and folly, rest on Mexico alone. And possessed as it was by a population which was in truth but a colonial detachment from our own, . . . their incorporation into the Union was not only inevitable, but the most natural, right and proper thing in the world—and it is only astonishing that there should be any among ourselves to say it nay. . . .

"California will, probably, next fall away from the loose affiliation which, in such a country like Mexico, holds a remote province in a slight equivocal kind of dependence on the metropolis. Imbecile and distracted, Mexico can never exert any real governmental authority over such a country. The impotence of the one and the distance of the other, must make the relation one of virtual independence, unless, by stunting the province of all natural growth, and forbidding that immigration which alone can develop its capabilities and fulfill the purposes of its creation, tyranny may retain a military dominion which is no government in

the legitimate sense of the term. In the case of California this is now impossible. The Anglo-Saxon foot is already on its borders. Already the advance guard of the irresistible army of the Anglo-Saxon emigration has begun to pour down upon it, armed with the plough and the rifle, and making its trail with schools and colleges, courts and representative halls, mills and meeting-houses. A population will soon be in actual occupation of California, over which it will be idle for Mexico to dream of dominion. They will necessarily become independent. All this without agency of our government, without responsibility of our people—in the natural flow of events, the spontaneous working of principles, and the adaptation of the tendencies and wants of the human race to the elemental circumstances in the midst of which they find themselves placed. . . .

"Whether they will then attach themselves to our Union or not, is not to be predicted with any certainty. Unless the projected rail-road across the continent to the Pacific be carried into effect, perhaps they may not; though even in that case, the day is not far distant when the Empires of the Atlantic and the Pacific would again flow together into one. . . . But that great work . . . cannot remain long unbuilt. Its necessity for this very purpose of binding and holding together in its iron clasp our fast settling Pacific region with that of the Mississippi valley . . . gives assurance that the day cannot be distant which shall witness the conveyance of the representatives from Oregon and California to Washington within less time than a few years ago was devoted to a similar journey by those from Ohio. . . .

"Away, then, with all idle French talk of *balances of power* on the American Continent. There is no growth in Spanish America! Whatever progress of population there may be in the British Canadas, is only for their own early severance of their present colonial relation to the little island three thousand miles across the Atlantic; soon to be followed by Annexation, and destined to swell the still accumulating momentum of our progress. And whatsoever may hold the balance, though they should cast into the opposite scale all the bayonets and cannon, not only of France and England, but of Europe entire, how would it kick the beam against the simple solid weight of two hundred and fifty or three hundred millions . . . destined to gather beneath the flutter of the stripes and stars, in the fast hastening year of the Lord 1945?"

true to his Jeffersonian states' rights principles, promptly vetoed it. In short order his entire cabinet, except Secretary of State Daniel Webster, who still had important diplomatic business to complete, resigned in protest. Thereafter, Tyler and the congressional Whigs remained at loggerheads. The president vetoed two Whig efforts to raise the tariff and signed the Tariff Act of 1842

only after Henry Clay's pet scheme to distribute the federal surplus to the states had been cut out of the bill.

In foreign affairs, where the Constitution allows the executive a relatively freer hand, Tyler was more effective. The president was a moderate expansionist. As a southerner, he craved new territory within slavery's supposed "natural limits"—

the region where cotton, sugar, rice, and other warm-climate, slave-grown crops could flourish. Such a place was Texas, where the American settlers were already using slave labor to produce bumper cotton crops. Tyler was indifferent to expansion elsewhere.

The president's attitude affected the course of negotiations with Britain over the disputed boundary between Canada and the states of Maine, New York, Vermont, and New Hampshire. In 1838 this disagreement had produced a violent clash when Maine tried to eject British subjects from parts of the Aroostook district claimed by the Canadian province of New Brunswick. For a while an undeclared Aroostook War raged between American and Canadian lumbermen and trappers in the dense forest along the boundary. Fortunately, more serious fighting was avoided when the Maine and New Brunswick authorities agreed to desist temporarily from further settlement.

The boundary dispute continued to fester, however, while other arguments with Britain accumulated. The unwillingness of the United States to join the British in suppressing the illegal Atlantic slave trade deeply offended British antislavery opinion. There was also the affair of the *Caroline*, an American-owned steamship hired by Canadian rebels to aid them in an uprising against British rule. Pro-British Canadian volunteers had crossed the border and destroyed the *Caroline* near Niagara Falls and, in the process, had killed one American citizen on American soil.

Rather than challenge the British in these matters, Tyler and Secretary of State Daniel Webster chose to be conciliatory. The British, too, preferred compromise, and the envoy they sent to negotiate with Webster, Lord Alexander Ashburton, was a pro-American banker married to an American woman. In a few short weeks the two men worked out a compromise in the Webster-Ashburton Treaty (1842). Under its terms the United States would keep about 4.5 million acres of the 7.7 million in dispute; New Brunswick would get the rest. In addition, the United States government agreed to join Britain in supporting a naval squadron off the African coast to capture slave ships attempting to bring Africans to the Americas. In a supplementary exchange of notes Ashburton in effect also apologized for the *Caroline* incident.

Before the treaty could be adopted, however, Maine had to be satisfied. Webster accomplished this by showing the state authorities a long-lost map, supposedly drawn at the time of the 1783 peace treaty with Great Britain, that depicted the Canadian border as dipping far south into Maine.

The United States, Webster observed, had made a better bargain than it deserved. Confronted by this information, Maine authorities withdrew their objections and the treaty was confirmed. Still, many northerners felt that the administration had been too weak, and they were right. A map discovered in 1933 clearly demonstrated that Maine's original claim was valid and that the United States had unnecessarily given away over 3 million acres of the national domain.

Tyler's rather tepid interest in northern real estate also applied to Oregon. Many Americans, especially northern Democrats, insisted that the United States rightfully owned all the Oregon country from the northern boundary of California at 42° north latitude to the southern boundary of Russian America at 54° 40′ north latitude. Tyler proposed to the British that Oregon be divided at the forty-ninth parallel. He would accept even less territory, he told them, if they would pressure Mexico to give the United States the excellent Pacific port of San Francisco. The British were unwilling to accept this arrangement, and the Oregon dispute remained unsettled.

Victory for Tyler. Tyler's major diplomatic success came in Texas. No sooner had they achieved independence than the Texans sought admission to the Union. Many Americans, especially Whigs, heartily opposed the annexation of Texas. Eager to centralize national power within the existing limits of the United States, the Whigs opposed any dispersion of that power over a broader area. Many northerners, including some Democrats, feared that Texas, which would surely enter the Union as a slave state or even a number of slave states, would reinforce the "slave power" in the national government. A group of antislavery congressmen, led by former President John Quincy Adams, called the effort to annex Texas a "slavocracy" plot to add to southern power in Congress. Still other citizens feared war. The Mexican government had refused to recognize the independence of Texas and had even tried unsuccessfully to reconquer its former province. Annexation, these opponents felt, might well goad the Mexicans into attacking the United States.

With so many Americans hostile to slavery, skeptical of expansion, or fearful of war, the Texas annexation issue seemed like a hot potato; and for most of a decade the American government gingerly avoided it. In early 1837, just before leaving office, Jackson officially recognized Texas, and during the next few years Americans established trade relations with the "Lone Star Republic." Annexation, however, remained stalled.

Various forces soon goaded the Americans to action. Discouraged by American indifference, the Texans began to dicker with England and France for recognition and loans in exchange for free trade in cotton and generous land grants to French and British subjects. This flirtation with the major European powers, intended to force Congress's hand, disturbed many Americans. Slaveholders feared that Britain, which had abolished slavery in its colonies in the 1830s, might acquire Texas and end slavery there, exposing the South's western flank to abolitionist influence. Other Americans, although reluctant to incorporate Texas into the Union, objected even more to allowing her to become part of the British Empire. Proannexation sentiment was further reinforced by an influential group of capitalists who owned Texas bonds and Texas lands and who believed that annexation would guarantee the safety and profits of these investments.

Tyler cleverly played on the interests of all these groups to secure annexation. To the proslavery southerners he pointed out the dangers of British abolitionism in Texas. To Anglophobes and patriots he suggested that British interest in Texas was part of a plot to encircle the United States. Through a personal friend, Senator Robert J. Walker of Mississippi, he promised Pacific ports to the commercial men of the Northeast interested in the China trade.

Despite Tyler's and Walker's efforts, the Senate defeated an annexation treaty in 1844, and Texas remained outside the Union almost to the end of Tyler's term. Annexation and Oregon became major issues in the 1844 presidential contest. By this time Tyler had completely lost the support of his nominal party and was not seriously considered for renomination. Instead the Whigs turned to Henry Clay, who opposed annexation on the grounds that it would mean war with Mexico. Rather than repudiate their candidate's stated principles, the Whigs avoided any mention of Oregon or Texas in their platform and thus maintained party harmony. The Democrats, as usual, became embroiled in a lengthy battle over men and policies. Martin Van Buren considered himself the party's titular leader despite his defeat in 1840, but he was opposed to annexation, and most of the party favored it. Annexationists successfully blocked his nomination, but they deadlocked the convention in the process. Maneuvering went on for days until, on the ninth ballot, James K. Polk of Tennessee, former speaker of the House of Representatives, received the prize. The Democratic platform, written by Senator Walker, called for the "reoccupation of Oregon and the reannexation of

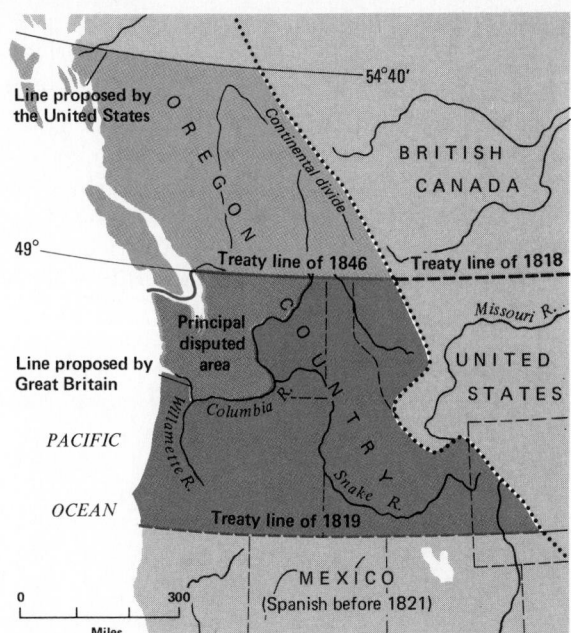

The Oregon controversy, 1818–1846

Texas at the earliest practicable period." The suggestion in this wording—that the United States was merely exerting clear preexisting rights in these regions—was dubious history, but it accurately expressed expansionists' convictions.

The Democrats went on to victory, but just barely. The tariff and Texas were the major campaign issues, and on both, the candidates wavered and waffled—to the public's general disgust. In the end Polk won, but only because James Birney, candidate of the tiny Liberty party, drew enough antislavery voters from Clay to give Polk New York by 5,000 votes and a paper-thin electoral majority.

Polk's election was not, then, a strong mandate for annexation. Nevertheless, many formerly undecided citizens, now concluding that annexation was inevitable, gave it their support. To Tyler this was a cue to renewed efforts. Rather than submit yet another annexation treaty, which would require the approval of two-thirds of the Senate, he asked Congress for a joint annexation resolution, which would need only a bare majority of both houses for adoption. This approach worked. By heavily Democratic votes in both houses Congress approved the resolution. On March 1, 1845, in the closing hours of his administration, Tyler signed the joint resolution. Texas entered the Union as a slave state in December 1845, but only after another heated debate in Congress with Adams and other antislavery Whigs leading the opposition.

MOVING TOWARD WAR

For many months the Mexican government had been threatening retaliation if the United States absorbed Texas. Now, in the wake of the joint resolution, the Mexican minister to Washington asked for his passport and returned to Mexico City eager to tell his superiors that the Americans had no stomach for war and could be easily intimidated.

The minister had not taken the correct measure of James K. Polk. A slight man of forty-nine with cool gray eyes and thin-lipped mouth, the new president was not impressive physically. Nor did he loom much larger intellectually. Polk's talents and mind were both mediocre. But he was a remarkably strong-willed man, in his aggressive spirit and willfulness resembling his hero and sponsor, Andrew Jackson. Determined to make his mark, he mastered the details of government through sheer energy. He soon became so adept at department routines that at one point he bet his secretary of state, James Buchanan, several bottles of champagne that the latter had made a mistake in a diplomatic note. Polk won the wager. It is the measure of the man's humorless personality that he refused to collect his prize.

Manifest Destiny. Like many Americans of his day, Polk was imbued with the mystique of Manifest Destiny. First given this name by John L. O'Sullivan, a New York Democratic magazine editor, the doctrine proclaimed that the American people had the God-given right to subdue and spread their benevolent institutions over the entire continent. This process could not be stopped until the nation reached from the Atlantic to the Pacific, its "natural boundaries," for it was ordained and irreversible. "Make Way for the Young American Buffalo," declaimed a bombastic New Jersey defender of American destiny:

> He has not got land enough. . . . I tell you we will give him Oregon for his summer shade, and the region of Texas as his summer pasture. Like others of his race, he wants salt, too. Well, he shall have the use of two oceans—the mighty Pacific and the turbulent Atlantic shall be his.

Manifest Destiny was not a new doctrine. It can be traced back as far as the Puritans of Massachusetts Bay, who felt that they had a special "mission" in America. Reinforced by the tremendous national energies unleashed following independence and by the aggressive economic opportunism and buoyant confidence that accompanied pre–Civil War economic growth, Manifest Destiny reached a climax in the 1840s. It was a self-serving ideology. Like the French, British, German, and Japanese rationalizations of territorial ambitions at other times, it sought to justify policies that were based on selfish national interest. Certainly the peoples and nations who stood in the way of America's expansionist urge found it difficult to see American growth as divinely inspired and benevolent. Their skepticism was not misplaced. All too often Manifest Destiny would serve to excuse the most brutal disregard of the rights of others. It also contained a large element of cultural and racial arrogance. Its implicit theme was that American civilization and "Anglo-American" stock were superior to any other; at times it revealed explicit contempt for the nonwhite and Hispanic peoples of North America.

Yet American expansionism differed from its Old World equivalent in at least one important way. Americans have never been comfortable with colonies. The Northwest Ordinance of 1787 had established the precedent that all new territory acquired by the United States would eventually be organized into self-governing states to be incorporated into the Union as equals of the others. This principle served as a check on American expansionism. Whether out of prejudice against other cultures and races or merely in recognition of cultural disparities, Americans have been reluctant to annex densely populated regions of peoples with different traditions, customs, and beliefs. In 1846 this attitude would help put a damper on the "All Mexico!" movement that followed the war that was about to begin.

Polk and his cabinet endorsed the premises of Manifest Destiny. In Oregon the president seconded his followers' cry of "Fifty-four forty or fight." He also believed that Britain coveted the rich province of California and was planning a takeover. We now know that England had no such plan, but the weakness of Mexico's hold on California and the intrigues of local British diplomatic agents made Polk and his advisers understandably uneasy and anxious to beat England to the punch. Polk's expansionism also led him to support the Texas claim to territory reaching southwest to the Rio Grande. The Mexican government insisted that the province extended only to the Nueces River many miles to the northeast, and the precedents for this position were strong ones. Polk never questioned the Texans' claims, however, and was willing to use force to make them good.

Debate on Expansionism. Not all Americans accepted Polk's ambitious territorial goals. In New England and parts of the Northeast where antislavery sentiment was strong, there were few expansionists. Southerners, though eager for Texas, cared little about Oregon. Americans as a whole felt that California and the Southwest, with their mixed races and large stretches of barren desert and craggy mountains, were probably more trouble than they were worth.

Expansionist feelings were strongest in the Northwest and parts of the Northeast. In Pennsylvania and New York commercial men and industrialists looked forward to continental markets and the access to the Far East that Pacific ports might bring. The business community was small, but its views counted politically. In the upper Mississippi Valley land hunger was the basis for expansionism. Many people in this vast, lightly settled region already feared the disappearance of cheap land and looked to the Far West as a reservoir for future generations.

Still, politics probably influenced attitudes toward expansion more than sectional and occupational interests. Whig voters tended to see politics as an extension of morality: since expansion favored slavery, it was unethical. Democrats were less inclined to treat politics as a moral arena: they either considered the expansion of slavery an irrelevant issue or, in the South, actually welcomed it. Moreover, the two parties had different traditions regarding territorial growth. The Democrats were largely the heirs of the Jeffersonian Republicans, who had acquired Louisiana and Florida. On the other hand, the Whigs, as a party, were largely descended from the Federalists, who had preferred to avoid geographical expansion.

Age, too, affected how Americans thought about extending the nation's boundaries. Expansionists were generally youthful. Democrats associated with the "Young America" group led the movement for a totally American continent. Made up largely of political leaders like the thirty-two year-old Stephen A. Douglas of Illinois and such youthful journalists as twenty-six-year-old Walt

Columbia brings daylight to North America, laying railroad tracks and stringing telegraph wire, as Indians and buffalo flee her advance. Americans believed they were ordained by God to farm Oregon and Texas, mine California, and build ports on the Pacific coast.

Library of Congress; Collection of the Late Harry T. Peters

Whitman, Young America exhibited all the enthusiasm for great, bold deeds traditionally associated with vigorous young people. President Polk, who at 49 was the youngest man to hold presidential office up to that time, was temperamentally a member of this group.

Compromise with England. Although he desired expansion, Polk was not anxious to go to war for it. In his inaugural address he repeated the claim of the 1844 Democratic platform that the American title to Oregon was "clear and unquestionable." But in later months he blew hot and cold on Oregon, alternately threatening and appeasing Britain. Soon after his inauguration he proposed settling the Oregon dispute by extending the existing Canadian-American boundary, the forty-ninth parallel, all the way to the Pacific. When the British minister haughtily rejected this proposal, the angry Polk withdrew it. Several months later, in his first message to Congress, the president again demanded all of Oregon to the 54° 40' line and asked Congress to give the required one-year notice to Britain ending joint occupation of the region.

The threat of a direct confrontation with the United States startled the British, and they asked the American government to renew its forty-ninth parallel offer. The touchy president refused, but allowed Secretary of State Buchanan to tell the British that if *they* initiated a compromise, the American government would reconsider. In early June 1846 the London government proposed extending the boundary along the forty-ninth parallel to the Pacific, but reserving all of Vancouver Island for Britain. Polk now submitted the plan to the Senate. The bellicose Young Americans denounced it as a betrayal of American interests, but by a vote of 41 to 14, the Senate adopted it. The Oregon question, which had dragged on since the days of John Quincy Adams a generation before, had finally been settled by good sense and compromise.

And not a moment too soon. Polk had not expected war with Mexico when he first proposed a settlement to the British; but by the time the Senate approved the Oregon treaty, Americans and Mexicans were killing one another along the whole border from Texas to present-day Arizona.

The Slidell Mission. Polk blundered into war. He coveted Mexican territory; but as in the case of Oregon, he was reluctant to fight for it. In the fall of 1845 he had dispatched John Slidell to Mexico to see if the United States could get what it wanted by negotiation. Mexico had broken diplomatic relations with the United States at the time of the Texas annexation, and Mexican patriots were still outraged at what they considered the theft of one of their country's choice provinces. Anti-American Mexicans refused to accept negotiations and demanded war against the United States. Nevertheless, Polk remained hopeful of a peaceful settlement. Slidell was to say that if Mexico recognized the Rio Grande as the southern boundary of Texas, the United States would pay the $3.25 million that Mexico owed to American citizens. He was also to offer $5 million for the province of New Mexico and $25 million more for California. He did not expect these negotiations to fail, Polk informed his envoy; but if they did, he would ask Congress "to provide proper remedies." Historians have interpreted this phrase as a threat of war, and it probably was. But Polk was certain that the negotiations would be successful, and he made it clear that he considered the use of force highly unlikely.

The Slidell mission went wrong from the very beginning. Mexican patriots, having gotten wind of Slidell's purpose, demanded that the Mexican people overthrow their own rulers lest they sell the entire country to the United States. At first the Mexican government of José Herrera was inclined to negotiate, but the pressures of public opinion made it hesitate and pursue a confusing policy. Although Slidell was permitted to enter Mexico, he was held at arm's length and not allowed to present his proposals.

Soon after Slidell reached Mexico City, the Herrera government fell. The new administration under Mariano Paredes attacked its predecessor for "seeking to avoid a necessary and glorious war" and began to negotiate with Great Britain for support against the United States if war should come. Disgusted with what he considered Mexican bad faith, Polk ordered General Zachary Taylor to move his troops to the north bank of the Rio Grande to occupy the disputed Texas border region and protect Texas against possible attack. The Mexican government, fearing public opinion, soon gave Slidell his walking papers.

Hope for a negotiated settlement faded with Slidell's dismissal. By the spring of 1846 Polk had concluded that war was unavoidable. On April 23 Paredes announced that Mexico had declared "defensive war" on the United States, and news soon reached Washington that the Mexicans were preparing to attack Taylor's army. Early in May Polk discussed a war declaration with his cabinet. All of his advisers except Secretary of the Navy George Bancroft agreed that a declaration was justified. But before Secretary of State Buchanan could prepare a statement of grievances against Mexico, news reached the capital that Mexican troops had crossed the Rio Grande and attacked a unit of Taylor's troops in the disputed region. Two days later Polk's war message was read to Congress. War was declared by a vote of 40 to 2 in the Senate and 174 to 14 in the House.

WAR WITH MEXICO

The war lasted almost two years, costing 13,000 American lives and $100 million. It was a remarkable triumph for American arms. This time, the combination of a small regular army and a mass of volunteers worked well. Men flocked to the recruiting offices. Many enlistees came from the Mississippi Valley, where the spirit of Manifest Destiny was at its most bellicose. To lead these troops the country had a cadre of well-trained officers, graduates of the military academy at West Point. Although few West Pointers had yet commanded large military units, their professionalism and overall competence made them quick and able learners. Besides skilled military leadership, the country also enjoyed excellent morale. Many Whigs remained skeptical of the war, and antislavery people strongly opposed it. But most Americans enthusiastically supported the armies in the field and cheered each victory.

Taking the Borderland. Never before, and not again until the Second World War, would American troops march and fight over so wide an area. In the north the Army of the West under Stephen Watts Kearny advanced from the Missouri River, captured Santa Fe, and took possession of New Mexico. A month later Kearny's forces thrust across the Mojave Desert to San Diego in southern California. In northern Mexico Zachary Taylor's army clashed with troops led by General Mariano Arista and twice routed them. Taylor soon advanced southward and seized Monterrey, capital of Nuevo León.

Meanwhile, events were happening at a hectic pace in California. Even before the formal outbreak of hostilities California had become a hotbed of anti-Mexican intrigue. In 1845 Polk had secretly authorized Thomas O. Larkin, the American consul in the California capital, to encourage a secessionist movement among the several thousand American settlers in the province. Before Larkin's plans could mature, however, a group of American settlers proclaimed the "Republic of California" and adopted a national flag prominently displaying a grizzly bear. At this point Captain John C. Frémont, in California with a contingent of United States troops ostensibly for exploring purposes, took over leadership of the Bear Flag Revolt. The hotheaded young officer and his men soon clashed with a force led by José Castro, the Spanish governor, and in a brief skirmish routed it. In mid-July 1846 Frémont occupied the northern California capital, while Castro fled south toward Los Angeles.

By this time the United States was officially at war with Mexico and had dispatched a fleet under the command of Commodore John D. Sloat to the California coast. Sloat arrived in July 1846 and claimed the province for the United States. In ill health, he was soon replaced by Robert Stockton, who tried to establish American authority in the province with Frémont's help. The task proved to be difficult. Mexican forces drove the Americans out of Los Angeles, Santa Barbara, and San Diego. Virtually the whole of southern California was back in Mexican control when Kearny arrived outside San Diego with his Army of the West. Combining forces with Stockton, he defeated the Mexicans and ended resistance to American authority in California by the autumn of 1846.

Victory in Mexico. The United States now controlled all the Mexican borderland from the Gulf of Mexico to the Pacific coast. But the war was not over. By this time Mexico was again under the leadership of Santa Anna. Exiled to Cuba after the Texas war, he had inveigled the Americans into returning him to Mexico by promising to make peace on American terms. Once safely home, however, Santa Anna repudiated his promise, overthrew Paredes, and prepared to march against his recent benefactors. By early 1847 he was camped with twenty thousand troops near San Luis Potosí, ready to attack Taylor. At Buena Vista his untrained troops attacked a much smaller force of equally untried American volunteers and were beaten.

Buena Vista ended the fighting in northern Mexico. But the Mexicans had no intention of surrendering. To crush Mexican resistance once and for all, Polk authorized General Winfield Scott to seize the port of Veracruz and from there move over land on Mexico City itself. In March 1847 Scott took Veracruz after a brief siege. Quickly leaving the malarial Mexican lowlands, he advanced toward the central Mexican plateau. In April he encountered Santa Anna at Cerro Gordo. In a brief but hard-fought battle Scott's men routed the Mexicans. Resuming his advance on Mexico City, Scott again defeated Santa Anna's armies at Contreras and Churubusco. The Mexi-

An Historical Portrait   John Charles Frémont

Whether John Charles Frémont, explorer, military man, and politician, was a pathfinder, a pathmarker, or a pathfollower is open to question, but there is no doubt that he is one of the more romantic figures in American history. His mother was Anne Beverly Whiting, a descendant of one of the Founding Fathers and member of a distinguished but impoverished southern family. His father was John Charles Frémont, a French royalist who fled from Napoleonic France on a ship bound to Santo Domingo and was captured by the British. After spending some months in a prison in the British West Indies, he was allowed to emigrate to the United States and ended up in Richmond in 1808.

It was in Richmond that the dashing French émigré met Anne, the childless and unhappily married wife of Major John Pryor, a tyrannical and wealthy man forty-five years her senior. After a showdown with the angry husband, the couple eloped without legal ceremony and set out on their honeymoon intending to study Indian tribes in the South. What little money Anne had quickly ran out and the Frémonts settled in Savannah, where Anne took in boarders and John Charles taught dancing and French. On January 21, 1813, their child, John Charles Frémont, Jr., was born.

The family moved to Nashville and then to Norfolk. There, mother and father were finally married after Major Pryor's death. John Charles Frémont, Sr., died of pneumonia in 1818, when his eldest son was only five years old. Gossip about the family scandal continued to haunt Mrs. Frémont, so she soon moved to the more cosmopolitan and less puritanical city of Charleston, where she supported her three children on a small inheritance, augmented by paying guests at her house.

Young John Charles was brilliant, handsome, and charming, and although his credentials were not impeccable by class-conscious antebellum standards, he made many friends among Charleston's best families. Charley also attracted patrons. The earliest of these was John W. Mitchell, a lawyer who gave him a clerkship in his office and sent him to be educated at a fancy preparatory school. At sixteen he was able to enter Charleston College as a junior, where he excelled in mathematics and natural science. Mitchell continued to help him financially, as did the rector of St. Philip's, Charleston's most socially prominent Episcopal Church. Unfortunately, he fell in love, neglected his studies, and cut classes. After several warnings he was expelled just three months short of his graduation for "habitual irregularity and incorrigible negligence."

Frémont was now forced to earn money to help support himself and his family. Luckily his intellectual reputation earned him a teaching position and a job in the library at a private school in Charleston. Through his teaching and library work he continued to meet and charm distinguished Charlestonians who were anxious to give him their patronage. One of these was Joel Roberts Poinsett, Jacksonian politician, member of St. Philip's, first United States minister to Mexico, and the man who introduced the red tropical flower, the poinsettia, to the United States. Poinsett helped Charley get a job as the mathematics teacher on the U.S.S. *Natchez,* then about to undertake a cruise down the coast of South America. Two years later, when the *Natchez* returned, Frémont passed the examination for professor of mathematics in the navy. While he was debating whether to accept this position, Poinsett got him a job with the United States Topographical Corps as an assistant engineer to survey the route of a projected railroad running from Charleston to Cincinnati. When Poinsett became secretary of war in 1837, he had Frémont commissioned as a lieutenant in the army and made second in command to Joseph Nicolett, a famous French scientist, on two surveys of the territory between the Mississippi and Missouri rivers. The two expeditions took Lieutenant Frémont from Fort Pierre on the Missouri to Fort Snelling on the Mississippi. When he returned to Washington in 1839, he and Nicolett collaborated on a series of maps and scientific reports.

In Washington the twenty-six-year-old Frémont was lavishly praised by his mentor, who also introduced him to Senator Thomas Hart Benton of Missouri, a leader of the expansionists in Congress and a supporter of government-sponsored exploration of the West. Frémont was soon eating dinner often at the Benton house and courting his host's beautiful and intelligent teenage daughter, Jessie. The Bentons were opposed to the match because of the age difference and Frémont's small income. When their lecturing failed to deter the young couple, the parents prevailed on Poinsett to order John Charles on another expedition.

By now Nicolett was ill, so Frémont was put in charge of the survey of the Des Moines River and Iowa Territory, a region being rapidly settled by farmers. Frémont spent the spring and summer of 1841 successfully exploring and mapping Iowa Territory, and by August he was back in Washington resuming his courtship. The couple could not overcome the Bentons' objections, so they were secretly married in October. In November they informed the senator, who finally accepted the situation when his daughter clutched her husband's arm tightly and quoted the words of Ruth: "Whither thou goest, I will go." Frémont had gained himself not only a rich and beautiful wife, but another powerful patron.

Through Benton's influence Frémont was chosen to head a series of major western expeditions. In 1842, with Christopher (Kit) Carson as his guide, he surveyed the area beyond the Mississippi as far as the South Pass in Wyoming. This trip produced a scientific map of the Oregon Trail and a report that praised the fertility of the land and furnished practical advice to emigrants. The following year Benton got Congress to authorize a second expedition to the mouth of the Columbia River. This trip was almost called off because Frémont decided to take with him a twelve-pound howitzer cannon. The War Department feared that it would be construed as a military venture against Mexico and dispatched an order asking Frémont to return to Washington. Jessie Frémont suppressed the order and sent a letter to her husband urging him to speed up his departure.

This expedition took Frémont into California. Instead of turning · back when he reached the Dalles in Oregon, he went south to explore the Great Basin between the Rockies and the Sierras and then crossed the mountains into California. Although this part of Frémont's trip was not authorized, Benton and his expansionist friends in the Senate were eager to learn all they could about this territory in case of war with Mexico, and it seems likely they knew of his plans. In January 1844 Frémont and his men began the dangerous midwinter journey across the Sierras. The cold, snow, and high elevations did not daunt them and luckily there were no severe blizzards like the one that wiped out the Donner party a few years later. At the beginning of March they reached Fort Sutter. Here they were treated generously by Captain John Augustus Sutter, who informed them of the weakness of the Mexican position in California and his own dreams of opening up this region to Americans. From Fort Sutter Frémont went south, exploring parts of Nevada and Utah before finally returning to Washington at the end of the year. During the winter of 1844–45 he and Jessie drafted his report on this second trip, emphasizing the fertility and beauty of the region and the viability of the Oregon Trail. This report was well received by Congress, which authorized a printing of 10,000 copies. These were eagerly read on both sides of the Atlantic.

In March 1845 the expansionist James Knox Polk was inaugurated president. Polk favored not only the incorporation of Oregon and Texas into the Union but also the annexation of California. He and other expansionists feared a British takeover of California if the United States did not act quickly. Soon after Polk's inauguration Benton and Frémont induced Congress to authorize a new western expedition. Like the others, the ostensible purpose of this trip was scientific, but Frémont later admitted in his *Memoirs* that "in arranging this expedition the eventualities of war were taken into consideration." Secretary of the navy George Bancroft, he declared, expected him to convert his band into a military force if he found that war had begun when he reached California.

Frémont and an armed party of sixty-two, including six Delaware Indians, blazed a new trail through Nevada and reached Sutter's Fort on December 9, 1845. From there they proceeded to Monterey on the pretext of gathering additional supplies, and contacted Thomas Larkin, the American consul. Deciding not to provoke the Mexican authorities further, Frémont set off for Oregon, but was met by a confidential messenger from Washington. He then turned back toward California, camping near Sonoma, where he helped ignite a revolt by a small group of American settlers against Mexico. These men hoisted a flag with a grizzly bear prominently displayed, founding the "Republic of California," nicknamed the Bear Flag Republic.

When news of war with Mexico reached California, Commodore Robert Stockton appointed Frémont major of the California Battalion, a force composed of expedition members and settlers. When the battalion captured Los Angeles, Stockton appointed him governor of California. This put Frémont on a collision course with General Stephen W. Kearny, who claimed he had official orders to take California and set up a government. With Stockton's support, Frémont disregarded Kearny's claims and served as governor for two months. He was then arrested by Kearny, whose orders had been confirmed, court-martialed, and found guilty of mutiny, conduct prejudicial to military discipline, and disobedience. Polk remitted his sentence of dismissal from the army, but let the verdict stand.

Frémont, hurt and indignant, resigned.

Shortly after, Senator Benton and some wealthy St. Louis friends financed a fourth Frémont expedition to survey routes for a Pacific railroad. Frémont arrived in California in time to be greeted by news of the discovery of gold. Providentially, before he had left the previous time he had purchased for $3,000 the Las Mariposas tract in the Sierra foothills as a future home. Soon after he reached his new lands, Mexican helpers discovered rich veins of gold ore on them. This strike made Frémont into a multimillionaire. He acquired real estate holdings in San Francisco, further developed Las Mariposas, and for several years lived an affluent life in Monterey with Jessie and his three children.

When California became a state in 1850, Frémont was elected United States senator, but served only until 1851, when he was defeated by a proslavery candidate. His vocal opposition to the Fugitive Slave Law and his support of a free-soil Kansas won Frémont nomination as the first presidential candidate of the Republican party in 1856. He lost to James Buchanan by an electoral vote of 174 to 114. When the Civil War broke out, Lincoln appointed him major-general of the Western Department, headquartered in St. Louis. His problems in his new post were almost insurmountable. He had little ammunition and few arms or other supplies. He had to organize an army in a slave state that had a strong group of secessionists and a small number of Union partisans. In addition, he made many enemies when he declared martial law in Missouri and issued his own emancipation proclamation for the state's slaves. His detractors accused him of extravagance and self-promotion and his defeats in three Missouri battles prompted Lincoln to remove him from command. The radical antislavery man resented his dismissal and Lincoln reappointed him head of the Mountain Department with headquarters in Wheeling.

(*continued on p. 272*)

An Historical Portrait John Charles Frémont (*continued*)

Frémont asked to be relieved of this command when he proved ineffective against Confederate General Stonewall Jackson. In 1864 he was again endorsed as a candidate for president by the radical wing of the Republican party. Though he was skeptical of Lincoln, he withdrew for the sake of party unity, declaring "my only consideration [is] the welfare of the Republican Party."

Frémont's life went downhill from this point on. He lost most of his money in unprofitable railroad ventures and he and Jessie were forced to live in a small cottage in Los Angeles. He was rescued from dire poverty by Jessie's writings and her activities in the movement to redeem his military career. In April 1890, while visiting Washington, Congress restored him to major-

general rank and awarded him a $6,000 a year pension. Soon after, on a visit to friends in New York, Frémont caught cold and died. Although his life ended in failure, he had helped conquer a western empire for America. Over twenty geographic place names, scattered across the nation, mark his achievements.

can leader, seeking a breathing spell, retreated to his capital and requested an armistice. Peace negotiations quickly broke down, however, and Scott marched on the city. After fierce fighting at Molino del Rey and Chapultepec, where the young cadets of the Mexican military academy fought with great gallantry, the American commander captured the city. On September 13, 1847,

the American flag was raised by a battalion of U.S. marines over the "halls of Montezuma." Santa Anna sought to resume the fighting, was defeated, and fled the country. The war was over.

The Peace.   As wars go, the Mexican conflict was brief. The peace negotiations, however, dragged on for five months. Although they were clearly

The Mexican War, 1846–1848

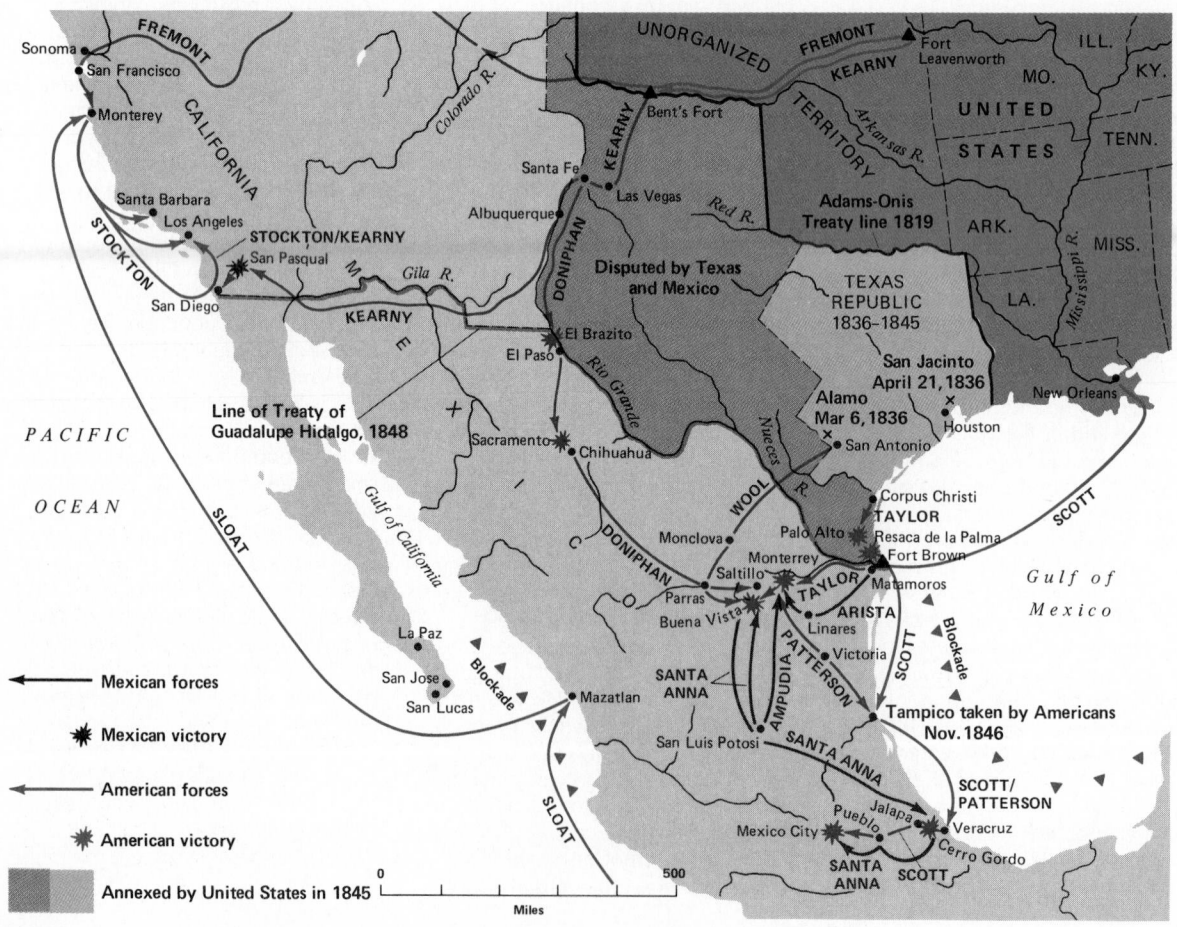

beaten by any military measure, the Mexicans refused to accept the consequences of defeat. Negotiations, begun by Nicholas Trist well before the capture of Mexico City and Santa Anna's flight, quickly broke down when the American commissioner discovered that Santa Anna would not consider surrendering any of his country's territory. Nor did matters improve once Santa Anna was ousted. For all his faults, Santa Anna had enjoyed wide popular support. Now it was difficult to find any Mexican leader with the authority and the will to accept defeat and the inevitable territorial concessions.

Within the United States indecision about how much territory the country should demand also impeded rapid settlement. At the beginning of the war the ambitions of most Americans were relatively modest: California and New Mexico. But with each new, dazzling victory, the national appetite grew until "All Mexico" became a powerful slogan and movement. As Lowell's skeptical farmer Biglow phrased it: "Our Destiny higher an' higher kep' mountin'."

For a while the All Mexico surge seemed unstoppable. Besides its appeal as the logical culmination of Manifest Destiny, it was attractive to the country's commercial interests. Ports on the Pacific at San Francisco or on Puget Sound were all very well, but overland transportation between the West Coast and the manufacturing and commercial centers of the East was time-consuming and expensive. For generations Americans had talked of building a canal across the narrowest part of the North American continent in Central America. With Mexico in its possession, the United States could build such a canal on its own territory at the Isthmus of Tehuantepec. By absorbing all of Mexico, enterprise, progress, and the glory and greatness of America and its institutions might all be furthered simultaneously.

But the All Mexico advocates did not reckon with the Mexicans themselves. In New Mexico and California, and in the Mexican heartland, the occupying American troops were soon being attacked by Mexican irregulars. At Taos, in New Mexico, Mexican and Indian guerrillas organized a revolt, killed the American governor, Charles Bent, and had to be put down by soldiers hastily brought in from Santa Fe. If the United States insisted on all of Mexico, it could expect more of this resistance. Who knew how long the fighting might last?

The All Mexico issue was ultimately decided by the reluctance of most Americans to take on the

In the midst of the Mexican War an American editor proclaimed it "our destiny to civilize that beautiful country and enable its inhabitants to appreciate some of the many blessings and advantages they enjoy." Here General Scott's forces storm Chapultepec, killing all its defenders—unseasoned teenage cadets.

STORMING OF THE CASTLE OF CHAPULTEPEC, BY THE AMERICAN ARMY UNDER GENERAL SCOTT, SEPT. 13, 1847.

New-York Historical Society

responsibility of governing a large non-English-speaking population with different institutions and traditions. Meanwhile, peace negotiations proceeded slowly. In October 1847 Polk recalled Trist, but the headstrong, ambitious Virginian, on the advice of General Scott, refused to return and continued to negotiate with Mexican officials. Fortunately for Trist, Santa Anna's successors, faced with the prospect of renewed fighting, finally concluded that they must make peace. On February 2, 1848, they signed an agreement with Trist at Guadalupe Hidalgo.

The Treaty of Guadalupe Hidalgo gave the United States the provinces of California and New Mexico and confirmed the Rio Grande as the southern boundary of Texas. The Mexican Cession included the present states of California, Nevada, and Utah, and parts of Arizona, New Mexico, Wyoming, and Colorado. In return, the United States agreed to pay Mexico $15 million and to assume the $3.5 million of American citizens' claims against the Mexican government.

These terms differed only marginally from those Slidell had been authorized to propose before the war, and some Americans favored rejecting them. After a costly and total military victory, why take only as much as you had asked for in the first place? Polk himself disliked the treaty because it had originated with Trist, whom he had relieved of his commission. But most Americans were inclined to accept it. "Admit all [the treaty's] faults," wrote one newspaper editor, "and say if an aimless and endless foreign war is not far worse. . . . *We are glad to get out of the scrape even upon these terms.*" This accommodating spirit prevailed when the treaty came before the Senate, and it was ratified by 38 votes to 14.

CONCLUSIONS

And so the war ended on a moderate and conciliatory note. The Mexican government could consider the $15 million an acknowledgment of American guilt; Americans could see themselves as forbearing and generous.

But what were the causes? The war was part of a process of territorial expansion over which Americans—and even more clearly their government—had relatively little control. Greed—or acquisitiveness, if one prefers—was part of the American character and could not easily have been checked by laws or moral exhortation, even if the United States government had wanted to. No agency could have kept American citizens from moving into the loosely held Mexican bor-

derland. Whatever Washington had done, it is likely that New Mexico and California would have taken the same course as Texas. American migration would have been followed by secession, demands for annexation, and eventual incorporation into the United States. No doubt war would have been part of the process.

The Mexican War, then, was in some ways almost inevitable. Had Mexico been a strong and stable country, Mexican-American relations would undoubtedly have taken a different course. We cannot blame the victim for his misfortunes, but it is hard not to conclude that Mexico's history, which found it after independence a poor, disorganized nation with a powerful, dynamic, and materialistic neighbor, was a crucial factor in its fate. A wise Mexican has observed: "Poor Mexico, so far from God, so near the United States!"

The joke, however, was on the Americans. At the war's start Ralph Waldo Emerson predicted that the United States would conquer Mexico, but that the victory would "poison us." As we shall see in Chapter 14, it almost did.

FOR FURTHER READING

Bernard De Voto. *Across the Wide Missouri* (1947)
> With evident delight, De Voto chronicles the Rocky Mountain fur trade that flourished in the 1820s and 1830s. He describes company rivalries, the carousals of the annual "rendezvous," and relations between fur trappers and Indians. Contains interesting sketches made on the scene in 1837–38 by the artist Alfred Jacob Miller.

Francis Parkman. *The Oregon Trail* (1849). Edited and introduced by Harry Sinclair Drago (1964)
> Parkman was only twenty-three years old and fresh out of Harvard when he and a cousin set forth in 1846 from St. Louis to live among the fur trappers and the nomadic Sioux Indians. The title of this book—the creation of an enthusiastic publisher—is misleading because Parkman never came within 500 miles of the Oregon Trail. This is a fascinating contemporary depiction of the trans-Mississippi West.

John David Unruh. *The Plains Across: The Overland Emigrants and the Trans-Mississippi West, 1840–1860* (1978)
> The best overall treatment of emigration by way of the various overland "trails" from the settled areas of the East to the West Coast before the Civil War. Written by a young scholar who died just before the book appeared.

Henry Nash Smith. *Virgin Land: The American West as Symbol and Myth* (1950)
> The westward drive of empire, the Wild West hero, and the West as "garden of the world" were common images in the American mind

during the era of westward expansion. Smith examines how the nineteenth-century West influenced the life and helped to shape the character of American society as a whole.

George R. Stewart. *Ordeal by Hunger: The Story of the Donner Party* (1936)

Stewart records the history of eighty-nine people on their way to California who were stranded in the High Sierra during the winter of 1846–47. All experienced terrible hardships; forty-four died, and some of the others survived only by resorting to cannibalism.

Ray Allen Billington. *The Far Western Frontier, 1830–1860* (1956)

Here is a colorful survey of the Far West in the generation before the Civil War. Billington deals with all of the important aspects of the trans-Missouri westward movement—political, social, and economic.

Frederick Merk. *Manifest Destiny and Mission in American History* (1963)

The best discussion of this important topic by one of the deans of western history. Covers more than just the period of this chapter.

David M. Pletcher. *The Diplomacy of Annexation: Texas, Oregon, and the Mexican War* (1973)

Treats the background of the Mexican War and the economic and political interests of the United States, Mexico, Britain, and France during the 1830s and 1840s. Pletcher avoids the easy moralizing that others often bring to the subject.

Norman A. Graebner. *Empire on the Pacific: A Study in American Continental Expansion* (1955)

Graebner hunts for the reasons behind the acquisition of Oregon and California. He concludes that it was not Manifest Destiny or the "pioneering spirit," but rather the desire of eastern commercial interests for ports on the Pacific.

Eugene Genovese. *The Political Economy of Slavery: Studies in the Economy and Society of the Slave South* (1965)

Most of this book deals with the profitability of slavery and so is relevant to Chapter 13. But it also deals with expansion. Genovese depicts expansionism as the effort of a southern planter elite to save slavery from a trap of soil exhaustion and declining profitability. When the North said no to any additional expansionism after 1848, the South seceded.

Otis Singletary. *The Mexican War* (1960)

A good, brief treatment of the war against Mexico.

Julie Roy Jeffrey. *Frontier Women: The Trans-Mississippi West, 1840–1880* (1979).

A fresh, entertaining discussion of women along the way to, and in, the Far West, from Oregon onward.

12 Americans Before the Civil War

What Were They Really Like?

1790 The geographic center of American population is east of Baltimore

1793 Congress adopts first fugitive slave law

1794 Black preacher Richard Allen establishes the congregation that becomes the first African Methodist Episcopal Church

1821 Emma Willard founds the Troy Female Seminary (the Emma Willard School) in New York

1825 Robert Owen founds New Harmony (Indiana)

1831 First issue of William Lloyd Garrison's *The Liberator* • Nat Turner's Rebellion in Virginia: 57 whites and about 100 slaves die

1833 American Anti-Slavery Society organized • Oberlin becomes the first college to admit women as full degree candidates

1837 Abolitionist editor Elijah Lovejoy, defending his printing press against a mob, is murdered in Illinois • Mary Lyon founds a women's academy, now Mount Holyoke College, in Massachusetts

1838 Sarah Grimké publishes *Letters on the Equality of the Sexes*

1840s "Potato famine" sends hundreds of thousands of Irish to the United States

1844 Protestants riot against Irish Catholics in Philadelphia

1848 John Humphrey Noyes founds Oneida Community (New York) • Lucretia Mott and Elizabeth Cady Stanton organize the first Woman's Rights Convention at Seneca Falls, New York

1849 Elizabeth Blackwell receives a medical degree from Geneva College

1850 Hawthorne's *The Scarlet Letter* published

1851 Maine passes the first state prohibition law • Melville's *Moby Dick* published

1855 First edition of Walt Whitman's *Leaves of Grass*

1865 The first all-women's college, Vassar, is established

I n the decades before the Civil War America fascinated people of other nations. Hundreds of educated Europeans visited the new country to see for themselves what manner of society was emerging on the North American continent.

Most European travelers were impressed by the social and economic democracy they encountered in the United States. Harriet Martineau, an English intellectual, observed after her 1834 visit that few in America were "very wealthy; few are poor; and every man has a fair chance of being rich." Alexis de Tocqueville, in his famous *Democracy in America*, wrote that in the United States people were "more nearly equally powerful, than in any other country of the world or in any other age of recorded history." Frances Trollope, who spent the years 1827–30 in Cincinnati, noted that in America maids and other domestics refused to consider themselves inferior to their mistresses, referring to themselves as "help" rather than "servants." Sir Charles Lyell remarked that in the United States "the spirit of social equality . . . left no other signification to the terms 'gentleman' and 'lady' but that of male and female individual."

Not every visitor agreed that Americans were democratic. Some detected a deep streak of snobbery in the United States. Isidor Löwenstern, a Viennese scholar who traveled through the country in 1837, observed that "distinctions of rank have their defenders in America as zealous as in the Old World. . . ." Women, he wrote, were especially snobbish. The ladies of Philadelphia, for example, took "infinite pains and all their cleverness to differentiate themselves, and as much as possible to avoid contact with inferior classes."

Foreign observers also disagreed about the much-touted American individualism. The Swedish novelist Fredrika Bremer considered it a prominent American characteristic that "every human being must be strictly true to his own individuality—must stand alone with God, and from this innermost point of view must act alone according to his own conscientious convictions." On the other hand, Martineau complained that Americans suffered from a "fear of singularity"; and Tocqueville believed that public pressure to conform constituted a "tyranny of the majority" in America almost as stifling as European despotism.

Still another disagreement among the foreign observers of pre–Civil War America was whether Americans were practical, hardheaded, and materialistic—or romantic, sentimental, and idealistic. Trollope, no slouch herself at seeking wealth, wrote that she never met an American who was not trying to increase his fortune. "Every bee in the hive is actively employed in search of that honey . . . vulgarly called money; neither art, science, learning, nor pleasure can seduce them from its pursuit." Yet Bremer noted that Americans respected books and learning, and she was surprised by how much social and charitable work they did. Individual Americans were often anything but hardheaded and practical, she noted. Nor did all observers believe that Americans worshiped money above all other things. Of all the cities of the world, wrote the Hungarian politician Ferencz Pulszky and his wife, Theresa, after their 1852 visit, Boston was "the only one where knowledge and scholarship" had "the lead of society." There a "distinguished author, an eminent professor, an eloquent preacher, are socially equals of the monied aristocracy."

What a confusing set of contrasts! Visitors saw equality; they saw snobbery. Americans were individualists; they were also conformists. A practical, materialistic people, they also seemed to be dreamers, poets, and philanthropists. How can we reconcile these conflicting views of antebellum Americans? Let us examine American culture, institutions, social structure, and values between 1815 and 1860. In this chapter we shall focus primarily on the North and the West, saving the South for separate attention in Chapter 13.

THE MOVING FRONTIER

Generations of scholars have seen the West, the area where the older society and culture of the East touched the primitive frontier, as the key to American character and institutions. Before 1860 the West was the fastest-growing part of the nation. Population increased rapidly in the Middle Atlantic states and parts of New England, too, but trans-Appalachian growth far outstripped the pace elsewhere. In the forty-five years following 1815 the West became home to 15 million Americans. By 1860, eleven years after the great Gold Rush, even distant California had almost 380,000 people. The country had over 31 million inhabitants when the first shots of the Civil War were fired, and half of them lived in states and territories where settled white communities had not existed at the time of Washington's inauguration.

Americans generally moved west along lines of latitude. Thus the heavy migration from New England first crossed the Berkshire Hills to central New York, then swept through the Mohawk Valley into northern Ohio, northern Illinois, and

The Huntington Library

In 1858 the raw town of Omaha on the Missouri River was an important jumping-off place for travelers crossing the Great Plains. In this contemporary watercolor two wagons, one bound for California and one for the new gold fields at Pike's Peak, are stocking up on provisions at Pundt & Koenig's "Outfitting house" and general store.

southern Michigan. One branch of the Yankee exodus reached out to distant Oregon. New Yorkers and Pennsylvanians tended to settle the middle portions of the trans-Appalachian region. Most southerners moved to the lower parts of the Old Northwest and to the newer slave states of Kentucky, Tennessee, and the Gulf region. Southern blacks as well as whites moved westward. Most blacks accompanied their masters to the cotton fields of the interior; others, however, were transported by slave dealers and sold to cotton planters in the new region. Meanwhile, the Indians were continually forced westward ahead of the encroaching white settlers.

The Migrants' Motives. What induced easterners to abandon familiar places, jobs, and families to expose themselves to the uncertainties of a new environment? Reasons for moving westward of course varied from person to person, group to group, and region to region. Some western pioneers were the "loners" of traditional romantic accounts who could not remain where they were once they had seen the smoke of a neighbor's fire on the horizon. Americans generally were a restless people. They suffered, one observer wrote, from a serious "disease of locomotion" that detached children from parents and separated neigh-

bor from neighbor. This physical restlessness infected not only rural people heading for the frontier but also city folk. In many mid-nineteenth-century cities and towns May 1 was "moving day," when almost all house and apartment leases expired and people changed their residences. On the day or two preceding the event, city streets were jammed with people, horses, carts, and wagons piled high with furniture, kitchen equipment, and personal belongings. "Move—move—keep moving—straw—soot—dust and ashes at every step—all confusion," wrote one disgusted pre–Civil War resident of Kingston, New York. "Everyone has his or her hands and arms full—all are in a trot—it is like the sacking of a city. . . ."

But restlessness was not the only reason why people "lit out for the territories." Some were refugees—people fleeing the law, their creditors, their spouses, or themselves. Married women and children went west without much choice because their husbands or fathers did. On the other hand, many single women regarded the West as a land of opportunity. Young western farmers needed wives, and unmarried women could easily find husbands and the security and social status that only marriage and a family of one's own could then confer.

Economic considerations, however, probably outweighed personal and social motives. New England's first emigrants streamed to the cheap lands of the Genesee country of western New York in the 1790s following the rapid rise in Yankee land prices. In the 1820s there was another New England exodus as the many tenants and agricultural laborers dislodged by conversion of arable land to sheep pasture moved west. In the next few decades further waves of New England migrants were inspired by competition from western grain and meat. Unable to undersell the cheap commodities of the fertile Mississippi Valley, many Yankee farmers from Massachusetts or Connecticut simply gave up and joined the exodus.

The people of the Middle Atlantic region, where soils were good, had less reason to move than their Yankee neighbors. By the 1840s and 1850s, however, many former New Englanders who had settled in central and western New York, or their children, began a second migration to Wisconsin and Iowa, responding once again to the lure of cheap, fertile land.

The older South also felt the economic attraction of the West. Declining soil fertility pushed people out of the Chesapeake region and the older cotton areas of South Carolina and Georgia, while the more fertile cotton lands across the mountains exerted a simultaneous pull. Whenever cotton prices rose, Virginia, Maryland, Carolina, and Georgia yeomen and planters sold their land and their buildings, put their families and household wares on wagons, and, with their slaves trudging behind, departed for the beckoning Southwest.

The Frontier Type. During the colonial period, as we have seen, the environment of the new World altered the Old World heritage of the earliest European immigrants. Did the West have similar effects on the eastern pioneers of the nineteenth century? Most scholars think it did. According to Frederick Jackson Turner, the late-nineteenth-century historian of the frontier, the West made pioneers from the East into new people—individualistic, egalitarian, and idealistic. The West, Turner declared, was "productive of individualism" because the frontier reduced society to its essentials and forced people to rely on their own unaided resources. "Complex society was precipitated by the wilderness into a kind of primitive organization based on the family. The tendency is antisocial. It produced antipathy to control, and particularly any direct control." The West was also egalitarian, Turner felt. Among the pioneers, "one man is as good as another. . . . An

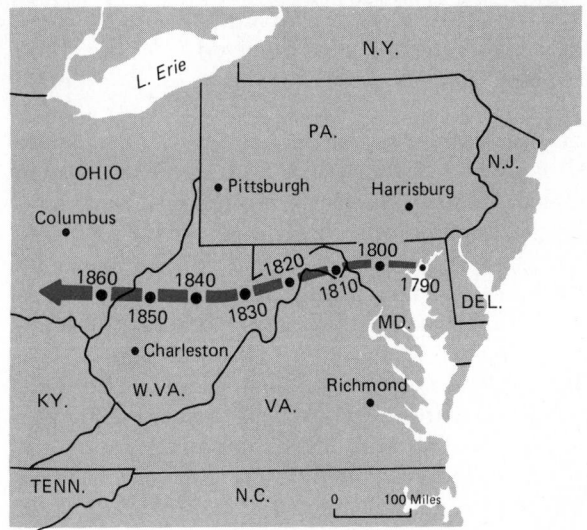

The geographic center of population, 1790–1860

optimistic and buoyant faith in the worth of the plain people, a devout faith in man prevailed in the West." Idealism was another characteristic that emerged from the westward movement. "From the beginning of that long westward march of the American people America has never been the home of mere contented materialism. It has continually sought new ways and dreamed of a new perfected social type."

Turner's interpretation of the West has left an indelible mark on Americans' perceptions of their past. The rugged-individualist hero—usually a sheriff, rancher, or gunfighter—with only his wits and his Colt .45 to defend himself and his cause, is a central figure of national mythology. He is not only self-reliant, he is also democratic and makes no distinction between ranch hands and ranch owners. By contrast, there is the "dude" from Boston or Philadelphia who has to learn the hard way that in the West clothes and manners do not make the man. And there is the posse or vigilante group to demonstrate the importance of spontaneous democratic social action.

The truth is more complex than this western myth. Western individualism was not unqualified. Community cooperation and social control existed on the frontier. Westerners joined in social activities and mutual-aid efforts like barn raising, fence building, cooperative harvesting, quilting bees, and assisting at childbirth. In politics westerners, like other Americans, rejected unqualified laissez-faire and seldom hesitated to pass laws to control the economic and social practices of their neighbors when regulation suited their purposes.

Turner also exaggerated the extent to which the movement westward involved individuals and isolated families. New Englanders often settled in groups, creating compact communities modeled on the traditional "towns" of Massachusetts and Connecticut. Villages like Kent and Ashtabula in Ohio's Western Reserve were physical replicas of colonial communities in southern New England. At times entire eastern communities pulled up stakes as an entity and headed west. The migration of the Latter-Day Saints (Mormons) from upstate New York to Ohio, Missouri, then back to Illinois, and finally to the plain near the Great Salt Lake is a particularly striking instance of group migration. The new Mormon "Zion," moreover, scarcely conformed to the stereotype of a community dominated by rugged individualists. Water shortages, the costs of sponsoring new waves of immigrants, the memories of recent persecutions by the "gentiles"—all created in Utah a tight-knit, closely regulated community in which decisions were made by elders and by Brigham Young, the charismatic Mormon leader.

Still, westerners were probably more individualistic than easterners. Spread more thinly over the land, without the steady support of close neighbors, they faced an unsubdued physical environment and had to be self-reliant or perish. The great distances between families also made it easier to be tolerant of differences. How your neighbors conducted their personal affairs was not very important when they lived a mile or more away.

Self-reliance and mutual toleration were the positive aspects of frontier individualism. Another, less attractive side was lawlessness. Westerners were much given to brawling and violent behavior. During the 1840s Iowans' use of the bowie knife made them world-famous for bloodthirstiness. Cutting, eye gouging, and nose biting were common ways of settling disagreements in the antebellum West. Although the use of vigilantes was an effort to impose law on lawless communities, it also expressed westerners' penchant for taking the law into their own hands.

In general, western compliance with social norms was rather poor by eastern or European standards. "I have rarely seen so many people drunk," wrote a traveler in the West in the 1830s. Tobacco chewing, spitting, and swearing were almost universal. Charles Dickens concluded after his American visit in the 1840s that westerners could scarcely speak without "many oaths . . . as necessary . . . words."

Turner's assertions about western egalitarianism and lack of concern for materialism must also be qualified. It is true that outside the Southwest, where the slave system imposed its strong stamp, the rural West achieved a rough equality of material condition. As we saw in Chapter 9, abundant land and a democratic, if imperfect, system of land distribution created a large body of farm owners of middle rank by 1860. Even more significant, however, is the fact that western *attitudes* were egalitarian. One westerner did not regard another as superior merely because the other possessed a better education or a more impressive pedigree. One high-bred English lady was surprised that people in the California mining camps of the 1850s considered themselves as good as she was. A westerner who dismissed distinguished ancestors as grounds for respect remarked: "It's what's above ground, not what's under, that we think on."

American Antiquarian Society

A REGULAR ROW IN THE BACKWOODS.

The pre-Civil War West was a violent place. This picture is a bit exaggerated, though there were moments when scenes like this one did indeed occur. Note the bottles and jugs on the ground. The artist was clearly making a statement about the source of much western mayhem and disorder.

But communities in the Southwest were also full of "cotton snobs" and newly minted gentlemen. In the fast-growing western cities class distinctions developed very quickly. Richard Wade asserts that social "lines sharpened, class divisions deepened, and the sense of neighborliness and intimacy weakened" in the major western cities between 1815 and 1830. And no matter how indifferent they were to ancestry, westerners were generally impressed by money. Pioneer farmers had come west to achieve modest independence at least, and to get rich if they could.

Turner's agreeable, positive picture, then, is an overstatement. Real westerners were cruder, more materialistic, and less egalitarian and individualistic in their behavior than he claimed. But their values were indeed individualistic and egalitarian.

NEW PRESSURES IN THE NORTHEAST

What about the rest of the country? Did the West's qualities mark Americans elsewhere as well? Turner claimed that they did. The West, he said, was the ultimate source of the democratic values of the nation as a whole. Attitudes and institutions developed on the frontier were carried back east, helping to make the entire country an open, democratic society.

Such an interpretation, however, leaves many things out of account. In the pre–Civil War years the Northeast was being engulfed in a rush of economic changes that turned farm people into factory wage earners and brought to America's shores thousands of newcomers from Europe. These changes had vital effects unrelated to the frontier experience of the West.

Problems of Urbanization. One social force that Turner ignored was urbanization. In 1800 the nation had only five towns with over 10,000 inhabitants: New York, Philadelphia, Boston, Charleston, and Baltimore. Although crowded with skilled craftsmen producing a wide range of manufactured goods, these small cities were primarily centers of foreign trade, shipping American grain, furs, lumber, tobacco, and other products of the land to distant places around the world. And even inland urban communities were mostly trading centers.

As the economy changed and grew, the new factories and mills attracted a wave of people to the older towns and created new ones such as Lowell, Fall River, Chicopee, and Nashua in the Northeast. Cities also sprouted or expanded in the West. By the 1850s substantial towns such as Louisville, Cincinnati, St. Louis, Chicago, and Lexington had grown up in the trans-Appalachian region.

Wherever located, cities brought people together in schools, concert halls, theaters, clubs, churches, libraries, political parties, and other associations, creating a sense of community and shared interests and values. But cities were also troubled places with many disruptive social problems. One was the lack of transportation. At first cities were so small that people could get around on foot. By the eve of the Civil War, however, Baltimore, Boston, Chicago, Cincinnati, St. Louis, and New Orleans all had over 100,000 people; Philadelphia had over 500,000; and New York–Brooklyn, over a million. Such metropolises required public transportation systems. Omnibuses—elongated carriages pulled by horses—came in the 1830s. But not until the arrival two decades later of the horse-drawn streetcar running on rails did the major towns acquire reasonably good transit systems.

Housing was another major urban problem, and it was never adequately solved. As middle-class people abandoned the city centers to move to newer districts, their dwellings were cut up into small apartments; many working-class newcomers were forced to take over this housing. Sometimes landlords built shacks in the gardens and backyards of older middle-class houses for the newcomers. By the 1850s most large cities had acquired the latest urban development: the slum.

The poor housing was matched by poor water supply, poor waste disposal, and poor health services. Early in the nineteenth century Philadelphia, Cincinnati, and Pittsburgh built aqueducts to bring pure country water into their cities, but it was midcentury before New York, Boston, and other towns abandoned use of polluted wells and streams. Waste disposal in most American cities was also primitive. Slop water from baths (infrequently taken), sinks, and "necessary houses" was often merely dumped into the streets. Where sewers existed, they were often connected to the same stream that supplied the community's drinking water. Scavenging pigs took care of much of the cities' garbage disposal. In the 1840s Dickens was amazed to see "gentlemen hogs . . . ugly brutes" trotting up New York's Broadway behind his carriage. Although the pigs performed a civic service by consuming some of the garbage, their droppings, along with those of horses by the thousands, were a major source of urban pollution. On a sweltering August day in 1852, one New Yorker

New York Public Library Picture Collection

*This 1835 illustration of the Cincinnati riverfront suggests how important
steamboats and rivers were to western urban development. At this time, the "Queen
City of the West" was not only an important river port, but also a major cultural
center boasting a medical college, an academy of fine arts, many libraries, and other
amenities. Despite these, an Englishwoman who visited the city in the late 1820s
called it "an uninteresting mass of buildings."*

noted, "the streets smell like a solution of bad
eggs in ammonia."

It is not surprising that health was poor in
the antebellum cities. Typhoid fever and typhus
were common. The cholera epidemics of 1832 and
1849–50 came from the infected water supplies.
Smallpox, yellow fever, and malaria were other
common urban afflictions. Although not all these
diseases were actually water-borne, doctors
thought they were, and the alarm they caused
moved public-spirited citizens to improve water
supplies and establish boards of health.

Crime and Violence. The traditional social restraints of America broke down in the antebellum
cities. They were jammed with people who had
few social ties to families and other groups; they
became catch basins for the antisocial. Newcomers who quickly succeeded in getting ahead
could avoid the cities' corrosive effects, but those
who failed or only found marginal places in the
urban economy often succumbed to temptations

or turned to antisocial occupations. Inevitably cities were full of burglars, footpads, pickpockets,
and ruffians who preyed on law-abiding citizens.
One 1858 estimate claimed that there was one
prostitute for every fifty men in American cities.

The general violence and disorder of antebellum American life was magnified in the cities.
But even small communities were not exempt. No
Fourth of July or election day passed without broken heads and blood in the streets of America's
country villages and hamlets. The metropolises
were worse, of course. City slums, like New York's
notorious Five Points, fostered gangs that conducted full-scale wars with one another and with
the police. Urban immigrant districts, crammed
with the poor and outcast, were especially vio-
lence-prone, a fact that led many native Americans
to conclude that the foreign-born were a danger to
society. Riots were frequent in antebellum cities.
In 1837 Boston volunteer firemen and Irish
mourners clashed violently at a funeral procession
on Broad Street and state militia had to be called

out to quell the mayhem. Still worse were the disturbances in New York in 1849 when the appearance of a British actor at the Astor Place Theater touched off a riot that left twenty-two dead. The cause: the Englishman had snubbed an American actor when he was on tour in Britain.

At first American cities had few means to deal with disorder. Until the 1840s the law was enforced by elected constables by day and a part-time "watch" at night. The increasing violence and rioting that marked these years of tensions between the native- and foreign-born and the urban erosion of rural-derived social controls made this antique system inadequate. In 1838 Boston established a professional daytime police force to supplement the night watch. In the following decade New York gave up the night watch entirely and established a twenty-four-hour-a-day police force. Before long most other large eastern cities had taken the same road to a modern police system.

Surging Immigration. Although Turner described America as an egalitarian society, increasing tensions between native Americans and recent immigrants clearly challenged the principle of equality. Immigration had been light during the half century following the Revolution. Then in the 1830s the number of new arrivals grew to almost 600,000; in the 1840s, to 1.7 million; and in the 1850s, to 2.3 million. The immigrants included Swiss, Netherlanders, Poles, Norwegians, Swedes, French, Russians, and Italians. Most, however, came from Britain, the south of Ireland, and Germany.

The two largest groups, the Irish and the Germans, did not fare equally well in America. The Irish came from a poorer land and brought less to America. For centuries the Catholic Irish peasants had suffered for their religion at the hands of the Protestant English. Denied economic and political rights, they lived as impoverished tenants on lands owned by rich Protestant landlords. In the late eighteenth and early nineteenth centuries the introduction of the potato permitted peasant families to raise more food on their small plots of ground, and Ireland's population soared. When the potato crop failed during the mid-1840s,

This New York City intersection—the "Five Points"—was the most notorious neighborhood in the antebellum United States. This picture was painted in 1829; when Charles Dickens observed the neighborhood in 1842, it was still "reeking everywhere with dirt and filth." Note the numerous "Groceries"; at the time, groceries frequently sold liquor to customers, who brought their own bottles to be filled.

New-York Historical Society

hundreds of thousands of Irish fled to escape starvation. Some went to England. Many more crossed the Atlantic with their few possessions to America.

Unable to buy land or pay the fare to the West once they arrived, Irish families usually stayed in the eastern cities, where they took the lowest-paying jobs—as construction workers, day laborers, factory workers, porters, handymen, and teamsters. To help make ends meet, many Irish women and girls worked part-time as laundresses or garment workers. Thousands became maids, cooks, and charwomen in the homes of middle-class native Americans. Eventually "Bridget" became almost a synonym for "domestic servant" in America.

The Germans were more fortunate. Most early-nineteenth-century German immigrants were farmers who, like the Irish, were seeking better lives in America. But the pressures on them to leave their homeland were not so severe. Many owned their own land, which they were able to sell for cash that they brought with them to the new land. They were also, on the whole, more skilled than the Irish; a larger portion were craftspeople, mechanics, printers, and the like. Some were even members of the middle class—lawyers, doctors, musicians, soldiers, college professors, and businesspeople—who were fleeing the antiliberal persecutions that followed the failure of the German Revolution of 1848. (The German immigrants of this period are often referred to as "forty-eighters.")

With more money for train fares and land, many of the German arrivals could leave the crowded labor markets of the large port cities for the cheap lands of Illinois and Wisconsin. Those who stayed in the East were often able to do better for themselves than the Irish. Every American city had German mechanics, printers, and craftsmen. The "forty-eighters" often made their mark in business, medicine, academic life, and even politics. Carl Schurz, Gustav Koerner, and other German political refugees rose to prominent positions in nineteenth-century American public life.

Discrimination. Most immigrants found America a mixed blessing. True, there were jobs, and for some, land. No one starved. Immigrant children could go to school. The more fortunate and enterprising could pull themselves up from unskilled laborers to small businesspeople, often providing services for their compatriots or selling them the old-country goods they craved.

Still, the social environment of their adopted land was not ideal. Americans talked about equality and took pride in the openness of their borders, but they disliked the immigrants and often treated them harshly. During the fifty-year period of slack immigration following the Revolution, white Americans had become a relatively homogeneous group. Unused to large blocks of aliens in their midst, native-born Americans were overwhelmed by the deluge of newcomers after 1830. Many viewed the immigrants as lawbreakers and tipplers, clannish people who refused to adopt the customs of their new country. Also, the newcomers were often poor. Confusing causes with consequences, native Americans frequently held the immigrants responsible for their squalid housing, their raggedness, their bad health, and the unsanitary conditions in which they lived.

Native-born Americans also reacted negatively to the immigrants' religion. Thousands of new arrivals, including virtually all the Irish and many Germans, were Catholic. Protestant Americans had a long tradition of anti-Catholicism derived from the religious conflicts of the English Reformation. Although there were Catholics in the United States before 1830, the Catholic community had been small, unobtrusive, and assimilated. It was generally accepted by its neighbors. With the deluge of the 1830–60 period, however, there suddenly appeared in every town and city Catholic churches, schools, convents, hospitals, and seminaries. A central Catholic hierarchy soon took shape. For the first time Americans encountered on their streets the unfamiliar sight of priests and nuns in black garments. They also encountered the "Continental Sunday," which turned the sober Protestant Sabbath into an exuberant day of visiting, picnicking, athletics, and drinking.

Latent anti-Catholicism soon became active anti-Catholicism. Protestant laymen and ministers, used to their own loose congregational system of church government, accused the highly centralized Catholic Church of antidemocratic tendencies. Catholics, moreover, were undermining the public school system, they said, by establishing parochial schools and demanding that the state support them. A few bigoted extremists even revived the time-worn accusations of rampant vice and immorality among Catholic priests and nuns.

Encouraged by such propaganda, antiforeign feeling increased dramatically, and between 1830 and 1860 the nation's cities witnessed violent confrontations between immigrant Catholics and militant native Protestants. More common, however, was the day-to-day discrimination that immigrants encountered. Landlords often would not rent to foreigners, especially the Irish. During the 1850s newspaper help-wanted ads frequently carried

Library of Congress

Philadelphia's police attempt to stop a riot between Catholics and bitterly anti-Catholic "nativists" in 1844. Fierce nationalists, the nativists objected to the Catholics' tie to a foreign authority: "the bloody hand of the Pope."

the warning "Irish Need Not Apply." If more of the immigrants did not find economic life intolerable, it was because the acute American labor shortage often gave employers little alternative to offering them jobs.

In the 1850s, when immigration was at its height, antiforeign, anti-Catholic feelings spawned a political movement based on bigotry. During the 1840s antiforeign, "nativist" societies had acted as pressure groups seeking to exclude foreigners from America or reduce their influence in American life. About 1850 one of these, the secret Order of the Star-Spangled Banner, began to be called Know-Nothings since, when asked about the organization, members denied any knowledge of it. In the next few years the Know-Nothings abandoned their secrecy and, as the American party, became active in the country's political life. Their platform called for restricting officeholding to native-born Americans and discouraging immigration by extending to twenty-one years the residential qualification for citizenship. In 1855 the Know-Nothings elected six state governors and sent a large delegation to Congress. The new party fell as quickly as it rose, splitting into factions when it was unable to deal with the urgent problem of slavery's extension. By 1858 it was all but dead, but it had left behind an unhappy legacy of political nativisim.

Free Blacks. Even more than religion and nationality, race tested American egalitarian ideals. Two hundred thousand free blacks, largely the descendants of slaves freed after the Revolution, lived in the northern and western states in 1850.

The free black community of the North included many talented men and women. Starting as an errand boy in Philadelphia, James Forten amassed a fortune as a sail maker. His granddaughter, Charlotte Forten, was a teacher, diarist, and prominent abolitionist. Some of the most stylish restaurants, barbershops, and catering establishments in northern cities were run by blacks. The larger cities also sheltered able black ministers and journalists. But these people were exceptional. The great majority of northern free blacks were unskilled laborers at the bottom of the social pyramid.

Bigotry deeply affected the life of almost every free black. White Americans everywhere treated black Americans with contempt and were so firmly convinced of their inferiority that even the white enemies of slavery often found the presence of blacks discomforting. Denied education in many places, blacks were also denied citizenship in most northern states. In the Northwest state "black laws" sought to exclude them from residence. In many northern communities Jim Crow laws (the name derived from a popular blackface minstrel show) required separate public facilities for blacks and whites. Even in Massachusetts, the only state where blacks enjoyed complete civil equality, prejudice penalized them.

Their exclusion from many spheres of the larger community's life inspired some free blacks to creative solutions. When, for example, the white officials of St. George Methodist Church of Philadelphia tried to segregate the many blacks who came to hear the popular black preacher Richard Allen, Allen organized the Free African Society. In 1794 he established the African Method-

Massachusetts Historical Society, Boston

Elizabeth Freeman was a black Massachusetts woman who successfully sued for her freedom in 1783. Her victory, under Massachusetts constitution that declared "all men are born free and equal," established a precedent. Thereafter slavery ceased to exist in the commonwealth. Freeman lived to a ripe old age, residing in a house she bought with the wages she earned.

ist Episcopal Church, which eventually had thousands of communicants all through the North and South. Free black Christians of other denominations likewise established separate churches rather than accept inferior status within white ones. Blacks also founded separate Masonic, Odd Fellows, and other fraternal lodges when they were not admitted to full equality in existing white associations.

As the years passed, things got worse rather than better for free black Americans. Before the 1830s there had been a place, if a lowly one, for blacks in the northern economy. With the influx of immigrants, their lot deteriorated. Employers preferred native Americans above all, but would hire newly arrived Germans and Irish before free blacks. The immigrants themselves, especially the Irish, were hostile to blacks, seeing them as competitors in the labor market. At times immigrants made blacks scapegoats for their own frustrations and disappointments. Tensions between blacks

and Irish sometimes erupted into savage riots in which scores of people were injured.

Women. Not only was American equality marred by racial, religious, and ethnic discrimination; it was also limited by discrimination based on sex. Antebellum America, like every other Western society, was male-dominated. Especially in the early years of the century women's legal status was inferior to men's. It was difficult for any woman, except perhaps a strong-willed and self-sufficient widow, to live independently of a man, whether father, husband, or brother. Under the law women were treated as minors. The earnings and property of married women belonged to their husbands. They could not sign legal papers. Their husbands could beat them without the law's intervention except in unusual cases. Their children were not their own in a strict legal sense, and in a divorce they usually lost all claim to their offspring. Nor were matters much better in public realms. Women could not hold office or vote. Virtually all the professions were closed to them except schoolteaching, and as we have seen, women schoolteachers were paid lower salaries than men. Indeed, most women's work outside the home tended to be unskilled or poorly paid or both.

Few married women worked for wages in this era. Working women usually were either young, unmarried girls waiting for husbands and families, or older spinsters or widows who had no choice but to support themselves. This meant that the life of a typical American woman was conditioned largely by her role and function in her family household. Here matters were improving somewhat in these pre–Civil War years, especially for middle-class women. For the wives of businessmen, professionals, and highly skilled workers, there were servants, usually young immigrant women, to help with the heavy chores of the typical household in the pre-electric, pre–running water, pre–telephone era. In addition, the burden of raising children began to lift as birthrates fell. Although birth control methods were crude, by the eve of the Civil War the numbers of children born each year per family had dropped about 40 percent from the 1800 levels.

Other improvements came for middle-class women as new working conditions took men out of the household. In former years, when over 90 percent of all Americans lived on farms, whole families worked together. In many of the early textile mills, especially those of Rhode Island, work continued to be a concern of the whole family. But increasingly among middle-class city people, fathers went to work in the morning, leaving wives and children at home. This emerging pattern encouraged a belief in a distinct women's "sphere"—the family circle—where their role was supreme. Reinforced by the idea that in a free republic women educated the sons who led the nation, the concept of a distinct women's sphere raised the status of women within the family. Women were still their husbands' inferiors, but in the nursery they were supreme.

Despite some advances in status, women continued to suffer from male condescension. Male-dominated society claimed to honor women, but often treated them as emotional and physical invalids. Women were thought to be frail creatures, dominated by their wombs, which made them nervous and sickly and not competent to bear the full burdens of adulthood. As protection, society surrounded them with a wall of stifling conventions and expectations, epitomized in the "cult of true womanhood." A true woman was sweet and gentle, modest and nurturing, pious and reverent, and irreproachably chaste. Even

This portrait, painted in Maryland in about 1830 by Elizabeth Glaser, epitomizes the contemporary "cult of true womanhood." The doll-like woman seems unsuited for anything more demanding than watering flowers. The painting attests to another pursuit allowed young ladies—painting itself, especially in a delicate medium like watercolors.

Sotheby's

within the bonds of marriage, women were expected to be "pure" and dampen their "animal" urges.

There were perhaps some advantages to these misconceptions and myths. Some women, especially those of the middle class, were spared heavy physical chores and the pressures of making a living. Some scholars have recently argued that women used prudery as a way of retaliating against male superiority. But no matter how intended or used, the practice of treating women like children diminished their lives and deprived the nation of their talents.

THE ARTS IN ANTEBELLUM AMERICA

Just as the egalitarian sentiments Turner found in America were limited by biases, the idealism he praised was not total. Materialism was rampant in antebellum America, especially in the North. Foreign travelers invariably commented that American men seemed capable of talking about nothing but prices, business, and get-rich-quick schemes. Southerners, too, often attacked Yankee materialism and contrasted it unfavorably with the supposed easy graciousness of their own region's life. Yet there was another side to the nation's values. Americans were an artistic, imaginative, and creative people who would make major contributions to the arts in the antebellum years. By 1860 American literature, architecture, and painting could be compared with the best that contemporary Europe could offer.

An American Literature. "Who reads an American book?" sneered the English critic Sydney Smith in 1820. By the time he uttered his famous insult, many educated Europeans were doing that very thing.

Americans themselves have always been readers. During the colonial period they read practical manuals, almanacs, and religious works. In the half century following the French and Indian War, while the British Empire was being torn apart and the young nation was struggling for survival, Americans devoured newspapers, pamphlets, and books dealing with political themes. Only after 1815, however, when Americans turned to matters besides politics, did the audience for "polite letters" expand sufficiently to encourage talented men and women to make careers as novelists and poets.

At the beginning of the nineteenth century

Americans were apologetic about their lack of literary distinction. During the earliest years of the republic the air resounded with voices calling for a national literature that would use American themes and avoid slavish imitation of Europe. Energy and enthusiasm were not enough to produce such a literature, however; genius was required. Suddenly two New Yorkers—Washington Irving and James Fenimore Cooper—provided it.

Both men were deeply affected by the romantic revolution that had swept the Western world toward the end of the eighteenth century. In the arts romanticism brought the rediscovery of emotion after the long reign of reason and intellect. Whether in words, paint, sound, or stone, romantic artists celebrated feeling, especially their own. They probed individual personality, and were fascinated by eccentricity and extreme situations and emotions. Death, ecstasy, horror, and crime seemed proper subjects for their talents. So, too, did the quaint and the "picturesque." Romantic artists were especially sensitive to the beauties of nature.

Irving's first important work was his contribution to the *Salmagundi Papers* (1807), charming graceful essays in an eighteenth-century style that delighted polite society. Over the next decades Irving composed many essays, short stories, histories, and biographies that assured his reputation as the first major American author. In his three most popular works—the classic "The Legend of Sleepy Hollow" (1820), "Rip Van Winkle" (1820), and *Diedrich Knickerbocker's A History of New York* (1809)—Irving made his settings the colorful and picturesque Hudson Valley with its stolid Dutch burghers and the misty green Catskill Mountains with their intriguing myths and legends. This was authentic American material that answered the call for a native American literature.

Still more "American" were the novels of James Fenimore Cooper. The first of the Leatherstocking Tales, *The Pioneers* (1823), recounted the adventures of Natty Bumppo, the typical American frontiersman. Natty was the untutored "natural" man who expressed Cooper's own disdain for the commercial civilization of the country's eastern cities. The frontiersman's home was the great unspoiled forest, where he pitted his skills and sinews against the dangers of wild nature and wild men. In his struggles he seldom had company—at most one or two men like himself. The five Leatherstocking Tales, including *The Last of the Mohicans* (1826), concern the proud individual testing himself against powerful human and physical forces. They were cast from the same mold as the later cowboy novel and Hollywood western.

The New England Renaissance. Irving and Cooper made New York the national literary capital during the 1820s. By the following decade there were major writers elsewhere as well. In the South Edgar Allan Poe, born in Boston but raised in Virginia, practiced his somber art. As a poet he was a minor figure, but his short stories—including "The Gold Bug," "The Fall of the House of Usher," "The Murders in the Rue Morgue," and "The Pit and the Pendulum," among others—make him an author of world renown. To us, Poe often seems less "American" than writers like Irving and Cooper. Yet in his fondness for hoaxes, mysteries, and violence he was very much in the national temper. His great talent notwithstanding, few Americans of the day considered this tortured, morbid, hard-drinking man an adornment of the country's cultural life. Far more consistent with American pride were the literary giants who burst forth in New England, especially in and around Boston.

In the generation before the Civil War the Massachusetts capital was the ideal seedbed for an impressive literary flowering. A relatively small community of under 100,000 in 1840, Boston was a "walking city." People could easily attend to their affairs on foot, and face-to-face contact among those of like mind and taste was common. Boston also had a tradition of learning based on the proximity of Harvard and the heritage of a scholarly and intellectual New England clergy. The city had an educated elite with money and leisure to patronize and encourage authors.

Boston's literary renaissance owed much to the philosophy of transcendentalism—an approach to God, humanity, and nature compounded of diverse elements. Although it borrowed heavily from European romanticism and oriental mysticism, transcendentalism was distinctly American. It was optimistic: humans were perfectible and God was forgiving. It was individualistic: each person must follow his or her own bent. And it was democratic: all men and women had within them part of the divine spark. Transcendentalism was certainly not materialistic; it was high-minded and humane.

The transcendental mood was best expressed in the essays—actually, sermons in print—of Ralph Waldo Emerson. Emerson's calm optimism, reasonable and humane views, social generosity, pure motives, and high-mindedness seemed noble and reassuring. He respected American practicality and praised self-reliance, but at the same time deplored excessive concern with material progress. The "invasion of Nature by Trade with its Money, its Credit, its Steam, its

National Portrait Gallery, Smithsonian Institution

Ralph Waldo Emerson looking the part of the sensitive, clearheaded, optimistic philosopher.

Railroad," he wrote, "threatens to upset the balance of man, and establish a new, universal Monarchy more tyrannical than Babylon or Rome."

In Concord, the semirural community outside Boston where he made his home, Emerson was surrounded by a group of talented and idealistic men and women, including Bronson Alcott, Henry David Thoreau, George Ripley, William Ellery Channing, Margaret Fuller, Elizabeth Peabody, and—for a time—Nathaniel Hawthorne. At Emerson's Tuesday evenings these people discussed their host's ideas and those of congenial European writers and thinkers. Their thoughts reached the cultured public through a small magazine, *The Dial,* first published in 1840. In the early 1840s Ripley and a few others of the Emerson circle established Brook Farm, a cooperative experimental community at West Roxbury, Massachusetts, a venture that tested their utopian belief in human perfectibility and innate goodness.

Emerson was the theorist of transcendentalism, but Thoreau acted on it. Thoreau was living refutation of the charges that Americans were materialists and conformists. A native of Concord, he loved nature, disdained material values, and possessed a social conscience unusually sensitive to injustice even in this age of reform. In 1845 he put his own precepts to the test by going to live in the

woods at Walden Pond. There he discovered the essentials of existence and concluded that human beings needed very little to be happy. Thoreau was also a courageous individualist, defying the authorities during the Mexican War by refusing to pay his taxes to support what he felt was an unjust attack on America's weaker neighbor.

Nathaniel Hawthorne, the most talented of the Boston group, rejected many of its teachings. In fact, he was a conservative Democrat. But he, too, refused to accept the materialistic values of commercial-industrial America. Hawthorne's spirit harked back to the dour, pessimistic mood of early Puritanism when New Englanders were certain that all men and women were sinful and most were damned. Unlike his Concord acquaintances, he was a sardonic, skeptical man with a strong sense of the human capacity for evil. These qualities and perceptions he incorporated into many

The title page of the first edition of Thoreau's Walden. Our modern image of Thoreau is of a solitary, plainspoken man, but he wrote and revised his work with extreme care, and during his stay in the woods he visited or had visitors from Concord almost every day.

The Thoreau Lyceum

National Portrait Gallery, Smithsonian Institution

Walt Whitman as patriarch, in 1887, five years before his death.

memorable short tales, and into the longer works *The Scarlet Letter* (1850) and *The House of the Seven Gables* (1851). Hawthorne's disagreements with some members of Emerson's group prompted him to satirize the impracticality of their social experiments in *The Blithedale Romance* (1852), a novel about Brook Farm.

Melville and Whitman. Emerson's transcendentalism was even less acceptable to another great American writer: New Yorker Herman Melville. Melville began his writing career after seven years at sea. His first novels—*Typee* (1846), *Omoo* (1847), and *Mardi* (1849)—related his adventures among the natives of the South Seas. In 1850 he began *Moby Dick*, in outward form a sea adventure, but actually a far more profound book. In his study of Captain Ahab and Ahab's single-minded determination to destroy the white whale, Melville created a powerful allegory of human obsession. *Moby Dick,* with its dark and complex themes, was not as enthusiastically received by antebellum American readers as Melville's earlier work, but today it is thought to be one of America's greatest novels.

Like Melville, Walt Whitman was not fully appreciated until this century. A writer of distinctly American character, Whitman carried individualism to the point of egotism. His "Song of Myself" begins with the lines:

> I celebrate myself and sing myself,
> And what I assume you shall assume,
> For every atom belonging to me as good belongs to you.

In this mood he reveals the boastfulness that we associate with the American frontier, although he himself spent much of his life in Brooklyn and Camden, New Jersey. Whitman was also a sensualist; whatever Americans of this generation did in private, few if any ever publicly proclaimed their lustiness, their admiration of personal beauty, and their delight in physical love as he did. Much of his poetry, incorporated into successively enlarged editions of *Leaves of Grass* (1855–92), shocked its readers both for its arrogance and for its sexual explicitness. In his prose, most notably *Democratic Vistas* (1871), Whitman was the advocate of a vigorous and vital democracy that would enable people to fulfill themselves spiritually in spite of material abundance.

Popular Literature. The Boston and New York writers were on the whole skeptical of American materialism. Several exhibited a streak of pessimism that ran against America's postcolonial tendency to envision a bright future. They were the first group of American intellectuals at war with the dominant values of their society. Popular literature, however, frankly endorsed getting ahead, materialism, and conformity. During the antebellum period presses poured out a flood of inexpensive novels that reinforced American folk attitudes. Patriotism was one profitable theme. Joseph Holt Ingraham's *The Pirate of the Gulf* (1836) was a blood-and-thunder thriller about the pirate Jean Lafitte, who had aided Jackson at New Orleans. Ingraham's success with patriotic adventure novels was matched by that of George Lippard and "Ned Buntline" (Edward Zane Carroll Judson), authors of tales of crime and punishment. Another successful type was the religious novel of faith challenged and ultimately preserved.

Popular literature presented one of the few opportunities for middle-class women to earn their living at something besides schoolteaching, and they took advantage of it. Mary Agnes Fleming, Catharine Maria Sedgwick, Susan Warner, Sarah Payson Willis, and other women turned out countless novels praising domesticity, chastity, true love, and assorted household virtues. These works were cloyingly sentimental. To sustain interest the authors included such melodramatic characters as "the other woman," "the weak husband," "the dying child," and "the martyred wife." In the end justice triumphed, and no one but the villain—or villainess—got hurt. Meanwhile, on the way to the denouement, the reader was exposed to only the sweetest, noblest, and most conventional sentiments.

The public lapped these works up. Warner's

Wide, Wide World (1850) earned her the then-remarkable sum of $35,000 in royalties. In 1853 Willis's *Fern Leaves from Fanny Fern's Portfolio* sold 70,000 copies; during the same period Hawthorne's *Mosses from an Old Manse* (1846) brought him only $144. Not surprisingly, Hawthorne was bitter. "America," he wrote, "is now wholly given over to a damned mob of scribbling women." The great novelist was being unfair in singling out women, for men also contributed prodigiously to the mass of writing that affirmed the popular values of the day.

The literature of antebellum America thus expressed many of the contradictions of the nation. Most of the better writers were skeptical of commercial values. They celebrated the individualism of the nonconformist who resisted the dominant teachings of the day or defied nature. In Melville, Poe and Hawthorne we also detect despair and pessimism, attitudes scarcely approved by Americans or ascribed to them by most foreign observers. Popular literature, on the other hand, sang the praises of family, country, and traditional virtue and refused to carp at darker American characteristics, commercial or otherwise.

Painting. The other arts are equally suggestive of the nation's inner contradictions. American artists achieved a high level of technical proficiency

and produced excellent work during these years. But many American painters disliked their country and considered their fellow citizens unappreciative materialists with philistine attitudes toward art. John Vanderlyn, a painter of elegant nudes, insisted that "no one but an artistic quack could paint in America." Washington Allston, like Vanderlyn trained in Europe, returned to the United States to experience the frustration that eventually led to his emotional breakdown and the collapse of his promising career. Later critics of the United States would cite Allston as a victim of the blighting effect of American materialism and lack of true appreciation for "culture" and the fine arts.

None of these dissenters, however, made dissent the subject of his art, and on the whole they were outnumbered by the celebrators of America. Thomas Cole, Asher B. Durand, and the lesser artists of the Hudson River school chose as their subjects the American countryside, especially the scenery of the Northeast. Their work was idyllic and romantic rather than realistic, but it avoided the artificiality of Allston and Vanderlyn. Still closer to the popular taste were painters like William Sidney Mount and George Caleb Bingham, whose scenes of rural life and homey anecdotes in paint resembled the sentimental popular novels but excelled them in quality.

William Sidney Mount was the Norman Rockwell of his day. His America was the happy republic where everyone and everything—including the pig in this 1842 painting—wore a smile.

New York State Historical Association, Cooperstown

George Catlin and John Audubon were less mannered and less sentimental about the American environment. Catlin's superb pictures of American Indians have enough accuracy and detail to delight an anthropologist. Audubon, of course, was a great naturalist as well as an excellent draftsman, and his watercolor and crayon sketches of American birds are scientific documents as well as objects of great beauty.

The Romantic and the Practical in Architecture. Americans between 1815 and 1860 were both practical house builders and romantic artists in stone, brick, and wood. The characteristic American innovation in domestic architecture was the balloon-frame house, so-called because it was light and usually impermanent. Instead of using the heavy joined timbers that had made earlier house construction resemble fine cabinet making, the builders of balloon frames put up a light skeleton of uprights and cross members attached by nails. Over it they placed a siding of boards or shingles and a roof, often of the same material. The resulting building was well suited to a fast-growing society that needed enormous amounts of new housing, had abundant timber, and was willing to sacrifice individuality for speed and cheapness.

Of course, there were people in both town and country who wanted more than a box with a roof to live in. In this era they commissioned workers in the Greek revival style to build gracious mansions. Greek revival also became the idiom for public architecture. Americans felt indebted to Rome and Athens for their institutions and found the new architecture so congenial that they used it in the Capitol in Washington.

Competing with the Greek revival style for the affection of the prosperous and sophisticated was the nostalgic romanticism of the Gothic style. Gothic was better suited to churches and homes than to public buildings, though James Renwick's Smithsonian Institution buildings are a distinguished exception. For churches Gothic was a natural style, and the traditions of the great European cathedrals and English parish churches were continued beautifully in such structures as Richard Upjohn's Trinity Church and Renwick's Grace Church in New York. It was in private homes, however, that the Gothic style flourished best. It lent itself not only to mansions; in some ways it was even more suitable for wooden cottages.

Greek revival and Gothic were the romantic sides of American architecture during these years; the balloon-frame house shows the practical, materialist one. The romantic side searched for an American past that never was, whether in the austere dignity of the classical age or in the mystery, myth, and chivalry of the Middle Ages. The practical side sought a solution to the era's housing problem. Together they neatly bracketed the extremes of American national character before the Civil War.

THE PERFECT SOCIETY

The social scene of the pre–Civil War North, like the cultural flowering, contained elements that contradicted the charges of American materialism and conformity. Northern society exhibited a degree of dissent, a willingness to confront established social institutions and a zeal for tearing them down and replacing them with new ones, that could be found almost nowhere else in the world. This was a time when, according to Emerson, "madmen, madwomen, men with beards, Dunkers, Muggletonians, Comeouters, Groaners, Agrarians, Seventh Day Baptists, Unitarians and Philosophers—all came successively to the top, and seized their moment, if not their hour, wherein to chide, or pray, or preach, or protest."

Emerson was making fun of the more extreme reformers, but it is true that the reform impulse produced a confusion of voices and actions. Reformers worked at changing prisons, improving

The Metropolitan Museum of Art; Harris Brisbane Dick Fund, 1934

American architecture ranged from Egyptian, Greek, Gothic, and even Chinese forms to the purely practical, shown here. Derisively called "balloon frames" because of their lightness, such houses were cheap and required "about as much mechanical skill as it does to build a board fence."

treatment of the mentally disturbed, enforcing temperance, carrying Christianity to the "heathen," ending warfare, preventing prostitution, extending women's rights, abolishing slavery, and creating utopian communities. Indeed, wherever sensitive and compassionate antebellum Americans encountered misery, vice, and injustice, they seemed determined to end them through collective effort.

Religious Roots of Reform. The reform movements of the years preceding 1860 drew some of their energy and substance from the new religious spirit that swept the nation. At the beginning of the nineteenth century American Protestantism was languishing. Most Americans considered themselves Christians, and many attended one of the numerous Protestant churches on Sunday. But compared with the past, or so believers held, piety had declined drastically both on the frontier and in the East. In some Connecticut towns in the 1790s Congregational churches added only four or five new members a year. In New England and in those parts of upstate New York and the Great Lakes states where Yankees had immigrated, ministers worried that "the Sabbath would be lost, and every appearance of religion vanish."

Before long, the religious pendulum swung back the other way, to renewed religious fervor. During the first half century of the republic a second Great Awakening, led by traveling bands of Methodist, Baptist, and Presbyterian evangelists, induced thousands of Americans to consider their sins, contemplate a new life, affirm or reaffirm their faith, and join the church. Vast outdoor revivals drew great numbers of rural citizens to marathon preaching sessions, where eloquent evangelists like Charles Grandison Finney, Francis Asbury, and Peter Cartwright exhorted sinners to abandon their evil ways and find salvation in God's everlasting love. The most memorable revival meeting of all took place at Cane Ridge, Kentucky, where for almost a week between 20,000 and 40,000 participants listened to 40 ministers. At one time more than 100 exhausted, repentant sinners lay prostrate amid the "solemn hymns, the empassioned exhortation, the earnest prayers, and the sobs, shrieks, or shouts bursting from persons under intense agitation."

The revivals were welcomed by many good Christians. In the wake of each visiting evangelist, new members poured into the Methodist, Presbyterian, and Baptist churches. Many of the "saved" joined new denominations. Western New York, called the "burnt-over" district for the wave after wave of revivalism that swept across it, became a religious hothouse that fostered a score of new sects, among them the Latter-Day Saints (Mormons), Adventists, and Shakers.

On the other hand, leaders of the more sedate groups like the Episcopalians and Congregationalists attacked the new preachers as ranters and dangerous inciters of undignified emotional display. Orthodox Calvinists deplored their rejection of predestination. But orthodox Calvinism was also at war during these years with Unitarianism, an offshoot of Congregationalism that had divested itself of Calvinist pessimism along with the orthodox Christian belief in the Trinity. Unitarians were heirs of Enlightenment rationality who accepted a general Christian benevolence but rejected what they considered the supernatural and irrational in traditional Christian belief.

Unitarianism and evangelicalism attracted different sorts of individuals. The first appealed to educated merchants and professional people, especially in the Boston area; the second made greater headway among farmers and lower-middle-class artisans and tradespeople. For all their social differences, however, Unitarians and evangelicals agreed that men and women could effect their own salvation and perfect both themselves and their society. The converted, proclaimed Finney, "should aim at being holy and not rest till they are as perfect as God." Sin was selfishness; virtue, selflessness and benevolence toward others. Sin, said the new breed of religious leaders, was voluntary; humanity could reject it; and collective sin—what we call social evils—could be rooted out by human will, education, and cooperative public actions.

This "Perfectionist" doctrine quickly penetrated organizations already involved in efforts to improve society. By 1820 these groups were in close contact with one another and constituted an informal "benevolent empire" that devoted its attention to world peace, temperance, foreign missions, antislavery, and other good causes. The benevolent societies usually had limited, practical goals. The most zealous of the new reformers, inspired by the evangelists, believed that evil must be ripped out root and branch, as soon as possible. Not all reformers were so ambitious. Nevertheless, Perfectionism gave to the wave of humanitarian reform that swept the North and the West a passion, and at times a fanaticism, that it had lacked before.

The Desire for Social Control. Other impulses besides Perfectionism inspired the reformers' zeal to change the world. Many believed that society in this era of emerging industrialization and urban-

The Whaling Museum, New Bedford, Mass.

The second Great Awakening fostered reform movements such as abolitionism, women's rights, and prohibition. After revivalist preachers "knocked out the (cork) and let nature caper," their flock "got religion" and rolled in the aisles, jerking about, even barking in ecstasy.

ization was experiencing a severe breakdown, and feared that social chaos would result if something were not done to check the collapse. Reformers of this sort often blamed society's plight on family failure. According to the Boston Prison Discipline Society, it was the "confession of many convicts . . . that the course of vice, which brought them to prison, commenced in disobedience to their parents, or their parents' neglect." Insanity and alcoholism were also thought to stem from families' increasing inability, in an industrializing society, to discipline and train their members. To men and women who held such views, "asylums," where victims of their family's failings could find havens from the harsh new world and learn to cope with their difficulties, seemed the solution.

Penitentiaries were one form of asylum that reformers of this kind sought to establish. Clearly, existing jails and prisons were deplorable. They were unsanitary places with bad food, where first

offenders were mixed with hardened criminals. They did nothing to rehabilitate lawbreakers. The reformed system of penitentiaries endorsed by Louis Dwight, Elam Lynds, and others separated first offenders from repeaters, provided better sanitation, and allowed prisoners some privacy. But as a would-be substitute for family discipline, it also imposed solitary confinement, hard physical labor, and regimentation. In the Auburn system of New York, established in 1816, prisoners were strictly regimented, marched to and from work in tight lockstep, and flogged for violating prison rules. It is not easy today to detect the humanitarianism of the penitentiary system, and in the end it failed in its primary aim of rehabilitating criminals. Yet the changes were considered models of enlightenment in their day, and dozens of European observers came to view the American system and learn.

Dorothea Dix's efforts to improve the treatment of the insane also called for asylums. The problem of the insane in antebellum America was clearly serious. In an earlier era "lunaticks" had been kept at home in the care of their families. They were seldom cured, but at least they were usually well treated. Increasingly, however, the physical mobility of American families and their growing reluctance to carry the burden of unproductive relatives forced the community to care for the mentally disturbed. Unfortunately, there were few mental hospitals, and the insane were often treated like animals. When the passionately idealistic young Massachusetts reformer first observed how the insane fared in her home state, she was shocked. Mental patients, Dix reported, were kept in "cages, closets, cellars, stalls, pens!" They were "chained, naked, beaten with rods, and lashed into obedience." Dix demanded that Massachusetts establish asylums to provide the insane with humane treatment. With the aid of Samuel Gridley Howe, Horace Mann, and Dr. Luther Bell, by 1860 she had induced almost every state to provide improved facilities for mental defectives and the insane.

Alcoholism was another deep concern of the reformers, though they seldom considered asylums the proper method of dealing with it. There can be no question that antebellum America had a temperance problem. Captain Basil Hall, an English visitor of the 1820s, noted the "universal practice of sipping a little at a time, but frequently . . . during the whole day." Americans themselves worried about their countrymen's drinking habits. Ministers asserted that drunkenness and "lewdness" went hand in hand. The guardians of public morals believed that alcoholism was especially prevalent among the working class and immigrants; but in fact, all classes had their share of drunkards who squandered their wages, beat their wives, neglected their children, and committed vicious crimes while under the influence of "demon rum."

The temperance reform movement developed two wings. The moderates wished to educate society on the evils of alcohol in order to reduce drinking. The "total abstainers" condemned all drinking as a sin and demanded state laws to outlaw the production, transport, and consumption of alcoholic beverages. The battles between these two factions split the American Society for the promotion of Temperance during the 1830s, and for several years the movement languished. Then, in the following decade, the total abstainers, or prohibitionists, under the leadership of Neal Dow, gained control. Dow's first success came in 1851 when Maine, his native state, passed

The Boston Athenaeum

This is an idealized portrait of Dorothea Dix, the advocate of better treatment for the insane. It captures the strong will and determination that made Dix so effective in persuading legislators to vote for the establishment of asylums.

the first statewide prohibition law. In the next few years a dozen states, mostly in the North and West, adopted the "Maine Law."

Growing Female Assertiveness. Many of the reformers were women. At one time scholars ascribed their large numbers within the reform movements to the "natural tenderness" or the intrinsic nurturing quality of women. Today we are more likely to seek an explanation in the social setting of the day, especially in the experience of middle-class women. The cult of domesticity had given mothers higher prestige and sanctioned better education for women. Yet society still believed that women's proper sphere was the home and family. To the young women pouring out of the new seminaries, or otherwise affected by the new partial liberation, the countless remaining restraints on women's public role seemed increasingly galling.

At first women found it very difficult to assert their own rights. Striving for the betterment of others seemed more acceptable, for these efforts were related to women's traditional helping role. Dorothea Dix's work for the insane may be seen as

Library of Congress

Though here she looks prim in a mid-Victorian way, Elizabeth Cady Stanton fought for women's rights. Born in 1815, she died in 1902, less than two decades before the Nineteenth Amendment granted women the vote.

an instance of such displacement. Many reform-minded middle-class women also turned to the problems of working girls forced into prostitution in order to eke out a living in the cities. Hundreds of middle-class women during these years also joined missionary societies to bring the message of Jesus to benighted westerners, and to the Chinese, Hawaiians, Burmese, and Africans overseas.

Women also participated in record numbers in the ranks of the American Peace Society, which opposed recourse to war as a means of settling disputes among nations. Although it attacked all wars, the society especially denounced offensive wars. This approach did not please true pacifists, who believed defensive as well as offensive wars evil. Led by William Lloyd Garrison, Angelina Grimké, Abby Kelly, Bronson Alcott, and others, the radicals seceded and formed the Non-Resistance Society, which rejected all submission to national interests that required violence. "We allow no appeal to patriotism, to revenge any national insult or injury," declared its Declaration of Principles. "We conceive that a nation has no right to defend itself against foreign enemies, or . . . punish invaders. . . ."

The antislavery movement also attracted women reformers, and their experience in the momentous attack on black bondage was a key catalyst in overcoming their reluctance to aid themselves. Within the antislavery movement few objected to women helping to raise money through bazaars or cake sales. But at least a few

bolder women wanted to take more active roles as speakers and organizers. The first woman to put such urges into practice was Sarah Grimké, who left the South in 1829 with her more retiring sister, Angelina, when they could no longer stand the scourge of slavery. In 1837, after becoming Quakers, the sisters began to give antislavery talks to small groups of women who came to hear about the "peculiar institution" from those who knew it firsthand. Men soon began to attend, and before long Sarah was addressing large gatherings of both men and women in New York and New England.

For women to speak before "mixed" audiences was a shocking break with tradition. In addition to attacks from those opposed to the antislavery movement, Grimké's speeches were decried by abolitionist leaders who deplored the growing participation of women in the antislavery movement and fought such men as William Lloyd Garrison and the black abolitionist Frederick Douglass who endorsed female activism.

Despite, or perhaps because of, such opposition, Sarah Grimké moved on to become one of the earliest feminists. In 1838 she published *Letters on the Equality of the Sexes,* in which she denounced the traditional education and indoctrination of women. Women should be treated as full human beings. "Whatsoever it is morally right for a man to do," she announced, "it is morally right for a woman to do."

Grimké's example by itself was electrifying to many women. Meanwhile, the antislavery movement helped turn other women toward considering their own bondage. When in 1840 the World's Antislavery Convention in London excluded nine American female delegates from its deliberations, two of these, Lucretia Mott and Elizabeth Cady Stanton, resolved to launch a new organization dedicated to personal liberation for women. In the summer of 1848 Mott and Stanton brought together 250 people for a convention at Seneca Falls, New York, to consider women's rights. Most of the delegates were women, but there were also male Quakers and reformers, including black abolitionist Frederick Douglass. Seneca Falls marked the true beginning of the women's rights movement. The delegates issued a Declaration of Sentiments modeled after the Declaration of Independence and indicting "man" as the oppressor. The declaration was followed by resolutions urging women to organize and fight for their rights. The most radical demand, the one that most clearly violated the notion of women's "proper sphere," was for the "elective franchise."

Efforts at this time to organize a permanent national women's rights body failed, but the wom-

Women's Rights

Lucy Stone was a founder of the pre–Civil War women's rights movement. Determined to get an education at a time when women were considered incapable of exercising the higher faculties, she was fortunate when Oberlin College in Ohio opened its doors to women and blacks. In 1847, soon after earning her degree, she joined the abolitionist movement and for several years worked for the American Antislavery Society. For Lucy Stone, as for other women, abolitionism served as a bridge to the women's rights movement. In 1850 she helped to organize the first national women's rights convention at Worcester, Massachusetts, and eventually became a leader of the women's suffrage movement as well. During her lifetime she was notorious for keeping her maiden name after marriage to Henry B. Blackwell. Other feminists who imitated her came to be called Lucy Stoners.

The selection below is part of a speech Lucy Stone delivered extemporaneously at a women's rights convention in Cincinnati in 1855. It is a remarkable capsule summary of women's grievances and aspirations during the antebellum era as perceived by the feminists of the day.

"The last speaker alluded to this movement as being that of a few disappointed women. From the first years to which my memory stretches, I have been a disappointed woman. When, with my brothers, I reached forth after the sources of knowledge, I was reproved with 'It isn't fit for you; it doesn't belong to women.' Then there was but one college in the world where women were admitted, and that was in Brazil. I would have found my way there, but by the time I was prepared to go, one was opened in the young State of Ohio—the first in the United States where women and Negroes could enjoy opportunities with white men. I was disappointed when I came to seek a profession worthy an immortal human being—every employment was closed to me, except those of the teacher, the seamstress, and the housekeeper. In education, in marriage, in religion, in everything, disappointment is the lot of woman. It shall be the business of my life to deepen this disappointment in every woman's heart until she bows down to it no longer. I wish that women, instead of being walking show-cases, instead of begging of their fathers and brothers the latest and gayest new bonnet, would ask of them their rights.

"The question of Woman's Rights is a practical one. The notion has prevailed that it was only an ephemeral idea, it was but women claiming the right to smoke cigars in the streets, and to frequent bar-rooms. Others have supposed it is a question of comparative intellect; others still, of sphere. Too much has already been said and written about woman's sphere. Trace all the doctrines to their source and they will be found to have no basis except in the usages and prejudices of the age. This is seen in the fact that what is tolerated in woman in one country is not tolerated in another. . . .

"I have confidence in the Father to believe that when He gives us the capacity to do anything He does not make a blunder. Leave women, then, to find their sphere. And do not tell us . . . that our province is to cook dinners, darn stockings, and sew on buttons. We are told woman has all the rights she wants; and even women, I am ashamed to say, tell us so. They mistake the politeness of men for rights—seats while men stand in this hall tonight, and their adulations; but these are mere courtesies. We want rights. The flour-merchant, the house-builder, and the postman charge us no less on account of our sex; but when we endeavor to earn money to pay all these, then, indeed, we find the difference. Man, if he has energy, may hew out for himself a path where no mortal has ever trod, held back by nothing but what is in himself; the world is all before him, there to choose; and we are glad for you, brothers, men, that it is so. But the same society that drives forth the young man, keeps woman at home—a dependent—working little cats on worsted, and little dogs on punctured paper; but if she goes heartily and bravely to give herself to some worthy purpose, she is out of her sphere and she loses caste. Women working in tailor-shops are paid one-third as much as men. Some one in Philadelphia has stated that women make fine shirts for twelve and a half cents apiece; that no woman can make more than nine a week, and the sum thus earned, after deducting rent, fuel, etc., leaves her just three and a half cents a day for bread. Is it any wonder that women are driven to prostitution? Female teachers in New York are paid fifty dollars a year, and for every such situation there are five hundred applicants. I know not what you believe of God, but I believe He gave yearnings and longings to be filled, and that He did not mean all our time should be devoted to feeding and clothing the body. The present condition of woman causes a horrible perversion of the marriage relation. It is said of a lady, 'Has she married well?' 'Oh, yes, her husband is rich.' Woman must marry for a home, and you men are the sufferers by this; for a woman who loathes you may marry you because you have the means to get money which she cannot have. But when woman can enter the lists with you and make money for herself, she will marry you only for deep and earnest affection. . . ."

en's rights advocates scored some early successes. After a bitter fight that split the American antislavery movement, women won the right to address antislavery meetings of the Garrison-dominated American Antislavery Society. Also under feminist pressure several states passed laws giving married women greater control over their own property and equalizing and liberalizing divorce proceedings. But the going was hard. Feminists were mocked, snubbed, and jeered at. They were spared physical attack, but that was virtually all they escaped.

In addition to organized group efforts to resist male domination of society, many women strove individually to improve their position. The first barrier to achievement, the inaccessibility of higher education to women, was breached when Oberlin in 1833, and then other colleges, admitted women as full degree candidates. In 1865 the first all-women's college, Vassar, was established.

With degrees in hand, women could now take on the professions. In 1850 Antoinette Brown took a theology degree at Oberlin and became the first ordained woman minister. The female breakthrough in medicine came with the Blackwell sisters, who earned their degrees at Geneva College, the only school that would admit them for medical training. Other women began to take law courses and set up practices as attorneys. In almost every case women professionals encountered resistance and ridicule in these years. But by the Civil War women had at least broken the crust of male domination of the public sphere, and it was apparent that more advances would follow.

Antislavery Sentiments. The antislavery movement was a momentous and controversial focus for reform in its own right. We have already seen how the Revolution undermined slavery north of the Mason-Dixon line. In succeeding decades the Quakers continued to oppose slavery, although they avoided harsh attacks on slaveholders. Antislavery groups remained active in many places for a time after 1783, even in the South itself.

One expression of antislavery sentiment in this period was the colonization movement dedicated to returning free blacks to Africa. Some members of the American Colonization Society (founded in 1817), especially southerners, saw their movement primarily as a means of getting rid of a dangerous group that threatened the survival of slavery. Recognizing white southerners' fears that if slavery were abolished, the South would have an enormous problem adjusting to a vastly expanded free black population, others believed that returning blacks to Africa could serve as a first step in eventually freeing all the slaves. Whatever their motives, promoters of colonization did not take into account the costs of transporting millions of blacks to Africa, southern resistance to liquidating hundreds of millions of dollars' worth of property, or the feelings of black Americans themselves. This was their native land, most blacks said; Africa was not their country. Under the auspices of the Colonization Society, a few thousand free blacks, former slaves, and Africans taken from

illegal slave ships were sent to Liberia, a new black republic founded on the West African coast. But as a serious solution to the slavery problem, colonization remained unworkable.

During the late 1820s the antislavery movement took on a new dimension when it linked up with religious Perfectionism and was converted into a crusade for immediate and total abolition. The instigator of the change was William Lloyd Garrison, a pious young printer from Newburyport, Massachusetts. After editing the *National Philanthropist,* the first temperance newspaper, and turning it into a journal of general moral reform, Garrison developed a white-hot determination to drive slavery from the land. Garrison's "immediatism" rejected the quiet tone and step-by-step approach of the Quakers as dealing too gently with sin. Now was the time to demand abolition—if necessary, in a way that did not spare people's feelings.

On January 1, 1831, the first issue of Garrison's *Liberator* appeared. It rang with the fervor for liberty and the righteous determination to end the evil of slavery that would make its editor the hope of the oppressed and the despair of moderates. In words that still inspire, Garrison wrote:

> I *will be* as harsh as truth, and as uncompromising as justice. On this subject, I do not wish to think, to speak, or write with moderation. . . . I am in earnest—I will not equivocate—I will not excuse—and I will not retreat a single inch—AND I WILL BE HEARD.

Despite its militant tone the *Liberator* at first attracted little attention. Then in August 1831 Nat Turner, a slave preacher, instigated a slave uprising in the Virginia tidewater that led to 57 white and 100 slave deaths. A wave of horror rolled across the South. Though Garrison had had nothing to do with the revolt, southerners were certain that he had inspired Turner. They demanded that he and his fellow abolitionists be stopped by every means possible. Garrison was not deterred. As the years passed, he became even more uncompromising and intransigent. A thorough Perfectionist, he became convinced that the criminal code, war, and government itself were all efforts to coerce human beings and were equally evil. By condoning slavery, the federal Constitution seemed particularly wicked, and in 1843 Garrison began to place at the head of his editorial column the words:

> Resolved, that the compact which exists between the North and South is a "Covenant with Death, and an agreement with Hell,"—involving both parties in atrocious criminality,—and should be immediately annulled.

Racism in action in the free North. This 1839 woodcut from The Anti-Slavery Almanac *probably depicts the attack by white bigots on Prudence Crandall's school for black girls at Canterbury, Connecticut.*

Not all abolitionists were as militant as Garrison. In the West another group of antislavery leaders spoke in more moderate voices. There Oberlin College quickly became a center of antislavery sentiment and its students active missionaries in the antislavery cause. Led by the dynamic Theodore Weld, the Oberlin abolitionists refused to adopt the extreme positions and language of the Garrisonians. They were also not as certain as Garrison that women's rights and other reforms were the proper concern of abolitionists. In 1840 the Weld-Tappan group split from the Garrisonians to form the American and Foreign Antislavery Society with headquarters in New York, leaving the Garrisonians in possession of the American Antislavery Society with headquarters in Boston.

In addition to facing conflicts within their movement, abolitionists were often assailed by conservatives even in the North, who saw them as dangerous to social and political order. Mobs attacked Garrison in Boston, and antislavery leader Elijah Lovejoy was murdered in Alton, Illinois. When not subject to physical violence, abolitionists were denounced as fanatics, dangerous agitators, and heretics. They were frequently denied basic constitutional rights. When Prudence Crandall attempted to admit a black girl to her Connecticut school in 1833, local whites broke her windows and contaminated her well. Eventually, despite abolitionists' efforts to defend her legal rights, she was driven from the state. Antiabolitionist feeling penetrated to the highest levels of public life. President Andrew Jackson attacked the antislavery advocates as extremists bent on instigating slave insurrections; his postmaster general denied abolitionists the use of the mails to distribute their newspapers, books, and pamphlets. In 1836, Congress adopted the "gag rule"

placing all antislavery petitions of abolitionists "on the table," where they were simply ignored.

The physical, verbal, and legal assaults did not keep men and women from joining the antislavery movement. In fact, by converting abolitionism into an issue of free speech, the attacks may have created sympathy and attracted recruits. Hundreds of men and women—many of New England ancestry, though there were occasional southerners like the Grimké sisters and Alabama planter James G. Birney—flocked to the antislavery organizations. A majority of prominent abolitionists were white, but many free blacks also joined the movement. Unfortunately, blacks within the antislavery societies were often snubbed by white abolitionists who defended human equality in the abstract but could not overcome their actual prejudice against black people. Yet, despite the prejudice of whites, Frederick Douglass, the brilliant black editor of the antislavery *North Star*; Henry Highland Garnet, an eloquent black preacher; and Sojourner Truth, an illiterate woman and former slave who spoke with effective simplicity for the cause of freedom—all became prominent members of abolitionist societies.

Utopian Socialism. Each of these movements—prison reform, improved treatment of the insane, temperance, women's rights, abolitionism—was an attempt to cure some supposed ill of American society while leaving the main structure untouched. There were Americans in these years, however, who rejected the very foundations of their society and chose to withdraw from it almost entirely or to change it from the bottom up.

These people deeply deplored the social and moral climate of their country: America was too

An Historical Portrait Frederick Douglass

The expression "a credit to his race" used to be applied to a certain kind of well-educated black man who conformed to white expectations. Such people had acquired an education, taken on the white man's speech, and dressed in a white-middle-class way. Above all, they accepted the racial status quo and did not seek to change it. Frederick Douglass was "a credit to his race" by all but the last criterion. He did not accept the way blacks were treated in the United States. Indeed, he was one of the boldest, most resolute enemies of the cruel racial regime that, whether in slavery or "freedom," white America imposed on his people.

Douglass was born in 1818 in Maryland, son of a slave mother and an unidentified white father. Like all North American blacks, he followed his mother's condition, and like her was the property of Aaron Anthony, a Maryland planter with thirty slaves and three farms.

Frederick's mother died while he was still a young child and he went to live on a distant plantation owned by Anthony. Here he observed floggings for the first time and learned that the violence done to blacks by their white masters sometimes made them cruel to one another. Fortunately his stay on the Anthony plantation was brief. In 1825 Frederick was sent to Baltimore to be the companion of the son of Hugh and Sophia Auld. Mrs. Auld was a kind woman and taught the boy to read and write. Her husband, however, was meanspirited and disapproved of her act. Literacy, he shouted, would "spoil the best nigger in the world." Mrs. Auld never again taught the bright slave boy anything.

Yet Frederick never gave up his quest for learning. When he left the Aulds' household to work in a Baltimore shipyard, he continued to read. The white South was right to forbid slave literacy. At the age of thirteen Frederick bought a book of rhetoric that contained model speeches by the great orators declaiming the principles of freedom and even of slave emancipation. From this work he learned many of the skills and eloquent arguments he would later use with devastating effect against the "peculiar institution."

Following Hugh Auld's death, Frederick was shunted around from one heir to another and employed as a field hand far from the stimulating life of the city. His resentment of his new condition finally induced his latest master to return him to Baltimore, to be apprenticed to a trade and freed when he reached twenty-one.

But Douglass could not wait till then. In September 1838, dressed as a seaman, he hopped a train northward and arrived in New York soon after. In New York he was befriended by the black abolitionist Charles Ruggles, who gave him shelter. Ruggles also helped him contact Anna Murray, a freeborn blackwoman Douglass had met in Baltimore, and it was in Ruggles's house that Frederick and Anna were married.

Soon after, at Ruggles's urging, the young couple left for New Bedford, Massachusetts, a community where they believed Frederick was less likely to be betrayed as a fugitive slave than in New York. It was in New Bedford that Frederick abandoned his slave name and took "Douglass" as a further disguise.

A new life began for Douglass in New England. He soon came to the attention of the prominent abolitionist leader William Lloyd Garrison, and in August 1841 he was invited to speak at an antislavery convention. Douglass created a sensation. Even abolitionists seldom knew educated blacks and at times they, too, exhibited race prejudice and condescension. But no one could doubt that this imposing, eloquent black man was a superior being and a living reproach to slavery. The lesson must be spread. Douglass was immediately hired at $450 a year as speaker for the Massachusetts Antislavery Society.

During the next three years Douglass toured the North, denouncing slavery at dozens of abolitionist meetings. His effect on his audiences was powerful but, like many abolitionists, he was also heckled and even attacked physically. In 1845 Douglass published the first of three autobiographies recounting his life as a slave and harshly condemning slavery. Soon after, he took ship for England under the sponsorship of the American Antislavery Society to bring his message to the many friends of black emancipation in Europe.

Like many black Americans during slavery days—and after— Douglass found his contact with Europe liberating. Europeans had little of the color prejudice of white Americans. Douglass found he could go anywhere in Europe, speak to anyone, and never be treated as an inferior.

Despite this exhilarating experience, in 1847 Douglass concluded that he must return to his native land. Recognizing the danger that he would be recaptured as a fugitive when he set foot on American soil, his English friends purchased his freedom from his legal owner. Douglass arrived back in the United States in April 1847 at the age of thirty, a free man for the first time in his life.

Back home, Douglass decided to establish a newspaper to expound his views. His friends in the abolitionist movement tried to dissuade him, arguing that there were already

competitive and individualistic, too given over to the pursuit of wealth and too severely marred by inequality and exploitation. Yearning for a society closer to human scale where men and women could deal with one another face to face, eager to erase the distinctions between rich and poor, hopeful of replacing competition with cooperation, and determined to eliminate human drudg-

too many abolitionist papers and that if he failed, it would reflect on the capabilities of his race. But Douglass was now unwilling to accept white direction; blacks, he believed, must have an independent voice in the movement. His persistence led to a break with Garrison, though not with the less doctrinaire white abolitionists. With their help Douglass began publishing the *North Star* out of Rochester, New York, in 1847.

He soon discovered how hard it was to run a newspaper, and there would be many times in the next dozen years when he would consider abandoning the enterprise. But the paper afforded a far better outlet for Douglass's views than the lecture platform. The *North Star*'s columns and editorial pages covered not only the antislavery movement but also temperance, discrimination against free blacks, and national politics. Douglass and his paper were particular friends of women's rights. He was one of the sixty-seven men who attended the historic Seneca Falls Convention in 1848, which effectively launched the women's rights movement, and throughout his career he remained a strong supporter of Susan B. Anthony and Elizabeth Cady Stanton, the women's rights leaders.

As the country approached the final sectional crisis, Douglass became increasingly critical of Garrison's antipolitics position. He supported the Liberty party and its successor, the Republican party. In 1860 he endorsed Lincoln, though he had no illusions that the rough-hewn man from Illinois would attack slavery head-on. Douglass considered the war that followed Lincoln's election providential. Here was the opportunity to finally strike slavery a mortal blow. But this result could not be left to chance. Through the early months of the

war Douglass hammered away in print and from the platform at the necessity of destroying slavery in order to put down the rebellion. He was jubilant when the president announced in September 1862 his intention to issue the Emancipation Proclamation.

On the night of December 31, 1863, Douglass and 3,000 other antislavery men and women gathered in Boston's Tremont Temple to await word from Washington that the Proclamation was finally in force. At 10 P.M. a man came running through the crowd shouting: "It is coming! It is on the wires!" The crowd burst into spontaneous cheers. Prayers were offered up and joyous speeches continued until dawn. After two and a half centuries the evil institution was dead.

Douglass would live for thirty more years. During the Reconstruction era he would demand "immediate, unconditional, and universal enfranchisement of the black man in every State in the Union." He was one of the black leaders who visited Andrew Johnson in the White House in February 1866 to ask the president's support for giving freedmen the vote. The outspoken Douglass offended Johnson, who later told one of his private secretaries that he was "just like any nigger, and he would sooner cut a white man's throat than not." The suffrage issue put strains on the alliance of blacks and women. Susan B. Anthony and Elizabeth Cady Stanton wanted Douglass to support the simultaneous enfranchisement of women and blacks, but Douglass refused on the grounds that such linkage would jeopardize votes for blacks. It was now, he said, "the Negro's hour."

In 1872 Douglass and his family moved to Washington, where, during the administrations of Hayes and Garfield, he held minor but

well-paying patronage jobs with the federal government. Republican preferment, plus the added years, cooled Douglass's ardor for change and curbed his critical pen and tongue. So much had been accomplished since slavery days for black people; it was hard to carp at the many inequalities that remained. Fortunately, successive versions of his autobiography sold well and provided the income he needed to live comfortably in the capital.

In 1882 Anna, Douglass's wife of forty-four years, died. Theirs had not been a happy relationship; Frederick was too public a man and had too many admirers, many of them female. He was a doting father to his three children and helped them whenever he could, but none of them achieved independence or conventional success. In 1884 Douglass scandalized blacks and whites alike by marrying a white woman. Yet despite the uproar, in 1889, when he was seventy-one, President Benjamin Harrison appointed him minister to the black republic of Haiti. Douglass disliked the climate and soon resigned.

He lived until February 1895, and in his last years regained some of his zeal for the black man's cause. Among his last writings was a series of attacks on the new epidemic of lynching that was sweeping the South. Seven months after he died another black leader would rise to speak at the Atlanta Cotton States Exposition. Booker T. Washington would make a pact with white America that would freeze the racial status quo for fifty years. A later generation of black leaders would condemn the Atlanta Compromise, but in all likelihood, his latest biographer believes, Frederick Douglass, who had waited so long to see even a flawed freedom, would have approved.

---

ery, they went off to the woods or the frontier to found communities based on some idealistic economic, social, or religious philosophy.

Several of the new utopian communities

were inspired by the writings of Charles Fourier, a French thinker who opposed capitalism as inhumane and competitive. Fourier proposed in its place a system of small cooperative communities scattered about the countryside where men and women could work at farming and industry while living in a communal structure—a phalanx. No one would own the community's capital and collect its dividends. All would share both the labor and the profit. Government of each phalanx would consist of a Council of Seven, five of whom would be women.

Brook Farm, established near Boston by George Ripley, eventually adopted a Fourierist mode. It was a place of intellect and warmth where New England intellectuals taught, farmed, and played. Everyone who visited found it gay, charming, and pleasant. But, alas, the New England literary folk were far better at words than at farming. "Never," remarked one skeptic, were there "such witty potato-patches and such sparkling cornfields before or since." But, he added, there was a "lack of method," and that explained the community's eventual failure. In 1847, realizing that the enterprise was losing money, the founders closed their doors.

A communitarian experiment that owed as much to religious as to political principles was Oneida, a community led by John Humphrey Noyes, a Yale-educated minister who settled with his followers in western New York in 1847. At Oneida Noyes preached against what he called "the Sin system, the Marriage system, the Work system, and the Death system," combining religious evangelism and socialist economics. All work was reduced to what seemed essential and unavoidable. Women, particularly, were freed of drudgery by simplified methods of housekeeping. Men and women joined in the essential work of digging, building, and farming. To make this labor more comfortable, women adopted short hair and baggy trousers.

Noyes's most radical experiment was "complex marriage." He and his followers believed that monogamy (a single spouse) was selfish and interfered with a true sense of community. Instead, every man at Oneida was considered the husband of every woman and vice versa. Outsiders called this "free love" and condemned it as an utter breakdown of morality. But the Oneidaites responded that no one in the community was forced to accept sexual relations he or she did not desire. Though Oneida members practiced birth control, some children were born into the community; they were treated in an unusually permissive way, being allowed, for example, to sleep until awakened by the natural rhythms of their bodies. Unlike the typical schools of the time, which used memorization and awards and punishment,

Oneida schools sought to arouse curiosity and make learning a pleasure.

The Oneida community was an unusual success. It avoided the bickering that destroyed so many other communitarian experiments by a scheme of self-criticism whereby members could air their grievances before the whole group and work them out. Oneida also developed a firm economic foundation. Noyes, recognizing that industry was better suited to a community such as Oneida than agriculture, trained members in embroidery and silk making and mobilized their ingenuity in developing manufactures. The community basked in prosperity for many decades, becoming, ironically, the basis for a major commercial cutlery firm that is still in business.

There were many other experimental communities. During the nineteenth century, it is estimated, more than 100 such communities with 100,000 members were formed in the United States, most of them between 1820 and 1860. As Emerson wrote an English friend in 1840: "We are all a little wild here with numberless projects of social reform. Not a reading man but has a draft of a new community in his waistcoat pocket."

Most communities founded on some sort of political or philosophical plan were short-lived. New Harmony, a socialist experiment on the banks of the Wabash sponsored by the British philanthropist Robert Owen, lasted two years and then disbanded when internal bickering destroyed all chance of harmony. Icaria, designed as an experiment in communal ownership and use of capital, attracted a small group of French people to the new state of Texas in 1847. A year later it was defunct. The longest-lived of the Fourierist communities lasted only twelve years.

Communities with a religious base were generally more successful than ones founded on a political ideal. Among the most enduring "utopian" communities were those established by the English Quaker Mother Ann Lee, who came to America in 1774 and organized her first small "Shaker" settlement soon after. At first the Shakers expanded slowly from this core, but then, during the 1830–50 period, stimulated by the second Great Awakening, Shakerism experienced a great burst of energy. By the late 1840s there were about 6,000 Shakers living in a score or more communities scattered across the northern states.

In their trim, spare, simple villages the Shakers followed a life that combined economic cooperation with a pursuit of spiritual perfection that precluded sexual relations. Though their celibacy obviously limited expansion, the Shaker

Courtesy Oneida Ltd., Silversmiths

The sharp line between men's and women's spheres did not exist at the Oneida community, as this photo of a pea-shelling bee in the 1850s shows. At the far right, a woman wears the short (for the day) skirt over pantaloons typical of Oneida women. This outfit preserved female modesty while allowing women to work at "masculine" jobs.

communities overcame this natural barrier to continuity by recruiting a steady stream of men and women who disliked the competitive, individualistic life of the larger society. Shakers prospered collectively by selling seeds, medicinal herbs, bonnets, cloaks, and cabinetwork, and lasted as a group well into the twentieth century.

There were many other long-lived religious communities. The various Rappite villages founded by German Pietists around 1805 continued until 1900. The Pietist Amana Society, also German in origin, established its first villages in western New York in the 1840s. It, too, survived into the twentieth century, growing prosperous on weaving and blanket making. It still exists today, though it is now a successful manufacturer of electrical appliances.

The commercial success of the religious communities illustrates the paradoxes of antebellum America. Secular faiths were unable to deal with the craving for brotherhood and cooperation. During the pre–Civil War era no political or economic philosophy could overcome the acquisitiveness and individualism of the larger society. A religious perspective was more effective. But to survive, the religious communities found it necessary to become successful economic enterprises.

CONCLUSION

What were pre–Civil War Americans in the North and West truly like, then? Americans were competitive and individualistic; they were crude, bad-mannered, violent, and bigoted. They were also humane, romantic, creative, and socially speculative. It seems fitting to call them, as one historian has, "people of paradox."

These inconsistencies can be traced to the special circumstances of the northern part of the nation in these years. The whole region north of Dixie was in a state of extraordinary flux. Still agricultural and rural, it was rapidly becoming industrial and urban. Still largely composed of native-born Protestants whose forebears had arrived in the colonial era, it was experiencing a deluge of newcomers from Europe, many of whom were Catholic. Besides the tensions these changes created, there were antagonisms between East and West. Easterners often disliked western manners and practices, yet they themselves were moving west in vast numbers and learning to adjust to western economic competition. These transplanted easterners were undoubtedly influenced by the western practices they deplored.

One important fact should be kept in mind as

we consider the country's evolution: virtually all the changes we have considered in this chapter followed lines of latitude. In shifts of people, institutions, values, and problems, Northeast mixed with Northwest. This is not to say that the two sections did not retain many distinctive features, but by 1860 Northeast and Northwest were far more alike than either was to the South. This development of distinctive North-South sectional identities would have momentous consequences for the nation.

FOR FURTHER READING

Roger Brown. *Modernization: The Transformation of American Life, 1600–1865* (1976)
> This book is an attempt to place social change in America within the framework of modernization. A modern society is one in which custom and personal, face-to-face relations among people are replaced by impersonal, contractual relations. A modern society is subject to rapid and continuous change; traditional society is static. The North, in effect, modernized by 1865; the South did not.

Keith Melder. *The Beginnings of Sisterhood* (1977)
> A fine, brief treatment of the social background and early course of the women's rights movement. Deals with the changes in women's status during the antebellum period and how they affected women's public roles in America.

Nancy Cott. *The Bonds of Womanhood: "Women's Sphere" in New England, 1780–1835* (1977)
> Sees women's lives being transformed by the growing separation of family and work during the early years of the republic. An important book, but one that perhaps exaggerates the extent to which the social change characteristic of our own day can actually be found in this earlier period.

Linda Gordon. *Woman's Body, Woman's Right: A Social History of Birth Control in America* (1976)
> A book with a strong thesis: "Birth control represented the single most important factor in the material basis of woman's emancipation in the course of the last century." Professor Gordon describes the often gruesome measures used by nineteenth-century women to limit their families, including makeshift abortion and infanticide.

Russel B. Nye. *Society and Culture in America, 1830–1860* (1974)
> A superior intellectual and cultural history by a scholar who has made every aspect of American cultural life, from high to low, his life's study.

Oscar Handlin, editor. *This Was America* (1949)
> Contains excerpts from many of the accounts by foreign travelers that scholars have used to paint antebellum America's portrait.

Ray Allen Billington. *America's Frontier Heritage* (1966)
> Billington is the outstanding historian of the frontier and the author of a major biography of Frederick Jackson Turner. In this book he examines Turner's frontier thesis and revises it in light of recent scholarship.

Oscar Handlin. *Boston's Immigrants, 1790–1880* (1968)
> This study of Boston's "old immigrants" catches the essence of the urban immigrant experience in microcosm. Handlin has brought the story up to 1880 in this revised edition, but the emphasis remains on the years before the Civil War.

Ray Billington. *The Protestant Crusade, 1800–1860: A Study of the Origins of American Nativism* (1938)
> This case study of mass reaction describes the development of anti-Catholic and antiforeign feeling that reached its peak in the 1850s. An older book that is still valuable and readable.

Leon F. Litwack. *North of Slavery: The Negro in the Free States, 1790–1860* (1961)
> Litwack's thesis is that by 1860 most blacks in the states where slavery was forbidden were segregated from whites, economically oppressed, and without civil rights. Topics of special interest include black-Irish relations, the role of black religious leaders, and the efforts of black leaders and white abolitionists to improve conditions.

Alice Felt Tyler. *Freedom's Ferment: Phases of American Social History to 1860* (1944)
> Still the best narrative history of the antebellum reform impulse. Covers everything from socialism to women's rights.

David Rothman. *The Discovery of the Asylum: Social Order and Disorder in the New Republic* (1971)
> Rothman sees the origin of much of the antebellum reform impulse in the attempt by society to make up for the deficiencies of the American family. In his view, the penitentiaries, the poorhouses, and the institutions for the insane were established largely to prevent disorder and impose social control; the humanitarian element was secondary. An important book but one that exaggerates one side of the pre–Civil War reform movement.

Richard Wade. *The Urban Frontier: The Rise of Western Cities, 1790–1830* (1959)
> Wade makes the point in this study of a group of Mississippi Valley cities during their pioneer phase that the antebellum West was not only a region of farms. It also consisted of fast-growing urban centers.

Leonard Arrington. *Great Basin Kingdom: An Economic History of the Latter-Day Saints, 1830–1900* (1958)
> An economic history of the Mormons from their beginnings in upstate New York to the twentieth century. Emphasizes their economic theories and practices as they were put into effect in Utah after 1846.

13 | The Old South

What Is Myth and What Was Real?

1807 Congress prohibits the slave trade with Africa, but illegal importation of black slaves continues

1822 Denmark Vesey and thirty-five slaves are hanged for planning a slave rebellion in South Carolina

1831 Nat Turner leads an unsuccessful slave rebellion in Virginia • Tariff of Abominations precipitates nullification crisis in South Carolina

1832 In response to Turner's rebellion the Virginia legislature debates the abolition of slavery

1836 Under pressure from southern congressmen, the House of Representatives adopts a "gag rule" prohibiting discussion of all abolitionist petitions

1849 John Calhoun writes *Disquisition on Government*: he states his theory of the "concurrent majority" in the Senate the following year

1852 Harriet Beecher Stowe's *Uncle Tom's Cabin* is published

1857 Hinton R. Helper's *The Impending Crisis of the South* is published

1858 James Hammond in a famous speech declares there has to be a "mud sill" upon which to erect a civilized cultured life

1860 Abraham Lincoln elected president • Slaves in the South number about 4 million, sixteen times the number of free blacks • South Carolina secedes from the Union

Magnolias and moonlight; white mansions with tall colonnades; beautiful hoop-skirted ladies and handsome, dignified gentlemen; thoroughbred horses; rich laughter and song drifting up from the slave quarters; waltzes and witty talk in the big plantation house. This was the Old South—a society that achieved for a brief moment a brilliance and happy harmony based on the mutual respect of classes, an ideal of excellence, and good prices for cotton.

Or was it? There is another picture that is almost the complete opposite. In this view the Old South—the slave states in the half century before 1860—was a benighted region where a privileged minority lorded it over millions of black slaves and "poor white trash." The typical elite planter was a newly rich "cotton snob," who abused his black chattels and showed contempt for the nonslaveholding class he himself had so recently left behind. The poor whites, in turn, were supposedly shiftless, dirty, violent, and ignorant people

who lived by a little desultory farming and by hunting, fishing, and trading whiskey with the slaves for stolen plantation goods. Beneath the poor whites were the oppressed and exploited blacks. Subjected to a regime of terror and physical violence, they lived in fear and fought their oppressors by laziness, deceptiveness, flight, or violence.

What was the Old South really like? Are both descriptions essentially fables? Is one fable truer than the other? Or is there some truth in both?

AN UNEXPECTED DIVERSITY

One myth about the Old South is that it was utterly distinct in its climate and geography. The Deep South indeed was warmer than the rest of the nation, and this made a difference economically. Short-fiber cotton and sugarcane need a long growing season—at least 200 days—and such a frost-free period could be found only in the region

Slavery and agricultural production

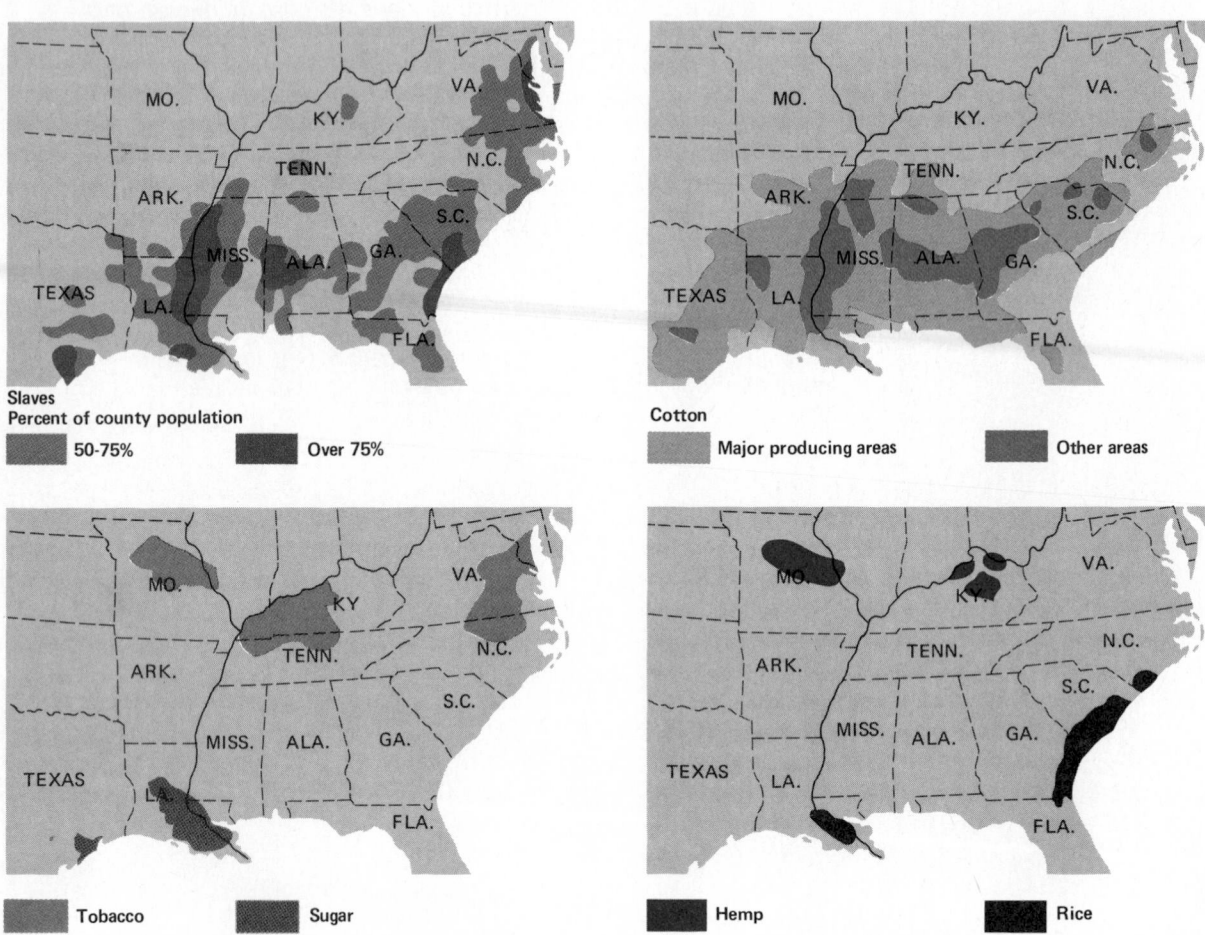

Slaves
Percent of county population
■ 50-75%   ■ Over 75%

Cotton
■ Major producing areas   ■ Other areas

■ Tobacco   ■ Sugar

■ Hemp   ■ Rice

from North Carolina south through Florida and then west in a wide band along the Gulf of Mexico as far as Texas. Much of the Deep South was too warm for wheat; its chief grain crop was corn. It had poor pasturage; the corn-eating hog, rather than the grass-eating cow was the basis of its animal husbandry. Thus climate helped distinguish part of the South from most of the North.

But the climatic distinction must not be exaggerated. There was little difference between the climate of Kentucky and Virginia and, say, that of Ohio and Pennsylvania—and yet the first two states were parts of the Old South, the second two of the North. Nor was the South's topography unique. The Appalachian plateau, the Atlantic coastal plain, and the Mississippi Valley were geographical features shared by the two sections. In short, it was not primarily the natural environment that defined the Old South.

Southern Agriculture. Another myth is that the Old South was a single agricultural unit. When we think of Dixie in this period, we imagine a gigantic cotton field. Yet cotton was only one of the region's many crops, and not even the most valuable. Corn, which grew everywhere, fattened the region's farm animals and, in the form of "pone," "hominy," and "roasting ears," fed most of its people. The southern corn crop was valued at $209 million in 1855; the cotton crop, at only $136 million.

Although cotton was second in total value, it was the great cash crop. Unlike corn, it was exported to the North and to Europe in vast quantities—almost a million bales in 1860—and it paid for the South's manufactures. It also made the South's fortunes. No one became rich by growing corn, but cotton was white gold that brought wealth to the efficient and lucky planter. On the eve of the Civil War the newer cotton-growing region of the Gulf states, the lower Mississippi delta, and eastern Texas was the richest part of the slave states.

Other staple crops brought in cash. Kentucky hemp, Louisiana sugar, Carolina rice, and Virginia, Maryland, and Kentucky tobacco were important in their regions. Although none even came close to cotton as a source of income, they contributed to the region's remarkable diversity.

Industry. Another myth about the Old South is that it was economically backward. Until recently historians said that cotton growing was actually an unproductive enterprise. It exhausted the soil, so that by the eve of the Civil War large sections of the older South consisted of worn-out lands. Only

by constant expansion into virgin soil could the planter ensure himself a decent profit. And cotton supposedly deflected capital from more productive enterprise. Planters poured their capital into new land and slaves rather than into machines and factories.

And even if southerners had been willing to invest in industry, the older view went, the slave system would have prevented it. Slaves lacked the necessary skills, incentives, and education for industrial work. Moreover, to set up successful industrial enterprises where the labor force was property was too great a burden for would-be investors. In addition to buildings and machines, they would have had to purchase their workers. Finally, a slave society inevitably encouraged aristocratic values and contempt for hard physical work—attitudes at odds with successful industrialization. Given all these qualities of a slave society, historians once declared, it was not surprising that the South remained bound to agriculture and achieved a slower rate of economic growth than the rest of the nation.

Few scholars today accept these ideas without serious qualifications. It is true that the Old South developed its manufacturing potential more slowly than the Northeast and a few of the most advanced European countries. But the reasons have little to do with slavery. Most slaves were field hands, performing jobs that did not require much skill. Yet even among the slaves who worked in the fields, some who showed managerial talent served as "drivers" or even overseers supervising large work gangs. Moreover, many slaves were skilled craftspeople. Plantations needed coopers, masons, carpenters, brick makers, gardeners, and the like. Slaves filled these jobs, which was one reason European immigrants generally avoided the Old South. On the sugar plantations of Louisiana black experts supervised most of the delicate operations of sugar refining. Slave women were often skilled seamstresses, weavers, cooks, and midwives. Some even practiced medicine, on white as well as black patients. Clearly slaves could have been the work force for an industrial economy.

Nor did prospective factory owners in the South have to buy their employees. Many planters, unable to employ all their slaves full-time, hired them out at prevailing wage rates. Hired slaves worked as municipal workers in southern cities; they worked by the day for southern householders. They also worked in southern factories and industries. In the pine forests of the Carolinas several thousand blacks labored in the lumber and turpentine industries. Hired slaves

Harper's Monthly

We think of slaves as toiling in fields of cotton, but some 400,000 were part of the South's urban industrial work force. Virginian tobacco factories such as this one relied almost exclusively on hired slaves, whose wages went to their masters.

were miners in Virginia, Kentucky, and Missouri. Deck hands on the river steamers of the Old South were generally black bondsmen, as were the construction workers on railroads and canals. Cotton mills in South Carolina, Alabama, and Florida used slave "operatives," and in Virginia slaves worked in tobacco factories. The Tredegar iron mills of Richmond, which would produce most of the Confederacy's artillery, were manned exclusively by hired slaves after 1847.

White society in the Old South, 1860

Note: The Old South is here assumed to be all states in which slavery was legal in 1860. Slaveholders are defined as members of families owning slaves. Source: *Eighth Census of the United States, 1860: Population by Age, Sex, Race and Agriculture of the United States.*

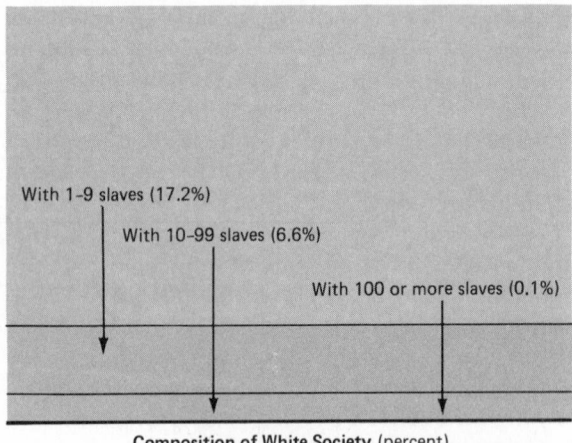

With 1-9 slaves (17.2%)

With 10-99 slaves (6.6%)

With 100 or more slaves (0.1%)

Composition of White Society (percent)

Nonslaveholders (78.1%)

Slaveholders (23.9%)

Clearly, then, the slave labor system did not exclude industry and business from the Old South. Neither did southern values. Dixie planters were not a collection of feckless romantics. Most of them were practical men who managed their plantations rationally, studied agriculture as a business, encouraged experimentation in crops and animal breeding, and organized their labor force efficiently. Through their overseers, or sometimes directly, they supervised their slaves' performance in the fields. The historian Jacob Metzer calls the pre–Civil War southern plantation "a modern business organization, and possibly even a leading business organization of its time."

The final proof that slavery was not incompatible with industry, however, is the actual industrial performance of the pre–Civil War South. The Old South was a remarkably industrialized part of the world for its day, ahead of all but a very few European countries in cloth output and railroad mileage—important measures of economic growth. In 1860 there were almost 200 textile mills scattered through the region, plus hundreds of tobacco factories, flour and lumber mills, and other manufacturing establishments that processed the section's agricultural products.

Still, it remains true that Dixie fell behind the Northeast in industrial development despite its natural endowments of waterpower, coal, iron, and cotton—all basic resources of the early industrial revolution. The explanation for this relative lag, however, lies not in the section's labor force or values but in certain economic realities. Southern capitalists concentrated on agriculture to the relative neglect of trade and industry because they could make larger profits by doing so. Perhaps if prices for cotton and the South's other staples had not been so high during much of the late pre–Civil War period, planters would have been driven to shift their labor, capital, and skills to manufacturing. But prices *were* high, and a dollar invested in land and slaves in the Mississippi delta, the Louisiana bayou country, or the Kentucky bluegrass yielded a very good return. It was not an aristocratic contempt for "trade"—though at times southerners professed disdain for commerce and manufacturing—but a rational estimate of profits on investment that led planters to put their money into agriculture rather than industry. And the results of the South's concentration on commercial agriculture were not meager. If the South in 1860 is considered as a separate nation, its per capita income was fourth among the countries of the world, exceeded only by Australia, the remainder of the United States, and Great Britain.

Social Diversity. The Old South's social system has also been misperceived. In the past, few scholars questioned the existence of a three-tiered society of great planters, black slaves, and poor whites. But that scheme does not correspond very closely to reality. Each layer was far more complex than this view suggested.

The top layer was very thin indeed. In 1860 only 2,200 southerners owned 100 or more slaves, and these 2,200 made up less than 1 percent of the 383,000 slaveholding families in that year. The lordly domain—and the equally lordly agrarian aristocrat—was a rarity in the Old South.

The typical slaveholder was a member of the middle class. Seventy-one percent of slaveholders—almost 200,000—had fewer than 10 slaves. These small farmers could scarcely maintain the style and pace of the planter elite. They ate plain food and lived in houses that were little more than enlarged balloon-frame structures or even modified log cabins. They were often rough in their speech and in their ways. Although aspiring to wealth and gentility, they had far to go before they could claim either.

Even more numerous was the nonslaveholding yeomanry, consisting of white farmers who worked their acres themselves, helped by their grown sons and some occasional hired labor. Professor Frank Owsley and his students at Vanderbilt University have recently painted a picture of the Old South's yeomen that resembles a sentimental Currier and Ives print. Sturdy, independent, democratic, they lived comfortably but simply. Their daily rounds were punctuated by hoedowns, camp meetings, cabin raising, corn shucking, and other assorted happy social activities. They were also politically influential, and like their counterparts in the North were often deferred to by the elite at election time.

Owsley's effort to redress the picture of the nonslaveholding whites is long overdue. The white yeomanry was indeed a substantial group and was particularly numerous in hilly upland regions and the "pine belts," away from the river bottomland. The soil of the river edges was fertile and, when drained and cleared, ideally suited to cotton culture. It was therefore in the Mississippi delta and the valleys of the Tombigbee, Pearl, and Suwannee rivers that the great plantations flourished. But since the bottomland was both malarial and expensive, the yeomen gave it a wide berth. Yet even in the delta regions of Mississippi and Alabama, small farmers could be found.

The yeoman class also wielded considerable political power. Voting rights in many parts of the Old South were as broad as elsewhere in the country, and southern politicians had to heed the yeomen's wishes. Moreover, in some areas the yeoman–small planter class was able to manipulate election districts so that counties where the white population was proportionately greatest—where the small farmers predominated—could control the state legislatures.

But in revising the traditional view, we must not go too far. Wealth in the South was more concentrated than in the North, where there was no agricultural elite that owned much of the best land. Southern yeomen, however numerous, were also probably poorer than their northern counterparts. Travelers in the antebellum South often emphasized the yeoman's rather primitive existence. Frederick Law Olmsted, a northern gentleman farmer and well-known landscape architect, described his encounter with one central Mississippi white farm family in 1854 as follows:

> The house was all comprised in a single room, twenty-eight by twenty-five feet in area, and open to the roof above. There was a large fireplace at one end and a door on each side—no windows at all. Two bedsteads, a spinning-wheel, a packing-case, which served as a bureau, a cupboard, made of rough hewn slabs, two or three deer-skin seated chairs, a Connecticut clock, and a large poster of Jayne's patent medicines, constituted all the visible furniture.
> . . . A little girl, immediately, without having had any direction to do so, got a frying-pan and a chunk of bacon from the cupboard, and cutting slices from the latter, set it frying for my

Library of Congress

A southern yeoman farmer and his family. Such people often eked out a living on the South's hilly lands, and without the help of slaves.

supper. The woman of the house sat sulkily in a chair tilted back and leaning against the logs, spitting occasionally at the fire, but took no notice of me, barely nodding when I saluted her. A baby lay crying on the floor. I quieted it and amused it with my watch till the little girl, having made "coffee" and put a piece of cornbread on the table with the bacon, took charge of it.

Central Mississippi was still almost a frontier when Olmsted visited it; nevertheless, it seems clear that the level of comfort among the southern yeomanry was inferior to that of their northern counterparts. Nor is there any point in denying that there was a southern white lower class. Particularly in the pine barrens and in the hill country, where poor soils and steep, sloping terrain made farming difficult, small groups of white families made a precarious living by growing corn, raising pigs, and hunting. These rural poor were often despised. Fanny Kemble, a visiting English actress, called them "the most degraded race of human beings claiming an Anglo-Saxon origin that can be found on the face of the earth." Kemble was not an impartial observer: she hated slavery and sought to demonstrate that it degraded whites as well as blacks. But it is clear that whether explained by slavery, nutritional diseases like pellagra, or natural selection, there was indeed a group of wretched whites who inhabited the rural nooks and crannies of pre–Civil War southern society.

Nor can we fully accept Owsley's view of the Old South's middle-class democracy. Although the South's yeomen had to be heeded politically, they did not wield most of the region's political power. In the older parts of the South—the Carolinas, Georgia, Maryland, and Virginia—voting was rigged in favor of the plantation areas. In the newer states slaveholders often enjoyed special advantages such as relatively low property taxes. And even where the yeomen made their numbers felt, they often deferred to the planters. In many parts of the Old South, as in colonial times, the aristocracy occupied positions of influence far beyond their formal power. Talented sons of the yeomanry with political ambitions had to acquire land and slaves to succeed in public life. Jefferson Davis, whose father was an unsuccessful small slaveholder, had to marry into the planter class to become a United States senator, secretary of war, and finally president of the Confederate States of America. John C. Calhoun, whose father was a farmer with no slaves, married a Carolina rice heiress whose fortune freed him to pursue politics. Andrew Jackson, too, became important enough to be considered for Congress only after he became a prosperous planter.

Not everyone in the South admired the planter elite. Some of the South's white, nonslaveholding yeomen resented slavery and planter leadership. The spokesman for this generally inarticulate group was Hinton R. Helper of Heidelberg in western North Carolina. His book, *The Impending Crisis of the South* (1857), is a blistering attack on the planter class. These men, he claimed, had retarded the South's growth and oppressed its yeomen. As a group, they were "so depraved that there . . . [was] scarcely a spark of honor or magnanimity to be found among them." Helper, like many whites of his class, also despised blacks, but he was willing to use fire to fight fire. To destroy the power of the planters, he proposed to rally the nonslaveholders against them—with the help, if need be, of the slaves.

Helper's was a minority voice in a minority section. Most of the South's small farmers would wait fifty years before they would consider challenging the leadership of their "betters." Still, his *Impending Crisis* is an interesting glimpse beneath the mythology of antebellum southern society.

LIFE UNDER SLAVERY

Like the white South, the black South has long been covered by a thick crust of myths. The older legend depicts "happy darkies" singing in the fields. Lovable but childlike creatures, they did not feel the oppression of slavery the way white people would. Of course slavery deprived black people of a fundamental right, these apologists admitted, but on a day-to-day basis it was a rather benign institution, and masters and slaves found it possible to develop mutual respect and to live comfortably with the inequality. There is a newer picture that is the diametric opposite. Slavery, it says, was a system of organized terror that either broke the spirit of black people or drove them to blind fury against their oppressors. Slaves were often whipped or maimed and were consigned to an incessant round of brutal, degrading labor. Worst of all, masters broke up the slaves' families and violated black women.

The truth is far more complex than either description allows. Slave life was very diverse. Like most white southerners, most blacks were employed in agriculture. Only a small portion of the southern population in 1860 was urban, and only about 17 percent of the total city population of the slave states was black. Yet black urbanites provided the black community with much-needed leaders and were an important element in the general cultural life of cities like New Orleans and Charleston.

Most southern blacks were slaves; but on the eve of the Civil War about 250,000—the same number as in the North—were free. Free blacks lived predominantly in the upper South, especially in Maryland, Kentucky, Delaware, Missouri, and Virginia, many in cities. In 1860 Baltimore's free black population out-numbered its slaves ten to one; Washington, D.C., had over 9,000 free blacks and fewer than 1,800 slaves.

Wherever free blacks lived in the South, their lot, as in the North, was not enviable. A few were successful in business, the skilled trades, the professions, or agriculture. Some free blacks even owned slaves of their own, and a tiny number were planters with considerable property, including slaves. Most, however, were unskilled laborers who huddled in the slums of the large southern towns, worked at menial tasks, suffered the contempt of whites, and were denied fundamental civil rights.

The South's slaves numbered about 4 million in 1860, sixteen times the number of free blacks. The great majority worked the soil. Whereas whites were mostly associated with small farm units, almost three-fourths of the South's slaves were found on relatively large plantations.

Working on a large plantation had some advantages. Where there were many slaves, there were many different jobs. On the large plantations slave women found employment as seamstresses, cooks, nurses, or maids in the master's house;

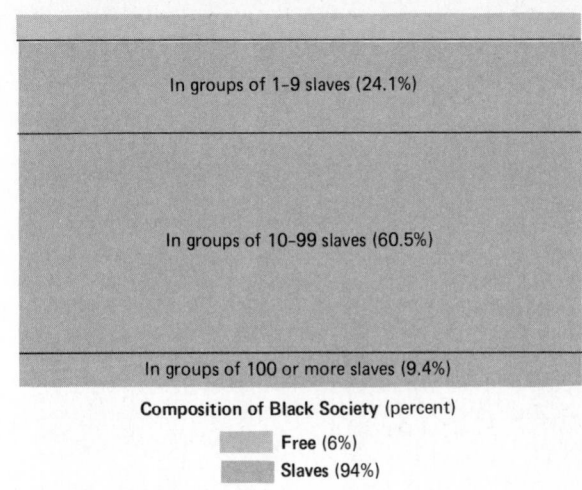

Black social structure in the Old South, 1860

Note: The Old South is here assumed to be all states in which slavery was legal in 1860.

Source: *Eighth Census of the United States, 1860: Population by Age, Sex, Race* and Lewis C. Gray, *History of Agriculture in the Southern United States* (1933).

slave men worked as butlers, coachmen, and valets. Black house servants were not free, but they were the envy of other slaves. Their jobs kept them out of the fields and brought them into contact with the more interesting world of the "big house." It also enabled them to control their working conditions to some degree. Few white masters or mistresses wanted to offend a good cook or laundress: it might ruin dinner or make it impossible to get a shirt properly ironed. And on large plantations even slaves who were not house servants still enjoyed some advantages. Besides working in the field, they might serve as drivers, skilled mechanics, or craftsmen. Because skilled workers were often hired out in towns and were sometimes allowed to negotiate their own terms of hire, these slaves were unusually free—for slaves, that is.

Even the field hands on the large plantations were better off than those on smaller establishments. It is true that the labor was often intense. Worked in gangs under close supervision, the slaves were expected to be productive, and they were. The output per worker on large plantations was consistently higher than on small ones. But force was not the most effective means of encouraging hard work; generosity was sometimes a better method. Planters usually perceived this and acted accordingly. Where an absentee master employed a white overseer to manage his plantation, the slaves were sometimes treated more severely. Still, the overall estimate that the workload was seldom excessive on large plantations remains valid.

The Slaves Speak Out

We have many surviving accounts of slavery from the inside, but virtually all of these were written by unusual people—literate black men and women who escaped from bondage and went north or to Canada. An exception is the collection of Slave Narratives made by the New Deal Works Progress Administration (WPA) during the 1930s. The WPA workers interviewed several hundred elderly southern blacks who had lived under the slave regime before 1863, and recorded their descriptions of personal experiences. The following selection is excerpted from the account of Mingo White of Burleson, Alabama, who at the time of the interview was between eighty-five and ninety years old.

"I was born in Chester, South Carolina, but I was mostly raised in Alabama. When I was about four or five years old, I was loaded in a wagon with a lot more people in it. Where I was bound I don't know. Whatever became of my mammy and pappy I don't know for a long time. I was told dere was a lot of slave speculators in Chester to buy some slaves for some folks in Alabama. I 'members dat I was took up on a stand and a lot of people came round and felt my arms and legs and chest, and ask me a lot of questions. Before we slaves was took to de tradin' post Old Marsa Crawford told us to tell everybody what asked us if we'd ever been sick dat us'd never been sick in our life. Us had to tell 'em all sorts of lies for our marsa or else take a beatin'.

"I was just a li'l thing, tooked away from my mammy and pappy, just when I needed 'em most. . . . My pappy and mammy was sold from each other, too, de same time I was sold. I used to wonder if I had any brothers or sisters, as I had always wanted some. . . .

"I weren't nothin' but a child endurin' slavery, but I had to work de same as any man. I went to de field and hoed cotton, pulled fodder and picked cotton with de rest of de hands. I kept up, too, to keep from gettin' any lashes dat night when us got home. In de winter I went to de woods with de menfolks to help to get wood or to get sap from de trees to make turpentine and tar. Iffen us didn't do dat we made charcoal to run de blacksmith shop with.

"De white folks was hard on us. Dey would whip us about de least li'l thing. It wouldn'ta been so bad iffen us a had comforts, but to live like us did was 'nough to make anybody soon as be dead. De white folks told us dat us born to work for 'em and dat us was doin' fine at dat. . . .

"De white folks didn't learn us to do nothin' but work. Dey said dat us weren't supposed to know how to read and write. Dere was one feller name E. C. White what learned to read and write even durin' slavery. He had to carry de chillen's books to school for 'em and go back after dem. His young marsa taught him to read and write unbeknownst to his father and de rest of de slaves.

"After de day's work was done dere weren't anything for de slaves to do but go to bed. Wednesday night they went to prayer meetin'. We had to be in de bed by nine o'clock. Every night de drivers come around to make sure dat we was in de bed. . . .

"On Saturday de hands worked till noon. Dey had de rest of de time to work dey gardens. Every family had a garden of deir own. On Saturday nights de slaves could frolic for a while. Dey would have parties sometimes and whiskey and home-brew for de servants. On Sundays we didn't do anything but lay round and sleep, 'cause we didn't like to go to church. On Christmas we didn't have to do no work, no more'n feed the stock and do de li'l work round de house. When we got through with dat we had de rest of de day to run round wherever we wanted to go. 'Course we had to get permission from de marsa. . . .

"[After the war] I married Kizi Drumgoole. Reverend W. C. Northcross perform de ceremony. Dere weren't nobody dere but de witness and me and Kizi. I had three sons, but all of 'em is dead 'ceptin' one and dat's Hugh. He got seven chillens."

The physical comfort of slaves on large plantations was better than on small ones. Every slaveholder was interested in making money and understood that profits depended in part on maintaining a healthy, contented, well-nourished labor force. But only large plantations could provide medical services, weather-tight cabins, and the varied diet needed to maximize the efficiency of slave workers.

The one out of four slaves living on farms or small plantations no doubt had closer contact with the white owner and his family. They often ate at the same table with the master and sometimes even slept in the same cabin. But slaves who lived in such close quarters with their owners were constantly subject to white scrutiny, always made aware of their inferior social status, and had less opportunity to meet other blacks. In addition, small farmers were more likely to run into financial problems and be forced to sell their slaves. Blacks then faced the grim prospect that their families would be broken up. An earlier generation of historians assumed that slaves benefited from the close association with whites that was possible on the smaller farm. But this conclusion ignores the cultural and physical poverty of small-plantation life and assumes the superiority of white to black culture.

Library of Congress

On large plantations, slaves were supervised by overseers like the man on horseback above. These men, pressured by owners to make a profit, often worked the field hands hard. As a result, they were hated and feared by the slaves.

Slave Culture. We now know that slavery did not prevent the development of a black American culture. This culture achieved a remarkable flowering in music and oral literature, particularly. Slaves sang about God and salvation, about their work, about love and passion, and about their daily lives. They composed humorous songs, bitter songs, and even rebellious songs that explicitly called for freedom. They also composed entertaining stories and poems. Talented black storytellers drew on the West African tradition of oral history, fable, and legend, combined it with Bible stories, and filled their tales with the animals and people of the southern environment. The stories, like the songs, often expressed the slaves' true feelings about their condition. One of the best-known group of tales featured Brer Rabbit, who manages to outwit stronger animals with his resourcefulness and trickery.

Music and oral literature comforted the slaves and helped them create a group identity. Religion played much the same role. West Africans accepted a supreme God, though they did not think of him as a jealous, exclusive deity. This belief enabled transplanted slaves to accept the Christian faith of their European masters. Blacks found the enthusiastic Protestantism of the Baptists and Methodists especially congenial, though they never fully accepted the Protestant emphasis on guilt.

Observers of the Old South never failed to comment on the deep religious commitments of black men and women and often noted that their piety put their "betters" to shame. Southern whites generally welcomed these religious feelings, and many planters employed white ministers to preach to their slaves, who seized the chance to attend religious services on the plantation. In the

Lightfoot Collection

A central component of slave culture was music. This slave boy's improvised "fiddle" suggests how strong the musical impulse was and how ingeniously some slaves were able to satisfy it.

towns they often went to white churches, though they had to sit in separate places in the back or in the gallery. But blacks preferred religious autonomy. Throughout the antebellum period black preachers, many of them self-taught and unordained, ministered to the needs of blacks, sometimes in secret. During slave days, as in more recent years, black clergymen frequently also served as the social and political leaders of their people.

Masters hoped that blacks would learn from Christianity the message of submission, obedience, sobriety, and what nineteenth-century white Americans considered seemly behavior. Black Christianity actually had very different consequences. Like black music and literature, it helped preserve a sense of black independence. Blacks took pride in their piety, which seemed to them more sincere and heartfelt than that of whites. They also found in their version of Christianity a message of hope and freedom. The popularity of spirituals like "Go Down Moses" suggests how closely the slaves identified with the Children of Israel and how eagerly they awaited liberation from bondage. Perceptive whites understood the subversive quality of black Christianity, and during times of slave unrest slaveowners often forbade religious meetings on the plantation.

Slavery as a Coercive System. Some masters accommodated the religious needs of their slaves and provided them with medical attention, decent food, and adequate housing. They also generally preferred to control behavior and encourage effort by rewards rather than punishments. Slaves were given time off to cultivate garden patches, to visit friends and relatives, and to hold parties. One of the most effective ways to guarantee obedience and hard work was to allow a slave to learn a craft or trade and so achieve the freedom of movement that came with "hiring out." In some cases owners conferred the ultimate privilege on skilled slaves: the right to buy their own freedom with the proceeds of their labor.

But slavery, however lenient in some places and times, remained a system grounded on coercion. Slaves were punished by having privileges withdrawn or extra work piled on. They were flogged for stealing, for disobeying orders, for running away, for fighting and drinking. Young males—the most rebellious members of any population—were more likely to be lashed than other slaves, but no group was exempt from physical punishment. At times slaves were whipped without apparent cause. Mary Boykin Chesnut, wife of a South Carolina planter-politician, admitted that "men and women are punished when their masters and mistresses are brutes, not when they do wrong." Even slaves who were not themselves physically chastised were deeply affected by it; to witness grown men or women being flogged was an intimidating experience that drove home the lesson that the white owner was indisputable master.

Slavery and the Family. One of the most affecting parts of Harriet Beecher Stowe's best-selling antislavery novel, *Uncle Tom's Cabin* (1852), is the account of how Arthur Shelby, a kindly Kentucky master, is forced to sell the little slave boy Harry to a crude and brutal slavetrader in order to pay his debts. Harry's mother, Eliza, flees with him before the sale and—in a scene that became one of the most famous in all sentimental literature—mother and child escape to free territory across the ice-choked Ohio River. *American Slavery as It Is*, an important abolitionist tract, not only depicted the physical abuse of slaves in nauseating detail but also denounced slavery's disregard of black family life, its encouragement of moral laxity, and the opportunity it afforded for the sexual exploitation of black women.

The Historic New Orleans Collection

John Antrobus, Plantation Burial *(c. 1860). Slaves preferred to bury their dead at night, and they took the opportunity to socialize as well as to mourn and pray. The presence of the master and mistress at the lower right increases the romantic feeling of the painting.*

Everything recorded in the antislavery tracts took place. Slave families were indeed broken up by sale; the experience of Eliza and Harry was not unique. Though no one really knows how often wives were separated from husbands and children from parents, the threat of separation was always a powerful weapon of social discipline. Slavery was at war with black family life in other ways. Nowhere in the Old South did the law recognize the sanctity of slave marriages; to have done so would have limited the power of slaveholders to dispose of slaves as they wished. On the other hand, the picture is not totally bleak. Masters often found it advantageous to encourage strong marriage ties among their slaves because they reduced rivalries and made for a more efficient work force. Generally speaking, slaves themselves preferred the married to the single state. But whether the initiative came from the master or from the slaves themselves, the result was a surprisingly large number of strong, loving, and permanent slave unions and stable slave families.

One of the most lurid charges leveled by abolitionists against the slave system is that it al-lowed white men to exploit black women sexually. There is truth to this accusation. Some slaveowners and white overseers had virtual harems. Less sensational, but more telling, the 1860 census records that 10 percent of the slave population had partly white ancestry. We must assume, given the disparity in power between white men and slave women, that the relationships that produced racially mixed offspring were frequently imposed on black women. Yet as Professor Eugene Genovese remarks: "Many white men who began by taking a black girl in an act of sexual exploitation ended by loving her and the children she bore. They were not supposed to, but they did. . . ."

Miscegenation—mating across racial lines—was rare on the well-run plantation, though less unusual in cities and towns. Wherever it took place, it was considered scandalous. Harmful to slave discipline and deeply resented by both slave men and women, it was also condemned by white society, which held that all sexual relations outside marriage were deplorable. Slave families, whose solidarity was formidable considering the

The Old South   315

Library of Congress

Historians long believed that slavery left blacks with little sense of family. But plantation slaves usually lived with their families and had strong ties to them. Here, three generations pose for a family portrait.

trying conditions, were disrupted by the practice. White women, particularly, considered it a threat to their families, which explains why southern white women were often hostile to slavery. But miscegenation did take place, and it must be considered another count in the indictment of slavery.

The "Bottom Line" of Slavery. The most recent data on slavery seem to refute the grimmest assertions of its critics. Physical cruelty was not the universal experience of the average slave. The slave family survived. Slaves were able to express themselves in music, religion, and literature. Within the slave system there was some opportunity for the enterprising and the able to improve their economic well-being. Nevertheless, slaves were not the "happy darkies" of myth.

The most obvious evil of slavery was its denial of individual freedom. Ultimately, the slaves' lives were not their own. Slaves were not free to move. They could not withhold their labor or benefit from it directly. They could not express their personalities fully. The peculiar institution also directly repudiated those sacred rights of life, liberty, and the pursuit of happiness that all Americans professed to cherish. Slaves knew of white America's professions, and the disparity between principles and performance undoubtedly made the pain of bondage all the greater.

And there was much else. Slavery provided no effective remedy for cruelty. There were laws against sadistic torture and mutilation of slaves; but the laws could not be easily enforced because the slave was a legal nullity who could not testify

against whites in court. Masters might prefer to preserve slave families; but since nothing required them to do so, they did not when keeping families intact conflicted with their pressing financial interests. Slavery also denied black people the full use of their abilities. Opportunities to become drivers or to acquire some skill were no substitute for the ability to reach the highest levels of business or the professions. In addition, it was illegal to teach slaves to read and write. Some masters ignored the law and themselves instructed their slaves to read or permitted literate blacks to teach their fellow bondsmen. Yet in 1860 more than nine out of ten slaves could not read, a condition that severely limited their access to many areas of knowledge and experience. When talented slaves like Josiah Henson, Solomon Northup, and Frederick Douglass were free to tell their stories, they utterly condemned the system that denied them their humanity. Slavery, wrote Frederick Douglass in his *Autobiography*, "could and did develop all its malign and shocking characteristics." It was "indecent without shame, cruel without shuddering, and murderous without apprehension or fear of exposure, or punishment."

Finally, slavery reinforced racism. It was a mark of inferiority that affected all black men and women and did not disappear even when black people secured their freedom. Slavery accordingly amplified the original racial antipathies of white Americans and made black skin a stigma strong enough to survive even the destruction of the peculiar institution itself.

THE SOUTHERN MIND

Perhaps the most beguiling myth about the Old South is that it was a genial, cultivated society. There is some truth in the picture. Among the planters there were kindly and charming ladies and gentlemen who read the classics, appreciated music, and kept in touch with the best thought of England and Europe. Samuel Walker, a Louisiana sugar planter, was an avid reader of Charles Lamb and Jeremy Taylor and named his plantation Elia, the pen name of his favorite English essayist. Walker had literary talent and devoted his time to writing a novel. He valued education and sent his children to good schools rather than rely, like many of his neighbors, on tutors. The region also had many literate, upright yeomen whose natural dignity, independence, and generous hospitality would have warmed the heart of Jefferson. Nor were all southern whites hostile to change. The

South, for example, joined the crusade against demon rum and against mistreatment of convicted felons. It was even a little ahead of the North in showing concern for the insane. During the 1820–50 period, moreover, many southern states adopted the principle of universal white-male suffrage. Yet by 1860 the white South had also become a land of fear and suspicion where dissent seemed treason and those who denied the region's superiority over all other societies were cruelly ostracized or brutally driven out. In such an atmosphere culture languished or became the servant of self-defense, and all chance of reform ended.

Slave Revolts. The South's fears were directly related to slavery. Although most southerners refused to acknowledge that slavery was a cruel and exploitative system, many recognized that the slaves resented their bondage and would end it if they could. Slaves revealed their hatred of the system by the day-to-day resistance of ignoring directions, engaging in slowdowns, and running away. Occasionally a male slave would attack his master or overseer.

The most feared of all forms of slave resistance was the slave revolt, and several of these took place in the South. Early in the nineteenth century a slave named Gabriel Prosser was foiled in his attempt to capture the city of Richmond. A decade later 500 slaves began a march on New Orleans and had to be dispersed by troops. In 1822 Denmark Vesey, a free black from Charleston, organized a slave insurrection that was betrayed by a fellow slave. Vesey and thirty-four other blacks were hanged. Most frightening of all, however, was the Nat Turner uprising in the Virginia tidewater in 1831. Turner, a slave foreman and preacher inspired by the Bible, decided to strike a blow for freedom. On August 27, aided by a few other slaves, Turner killed his master and his family. Then, with seventy fellow bondsmen gathered along the way, he marched through the countryside, killing and burning. Before the rebellion was put down by state and federal troops, sixty whites had lost their lives. Most of Turner's party were either captured or killed in skirmishes with the soldiers during the first forty-eight hours, and thirteen slaves and three free blacks were later hanged. It took an additional two months to capture the resourceful Turner, who then was tried, convicted, and executed.

Though slave revolts were far less common in the American South than in other New World slave societies, they revealed the true feelings of blacks in a particularly dramatic way and sent a chill through the hearts of white southerners. There were times when southerners seemed positively obsessed with the fear of a "servile insurrection" that might result in the mass destruction of white lives and property. This nervousness fed on itself; for each instance of actual slave unrest in the antebellum South, there were a hundred rumors of slave plots.

Quieting the Opposition. At times southern fears led to honest soul-searching. Soon after the suppression of Nat Turner's insurrection, when slavery had not yet become sacred and untouchable, the Virginia legislature conducted a frank debate on the possible abolition of slavery in the state. Some representatives, primarily from the state's western, nonslaveholding districts, attacked the

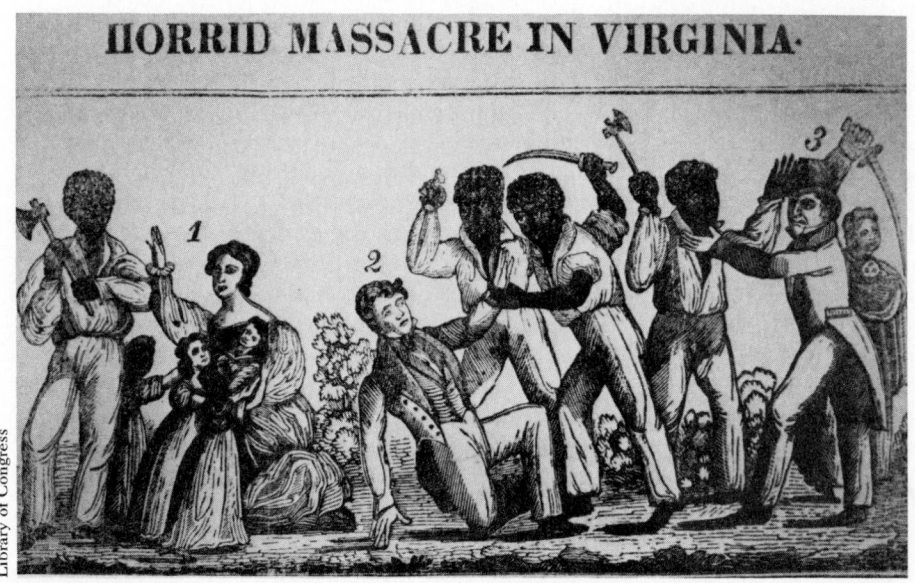

HORRID MASSACRE IN VIRGINIA·

Library of Congress

This 1831 woodcut was inspired by Turner's rebellion. The uprising alarmed white southerners because it was directed against slavery itself, not against a particularly brutal master. That meant that even the gentlest, fairest slaveholder might be murdered in his bed one night.

peculiar institution as "offensive to the moral feelings of a large portion of the community," "ruinous to the whites," degrading to labor, and a danger to the social order of the South. In the end, unfortunately, the debate led nowhere; slavery in Virginia, as elsewhere, was by now so intertwined with the culture and economy of the community that abolition seemed a cure worse than the disease.

This 1832 debate was the last serious public discussion of abolition in the South. Thereafter the response to slave unrest was repression. Laws requiring slaves to carry passes when they were away from their masters were more carefully enforced, especially following slave troubles or rumors of troubles. The patrol system, requiring groups of men to travel about checking on slaves off the plantation, was tightened. After 1832, in scores of southern communities innocent slaves were jailed or even executed in panicky reaction to anticipated slave uprisings.

These fears cast a pall over the political and intellectual life of the South. Many southerners became convinced that the restlessness of the slaves was the work of outside agitators: free blacks, black merchant seamen, and—above all—northern abolitionists. To deal with the problem southern legislatures passed laws that made manumission—the freeing of slaves by their owners—increasingly difficult and restricted the rights and movements of free blacks. Several states even sought to expel free blacks from their limits. In Maryland and Missouri the state legislatures appropriated sums for the purpose of returning ("colonizing") free blacks to Africa. South Carolina tried to prevent slaves from being "contaminated" by black merchant seamen working for northern and foreign firms by forbidding black sailors to set foot on state soil.

The fiercest southern response was reserved for the abolitionists. Of all the outside groups that endangered the peace and safety of the South, they seemed the worst. Governor John Floyd of Virginia accused the abolitionists of fomenting the Nat Turner revolt and labeled them "unrestrained fanatics." To other southerners they were "a pestilent sect," "ignorant and infatuated barbarians." Even though they were federal employees, postmasters throughout the South refused to deliver abolitionist newspapers and books. When antislavery activists denounced this as censorship of the mails, Postmaster General Amos Kendall, a Kentuckian by adoption, refused to intervene. "We owe an obligation to the laws," he conceded, but "we owe a higher one to the communities in which we live."

Censorship of the mails was the mildest of the South's efforts to preserve its system by cutting off the free exchange of ideas. After the Virginia debate of 1832 the subject of abolition was considered closed. Almost everywhere in the slave states toleration for social and intellectual dissent weakened. White southerners who refused to go along with the majority view, like James G. Birney of Alabama, Angelina and Sarah Grimké of South Carolina, and Cassius M. Clay of Kentucky, were denounced, threatened, and eventually driven from the South. Southern leaders sought to suppress abolitionist agitation elsewhere as well. In 1836, as we have seen, the southern delegation in Congress, annoyed at the barrage of petitions asking for abolition of slavery in the District of Columbia, induced the House of Representatives to adopt a rule automatically laying such petitions "on the table" without action. This "gag rule" remained in force for eight years despite attacks by antislavery advocates and civil liberties champions, who assailed it as a denial of free speech and a violation of the constitutional right of petition.

Arguments in Favor of Slavery. The South also mounted a counterattack on its critics that produced some interesting—and generally deplorable—results. In the eighteenth century southerners seldom defended slavery in the abstract. Though they were quick to defend the agricultural interests that depended on it, they often conceded that, ideally speaking, slavery was a violation of human rights. Its ultimate justification was necessity: the South could not survive without black laborers, and since it was unthinkable that blacks could be anything but social and economic subordinates, they must remain slaves. Still, however unavoidable, slavery seemed clearly wrong to most thinking southerners.

After about 1800, however, southern leaders and publicists ceased to question the institution of slavery; indeed, they began to defend it. Slavery, they said, was sanctioned by the Bible and the Christian faith. In the Old Testament God made Ham, the second son of Noah, a servant of his two brothers. Ham's descendants, the dark races, must therefore serve the light-skinned progeny of Shem and Japheth. The New Testament supported the peculiar institution by enjoining "servants" to be obedient and dutiful to their masters. It is difficult to tell how seriously white southerners took the biblical defense of slavery. It was possible to extract other meanings from the Bible, as both black and northern abolitionists had reason to know. For those already disposed to defend the peculiar institution on more practical grounds, it was nevertheless comforting to have the Lord's reinforcement.

In the thirty years before the Civil War, apologists for slavery also constructed a "scientific" defense. Blacks, they maintained, were biologically inferior to whites. They had smaller cranial capacities and a more limited intelligence. They were also closer to "brute creation" than the more intellectual and spiritual white race, as evidenced by the supposedly greater physical endurance and sexual prowess of Africans.

The most sophisticated proslavery argument, however, was sociological. In the writings of the brilliant but bigoted Virginian George Fitzhugh, slavery was converted from a necessary evil to a "positive good." Fitzhugh considered the North's vaunted freedom a failure. It had not brought comfort and security to the white masses: it had brought them slums, social dislocations, and grinding "wage slavery." By rejecting egalitarianism and individualism and accepting the idea of social hierarchy, the South had avoided the cruelty of a competitive society. Slaves, unlike free white laborers, were not tossed on the human rubbish heap after they had ceased being useful to their employers. The South, moreover, was free of such taints as Mormonism, Perfectionism, Fourierism, trade unionism, and other disgusting and deplorable consequences of freedom. "In the whole South," Fitzhugh asserted, "there is not one Socialist, not one man rich or poor, proposing to subvert and reconstruct society."

Fitzhugh's attack on northern society and its democracy quickly became a commonplace of southern opinion. It was repeated by Calhoun on the floor of the Senate. It filled the pages of newspapers, books, and pamphlets, and was heard from pulpits throughout Dixie. Senator James Hammond of South Carolina gave it classic form in his famous speech of 1858, in which he declared that there had to be a "mud sill" upon which to erect a civilized, cultured life. This mud sill was a class "to do the menial duties, to perform the drudgery of life . . . a class requiring but a low order of intellect and but little skill." Far better, said Hammond, that these people be black, as in the South, than white, as in the North.

Romance and Culture. The need to justify the South's way of life profoundly affected southern culture and social values. Influenced by the novels of Sir Walter Scott, literate southerners came to equate their society with medieval and early modern Europe. Southerners of the best sort, they asserted, were true gentlemen whose forebears

were the cavaliers who fled England after the defeat of Charles I by Cromwell. They were, claimed one Alabaman, "directly descended from the Norman Barons of William the Conqueror, a race distinguished . . . for its warlike and fearless character, a race at all times . . . renowned for its gallantry, chivalry, honor, gentleness and intellect. . . ." Northerners, by contrast, were descended from Cromwell's Puritan Roundheads, people without breeding or gentility who, to top it all, exhibited the "severe traits of religious fanaticism."

This fantasy permeated upper-class southern life. Plantations became feudal manors, planters became chivalrous knights, slaves became respectful serfs. Southerners came to idealize the warrior virtues. They esteemed horsemanship and adopted fox hunting as a plantation sport. They held tournaments where young gallants jousted for prizes while lovely belles showered them with roses from the sidelines. In time only a military career could compete with planting as a proper calling for a gentleman.

Upper-class southern women were an essential part of the cult of chivalry. Southern "ladies" were placed on pedestals and treated with elaborate gallantry and outward deference. The reality of the southern white woman's life was often quite different, however. Most were not plantation mistresses, but the wives and daughters of common farmers. There was little pampering or chivalry in the lives of these women. And even the mistress of a great plantation often worked hard. Managing a large household and many house slaves was a complex and demanding job full of emotional conflict. The house slaves were often "part of the family" and the tension between women's familial feelings for their servants and their need to exploit them for their own comfort was often evident in the diaries of southern ladies. Meanwhile, the myth of female helplessness and need for protection limited the freedom and autonomy of southern women even more than "women's sphere" restricted their contemporary northern sisters.

It is not surprising that the forces that encouraged the flowering of this social mythology tended to stifle artistic growth in the antebellum period. William Gilmore Simms and Edgar Allan Poe aside, few southern writers rose above mediocrity. After Jefferson's death in 1826 there were few creative southern architects. All the important American painters of the antebellum years either were northerners or lived in the North or Europe. Although many popular songs—like Stephen Foster's "Swanee River," "My Old Kentucky Home," "Old Black Joe," and "De Camptown Races"—

An Historical Portrait William Gilmore Simms

It is ironic that William Gilmore Simms failed to gain from Charleston, South Carolina, his beloved birthplace, the appreciation and recognition that his achievements deserved. In the years between 1833 and the outbreak of the Civil War, Simms published more than thirty works of fiction. Most of these dealt with the South's heroic exploits during the colonial period or the nobility of the settlers on the frontier of the lower South. They helped create the mythology by which the Old South explained itself to the world. And yet, though honored elsewhere and by posterity, during his lifetime he never won the approval he wanted from his hometown.

William Gilmore Simms was born in April 1806. Two years later his father, a Scotch-Irish immigrant, depressed by his wife's death and humiliated by his recent bankruptcy, left little William in the care of his maternal grandmother and went off to rebuild his life. Mrs. Gates, a "proper" Charlestonian, brought William up, sending him first to public schools and then, at the age of ten, to the College of Charleston.

His schools, however, were not as important as other forces in molding his literary imagination. Grandmother Gates captivated him with tales of his family's adventurous and courageous past. His great-great-grandfather had battled the British invaders of Charleston during the Revolutionary War, and his great-grandfather, fighting alongside Francis Marion, the "Swamp Fox," had helped liberate the city. A superstitious woman, his grandmother also had a store of shocking and supernatural stories, which William avidly listened to. Meanwhile, his father, in remaking his fortune on the frontier, had become a friend of Andrew Jackson and fought with him in the Creek War and at the battles of Tallahatchie and New Orleans. He wrote long letters to his son recounting his hairbreadth adventures in the borderlands and his exciting wartime experiences. The port of Charleston

was a third source of material for Simms's writing. After school, William sat on the docks, enthralled by visiting sailors' accounts of escapades in faraway places. When he was somewhat older he took advantage of Charleston's cultural and intellectual life, attending performances at the Broad Street Theater and joining the discussions at the Charleston Library Society.

In his early teens his grandmother apprenticed him to a druggist, hoping it would eventually lead to a career in medicine. Simms found pharmacology boring, however, and compensated himself for the dull work by reading all night. He soon abandoned medical studies and went to serve an apprenticeship with an attorney who also loved literature. By this time, his father had become a plantation owner in Georgeville, Mississippi. He invited his son to visit, in hope that he would come to live with him permanently. William traveled through the backroads and backwoods of the frontier, enjoying the time spent with his father and using his experiences as material for his Border Romances. But in the end he decided to return to Charleston, possibly because he had fallen in love with Anna Malcolm Giles, a local belle. His father advised him that he would be able to do more with his life if he stayed in Mississippi, that without connections and wealth he would never make a mark in Charleston. "I know it," he told his son, "only as a place of tombs." In later years Simms bitterly regretted this choice, feeling it had done him "irretrievable injury." "All that I have," he wrote, "has been poured to waste in Charleston, which has never smiled on any of my labors, which has steadily ignored my claims, which has disparaged me to the last. . . ." The entire South, and particularly his city, recognized only narrow avenues of success and were indifferent or hostile to those whose talents lay off the beaten track.

When he was nineteen and still studying law, Simms's first published poem appeared, a work

commemorating the death of Charleston native Charles Cotesworth Pinckney, soldier, Federalist leader, and diplomat. In 1825 also, Simms brought out his first volume of poetry and worked as editor of the *Album,* a short-lived literary and political magazine. The next year, having completed his law studies, he married Anna, the daughter of a city clerk. It was thought to be a love match, for many felt that Simms might have improved his standing in the community by choosing a girl from a "better" family.

He could not practice law until he was twenty-one. While he waited for admission to the bar, he continued to write poetry, publishing two more volumes, which were reviewed admiringly by critics and readers. His literary progress convinced him that he might make a career out of writing rather than law. Although he passed the bar in 1827 and practiced law successfully for a while, Simms was truly seduced by *belles lettres.* In 1830 he invested what was left of his maternal inheritance in the *Charleston City Gazette,* a daily newspaper, which he conceived of as a forum for the free exchange of important ideas.

The position he took in the nullification controversy bankrupted his paper and temporarily ruined him. He loved his nation as well as his state, and hoped that they could resolve their difficulties without resorting to extreme measures. Although he believed that the federal government was treading on the constitutional rights of South Carolina, he thought that the state's loyalty to the Union should triumph over its disagreements. "There are some . . . ," he declared, "who would destroy the body, to preserve a member—we are not of the class." He was viciously attacked by prominent politicians throughout the state. The mayor of Charleston suggested that he "confine himself to witticisms, poetry (good luck!) and literature for ladies (girls?). . . ." Eventually Simms lost most of his subscribers and all of his money. In 1832 he was forced to sell the *Gazette* at a loss.

The sale of his journal was not the only tragedy that befell Simms that year. Anna died, leaving him with a young daughter. By this time his father and grandmother had died as well. He had no desire to return to law, and with the Nullifiers in control of Charleston, he decided to go north. There he met the poet and journalist William Cullen Bryant, who introduced him to the New York literary scene. These writers, publishers, and editors were members of "Young America," a group that favored a cultural declaration of independence from Europe and the creation of a distinctive American literature.

In New York Simms published a long poem, "Atalantis," and a maritime adventure; wrote for the *American Quarterly Review;* and worked on his first novel, *Martin Faber,* a Gothic romance about a young frontiersman whose lust for status and money results in murder. Readers liked it, buying all but one of the printed copies. He soon followed with *Guy Rivers,* a "tale of Georgia . . . of a frontier and wild people, and the events [that] . . . may occur among a people & in a region of that character." Critics, who praised it, remarked on the uniqueness of the locale and requested that the author write more about those "untrodden paths" of fiction.

In 1835 Simms published *The Yemassee,* a fictional biography of a colonial governor of South Carolina and an account of the British conquest of the Yemassee Indians. The book also contains the first in a long series of upright, brave, imaginative, and ambitious southern heroes and virtuous, virginal (but physically alluring), intelligent southern women, the future mothers of a "Noble Race." In this book, which is the best known of all Simms's works and still in print, he praised slavery as a necessary and beneficial system and argued that slaves were content with their lot. In the same year he also brought out a romantic history of the Revolution-

ary era called *The Partisan.* The critical and commercial successes of these volumes finally convinced Simms that his destiny was to be a professional writer.

Although he had made many friends and found success in New York, he longed to return to South Carolina. He came back on a visit, which had fortunate consequences for him. In 1836 he met and married Chevillette Roach, whose father owned two plantations near Charleston. One of these was "Woodlands," which stood on property of almost 3,000 acres. Here Simms and his wife lived for nearly twenty-five years during the months from October to May. They spent the summers either in Simms's house in Charleston or in New York or New England. While he lived at Woodlands, Simms spent long mornings in the library writing, afternoons managing the plantation, and the evening hours entertaining guests at dinner. A visitor described Simms's new life: "For a whole morning have I sat in that pleasant library . . . watching . . . the tall, erect figure at the desk, and quick steady passage for hours of the indomitable pen across page after page—a pen that rarely paused to erase, correct, or modify. . . . At dinner he talked a great deal, joked, jested, and punned, . . . or, if a graver theme arose, he would often declaim. . . ."

Now that Simms was a member of the planter class, his sectional sympathies became more pronounced. He wrote a review for the *Southern Literary Messenger* attacking *Society in America* by Harriet Martineau, a British social observer. In Simms's view, Martineau had not only ignored the North's social problems while criticizing slavery, but she had also failed to observe that the southern system was in fact ethically superior. The slaveholder actually bettered the lives of his slaves by improving their morals and intelligence. Someday, Simms promised, when blacks had been elevated to the proper level, they would be freed. Martineau had claimed that since the manufactur-

ing North dominated the country's finances, the South was totally dependent on the North for its economic well-being. Not so, Simms declared. Northern industry could not operate without the South's cotton; therefore, slavery was the financial backbone of the whole nation. This article was acclaimed throughout the South. A version of what came to be called the "King Cotton" argument, it was widely reprinted and became a leading apology for slavery.

Simms, pleased by his success, continued to defend slavery and publicize the South's unique image. He compiled a history and geography of South Carolina. He wrote biographies of representative southern figures. He edited the *Southern Quarterly Review* and established *Simms Magazine.* Between 1844 and 1846 he was a member of the South Carolina legislature, and in the 1850s he actively advocated secession. But he did not give up on fiction. In these years before the Civil War he wrote nine novels, each in its own way glorifying his section and its people.

The era of the Civil War was a tragic one for Simms. The year before the war started, two of his sons died of yellow fever. Then his oldest son and namesake was wounded in battle. In 1863 his wife died at the age of forty-seven, having given birth the year before to her thirteenth child. Simms himself became mentally and physically ill for many weeks. In 1865 General William Sherman's men torched Woodlands and destroyed his art gallery and 10,000-volume library. Two weeks later he was an eyewitness to the burning and pillaging of Columbia, South Carolina, which affected him violently. At the end of the war he wrote to a friend: "Of all that I had . . . I have nothing left. . . ."

Yet he persisted in writing and turned out many poems, articles, and stories, earning money to rebuild his house and support his children. He wrote "Sack and De-

(*continued on p. 322*)

struction of the City of Columbia, S.C.," describing vividly his experiences on "Black Friday," the day the beautiful old town went up in flames. In addition, he composed three more book-length southern romances. A month before his death he delivered the opening speech at the Charleston County Floral Fair.

Simms died on Saturday, June 11, 1870. Charleston appreciated

him more in death than in life. The bells of St. Michael's tolled in his honor, and all sectors of the Charleston community sent condolences to his family. The *Charleston Courier* printed an appreciative editorial on Monday, the day of his funeral, when throngs of mourners came in a driving rain to pay their respects. But his best tribute had been written a decade earlier in

DeBow's Review of New Orleans: Simms, this article declared, "reflects . . . the spirit and temper of Southern civilization; announces its opinions, illustrates its ideas, embodies its passions and prejudices, and betrays those delicate shades of thought, feelings, and conduct, that go to form the character and stamp the individuality of a people. . . .''

---

had southern themes, the composers, including Foster himself, were mostly northerners. Even the minstrel show, which fused theater, comedy, and music into a unique form of entertainment, was basically a northern white commercialization of southern black folk culture and owed little to the white South.

Southern defensiveness also affected intellectual life. On the whole, the colleges and universities of the Old South were not great centers of learning, though for a while, in the 1830s, the best university in the country was Jefferson's University of Virginia, and South Carolina College had the most distinguished social science faculty. Nevertheless, many young southerners went to Harvard, Yale, or Princeton. By the 1850s the growing fear of dissent had brought hundreds of

Plantation houses like the Hermitage stand as monuments to the South's image of its culture. Here, civilization and wealth mingle harmoniously; riches are displayed with quiet good taste. The estate's leisured openness suggests unhurried cultivation of moral and intellectual sensibilities.

Georgia Historical Society

southern students back home. The increasing restrictions on free inquiry meanwhile drove such interesting social thinkers as Francis Lieber of South Carolina College and Henry Harrisse of the University of North Carolina to move north. Harrisse, before his departure, trenchantly attacked the intellectual intolerance he saw all around him.

> You may eliminate all the suspicious men from your institutions of learning, you may establish any number of new colleges which will relieve you of sending your sons to free institutions. But as long as people study, and read, and think among you, the absurdity of your system will be discovered and there will always be found some courageous intelligence to protest against your hateful tyranny.

By contrast with the fertile, innovative contemporary North, the South, then, was a cultural backwater. It was a region turned inward and intent on building up a false self-image and a false self-confidence.

Southern Ideology. Although it may not be enough to fuel a creative revolution, defensiveness has its uses. Southerners were able to detect the flaws in the individualistic, liberal capitalism that had appeared in the North and raise questions about democracy's political values. Like so much else in the Old South, this conservative critique was a defense mechanism, but it raised some valid and interesting questions.

The southern critique of northern political ideology was primarily an attack on majoritarian democracy. Although most southern states had established universal white-male suffrage, some of the most articulate southerners continued to doubt the wisdom of majorities. Pure and simple majority rule was obviously a disadvantage to the South. If mere numbers were considered in making political decisions, the South would have been consigned to certain defeat. Well before 1860 it had fallen behind the North in population and hence in congressional representation. Until the 1850s a sectional parity had been maintained in the United States Senate by admitting into the Union one slave state for each free one. But almost certainly more free than slave states would eventually be carved out of the western territories; and when this took place, the South would lose its fragile political equality with the North.

Southerners worried about their section's decline and sought to discover its causes. A number—including J. D. B. De Bow, William Gregg, and Edmund Ruffin—concluded that the cause was slow economic growth owing to the South's vassalage to the North. During the late 1820s and early 1830s southerners blamed the tariff for their dependent status. But after the mid-1830s, when southern political victory had removed the tariff from center stage, the attack shifted to the North's commercial dominance. Virtually every aspect of the South's economy except the raising of crops, the apostles of commercial independence claimed, was dominated by northern businessmen. Much of the South's shipping was done in northern vessels. Almost all imports came through New York, and until the 1850s even the cotton crop generally went to New York before being shipped to Europe. Northern capitalists and their agents also controlled most of the South's banking. Northern cotton "factors" (agents) residing in the South dominated agriculture, extending credit to planters and farmers, sending crops to market, and buying supplies their customers wanted. They were useful to the southern economy, but the price they exacted for their services, southerners insisted, was excessive.

The picture of northern dominance painted by the critics was exaggerated. Not all the South's business was handled by outsiders; the section produced a substantial crop of home-grown merchants, bankers, and manufacturers who often combined town business with plantation ownership. Yet most southerners assumed northern dominance, chafed under it, and periodically determined to end it. Gregg, a successful textile magnate, constantly urged his fellow southerners to invest their capital in manufactures to make their section independent of the North and Europe. The publicist and editor De Bow used his *Review* to call for southern economic independence. "Action, Action, Action!!!" the *Review* demanded. "Not in the rhetoric of Congress, but in the busy hum of mechanism, and the thrifty operators of the hammers and anvil." Ruffin condemned southern farming practices and advocated improved agricultural methods to stem the flow of yeomen from the South and to help equalize free- and slave-state populations.

Beginning in 1837, southern merchants and publicists convened in various cities to consider ways to liberate their section from its supposed economic bondage to the North. These conventions proclaimed the need for the South to do its own importing and exporting as well as its own banking. Delegates discussed at great length how to end "the abject state of colonial vassalage" to the North by such devices as direct shipping of cotton to Europe from southern ports. The conventions achieved few concrete results, but they were effective forums for the display of antinorthern feelings. Toward the end of the 1850s, when sectional antagonisms reached their peak, the conventions went on record against northern books, magazines, and teachers and passed resolutions demanding the reopening of the transatlantic slave trade, which had been closed since 1808.

The growing imbalance of population and total wealth between the two sections of the country

Prized, pampered, and put on a pedestal—the southern belle. Whatever she was in fact, the southern woman (here, Sarah Knox Taylor, daughter of president Zachary Taylor and first wife of Jefferson Davis) was mythologized as the incarnation of the aristocratic virtues of plantation life.

Louisiana State Museum

was an unpleasant fact of life that southerners had to face. Perhaps manufactures, improved agriculture, and direct trade with Europe could stem the relative decline and even reverse it. But what if they could not? How could the South remain a part of the Union and, as the weaker partner, defend its unique and controversial interests?

This problem obsessed John C. Calhoun in his later years. During the tariff crisis of 1831–32 Calhoun had resurrected the theory of nullification first raised in the 1790s as part of the Kentucky Resolution. But nullification seemed more and more inadequate. Between the 1830s and his death in 1850, the South Carolinian sought a new formula to protect his section's minority interests. In a succession of treatises, speeches, and letters, Calhoun's solution slowly evolved into a critique of the democratic concepts of the age. People were not all equal, he declared. The Declaration of Independence expressed a noble theory, but an invalid one. The best societies, like those of classical Greece and Rome, recognized the inherent inequality of human beings and exploited the inferior groups to construct great civilizations. If people were unequal, it stood to reason that some should lead and others follow, otherwise the inferior many would impose their will on the superior few and the result would be a tyranny of the ignorant. In the United States a despotism of numbers would result in sectional oppression: the North with its greater population would trample on the rights of the South.

How could those rights be protected? A "concurrent majority" was Calhoun's solution. Before any law that vitally concerned the interests of either section went into effect, let it be ratified by both sections of the country. This arrangement could be guaranteed by a dual presidency, with one president selected by the North and the other by the South. Both would have to approve any important measure passed by Congress before it became law. In this way the South could exercise a veto over a domineering North and check the normal tendency of a majority to ride roughshod over the rights of a minority.

John C. Calhoun died before the inner logic of his theories was expressed in deeds. He had not wished to see the Union destroyed; he hoped to preserve it by finding an accommodation that the South could live with. It is fitting, however, that when the people of Charleston received news of South Carolina's secession from the Union in 1860, they unfurled a banner bearing Calhoun's image.

CONCLUSIONS

The Old South was neither a hell nor a paradise. Though upper-class southerners sought to create a fantasy land of modern chivalry, moonlight, and magnolias, they were at best only partially successful. The Old South was ruled by a planter elite, but only with the consent of a substantial yeomanry and through the mechanism of universal white-male suffrage. Under the veneer of gracious plantation life, moreover, was the firm reality of profits and the managerial skill that helped create them. And insofar as the romantic myth succeeded in convincing southerners, it served to stifle artistic creativity and enslave southern women even more thoroughly than their northern sisters.

On the other hand, the Old South was not solely the land of "the whip and the lash" depicted by its enemies. Slavery was coercive by its very nature and represented a tragic waste of human potential. It was designed to bring wealth to the planter class and it did. Yet southern slavery avoided the worst abuses possible in a system of forced labor. Black men and women were able to create some social room for themselves and find joy and pleasure in life and in their families.

In the end slavery became a threat to the entire nation. Southerners eventually concluded that they could not maintain slavery and share the liberal values of the age, and they reacted with a mixture of defensiveness and intolerance that revealed their uneasiness. To the very end the South would continue to be typically American in many of its values and qualities. Yet with each passing year it diverged more and more from the liberal mainstream of the United States. Before long southerners would consider themselves a separate people. The consequences would be tragic.

FOR FURTHER READING

William R. Taylor. *Cavalier and Yankee: The Old South and American National Character* (1961)
> The author examines the myth of the southern Cavalier—a symbol of the agrarian South and the opposite, supposedly, of the money-minded, unchivalrous Yankee. In the popular fiction of the time Taylor finds evidence that the planters' confidence gradually eroded into self-doubt as 1860 approached.

Frederick Law Olmsted. *The Cotton Kingdom: A Traveler's Observations on Cotton and Slavery in the American Slave States* (1861). Edited and introduced by Arthur M. Schlesinger, Sr. (1953)

Inspired by a discussion with William Lloyd Garrison, the planner of New York's Central Park went south in 1853 to write on the slave economy for *The New York Times*. In his colorful report, long a source of information for scholars and historical novelists, Olmsted demonstrates, to his own satisfaction at least, that dependence on slave-grown cotton fostered "lazy poverty" and was a barrier to the South's broad economic progress.

Benjamin A. Botkin, editor. *Lay My Burden Down: A Folk History of Slavery* (1945)
This one-volume oral history was compiled from the Slave Narrative Collection made during the 1930s. Former slaves—75 to 105 years old when interviewed—describe slavery and their feelings about emancipation.

John W. Blassingame. *The Slave Community: Plantation Life in the Ante-Bellum South* (1972)
This is a compact, readable study of Old South slavery as seen from inside the system. The author demonstrates the extent to which slaves were able to create islands of freedom in which to conduct their personal lives.

Robert W. Fogel and Stanley L. Engerman. *Time on the Cross: The Economics of Negro Slavery* (1974)
An econometric study of Old South slavery that has drawn a lot of criticism both for its methods and for its conclusions. Using statistical data, the authors try to show that slavery was profitable and relatively benign. An interesting book, but one that must be read with care.

Herbert Gutman. *The Black Family in Slavery and Freedom, 1750–1925* (1976)
An important study of the evolving black family from the colonial era until well after emancipation. Gutman supports the view that black slave families were strong units.

Eugene Genovese. *Roll Jordan Roll: The World the Slaves Made* (1974)
Makes some of the same points as Gutman and Blassingame. According to Genovese, American slaves did more than merely survive; they formed a "black nation" in the South based on religion and strong family ties. The writer is a leading Marxist scholar.

Clement Eaton. *Freedom of Thought in the Old South* (1940)
This older but still useful work presents a critical view of antebellum southern intellectual life. Eaton traces a progressive retreat from free inquiry and tolerance in the Jeffersonian period to conformity and repression in the years immediately before 1860.

Ulrich B. Phillips. *Life and Labor in the Old South* (1929)
This older book is the nearest thing we have to a scholarly version of the moonlight and magnolias view of the Old South. A Georgian, Phillips loved his native region, and expressed his love well here.

Frank Owsley. *Plain Folk of the Old South* (1949)
The best summation of the Owsley-Vanderbilt school of southern history, which emphasizes the small farmers rather than the slaves and large planters. Written with great affection for its subjects, it is a lively, readable—and short—book.

Ann F. Scott. *The Southern Lady from Pedestal to Politics, 1830–1930* (1970)
A brief survey of that social phenomenon, the southern lady. Written from diaries, letters, and memoirs, Scott's book makes the point that in the Old South white middle-class women were indeed pampered and patronized.

William Styron. *Confessions of Nat Turner* (1967)
Nat Turner, the black preacher who instigated the 1831 Virginia slave uprising, tells his own story in this widely acclaimed historical novel.

14 The Coming of the Civil War

What Caused the Division?

1780   Pennsylvania becomes the first state to prohibit slavery

1787   The Northwest Ordinance prohibits slavery north of the Ohio River and west of Pennsylvania

1812   Louisiana is admitted into the Union as a slave state

1820   The Missouri Compromise

1832–34   The South Carolina nullification crisis

1839   Activist abolitionists found the Liberty party

1846   Congressional debate on the Wilmot Proviso worsens sectional controversy

1848   The California Gold Rush • Formation of the Free-Soil party • Zachary Taylor elected president

1850   The Compromise of 1850, including passage of the Fugitive Slave Act

1852   Harriet Beecher Stowe's *Uncle Tom's Cabin* published • Franklin Pierce elected president

1854   The Kansas-Nebraska Act • The Republican party is formed by antislavery Whigs and Democrats

1856   John Brown murders five proslavery settlers in Kansas • James Buchanan elected president

1857   *Dred Scott* decision • Buchanan accepts Kansas's fraudulent constitution

1858   The Lincoln-Douglas debates focus national attention on the Illinois election for United States Senator

1859   John Brown's raid on Harpers Ferry

1860   The Democratic party breaks up at its national convention • Abraham Lincoln is nominated by the Republican national convention; he is elected president

1860–61   South Carolina, Georgia, Louisiana, Mississippi, Florida, Alabama, and Texas secede from the Union

1861   Delegates of six seceded states adopt a constitution and elect Jefferson Davis president • Lincoln says the federal government will hold its property in the South; Confederates fire on Union-held Fort Sumter • Arkansas, North Carolina, Virginia, and Tennessee secede

The Civil War was the greatest crisis that ever befell the United States—the only one that threatened the very survival of the nation. No sooner had the fighting broken out than thoughtful citizens urgently asked: Why? Why had a union so promising, so prosperous, so self-confident, so triumphant after 1848, come to this terrible pass? Students of American history still ask the question today.

The schism, as we shall see, was directly and immediately related to sectional battles that grew out of the victory over Mexico in 1848. But these confrontations, in turn, were the surface manifestations of the deepest social and intellectual currents of the preceding half century or more.

A HOUSE DIVIDED

On the eve of the Revolution an outspoken Massachusetts citizen would not have felt seriously out of place culturally or intellectually in South Carolina. And southerners visiting the North could speak their minds without shocking or offending their hosts. North and South in, say, 1770 were not very far apart in their economic or labor systems. Agriculture was the chief occupation of all Americans, from Maine to Georgia, by a wide margin. Slavery existed in every colony. There were more slaves in the South, of course, but a considerable part of the work force in such colonies as New York and Pennsylvania consisted of only half-free indentured servants. By 1800 even the religious differences that had separated Puritan New England from the Anglican South receded as both regions felt the effects of declining orthodoxy and growing religious diversity.

Then, in the generation and a half following the War of 1812, differences between North and South grew. As we saw in Chapters 9 and 12, the North began to industrialize and develop into a society marked by cultural diversity. Meanwhile, the South confirmed its stake in plantation agriculture and adopted the social orthodoxy and defensiveness we described in Chapter 13.

Ideological Differences. We must not impute single-mindedness or cultural uniformity to either section. Both North and South were very complex societies with a bewildering variety of dissenters. Only a minority of northerners were abolitionists, transcendentalists, or Perfectionists; many considered such people meddlers or fanatics. And the North was full of "doughfaces"—northern men with southern principles—who supported the southern position in the evolving sectional debates. The South, too, was divided. Southerners like D. B. De Bow and William Gregg urged emulation of the North's success in commerce and manufacturing, while among the small farmers, especially in the upland regions and the backcountry, there were those who despised slavery and the planter class.

Yet despite these persistent intrasectional divisions there gradually emerged two distinct sectional outlooks, which each year grew further apart and more antagonistic. In the South, as we saw in Chapter 13, political and intellectual leaders came to deliberately and effectively glorify an agricultural society based on slavery. They condemned dissent, rejected crass pursuit of profit, and denied the value of change. Although not every southerner accepted this ideology, it became ever more difficult for dissenters to speak out against the overwhelming weight of majority opinion.

The North also developed distinctive guiding beliefs in these years, though they evolved more slowly and never became so universal as the South's. The heart of the emerging northern ethos was freedom. This term meant many things to many people. To northern reformers it meant freedom to initiate social experiments. To northern intellectuals it meant freedom to speculate and criticize. To northern manufacturers it meant freedom from government control—though not exemption from government aid. To northern farmers it meant freedom to take up land in the West. To northern wage earners it meant freedom to move wherever opportunity offered, and to advance in life. At no time in the antebellum North did northern opinion leaders or officials attempt to impose these sentiments on the people. Nevertheless, the whole thrust of northern society created an increasing consensus on "free" values and attitudes.

Economic Conflict. The widening gap between the predominant northern and southern value systems has often been seen as a reflection of fundamentally competing economies: northern commerce and industry versus southern agriculture. There is no question that the differing economic interests of the antebellum North and South pushed them into frequent political battles along a wide-ranging front. We have seen in Chapter 10 how, during Jackson's presidency, the tariff issue provoked the South into fierce opposition and created a dangerous constitutional crisis. During the 1840s southern political leaders, working through the Democratic party, were able continually to lower customs duties on manufactured goods. So great was their success that by the end of the following decade, duties on imports offered almost no protection to northern industry. By the eve of the Civil War, the tariff had once again become a political issue; but this time it was the North that felt rebellious.

The tariff was not the only cause of conflict growing out of economic differences. Northern commercial interests favored federal subsidies to the American merchant marine; southerners saw little benefit to themselves in such measures and opposed paying the required taxes. Northern manufacturers wanted cheap labor for their factories and asked for a bill that would enable them to arrange abroad for foreign workers; southerners, seeing no reason to encourage northern population growth, resisted it. Northern merchants and manufacturers wanted large federal appropriations for dredging rivers and harbors; southerners, believing that they would benefit from these projects less than northern citizens, fought the appropriations.

There were at least two other economic issues that roiled sectional relations during the generation preceding 1861: a Pacific railroad and a

John C. Calhoun in old age, at about the time of the Compromise of 1850. It catches the man's austerity and something of his fierce determination—to defend his beloved South against detractors and enemies.

Library of Congress

homestead act. By the early 1850s most public-spirited Americans, northern and southern, strongly endorsed a railroad to connect the more settled parts of the country with the newly acquired Pacific coast. In both sections, moreover, people generally assumed that building a railroad across hundreds of miles of empty country would require a large federal subsidy. Yet despite this general agreement, the Pacific railroad produced sharp sectional controversy. Southerners wanted to link New Orleans with San Diego, or Memphis with San Francisco. Northerners demanded a route that would connect the Great Lakes at Chicago or Milwaukee with either San Francisco or Puget Sound. The constant bickering produced an impasse. In 1853 Jefferson Davis, secretary of war in the prosouthern administration of Franklin Pierce, arranged to buy the Gadsden Purchase (named after James Gadsden, the American commissioner who negotiated it) from Mexico. This strip of some 30,000 square miles in lower New Mexico and Arizona was the most feasible terrain for a New Orleans-to-San Diego railroad. After the real estate was acquired, however, northern congressmen vetoed the route. Southerners, in turn, were able to frustrate the choice of a central or northern connection.

The two sections also battled over a homestead bill. Both northerners and southerners were interested in acquiring free farms in the West, and at first the South did not object to homestead legislation. By the end of the 1850s, however, free land for western settlers seemed to promise greater benefits to free agriculture and the free states than to slavery and the South, and southern leaders sharply reversed their stand.

The Role of Slavery. These clashes over economic policies, though at times bitter, are not sufficient to explain the Civil War, however. At least half the battling was between competing groups of businessmen—as in the case of a Pacific railroad—rather than between southern planters and northern industrialists. Such conflict did not touch the fundamental economic interests of either northern or southern society and could have been reconciled. Furthermore, sectional conflicts over economic policy had existed before 1840 and continued after 1865; yet only in the years immediately preceding 1860 did divisive forces actually threaten the Union. In the nullification crisis of 1832 the whole South was presumably hurt by the Tariff of Abominations, but disunionist sentiment was strong only in South Carolina. A generation later eleven states left the Union when confronted with an apparent threat to the South's "rights."

Clearly, new forces must have intervened to forge a stronger bond among the southern states and create a weaker collective tie to the Union.

Beneath the sectional economic and intellectual differences lay another, more fundamental, factor: slavery. In the final analysis it was slavery that defined the South. A region diverse in climate, crops, and topography, the South's sense of cohesiveness came from its common labor system. Little beyond this shared institution could unite Virginia with Mississippi or Texas with South Carolina. It is true that Missouri, Kentucky, Maryland, and Delaware also had legal slavery and yet did not join the Confederacy. But in each of these "border states" slaves were few, and in the end, it required federal troops to hold them in the Union.

The role of slavery in creating a sense of southern distinctiveness depended largely on the Western world's reaction to the peculiar institution. Had slavery continued to prosper in the British Empire, had Europeans and northerners remained indifferent to its existence, it might not have served to bind together the diverse elements that constituted the southern United States. But as we saw in Chapter 13, foreign and domestic critics attacked slavery so fiercely after 1830 that southern society closed ranks, hardened its attitudes, and turned on its critics with a savage counterattack. It would be unfair to blame the Civil War on the abolitionists, as some apologists for the Old South have done. Nevertheless, their attacks increased sectional tensions and helped reinforce the southern sense of apartness and cohesiveness. Creating further anxiety in the South was the steady erosion of slavery in the border states. If Missouri, Kentucky, Maryland, and Delaware became free, who knew what states would follow?

Slavery also created a moral gulf between the two sections. Slaveholders by 1860 considered the peculiar institution a positive good that made possible what southern defenders perceived as the South's gracious and cultivated life. Northerners increasingly came to see slavery as a *sin*—a breaking of God's law—like intemperance, cruelty to prisoners, and mistreatment of the insane. To abolitionists, at least, it was intolerable for society to let this offense continue.

Before long the moral indignation against slavery had become politicized. In 1839 a group of antislavery leaders organized the Liberty party, dedicated to stopping the "slave power" and turning back the southern political influence that had, they said, made the North a "conquered province." The new party never attracted more than a small minority of northern voters, but it placed on the nation's political agenda the issues that the major parties would eventually be unable to evade.

THE DILEMMA OF TERRITORIAL GROWTH

The country's geographical expansion in the antebellum period aggravated the differences between the sections. If the nation had not been confronted time and again after 1846 with the question of whether new territory should be slave or free, the sections might have been able either to settle their differences or to ignore them. But such was not to be. Ever since Pennsylvania became the first state to declare slavery illegal in 1780, Americans had drawn sharp distinctions between regions where they would permit slavery and those where they would forbid it. State actions during and shortly after the Revolution established the line between slave and free territory among the thirteen original states at the southern boundary of Pennsylvania—the Mason-Dixon line. In the Northwest Ordinance of 1787 the Confederation Congress excluded slavery from the Northwest Territory, the unorganized region of the nation west of Pennsylvania and north of the Ohio River. In the Southwest, Congress agreed, "no regulation made . . . shall tend to emancipate slaves," thereby allowing slavery in that region by default.

As new territory was added to the nation, it became necessary to extend the boundary between slavery and freedom. Slavery already existed in parts of the Louisiana Purchase when the United States bought it, and Congress let it remain. In 1812 the most southerly part of the territory entered the Union as the slave state of Louisiana. Then, in 1819–20, a sharp but brief crisis erupted when another part of the Louisiana Purchase, Missouri, applied for admission to the Union.

In February 1819 Representative James Tallmadge, Jr., of New York proposed that Missouri be admitted only if "involuntary servitude be prohibited." The halls of Congress echoed with angry debate as northerners and southerners, concerned with the balance of congressional power between the sections and whether southerners could bring their slave property wherever they wished, attacked or defended the Tallmadge amendment. Southerners warned that if slavery were excluded from Missouri, the Union would be torn apart. Even the aging Jefferson considered the Tallmadge amendment ominous. The Missouri debate was a "fire bell in the night," he wrote, that warned of grave danger ahead for the Union.

After some months of heated wrangling, calmer voices prevailed. Under the Missouri Compromise of 1820, proposed by Senator Jesse B. Thomas of Illinois, Congress admitted two states—Maine and Missouri—to the Union. The first, carved out of Massachusetts, was admitted as a free state; Missouri came in as a slave state. The compromise further provided that in the rest of the Louisiana Purchase the southern border of Missouri (36° 30' north latitude) would divide future slave from free territory.

The Wilmot Proviso. The whole of the existing United States had now been assigned to one labor system or the other. For fifteen years after the Missouri Compromise, the territorial limits of slavery ceased to trouble Americans. Then, in 1835, Texas revived the issue. Many opponents of annexation feared that Texas would tip the balance between northern and southern power. Eventually, in 1845, Texas was admitted to the Union as a slave state. But Texas was only the beginning. The simmering pot was brought to a boil by the sudden addition to the United States of Oregon and the Mexican Cession regions of California and New Mexico.

No one expected slavery to be transplanted successfully to Oregon. That region of fog, forests, and furs seemed totally unsuited to staple crops and plantations and therefore unlikely to shelter a slave labor system. But what of the California–New Mexico region? Daniel Webster, among others, considered the Far Southwest equally uncongenial to slavery, but not all southerners agreed. In any case, they asked, why should slavery be legally and arbitrarily denied the chance to take root in the region? When, in August 1846, Congressman David Wilmot of Pennsylvania submitted a resolution requiring that slavery be excluded from every part of the territory that might be acquired from Mexico, he set off an explosion that shook the nation. Wilmot's proviso seemed to southerners an outrageously unfair attempt to exclude them from the benefits of the common vic-

The Missouri Compromise, 1820

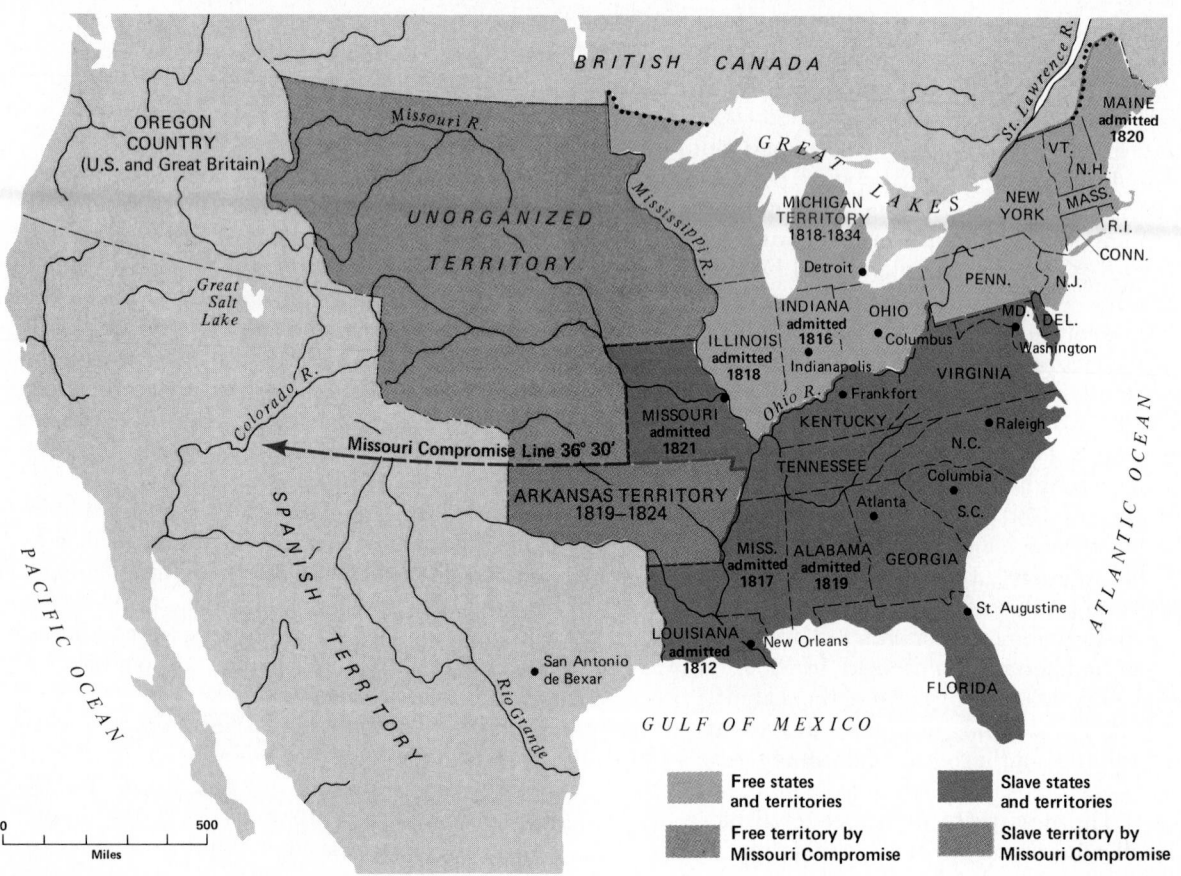

tory over Mexico. Some northerners agreed with the South, but most took a very different view. The more adamant opponents of slavery saw any extension of slavery as a concession to evil. Other northerners perceived it in narrower, but no less negative, terms. "If slavery is not excluded by law" from the national territories, Senator Preston King of New York pointed out, "the presence of the slave will exclude the laboring white man."

For months following the introduction of the Wilmot Proviso, the country remained in a fever of excitement. The aging Calhoun, once a strong Unionist but long since the great champion of southern interests, countered the proviso with resolutions denying that Congress had the power to exclude slavery from the territories. Southerners, though slow to catch fire, were soon denouncing the North. "The tocsin, 'the fire bell at night,' is now sounding in our ears," the Richmond *Enquirer* proclaimed, echoing Jefferson's words. The "madmen of the North and the Northwest have . . . cast the die, and numbered the days of this glorious Union." "Do the wicked men of the North imagine that we will be silent or inactive when enactments are proposed incompatible with our existence as freemen?" Southern strength in the Senate kept the Wilmot Proviso from passing, but this victory did not still the furor. The proviso remained in reserve, ready at any time to arouse sectional rivalries and hostilities.

Free Soil. The Wilmot Proviso inevitably colored the 1848 presidential campaign. Both major parties had free-soil wings that opposed allowing new slave states and territories into the Union and anti–free-soil factions that favored either leaving slavery alone or protecting it in the territories by enacting a federal slave code. At their nominating convention the Whigs papered over the potentially disruptive conflict by choosing "Old Rough and Ready," the hero of Buena Vista—Zachary Taylor—without a platform. The Democrats were less successful in dodging the slavery issue. Polk had pledged to serve only a single term, and was worn down by the cares of office; he refused renomination. In his place the Democrats chose Lewis Cass of Michigan, an aging party warhorse of indolent temperament and woeful countenance who opposed the Wilmot Proviso and favored "popular sovereignty," or "squatter sovereignty," a formula that would allow the residents of an organized territory to decide for themselves whether slavery would be admitted or excluded.

But Cass's nomination did not avert party dissension. By the time the Democratic convention met, northern Democrats were being wrenched in opposing directions, with one group strongly committed to the Wilmot Proviso and free soil and the other opposed to both. The powerful New York Democrats sent two delegations to Baltimore. One was made up of free-soil Barnburners (who vowed to "burn down the barn" if they could not control the party), the other of prosouthern Hunkers (who "hunkered" or "hankered" after office). The indestructible Martin Van Buren was the Barnburner hero. When the convention voted to seat both factions, he and his followers left in a huff.

The rift cast Van Buren in a stronger free-soil role than he deserved. After the Baltimore walkout the Barnburners met again at Utica, where they nominated Van Buren on a separate Barnburner ticket. This move was the beginning of a major realignment of the old national parties on the basis of section.

Free-soilers were generally skeptical of Van Buren but were attracted by his name. A figure of great national prominence might accomplish what an obscure abolitionist like James G. Birney, the Liberty party's candidate in 1840 and 1844, could not: win a large national following. Besides, what were the alternatives? Free-soil ("conscience") Whigs disliked the slaveholder Taylor. Free-soil Democrats were no happier with the straddler Cass. Meeting at Buffalo with the Barnburners, the antislavery rebels of both major parties organized the Free-Soil party. This new party nominated Van Buren and Charles Francis Adams (son of John Quincy Adams) as their candidates on a platform that demanded "free soil, free speech, free labor, and free men." The delegates left Buffalo convinced that the new party would make an impressive showing in the fall and mark the beginning of slavery's downfall.

Unfortunately, the slaves' deliverance would have to wait until another day. Taylor won an electoral as well as a popular majority. Van Buren's meager 300,000 votes came mostly from upstate New York, Massachusetts, the Western Reserve of Ohio, northern Illinois, and southern Wisconsin. These regions were inhabited by people with roots in New England and had been fertile grounds for revivalism in the preceding decades. They were, therefore, unusually susceptible to the antislavery appeal. Still, the election of 1848 was a portent of the future. Despite Van Buren's defeat, the Free-Soilers elected ten members of Congress who would be outspoken antislavery advocates in the bitter debates to come. Moral zeal and politics were beginning to merge in a new way, one that promised an eventual victory for free soil. But that was some time away. In 1848 most northern voters were still not ready for a single-issue, free-soil party.

Gold in California.

Taylor, though a southerner and a slaveholder, proved to be the bulwark of the Union. His strong unionism was a happy accident, for it would be needed in the months ahead. The immediate problem was California. In January 1848 an American working for John Augustus Sutter, a Swiss businessman long settled in the Mexican province, found gold while constructing a watermill channel near Sacramento. Sutter tried to keep the discovery a secret, but the news soon leaked out. In December 1848 President Polk confirmed the lucky strike in his annual message to Congress, setting off a mad rush to the gold fields. By January 1849 over sixty ships packed with gold seekers were on their way to California. In the spring thousands of others set out overland by way of the California Trail established by settlers earlier in the decade. By the summer the talk everywhere—in the newspapers, on the front porches, in the parlors, and around the cast-iron stoves at the general store—was mostly of California and gold. It seemed that the whole country was singing a new version of Stephen Foster's song:

> Oh Susanna, don't you cry for me
> I'm a-gwine to California with a banjo on my knee.

The fate of the 1849 California argonauts was often a harsh one. Hundreds sickened and died aboard ship or along the trail, although most eventually reached the land of gold. There, however, few struck it rich, at least at the gold streams. Some gave up and returned home. Others settled down in the new country and became farmers, laborers, storekeepers, or professionals, often making more money than the miners. By mid-1849 thousands of Americans from every state, section, race, and nationality had made California their home, including several hundred free blacks, who seemed to have survived the trip west better than most.

Taylor immediately grasped the need for some better form of government in California than the existing military regime. He also saw that allowing the turbulent community to pass through a lengthy territorial stage was potentially disruptive, since it would permit the free-soil forces in Congress to raise the issue of the Wilmot Proviso once again. To avoid further bitter debate on slavery in the territories, he urged the Californians to apply directly for entrance as a state, taking the slavery issue out of Congress's hands. In September 1849 a convention met in Monterey, drew up a constitution barring slavery, and sent it with an application for statehood to Washington.

Divisive Issues in Congress.

Taylor's scheme to avoid strife was well meant, but it did not work. The Thirtieth Congress was a deeply divided body in which sectional feeling ran high. The lower house consumed the session's first seventeen days in angry squabbling between southerners and northerners over the choice of a speaker of the House. For sixty-three ballots the representatives remained deadlocked, with congressmen threatening each other and southerners speaking ominously of disunion if they did not get their way. In this charged atmosphere it is not surprising that California's statehood application, which threatened the precarious balance of free and slave states, tripped off a fierce controversy.

California was not the only source of sectional friction. For years opponents of slavery had demanded that the slave trade in the District of Columbia be abolished. The capital of the nation, they insisted, must not be disgraced by the presence of slave pens and auction blocks. For their part, southerners fumed over the ineffectivenss of the federal fugitive slave law of 1793. The South was suffering great losses, they claimed, because northern state officials refused to cooperate with federal authorities in suppressing the so-called Underground Railroad; that allowed antislavery northerners to spirit hundreds of escapees to Canada by hiding them in houses, barns, and cellars on their way north. The southerners were mistaken: slave losses by escape were slight. But what people believed was more important than reality in influencing the events of these years.

Texas, too, figured in the reemerging sectional conflict. A slave state, it claimed part of eastern New Mexico. Militant southern rights advocates supported the state's claim; free-soilers opposed it. Moreover, the Lone Star State had joined the Union with unpaid debts amounting to several million dollars. Texas's creditors included many leading politicians and businessmen, some of them open to any deal that would make the debt secure.

Finally, there was the unresolved status of New Mexico. Unlike California, it was not ready for statehood; but it, too, needed some sort of government. Did Congress have the right to decide the slave question in that region while it was a territory? And if it had the right, should it exercise it? Or should the people of the territory, as Cass and the popular-sovereignty champions believed, be allowed to make that decision for themselves?

The Compromise of 1850. With the battle over the speaker finally resolved (Howell Cobb of Georgia was chosen), Congress went to work in a contentious and disorganized fashion to settle the other sectional problems. Fortunately for the Union, two leaders—Henry Clay and Stephen Douglas—quickly took matters in hand and forged an agreement that both sides could accept temporarily.

Clay, the aging Whig master of accommodation and compromise, was determined to frustrate the disunionist attitudes of his former ally Calhoun and those who accepted Calhoun's leadership. Clay was a Kentuckian and a slaveholder, but he had built his career on a broad-gauged nationalism. Now, in his seventies, he did not intend to see his beloved Union torn apart. Across the Senate aisle was another devoted Unionist, Stephen A. Douglas of Illinois. Douglas, thirty-seven years old, was at the beginning of his career. Originally from Vermont, he had gone to Illinois in his twenties, when it was still a young community, and had grown up professionally with the West. Historians have often judged this stubby, dynamic man an opportunist who would do anything to become president. Events would actually show that the ambitious "Little Giant" loved the Union and, when necessary, would put its welfare before his own. In trying to prevent a sectional showdown, Clay and Douglas had the help of Daniel Webster, Whig elder statesman from Massachusetts, and two Democrats, Thomas Hart Benton of Missouri and Sam Houston of Texas.

Few members of the Thirtieth Congress desired a disastrous confrontation, but many adopted such unyielding positions that one seemed unavoidable. On the southern side, looming above the rest, was Calhoun, a fierce partisan for his beloved South, though in poor health and visibly declining. Equally stubborn on the militant northern side were Salmon Chase of Ohio and Charles Sumner of Massachusetts, both Free-Soilers. More influential than these two political novices, however, was the former Whig governor of New York, the affable, cigar-smoking William Henry Seward. Despite his easygoing ways, Seward was at this point a radical antislavery man who seemed more devoted to freedom than to the Union.

In 1850 the cause of the Union proved stronger than southern rights, antislavery, or free soil. In January Clay presented a package bill to the Senate designed to settle all the outstanding sectional issues simultaneously. Clay's bill included six separate proposals: California was to be admitted to the Union as a free state; New Mexico was to be given a territorial government without

National Portrait Gallery, Smithsonian Institution

Stephen Douglas, the "Little Giant," sought to prevent southern secession by endorsing the principle of popular sovereignty. Although "the great persuader" managed a compromise in 1850, southern and northern Democrats were unwilling to allow the question of slavery to be resolved by popular votes in each new state.

mention of the slavery issue; Texas was to be denied its western boundary claims, but would have its debts assumed by Washington; slavery in the District of Columbia would be affirmed, but the District of Columbia slave trade would be abolished; and finally, Congress would adopt a new, more effective fugitive slave law. During the debate that soon swirled around Clay's Omnibus Bill, it became clear that although many congressmen would support separate parts of it, few could bring themselves to endorse the whole. In late July 1850, after almost six months of discussion, and despite the magnificent appeal of Webster for sectional forbearance and accommodation in his seventh of March speech, the Omnibus Bill was defeated.

By this time President Taylor had died. A

southerner, he nevertheless had worked behind the scenes in ways that southerners interpreted as unfriendly to their section. His death placed Millard Fillmore, a New Yorker, in the White House. Ironically, Fillmore, though a northerner, was more inclined to compromise with the South than Taylor had been. Equally helpful in striking a sectional bargain was Douglas. After the failure of the Clay's Omnibus Bill, the Little Giant took over management of the compromise measures. In September he ushered five separate bills through Congress—admitting California as a free state; organizing New Mexico and the adjacent Mormon settlements in Utah as territories, with their legislatures free to prohibit or allow slavery; settling the Texas–New Mexico boundary and awarding Texas $10 million to pay its creditors; abolishing the slave trade in the District of Columbia; and enacting a stiffer fugitive slave law. Southerners disliked California's admission and the bill ending the slave trade in Washington. Northerners disliked the Fugitive Slave Act and the organiza-

tion of New Mexico and Utah without slave-exclusion clauses. But enough congressmen from each side suppressed their prejudices to pass the individual laws. What Clay could not achieve with a single bill had now been accomplished with five.

The Compromise of 1850, as these measures are collectively called, heartened Unionists all over the country. Congress, profoundly relieved at having avoided disunion, celebrated the end of the unruly session with an exuberance that left many members with severe hangovers the next day. Jubilant crowds surged through the streets of Washington toasting Clay, Douglas, and Webster. In the country at large moderates gained confidence, as many citizens agreed with Cass that the slavery question was finally "settled in the public mind." Soon after the passage of the compromise measures, a convention of slave states at Nashville, Tennessee, called to secure redress of southern grievances, adjourned without taking the strong disunionist action that many had feared it might.

The Compromise of 1850

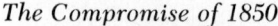

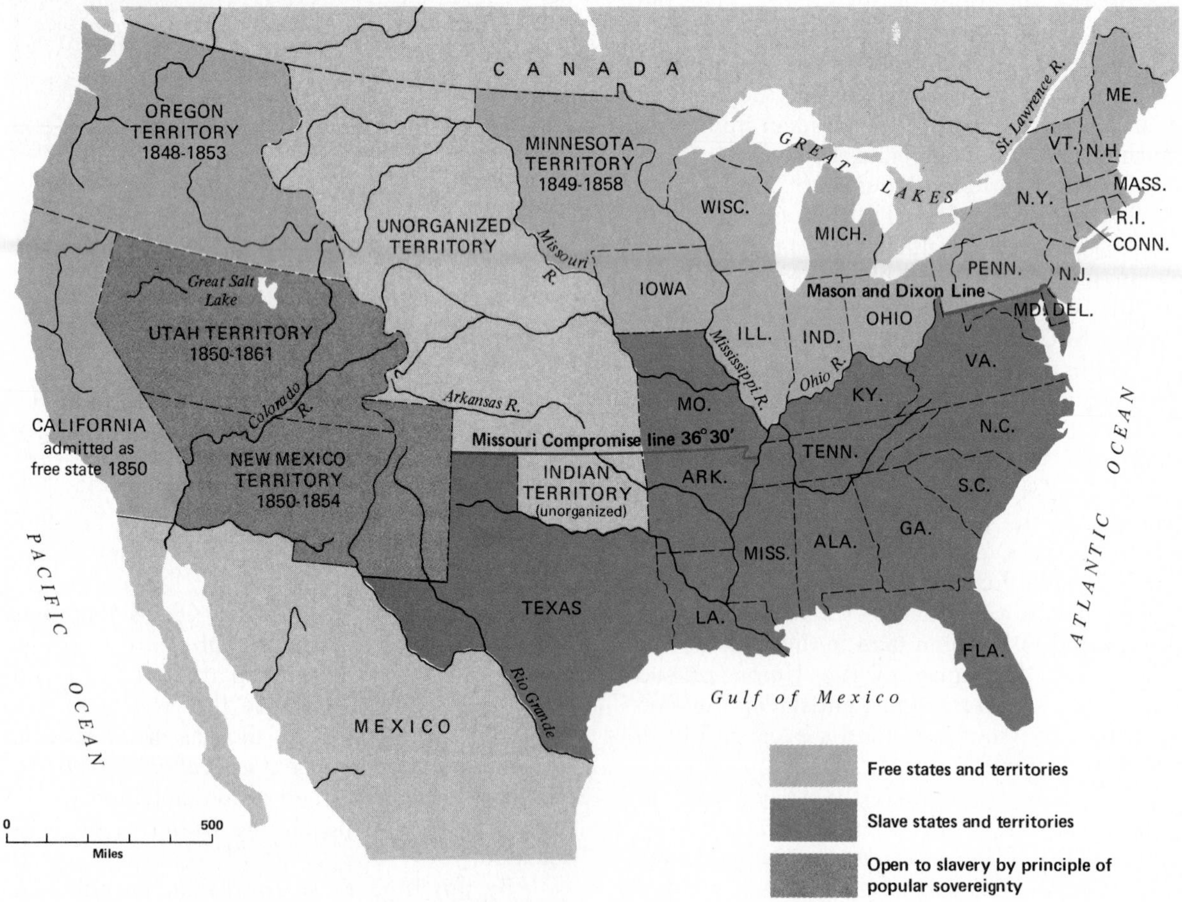

Free states and territories

Slave states and territories

Open to slavery by principle of popular sovereignty

The Fugitive Slave Act of 1850. The Union had once more been saved—or so it seemed. But southern fire-eaters and radical antislavery advocates disliked the compromise, and as the months passed, it became clear that it had not put an end to sectional discord. Indeed, one provision of the compromise, the Fugitive Slave Act of 1850, seemed only to inflame northern resentment against the South.

The new law was hard for many northerners to swallow. It deprived suspected runaway slaves of virtually every right normally granted to those accused of violating the law. By merely submitting an affidavit to a federal commissioner, a slaveowner could initiate claim to an avowed fugitive. The commissioner might reject the affidavit, but if he did, he received a fee of only $5; if he ordered the fugitive's return, he pocketed $10. While his case was being considered, the accused runaway was denied a jury trial. The law required that state officials and private citizens help the federal authorities capture escapees, a provision that many northerners regarded as an unprecedented federal violation of state sovereignty in addition to being inhumane. Anyone who refused to cooperate with the law could be fined or imprisoned. In effect, the law made every American a potential slave catcher.

The sight of black men and women being dragged off to jail by state or federal authorities, and ultimately returned to bondage, made thousands of indifferent citizens antislavery converts overnight. In many northern communities people actively resisted efforts to enforce the law. In Syracuse, Boston, Oberlin (Ohio), New York City, and even Baltimore, the commercial capital of a slave state, citizens hid escapees, attacked slave-catching officials, removed fugitives from jails, and whisked them away to Canada. In Lancaster County, Pennsylvania, irate citizens murdered at least one slaveholder pursuing an escapee from bondage. So aroused was public opinion in some parts of the North that several state legislatures enacted "personal liberty" laws making it a crime for state officials to abet owners and federal authorities in recovering fugitives. In effect, these states were nullifying a federal law that they found offensive.

Few southerners saw the faults of the Fugitive Slave Act. Quite the contrary: they considered the law the only reasonable way to protect their property and concluded that by defying it, northerners were repudiating their part of the 1850 bargain. The act placed traditional northern and southern constitutional positions in an ironic light. Southern politicians, by demanding a stronger

Library of Congress

The Fugitive Slave Act, part of the Compromise of 1850, led to bitter sectional antagonism. Shocked into active disobedience of the law, many northerners did what they could to warn and protect freedmen and fugitive slaves. This obstructionism was a prime cause of the South's grievances.

federal law and denouncing state efforts to block a locally unpopular measure, were implicitly repudiating their states' rights position. Northerners were endorsing measures that resembled Calhoun's nullification. Obviously both sides were willing to sacrifice their traditional constitutional positions rather than surrender an important sectional interest.

One northerner infuriated by the Fugitive Slave Act was Harriet Beecher Stowe. Stowe had little direct contact with slavery, but she thought she knew sin when she saw it. As a little girl she had wept when her father, the Reverend Lyman Beecher, prayed for "poor, oppressed, bleeding Africa," and as a young woman she had been shocked at the sight of escaped slaves being plucked off the streets of Cincinnati to be returned to their masters. In 1851 she wrote a series of slave-life sketches for an abolitionist journal, *Na-*

New-York Historical Society

In the most sensational scene from the most sensational book of the 1850s, Eliza flees the cruel Simon Legree and slavery by crossing the Ohio River at night in the dead of winter, on foot—hopping from ice floe to ice floe. This picture comes from the title page of a children's edition of Uncle Tom's Cabin.

WORSENING TENSIONS

Lincoln was exaggerating: *Uncle Tom's Cabin* only accelerated a process of national division already well under way. If in 1850 it seemed that Clay, Douglas, and Webster had finally checked the process, appearances were deceiving. Within three years the two older men, Clay and Webster, would be dead. Douglas would remain, but events would show that he lacked the skill of his seniors.

But for four years, notwithstanding the fugitive slave question, relative peace prevailed between the sections. The Compromise of 1850 had put to rest the slavery issue in the Mexican Cession, the only part of the country where the legality of slavery remained uncertain. After 1850 the whole country seemed to be staked out once and for all as either free or slave territory. There was nothing left to fight over.

Unfortunately for sectional peace, some refused to let the issue of slavery extension alone. In the North abolitionists continued to find slavery intolerable and to demand its eradication. Some southerners believed that slavery had to expand or die—a view, as we shall see, shared by some antislavery northerners. "We of the South," declared Jefferson Davis of Mississippi, "are an agricultural people, and we require an extended territory. Slave labor is a wasteful labor, and it therefore requires a still more extended territory than would the same pursuits if they could be prosecuted by the more economic labor of white men." Such leaders saw the territorial gains of the Mexican War as a mere appetizer, too small a morsel to satisfy the nation's geographical hunger. Some of these "ultras" looked to Mexico for further territorial gains, and during the late 1850s the Democratic administration of James Buchanan would try to buy several of Mexico's northern states. Others supported adventurer William Walker's "filibustering" efforts to seize a part of Central America in hopes that the region would provide an opportunity for slavery to expand. It was Cuba, however, that attracted the attention of most proslavery expansionists. The "Pearl of the Antilles," which already possessed a flourishing slave-plantation economy based on sugar, was Spanish, but this did not deter the expansionists. In 1854 three proslavery American ministers abroad—Pierre Soulé, John Y. Mason, and James Buchanan—with the support of President Franklin Pierce, issued the so-called Ostend Manifesto inviting Spain to sell Cuba to the United States. If it did not, "then by every law, human and Divine," proclaimed the three ministers, "we shall

tional Era. She soon expanded these into a novel that appeared in 1852 as *Uncle Tom's Cabin.* The book was a colossal success. In sentimental fashion it recounted the history of a lively and vivid cast of characters, black and white, all enmeshed in the tragic web of slavery. By the end of its first year the book had sold 300,000 copies, and eight presses were running day and night to keep up with the demand.

Southerners denounced *Uncle Tom's Cabin* and called Stowe an ignorant and dangerous woman. But in the North and in Europe, the novel was hailed as a masterpiece. It aroused such strong sympathy for slaves and such utter detestation of slavery that it heightened sectional confrontation. Contemporaries acknowledged its importance. Legend has it that when President Lincoln met Harriet Beecher Stowe during the Civil War, he remarked: "So this is the little lady who wrote the big book that caused the big war!"

be justified in wresting it from Spain." Nothing came of these expansionist gestures; but to many northerners it seemed clear that if the South had its way, it would goad the country once more into an expansionist course for the sole purpose of bolstering its peculiar institution.

The Kansas-Nebraska Act. Even more disastrous to sectional harmony was the work of Stephen Douglas. A sincere Unionist who had done much to cool sectional angers in 1850, he undid his good work in January 1854 when he introduced a bill to establish a territorial government in the Nebraska country based on popular sovereignty. The Kansas-Nebraska Act proposed to divide the Nebraska region into two territories. Under the 1820 Missouri Compromise the whole area should have been free-soil. The Douglas bill proposed to repeal this restriction. Instead, popular sovereignty would decide whether slavery was permitted in, or excluded from, the two territories. Eventually, the South might look forward to at least one slave state joining the Union from a part of the country where slavery had long been prohibited.

Why did this devoted friend of the Union reopen an obviously divisive issue that had already been settled? Douglas's motives were mixed. The Illinois senator, an enthusiastic expansionist during the 1840s, was deeply committed to the economic growth of the West. As chairman of the Senate's Committee on Territories, he believed that organizing the Nebraska country would encourage its settlement and development. This process would in turn increase the chances that Congress would choose a central route for the proposed Pacific railroad, because with farms, towns, and homes springing up in the new region, a central route through Chicago would provide much more business than any other proposed east-west right-of-way.

A Symbolic Issue. Douglas might have pushed for a measure to organize the Nebraska region without mentioning slavery, but he could not get

The United States in 1854

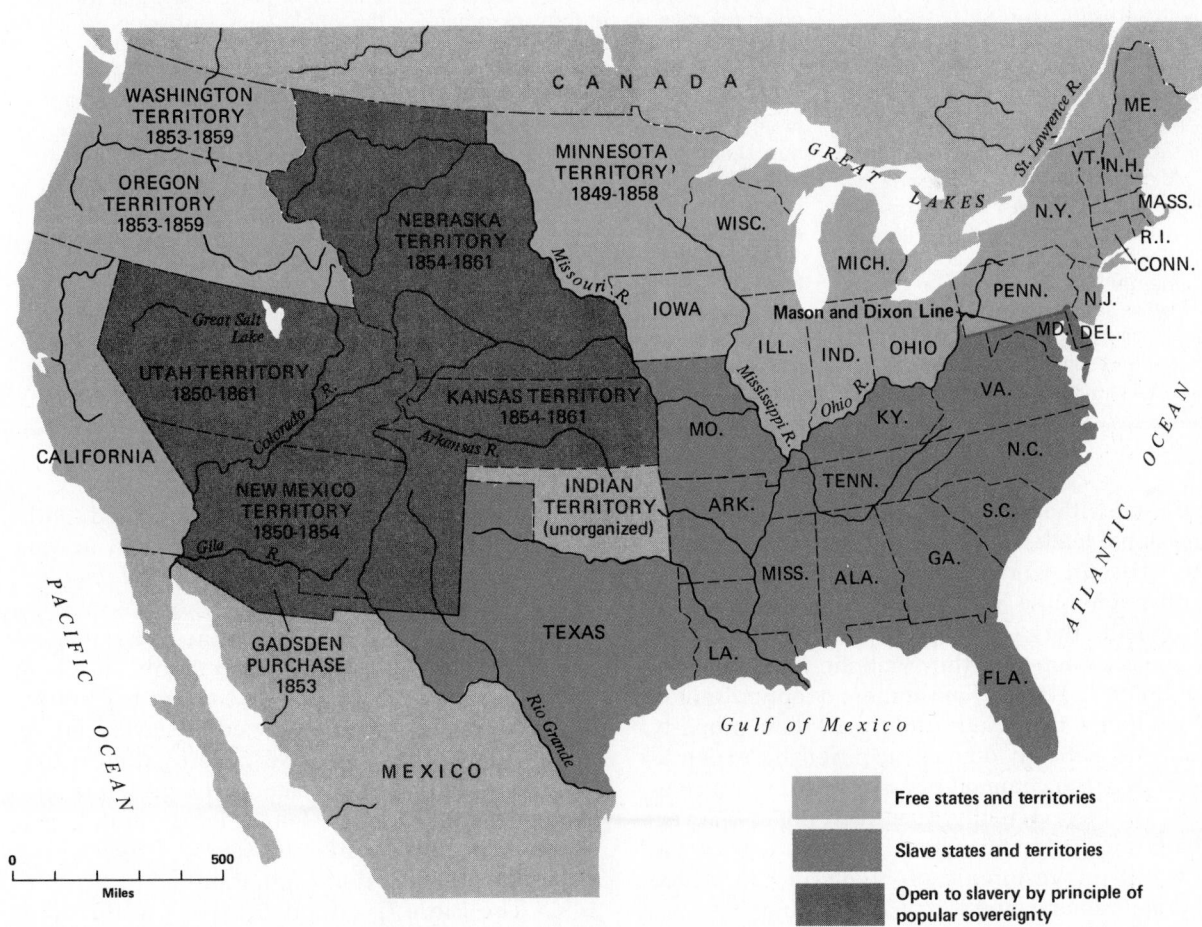

The Coming of the Civil War   337

An Historical Portrait Stephen A. Douglas

They called Stephen Douglas the "Little Giant" in part because of his appearance—he was only five feet four inches tall, with a massive head, deep chest, and broad shoulders—but also because he played a giant role during one of the most crucial decades in his nation's history.

Douglas was born in 1813 in Brandon, Vermont, a corner of New England that was Jeffersonian rather than Federalist in its politics. Douglas learned his egalitarian values in Brandon, but rural New England was a stifling place for an ambitious and able young man, and in 1830 he joined the Yankee exodus to the West.

Douglas's first stop was Canandaigua in the Burned-Over District of New York. Here he studied law with one of the town's leading attorneys. But Douglas had neither the time nor the money to meet the New York requirement that an attorney have four years of classical education and three years of legal study to qualify for practice. In June 1833, with $300 and several letters of recommendation in his pocket, he set out for the open, vibrant West.

After six months of wandering, Douglas settled down in Jacksonville, Illinois, in the center of the state, where streams of Yankees and southerners had converged to create a diverse and sometimes conflicting mix of values, politics, and customs. He resumed his law studies and in a few months passed the perfunctory oral examination to become a licensed attorney. Going west had been the right move. At the age of twenty-one Douglas was a full-fledged lawyer with a bright future ahead.

The promise was quickly fulfilled. Within a year Douglas had been elected state's attorney for the first judicial district. The appointment was political and a reward for his loyalty to Andrew Jackson and for his work in establishing the Morgan County Democratic party. In 1836 Douglas was elected as a Democrat to the state legislature. In 1840 he was appointed Illinois secretary of the state, and then served briefly as judge of the state supreme court. In 1843 he was sent to Congress for the Fifth District.

During his two terms in the House of Representatives Douglas became a leading champion of the West and its needs, an ardent defender of Manifest Destiny, and a powerful advocate of the Jacksonian principle that the people's voice, expressed through majorities, was sovereign. During his second term he first broached the idea that the new steam railroad would help make the United States "an ocean-bound republic," occupying the entire continent.

Meanwhile, the Little Giant had taken a wife. Douglas was not attractive to women; one Washington belle described him as "short, stout, and thick." He tried to compensate for his unimpressive appearance by a boisterous manner that many women considered coarse. What seemed like confirmed bachelorhood ended, however, in 1847 when he married Martha Martin, an attractive and witty North Carolina woman whose father was owner of 2,500 acres of prime Mississippi cotton land and over 100 slaves. Shortly after their marriage Douglas and Martha established their official residence in Chicago, the exploding metropolis on Lake Michigan. In 1848 Colonel Martin died and bequeathed Martha his Mississippi plantation and slaves.

The year of his marriage also saw Douglas's election to the United States Senate. As head of the Senate Committee on Territories he sought to further the growth and prosperity of the West. Personal interest reinforced his sectional loyalties. His new home, Chicago, was already a major railroad center and might become the gateway to the whole trans-Mississippi region if a Pacific railroad were to be constructed along a central route.

Douglas was also a dedicated Unionist. He had no patience with those who placed either sectional "rights" or antislavery above the continued existence of a prosperous, united nation. Though a northerner, he did not sympathize with people who saw slavery as an evil so great that everything must be sacrificed to destroy it. His opponents often blamed his indifference to slavery on his stake in the pecu-

it passed without southern support. Southern congressional leaders had let him know that repeal of the Missouri Compromise was a long overdue concession to the South and that without such inducement they would not support his bill. Douglas understood the symbolic importance to the South of repeal. Southerners deeply resented any attempt to exclude them and their property from the national domain acquired by expenditures from the common treasury or won by a common sacrifice. Actually, few liked popular sovereignty any better than free soil, but at least the Douglas bill restored their rights in part of the national domain, and that was important.

If rational interest alone had governed southern attitudes, the Kansas-Nebraska question would never have arisen at all. Few slaveholders were willing to go to an area unsuited to plantation agriculture and from which the free-state people, if they took control, would certainly oust them and their human property. According to the census of 1860, after being opened to slavery for six years, Kansas had two slaves. But by their nature symbolic issues are debates over principle, not substance, and the freedom to move their "peculiar species of property" to Kansas if they so desired appeared vital to southerners.

The Little Giant failed to foresee that Kan-

liar institution through his wife's Mississippi property. During his first Senate session Douglas fought for a Union-preserving compromise on the issues of admitting California to the United States, organizing New Mexico, and the other accumulated sectional disputes, and helped carry the Compromise of 1850 through to victory.

The forces and drives that moved Douglas throughout his career—love of the Union, respect for majorities, political ambition, and the desire to advance the interests of the West—were all incorporated into the 1854 Kansas-Nebraska Act. They proved incompatible. His bill to organize the Nebraska region of the Louisiana Purchase was intended to stimulate western development along the best central railroad route to the Pacific. He hoped that the issue of slavery in the new territories of Kansas and Nebraska could be settled by the principle of popular sovereignty that would allow the voters, rather than Congress, the right to decide for or against slavery. As applied to the Nebraska country, such a rule, in effect, would have nullified the Missouri Compromise, which had forbidden slavery for all time in the region. But Douglas's original bill was not direct enough for a group of southern senators, who threatened to defeat it unless an explicit repeal of the Missouri Compromise was included. Insufficiently sensitive to the

moral dimensions of the slavery issue, Douglas went along with their demand.

The political storm that followed passage of the revised bill helped tear the country apart and destroyed Douglas's career. Northern political leaders attacked the Kansas-Nebraska Act as a surrender to the "slavocracy." Northern Democrats and Whigs began to desert their parties and link up with various "anti-Nebraska" groups that eventually coalesced as the free-soil Republican party. The act soon produced a civil war in Kansas between free-state and slave-state supporters that further polarized the nation. Before long southerners were demanding that the federal government provide positive protection for slavery in the territories or else they would leave the Union.

Douglas stuck by his popular-sovereignty guns. Though at first it had been largely an expedient formula for avoiding the slavery issue in the West, increasingly it became in his eyes a sacred principle. He attacked the Pierce and Buchanan administrations' attempts to subvert it in "bleeding Kansas" to benefit the anti–free-soil groups. At Freeport, Illinois, during the 1858 debates with his Republican rival for the Senate, Abraham Lincoln, Douglas announced a formula to preserve the popular-sovereignty position against the Supreme Court's Dred Scott decision that offended southern Democrats.

Thereafter, Douglas was repudiated by most southern political leaders as a possible candidate for president. At the 1860 Charleston convention southern Democrats walked out rather than see him and popular sovereignty win the party's support. Though Douglas eventually won the northern wing's endorsement as the Democratic presidential nominee, he would have to run against a southern candidate as well as the Republican candidate, Lincoln.

The last months of Douglas's life were sad. After being defeated in the 1860 election, he was forced to witness the secession of the South. He had no more affection for the "Black Republicans" than for the Democratic fire-eaters who had denied him the nomination of a united party, but he offered his support to Lincoln when the new president rallied the North to put down the rebellion. "There can be no government without coercion," Douglas replied to those who opposed secession but also the use of force to prevent it. His last public act was to undertake, at Lincoln's request, a tour of the border states and the West to urge their people to support the president and the Union. He ended his trip in Chicago in May 1861. There he contracted typhoid fever and soon after died. He was buried on the shore of Lake Michigan, in the heart of the West that had nurtured his career and made him a national figure.

sas-Nebraska was an extremely important symbolic issue to the North as well. It did not matter that slavery was never likely to take root on the prairies. That had been one of Webster's major points in his great 1850 speech defending Clay's Omnibus Bill, but neither Webster nor Douglas saw that merely allowing the possibility of slavery's extension was enough to outrage even moderate antislavery people.

In this fevered atmosphere only a few people besides Douglas could keep their intellectual balance. For four raucous months Congress debated the Kansas-Nebraska bill. President Franklin Pierce, another northerner strongly inclined to

accommodate the South, supported the measure and put intense pressure on reluctant northern Democrats to endorse it. The president's intervention proved crucial, and the bill passed at the end of May 1854 by a majority composed of an almost solid South—both Whigs and Democrats—and proadministration northern Democrats.

National Parties Break Up. The Kansas-Nebraska Act put unbearable strains on the American party system. Months before its passage a group of congressional free-soil Democrats led by Senator Salmon Chase issued the so-called Appeal of the Independent Democrats. This manifesto branded

Kansas State Historical Society

Beginning with the Missouri Compromise in 1820, United States expansion was irrevocably linked with the conflict over slavery expansion. The Kansas-Nebraska Act, in Charles Sumner's words, put "slavery and freedom face to face, and bids them grapple." These Kansas antislavery supporters are ready for the confrontation.

the measure a "gross violation of a sacred pledge," a "criminal betrayal," and part of an "atrocious plot" to make the Nebraska country "a dreary region of despotism inhabited by masters and slaves." The appeal awakened a resounding echo in the North. From Maine to California Democratic newspapers screamed in outrage at Douglas's action. In many northern cities Douglas's opponents called rallies and passed resolutions bitterly condemning the bill. Party loyalists defended Douglas and Pierce, but many northern Democrats worried openly that northern votes would respond to this apparently prosouthern bill by repudiating them at the polls.

Whig divisions went even deeper. In the free states the Whig party was already in serious trouble. The deaths of Webster and Clay in 1852 left their old party without forceful leaders. In that year, too, the Whig candidate for president, General Winfield Scott, had been decisively defeated by Pierce. Even more than the Democrats, the Whigs found it impossible to contain the sectional forces that were now building. Northern Whigs, more strongly antislavery than their Democratic counterparts, were less willing or able to compromise with the southern members of their party. The pro–Kansas-Nebraska stand of the party's southern wing had profoundly disillusioned such men as Horace Greeley, a "conscience Whig" whose antislavery principles clashed with the

"cotton Whig" sentiments of his party. Through his powerful *New York Tribune*, Greeley attacked the measure, proclaiming that the unanimous sentiment of the North was "indignant resistance." In February 1854 Seward, leader of the conscience Whigs, repudiated the Nebraska bill in a three-hour Senate speech that warned the South that its demands for equal rights in the territories would tear the country apart.

In a matter of months the Whig party began to crumble. For a while many Whigs took refuge with the Know-Nothings, an antiforeign political group dedicated to excluding nonnatives and Catholics from public office. Appealing to many of the same pietistic Protestant groups that had traditionally supported the Whigs, the Know-Nothing party in 1854 cut sharply into Whig strength in the North. For a while it looked as if it would become the Whigs' successor. The new party, however, repelled as many voters as it attracted. Democrats, many of whom were Catholic, predictably attacked it. Even many Whigs were appalled by its hatred of foreigners and its religious bigotry. "As a nation," wrote the Illinois Whig Abraham Lincoln, "we begin by declaring that 'all men are created equal.' We now practically read it, 'all men are created equal except Negroes.' When the Know-Nothings obtain control it will read: 'All men are created equal except Negroes, foreigners and Catholics.'"

Happily for those stranded Whigs who could not stomach the Know-Nothings, there was an alternative. In the wake of Douglas's ill-advised measure, various anti-Nebraska organizations quickly sprang up in the Northwest and Northeast. At a meeting at Ripon, Wisconsin, in February 1854, the label *Republican* was first used to describe these groups. Several months later another anti-Nebraska assemblage at Jackson, Michigan, gave the Republicans their platform when they demanded that the territories be kept free of slavery, that the Kansas-Nebraska and Fugitive Slave acts be repealed, and that slavery itself, not merely the slave trade, be abolished in the District of Columbia. The Republicans rapidly grew in strength as northern Whigs and many northern Democrats were drawn to the new party by its central principle of free soil. Before long, many erstwhile Know-Nothings also joined the party, convinced that it was more reliably Protestant and native-American than its Democratic rival.

"Bleeding Kansas." The rise of the Republicans was accelerated by the outbreak of a vicious guerrilla war in Kansas. Within weeks of passage of the Kansas-Nebraska Act, advocates and opponents of slavery in the territory were at one another's throats: ambushes, arson, and even murder quickly became the order of the day in "bleeding Kansas." The struggle in Kansas was not over slavery alone. The government's failure to properly extinguish Indian titles or make land surveys in the territory created an extraordinary confusion that increased the new arrivals' inclination to violence. Men with opposing views on slavery were all the more inclined to fight when they also had conflicting land claims.

Outsiders, however, tended to see the conflict entirely in sectional and ideological terms and acted accordingly. The New England Emigrant Aid Company, organized by Eli Thayer, a Massachusetts free-soiler, raised funds and sent several thousand antislavery emigrants to Kansas. Many of these settlers came equipped with Sharps rifles, called Beecher's Bibles after the well-known Brooklyn antislavery minister, Henry Ward Beecher. Free-soil efforts in turn incited large numbers of Missourians to cross the river into the new territory. Called by their opponents "border ruffians," the Missourians were mostly white yeoman farmers. Many were proslavery, but on the whole their interest in Kansas's rich land differed little from that of most northern settlers.

Early in 1855 the proslavery group rigged elections to the territorial legislature, seized control of the local government, and promptly adopted a drastic slave code. Governor Andrew Reeder clashed with the proslavery leaders, and President Pierce, anxious to give the South what it wanted, soon recalled him. The president replaced Reeder with a succession of appointees, all of whom found the situation unmanageable and either resigned or were fired. Meanwhile, the free-staters had made their move. In October they called a convention at Topeka, adopted a constitution outlawing slavery, and ratified it by a popular vote in which slave-state men refused to participate. Now there were two rival governments in the territory—one claiming to represent a slave state, the other a free one.

Among those who turned to violence in Kansas was one John Brown of Osawatomie, a full-bearded patriarch sworn to free Kansas from slavery. Born in Connecticut, Brown spent most of his life wandering with his family from place to place, trying to make a living and establish a home. He had failed in virtually everything and had become an embittered and angry man. A fanatical abolitionist, he identified his own sufferings with those of the slaves and had come to see himself as an instrument of an avenging God to smite the slaveholders and destroy them. In Kansas Brown and his sons immediately associated themselves with the free-state forces. Angered by a proslavery group's attack on free-state headquarters at Lawrence, Kansas, in May 1856, Brown and a small band of followers took revenge by murdering five proslavery settlers in cold blood near Pottawatomie Creek.

News of the massacre spread quickly throughout the country. Southerners considered it proof that northerners would stop at nothing to "abolitionize" the country. In the North many people deplored the massacre; yet some uncompromising opponents of slavery saw it as a fitting response to the border ruffians' attacks on free-state settlers. In Kansas itself extremism begat further extremism and set off a virtual civil war, with mayhem and outrage on both sides. As atrocity succeeded atrocity, even moderate Americans found it increasingly difficult to avoid hating people of the other section.

The Sumner-Brooks Incident. In this overheated atmosphere bizarre and outrageous things happened. One of the more intemperate antislavery leaders in Congress was the junior senator from Massachusetts, Charles Sumner. A Puritan in politics, Sumner felt a zealot's need to right wrongs. No one in Congress was a more stubborn and courageous defender of blacks. At the same time, few members of Congress were as dogmatic, as certain

Library of Congress

A learned and courageous but often intemperate man, Charles Sumner represented the new breed of antislavery men the North began to send to Congress in the 1850s.

of the unfailing rectitude of their positions, or as unwilling to give their opponents credit for honesty or good intentions. Like many northern antislavery partisans, Sumner had watched the struggle over Kansas with growing dismay. On May 19, 1856, he rose in the Senate to deliver a blistering denunciation of the South in a speech he entitled "The Crime against Kansas." Well prepared, sonorous, full of learned allusions, the address also descended to personal attack, pillorying Douglas, the President, Senator David Atchison of Missouri, and others. But Sumner reserved his sharpest barbs for Senator Andrew Butler of South Carolina, calling him a Don Quixote, a foolish blunderer, and a liar. When Sumner sat down, there were few men even among his closest allies who did not feel he had gone too far.

Southerners, of course, considered the speech especially outrageous. Butler's nephew Preston Brooks, a hotheaded young congressman from South Carolina, resolved to avenge this insult to his kinsman and his section. Three days later Brooks entered the Senate and informed the seated, unsuspecting senator that his speech was a libel on South Carolina and Senator Butler.

Brooks then struck Sumner on the head repeatedly with a cane, and stopped only when other senators forcibly intervened.

The South considered Brooks's attack the just chastisement of a blackguard. But it shocked most northerners. Antislavery partisans called mass meetings to protest the assault, while the Massachusetts legislature passed resolutions declaring the beating "a gross breach of Parliamentary privilege—a ruthless attack upon the liberty of speech—an outrage of the decencies of civilized life, and an indignity to the Commonwealth of Massachusetts." Small in itself, the Brooks-Sumner affair confirmed northerners' skepticism of southern "chivalry" and convinced many that something must be done to curb "the arrogant and aggressive demands" of the "slave power."

REPUBLICANISM AND THE WORSENING CRISIS

Bleeding Kansas, the Sumner-Brooks affair, and *Uncle Tom's Cabin* all garnered recruits for the Republican party. The new organization was a frankly sectional party pledged to contain slavery. A few Republicans—the "Radicals"—were out-and-out abolitionists. Most believed that the federal government could and should prevent slavery from expanding. Some Republicans hoped that slavery, if contained, would retreat and eventually die. Others were indifferent to the fate of slavery in the Old South; it was sufficient that the western territories be kept open for free labor. "The policy of the Republican party," declared Senator James Harlan of Iowa, "invites the Anglo-Saxon . . . and others of caucasian blood to enter and occupy [the territories] and by the exclusion of slavery it will practically exclude the negro." Republicans of this stripe often seemed as hostile to slaves as to slaveholders.

The new party at first attracted few merchants, bankers, or manufacturers. Most business-people saw it as a divisive influence and feared that its success would disturb the country's economy. Those who joined did so because, like other citizens, they feared the "slave power" and wanted slavery checked and rolled back.

The Republicans' first presidential race was in 1856, when they nominated the California hero John Charles Frémont and called on Congress to exclude from the territories "those twin relics of barbarism, polygamy [practiced by western Mormons] and slavery." The Democrats chose former Pennsylvania Senator James Buchanan, largely because alone among prominent Democrats he had been out of the country—serving as minister to England—during the worst months of "bleeding Kansas" and so had escaped blame for any share in the atrocities. A third candidate, ex-President Fillmore, ran on the Know-Nothing ticket.

The Republicans campaigned enthusiastically for their candidate, "the pathfinder." But no amount of zeal could make up for the support that Buchanan received from voters who feared to disrupt the Union by supporting a purely sectional party. Buchanan took the election, carrying fourteen slave and five free states. Fillmore carried only Maryland, a result signaling the end of the Know-Nothing party. Frémont, however, carried eleven free states, a showing that alarmed southerners, who now viewed the 1860 presidential contest with deep foreboding.

Buchanan's Policies. Buchanan was not the man to guide the country through the four difficult years that followed. He was well-meaning but indecisive and weak, and his talents lay in the traditional maneuvering of American party politics. Republicans sized him up as another doughface Democrat, subservient to the South, and his choice of many southerners and doughface northerners for his cabinet confirmed their judgment.

Even before his inauguration Buchanan set out to undermine the free-soil position by intruding into the pending case of a Missouri slave, Dred Scott, then before the Supreme Court. Through the auspices of antislavery advocates, Scott was suing for his freedom on the grounds that he had resided in free territory, including the region closed to slavery by the Missouri Compromise. The case might have been decided on the basis of whether as a slave Scott had a right to sue in the federal courts, or whether under Missouri law his plea for freedom was valid. Instead, the Court chose to rule on the constitutionality of the Missouri Compromise. Most legal historians believe that there was no need for the Court to raise this issue. That it did was at least in part due to the wish of the president-elect, who believed that the Court should take up the question of congressional power over slavery in the territories and decide it once and for all. Urged on by Buchanan, five southern judges, including Chief Justice Roger Taney, and one northern justice concluded that Congress could only protect slavery in the territories, not prohibit it. If slavery was to be excluded from any part of the nation, it would have to be by state law; neither Congress nor a territorial legislature could do so.

The Dred Scott decision was a blow to the Republicans because it seemed to make their major plank—the exclusion of slavery from the territories by congressional action—meaningless. The decision also dismayed the popular-sovereignty advocates, because it appeared to nullify their fundamental principle that citizens of a territory could decide whether to admit or exclude slavery long before the statehood stage.

Buchanan soon gave the Republicans and the popular-sovereignty element in his own party further grounds for anger when he accepted the unfair proslavery constitution for Kansas adopted in 1857 by southern forces at Lecompton. His own appointee as governor in Kansas considered the Lecompton constitution fraudulent. It had been drawn up exclusively by proslavery voters, and free-state sympathizers had boycotted the referendum held for its approval. But Buchanan ignored the governor's advice and recommended that Congress accept the Lecompton document as the basis for admitting Kansas as a state. Congressional Republicans, predictably, refused; and Douglas, leader of the northern Democrats, called the constitution a fraud that perverted his principle of popular sovereignty. Douglas's stand won the admiration of Republicans, but he alienated the Buchanan administration and the proslavery Democrats. After being passed by the Senate, the bill to admit Kansas under the proslavery constitution was blocked in the House. By compromise, the Lecompton constitution was resubmitted to the Kansas voters. This time, with free-state voters participating, it was decisively rejected.

The Emergence of Lincoln. The troubles of the Buchanan presidency were compounded by the Panic of 1857. Although the depression was probably the cyclical downturn to be expected after ten years of booming growth and speculation, the North blamed it on southerners in Congress for lowering their tariff protection. Southerners, largely unaffected by a falling stock market and urban unemployment, saw the panic as a vindication of the slave economy. Buoyed by high world cotton prices, they took heart from the misfortunes of northern business and industry.

Midway through Buchanan's term, politicians were already looking ahead to the election of 1860. Douglas was the obvious front-runner for the Democrats. But the Little Giant had hurt his chances with proslavery Democrats by his disapproval of the Lecompton constitution. They were now demanding that Congress pass a federal slave code to protect slavery in the territories. When Douglas neither would nor could give them the support they wanted, they determined to defeat him at any cost.

Among the Republicans there was no lack of talent or political ambition as 1860 approached. The party's radical, antislavery wing supported either Seward or Chase. The most conservative Republicans preferred men like Edward Bates of Missouri—a border state with a substantial free-soil element in the half-northern city of St. Louis—or Supreme Court Justice John McLean of Ohio, who had voted against the majority in the Dred Scott case. Moderates were becoming more and more interested in Abraham Lincoln of Illinois.

We who know of Lincoln's greatness may find it hard to see him as he was in the late 1850s. The lanky prairie lawyer was pithy and shrewd, and combined keen realism with idealism. But as yet he gave little sign that he was capable of leading the nation through trying times. Men of wealth and refinement looked at his ungainly, craggy exterior, heard his plain speech, and put him down as a crude frontier politician.

Only gradually did he become "available." Following his single term in the House of Representatives (1847–48), Lincoln had returned to Springfield, Illinois, and his private law practice.

Lincoln received the Republican party's nomination in May 1860. This photograph, taken a month later, pleased the candidate. "That looks better and expresses me better that any I have ever seen; if it pleases the people, I am satisfied."

Library of Congress

For the next few years he devoted his time to defending slanderers, petty thieves, and the Illinois Central Railroad before the courts. All the while he kept up his connections with the Illinois Whigs and shared their doubts and anxieties when their party began to collapse. He did not formally become a Republican until his law partner without authority signed his name to a call for a local Republican convention. In 1856 he campaigned for Frémont.

Lincoln might have remained a provincial politician indefinitely if the Illinois Republicans, impressed by his oratory and past services to the Whigs, had not given him the party's senatorial nomination in 1858. The contest, pitting him against Douglas, attracted national attention. To remain in the presidential race, Douglas had to confirm his support at home by defeating Lincoln. People from all over the country watched to see what would happen, and their interest gave Lincoln invaluable free publicity. The contest was made all the more intriguing by its format. Soon after their nomination the two candidates agreed to debate face to face. Beginning in Ottawa in northern Illinois in late August 1858, they would travel through the state, finishing at Alton in mid-October. In seven communities the two candidates would appear on the same platform and direct questions at one another while the public looked on.

Although the debate was unusual, the open-air political rally had long been a major midwestern entertainment, and thousands came to watch the Lincoln-Douglas debates. Present also were reporters from the Illinois papers and from several eastern cities who hoped to see how well Douglas performed and incidentally to observe his opponent. The holiday atmosphere encouraged banter and name calling, but generally the level of discussion was high. At Freeport Lincoln tried to embarrass Douglas by asking him what was left of his policy of popular sovereignty now that the Dred Scott decision had declared that only the people of a state, not a territory, could exclude slavery. Douglas replied that because the peculiar institution required positive protection to flourish, all a territorial legislature need do was refuse to enact a slave code to protect slavery, and it would be effectively squelched. Thus, no matter what the Supreme Court had said, a territorial legislature could still keep slaves from entering its jurisdiction. This Freeport Doctrine offended southerners, who could only consider it a way to frustrate their Dred Scott victory. By this time Douglas had already lost most of the proslavery group's support, however, and the Freeport Doctrine preserved the middle, popular-sovereignty ground on which he had built his career.

Douglas won in Illinois and became the front-runner for the Democratic nomination in 1860. But even more fateful, Lincoln, though he had lost, was now a national figure. In February 1860 he journeyed east to speak at the Cooper Union in New York City. His careful, eloquent address impressed his distinguished audience. Old Abe would now be a major contender, too—on the Republican side.

Harpers Ferry. But first the country would have to undergo another ordeal of violence over slavery, and once again John Brown would be the instigator. After the Pottawatomie massacre Brown left Kansas and went east, where he met other antislavery leaders and wealthy supporters such as Gerrit Smith and Amos A. Lawrence. Some of these people doubtless knew of Brown's murderous activities in Kansas; others did not. In any case, when he asked for money to strike another blow against slavery, they gave it without asking for details.

In late 1859 Brown, his sons, and a small band of black and white supporters bought guns and drew up plans for an assault on the federal arsenal at Harpers Ferry, Virginia (now West Virginia). Brown apparently hoped to foment a major slave revolt that would topple the peculiar institution throughout the South. The capture of the federal post, he told his followers, would be the spark that would ignite the uprising. On the night of October 16, 1859, they seized the arsenal. But the slaves of Virginia and neighboring Maryland did not rise at news of the attack. Instead, a military force commanded by Colonel Robert E. Lee surrounded the arsenal and captured the surviving members of this implausible revolt. Brown and his band were hurriedly tried and hanged for treason against Virginia.

Brown's raid raised sectional feelings once again to a fever pitch. Many northerners condemned the attack, and even Lincoln and Horace Greeley believed Brown misguided. Others called Brown a hero. Thoreau compared him to Jesus, and novelist Louisa May Alcott named Brown "Saint John the Just." To southerners, who lived in constant dread of slave revolt, the raid was traumatic. Hundreds of southern students at northern colleges packed their bags and returned home. Georgians attacked the crew of a Yankee ship at Savannah, and a New Yorker newly installed as president of an Alabama college was forced to flee for his life. To many southerners the message seemed clear: the South was no longer safe in the Union.

The Party Conventions of 1860. Harpers Ferry kept the country in an uproar well into 1860, and by that time the nation was in the midst of the most fateful election campaign of its history. As the Democratic convention assembled in April 1860 at Charleston, South Carolina, the handsome seaside city was already heavy with summer heat. The blanket of tropical air made everyone uncomfortable and irritable. Charleston was the heart of secession country, and the city's usually charming

Boston Athenaeum

The Metropolitan Museum of Art, Gift of Mr. and Mrs. Carl Stoeckel

Two views of John Brown: an 1856 photograph, and an idealized painting of him on the way to the gallows three years later. The first picture suggests Brown's fanaticism and capacity for cruelty; the second, by an abolitionist artist, suggests his love for the suffering slave. Brown was both of these at once.

John Brown's Last Speech

On the evening of October 16, 1859, John Brown of Kansas and his band of eighteen men attacked the federal arsenal at Harpers Ferry in Virginia. Brown's plan, apparently, was to seize the stored weapons and escape to the mountains, where he would proclaim a freedman's republic and attract runaway slaves from the lowland areas. In the vastnesses of the Blue Ridge he would, with the captured guns, beat off all attack. Slavery would crumble and the nation would be finally purged of the great evil.

The scheme failed. Brown and his men captured the arsenal, but made little provision for escape or even for defending themselves. The authorities quickly rallied and sent militia and U.S. marines against the raiders. In the ensuing fight most of Brown's men, including two of his sons, were either killed or wounded; Brown and the rest were captured.

Tried for treason against the state of Virginia, in early November Brown was convicted and sentenced to death. When asked, in the legal formula of the time, why sentence should not be pronounced, he was taken aback since he had not expected the question that day. The following is the response he gave to the court. It captures the essence of the extreme antislavery position. Its eloquence also explains why Brown became a hero and martyr to so many in the North. The speech was extemporaneous, though Brown had used certain phrases previously in answering the many letters he had received while in jail.

"I have, may it please the court, a few words to say.

"In the first place, I deny everything but what I have all along admitted—the design on my part to free the slaves. I intended certainly to have made a clean thing of that matter, as I did last winter, when I went into Missouri and there took slaves without the snapping of a gun on either side, . . . and finally led them to Canada. I designed to have done the same thing again, on a larger scale. . . . I never did intend murder, or treason, or the destruction of property, or to excite or incite slaves to rebellion, or to make insurrection.

"I have another objection: and that is, it is unjust that I should suffer such a penalty. Had I . . . so inter-fered on behalf of the rich, the powerful, the intelligent, the so-called great, or in behalf of any of their friends, . . . and suffered and sacrificed what I have in this interference, it would have been all right; and every man in this court would have deemed it an act worthy of reward rather than punishment.

"This court acknowledges, as I suppose, the validity of the law of God. I see a book kissed here which I suppose to be the Bible, or at least the New Testament. That teaches me that all things whatsoever I would that men should do to me, I should do even so to them. It teaches me further, to 'remember them that are in bonds, as bound to them.' I endeavored to act up to that instruction. I say, I am yet too young to understand that God is any respecter of persons. I believe that to have interfered as I have done . . . on behalf of His despised poor, was not wrong, but right. Now, if it is deemed necessary that I should forfeit my life for the furtherance of the ends of justice, and mingle my blood further with the blood of my children and with the blood of millions in this slave country whose rights are disregarded by wicked, cruel, and unjust enactments,— I submit; so let it be done!

"Let me say one word further.

"I feel entirely satisfied with the treatment I have received on my trial. Considering all the circumstances, it has been more generous than I expected. But I feel no consciousness of guilt. I have stated from the first what was my intention, and what was not. I never had any designs against the life of any person, nor any disposition to commit treason, or excite slaves to rebel, or make any general insurrection. I never encouraged any man to do so, but always discouraged any idea of that kind.

"Let me also say a word in regard to the statements made by some of those connected with me. I hear it has been stated by some of them that I have induced them to join me. But the contrary is true. I do not say this to injure them, but as regretting their weakness. There is not one of them but joined me of his own accord, and the greater part of them at their own expense. A number of them I never saw, and never had a word of conversation with, till the day they came to me; and that was for the purpose I have stated.

"Now I have done."

---

and hospitable hostesses were notably unfriendly to the northern, Douglas men. So, too, were most of the southern delegates. Some of these, led by the fiery William Yancey of Alabama, had already concluded that there was no hope for the South in the Union. Rather than see Douglas and a popular-sovereignty platform triumph, many were prepared to walk out of the convention.

The convention majority of westerners and Douglas men, aware that they could not win in November on a platform demanding a federal code to protect slavery in the territories, refused to yield to southern demands. Yancey and fifty pro-slavery men departed. The majority continued the proceedings, but the remaining southerners were able to keep Douglas from getting the two-thirds majority needed for nomination under Democratic rules. After sixty ballots the delegates adjourned to try again at Baltimore six weeks later.

They were no more successful there. The seceders, now back, contested new, pro-Douglas delegations from the lower South; when they were defeated, they once more stomped out in a huff. Now the remaining delegates nominated Douglas on a popular-sovereignty platform. Soon after, the Yancey men met separately and chose John C. Breckinridge of Kentucky and a platform calling for a federal code that would protect slavery in the territories.

The breakup of the Democratic party was ominous for the Union. No matter how often Democrats had squabbled, they had always managed to reconcile their differences. By 1860 most of the other formal national institutions, including the Protestant churches, had become sectionalized over slavery. Southerners and northerners still maintained personal and business relations, but now the last agency by which sectional compromise might be achieved had been torn apart. The Whigs were gone. The Republicans were a purely sectional party. What would now hold the country together?

The remaining Whigs and a surviving fragment of the Know-Nothings tried to supply some sectional glue. They established the Constitutional Union party and nominated former Whigs John Bell of Tennessee and Edward Everett of Massachusetts on a platform of undying support for the Union. The Constitutional Unionists would win some support in November, but hardly enough to keep the nation from flying apart.

On May 16 the Republicans met in Chicago, confident of victory. As the delegates gathered, the Republican front-runner seemed to be William Seward, the New York senator. But Seward had once made a speech declaring the North and South engaged in "an irrepressible conflict" that must end with the United States becoming "either entirely a slave-holding nation, or entirely a free-labor nation." Republicans, realizing that they would need much moderate northern support to win, could not nominate a man who had so bluntly thrown down the gauntlet to the South. Most other candidates also seemed to have drawbacks. The Lincoln forces made much of these weaknesses and pictured their candidate as the perfect balance between moderation and radicalism—and a friend of the foreign-born to boot. He was also from Illinois, in the old Northwest Territory, a region the Republicans had to carry to win the presidency. Skillful intriguers, the Lincoln managers also packed the galleries with enthusiastic and noisy Lincoln supporters. Old Abe won the nomination on the third ballot. His running mate was Hannibal Hamlin of Maine; the Republicans were putting up a frankly sectional ticket. By contrast, each of the other three presidential tickets was balanced between North and South.

Lincoln's nomination was a victory for the moderate Republicans. The party platform demanded the limitation of slavery; but it did not specify how, in light of the Dred Scott decision, this end was to be achieved. It also deplored disunion, attacked the fanaticism of John Brown, and endorsed the right of each state to control its local institutions, including slavery. The nomination was also, in some ways, a victory for the industrial-commercial interests of the Northeast. As Horace Greeley had written before the convention: "An Anti-Slavery man *per se* cannot be elected; but a Tariff, River-and-Harbor, Pacific Railroad, Free-Homestead man *may* succeed *although* he is Anti-Slavery." Greeley reflected the views of eastern laborers, New England and Pennsylvania manufacturers, and western farmers—groups long frustrated in their economic goals by the alliance of southerners and northern Democrats. Now was the time, they felt, to defeat that coalition and enact measures for economic progress. True to these hopes, the party platform endorsed a homestead law, a protective tariff, a northern-route railroad to the Pacific, and federal aid for internal improvements. Far more than in 1856, the Republicans of 1860 wore the mantle of Henry Clay and Alexander Hamilton.

The Union Dissolves. No candidate advocated secession. Douglas, of course, was a Unionist, and Bell's sole platform was "the Constitution of the country, the Union of the States and the enforcement of the laws." Lincoln and the Republicans soft-pedaled the slavery issue to avoid increasing sectional discord. Even Breckinridge decried secession, though as Douglas noted, every secessionist voter rallied to his support.

The election was scarcely an endorsement of extremism. Lincoln won a clear electoral majority, getting 180 electoral votes and carrying every free state except New Jersey, where he split the electoral vote with Douglas. He achieved this victory with only 39 percent of the popular vote, almost all from the free states. Douglas was next in popular votes, with 29 percent. However, in every state but Missouri he was second to someone else: to Bell in the border states, to Lincoln in the North, and to Breckinridge in the Deep South. Thus he won only 12 electoral votes. Together, the Little Giant and Bell—both strong Unionists—won more popular votes in the slave states than Breckinridge. So even if we assume that Breckinridge's vote was primarily secessionist, we cannot consider the 1860 election a mandate for southern disunion.

Yet the results did not stop the southern ul-

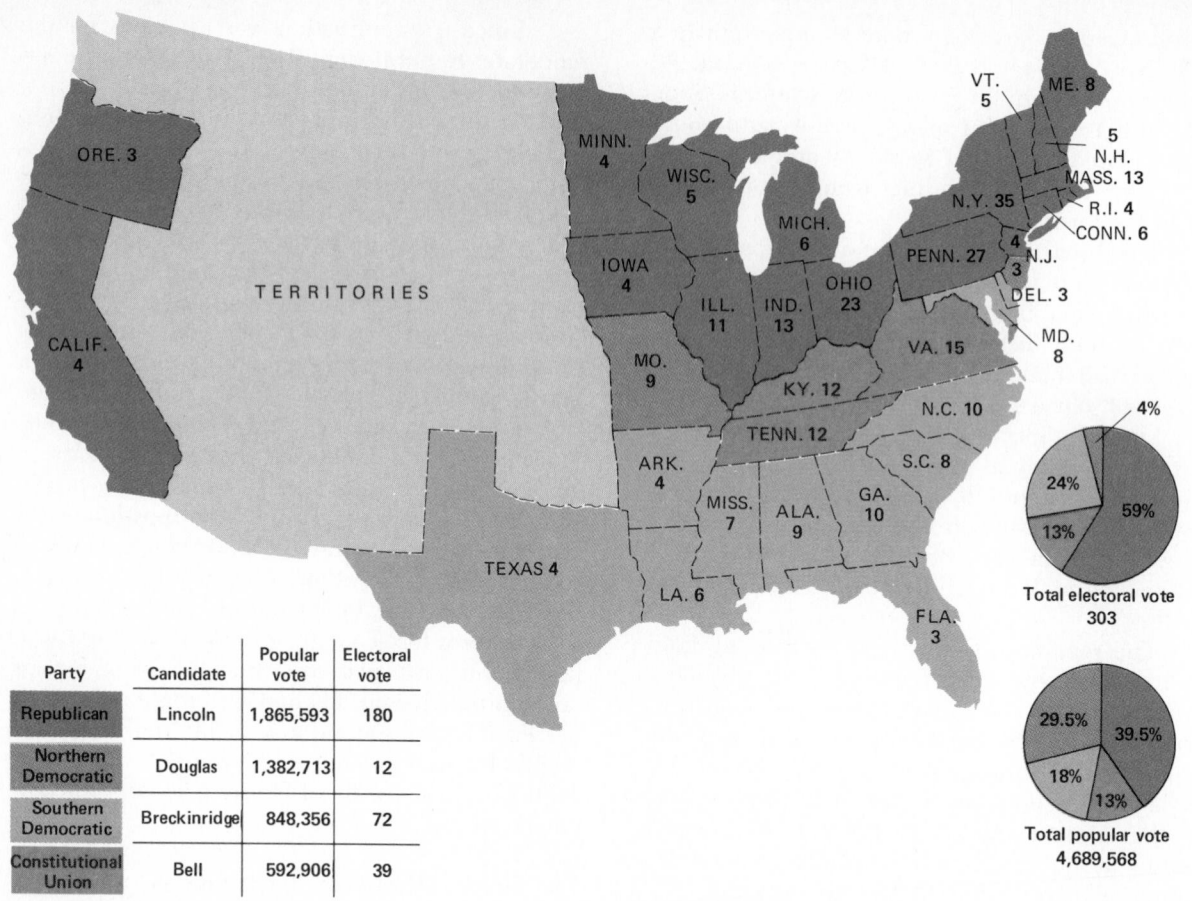

Party	Candidate	Popular vote	Electoral vote
Republican	Lincoln	1,865,593	180
Northern Democratic	Douglas	1,382,713	12
Southern Democratic	Breckinridge	848,356	72
Constitutional Union	Bell	592,906	39

The election of 1860

tras. By now southerners' fears verged on panic. Some saw slavery as gravely endangered. Weeks before the results were in, the *Charleston Mercury* predicted that if Lincoln won, "thousands of slaveholders will despair of the institution." In the border states, it was predicted, many would rush to sell their slaves, forcing down the price all over the South and possibly turning the states of the upper South into free states. Other journals and politicians warned that the new Republican president would appoint abolitionist federal officials in the South who would work to undermine the peculiar institution at every turn. Slavery would eventually collapse and white farmers and wage earners would be forced to compete with the cheap labor of freed blacks. The former slaves would also damage the social status of landless whites. Once free, what would distinguish them from white men?

Seething with such fears and anxieties, the South moved quickly when it learned of Lincoln's victory. News of the results found the South Carolina legislature in session. Brushing aside the de-

mand of moderates that the state wait for unified southern action, it immediately voted to call a secession convention. On December 20, 1860, by a unanimous vote, this convention declared that the "union now subsisting between South Carolina and other States . . . is hereby dissolved." In the next few weeks six more states—Alabama, Mississippi, Florida, Georgia, Louisiana, and Texas—joined South Carolina. At each state secession convention there were a few opponents of secession and even more delegates who favored waiting for united southern action. All through the South, however, the secessionists—representing the counties that were richer, more closely tied to slaves and cotton, and traditionally more Democratic than Whig—prevailed over their opponents. By February 1, 1861, the entire lower South was out of the Union, or claimed to be.

Secession Winter. People who lived through "secession winter"—the months between the election and Lincoln's inauguration—remembered it vividly as a period of acute tension and anxiety.

Southerners hovered between hope and apprehension, not knowing how the federal government would respond to secession and fearful that the confusion of the time would encourage slave insurrection. Meanwhile, the self-proclaimed independent state governments seized federal property, taking over customhouses, post offices, mints, arsenals, and forts. Many federal officials of southern birth transferred their allegiance to their native states. More ominous, southern army officers by the hundreds resigned their commissions and cast their lot with their home states.

In early February six of the seceded states sent delegates to Montgomery, Alabama, and established the Confederate States of America. Choosing Jefferson Davis of Mississippi as president and Alexander Stephens of Georgia as vice president, the delegates adopted a frame of government that in most ways resembled the federal Constitution. The Confederate constitution, however, declared slavery everywhere protected by law and forbade government bounties, subsidies, and protective tariffs. In Washington, beginning in December, the remaining Deep South congressmen resigned one by one, after impassioned speeches of regret and defiance.

Northerners, too, were uncertain and apprehensive. In Washington rumors circulated that the Confederates intended to seize the capital. News from New York City that Democratic Mayor Fernando Wood was planning to take the city out of the Union if its commercial allies, the southern planters, successfully seceded deeply disturbed northern citizens. Many northerners urged their political leaders to adopt a conciliatory course. Northern businessmen, worried that they would be unable to collect southern debts and fearing that severing business relations with the South would plunge the nation into deep depression, supported compromise to heal the breach before it became irreparable. Most Democrats also called for a generous northern response to restore unity.

Meanwhile, the lame-duck Buchanan administration drifted. Buchanan did not approve of secession, but neither did he believe in taking coercive measures to save the Union. Not only would they be unconstitutional; they might also drive out the eight slave states that still remained in the Union: Virginia, Tennessee, Arkansas, Missouri, Maryland, North Carolina, Kentucky, and Delaware. Strongly influenced by his southern advisers, the president preferred to do nothing while bemoaning the nation's plight and blaming the "Black Republicans" for the debacle.

Republicans themselves were divided. Horace Greeley, as strong an opponent of slavery as any, at first advised letting "the erring sisters go in peace." Delighted at the prospect of freeing the country of the slave stigma, the Garrisonian abolitionists seconded Greeley. But Republicans and antislavery advocates generally were determined to prevent secession. Strong Unionists, if only on their own terms, they could not contemplate the breakup of the nation. If the lower South could go, why not the upper South, and then perhaps the West? And then what? Could anything stop total national dissolution once it began? And for what? The South had been defeated in a constitutional and legal political contest. Could it now cry foul? Secession was not rebellion against tyranny, as in 1776, but against the most benign, most benevolent, most liberal government the world had ever seen. And how could the separation be effected? The new Confederacy would control the mouth of the Mississippi, on which the Northwest depended for its export trade. Could this vital site be allowed to fall into foreign hands? And the territories—who would get them?

During the months between the election and the inauguration, the eyes of the country inevitably turned to Lincoln. Many sincere Unionists urged the president-elect to make some major conciliatory gesture on the slavery question. Lincoln was unwilling to do so. He would keep hands off slavery in the states and support a constitutional amendment to that effect if it would reassure the South, he stated. He would even agree to enforce the Fugitive Slave Act faithfully if it were made fairer. But he could not surrender the heart of his party's platform: the restriction of slavery. If he did, the issue would only have to be fought all over again in the future. As he told a fellow Republican: "The tug has to come, and better now than any time hereafter."

Meanwhile, desperate efforts were under way in Congress and in the states to patch together yet another sectional compromise. The scheme proposed by Senator John J. Crittenden of Kentucky to extend the Missouri Compromise line of 36° 36' north latitude through the remaining federal territory seemed the most promising, but along with others it failed—largely because it required that both Republicans and ardent southern rights advocates surrender some principle they considered essential. During the sectional crises of 1820, 1833, and 1850, politicians had arranged compromises that preserved the Union. This time the divisions were too irreconcilable.

Major Anderson's Ordeal. With each passing day the crisis deepened. Increasingly, the attention of both sections focused on the two military posts in

The Confederate flag flies over Fort Sumter. Exactly four years later, on April 14, 1865, Major Anderson would return to raise the Stars and the Stripes. On that day slavery and the Confederacy would be dead. Lincoln would be dead by the new morning.

Confederate territory still in Union hands: Fort Sumter in Charleston harbor, and Fort Pickens at Pensacola, Florida. Their status, like so many issues during the previous fifteen years, had become charged with tremendous emotional and symbolic importance. Even President Buchanan was unwilling to give up the forts, though he had done little to prevent other seizures of federal property. In January he had dispatched the merchant steamer *Star of the West* with munitions and 200 armed troops to reinforce the beleaguered Major Robert Anderson at Fort Sumter. The vessel had been fired on in Charleston harbor and forced to turn back, leaving Anderson's garrison as desperate as before.

By Inauguration Day, March 4, 1861, nothing had been settled. Lincoln's inaugural address adopted a conciliatory tone. He would not insist on delivering the federal mails if such service were "repelled," nor would he appoint "obnoxious strangers" to federal offices in the South. But he promised to "hold, occupy, and possess the property and places belonging to the government." To surrender them, he believed, would be to recognize the virtual independence of the Confederacy.

Aware that Anderson's supplies were fast giving out, Lincoln, once in office, directed Cap-

tain Gustavus Vasa Fox to resupply Sumter with food and fuel. At the same time he dispatched an emissary to South Carolina to inform the state authorities that he intended to send provisions but no arms or troops to Anderson. If South Carolina did not attack the relief expedition or the fort, the federal government would not try to strengthen the Sumter garrison.

To the officials in Charleston, Lincoln's scheme appeared to be a ruse to rearm and reinforce Major Anderson. Davis and his cabinet resolved not to allow it. Soon after Lincoln's message reached the city, Confederate commander General Pierre Beauregard, acting under orders from the Confederate government, delivered an ultimatum to Anderson to evacuate or be fired on. Anderson rejected the ultimatum but told Beauregard frankly that his supplies were low and he would not be able to hold out for long. Beauregard decided that this reply was unsatisfactory. At 4:30 on the morning of April 12, 1861, the first cannon shot arced over the harbor to land on Sumter. For forty hours the bombardment continued, breaching the fort's walls and starting some fires. True to his pledge to hold his post, Anderson returned the fire. On the afternoon of April 13, with his ammunition exhausted, he lowered his flag and surrendered.

CONCLUSIONS

And so the war came. For the next four years the nation would suffer the agonies of fratricidal strife and skirt the edge of dissolution. What had brought the United States to this disastrous result?

The element that by itself comes closest to explaining the origins of the Civil War is slavery. But it was not moral outrage over the peculiar institution that set northern armies on the march to crush the Confederacy. Only a small minority of northerners saw the war at the outset as a crusade against a fundamental social evil. The actual role of slavery was far more subtle and diffuse. Southerners had developed a deep psychological stake in the peculiar institution and feared social and economic cataclysm if it collapsed. They also regarded northern antislavery agitation as an attempt to deny them a fundamental "right." Northerners, meanwhile, had come to fear an aggressive and demanding "slave power" that would ride roughshod over the rights of free men. Slavery defined the South and set it off against the North. Deeply woven into the fabric of southern life, it helped to create a southern sense of apartness. This sense, in turn, produced a combination of sectional aggressiveness and defensiveness that manifested itself in many realms and charged each with divisive power. Thus the clash of sectional economic interests became far more bitter than it might have been. Slavery also converted the Mexican Cession—an acquisition that would normally have been considered a national boon—into a constant source of friction that eventually cracked open the existing political parties and destroyed the last remaining bond between North and South.

We must not blame the schism on slavery alone, however. Sectional conflict might have been contained if this generation of Americans had possessed the statesmanship necessary for adroit compromise. Douglas, who might have filled the role played by Webster and Clay in the past, badly miscalculated in 1854, and inadvertently helped to wreck the Union, as well as his own career. The other leaders of the decade, many of them talented men, were far too closely tied to sectional interests to bridge the chasm that was opening between North and South.

By whatever indirect route it was reached, now began the nation's greatest ordeal.

FOR FURTHER READING

Michael Holt. *The Political Crisis of the 1850s* (1978)
Holt's thesis is that the breakup of the Union can be ascribed to the need of the two parties to define themselves in different and opposed ways. To make the distinctions, unfortunately, they then polarized the nation along sectional lines.

Holman Hamilton. *Prologue to Conflict: The Crisis and Compromise of 1850* (1964)
Hamilton provides a dramatic and incisive analysis of the strategy of the factions that drew up the Compromise of 1850.

David Potter. *The Impending Crisis, 1848–1861* (1976)
A masterful analysis of the political turmoil that ended with the secession of the South. This is the last book by one of the most acute and judicious minds devoted to the scholarship of the Civil War era.

Robert E. May. *The Southern Dream of a Caribbean Empire, 1854–1861* (1973)
May concludes that sectional conflict increased when the Republican-controlled Congress refused to support southern expansion into Central America and the Caribbean. He details the exploits of southerner William Walker, who actually ruled Nicaragua for a time, and describes various attempts to obtain Cuba for the United States and slavery.

Eugene Berwanger. *The Frontier Against Slavery: Western Anti-Negro Prejudice and the Slavery Extension Controversy* (1967)
Many opponents of slavery, especially in the West, fought it because of race prejudice: blacks, whether slave or free, must not be allowed in the new lands. The author weighs the effects of this bigotry on the laws and politics of the old Northwest, as well as Iowa, Kansas, Nebraska, Oregon, and California.

James A. Rawley. *Race and Politics: "Bleeding Kansas" and the Coming of the Civil War* (1969)
The role of the Kansas-Nebraska question in national politics. In this analysis of the free-soilers' motives, Rawley—like Berwanger—emphasizes their race prejudice.

Eric Foner. *Free Soil, Free Labor, Free Men: The Ideology of the Republican party Before the Civil War* (1970)
Ideology, Foner says, played a major role in bringing on the Civil War. The Republican leadership, less bigoted and more idealistic in its antislavery views than some scholars have claimed, viewed the North-South conflict as one between two very different societies. Foner believes that secession was the logical response to the election of Lincoln since he and his party were real threats to slaveholders.

Stephen B. Oates. *To Purge This Land with Blood: A Biography of John Brown* (1970)
Oates depicts Brown as a nineteenth-century Calvinist in a time made violent and fanatic by the slavery controversy.

David H. Donald. *Charles Sumner and the Coming of the Civil War* (1960)
An excellent, perceptive biography of a major

figure in the rise of political antislavery. It is critical of Sumner as intolerant, ambitious, and at times self-deceived.

Harriet Beecher Stowe. *Uncle Tom's Cabin* (1852)

This enormously popular novel about slavery sold a million copies in the United States by the Civil War. Stowe's major theme is not—as many believe—the day-to-day brutality of slavery, but its more indirect consequences in the breakup of black families and the corruption of slaveholders themselves. The book has the reputation—undeservedly—of being naive and foolishly sentimental.

J. Mills Thornton III. *Politics and Power in a Slave Society: Alabama, 1800–1860* (1978)

This recent book is broader in its significance than its title suggests. Thornton believes that Alabama's secession in 1860 ultimately derived from its white citizens' fear that the North's actions endangered equality and freedom for the South's white people. A difficult but rewarding book.

William L. Barney. *The Secessionist Impulse: Alabama and Mississippi in 1860* (1974)

Barney ties the secession of two key slave states to fear of abolitionist plots, racial anxieties, the work of firebrands, and uneasiness over severe food shortages during the months of crisis.

Kenneth Stampp. *And the War Came* (1950)

A close analysis, by an outstanding Civil War scholar, of the final secession crisis and Lincoln's part in it.

15 The Civil War

How Did the War Change the Nation?

1861   Confederates fire on Fort Sumter • President Lincoln calls up 75,000 state militia • Lincoln suspends *habeas corpus* for the first time and endorses severe penalties for treason • The First Battle of Bull Run • Congress grants Lincoln power to take over railroads and telegraphs, imposes internal revenue taxes on manufactures, and passes a personal income tax law • The Second Confiscation Act

1862   The Union treasury begins to issue $450 million "greenbacks" • Ironclads *Monitor* and *Merrimac* battle • Albert S. Johnston stops Grant's advance in the West at the battle of Shiloh Church, Tennessee • Union forces capture New Orleans • The Confederate States of America institute a draft • The Homestead Act • George McClellan's peninsular campaign is checked by Robert E. Lee • The Morrill Land Grant College Act • The first black Union regiments are authorized • Congress passes the first of two Pacific Railway Acts • The Second Battle of Bull Run • McClellan stops Lee's advance at Antietam Creek, Maryland • Lincoln issues the Emancipation Proclamation

1863   The Emancipation Proclamation goes into effect • Congress adopts a draft for the Union army • Joseph Hooker is defeated by Lee and "Stonewall" Jackson at Chancellorsville, Virginia • Democratic Congressman Clement Vallandigham is arrested and eventually banished to the South • Fifty pro-Union counties in Virginia are admitted into the Union as West Virginia • Battle of Gettysburg, Pennsylvania, the turning point of the war • Grant captures Vicksburg, Mississippi, and ensures Union control of the Mississippi River • The New York draft riots

1863, 1864   National Banking Acts establish uniform banking and currency practices

1864   Sherman captures Atlanta, Georgia, and marches to the sea • Second Pacific Railway Act passed by Congress • Lincoln reelected

1865   Lee asks Grant for terms of surrender; they conclude a peace at Appomattox Court House • Lincoln is assassinated by John Wilkes Booth, and Andrew Johnson becomes president

ew Americans who lived through the Civil War doubted that it had made an enormous difference in the life of their nation. Aside from the wholesale killing and maiming, the two warring governments had spent billions of dollars on arms, supplies, and services. Vast armies had been mobilized and millions of men exposed to places and experiences they would otherwise never have encountered. The war had destroyed slavery and decisively shifted power to the North. It also seemed to mark a great divide between a sleepier agrarian America and a bustling America of great factories and giant cities. As they looked back on the events of 1861–65, both ex-Yankees and ex-Confederates were certain that they had witnessed a profound transformation of the nation.

More recently some scholars have begun to have doubts about the extent of this change. The Civil War, they say, may have formally destroyed the peculiar institution, but it did not really free the nation's black people. Blacks had to wait until our own day for anything resembling real freedom and equality. Furthermore, the war, in this view,

did not promote the economic growth of the United States nor represent the great watershed between an agrarian and an urban-industrial world. In fact, some historians believe it retarded economic development and slowed the shift from agriculture to industry and from country to city.

How *did* the war affect the nation? As we discuss the awesome "brothers' war," we must, if we are to answer the question, consider not just the battles and campaigns but also the social, political, and economic changes that accompanied the strife and carnage.

NORTH AND SOUTH

The Civil War was a military contest, a confrontation of two economies, an ideological battle, and a war between two state departments, two congresses, and two chief executives. With the advantages of hindsight, we might assume that in each of these the Union had the advantage. But few Americans living in 1861 perceived it this way, and the fact that the war lasted so long and cost the

During the weeks following Fort Sumter, the martial spirit affected everyone: notice the enthusiasm as New York's Seventh Regiment leaves for the front. So many northerners tried to enlist that the United States turned down thousands.

Library of Congress

Union so much suggests that contemporary perceptions were not completely wrong.

The Balance of Forces. An objective, neutral observer making up a Confederate-Union balance sheet in April 1861, as the contest was about to begin, would probably have bet on the South. True, with 9 million people, the seceded states had less than half the population of the North. Furthermore, 3.5 million of its people were blacks, whom southerners were unwilling to arm—at first. The South also seemed outclassed economically. In 1860 the whole of what became the Confederate States of America had only 18,000 manufacturing establishments, employing 110,000 workers. The North had over 100,000 factories and shops, with 1.3 million employees. New York, Massachusetts, and Pennsylvania each produced industrial goods worth more than the output of the entire South. In the means to transport goods and men, the North was also far ahead of the South, with more than 70 percent of the nation's railroad track and twice as many horses and mules as the Confederacy.

Yet many other factors seemed to favor the Confederacy. The southern economy had its strengths. One was an abundance of food to feed its citizens, its draft animals, and its armies. Another was cotton. Cotton was useful for cloth and uniforms; but more important, it was the keystone of Confederate diplomacy. Without cotton, southerners thought, Europe's great textile industry, particularly Britain's, would shut down. To save itself from industrial ruin, England would have to intervene on the South's behalf to restore a dependable supply of American cotton. To guarantee that Britain would feel the pinch, early in the war southern states embargoed cotton, and patriotic Confederate citizens pressured planters to limit the amount of cotton they planted. Some cotton was even burned. The campaign cut the South's 1862 output to a third of its prewar volume.

The Confederacy also had important strategic advantages. For the South to win, it only had to survive; for the North to win, it had to conquer. The Confederacy, therefore, could use the less demanding and less expensive strategy of defense. The North, by contrast, had to accept the high costs of attack. Defense also provided supply advantages. The South had "interior" lines of communication; retreat would only make it easier to supply Confederate troops in the field. The North faced the opposite situation. As its armies pushed farther and farther into the South, it would experience the growing difficulties and breakdowns of constantly elongating supply lines. In the end, if only the war's price to the Union could be made high enough, southern independence seemed guaranteed.

For such a strategy to succeed, the North's morale and will to fight eventually would have to crack under the strain. Southerners, and many Europeans, were certain that here, too, the Confederacy had the edge. Paradoxically, the South—a slave society—in its own estimate was fighting for freedom. Mississippi, proclaimed Jefferson Davis in his farewell to the United States Senate, had left the Union only "from the high and solemn motive of defending and protecting the rights we inherited, and which it is our duty to transmit unshorn to our children." By contrast, most southerners, and some northerners, were certain that only the desire to dominate, to assert its power, and to achieve selfish economic and political ends lay behind the North's refusal to let the seceded states leave the Union. Did a society thus bent on conquest have the fortitude and determination of one committed to freedom? To southerners, the answer seemed clearly no.

The South also possessed superior military talent. Secession deprived the United States Army of a third of its officers, and the best third at that. Men like Joseph E. Johnston, Edmund Kirby-Smith, and—above all—Robert E. Lee took commissions in the Confederate armed forces only after great personal anguish. Their choice made, however, they supported the southern cause with dedication and skill; especially in the early months, before the Union discovered its own talented leaders, they contributed immeasurably to Confederate successes.

At the level of the common soldier, too, it seemed that the Confederacy had the edge. Southerners were an outdoor people, accustomed to hunting and fishing. They knew how to use rifles, and they were better adapted to physical hardship. Confederate sympathizers, certainly, had little doubt that young southern farm boys would make far better soldiers than the hollow-chested Yankee clerks from the counting-houses of New York, Philadelphia, Cincinnati, and Chicago.

Leadership. Despite these appearances, we can now see that almost all the real advantages lay with the North. The man who led the Union during these trying years was, without question, the Union's greatest single asset. Abraham Lincoln was a consummate politician. For four of the most dangerous years the nation ever faced, he managed to make the right political decisions. The mobilization of Union resources to fight a great—and in many quarters unpopular—war required prodigious political juggling. State governors, even Republicans, were jealous of their powers; they often clashed with the federal authorities, especially over military recruiting. Within his own party Lincoln had to deal with both radicals and conservatives. At times he felt compelled to limit civil liberties to preserve order and to prevent "agitators" from discouraging enlistment. He also faced the problem of the border states, which remained in the Union only precariously and had to be dealt with delicately to avoid pushing them into the Confederate camp. Finally, there was slavery: emancipation was the North's moral trump, but should it be played? If so, when?

The president also had sound military instincts, often better ones than those of the professionals. His chief claim to military leadership, however, was his choice of men. He was not always right, but he was capable of learning. Eventually he recognized the military genius of Ulysses S. Grant and William T. Sherman and gave them a free hand in managing the Union armies. The combination of their talents was an important step toward victory.

He looked the part of a president—far more so than his chief antagonist, Lincoln—but Jefferson Davis did not have Lincoln's extraordinary capacity to inspire people and make his government's cause appear just and valid.

National Portrait Gallery, Smithsonian Institution

Lincoln's selection of civilian subordinates was also, on the whole, wise and successful. As secretary of state, William Seward was ultimately an excellent choice. Early in 1861 Seward proposed that Lincoln transfer some of the president's powers to himself and at the same time provoke incidents with Britain and France that would bring the South rushing to defend the Union against foreign attack. Lincoln gently rebuked Seward for this preposterous idea, and thereafter the secretary recognized his chief's authority. The secretary of the treasury was the high-principled, aloof, ambitious, and humorless Salmon Chase. Although he had no significant experience in finance, Chase guided the government through some of the most difficult financial shoals it would ever encounter. Lincoln's choice of Simon Cameron, the powerful Republican leader of Pennsylvania, as secretary of war was a mistake. Cameron was both corrupt and incompetent. Fortunately, Lincoln quickly discovered his error, sent Cameron to Russia as American minister, and chose Ohio Democrat Edwin Stanton for the post. Although Stanton was often caustic and intolerant, he was a prodigious worker and a passionate and skilled defender of the Union cause.

Lincoln's preeminent success, however, was as a symbol of the Union's determination to survive. He was a master of English prose, and his major state papers and addresses rank among the most inspiring evocations of the democratic spirit. Taking what could easily be interpreted as a war of conquest indistinguishable from the British effort to suppress the colonists eighty years before, he converted it into a struggle for the noblest aspirations of the American people. The Union, the president persuaded his fellow citizens, was humanity's "last, best hope." If it should be defeated, democracy would fail, and the forces of darkness and tyranny triumph. If, however, the Union prevailed, government "of the people, by the people, for the people" would "not perish from the earth."

And what of the Confederacy's leader, Jefferson Davis? A West Point graduate, commander of the Mississippi Rifles in the Mexican War, Pierce's secretary of war, and former United States senator from Mississippi, Davis seemed eminently suited to guide the besieged Confederacy. He was honest, courageous, and intelligent; and his sharply etched lean features and dignified bearing gave him the look of a national leader. Davis's performance, however, was not as impressive as his credentials and appearance. He had to have his hand in everything, both civilian and military, and often he botched the job. According to

Stephen R. Mallory, Davis's secretary of the navy, the Confederate president "neither labored with method or celerity himself, nor permitted others to do so for him." He was also argumentative and, unlike his northern counterpart, insensitive to public opinion. Although many Confederate setbacks were the fault of others or were inherent in the South's situation, Davis's weaknesses clearly contributed to the South's defeat.

THE WAR BEGINS

The first responsibility of each president was to raise an army. Immediately after the attack on Fort Sumter Lincoln had called for 75,000 state militia to join the small regular army for three months' service. The war, he expected, would be brief, and the troops would be home for late spring planting. Except in those slave states still in the Union, the response was quick and enthusiastic. Young

northerners regarded the war as a glorious lark, and they flocked to recruiting offices. State quotas were quickly oversubscribed; and militia regiments, many composed of untrained men without rifles or proper uniforms, rushed off for Washington to meet their country's call.

Lincoln's move to put down the rebellion tripped off a furious reaction in the uncommitted slave states. Between April 17 and May 20 four more states—Virginia, Arkansas, Tennessee, and North Carolina—seceded and joined the Confederacy. It also propelled thousands of southerners into the army to defend southern rights. The Confederacy had the opportunity to make a formidable force out of this raw material, but it let the chance slip. President Davis, now residing with his government in the Confederate capital of Richmond, expected a long and difficult war, but his voice went unheeded. Like Lincoln, the Confederate Congress believed the war would end by winter, and it accepted many short-term volunteers who soon had to be replaced.

The United States on the eve of the Civil War

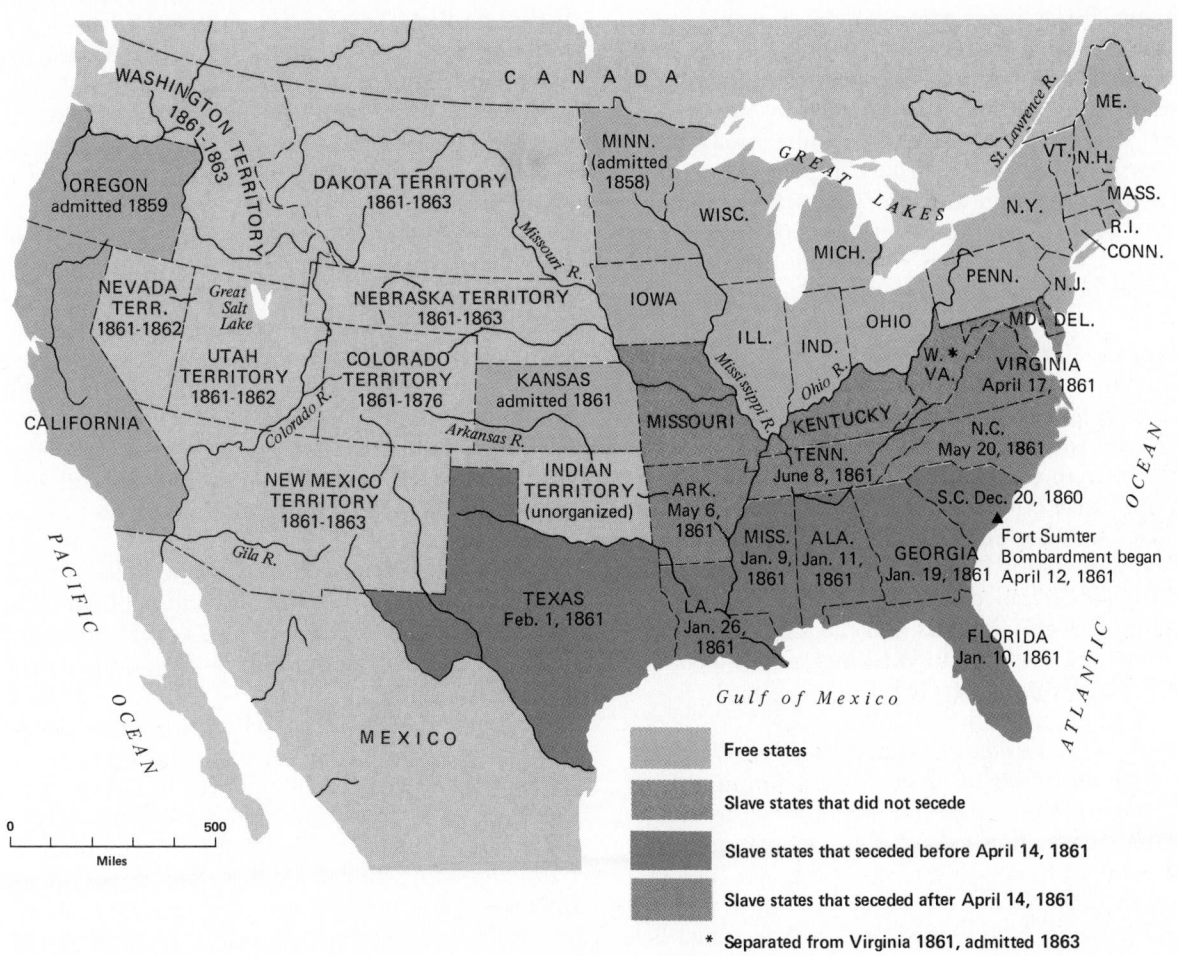

Bull Run. In this case Davis was right and Lincoln was wrong. The fighting was bloody, bitter, and interminable. The first major military confrontation between Union and Confederate troops took place in July 1861 at Bull Run, a small tributary of the Potomac twenty miles south of Washington. There 30,000 men under Union General Irvin McDowell, advancing on Richmond, met a Confederate force under Pierre Beauregard. The Confederates were outnumbered and outgunned but better led and better coordinated. For a while the Union forces held the upper hand, but the green Yankee troops panicked when the Confederates counterattacked. Disheartened and disorganized, they abandoned their rifles and artillery and fled pell-mell to the safety of Washington. Accompanying them in their head-long retreat was a motley array of civilians, including several congressmen and many ladies who had come out from the Union capital to watch what they expected to be a rebel rout.

Bull Run was a healthy antidote to northern overconfidence. Republican governors from all over the North telegraphed the War Department offering new regiments to protect the capital and prepare for a resumption of the march south. These men, moreover, would be enlisted for three years or the duration of the war. Patriotism, the glamor of a uniform, and the love of adventure were still potent stimulants to enlistment. With the early naive optimism now replaced by stubborn determination and not yet undermined by doubt and gloom, another 75,000 volunteers streamed into Washington training camps, prepared to put down the "rebellion."

Lincoln's Early Commanders. The man who took charge of this force was George B. McClellan. As a young officer, Little Mac had served in the Mexican War; but he had spent most of his military career in the Corps of Engineers, and when the war broke out, he was a civilian railroad director. His training and experience as an organizer and administrator helped him pull the army together. McClellan drilled his troops rigorously, welding the new arrivals and the ragged, dispirited mob that had fled to Washington into a confident, spit-and-polish army.

Organizing abilities, however, are not enough for a successful military leader. Despite the early minor victories in western Virginia that had brought him to the administration's attention, McClellan was not a good field commander. He took months to equip and train his men before resuming the attack. Finally, after insistent urging by Lincoln, in March 1862 McClellan's magnificent army of 130,000 set out for Richmond from Hampton Roads. At Williamsburg, in early May, McClellan first encountered the enemy. The engagement was a draw. For the next two months McClellan fought a series of battles—the Peninsular Campaign—against two of the South's ablest military leaders, Robert E. Lee and Thomas J. ("Stonewall") Jackson. He managed to avert defeat; but his army returned to Washington in June bruised and badly battered. Nothing had been achieved.

In the West Union forces under the Virginian George H. Thomas and the shaggy, hard-drinking Ulysses S. Grant were having better luck. In late January Thomas defeated the Confederates at the Battle of Mill Springs in Kentucky. Several weeks later Grant captured Fort Donelson on the Cumberland River, taking 14,000 Confederate prisoners. Soon Nashville fell to Union forces. Grant believed that he was now in a position to crush the Confederate army in the West decisively, but he underestimated the recuperative powers of his foe. On April 6, 1862, Albert Sidney Johnston attacked the exposed Union position near Shiloh Church (a meetinghouse near Pittsburg Landing, Tennessee) and pushed back the federal troops commanded by William Tecumseh Sherman. A confused two-day battle brought heavy casualties to both sides, including the death of the Confederate commander. Ultimately, Grant's army held, but the Union advance was stopped dead.

McClellan's lack of offensive zeal disturbed Lincoln. In addition, the general was becoming a political liability. A moderate Democrat, he was thoroughly detested by the "Radicals" in the Republican party, who advocated abolition of slavery and a more aggressive war policy to defeat the South. In July 1862 the president replaced McClellan as field commander in the eastern theater with General John Pope, simultaneously elevating Henry W. Halleck to general in chief of the Union armies.

For the next year the tide of war swept back and forth, with Lincoln unable to find a field commander to match Lee. After Pope's drubbing at the hands of Lee and Jackson in the Second Battle of Bull Run (August 29–30, 1862), Lincoln turned once again to McClellan, who once again disappointed him. Cocky and arrogant in manner and speech but timid in action, McClellan stopped Lee's advance into Maryland at Antietam (September 17, 1862) but lost the opportunity of decisively defeating the far smaller Confederate force. In November Lincoln decided to replace McClellan with Ambrose E. Burnside. The choice was

The Civil War was not all battles and bullets. At times it wore a festive aspect, and civilians often came out to the camps and battlefields to see the sights. The woman here is Kate Chase Sprague, daughter of treasury secretary Salmon P. Chase and wife of Rhode Island's millionaire governor, William Sprague.

unwise. In December 1862 at Fredericksburg, Virginia, the new Union commander sent massed infantry against entrenched Confederate troops whose rifles and artillery slaughtered the charging blue-clad federals. Lincoln replaced Burnside with Joseph Hooker, who quickly demonstrated that he was no better. At Chancellorsville, Virginia (May 2–4, 1863), Lee and Jackson severely mauled Hooker's Army of the Potomac. The only consolation for the Union forces was that Jackson was accidentally killed by his own men.

Union Strategy. The Union was not only slow in finding a competent commander; it also had difficulty evolving a clear, overall military strategy. At first "On to Richmond" had seemed enough of a plan. When Richmond proved to be far more difficult to reach than anyone expected, the Union administration and the field commanders looked for other approaches. Early in the war the aged commander in chief, General Winfield Scott, conceived the Anaconda Plan. Scott proposed that the Union armies, like the great anaconda snake that crushes its victims, should advance on all fronts and slowly, but inexorably, squeeze the South to death. Scott's strategy was too slow to suit Lincoln and the northern public, however, and it was never officially adopted. Nevertheless, the ap-

proach that eventually emerged had many of the Anaconda Plan's features. On land, northern armies would push farther and farther into the South, slicing into its vital communications. At sea, the Union navy would cut off Confederate access to foreign munitions, guns, and manufactures.

Early in 1862 the Union armies launched an offensive to cut the Confederacy in half along the Mississippi River. In April Union land and sea forces under Benjamin F. Butler took New Orleans, the South's largest city and the control point for access to the river. Bit by bit the Union forces advanced up and down the banks of the Mississippi. In the summer of 1863 the final Confederate positions on the river fell when Grant, aided by David Porter's river gunboats, took Vicksburg, Mississippi, and Port Hudson, Louisiana. The Confederacy was now cut in two.

The Naval War. The squeeze tactics were especially effective at sea, where each month the northern naval blockade grew tighter. In early 1862 the *Merrimac*, a Confederate ironclad converted from a scuttled United States naval vessel, threatened to break the Union blockade of Hampton Roads, Virginia. The federal navy rushed its own ironclad, the *Monitor*, to the scene. The two vessels battled to a draw, and the southern ship

The Civil War   359

Major battles of the Civil War, 1861–1865

retired, never again to challenge Union naval supremacy.

Its naval advantage was to stand the North in good stead. In the western theater federal gun-

boats on the Mississippi and its tributaries supported Union military operations with their canon and by keeping river supply lines open. Along the Atlantic and Gulf coasts the seagoing Union fleet made possible successful amphibious attacks against southern ports like New Orleans, Mobile, Savannah, and Port Royal. The most useful naval action, however, was the coastal blockade. Each month, as the number of available ships grew, the sea noose around the South drew tighter. In 1861 the federal navy captured one Confederate vessel in ten that tried to escape to the open sea; by 1865 its record had improved to one in two, and growing Confederate shortages of many products hitherto imported from Europe attested to the mounting effectiveness of the blockade.

The Confederates also had their moments of glory at sea. Many Confederate blockade-runners—swift, shallow-draft vessels—successfully evaded Union ships and dashed to Bermuda or some other British-American port. There they loaded Enfield rifles, medicines, and lead, as well as scarce luxury items; if they were lucky, they brought their cargoes back to the besieged Confederacy. On the high seas the *Alabama* and other Confederate raiders destroyed millions of dollars' worth of Union shipping. To protect themselves against disastrous loss, northern ship owners transferred their vessels to foreign registry or paid high insurance rates. Despite these successes, the Confederates were never able to challenge the Union navy on the waters, and each month saw the northern advantage grow as its shipyards turned out scores of new vessels to augment Union naval strength. In June 1864 the United States Navy's *Kearsarge* finally caught up with Captain Raphael Semmes of the *Alabama* off Cherbourg, France, and put an end to his spectacular raiding career.

The Diplomatic War. Europe's need for cotton had promised the Confederacy a chance to secure diplomatic recognition and possibly military help from Britain and France. The South could also count on Europe's upper classes, who felt they had more in common with the southern planter elite than with the crude, money-mad Yankees. Besides, nothing would suit British policy better than cutting the bumptious United States down to size by helping divide it in half. The French, for the most part, followed Britain's anti-Union lead. But, after establishing a puppet regime in Mexico that violated the Monroe Doctrine, they had their own reasons for favoring a Yankee defeat and an enfeebled United States.

In the end cotton diplomacy proved to be a disappointment. The British imported cotton from Egypt and India to replace some of the lost southern supply. And northern wheat, which England needed, gave the Union a similar, though less powerful, lever on British policy. The North

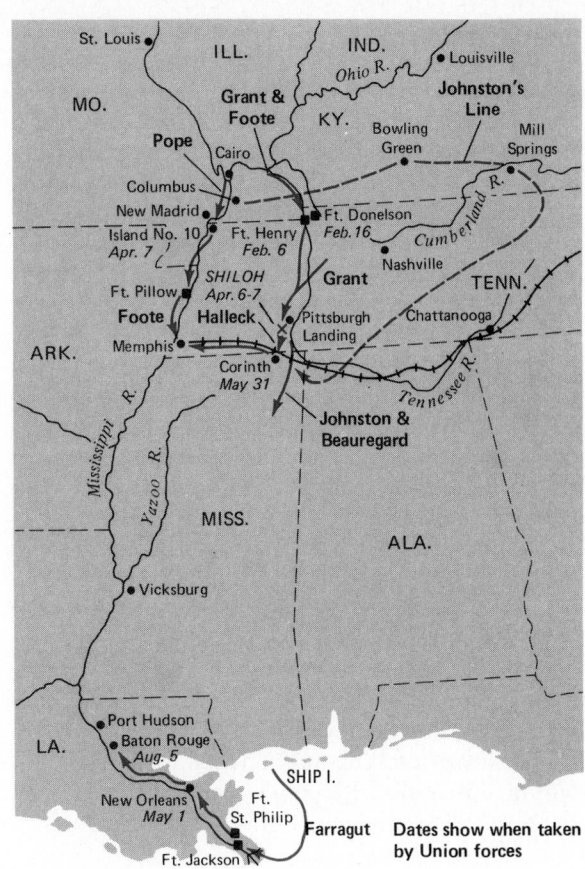

War in the West, 1862

also had one high card that its enemy lacked: the prospect of emancipation. Though they might not be averse to southern independence, the British middle and working classes could not morally support the slave system. If the North could convince the British people of its antislavery intentions, the London government would find it difficult to throw its weight against the Union.

For three years, however, the Union and the Confederacy fought desperately to curry favor with the British. The South won the early diplomatic rounds. Late in 1861 the Confederate commissioners to France (John Slidell) and England (James M. Mason) ran the Union blockade and reached Havana, where they boarded the *Trent*, a British vessel, for passage to Europe. On November 7 Captain Charles Wilkes of the U.S.S. *San Jacinto* intercepted the *Trent*, arrested Slidell and Mason, and took them to Boston. The furious British demanded their release, as well as reparations and an apology. With Union sentiment hostile to Britain, Lincoln and his secretary of state, William Seward, sat on the situation for a time, then quietly returned the commissioners with an apology. But the *Trent* affair gave the Confederates an edge. Early in 1862 the British government permitted the Confederates to use British shipyards to build and outfit the *Alabama* and other raiders, and soon after allowed the Confederate navy to contract with the Laird shipbuilding firm in Scotland for several powerful, ironclad "rams." For a while, too, English investors were receptive to lending money to the Confederacy.

The tide turned, however, when British friends of the United States, led by Richard Cobden and John Bright, appealed to antislavery British opinion and succeeded in creating a strong pro-Union current. The efforts of these sympathetic Britons, the tireless maneuvering of Lincoln's minister to England, Charles Francis Adams, and Union victories on the battlefield combined to shift British opinion in favor of the North. In October 1863 the British government seized the Laird rams before the Confederates could take delivery, ending their threat to the Union blockade. Though the North's worst diplomatic fears were allayed by the end of 1862, the possibility of a falling-out between Britain and the Union threatened Lincoln's war effort and gave hope to the South almost to the end of the war.

WAR AND SOCIETY

The titanic military, naval, and diplomatic drives of North and South were sustained by equally stu-

pendous efforts of their respective home fronts. The raising of troops, the marshaling of financial and economic resources, and the management of internal dissent were all vital parts of the great struggle on both sides to achieve victory.

Conscription. Throughout the war both combatants relied primarily on volunteers to fill their military ranks. For the first half of the war it worked, but it could not last. A few months of bitter fighting, growing casualty lists, and news of the danger, the anguish, and the hard work of soldiering dampened youthful enthusiasm; fewer and fewer volunteers turned up at the recruiting offices. Yet the war consumed manpower at a frightful rate. Local communities, seeking to meet the quotas assigned by Washington or Richmond, resorted to bonuses to encourage enlistment. In 1862 Buffalo offered each new Union recruit $80 to enlist. Orleans County, New York, gave a cow to the wife of every man who joined the army. Many communities provided monthly stipends to the families of volunteers. The Confederate Congress offered bounties and generous furloughs to volunteers who reenlisted.

By the middle of 1862, however, neither glory nor material incentives were enough to fill Confederate and Union ranks; both governments were forced to resort to conscription. The draft laws on each side contained many inequities. The Confederate measure provided that anyone who supervised twenty slaves or more, whether as owner or overseer, was exempt from service. The

Library of Congress

The wounded near Fredericksburg. The emptiness and despair on these soldiers' faces contrast with the confidence and optimism of the early volunteers. With inadequate food, shelter, and sanitation, the ideals of glory and victory gave way to the realities of pain and death.

Union law allowed a man to avoid the army if he could find and pay for a substitute or gave the government $300. The exemptions in both conscription systems were defended on the grounds of national interest or compassion, but they favored the affluent and encouraged critics in the North and South to charge that it was "a rich man's war and a poor man's fight." In the Union, particularly, opposition to the draft took violent forms, culminating in four days of rioting, looting, arson, and attacks on blacks and abolitionists in New York City in mid-July 1863.

Conscription was a novel exercise of central government power. The three previous American wars had been fought by volunteers. Now, under the goad of necessity, both Union and Confederate governments had asserted a right never claimed before, the right to compel men to risk their lives for the nation. But this innovation was only one of many, all pointing to enhanced national over local power and all increasing the physical and institutional integration of the country.

The Beginnings of Modern National Finance.
Paying for the war was a major challenge for both governments. In 1861, after three generations of independence, Americans were still not used to heavy taxes. But the war cost both governments enormous sums. At one point the Union treasury was paying out $2 million a day for munitions, supplies, military pay, and other public expenses.

The Confederacy initially tried to meet most of its costs with money borrowed from foreign and domestic sources. This approach yielded little, for few capitalists at home or abroad would lend money to the South except at outrageous interest rates. As early as 1861, following the precedent of the Revolution, the Confederate treasury turned to paper money. Since there was little gold in the South, this was "fiat" money, mere IOUs.

Though the Confederate printing presses spewed out over $1.5 billion in paper money during the war, even that proved inadequate for the Confederacy's needs. Before many months the value of Confederate currency had fallen so low that the government was forced to adopt other means for paying its bills. Eventually the Richmond authorities were compelled to bypass private enterprise and invade property rights to get the means to fight. In early 1863 the Confederate Congress authorized the impressment of slaves for the building of fortifications and for other government work. It also empowered the government to detail soldiers for work in vital war factories. And in April 1863 it assumed the authority to take from

Library of Congress

As enthusiasm for the war waned, both Confederate and Union governments went to greater lengths to attract new men, as this poster illustrates. In 1862 a northerner could receive $300 or more for enlisting; the same sum could buy his exemption from the draft.

each farmer a tenth of all the major crops he produced. The levy on crops, though unwieldy, was the best expedient a desperate Confederate government could design.

In the North the need to supply the military forces led to a parallel, though less drastic, inflation of national power, and since it was the Union government that survived, that growth was momentous for the nation's future. With access to the markets of Europe, the gold of the West, and most of the country's banking capital, Union Secretary of the Treasury Salmon Chase was better able than his Confederate counterpart to tax and borrow. By 1865 Congress had imposed internal revenue taxes on hundreds of manufactured items, created a Bureau of Internal Revenue to administer the tax laws, and established America's first income tax. Using the excuse that heavily taxed American manufactures must be protected against cheaper foreign wares, the Republican Congress also raised tariff rates to levels never before reached, drastically reversing the prewar trend under the Democrats.

Internal taxes and import duties were not enough, however, and the Union, too, resorted to borrowing. Under Chase's prompting, Congress authorized the sale of several hundred million dollars of bonds, paying 6 percent interest in gold. The treasury's chief agent, Philadelphia banker Jay Cooke, advertised this issue in every northern newspaper and sent his subagents all over the country to peddle the securities from door to door. Eventually he sold $362 million in bonds. By the war's end these bond sales and others had pushed the Union debt to the immense figure of $2.5 billion.

The treasury's financial needs produced a major revolution in the country's banking system. The state banks that had supplied the country's currency and credit needs since the demise of the Second Bank of the United States in 1836 proved inadequate to meet the country's political emergency. Matters were brought to a crisis in December 1861, when public hoarding of gold and excessive treasury borrowing from the banks forced the banks to cease redeeming their notes in specie. With the need to keep a gold reserve no longer limiting their paper money issues, the banks were free to turn on the printing presses. The country now faced the prospect of a deluge of worthless paper bank notes to meet its day-to-day currency needs.

To end this chaotic situation and at the same time tap the banks for funds, Chase proposed a national currency backed by government bonds and issued by a new system of federally chartered banks. Under the National Banking Acts of 1863 and 1864, businessmen who bought a specified amount of federal bonds could organize new banks and issue bank notes backed by the government securities. Now, instead of a multitude of privately issued bank notes unsecured by gold, the country would have a uniform paper money system under strict federal control. And after the war these notes would be doubly safe, for then, it was assumed, gold would once more return to normal circulation and the government and the banks would be able to redeem their obligations in "specie" on demand.

The national banking system would prove less of an economic boon than its sponsors had hoped, but it did help the treasury finance the war. By June 1863 there were 450 national banks in existence, with millions of dollars' worth of federal bonds in their reserves, representing large revenues to the federal government. More impor-

tant, however, the national crisis had broken the stiff resistance to a federal banking system. For the first time in a generation Washington was back in the business of regulating the country's banking affairs.

The national banking system helped ease the Union's financial problems and at the same time provided a new sort of paper money for the nation's commercial needs. Still, this was not enough. Long before the bond sales and the new taxes produced results, the treasury was empty. There seemed no alternative to the intolerable situation but treasury-issued paper money, as had been done in the South, with its value shored up by a vague promise to redeem the "greenbacks" in gold after the war. The Union's superior resources, however, allowed it to limit the issue of greenbacks to $450 million and prevented their severe depreciation. By late 1864 northern prices were about two and a half times those of 1860. In the South price levels had risen fiftyfold.

The Spreading Rail System. The expansion of the government's role in finance was matched by its growing involvement in transportation. In 1861 the Union had 22,000 miles of railroad track. This was already the most extensive railroad network in the world, but it was not an integrated system. Many smaller communities had no railroad connections, and different track gauges prevented rapid through-traffic on many routes. The most glaring defect of all was the lack of rail connections to the West Coast.

The war reduced each of these deficiencies. After 1860, with the South out of the Union, Congress passed a measure to subsidize a transcontinental railroad. The Pacific Railway Act of 1862, as supplemented in 1864, gave the private promoters of the Central Pacific, building east from Sacramento, and those of the Union Pacific, building west from Omaha, 20 million acres of public land and a federal loan of $60 million in bonds. Little actual trackage was laid down during the war, but soon after Appomattox construction crews were pushing iron rails across the plains and mountains at a furious pace.

Meanwhile, the Lincoln administration pursued a vigorous and successful policy of controlling and coordinating existing railroads to meet war needs. In January 1861 Congress granted the president power to take over telegraph and rail lines. After May 1862 the railroads operated under overall government direction. In addition, the military superintendent of railroads arranged the construction of 650 miles of new track to link existing routes. The government's expanded role in transportation enabled the railroads to perform marvels in moving Union troops and guaranteeing that they always had what they needed to fight and live.

The Richmond government, in contrast, failed to mobilize southern railroads. Davis and his subordinates, though handicapped by the blockade and the South's inferior industry, did less than they might have to prevent locomotives and rolling stock from breaking down and tracks from wearing out. Scores of small private companies continued to set rail rates and make other decisions affecting the southern economy and war effort. Generally, troops arrived where they were needed, but goods moved slowly and at high cost. Because of railroad breakdowns, toward the end of the war southern troops were often shoeless, hungry, and ragged, while Confederate warehouses bulged with supplies and clothing.

Government Becomes Big Business. The demands of war enormously swelled the size of the Union government. Disbursements and tax collections brought an army of clerks to the stately Treasury Building across from the White House, while in the field hundreds of treasury agents fanned out to regulate the illegal cotton trade between northern buyers eager for scarce fiber and southerners eager for scarce goods. The War Department's scale of operation became even greater than the treasury's. Under Quartermaster General Montgomery Meigs, it performed prodigious labors in supplying the army. During the year ending June 30, 1865, alone, the Quartermaster Department purchased 3.4 million trousers, 3.7 million pairs of drawers, and 3.2 million flannel shirts, laying out for these and countless other articles over $431 million. To procure these items armies of government clerks and purchasing agents negotiated thousands of contracts with manufacturers and wholesalers. In 1861 the federal civil service had employed 40,000 people; by 1865 there were 195,000, a fivefold increase.

Government orders invigorated the North's economy. The gigantic War Department procurement did much to lower costs in private armories. It also stimulated production in a wide array of businesses directly connected to the war effort. In the boot and shoe industry, for example, it was reported in 1863 that "operatives are pouring in [to Lynn, Massachusetts, a major shoe center] as fast as room can be made for them; buildings for shoe factories are going up in every direction; the hum of machinery is heard on every hand." Frequently the scale of government orders encouraged standardization and mechanization of pro-

duction, establishing a model for postwar development. The canning industry was stimulated by government orders: when Gail Borden's condensed milk factory opened in early 1861, its entire output was "immediately commandeered" for the army.

Organizing Agriculture. In the South invading armies, the breakdown of transportation, and the erosion of the slave labor system led to agricultural decline. In the North agriculture burgeoned under wartime need. The process of mechanizing the American farm was already under way in 1860. The departure of thousands of young men from the farms precisely when the demand for farm products reached an all-time peak accelerated the acceptance of horse-drawn harvesters and mowers. During the decade of the 1850s American farmers had bought 100,000 of these machines; in 1864 manufacturers were turning out this many each year.

The expansion of northern farm output during the war was only obliquely a consequence of government action. But the government had an important direct impact on the social side of American agriculture. For years various northern and western farming groups had demanded favors of the federal government, only to see them blocked by Democratic and southern opponents. Now, with the South out of the Union and the Republicans in control of the government, the walls came down. In 1861 Congress authorized a department of agriculture within the Patent Office to be headed by a commissioner. In 1862 it enacted the Morrill Land Grant College Act, setting aside several million acres of federal land for support of agricultural and industrial higher education. The 1862 Homestead Act provided that any citizen or any alien who declared his intention of becoming a citizen and who was also head of a family and over twenty-one might claim 160 acres of land on specified surveyed portions of the public domain. After residing on this land, adding improvements, and paying a small registration fee, he would become its owner, with no further obligation except the usual local taxes. The law would be less than perfect in the way it was applied, yet it represented a triumph of the yeoman ideal and a fulfillment of Republican promises to the West.

New Bonds Between Citizens. The war emergency that enhanced the role of government in many areas also strengthened the nation's private voluntary institutions. Before 1861 the United States was anything but united in the spheres of life that affected ordinary citizens. In fact, the

Library of Congress

The war experience transformed a people accustomed to improvising into a disciplined nation concerned with planning and control. Volunteer nursing and individual acts of kindness yielded to the large, impersonal United States Sanitary Commission staffed by paid workers.

growing sectional confrontation during the 1850s had torn apart what little connective tissue existed. The war made the North-South split still deeper, of course, but within the Union itself it stimulated the growth of new civic bonds and attachments.

Everywhere patriotic people came together to help with those tasks that were still not considered the legitimate responsibility of the government. The United States Sanitary Commission, raising money through numerous "sanitary fairs," assisted the army's medical department. The Christian Commission of the Young Men's Christian Association supplied Bibles to the troops, provided them with other reading matter, and helped them send money home to their families.

Voluntary associations also boosted civilian morale. The Loyal Publication Societies of New York and New England churned out pamphlets explaining and defending the Union cause. Many leading intellectuals, including Charles Eliot Norton, Ralph Waldo Emerson and Professor Francis Lieber of Columbia, joined the societies and lent their names and their writing skills to their work. The Union League, active in eighteen northern states by 1862, brought prominent northern businessmen, professionals, intellectuals, and politicians together to propagandize for the Union and promote policies to help defeat the South. After 1865 it became a permanent network of clubs that united an urban elite for the support of nationalist Republican policies.

The participation of northern intellectuals in organizations like these, along with the moral support of the Union demonstrated by writers and intellectuals, marked a reversal of the critical attitudes of America's thinkers toward their country's leading institutions and values. Northern youth, too, apparently developed a new faith in their society. President Julian Sturtevant of Illinois College noted at midpoint in the struggle: "We were evidently in need of some vigorous discipline. The element of reverence for rightful authority was slipping out of the national mind. Our young men were beginning to feel all authority is despotism, all government tyranny, and all submission and obedience servility." The war, he wrote, had ended these signs of rebelliousness among the young and forged a more cohesive society.

This new faith of intellectuals and educated young people would have long-lasting effects. Before 1860 their views had tempered the materialistic attitudes of Americans and supplied a critical ingredient to the northern ethos. After 1865 few voices would be raised to challenge the values of a commercial-industrial society. Only in the South would some people demur; but their skepticism, associated as it was with disloyalty, defeat, and poverty, would go unheeded. Meanwhile, the brashness and thrust of Yankee businessmen and promoters would come to epitomize the nation. The Civil War, then, would mark not only the triumph of northern arms but also the victory of the practical, go-ahead side of the prewar northern personality.

Dissent. Despite the war-kindled patriotism, dissent flourished in both the Union and the Confederacy. In each it would create serious difficulties for the government. Ironically, repression would be stronger in the North, which prided itself on its intellectual freedom, than in the South, with its tradition of intolerance.

Dissent in the North ranged from mild disagreement with Republican policies to violent opposition that bordered on treason. The so-called War Democrats often differed with Lincoln and the Republicans over the best ways of achieving victory, but they followed the lead of Stephen Douglas in offering their whole-hearted support to the Union. The Little Giant died in June 1861, depriving the War Democrats of their outstanding leader; but to the end of the struggle, they were among the Union's staunchest supporters. More critical of administration positions were the Peace Democrats, who favored a negotiated peace with the South: either Lincoln should allow the South back into the Union with its rights and institutions guaranteed, or he should permit it to leave without further war and bloodshed.

The Peace Democrats, called Copperheads by their opponents, were probably in a minority at first; but their numbers swelled as the war dragged on and the prospect of quick victory receded. Much of their support came from the Midwest, where many Democrats were appalled by the centralizing tendencies of the Republicans and the new federal powers and responsibilities. Men such as Clement Vallandigham and George Pendleton of Ohio, Daniel Voorhees of Indiana, and a host of other midwestern Democrats regarded the Lincoln administration as the agent of "revived Whiggery" and of high-tariff New England and Pennsylvania. In Congress the Copperheads fought the National Banking Act, the issuance of greenbacks, and the various internal revenue bills. They also resisted every attempt to make abolition a part of the Union cause and decried the administration's efforts to abridge individual freedom. Most Peace Democrats, no matter how skeptical of the Republicans, supported measures they considered necessary for the country's reunification. But at the far edge of dissent was a tiny extremist minority who favored the Confederacy and flirted with treason.

The Copperheads were not the only opponents of administration policies. In the slave states that remained in the Union—Delaware, Maryland, Kentucky, and Missouri—anti-Union sentiment was often intense. During the war several border states became battlegrounds between pro-Union and pro-Confederate groups. Neighbor fought neighbor with a viciousness that sometimes went beyond anything found on the battlefields. In Missouri full-scale guerilla war broke out between Union and Confederate sympathizers. The state soon resembled Kansas during the "bleeding" 1850s as roving bands of irregulars attacked innocent—and not-so-innocent—citizens of the opposite persuasion. In suppressing the disorders in Missouri and elsewhere in the border region, Union commanders frequently used harsh and arbitrary methods that further alienated the prosouthern populace and stirred up even greater dissatisfaction.

Inevitably, Lincoln had to consider how much dissent was permissible in a nation threatened with dissolution. The president was deeply compassionate and strongly committed to free speech. But his first responsibility, he felt, was to preserve the Union.

To head off his opponents and those he considered dangerous to the Union cause, Lincoln employed a combination of guile, persuasion, and coercion. Within his own party he had to contend with the Radicals, Republicans who fervently opposed slavery and believed that the president was not moving fast enough or firmly enough against the South. They particularly deplored his unwillingness to use the war as an opportunity to destroy slavery and his reluctance to employ blacks in the armed forces. Republican conservatives pulled the other way, saying that the war to restore the Union must not be "abolitionized." To attack slavery would only drive the border states out and confirm southern determination to resist. Lincoln dealt with the opposing wings of his party, as he explained at one point, by carrying "a pumpkin in each end of the bag." In his cabinet this meant balancing Seward against Chase and seeing to it that neither prevailed. In Congress this meant listening to all Republican voices, keeping his options open, and moving only when it helped the Union cause.

Dealing with dissenters outside the party was more difficult. The remaining Democrats in Congress were often a thorn in the president's side. Historian James A. Rawley has suggested that the presence of a functioning two-party system in the Union during the war was an important northern advantage over the South. His observation, however valid, is hindsight. To Lincoln, Democratic opposition often seemed indistinguishable from disloyalty, and it proved hard for him to resist using his authority as commander in chief to suppress his critics.

Civil Liberties During Crisis. Lincoln's most outspoken opponent was Vallandigham of Ohio. In May 1863 the former congressman demanded a negotiated peace with the South and accused the Lincoln administration of needlessly prolonging the war for the sake of liberating blacks and enslaving whites. General Burnside, then military commander in Ohio, promptly arrested him. Tried by a military commission, Vallandigham was convicted of disloyalty and attempting to undermine the government.

The affair embarrassed Lincoln. The Ohioan was a prominent Democratic leader, and arresting him made the administration appear despotic while converting the congressman into a free-speech martyr. On the other hand, the president did not see how he could ignore those who threatened Union survival. "Must I shoot a simple-minded soldier boy who deserts," he wrote a group of Union Democrats who protested the Val-

Lincoln on Slavery

Lincoln despised slavery, but he loved the Union even more. For months following Fort Sumter his primary concern, perforce, was to keep more states from joining the Confederacy and to bring back into the Union, by force if necessary, those that had left. Slavery could wait. Other Americans—the abolitionists and other strong antislavery people—reversed the priorities. On August 19, 1862, Horace Greeley, the editor of the prominent antislavery newspaper the *New York Tribune*, published an editorial, "The Prayer of 20,000,000 People," demanding that the president attack slavery head on, without worrying about the political consequences. Lincoln replied in the letter below three days later. It is the statement of a man with little doubt about where his first loyalty lay, and suggests to what extent the abolition of the "peculiar institution" was a by-product of the war.

"Executive Mansion. Washington
August 22, 1862

"Hon. Horace Greeley.

Dear Sir: I have just read yours of the 19th, addressed to myself through the New York *Tribune*. If there be in it any statements or assumptions of fact which I may know to be erroneous, I do not, now and here, controvert them. If there be in it any inferences which I may believe to be falsely drawn, I do not, now and here, argue against them. If there be perceptible in it an impatient and dictatorial tone, I waive it in deference to an old friend whose heart I have always supposed to be right.

"As to the policy I 'seem to be pursuing,' as you say, I have not meant to leave any one in doubt.

"I would save the Union. I would save it the shortest way under the Constitution. The sooner the national authority can be restored, the nearer the Union will be 'the Union as it was.' If there be those who would not save the Union unless they could at the same time save slavery, I do not agree with them. If there be those who would not save the Union unless they could at the same time destroy slavery, I do not agree with them. My paramount object in this struggle is to save the Union, and it is not either to save or to destroy slavery. If I could save the Union without freeing any slave, I would do it; and if I could save it by freeing all the slaves, I would do it; and if I could save it by freeing some and leaving others alone, I would also do that. What I do about slavery and the coloured race, I do because I believe it helps to save the Union; and what I forbear, I forbear because I do not believe it would help save the Union. I shall do less whenever I shall believe what I am doing hurts the cause, and I shall do more whenever I shall believe doing more will help the cause. I shall try to correct errors when shown to be errors, and I shall adopt new views so fast as they shall appear to be true views.

"I have here stated my purpose according to my view of official duty, and I intend no modification of my oft-expressed personal wish that all men everywhere could be free.

Yours,
A. Lincoln"

---

landigham arrest, "while I must not touch the hair of a wily agitator who induces him to desert?" Lincoln solved the problem by releasing Vallandigham and banishing him to the Confederacy.

The Vallandigham case was not an isolated instance of federal restraint of dissenters. Lincoln suspended habeas corpus (the traditional protection of accused parties against arbitrary imprisonment) in areas where disloyalty seemed to endanger the war effort. He also endorsed Congress's imposition of severe penalties on persons guilty of treason or conspiracy to commit treason. In September 1862 he signed a sweeping order making anyone who sought to discourage enlistment, resisted the draft, or engaged in other "disloyal" practices subject to trial by military commission. Yet at no time was he happy about what he felt compelled to do, and he frequently restrained excesses committed by subordinates. When the overzealous Burnside closed the Democratic *Chicago Times* for supporting Vallandigham, the president ordered the paper reopened.

The Emancipation Proclamation. The Lincoln administration's willingness to invade civil liberties and limit the rights of free speech are still further instances of war-inflated government power. The repressive policy proved a temporary lapse that did not outlast the war. But in another area, race relations, the use of government war powers worked a profound, permanent, and beneficent change.

Lincoln and the Radicals differed on the question of slavery. As part of a Union-first policy, the president initially tried to steer clear of the issue. So long as there was any danger that the border slave states might still join the South, Lincoln believed that he must focus the public mind on reuniting the nation rather than on ending the peculiar institution. When General John Frémont, the former Republican presidential candidate, proclaimed in late 1861 that all slaves held by rebels in his Missouri command were free, Lincoln overruled him. The president also refused to use a feature of the Second Confiscation Act of

1861 that provided that captured slaves employed by the Confederacy against the Union be freed. When Horace Greeley publicly criticized him for his inaction against slavery, Lincoln replied that his "paramount object" in the struggle was "to save the Union, . . . not either to save or destroy slavery."

But Lincoln and the Radicals were not free agents: both were at the mercy of circumstances. Nor were blacks passive observers of emancipation. In the North black abolitionists joined their white colleagues in asserting that the war was a struggle over slavery and that to win it the Union must destroy the hateful institution. Slavery, Frederick Douglass proclaimed, was "a tower of strength" to the Confederacy. "The very stomach of this rebellion is the negro in the condition of a slave. Arrest that hoe in the hands of the negro and you smite the rebellion in the very seat of its life."

Even more compelling than the words of northern blacks were the deeds of southern blacks. Despite the absence from the farms and plantations of thousands of young white men, the black population of the South did not seize the opportunity to rebel and liberate itself. Generally, slaves continued to work at their accustomed tasks: they did indeed serve as "the very stomach" of the rebellion.

The slaves failed to rebel because they saw that resistance in the heavily armed and militarized wartime South would have been suicidal. This did not mean that they acquiesced, however. When Union armies drew near, the odds changed dramatically, and blacks showed their real feelings. According to the outraged *Richmond Enquirer,* one black coachman, when told by federal troops in 1862 that he was free, "went straightly to his master's chamber, dressed himself in his best clothes, put on his best watch and chain, took his [walking] stick, and returning to the parlor where his master was, insolently informed him that he might for the future drive his own coach."

Black men and women generally voted against slavery with their feet. As Union armies advanced into the Confederacy, black refugees flocked to their lines. At first Union officials did not know what to do with these homeless and destitute people. The government initially had no legal mandate to help them. General Benjamin F. Butler shrewdly called them "contraband of war" and paid them to work as free laborers on military fortifications. Other military commanders, following Butler's lead, employed thousands of "contrabands" at military jobs. Other refugees were set to work growing cotton for northern mills or took

jobs with private employers for money wages. Long before the end of the war a substantial part of the South's slaves had, in effect, liberated themselves from bondage.

More than self-liberation was required to demolish the pernicious institution, however: the country needed a national policy. Lincoln originally hoped that compensated emancipation and colonization in either Africa or Central America would finish slavery. But blacks were hostile to colonization, and in the border states slaveholders proved unwilling to consider freeing their slaves even if paid. Lincoln now faced the prospect of simply ending slavery—an institution deeply embedded in American life and representing $4 billion worth of private property—by direct action under the presidential war powers. It was a momentous step to take, and for a while he was reluctant to act.

The hope that the destruction of slavery would shorten the war finally tipped the balance in favor of abolition by federal proclamation. Three considerations worked powerfully on the president. One was Frederick Douglass's point: the reliance of the Confederacy on slave labor. If the blacks of the South knew that the federal government intended to set them free, they would cease to be a source of strength for the Confederacy. Another consideration was the potential value of black soldiers. If the North could tap this human reservoir, it could offset the immense losses on the battlefields and the declining zeal of white volunteers. Multitudes of slave refugees might join the Union armies if they were offered their freedom in exchange for military service. A final factor was the moral advantage of turning the war for the Union into a war for human freedom. If the Union cause were identified with the destruction of slavery, it would be difficult for any European power to aid the Confederacy.

By July 1862 Lincoln had concluded that a proclamation of emancipation was "absolutely essential for the salvation of the Union." He postponed making his intentions known, however, fearing that if the news came at a time of military difficulties, it would be taken as an act of desperation. On September 22, following Lee's defeat at Antietam, he issued a preliminary emancipation proclamation declaring that on January 1, 1863, in every part of the South then still in rebellion, all slaves would be "thenceforward and forever free." As scheduled, on New Year's Day, 1863, the final Emancipation Proclamation took effect. Technically, it affected only those places where federal law could not be enforced—the Confederacy. It said nothing about slavery in the border

An Historical Portrait   Mary Boykin Chesnut

Mary Boykin Chesnut's fame rests on her Civil War diary. She kept it locked up and out of her husband's sight, but won renown in later years for the journal she worked on in secret. When *Diary from Dixie* was finally published, it was favorably compared to the famous diaries of Cotton Mather and John and John Quincy Adams.

Mrs. Chesnut's life was that of a privileged southern belle. Her family was prominent in South Carolina. At the time of her birth in March 1823, her father, Stephen Decatur Miller, was a state senator who, five years later, became governor and then United States senator. Mary was a precocious, intelligent child who responded to the politically active environment around her. In a letter written before her ninth birthday she told her father she was looking forward to reading his Senate speech on the tariff.

In 1833 Miller resigned his Senate seat and moved with his family to his cotton plantation in Mississippi. When Mary was twelve, she was sent back to Charleston to acquire a "finishing school" education at Madame Talvande's French School for Young Ladies. In addition to the "accomplishments" expected of every well-bred antebellum southern woman, she learned history, rhetoric, natural sciences, literature, and German, and became particularly fluent in French. She was an excellent student and a popular classmate, as well as a boisterous social leader who occasionally had to pay the price for her pranks. Her training at Madame Talvande's resulted in a life-long attraction to intellectual pursuits and literary conversation, and a love of music, novels, cities, the theater, and French culture.

Charleston, one of America's most gracious cities, became the scene of Mary's love affair. When she was a thirteen-year-old school girl, she went for moonlight strolls on the Charleston Battery, the walk skirting the harbor, with James Chesnut, Jr., of Mulberry Plantation, a twenty-one-year-old Princeton graduate. Mary was brought back to Mississippi to cool her romance, but her parents soon returned her to Madame Talvande's to finish her education. Following her father's death in 1838, she became formally engaged to Chesnut, who was planning to go to Europe to study and travel. He wrote his fiancée from Paris that he would try to "become worthy of the girl I love and honor." He had "no hopes that stir my soul, no visions bright . . . which amuse my fancy that are not colored with thoughts of you. . . ."

On June 23, 1840, when Mary was seventeen and Chesnut twenty-five, they married and went to live at Mulberry Plantation, where her husband's parents, a couple in their mid-sixties, still lived. Although Mary assumed she would soon become mistress of Mulberry, her in-laws, both physically and mentally energetic, lived into their eighties and continued to direct the operations of house and lands. While his parents ran the plantation, James practiced law in neighboring Camden and served in the state legislature as representative, senator, and president until 1858, when, like his father-in-law, he was elected to the United States Senate.

During these years, with her in-laws in charge of her home, her husband involved in politics, and unable to have children, Mary often felt restless and useless. She occupied her time by reading, taking care of her young nieces and neph-

ews, and visiting Charleston, Columbia, and the northern spas at Saratoga and Newport. She also acted as her husband's hostess and secretary and maintained her interest in politics. In 1845 she persuaded James to take her to London on a literary pilgrimage to the homes of Dickens and Thackeray, hoping that the sea journey would help her health and the mental stimulation of travel would lift her spirits. But these activities did not really fill the time or energies of this bright, vivacious woman, and her years at Mulberry Plantation were troubled by depression and poor health.

Her husband's election to the United States Senate in 1858 provided Mary with the opportunity to live in Washington. She was extremely happy during these two years. She made friends easily with both the politicians and their wives, and charmed everyone she met with her intelligence, sense of humor, and conversational skill. She was soon invited to all the capital's important social functions and became a close friend of Varina Davis, wife of Jefferson Davis, the distinguished senator from Mississippi.

Her Washington years came to an end, however, after Lincoln's election in 1860. James resigned from the Senate to help draft the South Carolina Ordinance of Secession and organize the Southern Confederacy. In 1861 Mary accompanied her husband to Montgomery, Alabama, seat of the new Confederate government, and ran a lively salon where the men politicked and planned the strategy of the new nation, and their wives, excluded from such weighty matters, gossiped and intrigued.

Mary began her diary at this

states, and had the Union lost the war, it would have become a symbol of futility. But the Union won, and the proclamation in the end effectively sounded the death knell for slavery all over the United States.

On the Home Front.   Behind the lines the war caused marked changes in civilian life. In the South it produced great hardship for virtually every citizen. As prices rose, as transport broke down, as the blockade took effect, southern living

time. She was in Charleston in April 1861 when Fort Sumter was attacked, and watched the proceedings from a rooftop. In her original account she wrote: "At half past four we heard the booming of the cannon—I started up—dress & rush to my sisters in misery—we go on the housetop & see the shells bursting. . . ." When the smoke had cleared hours later, the Union had surrendered the fort to the Confederates and it was revealed, to Mary's relief, that no lives had been lost. Mary joined the celebration of the victory.

The Chesnuts returned to Montgomery for the second session of the Provisional Confederate Congress and in June 1861 went to Richmond, the new Confederate capital. Mary hoped her husband would be appointed minister to France when he lost his bid for reelection to the Confederate Senate because she dreaded returning to isolated Mulberry where her tyrannical father-in-law still presided. No such foreign appointment saved her, and she was forced to spend a half year in Camden, where she frequently complained in her diary of her husband's lack of interest in the war. "If I had been a man in this great revolution—I should have either been killed at once or made a name & done some good for my country. Lord Nelson's motto would be mine—Victory or Westminster Abbey."

She was rescued from the plantation in January 1862 when her husband accepted the chairmanship of the South Carolina Executive Council in Columbia. In the fall Chesnut became an aide to Jefferson Davis, a position that brought the couple back to Richmond. In the Confederate capital Mary involved herself in both serious and frivolous things. The Chesnuts' quarters at the Arlington Hotel was the scene of dinners, parties, and amateur theatricals. They had frequent houseguests, including family and friends from all over the South. The Chesnuts and the Davises were devoted friends and visited each other constantly. Mary and her circle often chatted about personal affairs as well as news of the war and sometimes enjoyed a touch of scandal. "We discussed," read a diary entry for June 1862, "clever women who help their husbands politically. . . . These lady politicians—if they are young and pretty—always get themselves a 'little bit' talked about."

Behind the gay and gracious social screen, however, were more somber thoughts. Mary's diary for these war years reveals her underlying despair at the numbers of brave young men killed or maimed, the beautiful plantations destroyed, and the growing hardship of life in Richmond as the Yankee noose tightened. As early as March 1862 she would note that her "world, the only world we cared for," was being "kicked to pieces. . . ." In January 1865, with James away on military business, she was frightened. "Yesterday, I broke down—," she admitted, "gave way to abject terror. The news of Sherman's advance— and no news of my husband."

After Appomattox the Chesnuts moved back to Camden, living temporarily in one of her father-in-law's plantation houses that had been spared destruction. Mulberry itself had been sacked by Union soldiers and its cotton burned, but it survived, and was eventually restored. Mary continued her diary until July 1865. During the first months of Reconstruction she was ill with a heart condition and depressed by both the South's defeat and her isolation. But her natural vivacity reasserted itself and she took over the management of the household, kept financial records, helped oversee the affairs of the plantation and the farm, and ran a butter-and-egg business with her maid, Molly. In 1873 the Chesnuts moved into a new home, Sarsfield, built with bricks from the old kitchen buildings at Mulberry.

During the 1870s and early '80s Mary wrote fiction to make additional money. In 1881 she began to work on a book based on her wartime diaries. James became ill in 1884 and Mary took time off to nurse him. He died at the end of the year, and then a week later her mother died as well. James had so many debts that Mary lost most of the land to his creditors, keeping only Sarsfield and a small dairy business. She continued to work on *Diary from Dixie,* but died on November 22, 1886, of a heart attack before the book was published.

Mary Chesnut was a perceptive reporter who ably documented southern society during the Civil War. She had a sharp eye for the foibles of human nature and a keen understanding of life's contradictions. Her presence in the Confederate capital during the important years of the Civil War and her ability to record her observations of events and personalities make her *Diary from Dixie* an invaluable historical document. It is also a vivid personal portrait that reveals Mary Boykin Chesnut as an outstanding woman of her time and, in the words of Lyman Butterfield, editor of the Adams Papers, "a great lady."

standards deteriorated. In Richmond a clerk in the Confederate War Department complained bitterly in 1863 that the inhabitants of the city were "almost in a state of starvation" though there was abundant food in the Confederacy as a whole. In Mobile food riots, led by women carrying banners reading "Bread or Blood" and "Bread and Peace," broke out in 1863. All through the South tea and coffee, both imported items, became scarce; and southern consumers turned to parched wheat, corn, peanuts, and even acorns as substitutes. When commodities were available, they often sold at prices far beyond the means of the average consumer. Another Confederate War Department official noted in 1863 that his salary of $3,000 would "go about as far as $700 would in 1860. Flour $28 against $4 then, tea $15 against $1.25, bacon $1.25 against 20 cents, and other things in proportion."

Deprivation and hunger hurt southern morale and led to recriminations that further damaged southern fighting spirit. One of the most serious manifestations of the South's sagging determination was the increase in overt anti-Confederate feelings. Even at the beginning of the war Unionist sentiment was strong in the hill country and in pockets all over the South. In the mountainous western counties of Virginia, in fact, anti-Confederate feeling produced a powerful secession movement that established a separate state government with its capital at Wheeling. In April 1863 Congress admitted the fifty rebellious counties to the Union as the new state of West Virginia.

As military and civilian conditions worsened in the Confederacy, southern Unionists and dissenters became bolder and ever more willing to express their opposition to continuing the war. They were soon attacking southern leadership and insisting that local and state needs came before those of the new nation. Governors Joseph E. Brown of Georgia and Zebulon Vance of North Carolina, in particular, fought the Davis administration at every turn when they felt that the rights and prerogatives of their states were being ignored by the Richmond authorities. In order to meet local needs, they refused to contribute men, money, and supplies to the central government, making the logistical problems of the Confederacy worse than ever.

As living conditions deteriorated in the South, they improved in the North. "Secession winter" and the first months of the war had been a time of economic crisis for northern citizens and businessmen. But then war orders began to pour in. True, prices rose and many people found it hard to make ends meet. Nevertheless, by 1863 the North as a whole wore an air of bustling prosperity. In the cities the stores were jammed with shoppers, many of them buying silk goods and expensive imported luxuries from France and England. City theaters were thronged with avid pleasure seekers. In eastern Pennsylvania the newly opened oil regions experienced a boom comparable only to that in the Gold Rush areas of California a decade before. Businessmen everywhere enjoyed exceptionally good times. On the farms of the North, too, prosperity prevailed. Unprecedented high farm prices stimulated output, and thousands of new prairie acres were plowed to meet the urgent demands of civilian and military markets.

Several northern groups benefited particularly from the war. Before 1861 employment opportunities for women had been limited. With thousands of able-bodied men now in the Union armies, traditional sex barriers weakened. Many women joined the vastly expanded War and Treasury departments as secretaries, copyists, and clerks. In the private sector the number of women factory operatives, schoolteachers, and clerical workers also increased.

One of the most important breakthroughs for women was the creation of a female nursing profession. Florence Nightingale, an Englishwoman, had already proved the competence of women as military nurses during the Crimean War; but men in authority resisted the use of women in Union military hospitals. They did not count on the determination and patriotism of strong-willed women like Clara Barton and Dorothea Dix, who insisted on sharing the work and sacrifices of the war effort.

Though women on both sides organized societies to aid the war effort, only in the North were they carried beyond the local level. The most powerful of these societies was the Women's Central Association of New York City. Organized by Dr. Elizabeth Blackwell, the association eventually founded the American Sanitary Commission in 1861. Through several thousand local ladies' aid societies in the North, the commission organized the diet, cooking, clothing distribution, medical transport, military hospital, medical supply, and relief services for soldiers and their families. Dorothea Dix was appointed superintendent of women nurses for the Union army. Some 10,000 white women served as nurses, receiving $12 a month in the North. About 4,000 black women worked for the Union as practical nurses, cooks, laundresses, and orderlies at $10 a month.

Many of the gains in paid employment for women were temporary. After 1865, as government departments contracted and men returned to civilian life, women were forced back into their drawing rooms or kitchens. But not all the advances were lost. The Civil War did much to establish nursing as a profession for women and to develop formal training and certification in that field. Clara Barton, who founded the American Red Cross twenty years after the Civil War, noted that by the time the war ended, "woman was at

American Antiquarian Society

THE RECRUITING QUESTION—A HINT TO RAILCAR COMPANIES.

▓Fascinating Conductress of City Car (to surprised Passenger)—"Yes! you see my good man has gone to the war, and as the Company continue half his wages, I've come along to earn the other half—hurry up, sir, if you please."

The Civil War created an acute labor shortage in both sections, opening new opportunities to women, especially in the less conservative North. This cartoon, however, expresses a hope more than a reality. Women moved into government work and nursing; few, if any, became "fascinating conductresses."

least fifty years in advance of the normal position which continued peace . . . would have assigned her."

The land of "chivalry" did not accord women as much opportunity to contribute to the war as the North. The Confederacy, for example, had no central association of women's organizations to coordinate women's participation in the war effort. The South also had no place for women nurses. Yet southern women were able to do their part to fight the Yankees. They took on clerical and schoolteaching jobs, and even performed field labor on the South's farms to help meet the labor shortage. Legend has it that no one in the South so ardently defended the Confederate cause as "the ladies." The expression is patronizing, but it is nevertheless true that southern women were especially effective in spurring the patriotic ardor and enlistment rates of southern men.

THE LAST YEARS OF BATTLE

Until mid-1863 it still seemed possible for the South to win a military victory. Lee's defeat of Hooker at Chancellorsville in May—although it coincided with the death of one of the Confederacy's most gifted generals, Stonewall Jackson—encouraged the whole South. Lee now decided to take the offensive. By moving the war to the North and threatening Washington, perhaps even taking some major Union city like Philadelphia, he might shatter northern morale and force a negotiated peace. On June 15 General Richard S. Ewell's army crossed the Potomac under Lee's overall command. It was soon joined by the remainder of the Army of Northern Virginia, which moved swiftly northward into the Cumberland Valley of Pennsylvania. Lee's advance alarmed the entire Union. Lincoln hurriedly removed the unsuccess-

Library of Congress

The Civil War has been called "the war of brothers." On rare occasions brothers did fight on opposing sides. More common was the situation depicted here: the Union officer on the right is George A. Custer, of later Indian-fighting fame; the other man is a Confederate prisoner, James Washington, who was Custer's classmate at West Point.

ful Hooker and appointed Major General George G. Meade commander of the Army of the Potomac.

A Victor Emerges.

The choice was a good one. Though neither colorful nor aggressive, Meade was competent. Marshaling his forces in good order, he deployed them athwart Lee's advance at Gettysburg, a village fifty miles from the state capital at Harrisburg. Entrenched on ridges to the south of the town, Meade's 88,000 men not only outnumbered Lee's 75,000 but also had superior artillery.

The battle was a seesaw affair lasting three full days (July 1–3, 1863). Lee's forces came close to sweeping the federals off their perches several times. The fighting was exceptionally bloody, much of it hand to hand. The replacement of the smoothbore musket by the rifle as the standard infantry weapon gave the defense a tremendous advantage. In battle after battle during the war, masses of infantry attacking an entrenched army were ripped to pieces by the minié balls (rifle bullets with conical heads) of the defenders. And so it was at Gettysburg. Each brave charge of the gray-clad Confederates was sent hurtling back after fearful carnage.

On the last day of battle the Confederates launched 10,000 men under George Pickett against the Union center on ominously named Cemetery Ridge. The Confederates advanced across the field against murderous fire and swept to the top of the Union emplacement. Then they reeled back, leaving behind several thousand dead and wounded.

Pickett's charge was the last spurt of Confederate strength. Lee expected Meade to counterattack, but the federals were almost as exhausted as the Confederates and sat tight. Seizing this opportunity to disengage safely, Lee ordered a general retreat. Soon he and his ragged army were back in Virginia.

Lee's defeat at Gettysburg coincided with Grant's capture of Vicksburg following a long cam-

---

Fredericksburg to Gettysburg, 1862–1863

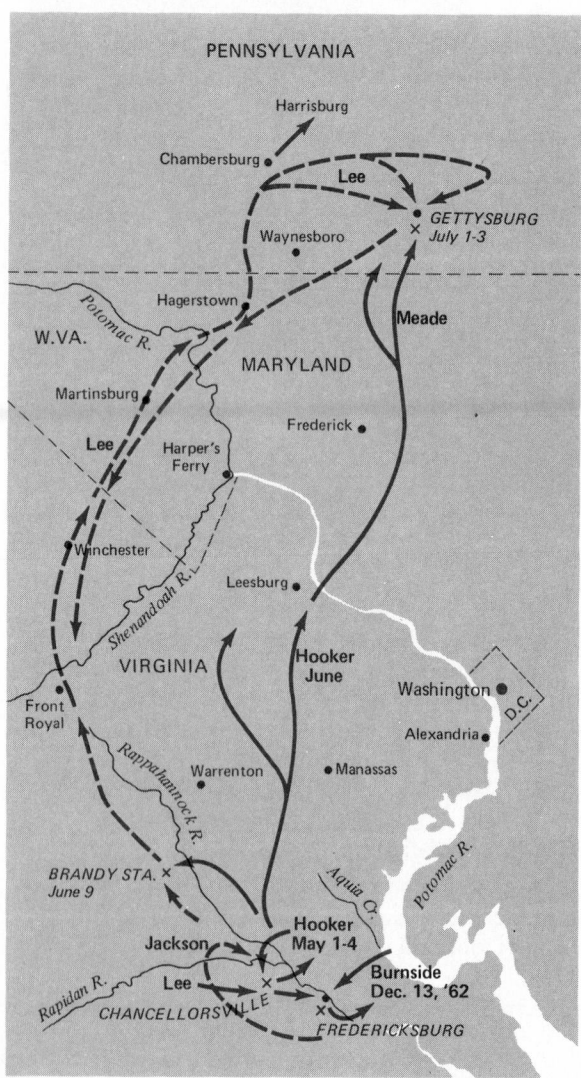

paign and costly siege. Then, in the fall of 1863, Grant and general George H. Thomas won the battles of Lookout Mountain and Missionary Ridge and finally pushed the Confederates out of ravaged Tennessee. Called to command all the Union forces, Grant came east in March 1864 to take over the Virginia front. In the next months he aimed massive sledgehammer blows at Lee and his lieutenants in the forested country between Washington and Richmond. The gains in ground were negligible, and the losses on both sides were appalling. Yet Grant realized that the attrition was easier for the Union to bear than for the enemy. Southern manpower was by now all but exhausted; the North, though weary, still had human reserves.

"Johnny Reb" and "Billy Yank." Although Gettysburg had been the war's turning point, many dismal months of fighting remained. The chief sufferers toward the end, as in the beginning, were the common soldiers of the Union and the Confederacy. Of the two, "Billy Yank" had the easier time, especially after the North's factories began to operate at high gear. The resources of the Union assured him enough food and clothing to keep the inner and outer man reasonably content. But his life was no picnic. Being a Union soldier involved long periods of hard foot-slogging over rough roads in every sort of weather, days of boredom in bivouac, followed, finally, by terrifying exposure to flying lead and iron. If wounded, his chances for survival were poor. Thousands of the injured died of shock, gangrene, or loss of blood. Many others were swept away by diseases picked up in unsanitary camps or as a result of exposure and exhaustion.

"Johnny Reb" suffered from all these afflictions and several others besides. The southern soldier often lacked adequate shoes, clothing, and food. Despite Confederate ingenuity in manufacture and supply, much of his equipment, including his rifle and ammunition, was captured from the Yankees. There was seldom enough to go around.

The men of both armies had their good moments. Many lifelong friendships were forged in the heat of battle. But however veterans later recalled their fighting days, soldiering was not an occupation that many men cared to stay at indefinitely, and in both armies the desertion rates were stupendous.

Black Soldiers. Two sources of northern strength largely denied the South were foreigners and blacks. About one of every four Union troops was foreign-born, mostly German or Irish. Several thousand foreign-born young men also fought with the Confederacy. But most European immigrants had avoided the South before 1861, and unlike the North, the Confederacy received few if any new arrivals after Fort Sumter.

The Union's most important manpower reserve consisted of northern free blacks and former southern slaves. At first race prejudice discouraged recruiting black soldiers. Then, as resistance to volunteering increased among whites, public opinion began to change. Why not share the burden of dying for the Union with one of the chief beneficiaries of the war, whites began to ask. The War Department relented and authorized black enlistments; soon thousands of young, eager black men began to don the Union blue.

These troops fought magnificently in many

Library of Congress

In 1861 Frederick Douglass advocated "carrying the war into Africa." Although Lincoln did not endorse black soldiers until January 1863, black troops—such as the 107th United States Colored Infantry Guard, shown here—fought in Louisiana, Kansas, Missouri, and along the Atlantic coast in 1862.

battles after August 1862, when the first black regiments were organized. Placed almost invariably under white officers and treated initially as second-class troops in matters of pay, bounties for service, and other benefits, black soldiers nonetheless established a record for bravery and enterprise equal to any group in the Union army. In March 1863 Lincoln called the black troops "very important, if not indispensable" to the Union war effort. By the end of the fighting, the Union army had enrolled over 178,000 black soldiers.

The valor of foreign-born and black troops had favorable effects on ethnic and racial attitudes in the North. Antiforeign sentiment declined. Racial bigotry continued, but the legal and social positions of northern blacks improved. Midwestern legislatures repealed state laws discriminating against free blacks or denying them the right to reside within state borders. Several cities ended the common practice of segregating blacks on streetcars and in schools. America scarcely became a racial paradise, but the shining record of black troops fighting for the Union made many white citizens reconsider their prejudices.

The Election of 1864. The lessening of ethnic conflict was not matched by a decline in political strife. By 1864 the Copperhead movement had lost its force, but normal political partisanship continued as usual. A presidential election was scheduled for 1864, and nobody suggested passing it over in the interest of national unity. At Baltimore the Republicans renominated Lincoln and chose Andrew Johnson, a Tennessee Unionist, as his running mate. The Democrats turned to General McClellan and George H. Pendleton of Ohio. Neither man was an extreme Copperhead, but both favored a negotiated peace.

For a while the Democrats hoped to ride to victory on the wave of discouragement that followed Confederate victories during the late summer. Lincoln himself was pessimistic and thought it "exceedingly probable that this Administration will not be reelected."

But the northern military picture abruptly improved. On September 2, 1864, General Sherman, who had launched his army of 100,000 southwest from Chattanooga in May, captured Atlanta, deep in the heart of the Confederacy. This brilliant campaign promised to cut the already divided South into two more pieces as soon as Sherman's "Bummers" cut their swath of destruction all the way to Savannah on the coast. Later that month Maine and Vermont, which then held early elections, gave Lincoln solid majorities. Northern and Republican morale revived. In November Lincoln swept the electoral college and won a popular majority of 400,000 votes over McClellan.

Sherman's march to the sea, 1864

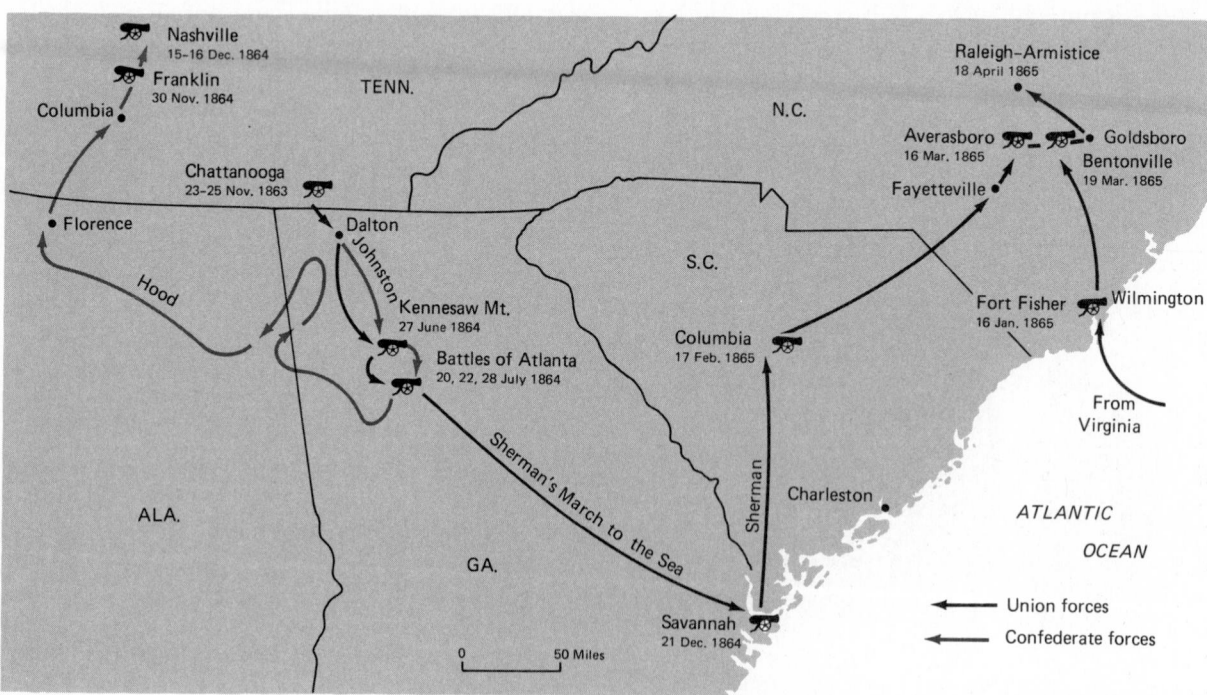

The Last Battles, the Last Casualty. The months following the election saw the rapid collapse of southern hopes. On December 22 Sherman reached the sea at Savannah and then turned north along the coast, heading for a rendezvous with Grant. In the West General Thomas smashed J. B. Hood's army in a two-day battle near Nashville. Meanwhile, after abandoning his effort to take Richmond from the north, Grant shifted his attack to the southeast around Petersburg, Virginia. On April 1, 1865, reinforced by the brilliant cavalry commander Philip H. Sheridan, he defeated Lee at Five Forks and forced him to abandon Petersburg. Southern morale now virtually collapsed. Davis tried to end seditious talk with a strict conspiracy law. He also proposed to recruit black soldiers to shore up the Confederate war effort. These men and their families would be granted their freedom if they fought for the South. But nothing helped, and on April 2 Confederate officials began to flee Richmond to avoid capture.

Lee—his army hungry, demoralized, and surrounded—asked Grant for terms on April 7. On Sunday, two days later, the two leaders met in the McLean House at the crossroads hamlet of Appomattox Court House. There they agreed on surrender terms. Grant was generous. The Confederate officers and men were to be released on their promise not to take up arms again. The Confederates would surrender all weapons and war materiel, but the men might keep their personal equipment, including their horses and mules. These, Grant said, they would need to help them "work their little farms." The brief ceremony over, 26,000 Confederates laid down their arms.

Lincoln came to the Confederate capital in early April to view the prize of four years of Union blood and treasure. In the next few days his mind ran much to the problems of political reconstruction, and after his return to Washington he made a major address on the subject. On April 14, 1865, the happy though tired chief executive went with his wife, Mary, and some friends to the theater to see the British comedy *Our American Cousin.* During the third act a dark-haired man entered the presidential box, fired a single shot at Lincoln, and leaped to the stage. Amid the confusion and the shrieks, he shouted something that sounded like "Sic Semper Tyrannis" ("Thus always to tyrants"), the Virginia state motto, and escaped. Early the next morning Abraham Lincoln died.

The assassin was John Wilkes Booth, an actor and Confederate sympathizer who, with a few other disgruntled southerners, had concocted a plot to destroy the man they held responsible for Confederate defeat. The plotters also intended to

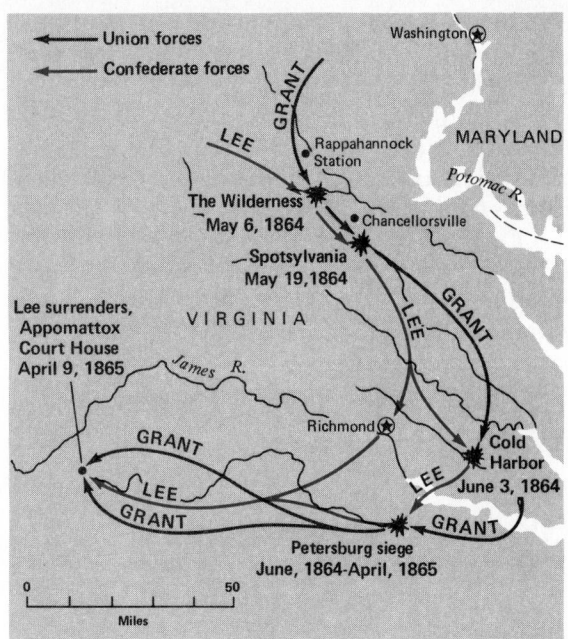

Appomattox, 1865

assassinate Seward, Vice President Johnson, and other high Union officials. Booth was cornered in Virginia on April 26 and either shot himself or was shot by a zealous Union soldier. He died before disclosing the full conspiracy; false rumors of complicity by Secretary Stanton or the Confederate leaders gained wide circulation.

CONCLUSIONS

The war was over; but was an era also over? How much difference would the war make in American life? Obviously it ended for all time the threat of national dismemberment through internal forces. Never again, not even during the most severe national crises, would any part of the United States threaten to secede. The war also fused the country into a more coherent social and economic whole. It made possible a transcontinental railroad, and created a national banking system and a new national currency. It trained thousands of men to manage large-scale operations and mass movements of people and goods—talents that when applied to private enterprise would help to create modern "big business" and further integrate the country. Though it took years beyond 1865 for the full effects to work themselves out, the war also helped to universalize the commercial values of the Northeast. The South would be slow to embrace the new ethos, but for good or ill the rest of the country would find Yankee enterprise and "get-ahead" more acceptable after 1865 than before. Even the intellectuals who had been emphatically critical before 1860 found liberal capitalist society more palatable after the experience of 1861–65.

Finally, the war destroyed slavery. It did not end problems between blacks and whites; they are still with us today. But it did sweep away an institution that rigidly prescribed the relations of the races and replaced it with alternatives that, however imperfect, permitted eventual reform and improvement.

FOR FURTHER READING

David H. Donald, editor. *Why the North Won the Civil War* (1960)
Five historians discuss the social and institutional structure of the Confederacy, the war-making potentials of North and South, northern political parties, military affairs, and Civil War diplomacy.

Benjamin P. Thomas. *Abraham Lincoln* (1952)
Still the best one-volume life of Lincoln. Catches the man as well as the political leader. Although critical where necessary, Thomas admires Lincoln deeply, and successfully conveys to the reader the reasons for his admiration.

Richard N. Current. *The Lincoln Nobody Knows* (1958)
Lincoln has meant many things to many people: both the abolitionist William Lloyd Garrison and the conservative Mississippi Senator James K. Vardaman claimed him as their own. What was he really like? Current discusses Lincoln's domestic life, religious views, and political goals.

Clement Eaton. *Jefferson Davis* (1977)
This is the best recent biography of the Confederate president. Written by a southern scholar, it is objective and fair. Eaton sees Davis's failure as a Confederate leader as the result of his inflexibility.

Bruce Catton. *Mr. Lincoln's Army* (1951); *Glory Road* (1952); and *A Stillness at Appomattox* (1956)
This trilogy is military history at its popular best. Catton captures the sights, sounds, and smells of battle, besides telling us what went on in the minds of the military commanders. The view is from the Yankee side of the line.

T. Harry Williams. *Lincoln and His Generals* (1952)
Lincoln was more than the civilian head of government. He was also commander in chief of all the Union's military forces. Williams's book deals with Lincoln "as a director of war and his place in the high command and his influence in developing a modern command system for this nation."

Adrian Cook. *The Armies of the Streets* (1974)
Spiraling inflation, racial and class resentments, and opposition to the new Union draft brought four days of looting, burning, and lynching of blacks to New York in July 1863. Cook's account of the New York draft riots makes good reading.

George M. Frederickson. *The Inner Civil War* (1965)
The war effected a transformation of northern intellectual life, according to Frederickson. Reformers rejected their anti-institutional, individualistic attitudes as "feeble sentimentalities" and came to favor an uncritical nationalism. After the war they were indifferent to social reform.

Frank L. Klement. *The Copperheads in the Middle West* (1960)
This study treats the Copperheads as the forerunners of Gilded Age agrarian dissenters. Their quarrel with Lincoln and the Republicans, Klement says, was as much over Republican policies favoring business and industry as over slavery and vigorous prosecution of the war.

Margaret K. Leech. *Reveille in Washington, 1860–1865* (1941)
A panorama of life, society, and politics in wartime Washington. Leech writes of high society, southern women prisoners, saloons, hospitals, the Lincoln family, Clara Barton, the famous detective Allan Pinkerton, the look of the capital's streets in wartime—and much else.

Bell I. Wiley. *The Life of Johnny Reb: The Common Soldier of the Confederacy* (1943); and *The Life of Billy Yank: The Common Soldier of the Union* (1952)
Until Wiley wrote these two composite biographies of Confederate and Union soldiers, most published accounts of the Civil War concerned high military officers and grand strategy. Drawn from ordinary enlisted men's letters, diaries, and other records, these are vivid, down-to-earth accounts of the amusements and inconveniences of camp life and the brutal experience of battle as it appeared to the ordinary soldier.

Benjamin Quarles. *The Negro and the Civil War* (1953)
According to Quarles, the real and lasting significance of the black Civil War experience was "the momentum it gave to the ideals of freedom and the dignity of man." The book deals with black Americans in both North and South, and with black soldiers as well as black civilians. Shows black Americans as active on behalf of their own freedom.

Emory M. Thomas. *The Confederate Nation, 1861–1865* (1979)
This recent study of the Confederacy claims that if the South had won its independence, it would have been as thoroughly transformed by the wartime experience as the North.

Martin Duberman. *Charles Francis Adams, 1807–1886* (1960)

An exemplary biography of a moderate anti-slavery leader, son of the sixth president, who became United States minister to England during the Civil War and Lincoln's most important diplomatic representative abroad during the years of Union crisis.

MacKinlay Kantor. *Andersonville* (1955)

This historical novel is about the infamous Confederate prison near Americus, Georgia, where almost 13,000 Union soldiers died in the last months of the war. Kantor is at his best in his compassionate portrayal of the perverse commandant, Henry Wirz, the only Confederate official executed at the war's end.

16 Reconstruction

What Went Wrong?

1863   Lincoln announces his "ten-percent plan" for reconstruction

1863–65   Arkansas and Louisiana accept Lincoln's conditions but Congress does not readmit them to the Union

1864   Lincoln vetoes Congress's Wade-Davis Reconstruction Bill

1865   Johnson succeeds Lincoln • The Freedmen's Bureau is established • Congress overrides Johnson's veto of the Civil Rights Act • Johnson announces his Reconstruction plan • All-white southern legislatures begin to pass "Black Codes" • The Thirteenth Amendment

1866   Congress adopts the Fourteenth Amendment, but it is not ratified until 1868 • The Ku Klux Klan is formed • Tennessee is readmitted to the Union

1867   Congress passes the first of four Reconstruction Acts • Tenure of Office Act • Johnson suspends Secretary of War Edwin Stanton

1868   Johnson is impeached by the House and acquitted in the Senate • Arkansas, North Carolina, South Carolina, Alabama, Florida, and Louisiana are readmitted to the Union • Ulysses S. Grant elected president

1869   Woman suffrage associations are organized in response to women's disappointment with the Fourteenth Amendment

1870   Virginia, Mississippi, Texas, and Georgia are readmitted to the Union

1870, 1871   Congress passes Force Bills

1875   Blacks are guaranteed access to public places by Congress • Mississippi "redeemers" successfully oust black and white Republican officeholders

1876   Presidential election between Rutherford B. Hayes and Samuel J. Tilden

1877   Compromise of 1877: Hayes is chosen as president, and all remaining federal troops are withdrawn from the South

By 1880   The tenantry system of agriculture is well established in the South

Almost no one has had anything good to say about Reconstruction, the process by which the South was restored to the Union. Contemporaries judged it a colossal failure. To most southern whites Reconstruction was a time when Dixie was subjected to a cruel northern occupation and civilization itself was submerged under an avalanche of black barbarism. For the ex-slaves—or freedmen, as they were called—the period of 1865–77 started with the bright promise of true freedom and prosperity, but ended in bitter disappointment with most blacks still on the bottom rung of southern society. Contemporary northerners, too, generally deplored these years. They had thought the Reconstruction program would change the South. But it had not succeeded, and most of them were relieved when the last federal troops withdrew in 1877 and the white South once more governed itself.

Americans in later years have not generally thought well of Reconstruction either. From the 1890s to the 1940s most historians assumed that the Republicans who controlled Washington and the southern state capitals were moved by the desire for revenge. Liberal scholars of the following generation, rejected this view, but they believed the chance to modernize and liberalize southern society had been missed because the North had neither will nor conviction sufficient to take the bold steps needed. Recently some younger historians have declared that by failing to provide land and power to the freedmen, the Reconstruction process nullified much of the advantage of emancipation. In this view, the North sold out the black people, leaving them little better off than before the Civil War.

Obviously, then, from almost every point of view, Reconstruction has seemed a failure. What went wrong? And was it as bad as most critics have believed?

THE LEGACY OF WAR

A month or so after Appomattox Whitelaw Reid, a correspondent for the Republican *Cincinnati Gazette*, went south to see what the war had done to Dixie. Strongly antisouthern, Reid was inclined to belittle claims of southern distress, but even he was struck by the devastation he encountered. Hanover Junction, near Richmond, Reid reported, "presented little but standing chimneys and the debris of destroyed buildings. Along the [rail]road a pile of smoky brick and mortar seemed a regularly recognized sign of what had once been a depot." Not a platform or water tank had been left, he wrote, and efforts to get the road in running order were often the only improvements visible for miles. Young pines covered the old fields of wheat and corn, and the crumbling remains of defense works could be seen everywhere.

Others gave similar descriptions. Wherever northern and southern armies had fought, every manmade object bore the scars. Interior South Carolina, hard hit by General Sherman's army, "looked for many miles like a broad black streak of ruin and desolation." In the Shenandoah Valley of Virginia between Winchester and Harrisonburg, scarcly a horse, pig, chicken, or cow remained

Library of Congress

The Confederate capital, Richmond, site of ironworks and munition factories, terminus of six railroads, lies in ruins. Charleston, Atlanta, Mobile, Vicksburg, and Galveston also knew these "dark Raven Days of sorrow."

alive. Southern cities, too, were devastated. Columbia, capital of South Carolina, was a blackened wasteland with not a store standing in the business district. Atlanta, Richmond, Selma, and other southern towns were also devastated.

Human losses were severe. Of the South's white male population of 2.5 million in 1860, a quarter of a million (some 10 percent) had died of battle wounds or disease. Most of these were young men who represented the region's most vigorous and creative resource. Of those who survived, some were maimed; many were worn out emotionally. "A more completely crushed country I have seldom witnessed," a Yankee officer in the occupation force wrote the United States attorney general.

The South's economic institutions were also wrecked. Its banking structure, based on now-worthless Confederate bonds, had collapsed. Personal savings had been wiped out as Confederate currency lost its value. Even more crushing, the region's labor system was in ruins. Slavery as an economic institution—and as a social one—was dead, but no one knew what to replace it with. Many blacks remained on the farms and plantations and continued to plant, cultivate, and harvest. Many others—whether to test their newfound freedom, hunt for long-lost relatives, or just to take their first holiday—wandered the roads or flocked to the cities, abandoning the land that had traditionally sustained the South's economy.

The physical and institutional destruction of the war was matched by its emotional damage. People in both sections harbored deep resentments. After struggling for independence against the "tyrannical government in Washington" and "northern dominance" for four years, white southerners could not help feeling apprehensive, angry, and deeply disappointed. Now, even more than in 1860, a weak South would be dominated by the North, whose arrogance and power were reinforced by victory and unchecked by any need to compromise. Northerners, for their part, would not easily forget the sacrifices and losses they had suffered in putting down what they considered the illegal and unwarranted rebellion; nor would they easily forgive the "atrocities" of the Confederacy. At Andersonville, Georgia, for example, during July 1864, 31,000 Union prisoners had been confined in a sixteen-acre stockade, sheltered only by tents and fed on scanty rations. As many as 3,000 prisoners had died in a month—100 a day. It did not matter that the prisoners' guards received the same rations, that southern prisoners in northern camps were not treated much better, or that bad conditions were made worse by Yan-

kee captives who preyed on their own comrades. To the northern public the Confederate officials, and especially the camp commandant, Captain Henry Wirz, were beasts who must be punished. Regarding the South as a whole, John Sherman, an Ohio Republican, spoke for many northerners: "We should not only brand the leading rebels with infamy, but the whole rebellion should wear the badge of the penitentiary, so that for this generation at least, no man who has taken part in it would dare to justify or palliate it."

The American people, then, faced a gigantic task of physical, political, and emotional restoration. By the usual measure, the period of restoration, or Reconstruction, lasted for some twelve years, until 1877. It was a time of upheaval and controversy, as well as new beginnings. In its own day the problems associated with Reconstruction dominated the political and intellectual life of the country, and they have fascinated and repelled Americans ever since.

ISSUES AND ATTITUDES

It is difficult even today to draw a balanced picture of Reconstruction. Many issues—racial inequality, southern poverty, sectional antipathies—are still with us. During Reconstruction people were even more deeply concerned with the role of blacks in the restored nation and the proper relation of the South to the rest of the United States. All agreed that racial and political readjustments were necessary. But how to make them deeply divided the American people, North and South, white and black, Republican and Democrat.

The positions that people took fell roughly into five categories: Radical Republican, northern moderate, southern conservative, southern Unionist, and southern freedmen. Let us allow each of these groups to speak for itself. The speeches that follow are fabricated, but they show what these groups of Americans felt about Reconstruction and wanted to see come out of it. Since they controlled so much of the process, let us start with the Radical Republicans.

Radical Republicans. "The South must be made to recognize its sins, and southerners must acknowledge that now that they have been defeated, they can no longer decide their own fate. It is now in the hands of the victorious North. Southerners can avoid our anger and show they are prepared to be readmitted as citizens of the United States in a number of ways. At the very least, they must reject their former leaders and choose new ones who have not been connected with the Confederacy. They can take oaths of loyalty to the United States. They can reject all attempts to repay the Confederate debt incurred in an unjust cause. Most important of all, they can accept the fact that the former slaves are now free and must be treated as the political equals of whites.

"Many former slaves worked and fought for the Union, and we must now help them through the difficult transition to full freedom. As to how this end can best be accomplished, not all of us are agreed. A few of us hold that it will be necessary for the freedmen to get land so they can support themselves independently. But all of us believe that at the very minimum the freedmen must have the vote and, during the early stages of the change, must be protected against starvation and exploitation. No doubt they will be grateful for the efforts of their Republican friends in defeating the slave power, destroying slavery, and defending them against those who will not accept the new situation. This gratitude will incline them to vote Republican. And that is all to the good. The Republican party is the great hope of the nation. It is the party of freedom and economic progress. It is not afraid to use government to encourage that progress. In a word, it is the party that has, since its founding, proved that it is the best embodiment of both the nation's moral and practical sense."

Northern Conservatives. "We, the northern conservatives, are generally of the old Democratic persuasion. Most of us opposed secession and supported the war. But we agree that now that the war is over and secession defeated, we must forget the past. Let southerners—white southerners, that is—determine their own fate. It is in the best American tradition to let local communities decide their own course without undue interference from the national government. Let us confirm this great principle of local self-determination, and short of a few guarantees for Unionists and blacks, let us allow the South back into the Union on its own terms.

"We must not try to force black suffrage or social equality down the throats of the former Confederates. Almost all white Americans believe that Negroes are ill-equipped to exercise the rights of citizens. The Radicals insist on giving them the vote only because they want to secure continued control of the national government. They want to guarantee the predominance of the values and goals of the Northeast, the nation's commercial-industrial capital, against the very different interests and goals of the country's agricul-

tural West and South. It is clearly hypocritical of the supposed champions of the freedmen to be so timid in supporting Negro suffrage in the northern states, where such a stand is politically unpopular and where there are too few Negroes to add to their voting strength. We must reject such hypocrisy and restore peace and tranquillity to the nation as quickly and completely as possible."

Southern Conservatives. "The war we fought and lost was for a noble cause, and it brought out the best in our southern people. We must never forget the sacrifice and heroism of the gallant men in gray. Perhaps secession was a mistake, but that fact will never diminish the tragic grandeur of our struggle.

"But let us now get back to the business of daily living. We of the South must be allowed to resume our traditional political relations with the rest of the states. We must be free to determine our own fate with a minimum of conditions. Above all, we must be permitted to steer our own course on race relations. The 'carpetbaggers' who come down from the North looking for easy money, and the southern renegade 'scalawags' lusting for power, are self-serving and contemptible. They do not understand or accept southern traditions.

"True, we must recognize that Negroes are no longer slaves and we must make certain concessions to their private rights, but in the public realm these must be limited by their capacities. Above all, Negroes must not be allowed to exercise political power. They are not the equal of whites. They are ignorant, lazy, improvident, and intellectually inferior. They can be duped and deceived by their professed 'friends' into supporting the Republican party, but actually their interests will be best served by those who have always been the leaders of southern society and who remain the Negroes' natural protectors. Nature dictates that the freedmen of the South remain in subordination, that they accept their humble economic stations and political inferiority, for that is the only way they can function at all."

Southern Unionists. "At long last we are free to speak our minds! For four long years we have been persecuted and intimidated by the secessionists. Now that they have been defeated, we deserve recognition and favor. Unfortunately the rebels are still in the majority. They say they have accepted the new circumstances of the South, but many of them have not, and we are in a vulnerable position. At the very least we must be protected by our northern friends against hostile unreconciled rebels. Moreover, we should be rewarded for our

Black Reconstruction

Black southerners were not passive participants in the Reconstruction process. In the South they joined the militia companies and the Union Leagues, as well as the Republican party. They also spoke out against their enemies and appealed to their white northern friends for support. The following is an early instance of such an appeal. It is a statement adopted by a black convention held in Virginia in August 1865, soon after the end of the war. Note how many of the things the delegates asked their white allies for were actually granted.

"We, the undersigned members of a Convention of colored citizens of the State of Virginia, would respectfully represent that, although we have been held as slaves, and denied all recognition as a constituent of your nationality for almost the entire period of the duration of your Government, and that by *your permission* we have been denied either home or country, and deprived of the dearest rights of human nature: yet when you and our immediate oppressors met in deadly conflict on the field of battle—the one to destroy and the other to save your Government and nationality, *we,* with scarce an exception, in our inmost souls espoused your cause, and watched, and prayed, and waited, and labored for your success. . . .

"When the contest waxed long, and the result hung doubtfully, you appealed to us for help, and how well we answered is written in the rosters of the two hundred thousand colored troops now enrolled in your service; and as to our undying devotion to your cause, let the uniform acclamation of escaped prisoners, 'whenever we saw a black face we felt sure of a friend,' answer.

"Well, the war is over, the rebellion is 'put down,' and we are *declared* free! Four fifths of our enemies are paroled or amnestied, and the other fifth are being pardoned, and the President has . . . left us entirely at the mercy of these subjugated but unconverted rebels, in *everything* save the privilege of bringing us, our wives, and little ones, to the auction block. . . . We *know* these men—know them *well*—and we assure you that, with the majority of them, loyalty is only 'lip deep,' and that their professions of loyalty are used as a cover to the cherished design of getting restored to their former relations with the Federal Government, and then, by all sorts of 'unfriendly legislation,' to render the freedom you have given us more intolerable than the slavery they intended for us.

"We warn you in time that our only safety is in keeping them under Governors of the *military persuasion* until you have so amended the Federal Constitution that it will prohibit the States from making any distinction between citizens on account of race or color. In one word, the only salvation for us besides the power of the Government is in the *possession of the ballot.* Give us this and we will protect ourselves. . . .

"We are 'sheep in the midst of wolves,' and nothing but the military arm of the Government prevents us and all the *truly* loyal white men from being driven from the land of our birth. Do not then, we beseech you, give to one of these 'wayward sisters' the rights they abandoned and forfeited when they rebelled until you have secured *our* rights by the aforementioned amendment to the Constitution. . . .

"Trusting that you will not be deaf to the appeal herein made, nor unmindful of the warnings which the malignity of the rebels are constantly giving you, and that you will rise to the height of being just for the sake of justice, we remain yours for our flag, our country, and humanity."

loyalty to the Union with an important place in the new order.

"We do not all agree about the role of the Negroes in the South's future, but many of us recognize that they are entitled to equal political rights now that they are free. Given the vote, they will inevitably—and rightly—look to us for leadership. Ex-rebels may call us scalawags and worse; that is to be expected. But we can help transform the South from a sleepy backward region dominated by the former planter class into a bustling, thriving region of farms, factories, and cities."

Southern Freedmen. "We are now free men and women and must be accorded all the privileges of free people as expressed in the Declaration of Independence. We contributed mightily to Union victory in war and have earned the right to be treated as equals. We are also the largest group in the South truly loyal to the Union. Southern whites, with few exceptions, cannot be trusted. They are unreconciled to defeat, and if the North fails to protect us and guarantee our rights as free men and women, these ex-Confederates will once more seize power and nullify the Union victory. The federal government, then, must continue for an indefinite period to wield a strong hand in the process of southern Reconstruction.

"We do not expect white southerners to accept us as social equals; but we must have legal equality and full civil rights, including, of course, the right to vote. We must also have economic independence, which means the right to sell our labor in the open market *and* the right to our own land. Thousands of the South's best acres, abandoned by disloyal owners during the war, are controlled either by the Freedmen's Bureau or by the army. Giving us this land would enable us to secure our independence and prevent our being kept in permanently subordinate positions. We also deserve access to education. Literacy is an important tool for achieving economic independence. If the cost of a public school system means that southern state taxes must rise, so be it."

Several of these positions overlapped. Radical Republicans and black freedmen, for example, often agreed on measures to guarantee a successful transition. The position of northern conservatives overlapped that of southern conservatives. But it would clearly be difficult to reconcile those people who wanted to return to prewar conditions as quickly as possible and those who hoped to make social transformation a requirement for readmitting the South to the Union. The diversity of opinion boded ill for the effort to bring together the nation's separated halves. In the next dozen years there would be fierce battles, some almost as passionate as the war itself, between the contending parties.

PRESIDENTIAL RECONSTRUCTION

Even before Lee's surrender at Appomattox in 1865, the Union government had been forced to consider the question of reconstruction. As Union troops advanced into the South, the Lincoln administration was confronted with the problem of how to govern the conquered territory. Military administration might suffice for a while; but it ran counter to the American tradition of civilian rule, and wherever possible the government sought to restore some civilian control.

Lincoln's Ten-Percent Plan. Lincoln tried to tailor his approach to each state's situation. In general, however, he started by appointing a civilian governor, supported by the military commander and whatever loyal residents the governor could find. In December 1863 he unveiled his "ten-percent plan," which provided that a former Confederate state would be readmitted to the Union when a number of citizens equal to 10 percent of those who had voted in the 1860 presidential election took an oath to support the Constitution and establish a state government that accepted the end of slavery.

Many Republicans felt that Lincoln was being too generous, and in July 1864 Congress responded to his scheme with the Wade-Davis Bill. This legislation would have required that before a new state government could be formed, a *majority* of the white male citizens must pledge to support

the federal Constitution. If they did so, the provisional governor would call a state constitutional convention. The governor could exclude anyone who had fought as a Confederate soldier or had held public office during the Confederate period. Lincoln vetoed the Wade-Davis Bill; but in his usual flexible—if confusing—way, he said that he did not object to it as an alternative to his own plan. Needless to say, no southern state chose to reorganize by the more stringent congressional blueprint. Tennessee, Arkansas, Virginia, and Louisiana accepted the terms of the ten-percent plan, however, and Lincoln proclaimed them back in the Union.

Johnson's Plan. Lincoln's assassination altered the course of political reconstruction profoundly. Had he lived, his standing, popularity, and flexibility might have induced Congress to accept major portions of his plan. Still, even he would have encountered difficulty. The war had swollen federal executive power, and at the end of the conflict Congress certainly would have reasserted itself by fighting to control so vital a program as Reconstruction. It seems unlikely that either side would have had its way entirely.

Lincoln's successor, Andrew Johnson, had to deal with this inevitable clash between Congress and the chief executive. Unfortunately, lacking Lincoln's prestige and political skill, Johnson handled the situation badly. Though he was the same age and from the same southern yeoman background as Lincoln, Johnson was a very different man. Lincoln's family left the slave South when he was a boy, and Abe grew up in the free state of Indiana. Later, as a respected Illinois lawyer, he developed a strong ego and came to appreciate the diverse views of a free society. Johnson, on the other hand, grew up in North Carolina, settled in yeoman-dominated eastern Tennessee, and worked as a simple tailor before entering politics. He was never personally secure, and his lack of self-confidence made him boastful of his humble beginnings and susceptible to flattery. His insecurity, combined with the antiblack and antiaristocratic sentiments of his home region, goes far to explain both his insensitivity to the plight of blacks and his initial hostility to the southern planter class. Johnson's pro–states' rights views also hampered his efforts to solve the unprecedented problems of the postwar period.

Moreover, Johnson was a rigid man, one who often lashed out at his opponents. He could be cajoled out of a position; but when defied directly, he refused to budge. This stubbornness, in turn, often forced his opponents into positions more ex-

Library of Congress

Andrew Johnson had much to do with the failure of Reconstruction. By tolerating the Black Codes and allowing the planter aristocracy to lead "Johnson governments," he drove moderate Republicans into the Radical camp and prevented coordinated and reasonable government action.

treme than their original stands. More than any other factor, Johnson's inability to compromise discouraged the moderates in Congress and drove many into the waiting arms of Radicals like Thaddeus Stevens, Charles Sumner, and Benjamin F. Wade.

The president's characteristics become apparent only gradually, however. At first Republican leaders responded to Johnson very favorably. Moderates and Radicals alike respected his plucky fight against secessionists when he was military governor of Tennessee. The Radicals, having heard him remark that "treason . . . must be made infamous and traitors . . . punished," were certain he would be tougher on the South than Lincoln. The "accession of Johnson will prove a Godsend to the country," Congressman George W. Julian wrote soon after Lincoln's assassination.

The new president's first important act of reconstruction was to pardon large groups of southerners who were willing to take an oath of loyalty to the Union. Excluded from the pardon was the planter class, defined as all those whose taxable property exceeded $20,000. Those excluded from

the general pardon could apply individually to the president, but the Radicals did not expect Johnson to be lenient. The power to pardon would prove important, for unpardoned southerners could not vote, hold office, or reacquire property seized by the federal government during the war.

During his first eight months of office Johnson had a free hand in formulating Reconstruction policy. Congress was not in session when Lincoln died in April, and was not due to meet until December. A wiser man, especially one who had served in both the Senate and House, as Johnson had, might have called Congress into special session and consulted its members about Reconstruction policy. But Johnson took the easy way out and acted on his own.

The president put his eight free months to good use. In May, on the same day he issued the general pardons, he also revealed his Reconstruction policy. The Johnson plan provided that a provisional governor, appointed by the president, would call a state constitutional convention whose delegates would be chosen by those who had taken the prescribed loyalty oath. Johnson made it clear that he expected the conventions to refuse to pay the Confederate debt, and he recommended that they give the vote to educated blacks. Otherwise he gave them almost a free hand to decide what sort of governments their states would have. Once having complied with these lenient conditions, the states would be readmitted to the Union. Congress, Johnson assumed, would accept the result when it assembled in December.

Within a few months of the day the president made his Reconstruction policy public, each of the unreconstructed states held elections for a convention and adopted a new state constitution. Each acknowledged the end of slavery and all, except South Carolina, pledged not to pay debts incurred in supporting the Confederate war effort. No state made a concession on giving blacks the vote, however. Soon afterward, they held statewide elections for governor and other officials and chose state legislators and delegates to Congress. Satisfied that the states had met his conditions, Johnson ordered that the powers exercised by his provisional governors be transferred to the newly elected state officials.

The Johnson Governments. In the next few months the "Johnson governments" operated without restraint from Washington. Their deeds dismayed many northerners, strengthened the Radicals, and destroyed any possibility that Congress would accept the president's Reconstruction policy.

Two things, especially, offended northern Republicans. In the elections for state and federal offices southern voters turned overwhelmingly to former Confederates for leadership. To the upcoming Congress they elected four Confederate generals, five Confederate colonels, six Confederate cabinet officers, fifty-eight Confederate congressmen, and Alexander H. Stephens, who had been vice president of the Confederate States of America. Many newly elected state and local officials, too, had been active in the secession governments. These men all qualified for office because they had received pardons from the president. Whatever the hater of the planter elite had originally felt, it was clear by the end of 1865 that Johnson could not resist the appeal of these men when they came to him hat in hand and asked for forgiveness.

It was natural for southerners to turn to former secessionists when choosing their leaders. To have done otherwise would have been to acknowledge a completely new order, a course that few communities ever accept willingly, and none in so short a time. But this blatant display of Confederate sympathies offended many northerners. Besides, it was only one of the "unforgivable" offenses resulting from the Johnson plan. Not only did the Johnson governments refuse to allow even a few blacks to vote; they also tried to permanently fix the status of blacks in southern society as an inferior one. In the so-called Black Codes the new state governments extended to the freedmen some rights previously reserved for the South's free population. Marriages between blacks, including earlier slave marriages, were legalized; freedmen were allowed to buy, own, and transfer property; and they were given the right, generally, to appear, plead, and testify in court. But the Black Codes also placed the freedmen in a position of distinct legal inferiority to whites. Blacks could not enter into work contracts freely: these were subject to elaborate regulations supervised by a judge. Blacks had to conform to prescribed agricultural work rules. Those who desired to work at a trade, or anything besides farming, had to meet strict apprenticeship standards and, in many areas, to obtain a license. Any black man not gainfully employed might be treated as a vagrant and imprisoned or sentenced to hard labor. In Mississippi fines were imposed for idleness and for a number of petty offenses; blacks who could not pay these might be hired out to anyone who would reimburse the local authorities for their labor. Blacks were also commonly forbidden to carry arms. They could be punished for a given crime more severely than white people. In some states the codes even restricted where they could live and own property.

Many northerners saw no essential difference betwen these laws and the prewar slave codes. Republicans were deeply angered. The *Chicago Tribune* declared that the people of the North would turn one of the worst offending states, Mississippi, into a "frog pond" before they would allow its Black Code "to disgrace one foot of soil in which the bones of our soldiers sleep and over which the flag of freedom flies." Another critic called the codes "an outrage against civilization." Even some white southerners feared that the new legislation had gone too far and would

Library of Congress

One of the real advances afforded by the emancipation was the legal recognition of black marriages. After 1865 black men and women seized the opportunity to solemnize relationships begun under slavery or to contract new ones. Officiating at this wedding is a chaplain from the Freedmen's Bureau.

An Historical Portrait   Thaddeus Stevens

His enemies in the South accused him of murder, adultery, misanthropy, and treason. His friends in the North considered him a defender of democracy and freedom. His admirers called him "the old Commoner" after the eloquent and witty William Pitt, leader of the British House of Commons. Detractors called him "old Clubfoot" because of his congenital deformity. This man who attracted scandal and controversy all his life was Thaddeus Stevens, leader during Reconstruction of the Radical Republicans in the House of Representatives.

Born in April 1792, Stevens was the second son of a sometime farmer, surveyor, wrestler, and shoemaker who disappeared permanently after the birth of his fourth son. His mother, Sarah, was a religious, strong-willed, and energetic woman who ran the farm and taught her sons reading from the Bible. It was she who showed Thaddeus how to fight failure and finally overcome it. She was a firm believer in the value of education, moving her four fatherless children to Peacham, Vermont, when an academy was founded there.

Thaddeus was a bright boy who justified his mother's faith in him. He was also rebellious, a trait that lasted his entire life. As a senior at the academy, he took part in a theatrical performance "by candlelight," an activity expressly forbidden by the stern puritan headmaster. After signing "articles of submission" stating that he regretted his misdeed, he was allowed to finish school. He graduated from Dartmouth in 1814, and in his commencement speech he defended luxury and wealth, claiming they were necessary for progress. Paradoxically, Stevens later attacked the South as a bastion of entrenched privilege and inequality.

In 1815 he went to York, Pennsylvania, where he taught for a year at the local academy and continued his study of law, begun in Vermont. Although the county insisted on a two years' residency requirement for admission to the bar, Stevens thought he was ready after a year because of his previous training. The lawyers of York did not like him and were unwilling to grant him a dispensation, so he crossed the border to Maryland. Here he answered a few questions on Blackstone's *Commentaries,* and a few on evidence and pleading, gave the judge two bottles of Madeira, and received his certification.

Stevens liked Pennsylvania, but did not want to return to York, where he had been snubbed. Instead, he opened his law office in Gettysburg. After a hard first year with few clients, he defended a mentally defective farmhand who had murdered a constable, using insanity as his plea. This was not a recognized defense at the time, and Stevens lost his case. He won himself a reputation for genius and boldness, however, and business poured into his office. He quickly bought himself a horse, a house and property in town, and a farm for his mother in Vermont. By 1830 he had become the largest property owner in the county, had invested in an iron business, and had been elected president of the Borough Council.

During his Gettysburg years Stevens survived an attack of typhoid fever that left him completely bald and added to his feelings of physical inferiority. Although he had many chances to marry, he rejected them all, feeling that his baldness and lameness made him unattractive and that any woman who wanted him must have reasons other than love.

Stevens also became an enthusiastic Anti-Mason, in part because of his rejection at Dartmouth and in York by secret societies. In 1831, in a speech at Hagerstown, Maryland, he attacked the Masons as corrupt, accused them of encouraging crime, and charged them with attempting to stop "the regular action of government." Jacob Lefever, a leading Mason and the owner of a Gettysburg newspaper, who had long been printing anonymous letters blaming Stevens for his supposed part in two recent murders, printed the Hagerstown speech in its entirety with a comment suggesting that Stevens had "blood" on his "skirts." Stevens sued him for criminal libel and damages. Lefever was sentenced to three months in jail and ordered to pay $1,500 in damages.

Despite the Masons' attacks, the Gettysburg townspeople elected Stevens to the state legislature, where he initiated much anti-Masonic legislation. He also made fiery speeches in behalf of an act to extend the free school system of Philadelphia to the entire state. His defense of education for all continued as long as he lived. Just a month before his death he introduced a bill in the House of Representatives "to establish a system of schools for the District of Columbia which shall serve as a model for similar institutions throughout the Union."

While still serving in the Pennsylvania legislature, Stevens became active in the antislavery cause, founding a colonization society and presenting a report in favor of abolishing slavery and the slave trade in the District of Columbia. At the state's constitutional convention in 1837 he refused to sign the final version of the constitution because it restricted suffrage to white males. He also acted as lawyer for fugitive slaves from other states hiding in the Pennsylvania hills. He was, by now, widely recognized as one of the state's foremost abolitionists.

In 1842 Stevens found himself at a personal low point. He had lost his seat in the state legislature and was deeply in debt because of business reverses, losses on massive election bets, and the failure of clients and friends to repay loans. To add to his troubles he was faced with a paternity suit brought by the father of an unmarried woman, a man whom he considerd a friend. He was eventually cleared of this charge, but was embittered by this betrayal and his experiences in Gettysburg generally. He moved his residence and law offices to Lancaster, where he regained his fortunes and his reputation as the state's most accomplished lawyer. Here he also acquired a mulatto housekeeper, Lydia Hamilton Smith, who worked for Stevens until he died. People speculated about their relationship; his enemies snidely referred to her as "Mrs. Stevens."

In 1848 Stevens was elected to

Congress as a Whig. In Washington he immediately gained a reputation as a firebrand. He denounced slavery as accursed, criminal, and shameful, and condemned northerners who permitted its continuance as fiercely as the southerners who practiced it. His House colleagues, from both sections, were often shocked at his abusive and offensive language, believing it better "suited to a fishmarket" than to the halls of Congress. He fought vigorously against both the Compromise of 1850 and the Fugitive Slave Act. After the shattering defeat of Winfield Scott, the Whig candidate for president in 1852, Stevens left Congress and returned to Lancaster to attend to his legal practice and iron business. Having no legitimate children of his own, he also devoted himself to his nephews, Thaddeus and Alanson.

Though out of Congress, Stevens remained involved in politics, taking an active part in the birth of the Republican party in Pennsylvania. In 1858 he was returned to Congress as a Republican, winning 75 percent of the votes in Lancaster County. In 1860 Stevens was a delegate to the Republican national convention. He was mentioned for a cabinet post after Lincoln's victory at the polls, but instead stayed in the House, where he became chairman of the powerful Ways and Means Committee. A month after Lincoln's inauguration Confederate troops fired on Fort Sumter, precipitating the War Between the States. Stevens's committee gave the administration staunch support on financial matters. He was largely responsible for the Internal Revenue Act of 1862, which taxed almost every article produced by the Union. He favored the greenback paper currency, issued directly by the United States and backed by the credit of the country rather than by gold.

During the war Stevens was remorseless toward the South. He favored confiscation of captured enemy property and called for war without mercy. Some thought this was in retaliation for the destruction of his iron works during Lee's invasion of Pennsylvania in 1863. He

introduced a bill calling for general emancipation, with compensation for loyal slaveholders and the freeing of slaves who wanted to leave their masters or who aided in "quelling the rebellion." Stevens favored generals who opposed slavery, believing that such men fought better. He hated George McClellan for his indecisiveness and was pleased when Lincoln fired him.

It was on Reconstruction that Stevens left his greatest mark. He and Charles Sumner were the two most prominent Radical Republicans—a group that favored strict terms for southern readmission to the Union, strong measures to guarantee the rights of the freedmen, and vigorous federal intervention to further economic progress. The Radicals had not been satisfied with Lincoln's lenient "ten-percent plan" for readmitting the seceded states to the Union. The harsher Wade-Davis Bill pleased Stevens no better; it was still too lenient.

When Andrew Johnson became president after Lincoln's assassination, Stevens hoped he would join the Radicals. On the surface, Johnson looked like an ally. A former senator from Tennessee, he had remained loyal to the Union and had fought against secessionists as military governor of the state. Both Stevens and Johnson had strong sympathies for the underdog, but where Stevens championed blacks, Johnson limited his compassion to poor whites. Less than two months after Johnson took office Stevens was permanently disillusioned with the president, considering his plans dangerous and his actions "insane." When Johnson proceeded to reconstruct the Union according to his own lenient design, Stevens and his fellow Radical Republicans determined to take over Reconstruction themselves.

On December 1, 1865, Stevens called together twenty-five supporters to propose a joint committee of both house of Congress on Reconstruction. The committee would study the condition of the "so-called Confederate States of America," and no member elected to Congress would be admitted until

the committee had made its report. When the full Republican caucus met the next night, it unanimously adopted this proposal. When Congress convened later that month, no southerner was seated and the Joint Committee of Fifteen on Reconstruction was established. As chairman of the House faction, Stevens was the dominant member of the committee. He intended to reduce the South to a "territorial condition" and treat it as a "conquered province" over which Congress would have complete control. He also was determined to guarantee the political and, if possible, the social rights of the freedmen. In 1865 and 1866 Stevens urged confiscation of land owned by rich ex-confederates and the transfer of forty acres of this property to each adult ex-slave. Not only would this provide the freedmen with a secure economic position in the South, it would also humble the proud southern elite that Stevens believed had brought the horrors of a brothers' war on the nation.

Stevens saw Johnson as the chief obstacle to the Radicals' policies and determined to get him. In early 1867 he secured passage of the Tenure of Office Act stripping the president of the authority to remove high officeholders who favored congressional Reconstruction. The Radicals also passed a measure requiring the president to issue orders to the army through the general of the army, Ulysses S. Grant, who could not be dismissed without the Senate's consent. The law was intended to filter all orders concerning Reconstruction through Grant, now a supporter of the Radical position.

This legislation set the stage for the impeachment of Andrew Johnson when the president refused to keep Edwin Stanton, a Radical, in his cabinet and ordered him to resign in February 1868. Stevens was in his middle seventies and in poor health by now, but he actively took part in the impeachment proceedings. He bypassed the Judiciary Committee and reported a resolution out of his own Committee on

(*continued on p. 390*)

An Historical Portrait Thaddeus Stevens (*continued*)

Reconstruction to impeach the president for violating the Tenure of Office Act. "Old Thaddeus Stevens," wrote a contemporary political commentator, "is still keeping himself alive only by the hope of sometime scalping Andrew Johnson . . . and watches with a feverish and bilious eye from behind the rampart of his Reconstruction laws the least movement of the enemy." The House voted for impeachment 126 to 47, but when the Senate tried Johnson for high crimes and misdemeanors, the necessary two-thirds majority for conviction fell short by one vote.

Stevens lived only ten weeks after the trial. Many said that his disappointment speeded his decline. This was not true, however. In the short period before his death he continued to work for Reconstruc-

tion, a free public school system for the District of Columbia, various railroad bills, and the purchase of Alaska. He died in August 1868 and rested in state in front of Lincoln's statue on the Capitol Rotunda, attended by an honor guard of black soldiers from Massachusetts. After his burial in Lancaster, the Republican party, in a spectacular gesture of respect, formally nominated him for Congress. So loyal were his constituents that he won in November!

Stevens made many fierce enemies during his lifetime. For many years after his death their views of him were widely accepted and he was remembered as an ill-tempered, vindictive, and punitive man who set back the course of sectional reconciliation. Now, following the "second Reconstruction" of the

1950s and 1960s, "the old Commoner" appears as a statesman ahead of his times and an often admirable defender of racial justice. He, of course, preferred to be seen as a great egalitarian. The inscription he chose for his tombstone testifies to his deep concern for all humanity, regardless of race:

I repose in this quiet and secluded spot,
Not from any natural preference for solitude
But, finding other Cemeteries limited as to Race by Charter Rules,
I have chose this that I might illustrate in my death
The Principles which I advocated Through a long life:
EQUALITY OF MAN BEFORE HIS CREATOR.

provoke the North into a harsh response. Meanwhile, congressmen were receiving almost daily reports from southern white Unionists that the former secessionists were crowing about how they once again had the upper hand and would make life difficult for their Unionist opponents.

CONGRESS TAKES OVER

By the time Congress assembled on December 4, 1865, the Republican majority—most moderates as well as Radicals—were seething with anger at the Johnson governments. Many were also beginning to have second thoughts about the president himself, who was showing too much sympathy for ex-Confederates. When the southern delegations appeared in Washington seeking admission to the Congress, its irritated leaders refused to seat them and determined to take over the task of managing Reconstruction.

On the first day of the session Congress established the Joint Committee on Reconstruction to oversee all measures concerned with restoring the South to the Union. This committee consisted of fifteen senators and representatives, three of them Democrats, whose views ranged all the way from moderate to radical. Under the leadership of the sardonic Thaddeus Stevens of Pennsylvania, it soon became a vehicle for the Radicals.

The first act of congressional Reconstruction was a bill to extend the life of the Freedmen's Bureau and widen its authority. Established in March 1865, the bureau provided aid to refugees, both white and black. It distributed rations, found employment for freedmen, and supplied transportation home for those who had been displaced by the war. It had established hospitals and schools and had drawn up guidelines for bringing ex-slaves into the free labor market. In enlarging the bureau's scope, Congress gave it "military protection and jurisdiction" over all cases involving discrimination against freedmen.

Republican moderates considered the Freedmen's Bureau Bill a relatively mild measure justified by the South's apparent stubbornness, but Johnson refused to sign it. His stated grounds were that the military provisions of the measure took away the authority of existing civilian agencies. Many Republicans correctly interpreted his veto as resistance to a strict Reconstruction policy and an attempt to retain executive control of the restoration process.

The fight over the Freedmen's Bureau was the opening round of a struggle that lasted until the end of Johnson's term, with each new battle driving more and more moderates into the Radical camp. Soon after his veto, Johnson further offended the Republican leaders by calling Stevens and Senator Charles Sumner of Massachusetts "traitors" and "opponents of the fundamental principle of government." Still the moderates continued to hope that the president would accept reasonable proposals to protect the freedmen. With this in mind, Lyman Trumbull of Illinois submitted a civil rights bill to Congress that defined United States citizenship to include blacks and declared that all citizens must be accorded the "full and equal benefit of all laws and proceedings for the security of person and property. . . ." Most Republicans considered the bill a judicious measure and endorsed it. Nevertheless, the president responded with another veto. This time virtually all Republicans thought the president had gone too far, and Congress promptly overrode the veto.

The Fourteenth Amendment. While Congress and Johnson were fighting for supremacy, the joint committee set to work on a comprehensive plan for reconstruction. The Thirteenth Amendment to the Constitution, adopted in December 1865, had confirmed Lincoln's Emancipation Proclamation of 1863 and officially abolished slavery, but it did nothing to make freedmen equal to whites under the law. The federal courts were clearly not too sympathetic to Republican policies. In the 1866

Milligan case, for example, they declared illegal the imposition of martial law on civilians in Indiana, a decision that went against the tough line Lincoln had taken toward antiwar Copperheads. The decision suggested that the courts were inclined to defend local rights against federal power. Who could say what they might do when they came to pass on Republican civil rights legislation? The joint committee's first effort, therefore, was to propose a Fourteenth Amendment to the Constitution that would define United States citizenship and guarantee individual rights. A constitutional amendment would place these rights beyond the power of contravention by the courts, the president, or the state governments.

As finally hammered out and submitted to the states, the Fourteenth Amendment was not all that the most radical of the Republican leaders desired. Congress had the chance to declare unconstitutional all political discrimination on racial grounds. Instead, it deferred to conservative opinion and continuing northern racial prejudice by passing an evasive measure. Rather than giving the vote to all men, it merely declared that whenever a state denied any portion of its adult male population the right to vote, the representation of

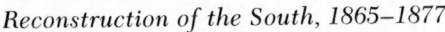

Reconstruction of the South, 1865–1877

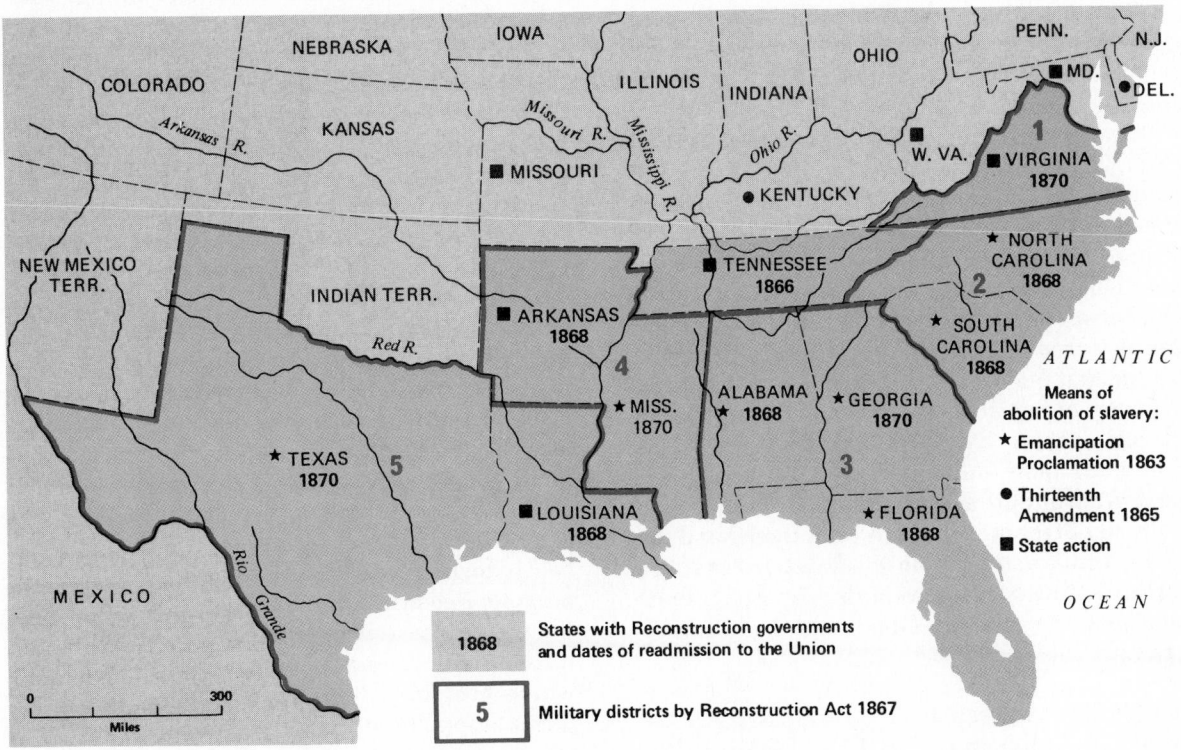

that state in Congress would be reduced proportionately. The South, with its large black population, would now have a powerful incentive to grant black men full voting rights, while the northern states, with few black residents, could continue to deny them their rights without serious penalty. Not until after the adoption of the Fifteenth Amendment (1870) were "race, color, and previous condition of servitude" eliminated as grounds for denying anyone the vote.

In addition to its voting provision, the Fourteenth Amendment defined national citizenship. It also excluded from state and federal office anyone who had taken an oath to uphold the Constitution and had then engaged in "insurrection and rebellion." Moreover, it declared the federal debt a sacred obligation of the American people. The most important clause of the amendment extended the protection of the Constitution to citizens whose rights might be threatened by state governments. The original federal Bill of Rights had limited the power only of the federal government over citizens. Now the Constitution would limit the states as well. No state, this immensely important provision declared, could "make or enforce any law which shall abridge the privileges or immunities of citizens of the United States; nor shall any state deprive any person of life, liberty, or property, without due process of law; nor deny to any person within its jurisdiction the equal protection of the laws."

In specifically restricting the franchise to males, the Fourteenth Amendment was a severe disappointment to women's rights reformers, many of whom had hoped that Union victory would result in suffrage for women as well as blacks. With ratification of the Fourteenth Amendment, the Constitution itself now implicitly denied women the vote, and a new amendment would be required to allow women to vote in federal elections. This setback split the women's rights advocates between those who supported black suffrage even if it was restricted to males and those who decided that they could no longer allow the struggle for racial justice to delay women's progress to full citizenship. By 1870 two women's rights groups, the more militant, New York–based National Woman Suffrage Association (led by Elizabeth Cady Stanton and Susan B. Anthony) and the more conservative, Boston-based American Woman Suffrage Association (led by Lucy Stone and Thomas Wentworth Higginson), had been organized.

The First Reconstruction Act.

The passage of the Fourteenth Amendment in June 1866 was fol-lowed by a concerted effort to compel the southern states to ratify it by making approval a condition of readmission to the Union. Despite congressional pressure, however, not until late July 1868 was the amendment ratified. Meanwhile, the supporters of congressional Reconstruction and the supporters of Johnson's plan vied for public endorsement. In the 1866 congressional elections the president adopted the unusual policy of stumping the North personally to win votes for his position. He did his cause little good. Wherever he went, his opponents heckled him mercilessly and goaded him into rash replies that seemed undignified. In the end the Radicals won a decisive victory—anti-Johnson Republicans carried Congress by a two-thirds majority. Radical legislation would now be veto-proof.

The new Congress quickly took advantage of its mandate. In March 1867, over the president's veto, Congress passed the Reconstruction Act. The most comprehensive piece of congressional Reconstruction legislation, this measure voided the Johnson governments and divided the South into five military districts, each under the jurisdiction of a general and each subject to martial law. The generals were to supervise a new constitution-making process in which blacks had to participate. Any constitution adopted by these conventions must uphold the principles that black men could vote but ex-Confederates would be excluded from both voting and officeholding. When a state had adopted a new constitution, and when it had ratified the Fourteenth Amendment and that amendment had become part of the federal Constitution, *then* that state would be allowed to seat its delegation in Congress. In the following months Congress passed several additional Reconstruction acts to reinforce the first and override southern delaying tactics.

Johnson Impeached.

Johnson did what he could to frustrate the Reconstruction Act of 1867. He appointed five military governors who he knew would interpret their powers narrowly in order to favor white conservatives rather than blacks and local Radicals. And he continued to use his pardoning power, enabling former rebels to regain control of lands that had been seized by the federal government.

Congress feared that Johnson would undermine its Reconstruction program through the hostile use of his executive powers. To hedge him in, it passed the Tenure of Office Act in March 1967, which prohibited the president from dismissing officials appointed with the advice and consent of the Senate without that body's approval. But its

Library of Congress

In August 1866 Johnson announced that "peace, order, tranquility, and civil authority now exist . . . in the United States." Dissatisfied with Johnson's idea of peace and order, the House voted his impeachment less than two years later. Here a packed gallery follows the trial of the century.

only sure weapon against the president's hostility was impeachment. The Constitution provides that all "civil officers" of the government can be removed from office "on Impeachment for, and Conviction of, Treason, Bribery, or other high Crimes and Misdemeanors." The machinery through which this action can be taken is unclear, but even murkier was whether Johnson could be accused of "high Crimes and Misdemeanors."

In December 1867 the Radicals attempted to pass an impeachment resolution. This failed when it became clear that there was no convincing evidence against the president. Well before the House voted on this first resolution, however, the situation had begun to change. During a congressional recess in August 1867 Johnson had suspended from office the Radical secretary of war, Edwin Stanton, in apparent violation of the Tenure of Office Act. The president restored Stanton in January 1868, when the Senate refused to accept his removal, but a month later he removed Stanton again. This defiance seemed to provide the grounds for impeachment that had not existed

when the first resolution had been proposed. On February 24, 1868, the House formally resolved to impeach the president.

The impeachment trial, conducted before the Senate sitting as a court, was the show trial of the century. The major charge against the president was his "unlawful" removal of Stanton. Attorney General Henry Stanbery, the president's counsel, based his defense on the fact that Stanton had been appointed by Lincoln, not Johnson. Consequently, Stanbery argued, he was not covered by the Tenure of Office Act. In any case, the law was probably unconstitutional, and it was the right of the president to test it by violating it and bringing it before the courts. Furthermore, Stanton was still in office (he had refused to leave), so no law had actually been broken.

During the six weeks of the trial intense excitement reigned in Washington and the country. Radicals insisted that acquittal would be a victory for rebels and traitors. The president had frustrated the clearly expressed will of the nation's duly elected legislators by pardoning rebels wholesale and by appointing officials to administer the Reconstruction Act who would not carry it out as they were required to. He must be stopped. Democrats and Johnson's remaining moderate supporters within Republican ranks claimed that conviction would mean that Congress had successfully usurped the power of the executive branch. The president's defenders also noted that his removal would have grave political consequences. The man next in line for the presidency was the president pro tempore of the Senate, the truculent Radical Benjamin Wade.

When the vote finally came on May 16, 1868, Johnson was acquitted by one vote. He should not have been impeached in the first place. There can be no question that he was stubborn, at times undignified, and that he used his executive power to impede Congress. Nor is there much dispute among scholars today that his policies were misguided. In a parliamentary system like Britain's he would probably have been removed by a legislative vote of no confidence. But the Founding Fathers had deliberately created an independently elected executive with the right to disagree with Congress. It therefore seems most likely that they intended impeachment to serve as a way to remove an official from office *only* for breaking the law or for gross incapacity. The Radicals, through impeachment, then, were actually seeking to change the Constitution.

RECONSTRUCTION IN THE SOUTH

Johnson's term came to an end soon after the impeachment trial. There is evidence that the president had been trying since 1866 to win the favor of the Democrats, his former party, in order to secure the Democratic nomination in 1868. But they turned to Horatio Seymour, the wartime governor of New York. The Republicans chose General Ulysses S. Grant. On a platform that simultaneously promised justice for southern Unionists and freedmen and peace between the sections, Grant won a decisive victory.

By the time the new president was inaugurated, the governments organized under the congressional Reconstruction acts—composed of white and black Republicans and decidedly Radical in temper—had been admitted to the Union, and the Fourteenth Amendment had been incorporated into the Constitution. In a narrow legal sense, Reconstruction was now complete. But in fact, the situation in the newly restored states remained uncertain and tense.

Economic Recovery. Several important changes had taken place in the South since April 1865. Physical reconstruction had proceeded at a furious pace. Southern railroads were quickly rebuilt after Appomattox and then extended to additional regions. Between 1865 and 1879, 7,000 miles of track were added to the southern rail network. Much of the needed capital was supplied by investors in the North and in Britain, who anticipated a more favorable business climate in the South. The southern state governments, both the Johnson regimes and the ones established under Congress's formula, also contributed, going heavily into debt to lend money to railroad enterprises. Industry also recovered. In 1860 southern cotton mills boasted 300,000 spindles. By 1880 these had increased to over 530,000. Between the same two dates southern manufactures as a whole increased in value almost 55 percent.

Many southerners had expected even more spectacular advances. Now that slavery was dead and the plantation class that had discouraged manufacturing was out of favor, the South, some felt, would flourish industrially. Until the 1880s such hopes were largely unrealized. Still, the rebound of industry and transportation from immediate postwar lows was remarkable.

During the period 1865–77 agriculture continued to be the chief element in the southern economy, and the war did little to shift southern agriculture from its traditional emphasis on corn

The economic recovery of former confederate states, 1870–1900
Note: Indexed at 1860 = 100
Source: *Twelfth Census of the United States, 1900: Agriculture.*

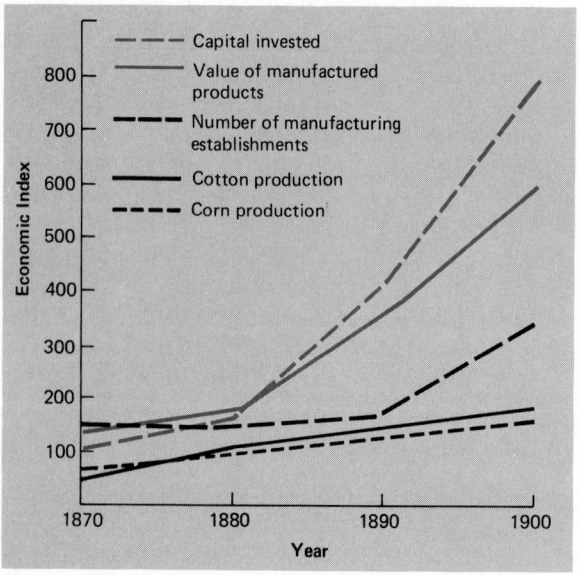

and cotton. If anything, cotton became even more important after 1865 than before the war. For a year or two after Appomattox cotton prices remained high. Though cotton was taxed heavily by the federal government—vengefully, southerners believed—high cotton prices helped put money into the pockets of a needy people. It took years to restore cotton production to prewar levels, but by 1878 the South's cotton output had almost reached its prewar peak. Thereafter, it grew steadily, and by the 1890s the region was producing twice as many bales as in 1859.

Tenantry and Sharecropping. By the end of the century the social basis of southern agriculture had been thoroughly transformed. Before the war defenders of slavery had denied that blacks could function in a free labor market. During the war the Treasury Department, under Secretary Chase's prompting, put this theory to the test in an interesting experiment in the South Carolina Sea Islands near Port Royal. The experiment demonstrated that when ex-slaves were given land, they made successful farmers. A similar experiment undertaken by Grant at Davis Bend, Mississippi, also proved successful. Unfortunately neither test benefited the freedmen. The Port Royal venture collapsed when the Treasury Department failed to transfer land title to the freedmen as it had promised, selling the abandoned Sea Island property to the highest bidder instead. The Davis Bend property was returned to planters armed with pardons from President Johnson.

The efforts to create a class of black farm owners in the South did not cease with these two instances. After 1865 Thaddeus Stevens and other Republicans in Congress advocated giving freedmen lands confiscated from "rebels" during the war. Only landowning could protect blacks against exploitation and keep them from being reinslaved, Stevens and people of like mind insisted. Former slaves themselves yearned to become landowners. "We all know that the colored people want land," a South Carolina carpetbagger declared. "Night and day they think and dream of it. It is their all and all." Whitelaw Reid in his trip south quoted an old black man: "What's de use of bein' free if you don't own land enough to be buried? Might juss as well stay slave all yo days."

Wishes were often transformed into vivid expectations. Many blacks, hearing the opinions of Stevens and his colleagues, came to believe that the government intended to give them "forty acres and a mule" and were bitterly disappointed when it proved untrue. A little acreage was turned over to freedmen. Radical-controlled South Carolina

set up a program to sell land on easy terms to ex-slaves. By 1890 the state Land Commission had given some 2,000 black families title to their own farms. In 1866 Congress passed the Southern Homestead Act, providing free land for blacks and whites alike on the federal domain in the former slave states.

In the end, however, a large black yeomen class failed to appear. The lands available in the South for homesteading were isolated and infertile, and few if any black families were able to make a success of farming them. Congress might have followed Stevens's advice and turned over all seized Confederate land to the freedmen. It might even have "nationalized" all southern land and redistributed it as various revolutionary governments have done in our time. But ultimately the Radicals were not so very radical, and their respect for private property rights—even those of ex-rebels—took precedence over their concern for the freedmen. Most were certain that the ballot offered sufficient protection to the freedmen; a social revolution was not needed.

There was another way that freedmen might have become landowners: black southerners might have accumulated some money and bought land. Southern land prices were low in the 1870s, and a few hundred dollars could have bought a black family a small farm. In 1865 Congress chartered the Freedmen's Bank to support such black self-help efforts. But the bank was poorly managed and could not withstand the financial Panic of 1873. When it closed its doors the following year, it took with it over $3 million of hard-won savings from thousands of black depositors.

Though few southern blacks ever became yeoman farmers, they did remain on the land. For a short while after Appomattox most worked for wages under contracts supervised by the Freedmen's Bureau. But this system pleased neither blacks nor their employers. Cash was difficult for landowners to find in the months following the war, so money wages were hard to pay. The bureau tried to guarantee payment, but employers often fell behind in their obligations anyway. The freedmen, of course, resented such treatment and also disliked the harshness with which some bureau agents enforced labor contracts against them. Still more unsatisfactory from the freedmen's point of view was the return to gang work and the planters' close supervision of every aspect of their labor and their lives. The system reminded them too much of slavery and seemed a mockery of freedom.

Out of this mutual dissatisfaction with wage-paid agricultural labor emerged a tenant farmer

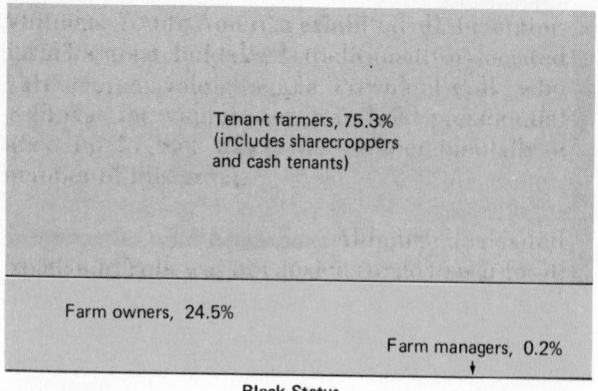

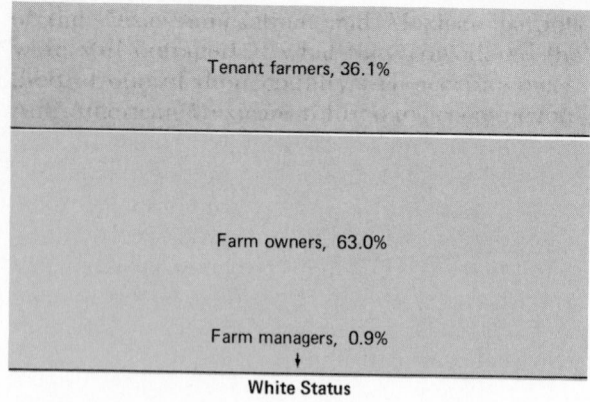

Black Status

White Status

The status of farm operators in former slave states, 1900

Source: Bureau of the Census, *Negro Populations of the United States 1790–1915* (1918) and *Negroes in the United States, Bulletin No. Eight* (1904).

system that by 1880 had become characteristic of the South. Tenantry took many forms and included whites as well as blacks. Thousands of Confederate privates returned home to become, not successful planters, but tenants on lands owned by former slaveholders. Tenants might pay rent either in cash or in part of the crop, typically cotton. Though the system was not as desirable as ownership, a cash tenant was at least free from constant supervision and sometimes could save enough to buy land.

The greater number of tenants farmers, however, especially among the freedmen, were sharecroppers, who turned over their crops to the landowners in exchange for either half the proceeds or perhaps two-thirds if the tenant did not have to borrow a mule and plow from the landlord. Linked to sharecropping was the crop-lien system, a credit arrangement by which a storekeeper (who sometimes was also the landlord) would extend credit to the tenant for supplies during the crop-growing season. When the harvest came and the cotton was sold, the tenant would then repay the debt. Buying on credit was expensive since it included an interest charge. It also gave dishonest storekeepers a chance to cheat. Since they kept the books, they had the upper hand and often juggled the debits and credits to suit themselves. Tenants who could not meet their debts could not change the merchant they dealt with; they remained tied to him almost like serfs.

The freedmen's lot represented a missed opportunity for the nation. This is not to say that freedom was no better than slavery. Some blacks managed to become landowners despite all the difficulties. Most were released from the degradation of close personal supervision by whites. Economically they were better off as sharecroppers

than as slaves. Roger Ransom and Richard Sutch conclude in a recent study that whereas slaves received in food, clothing, housing, medical attention, and so forth about 20 percent of what they produced for their masters, sharecroppers obtained a full half of their total output. In addition, blacks were now able to make decisions about their lives that they never were allowed to make before. Almost all decided that black women would no longer work in the fields; like white women, they would stay home and become proper housewives and mothers. Unfortunately these gains were a one-time advance, made just after the war. Thereafter, while the country as a whole became richer, black living standards remained stagnant.

Indeed, the sharecrop–crop-lien system proved to be an economic trap for the entire lower South. Since they did not own the land, sharecroppers had no incentive to improve it. Landlords, too, had little incentive, for they could only hope to recover a portion of the greater output that might come from additional capital investment. This arrangement also tied the South to a one-crop system and prevented diversification. As one sharecropper complained in the 1880s: "We ought to plant less [cotton and tobacco] and more grain and grasses, but how are we to do it; the man who furnishes us with rations at 50 percent interest won't let us; he wants money crops planted." Failure to diversify produced serious soil exhaustion that could only be offset by expensive additions of fertilizers. Worse still, cotton prices steadily declined for a generation after 1865, pulling down the entire cotton-tied Southern rural economy. Farms in the North and West, though they, too, had problems, came to look neater and more prosperous after 1865. Meanwhile, travelers in the rural South told of weed-choked farmyards, sagging unpainted shacks, and ragged, discouraged-looking people, black and white. With each year the South fell further behind the rest of the nation in almost every measure of material and social well-being: literacy, infant mortality, and per-capita income.

Cultural Change. Whatever the long-term economic trends, the end of slavery brought immense social and cultural gains for black Americans. Black men and women enjoyed a new freedom of movement, which some exercised by going to the cities or escaping to more prosperous parts of the country. At the end of Reconstruction several thousand blacks left the lower South and moved north or west. A particularly large movement of "exodusters" to Kansas after 1878 alarmed southern white leaders, who feared that they might lose their labor force.

The end of slavery freed blacks to express themselves as never before. Slavery had not destroyed black culture, but it had made it difficult for blacks to demonstrate the full range of their talents and to exercise their organizational abilities. The end of formal bondage released energies previously held in check. Blacks withdrew from white churches in large numbers and formed their own. Particularly successful were the Baptists and Methodists. By 1870 there were 500,000 black Baptists; in 1876 the African Methodist Episcopal church had 200,000 members. These churches gave talented former slaves an opportunity to demonstrate leadership beyond anything previously possible. Unlike politics, which was largely closed to talented black men after 1877, the ministry continued to provide leadership opportunities.

The end of slavery also expanded educational opportunities for blacks. Before the war slaves had been legally denied education. After 1865 northern philanthropists seized on Dixie as missionary territory. South Carolina needed only "freedom and education" to become "another Massachusetts," as one of these people remarked. In the months after Appomattox hundreds of Yankee teachers, hoping to uplift a benighted region, went South to establish schools and bring the blessings of literacy. The Freedmen's Bureau also labored to end illiteracy and sought to train blacks in trades. The most permanent impact was achieved by self-help. Before long every southern state, under Radical guidance, had made some provision for educating black children. The southern educational system long remained segregated (except for a time in the cosmopolitan city of New

Library of Congress

They were free, but the economic condition of most black sharecroppers and tenant farmers was little better than that of slaves. Redistribution of confiscated plantation lands might have improved their lot, but the government, which gave millions of acres to railroads, was not so generous to its newest citizens.

Orleans) and poor; yet the schools managed to make a dent in ignorance. By 1880 a quarter of all blacks could read and write; twenty years later the figure had risen to half. College training for blacks, nonexistent in the South before 1860, became available. No blacks were admitted to the established southern state universities, but southern state governments founded separate black colleges and universities. Meanwhile, the Freedmen's Bureau and white philanthropists helped charter such strong black colleges as Atlanta (now Atlanta University), Fisk in Tennessee, and Howard in Washington, D.C. Black education—indeed, all southern education—had a long way to go before it caught up with the North; but compared with the accomplishments before 1860, the gains of the generation following the war were truly impressive.

Yet segregation remained a central fact of life in the South. In 1875 Congress passed a strongly worded Civil Rights Act guaranteeing to all persons, regardless of color, "the full and equal enjoyment of all the accommodations . . . of inns, public conveyances . . ., theaters, and other places of public amusement"; but separation and social inequality persisted. In most communities trains, buses, and theaters had white and black sections. In private life the racial spheres were even more exclusive, and blacks were almost never invited to the homes of white people. Even southern Radicals seldom treated blacks as social equals.

Library of Congress

When the Freedmen's Bureau set up schools for blacks, former slaves of all ages flocked to them. Wrote Booker T. Washington, "It was a whole race trying to go to school." The Snow Hill School, here, abandoned classical education in favor of industrial training, which was more appropriate to black needs.

The Southern Radical Governments. To black Americans at the time, however, the greatest disappointment of Reconstruction was its political failure. Accepting blacks as political equals and even, in the case of black officials, as superiors was completely alien to the established values and customs of the white South.

Yet the governments set up under the 1867 Reconstruction Act allowed blacks an important role in local governments. They voted in the elections supervised by the five regional military commanders, and many were returned to office as state legislators and in other official capacities. Blacks did not, however, dominate the Radical Republican state regimes that congressional Reconstruction brought to power. Even in South Carolina, where blacks outnumbered whites in the total population, they held only a minority of leadership positions.

One of the persistent myths of Reconstruction is that black political leaders during the years of Republican rule were unusually corrupt or incompetent. Among the fifteen black southerners elected to Congress were a number of exceptionally intelligent, educated, and able men. Senator Blanche K. Bruce of Mississippi was an effective legislator who, had he been white, would have been a power in the land. On the level of state government black officials ranged from excellent to poor. All in all, as legislators and politicians, their record did not noticeably diverge from the contemporary white southern average.

It used to be said, too, that white Republicans were a deplorable bunch. This view is also invalid. Some of the white Radicals who ruled the postwar South were idealists who were committed to establishing a new order. Most were probably practical realists who believed it to the South's advantage to accept change. Carpetbaggers—northerners who came South to make money—were not all adventurers interested only in quick gains. Some had sincerely cast their lot with their new communities. And numbered among the native southern scalawags were many former Unionists and a large portion of the South's business class, as well as planters who before the war had voted Whig. They were attracted to the Republican party because they approved of its commercial and industrial programs, because of their traditional Whiggish differences with the Democrats, or because of humanitarian considerations. In any case, they were not the tiny minority of the white population that we would expect if they had been merely dissatisfied troublemakers. In 1872, for example, 20 percent of the South's white voters were Republicans.

In general, the Radical-dominated southern state governments were remarkably effective and reasonably honest. Of course, measured by the standards of the tightfisted prewar South, they were big spenders and ran up huge debts. But the job of rebuilding and adjusting to the new circumstances required a great deal of money. The new governments contributed freely to railroad and other businesses. They established the South's first state-supported school systems and sharply increased public spending for poor relief, prisons, and state hospitals. Though still far behind the North in providing social services, under Radical rule the South began to catch up with the nineteenth century.

The new Radical governments were also more democratic than the prewar regimes. The state constitutions adopted under congressional Reconstruction made many previously appointive offices elective and gave yeoman farmers better representation in the legislature than they had had before the war. They also gave the vote to white males who did not meet the old property qualifications. The new state governments reduced the number of crimes punishable by death, and granted married women more secure control over their property, as the North had done before 1860.

"Redemption." Despite these accomplishments, many white southerners despised the radical regimes and accused them of corruption. Some were in fact corrupt, but generally no more than was normal in state affairs during those years. Southern conservatives also disliked the reforms they initiated, because they were new, because they seemed to be Yankee-inspired, and because they were expensive. Landlords, in particular, denounced the new programs since they raised taxes on real estate. But above all, conservatives found it difficult to accept the Republican-dominated state governments because they were part of the new racial regime. After 250 years of regarding blacks as inherently inferior, the white South could not easily agree to changes that declared a black person the political equal of a white one.

A fierce struggle for political control soon developed in the South between the forces of the new era and those of the old. Radical Union Leagues helped to rally black and scalawag voters in support of Republican candidates for state and local offices. The Radicals also had influential friends in Washington, and after 1869, when Grant

became president, they had the support of the federal executive branch. For a while they succeeded in holding on to office, especially in states where they were most firmly entrenched—Alabama, Mississippi, Texas, Florida, Louisiana, and South Carolina. But in the end they could not match the experience, self-confidence, and ruthlessness of the defenders of bygone times, who hoped to "redeem" the South from "Black Republicanism."

A major weapon of the "redeemers" was the Ku Klux Klan. Formed in 1866 by young Confederate veterans primarily as a social club, the Klan quickly became an antiblack, anti-Radical organization. At the outset it used fear and superstition to intimidate blacks. Hooded, mounted Klansmen would swoop down at night on isolated cabins, making fearsome noises and firing guns. Later they resorted to more violent methods. They burned black homes, attacked and beat black militiamen, ambushed both white and black Radical leaders, and lynched blacks accused of crimes.

At its height in the late 1860s, the Klan went virtually unchecked. Then in 1870 and 1871 Con-

Secret societies like the Knights of the White Camelia, the Pale Faces, and the Knights of the Ku Klux Klan organized to frustrate Reconstruction. Describing itself as an "institution of Chivalry, Humanity, Mercy, and Patriotism," the Klan violently intimidated blacks.

Library of Congress

The Bettmann Archive, Inc.

Southern black voters after 1865 were alternately courted and coerced by white politicians. The Democrats found force more necessary than did the Republicans to win black votes. In this Radical Republican cartoon two Democrats (the one at right looking remarkably like Jefferson Davis) make no pretense of winning "hearts and minds."

gress passed three Force Bills, which collectively declared "armed combinations" and the Klan's terrorist activities illegal. Designed to enforce Reconstruction programs, the bills gave the president the right to prosecute in federal courts those who prevented qualified persons from voting. Grant invoked the measures in nine South Carolina counties, and soon hundreds were indicted for Klan activities.

The Klan quickly declined, but by the 1870s racism was thoroughly institutionalized in Democratic politics. The determination of southern conservatives to render blacks submissive and to take control of the South away from Radicals and their supporters persisted. The redeemers abandoned hooded robes and night rides, but not other forms of intimidation. Typical of their approach was the successful effort in 1875 to return Mississippi to conservative control. There the redeemers ostracized the scalawags and drove many white Republicans to abandon politics or change their party.

One who gave in to their tactics, Colonel James Lusk, told a black fellow Republican: "No white man can live in the South in the future and act with any other than the Democratic party unless he is willing and prepared to live a life of social isolation and remain in political oblivion."

Black voters could not be so easily forced to abandon the party that had served them so well, but here tougher tactics were often effective. Blacks who continued to vote Republican were denied jobs or fired from those they had. More stubborn black Republicans were threatened with violence. During the 1875 state election thousands of white Democrats armed themselves with rifles and shotguns, and then, to make the message clear, entered the names of black Republicans in "dead books." In Vicksburg, Yazoo City, and other Mississippi towns blacks were shot and killed in preelection fights.

The campaign worked. The Democrats captured the Mississippi legislature and elected the only state official up for election. The Republican governor, Adelburt Ames, faced with impeachment by the new legislature, agreed to resign. Mississippi had been "redeemed." Similar processes took place in most of the other states, so that by 1876 only Louisiana, Florida, and South Carolina remained under Republican administrations—and these regimes stayed in power only because they were protected by federal troops.

The End of Reconstruction. Clearly the redeemers were effective tacticians and organizers. But if the commitment of northerners to Radical rule in the South had not been weakening, the redeemers would not have succeeded. The decline of northerners' determination had several sources. To an increasingly large number of Republicans, it began to seem that the defense of the black man was merely an excuse for continued domination by the corrupt wing of their party. Whenever a new scandal was uncovered in the Grant administration—and there were many—it would be blotted out by an appeal to Republican unity against the ex-rebels, a process usually referred to as "waving the bloody shirt." The problem of how to deal with the blacks and their oppressors always seemed to justify continued Republican ascendancy. By the middle of the 1870s many who had once supported the Republican party concluded that abandoning the blacks and their friends in the South was better than continuing to uphold a corrupt party.

Fatigue and racism also played their parts. How long, many northerners asked, could the country invest energy and money to sustain a system that the "best elements" of southern society opposed? Clearly, they said, blacks would never make good citizens, and there was no point in continuing the hopeless battle. Such arguments were reinforced by a growing conviction among northern commercial and industrial groups that peace in the South would be better for business than the political agitation that constantly disturbed the nation.

The end came in 1876. In the presidential election of that year the Democrats nominated Samuel J. Tilden of New York, a stuffy and timid corporation lawyer. The Republican candidate

Election of 1876

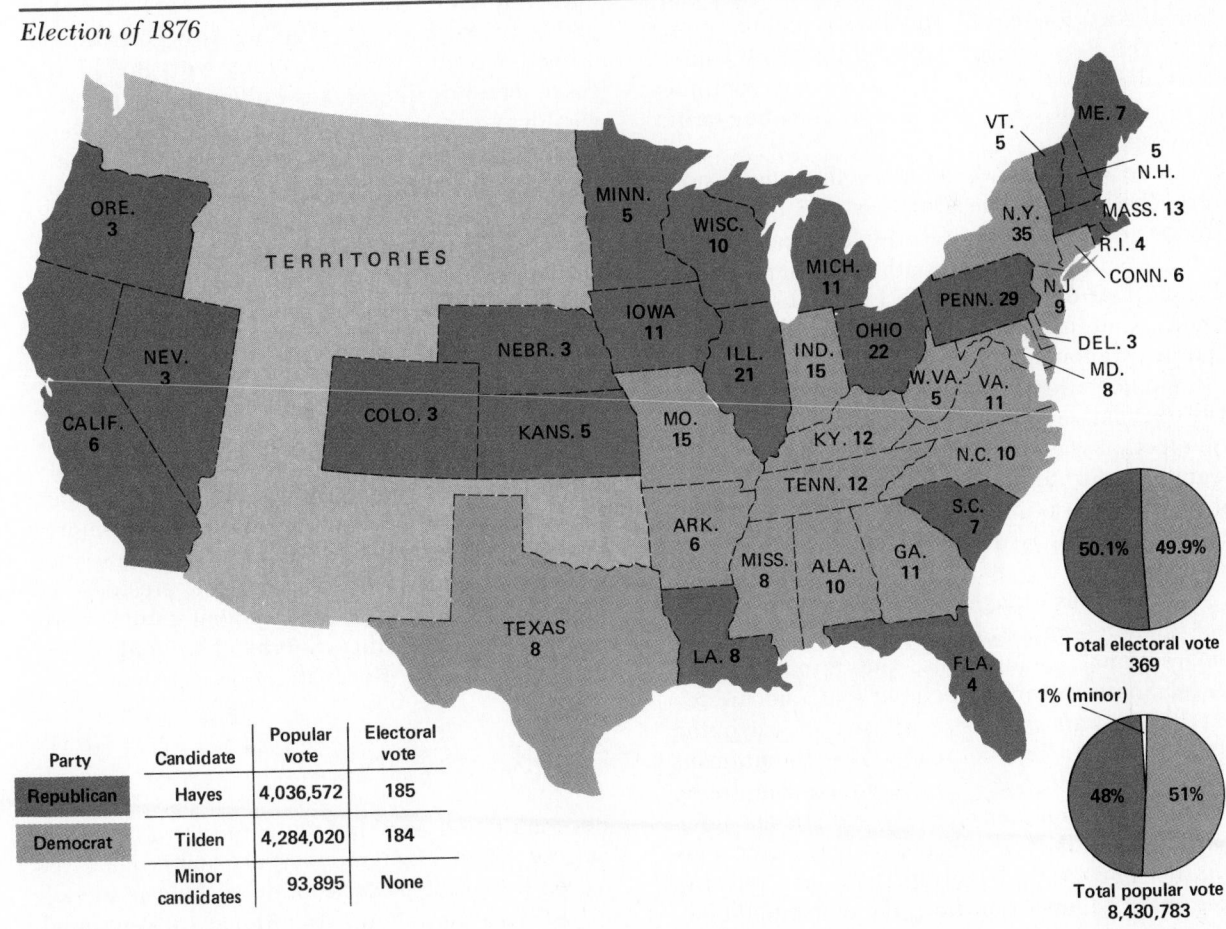

Party	Candidate	Popular vote	Electoral vote
Republican	Hayes	4,036,572	185
Democrat	Tilden	4,284,020	184
	Minor candidates	93,895	None

Total electoral vote 369

Total popular vote 8,430,783

New-York Historical Society

The Compromise of 1877 was a political deal; Hayes was only elected when he, in effect, made promises to end Reconstruction. Neither southern Democrats nor northern Republicans wanted their dealing made public, so they met in secret sessions like this.

was Rutherford B. Hayes, the equally upright and unapproachable governor of Ohio. The Democratic platform promised to withdraw federal troops from the South and endorsed traditional Democratic low-tariff, small-government positions. The Republicans declared that they would never abandon the black man and would continue to support positive government, a protective tariff, and "sound money."

The election was so close that the results were challenged. The Democrats claimed they had carried New York, New Jersey, Connecticut, Indiana, and the entire South. The Republicans insisted that the votes of Florida, Louisiana, and South Carolina—the "unredeemed" states—rightfully belonged to them. They also challenged one Democratic vote in Oregon, where electors had split between the two candidates. As in 1824, the election was thrown into the House of Representatives. For the next four months the country's political life was in an uproar as the politicians tried to settle the issue before Inauguration Day in March 1877.

Both sides brought every weapon to bear on the dispute—propaganda, legal maneuvering, congressional commissions, and threats of violence. Some historians believe that one hidden but vitally important issue during the disputed election period was railroads. The Republicans had favored land grants to encourage completion of the national rail network. The Democrats, however, disliked federal aid, and on many occasions leading northern Democrats had attacked the land-grant policy. At the time of the disputed elec-

tion, a major land grant of great importance to southern commercial and business interests was being considered in Congress. The Texas & Pacific Railroad, which would benefit from this grant, was supposed to connect New Orleans and other important southern cities with the Pacific coast. The rail link, it was believed, would bring wealth to many communities in the South. A Democratic administration, of course, would remove the troops from the remaining unredeemed states and end Reconstruction, but it would also oppose the Texas & Pacific project. This reasoning apparently led important southern leaders, many of them former Whigs who had little love for the Democrats, to bargain with the Republicans. In return for a promise to remove the troops, give some political rewards to southerners, and support a Texas & Pacific land grant, southerners in the House of Representatives agreed to support Republican Hayes. A number of important scholars believe that this bargain, known as the Compromise of 1877, gave Hayes the election. Soon after Hayes's inauguration as nineteenth president of the United States, the last federal troops were withdrawn from the South. The redeemers quickly moved in. Reconstruction was over.

CONCLUSIONS

Reconstruction was not an unrelieved disaster. During these momentous years southerners repaired the physical devastation of the war and re-established their states' traditional constitutional relations with the Union. Meanwhile, black southerners were able to create for themselves important islands of freedom—freedom to move, freedom to establish social and cultural insitutions of their own, freedom for black women to leave the fields. Also on the credit side were the Radical-sponsored Fourteenth and Fifteenth amendments. Once implanted in the Constitution, they would become the bases for a "second Reconstruction" in our own day.

Yet there is much that is dismaying about Reconstruction. In general, Americans of the era failed to meet the great challenges that faced them. Instead of a prosperous black yeomanry, the South would be left with a mass of impoverished semipeons who for generations would be a reproach to America's proud claims of prosperity and equality. Instead of political democracy, Reconstruction would bequeath a legacy of sectional fraud, intimidation, and shameless racial exclusion. Rather than accelerating southern economic growth, Reconstruction would chain the South to a declining staple agriculture and leave it ever further behind the rest of the nation.

Who was to blame for this debacle? One answer is that Americans were trapped by the past. Deep-seated prejudices and memories of slavery blinded most white southerners—and many northerners—to the need for racial justice. Traditional individualism and the commitment to self-help obscured the fact that the special circumstances of black dependence resulting from slavery called for imaginative government aid. And there were the accidents of events and personalities. Would Lincoln have seen realities more clearly? Certainly the succession of Andrew Johnson, a stubborn man of limited vision and conventional racial views, did nothing to solve the unique problems of the day. Refusing to recognize the North's need to exact some penance from the defeated South, he needlessly antagonized even moderates and drove them into the Radical camp. The result was a legacy of sectional hatred that poisoned American political life for generations.

Meanwhile, the nation was turning away from the intractable "southern problem" to what many citizens believed were more important matters. The South and Reconstruction became increasingly remote as the country at large experienced a surge of economic expansion that dwarfed anything of the past.

FOR FURTHER READING

Eric L. McKitrick. *Andrew Johnson and Reconstruction* (1960)

Andrew Johnson's personality is emphasized in this study of Reconstruction. McKitrick says that Johnson was easily flattered and irrationally stubborn when defied. Most serious of all his deficiencies, however, was that he failed to see that the North needed evidence of southern contrition before it could forgive and allow a return to normal relations between the sections.

Clement Eaton. *The Waning of the Old South Civilization, 1860–1880* (1968)

An excellent short summary of life among the common people and the planter elite in 1860, the effect of the war on southern culture, the postwar white adjustment to freed blacks, economic recovery, and the "cultural lag" especially evident in small towns and rural areas. Eaton concludes that the New South retained much of the old, especially its devotion to states' rights, white supremacy, and the cult of southern womanhood. In the brief generation since this book was written, much has changed, however.

Albion W. Tourgée. *A Fool's Errand: A Novel of the South During Reconstruction* (1879). Edited by George M. Frederickson (1966)

An autobiographical novel by a "carpetbagger" lawyer from Ohio who settled in North Carolina after the Civil War. As a Radical superior court judge, Tourgée was hated by white conservatives for his attempts to bring Ku Klux Klan leaders to justice. His estimate of the role of idealistic carpetbaggers is summed up in his title.

Allen W. Trelease. *White Terror: The Ku Klux Klan Conspiracy and Southern Reconstruction* (1971)

The big, definitive study of the first Klan after the Civil War. This is a potent indictment of the KKK and all its doings.

Joel Williamson. *After Slavery: The Negro in South Carolina During Reconstruction, 1861–1877* (1965)

In this detailed, interesting study of race relations in one key Reconstruction state, Williamson concludes that racial segregation was not wholly a product of "redemption." He also deals with efforts by South Carolina Radicals to provide "land for the landless."

Willie Lee Rose. *Rehearsal for Reconstruction: The Port Royal Experiment* (1964)

The efforts of the northerners who attempted to give the former Sea Island slaves their masters' land are tragicomic in Rose's account. Ultimately the ex-slaves lost the rich cotton lands to their former owners. Yet the temporary success of the Port Royal experiment tells us what might have been if the northern commitment to black freedom and racial justice had been stronger.

Roger Ransom and Richard Sutch. *One Kind of Freedom: The Economic Consequences of Emancipation* (1977)

An important book by two "cliometricians" about how emancipation affected the economic well-being of the freedmen and the South as a whole. Has an interesting discussion of the sharecrop–crop-lien system.

LaWanda Cox and John Cox. *Politics, Principles, and Prejudice, 1865–1866: Dilemma of Reconstruction America* (1963)

A study of presidential Reconstruction that gives the Radicals much credit for idealism and suggests how much politics actually entered into Andrew Johnson's decisions. Reverses the older pattern of blaming the Radicals and praising Johnson.

Leon Litwack. *Been in the Storm So Long: The Aftermath of Slavery* (1980)

Professor Litwack tells us—at somewhat excessive length—what black men and women felt about the new world of freedom after 1863. He shows that their reactions were amazingly diverse and often contradictory.

Herbert Gutman. *The Black Family in Slavery and Freedom, 1750–1925* (1976)

Excellent social history, not only of the slavery period, but also of the postslavery experience of black families.

Kenneth Stampp. *The Era of Reconstruction, 1865–1877* (1965)

An excellent overall view of the "new" Reconstruction history. Stampp attacks the myth that Reconstruction meant federal tyranny and "Negro rule." He considers the failure to redistribute property to the freedmen a mistake, but believes the Radicals were governed by idealism rather than greed or pure politics.

C. Vann Woodward. *Reunion and Reaction: The Compromise of 1877 and the End of Reconstruction* (1951)

The dean of southern historians concludes that the agreement to end the presidential election dispute of 1876–77 was not a bargain made purely in the interest of political peace and orderly government. Rather, it was a behind-the-scenes agreement to exchange continued Republican supremacy for major economic favors to southern business groups. Not all scholars buy his thesis.

Appendix

IN CONGRESS, JULY 4, 1776
The Declaration of Independence

The unanimous Declaration of the thirteen united States of America

When in the Course of human events, it becomes necessary for one people to dissolve the political bands which have connected them with another, and to assume among the powers of the earth, the separate and equal station to which the Laws of Nature and of Nature's God entitle them, a decent respect to the opinions of mankind requires that they should declare the causes which impel them to the separation.

We hold these truths to be self-evident, that all men are created equal, that they are endowed by their Creator with certain unalienable Rights, that among these are Life, Liberty and the pursuit of Happiness.

That to secure these rights, Governments are instituted among Men, deriving their just powers from the consent of the governed.

That whenever any Form of Government becomes destructive of these ends, it is the Right of the People to alter or to abolish it, and to institute new Government, laying its foundation on such principles and organizing its powers in such form, as to them shall seem most likely to effect their Safety and Happiness. Prudence, indeed, will dictate that Governments long established should not be changed for light and transient causes; and accordingly all experience hath shewn, that mankind are more disposed to suffer, while evils are sufferable, than to right themselves by abolishing the forms to which they are accustomed. But when a long train of abuses and usurpations, pursuing invariably the same Object evinces a design to reduce them under absolute Despotism, it is their right, it is their duty, to throw off such Government, and to provide new Guards for their future security.

Such has been the patient sufferance of these Colonies; and such is now the necessity which constrains them to alter their former Systems of Government. The history of the present King of Great Britain is a history of repeated injuries and usurpations, all having in direct object the establishment of an absolute Tyranny over these States. To prove this, let Facts be submitted to a candid world.

He has refused his Assent to Laws, the most wholesome and necessary for the public good.

He has forbidden his Governors to pass Laws of immediate and pressing importance, unless suspended in their operation till his Assent should be obtained; and when so suspended, he has utterly neglected to attend to them.

He has refused to pass other Laws for the accommodation of large districts of people, unless those people would relinquish the right of Representation in the Legislature, a right inestimable to them and formidable to tyrants only.

He has called together legislative bodies at places unusual, uncomfortable, and distant from the depository of their public Records, for the sole purpose of fatiguing them into compliance with his measures.

He has dissolved Representative Houses repeatedly, for opposing with manly firmness his invasions on the rights of the people.

He has refused for a long time, after such dissolutions, to cause others to be elected; whereby the Legislative powers, incapable of Annihilation, have returned to the People at large for their exercise; the State remaining in the mean time exposed to all the dangers of invasion from without, and convulsions within.

He has endeavoured to prevent the population of these States; for that purpose obstructing the Laws for Naturalization of Foreigners; refusing to pass others to encourage their migrations hither, and raising the conditions of new Appropriations of Lands.

He has obstructed the Administration of Justice, by refusing his Assent to Laws for establishing Judiciary powers.

He has made Judges dependent on his Will alone, for the tenure of their offices, and the amount and payment of their salaries.

He has erected a multitude of New Offices, and sent hither swarms of Officers to harrass our people, and eat out their substance.

He has kept among us, in times of peace, Standing Armies without the Consent of our legislatures.

He has affected to render the Military independent of and superior to the Civil power.

He has combined with others to subject us to a jurisdiction foreign to our constitution, and unacknowledged by our laws; giving his Assent to their Acts of pretended Legislation:

For quartering large bodies of armed troops among us:

For protecting them, by a mock Trial, from punishment for any Murders which they should commit on the Inhabitants of these States:

For cutting off our Trade with all parts of the world:

For imposing Taxes on us without our Consent:

For depriving us in many cases, of the benefits of Trial by Jury:

For transporting us beyond Seas to be tried for pretended offences:

For abolishing the free System of English Laws in a neighbouring Province, establishing therein an Arbitrary government, and enlarging its Boundaries so as to render it at once an example and fit instrument for introducing the same absolute rule into these Colonies:

For taking away our Charters, abolishing our most valuable Laws, and altering fundamentally the Forms of our Governments:

For suspending our own Legislatures, and declaring themselves invested with power to legislate for us in all cases whatsoever.

He has abdicated Government here, by declaring us out of his Protection and waging War against us.

He has plundered our seas, ravaged our Coasts, burnt our towns, and destroyed the Lives of our people.

He is at this time transporting large Armies of foreign Mercenaries to compleat the works of death, desolation and tyranny, already begun with circumstances of Cruelty & perfidy scarcely paralleled in the most barbarous ages, and totally unworthy the Head of a civilized nation.

He has constrained our fellow Citizens taken Captive on the high Seas to bear Arms against their Country, to become the executioners of their friends and Brethren, or to fall themselves by their Hands.

He has excited domestic insurrections amongst us, and has endeavoured to bring on the inhabitants of our frontiers, the merciless Indian Savages, whose known rule of warfare, is an undistinguished destruction of all ages, sexes and conditions.

In every stage of these Oppressions We have Petitioned for Redress in the most humble terms: Our repeated Petitions have been answered only by repeated injury. A Prince, whose character is thus marked by every act which may define a Tyrant, is unfit to be the ruler of a free people.

Nor have We been wanting in attentions to our British brethren. We have warned them from time to time of attempts by their legislature to extend an unwarrantable jurisdiction over us. We have reminded them of the circumstances of our emigration and settlement here. We have appealed to their native justice and magnanimity, and we have conjured them by the ties of our common kindred to disavow these usurpations, which, would inevitably interrupt our connections and correspondence. They too have been deaf to the voice of justice and of consanguinity. We must, therefore, acquiesce in the necessity, which denounces our Separation, and hold them, as we hold the rest of mankind, Enemies in War, in Peace Friends.

We, therefore, the Representatives of the united States of America, in General Congress, Assembled, appealing to the Supreme Judge of the world for the rectitude of our intentions, do, in the Name, and by Authority of the good People of these Colonies, solemnly publish and declare, That these United Colonies are, and of Right ought to be Free and Independent States; that they are Absolved from all Allegiance to the British Crown, and that all political connection between them and the State of Great Britain, is and ought to be totally dissolved; and that as Free and Independent States, they have full Power to levy War, conclude Peace, contract Alliances, establish Commerce, and to do all other Acts and Things which Independent States may of right do.

And for the support of this Declaration, with a firm reliance on the protection of divine Providence, we mutually pledge to each other our Lives, our Fortunes and our sacred Honor.

JOHN HANCOCK

NEW HAMPSHIRE
Josiah Bartlett
William Whipple
Matthew Thornton

MASSACHUSETTS BAY
Samuel Adams
John Adams
Robert Treat Paine
Elbridge Gerry

RHODE ISLAND
Stephen Hopkins
William Ellery

CONNECTICUT
Roger Sherman
Samuel Huntington
William Williams
Oliver Wolcott

NEW YORK
William Floyd
Philip Livingston
Francis Lewis
Lewis Morris

NEW JERSEY
Richard Stockton
John Witherspoon
Francis Hopkinson
John Hart
Abraham Clark

PENNSYLVANIA
Robert Morris
Benjamin Rush
Benjamin Franklin
John Morton
George Clymer
James Smith
George Taylor
James Wilson
George Ross

DELAWARE
Caesar Rodney
George Read
Thomas M'Kean

MARYLAND
Samuel Chase
William Paca
Thomas Stone
Charles Carroll,
  of Carrollton

VIRGINIA
George Wythe
Richard Henry Lee
Thomas Jefferson
Benjamin Harrison
Thomas Nelson, Jr.
Francis Lightfoot Lee
Carter Braxton

NORTH CAROLINA
William Hooper
Joseph Hewes
John Penn

SOUTH CAROLINA
Edward Rutledge
Thomas Heyward, Jr.
Thomas Lynch, Jr.
Arthur Middleton

GEORGIA
Button Gwinnett
Lyman Hall
George Walton

Resolved, That copies of the Delaration be sent to the several assemblies, conventions, and committees, or councils of safety, and to the several commanding officers of the continental troops; that it be proclaimed in each of the United States, at the head of the army.

The Constitution of the United States of America

Preamble

We the People of the United States, in Order to form a more perfect Union, establish Justice, insure domestic Tranquility, provide for the common defence, promote the general Welfare, and secure the Blessings of Liberty to ourselves and our Posterity, do ordain and establish this Constitution for the United States of America.

Article I

Section 1. All legislative Powers herein granted shall be vested in a Congress of the United States, which shall consist of a Senate and House of Representatives.

Section 2. The House of Representatives shall be composed of Members chosen every second Year by the People of the several States, and the Electors in each State shall have the Qualifications requisite for Electors of the most numerous Branch of the State Legislature.

No Person shall be a Representative who shall not have attained to the Age of twenty-five Years, and been seven years a Citizen of the United States, and who shall not, when elected, be an Inhabitant of that State in which he shall be chosen.

Representatives and direct Taxes shall be apportioned among the several States which may be included within this Union, according to their respective Numbers, [which shall be determined by adding to the whole Number of free Persons, including those bound to Service for a Term of Years, and excluding Indians not taxed, three fifths of all other Persons.][1] The actual Enumeration shall be made within three Years after the first Meeting of the Congress of the United States, and within every subsequent Term of ten Years, in such Manner as they shall by Law direct. The Number of Representatives shall not exceed one for every thirty Thousand, but each State shall have at Least one Representative; and until such enumeration shall be made, the State of New Hampshire shall be entitled to chuse three; Massachusetts eight; Rhode Island and Providence Plantations one; Connecticut five; New York six; New Jersey four; Pennsylvania eight; Delaware one; Maryland six; Virginia ten; North Carolina five; South Carolina five; and Georgia three.

When vacancies happen in the Representation from any State, the Executive Authority thereof shall issue Writs of Election to fill such Vacancies.

The House of Representatives shall chuse their Speaker and other Officers; and shall have the sole Power of Impeachment.

Section 3. The Senate of the United States shall be composed of two Senators from each state, [chosen by the Legislature thereof,][2] for six Years; and each Senator shall have one Vote.

Immediately after they shall be assembled in Consequence of the first Election, they shall be divided as equally as may be into three Classes. The Seats of the Senators of the first Class shall be vacated at the Expiration of the second year, of the second Class at the Expiration of the fourth Year, and of the third Class at the Expiration of the sixth Year, so that one third may be chosen every second Year; [and if Vacancies happen by Resignation, or otherwise, during the Recess of the Legislature of any State, the Executive thereof may make temporary Appointments until the next Meeting of the Legislature, which shall then fill such Vacancies.][3]

No Person shall be a Senator who shall not have attained to the Age of thirty Years, and been nine Years a Citizen of the United States, and who shall not, when elected, be an Inhabitant of that State for which he shall be chosen.

The Vice President of the United States shall be President of the Senate, but shall have no Vote, unless they be equally divided.

The Senate shall chuse their other Officers, and also a President pro tempore, in the Absence of the Vice President, or when he shall exercise the Office of President of the United States.

The Senate shall have the sole Power to try all Impeachments. When sitting for that Purpose, they shall be on Oath or Affirmation. When the President of the United States is tried, the Chief Justice shall preside: And no Person shall be convicted without the Concurrence of two thirds of the Members present.

Judgment in Cases of Impeachment shall not extend further than to removal from Office, and disqualification to hold and enjoy any Office of honor, Trust or Profit under the United States: but the Party convicted shall nevertheless be liable and subject to Indictment, Trial, Judgment and Punishment, according to Law.

Section 4. The Times, Places and Manner of holding Elections for Senators and Representatives, shall be prescribed in each State by the Legislature thereof; but the Congress may at any time by Law

[1] Bracketed material superseded by Section 2 of the Fourteenth Amendment.

[2] Bracketed material superseded by Clause I of the Seventeenth Amendment.

[3] Bracketed material modified by Clause 2 of the Seventeenth Amendment.

make or alter such Regulations, except as to the Places of chusing Senators.

[The Congress shall assemble at least once in every Year, and such Meeting shall be on the first Monday in December, unless they shall by Law appoint a different Day.]4

Section 5. Each House shall be the Judge of the Elections, Returns and Qualifications of its own Members, and a Majority of each shall constitute a Quorum to do Business; but a smaller Number may adjourn from day to day, and may be authorized to compel the Attendance of absent Members, in such Manner, and under such Penalties as each House may provide.

Each House may determine the Rules of its Proceedings, punish its Members for disorderly Behaviour, and, with the Concurrence of two thirds, expel a Member.

Each House shall keep a Journal of its Proceedings, and from time to time publish the same, excepting such Parts as may in their Judgment require Secrecy; and the Yeas and Nays of the Members of either House on any question shall, at the Desire of one fifth of those Present, be entered on the Journal.

Neither House, during the Session of Congress, shall, without the Consent of the other, adjourn for more than three days, nor to any other Place than that in which the two Houses shall be sitting.

Section 6. The Senators and Representatives shall receive a Compensation for their Services, to be ascertained by Law, and paid out of the Treasury of the United States. They shall in all Cases, except Treason, Felony and Breach of the Peace, be privileged from Arrest during their Attendance at the Session of their respective Houses, and in going to and returning from the same; and for any Speech or Debate in either House, they shall not be questioned in any other Place.

No Senator or Representative shall, during the Time for which he was elected, be appointed to any civil Office under the Authority of the United States, which shall have been created, or the Emoluments whereof shall have been encreased during such time; and no Person holding any Office under the United States, shall be a Member of either House during his Continuance in Office.

Section 7. All Bills for raising Revenue shall Originate in the House of Representatives; but the Senate may propose or concur with Amendments as on other Bills.

Every Bill which shall have passed the House of Representatives and the Senate, shall, before it become a Law, be presented to the President of the United States; If he approve he shall sign it, but if not he shall return it, with his Objections to that House in

which it shall have originated, who shall enter the Objections at large on their Journal, and proceed to reconsider it. If after such Reconsideration two thirds of that House shall agree to pass the Bill, it shall be sent, together with the Objections, to the other House, by which it shall likewise be reconsidered, and if approved by two thirds of that House, it shall become a Law. But in all such Cases the Votes of both Houses shall be determined by Yeas and Nays, and the Names of the Persons voting for and against the Bill shall be entered on the Journal of each House respectively. If any Bill shall not be returned by the President within ten Days (Sundays excepted) after it shall have been presented to him, the Same shall be a Law, in like Manner as if he had signed it, unless the Congress by their Adjournment prevents its Return, in which Case it shall not be a Law.

Every Order, Resolution, or Vote to which the Concurrence of the Senate and House of Representatives may be necessary (except on a question of Adjournment) shall be presented to the President of the United States; and before the Same shall take effect, shall be approved by him, or being disapproved by him, shall be repassed by two thirds of the Senate and House of Representatives, according to the Rules and Limitations prescribed in the Case of a Bill.

Section 8. The Congress shall have Power To lay and collect Taxes, Duties, Imposts and Excises, to pay the Debts and provide for the common Defence and general Welfare of the United States; but all Duties, Imposts and Excises shall be uniform throughout the United States;

To borrow Money on the credit of the United States;

To regulate Commerce with foreign Nations, and among the several States, and with the Indian Tribes;

To establish an uniform Rule of Naturalization, and uniform Laws on the subject of Bankruptcies throughout the United States;

To coin Money, regulate the Value thereof, and of foreign Coin, and fix the Standard of Weights and Measures;

To provide for the Punishment of counterfeiting the Securities and current Coin of the United States;

To establish Post Offices and post Roads;

To promote the Progress of Science and useful Arts, by securing for limited Times to Authors and Inventors the exclusive Right to their respective Writings and Discoveries;

To constitute Tribunals inferior to the supreme Court;

To define and punish Piracies and Felonies committed on the high Seas, and Offences against the Law of Nations;

To declare War, grant Letters of Marque and

4 Bracketed material superseded by Section 2 of the Twentieth Amendment.

Reprisal, and make Rules concerning Captures on Land and Water;

To raise and support Armies; but no Appropriation of Money to that Use shall be for a longer Term than two years;

To provide and maintain a Navy;

To make Rules for the Government and Regulation of the land and naval Forces;

To provide for calling forth the Militia to execute the Laws of the Union, suppress Insurrections and repel Invasions;

To provide for organizing, arming, and disciplining, the Militia, and for governing such Part of them as may be employed in the Service of the United States, reserving to the States respectively, the Appointment of the Officers, and the Authority of training the Militia according to the discipline prescribed by Congress;

To exercise exclusive Legislation in all Cases whatsoever, over such District (not exceeding ten Miles square) as may, by Cession of particular States, and the Acceptance of Congress, become the Seat of the Government of the United States, and to exercise like Authority over all Places purchased by the Consent of the Legislature of the State in which the Same shall be, for the Erection of Forts, Magazines, Arsenals, dock-Yards, and other needful Buildings;—And

To make all Laws which shall be necessary and proper for carrying into Execution the foregoing Powers, and all other Powers vested by this Constitution in the Government of the United States, or in any Department or Officer thereof.

Section 9. The Migration or Importation of such Persons as any of the States now existing shall think proper to admit, shall not be prohibited by the Congress prior to the year one thousand eight hundred and eight, but a Tax or duty may be imposed on such Importation, not exceeding ten dollars for each Person.

The Privilege of the Writ of Habeas Corpus shall not be suspended, unless when in Cases of Rebellion or Invasion the public Safety may require it.

No Bill of Attainder or ex post facto Law shall be passed.

No Capitation, or other direct, Tax shall be laid, unless in Proportion to the Census or Enumeration herein before directed to be taken.[5]

No Tax or Duty shall be laid on Articles exported from any State.

No Preference shall be given by any Regulation of Commerce or Revenue to the Ports of one State over those of another: nor shall Vessels bound to, or from, one State, be obliged to enter, clear, or pay Duties in another.

No Money shall be drawn from the Treasury, but in Consequence of Appropriations made by Law;

[5] Modified by the Sixteenth Amendment.

and a regular Statement and Account of the Receipts and Expenditures of all public Money shall be published from time to time.

No Title of Nobility shall be granted by the United States: And no Person holding any Office of Profit or Trust under them, shall, without the Consent of the Congress, accept of any present, Emolument, Office, or Title, of any kind whatever, from any King, Prince, or foreign State.

Section 10. No State shall enter into any Treaty, Alliance, or Confederation; grant Letters of Marque and Reprisal; coin Money; emit Bills of Credit; make any Thing but gold and silver Coin a Tender in Payment of Debts; pass any Bill of Attainder, ex post facto Law, or Law impairing the Obligation of Contracts, or grant any Title of Nobility.

No State shall, without the Consent of the Congress, lay any Imposts or Duties on Imports or Exports, except what may be absolutely necessary for executing its inspection Laws: and the net Produce of all Duties and Imposts, laid by any State on Imports or Exports, shall be for the Use of the Treasury of the United States; and all such Laws shall be subject to the Revision and Controul of the Congress.

No State shall, without the Consent of Congress, lay any Duty of Tonnage, keep Troops, or Ships of War in time of Peace, enter into any Agreement or Compact with another State, or with a foreign Power, or engage in War, unless actually invaded, or in such imminent Danger as will not admit of delay.

Article II

Section 1. The executive Power shall be vested in a President of the United States of America. He shall hold his Office during the Term of four Years, and, together with the Vice President, chosen for the same Term, be elected, as follows.

Each State shall appoint, in such Manner as the Legislature thereof may direct, a Number of Electors, equal to the whole Number of Senators and Representatives to which the State may be entitled in the Congress: but no Senator or Representative, or Person holding an Office of Trust or Profit under the United States, shall be appointed an Elector.

[The Electors shall meet in their respective States, and vote by Ballot for two Persons, of whom one at least shall not be an Inhabitant of the same State with themselves. And they shall make a List of all the Persons voted for, and of the Number of Votes for each; which List they shall sign and certify, and transmit sealed to the Seat of the Government of the United States, directed to the President of the Senate. The President of the Senate shall, in the Presence of the Senate and House of Representatives, open all the Certificates, and the Votes shall then be counted. The Person having the greatest Number of Votes shall be the President, if such Number be a

Majority of the whole Number of Electors appointed; and if there be more than one who have such Majority, and have an equal Number of Votes, then the House of Representatives shall immediately chuse by Ballot one of them for President; and if no Person have a Majority, then from the five highest on the List the said House shall in like Manner chuse the President. But in chusing the President, the Votes shall be taken by States, the Representation from each State having one Vote; A quorum for this Purpose shall consist of a Member or Members from two thirds of the States, and a Majority of all the States shall be necessary to a Choice. In every Case, after the Choice of the President, the Person having the greatest Number of Votes of the Electors shall be the Vice President. But if there should remain two or more who have equal Votes, the Senate shall chuse from them by Ballot the Vice President.][6]

The Congress may determine the Time of chusing the Electors, and the Day on which they shall give their Votes; which Day shall be the same throughout the United States.

No Person except a natural born Citizen, or a Citizen of the United States, at the time of the Adoption of this Constitution, shall be eligible to the Office of President; neither shall any Person be eligible to that Office who shall not have attained to the Age of thirty-five Years, and been fourteen Years a Resident within the United States.

[In Case of the Removal of the President from Office, or of his Death, Resignation, or Inability to discharge the Powers and Duties of the said Office, the Same shall devolve on the Vice President, and the Congress may by law provide for the Case of Removal, Death, Resignation or Inability, both of the President and Vice President, declaring what Officer shall then act as President, and such Officer shall act accordingly, until the Disability be removed, or a President shall be elected.][7]

The President shall, at stated Times, receive for his Services, a Compensation, which shall neither be encreased nor diminished during the Period for which he shall have been elected, and he shall not receive within that Period any other Emolument from the United States, or any of them.

Before he enter on the Execution of his Office; he shall take the following Oath or Affirmation—"I do solemnly swear (or affirm) that I will faithfully execute the Office of President of the United States, and will to the best of my Ability, preserve, protect and defend the Constitution of the United States."

Section 2. The President shall be Commander in Chief of the Army and Navy of the United States, and of the Militia of the several States, when called into the actual Service of the United States; he may require the Opinion, in writing, of the principal Office in each of the executive Departments, upon any Subject relating to the Duties of their respective Offices, and he shall have Power to grant Reprieves and Pardons for Offences against the United States, except in Cases of Impeachment.

He shall have Power, by and with the Advice and Consent of the Senate, to make Treaties, provided two thirds of the Senators present concur; and he shall nominate, and by and with the Advice and Consent of the Senate, shall appoint Ambassadors, other public Ministers and Consuls, Judges of the supreme Court, and all other Officers of the United States, whose Appointments are not herein otherwise provided for, and which shall be established by Law: but the Congress may by Law vest the Appointment of such inferior Officers, as they think proper, in the President alone, in the Courts of Law, or in the Heads of Departments.

The President shall have Power to fill up all Vacancies that may happen during the Recess of the Senate, by granting Commissions which shall expire at the End of their next Session.

Section 3. He shall from time to time give to the Congress Information of the State of the Union, and recommend to their Consideration such Measures as he shall judge necessary and expedient; he may, on extraordinary Occasions, convene both Houses, or either of them, and in Case of Disagreement between them, with Respect to the Time of Adjournment, he may adjourn them to such Time as he shall think proper; he shall receive Ambassadors and other public Ministers; he shall take Care that the Laws be faithfully executed, and shall Commission all the Officers of the United States.

Section 4. The President, Vice President and all civil Officers of the United States, shall be removed from Office on Impeachment for, and Conviction of, Treason, Bribery, or other high Crimes and Misdemeanors.

Article III

Section 1. The judicial Power of the United States, shall be vested in one supreme Court, and in such inferior Courts as the Congress may from time to time ordain and establish. The Judges, both of the supreme and inferior Courts, shall hold their Offices during good Behaviour, and shall, at stated Times, receive for their Services, a Compensation, which shall not be diminished during their Continuance in Office.

Section 2. The judicial Power shall extend to all Cases, in Law and Equity, arising under this Constitution, the Laws of the United States, and Treaties made, or which shall be made, under their Authority;—to all Cases affecting Ambassadors, other pub-

---

[6] Bracketed material superseded by the Twelfth Amendment.

[7] Bracketed material modified by the Twenty-fifth Amendment.

lic Ministers and Consuls;—to all Cases of admiralty and maritime Jurisdiction;—to Controversies to which the United States shall be a Party;—to Controversies between two or more States;—between a State and Citizens of another State;—between Citizens of different States;—between Citizens of the same State claiming Lands under Grants of different States, and between a State, or the Citizens thereof, and foreign States, Citizens or Subjects.[8]

In all Cases affecting Ambassadors, other public Ministers and Consuls, and those in which a State shall be Party, the supreme Court shall have original Jurisdiction. In all the other Cases before mentioned, the supreme Court shall have appellate Jurisdiction, both as to Law and Fact, with such Exceptions, and under such Regulations as the Congress shall make.

The Trial of all Crimes, except in Cases of Impeachment, shall be by Jury; and such Trial shall be held in the State where the said Crimes shall have been committed; but when not committed within any State, the Trial shall be at such Place or Places as the Congress may by Law have directed.

Section 3. Treason against the United States, shall consist only in levying War against them, or in adhering to their Enemies, giving them Aid and Comfort. No Person shall be convicted of Treason unless on the Testimony of two Witnesses to the same overt Act, or on Confession in open Court.

The Congress shall have Power to declare the Punishment of Treason, but no Attainder of Treason shall work Corruption of Blood, or Forfeiture except during the Life of the Person attainted.

Article IV

Section 1. Full Faith and Credit shall be given in each State to the public Acts, Records, and judicial Proceedings of every other State. And the Congress may by general Laws prescribe the Manner in which such Acts, Records and Proceedings shall be proved, and the Effect thereof.

Section 2. The Citizens of each State shall be entitled to all Privileges and Immunities of Citizens in the several States.

A Person charged in any State with Treason, Felony, or other Crime, who shall flee from Justice, and be found in another State, shall on Demand of the executive Authority of the State from which he fled, be delivered up, to be removed to the State having Jurisdiction of the Crime.

[No Person held to Service or Labour in one State, under the Laws thereof, escaping into another, shall, in Consequence of any Law or Regulation therein, be discharged from such Service or Labour,

but shall be delivered up on Claim of the Party to whom such Service or Labour may be due.][9]

Section 3. New States may be admitted by the Congress into this Union; but no new State shall be formed or erected within the Jurisdiction of any other State; nor any State be formed by the Junction of two or more States, or Parts of States, without the Consent of the Legislatures of the States concerned as well as of the Congress.

The Congress shall have Power to dispose of and make all needful Rules and Regulations respecting the Territory or other Property belonging to the United States; and nothing in this Constitution shall be so construed as to Prejudice any Claims of the United States, or of any particular State.

Section 4. The United States shall guarantee to every State in this Union a Republican Form of Government, and shall protect each of them against Invasion; and on Application of the Legislature, or of the Executive (when the Legislature cannot be convened) against domestic Violence.

Article V

The Congress, whenever two thirds of both Houses shall deem it necessary, shall propose Amendments to this Constitution, or, on the Application of the legislatures of two thirds of the several States, shall call a Convention for proposing Amendments, which, in either Case, shall be valid to all Intents and Purposes, as Part of this Constitution, when ratified by the Legislatures of three fourths of the several States, or by Conventions in three fourths thereof, as the one or the other Mode of Ratification may be proposed by the Congress; Provided that no Amendment which may be made prior to the Year One thousand eight hundred and eight shall in any Manner affect the first and fourth Clauses in the Ninth Section of the first Article; and that no State, without its Consent, shall be deprived of its equal Suffrage in the Senate.

Article VI

All Debts contracted and Engagements entered into, before the Adoption of this Constitution, shall be as valid against the United States under this Constitution, as under the Confederation.

This Constitution, and the Laws of the United States which shall be made in Pursuance thereof; and all Treaties made, or which shall be made, under the Authority of the United States, shall be the supreme Law of the Land; and the Judges in every State shall be bound thereby, any Thing in the Constitution or Laws of any State to the Contrary notwithstanding.

The Senators and Representatives before mentioned, and the members of the several State Legisla-

---

[8] This paragraph modified in part by the Eleventh Amendment.

[9] Bracketed material superseded by the Thirteenth Amendment.

tures, and all executive and judicial Officers, both of the United States and of the several States, shall be bound by Oath or Affirmation, to support this Constitution; but no religious Test shall ever be required as a Qualification to any Office or public Trust under the United States.

Article VII

The Ratification of the Conventions of nine States, shall be sufficient for the Establishment of this Constitution between the States so ratifying the Same.

DONE in Convention by the Unanimous Consent of the States present the Seventeenth Day of September in the Year of our Lord one thousand seven hundred and Eighty seven and of the Independence of the United States of America the Twelfth. IN WITNESS whereof We have hereunto subscribed our Names.

GEORGE WASHINGTON—President
and deputy from Virginia

NEW HAMPSHIRE
John Langdon
Nicholas Gilman

CONNECTICUT
William Samuel Johnson
Roger Sherman

NEW YORK
Alexander Hamilton

NEW JERSEY
William Livingston
David Brearley
William Paterson
Jonathan Dayton

PENNSYLVANIA
Benjamin Franklin
Thomas Mifflin
Robert Morris
George Clymer
Thomas FitzSimons
Jared Ingersoll
James Wilson
Gouverneur Morris

DELAWARE
George Read
Gunning Bedford, Jr.
John Dickinson
Richard Bassett
Jacob Broom

MASSACHUSETTS
Nathaniel Gorham
Rufus King

MARYLAND
James McHenry
Daniel of St. Thomas
Jenifer
Daniel Carroll

VIRGINIA
John Blair
James Madison, Jr.

NORTH CAROLINA
William Blount
Richard Dobbs Spaight
Hugh Williamson

SOUTH CAROLINA
John Rutledge
Charles Cotesworth
Pinckney
Charles Pinckney
Pierce Butler

GEORGIA
William Few
Abraham Baldwin

Attest: William Jackson,
Secretary

The Amendments

ARTICLES in addition to, and Amendment of the Constitution of the United States of America, pro-

posed by Congress, and ratified by the Legislatures of the several States, pursuant to the fifth Article of the original Constitution.

Article I

[Articles I through X, now known as the Bill of Rights, were proposed on September 25, 1789, and declared in force on December 15, 1791.]

Congress shall make no law respecting an establishment of religion, or prohibiting the free exercise thereof; or abridging the freedom of speech, or of the press; or the right of the people peaceably to assemble, and to petition the Government for a redress of grievances.

Article II

A well regulated Militia, being necessary to the security of a free State, the right of the people to keep and bear Arms, shall not be infringed.

Article III

No Soldier shall, in time of peace be quartered in any house, without the consent of the Owner, nor in time of war, but in a manner to be prescribed by law.

Article IV

The right of the people to be secure in their persons, houses, papers, and effects, against unreasonable searches and seizures, shall not be violated, and no Warrants shall issue, but upon probable cause, supported by Oath or affirmation, and particularly describing the place to be searched, and the persons or things to be seized.

Article V

No person shall be held to answer for a capital, or otherwise infamous crime, unless on a presentment or indictment of a Grand Jury, except in cases arising in the land or naval forces, or in the Militia, when in actual service in time of War or public danger; nor shall any person be subject for the same offence to be twice put in jeopardy of life or limb; nor shall be compelled in any criminal case to be a witness against himself, nor be deprived of life, liberty, or property, without due process of law; nor shall private property be taken for public use, without just compensation.

Article VI

In all criminal prosecutions, the accused shall enjoy the right to a speedy and public trial, by an impartial jury of the State and district wherein the crime shall have been committed, which district shall have been previously ascertained by law, and to be informed of the nature and cause of the accusation; to be confronted with the witnesses against him; to have compulsory process for obtaining witnesses in his favor, and to have the Assistance of Counsel for his defence.

Article VII

In Suits at common law, where the value in controversy shall exceed twenty dollars, the right of trial by jury shall be preserved, and no fact tried by a jury shall be otherwise re-examined in any Court of the United States, than according to the rules of the common law.

Article VIII

Excessive bail shall not be required, nor excessive fines imposed, nor cruel and unusual punishments inflicted.

Article IX

The enumeration in the Constitution, of certain rights, shall not be construed to deny or disparage others retained by the people.

Article X

The powers not delegated to the United States by the Constitution, nor prohibited by it to the States, are reserved to the States respectively, or to the people.

Article XI

[Proposed March 4, 1794; declared ratified January 8, 1798]

The Judicial power of the United States shall not be construed to extend to any suit in law or equity, commenced or prosecuted against one of the United States by Citizens of another State, or by Citizens or Subjects of any Foreign State.

Article XII

[Proposed December 9, 1803; declared ratified September 25, 1804]

The Electors shall meet in their respective states and vote by ballot for President and Vice-President, one of whom, at least, shall not be an inhabitant of the same state with themselves; they shall name in their ballots the person voted for as President, and in distinct ballots the person voted for as Vice-President, and they shall make distinct lists of all persons voted for as President, and of all persons voted for as Vice-President, and of the number of votes for each, which lists they shall sign and certify, and transmit sealed to the seat of the government of the United States, directed to the President of the Senate;—The President of the Senate shall, in the presence of the Senate and House of Representatives, open all the certificates and the votes shall then be counted;—The person having the greatest number of votes for President, shall be the President, if such number be a majority of the whole number of Electors appointed; and if no person have such majority, then from the persons having the highest numbers not exceeding three on the list of those voted for as President, the House of Representatives shall choose immediately, by ballot, the President. But in choosing the President, the votes shall be taken by states, the representation from each state having one vote; a quorum for this purpose shall consist of a member or members from two-thirds of the states, and a majority of all the states shall be necessary to a choice. [And if the House of Representatives shall not choose a President whenever the right of choice shall devolve upon them, before the fourth day of March next following, then the Vice-President shall act as President, as in the case of the death or other constitutional disability of the President.][10]—The person having the greatest number of votes as Vice-President, shall be the Vice-President, if such number be a majority of the whole number of Electors appointed, and if no person have a majority, then from the two highest numbers on the list, the Senate shall choose the Vice-President; a quorum for the purpose shall consist of two-thirds of the whole number of Senators, and a majority of the whole number shall be necessary to a choice. But no person constitutionally ineligible to the office of President shall be eligible to that of Vice-President of the United States.

Article XIII

[Proposed January 31, 1865; declared ratified December 18, 1865]

Section 1. Neither slavery nor involuntary servitude, except as a punishment for crime whereof the party shall have been duly convicted, shall exist within the United States, or any place subject to their jurisdiction.

Section 2. Congress shall have power to enforce this article by appropriate legislation.

Article XIV

[Proposed June 13, 1866; declared ratified July 28, 1868]

Section 1. All persons born or naturalized in the United States, and subject to the jurisdiction thereof, are citizens of the United States and of the State wherein they reside. No State shall make or enforce any law which shall abridge the privileges or immu-

[10] Bracketed material superseded by Section 3 of the Twentieth Amendment.

nities of citizens of the United States; nor shall any State deprive any person of life, liberty, or property, without due process of law; nor deny to any person within its jurisdiction the equal protection of the laws.

Section 2. Representatives shall be apportioned among the several States according to their respective numbers, counting the whole number of persons in each State, excluding Indians not taxed. But when the right to vote at any election for the choice of electors for President and Vice President of the United States, Representatives in Congress, the Executive and Judicial officers of a State, or the members of the Legislature thereof, is denied to any of the male inhabitants of such State, being twenty-one years of age, and citizens of the United States, or in any way abridged, except for participation in rebellion, or other crime, the basis of representation therein shall be reduced in the proportion which the number of such male citizens shall bear to the whole number of male citizens twenty-one years of age in such State.

Section 3. No person shall be a Senator or Representative in Congress, or elector of President and Vice President, or hold any office, civil or military, under the United States, or under any State, who, having previously taken an oath, as a member of Congress, or as an officer of the United States, or as a member of any State legislature, or as an executive or judicial officer of any State, to support the Constitution of the United States, shall have engaged in insurrection or rebellion against the same, or given aid or comfort to the enemies thereof. But Congress may by a vote of two-thirds of each House, remove such disability.

Section 4. The validity of the public debt of the United States, authorized by law, including debts incurred for payment of pensions and bounties for services in suppressing insurrection or rebellion, shall not be questioned. But neither the United States nor any State shall assume or pay any debt or obligation incurred in aid of insurrection or rebellion against the United States, or any claim for the loss or emancipation of any slave; but all such debts, obligations and claims shall be held illegal and void.

Section 5. The Congress shall have power to enforce, by appropriate legislation, the provisions of this article.

Article XV

[Proposed February 26, 1869; declared ratified March 30,1870]

Section 1. The right of citizens of the United States to vote shall not be denied or abridged by the United States or by any State on account of race, color, or previous condition of servitude.

Section 2. The Congress shall have power to enforce this article by appropriate legislation.

Article XVI

[Proposed July 12, 1909; declared ratified February 25, 1913]

The Congress shall have power to lay and collect taxes on incomes, from whatever source derived, without apportionment among the several States, and without regard to any census or enumeration.

Article XVII

[Proposed May 13, 1912; declared ratified May 31, 1913]

The Senate of the United States shall be composed of two Senators from each State, elected by the people thereof, for six years; and each Senator shall have one vote. The electors in each State shall have the qualifications requisite for electors of the most numerous branch of the State legislatures.

When vacancies happen in the representation of any State in the Senate, the executive authority of such State shall issue writs of election to fill such vacancies: *Provided,* That the legislature of any State may empower the executive thereof to make temporary appointments until the people fill the vacancies by election as the legislature may direct.

This amendment shall not be so construed as to affect the election or term of any Senator chosen before it becomes valid as part of the Constitution.

Article XVIII

[Proposed December 18, 1917; declared ratified January 29, 1919; repealed by the Twenty-first Amendment December 5, 1933]

Section 1. After one year from the ratification of this article the manufacture, sale, or transportation of intoxicating liquors within, the importation thereof into, or the exportation thereof from the United States and all territory subject to the jurisdiction thereof for beverage purposes is hereby prohibited.

Section 2. The Congress and the several States shall have concurrent power to enforce this article by appropriate legislation.

Section 3. This article shall be inoperative unless it shall have been ratified as an amendment to the Constitution by the legislatures of the several States, as provided in the Constitution, within seven years from the date of the submission hereof to the States by the Congress.

Article XIX

[Proposed June 4, 1919; declared ratified August 26, 1920]

The right of citizens of the United States to vote shall not be denied or abridged by the United States or by any State on account of sex.

Congress shall have power to enforce this article by appropriate legislation.

Article XX

[Proposed March 2, 1932; declared ratified February 6, 1933]

Section 1. The terms of the President and Vice President shall end at noon on the 20th day of January, and the terms of Senators and Representatives at noon on the 3d day of January, of the years in which such terms would have ended if this article had not been ratified; and the terms of their successors shall then begin.

Section 2. The Congress shall assemble at least once in every year, and such meeting shall begin at noon on the 3d day of January, unless they shall by law appoint a different day.

Section 3. If, at the time fixed for the beginning of the term of the President, the President elect shall have died, the Vice President elect shall become President. If a President shall not have been chosen before the time fixed for the beginning of his term, or if the President elect shall have failed to qualify, then the Vice President elect shall act as President until a President shall have qualified; and the Congress may by law provide for the case wherein neither a President elect nor a Vice President elect shall have qualified, declaring who shall then act as President, or the manner in which one who is to act shall be selected, and such person shall act accordingly until a President or Vice President shall have qualified.

Section 4. The Congress may by law provide for the case of the death of any of the persons from whom the House of Representatives may choose a President whenever the right of choice shall have devolved upon them, and for the case of the death of any of the persons from whom the Senate may choose a Vice President whenever the right of choice shall have devolved upon them.

Section 5. Sections 1 and 2 shall take effect on the 15th day of October following the ratification of this article.

Section 6. This article shall be inoperative unless it shall have been ratified as an amendment to the Constitution by the legislatures of three-fourths of the several States within seven years from the date of its submission.

Article XXI

[Proposed February 20, 1933; declared ratified December 5, 1933]

Section 1. The eighteenth article of amendment to the Constitution of the United States is hereby repealed.

Section 2. The transportation or importation into any State, Territory, or possession of the United States for delivery or use therein of intoxicating liquors, in violation of the laws thereof, is hereby prohibited.

Section 3. This article shall be inoperative unless it shall have been ratified as an amendment to the Constitution by conventions in the several States, as provided in the Constitution, within seven years from the date of the submission hereof to the States by the Congress.

Article XXII

[Proposed March 24, 1947; declared ratified March 1, 1951]

Section 1. No person shall be elected to the office of the President more than twice, and no person who has held the office of President, or acted as President, for more than two years of a term to which some other person was elected President shall be elected to the office of the President more than once. But this Article shall not apply to any person holding the office of President when this Article was proposed by the Congress, and shall not prevent any person who may be holding the office of President, or acting as President, during the term within which this Article becomes operative from holding the office of President or acting as President during the remainder of such term.

Section 2. This article shall be inoperative unless it shall have been ratified as an amendment to the Constitution by the legislatures of three-fourths of the several States within seven years from the date of its submission to the States by the Congress.

Article XXIII

[Proposed June 16, 1960; declared ratified April 3, 1961]

Section 1. The District constituting the seat of Government of the United States shall appoint in such manner as the Congress may direct:

A number of electors of President and Vice President equal to the whole number of Senators and Representatives in Congress to which the District would be entitled if it were a State, but in no event more than the least populous state; they shall be in addition to those appointed by the States, but they shall be considered, for the purposes of the election of President and Vice President, to be electors appointed by a State; and they shall meet in the District and perform such duties as provided by the twelfth article of amendment.

Section 2. The Congress shall have power to enforce this article by appropriate legislation.

Article XXIV

[Proposed August 27, 1962; declared ratified February 4, 1964]

Section 1. The right of citizens of the United States to vote in any primary or other election for

President or Vice President, for electors for President or Vice President, or for Senator or Representative in Congress, shall not be denied or abridged by the United States or any State by reason of failure to pay any poll tax or other tax.

Section 2. The Congress shall have power to enforce this article by appropriate legislation.

Article XXV

[*Proposed July 6, 1965; declared ratified February 23, 1967*]

Section 1. In case of removal of the President from office or of his death or resignation, the Vice President shall become President.

Section 2. Whenever there is a vacancy in the office of the Vice President, the President shall nominate a Vice President who shall take office upon confirmation by a majority vote of both Houses of Congress.

Section 3. Whenever the President transmits to the President pro tempore of the Senate and the Speaker of the House of Representatives his written declaration that he is unable to discharge the powers and duties of his office, and until he transmits to them a written declaration to the contrary, such powers and duties shall be discharged by the Vice President as Acting President.

Section 4. Whenever the Vice President and a majority of either the principal officers of the executive departments or of such other body as Congress may by law provide, transmit to the President pro tempore of the Senate and the Speaker of the House of Representatives their written declaration that the President is unable to discharge the powers and duties of his office, the Vice President shall immediately assume the powers and duties of the office as Acting President.

Thereafter, when the President transmits to the President pro tempore of the Senate and the Speaker of the House of Representatives his written declaration that no inability exists, he shall resume the powers and duties of his office unless the Vice President and a majority of either the principal officers of the executive department or of such other body as Congress may by law provide, transmit within four days to the President pro tempore of the Senate and the Speaker of the House of Representatives their written declaration that the President is unable to discharge the powers and duties of his office. Thereupon Congress shall decide the issue, assembling within forty-eight hours for that purpose if not in session. If the Congress, within twenty-one days after receipt of the latter written declaration, or, if Congress is not in session, within twenty-one days after Congress is required to assemble, determines by two-thirds vote of both Houses that the President is unable to discharge the powers and duties of his office, the Vice President shall continue to discharge the same as Acting President; otherwise, the President shall resume the powers and duties of his office.

Article XXVI

[*Proposed March 23, 1971; declared ratified July 5, 1971*]

Section 1. The right of citizens of the United States, who are eighteen years of age or older, to vote shall not be denied or abridged by the United States or by any State on account of age.

Section 2. The Congress shall have power to enforce this article by appropriate legislation.

Presidential Elections

Year	Candidates Receiving More Than One Percent of the Vote (Parties)	Popular Vote	Electoral Vote
1789	GEORGE WASHINGTON (No party designations)		69
	John Adams		34
	Other Candidates		35
1792	GEORGE WASHINGTON (No party designations)		132
	John Adams		77
	George Clinton		50
	Other Candidates		5
1796	JOHN ADAMS (Federalist)		71
	Thomas Jefferson (Democratic-Republican)		68
	Thomas Pinckney (Federalist)		59
	Aaron Burr (Democratic-Republican)		30
	Other Candidates		48
1800	THOMAS JEFFERSON (Democratic-Republican)		73
	Aaron Burr (Democratic-Republican)		73
	John Adams (Federalist)		65
	Charles C. Pinckney (Federalist)		64
	John Jay (Federalist)		1
1804	THOMAS JEFFERSON (Democratic-Republican)		162
	Charles C. Pinckney (Federalist)		14
1808	JAMES MADISON (Democratic-Republican)		122
	Charles C. Pinckney (Federalist)		47
	George Clinton (Democratic-Republican)		6
1812	JAMES MADISON (Democratic-Republican)		128
	De Witt Clinton (Federalist)		89
1816	JAMES MONROE (Democratic-Republican)		183
	Rufus King (Federalist)		34
1820	JAMES MONROE (Democratic-Republican)		231
	John Quincy Adams (Independent-Republican)		1
1824	JOHN QUINCY ADAMS (Democratic-Republican)	108,740	84
	Andrew Jackson (Democratic-Republican)	153,544	99
	William H. Crawford (Democratic-Republican)	46,618	41
	Henry Clay (Democratic-Republican)	47,136	37
1828	ANDREW JACKSON (Democratic)	647,286	178
	John Quincy Adams (National Republican)	508,064	83
1832	ANDREW JACKSON (Democratic)	687,502	219
	Henry Clay (National Republican)	530,189	49
	William Wirt (Anti-Masonic)	33,108	7
	John Floyd (National Republican)		11
1836	MARTIN VAN BUREN (Democratic)	765,483	170
	William H. Harrison (Whig)		73
	Hugh L. White (Whig)	739,795	26
	Daniel Webster (Whig)		14
	W. P Mangum (Anti-Jackson)		11
1840	WILLIAM H. HARRISON (Whig)	1,274,624	234
	Martin Van Buren (Democratic)	1,127,781	60
1844	JAMES K. POLK (Democratic)	1,338,464	170
	Henry Clay (Whig)	1,300,097	105
	James G. Birney (Liberty)	62,300	0
1848	ZACHARY TAYLOR (Whig)	1,360,967	163
	Lewis Cass (Democratic)	1,222,342	127
	Martin Van Buren (Free Soil)	291,263	0
1852	FRANKLIN PIERCE (Democratic)	1,601,117	254
	Winfield Scott (Whig)	1,385,453	42
	John P. Hale (Free Soil)	155,825	0

Year	Candidates Receiving More Than One Percent of the Vote (Parties)	Popular Vote	Electoral Vote
1856	JAMES BUCHANAN (Democratic)	1,832,955	174
	John C. Frémont (Republican)	1,339,932	114
	Millard Fillmore (American)	871,731	8
1860	ABRAHAM LINCOLN (Republican)	1,865,593	180
	Stephen A. Douglas (Democratic)	1,382,713	12
	John C. Breckinridge (Democratic)	848,356	72
	John Bell (Constitutional Union)	592,906	39
1864	ABRAHAM LINCOLN (Republican)	2,206,938	212
	George B. McClellan (Democratic)	1,803,787	21
1868	ULYSSES S. GRANT (Republican)	3,013,421	214
	Horatio Seymour (Democratic)	2,706,829	80
1872	ULYSSES S. GRANT (Republican)	3,596,745	286
	Horace Greeley (Democratic)	2,843,446	—*
	Other Candidates		63
1876	RUTHERFORD B. HAYES (Republican)	4,036,572	185
	Samuel J. Tilden (Democratic)	4,284,020	184
1880	JAMES A. GARFIELD (Republican)	4,453,295	214
	Winfield S. Hancock (Democratic)	4,414,082	155
	James B. Weaver (Greenback-Labor)	308,579	0
1884	GROVER CLEVELAND (Democratic)	4,879,507	219
	James G. Blaine (Republican)	4,850,293	182
	Benjamin F. Butler (Greenback-Labor)	175,370	0
	John P. St. John (Prohibition)	150,369	0
1888	BENJAMIN HARRISON (Republican)	5,447,129	233
	Grover Cleveland (Democratic)	5,537,857	168
	Clinton B. Fisk (Prohibition)	249,506	0
	Anson J. Streeter (Union Labor)	146,935	0
1892	GROVER CLEVELAND (Democratic)	5,555,426	277
	Benjamin Harrison (Republican)	5,182,690	145
	James B. Weaver (People's)	1,029,846	22
	John Bidwell (Prohibition)	264,133	0
1896	WILLIAM McKINLEY (Republican)	7,102,246	271
	William J. Bryan (Democratic)	6,492,559	176
1900	WILLIAM McKINLEY (Republican)	7,218,491	292
	William J. Bryan (Democratic; Populist)	6,356,734	155
	John C. Wooley (Prohibition)	208,914	0
1904	THEODORE ROOSEVELT (Republican)	7,628,461	336
	Alton B. Parker (Democratic)	5,084,223	140
	Eugene V. Debs (Socialist)	402,283	0
	Silas C. Swallow (Prohibition)	258,536	0
1908	WILLIAM H. TAFT (Republican)	7,675,320	321
	William J. Bryan (Democratic)	6,412,294	162
	Eugene V. Debs (Socialist)	420,793	0
	Eugene W. Chafin (Prohibition)	253,840	0
1912	WOODROW WILSON (Democratic)	6,296,547	435
	Theodore Roosevelt (Progressive)	4,118,571	88
	William H. Taft (Republican)	3,486,720	8
	Eugene V. Debs (Socialist)	900,672	0
	Eugene W. Chafin (Prohibition)	206,275	0
1916	WOODROW WILSON (Democratic)	9,127,695	277
	Charles E. Hughes (Republican)	8,533,507	254
	A. L. Benson (Socialist)	585,113	0
	J. Frank Hanly (Prohibition)	220,506	0
1920	WARREN G. HARDING (Republican)	16,143,407	404
	James M. Cox (Democratic)	9,130,328	127
	Eugene V. Debs (Socialist)	919,799	0
	P. P. Christensen (Farmer-Labor)	265,411	0

Year	Candidates Receiving More Than One Percent of the Vote (Parties)	Popular Vote	Electoral Vote
1924	CALVIN COOLIDGE (Republican)	15,718,211	382
	John W. Davis (Democratic)	8,385,283	136
	Robert M. La Follette (Progressive)	4,831,289	13
1928	HERBERT C. HOOVER (Republican)	21,391,993	444
	Alfred E. Smith (Democratic)	15,016,169	87
1932	FRANKLIN D. ROOSEVELT (Democratic)	22,809,638	472
	Herbert C. Hoover (Republican)	15,758,901	59
	Norman Thomas (Socialist)	881,951	0
1936	FRANKLIN D. ROOSEVELT (Democratic)	27,752,869	523
	Alfred M. Landon (Republican)	16,674,665	8
	William Lemke (Union)	882,479	0
1940	FRANKLIN D. ROOSEVELT (Democratic)	27,307,819	449
	Wendell L. Willkie (Republican)	22,321,018	82
1944	FRANKLIN D. ROOSEVELT (Democratic)	25,606,585	432
	Thomas E. Dewey (Republican)	22,014,745	99
1948	HARRY S. TRUMAN (Democratic)	24,179,345	303
	Thomas E. Dewey (Republican)	21,991,291	189
	J. Strom Thurmond (States' Rights)	1,176,125	39
	Henry Wallace (Progressive)	1,157,326	0
1952	DWIGHT D. EISENHOWER (Republican)	33,936,234	442
	Adlai E. Stevenson (Democratic)	27,314,992	89
1956	DWIGHT D. EISENHOWER (Republican)	35,590,472	457
	Adlai E. Stevenson (Democratic)	26,022,752	73
1960	JOHN F. KENNEDY (Democratic)	34,226,731	303
	Richard M. Nixon (Republican)	34,108,157	219
1964	LYNDON B. JOHNSON (Democratic)	43,129,566	486
	Barry M. Goldwater (Republican)	27,178,188	52
1968	RICHARD M. NIXON (Republican)	31,785,480	301
	Hubert H. Humphrey (Democratic)	31,275,166	191
	George C. Wallace (American Independent)	9,906,473	46
1972	RICHARD M. NIXON (Republican)	45,631,189	521
	George S. McGovern (Democratic)	28,422,015	17
	John Schmitz (American Independent)	1,080,670	0
1976	JAMES E. CARTER, JR. (Democratic)	40,274,975	297
	Gerald R. Ford (Republican)	38,530,614	241
1980	RONALD W. REAGAN (Republican)	42,968,326	489
	James E. Carter, Jr. (Democratic)	34,731,139	49
	John B. Anderson (Independent)	5,552,349	0
1984	RONALD W. REAGAN (Republican)	53,428,357	525
	Walter F. Mondale (Democratic)	36,930,923	13

* Greeley died shortly after the election; the electors supporting him then divided their votes among other candidates.

Chief Justices of the Supreme Court

Term	Chief Justice
1789–1795	John Jay
1795	John Rutledge
1795–1799	Oliver Ellsworth
1801–1835	John Marshall
1836–1864	Roger B. Taney
1864–1873	Salmon P. Chase
1874–1888	Morrison R. Waite
1888–1910	Melville W. Fuller
1910–1921	Edward D. White
1921–1930	William H. Taft
1930–1941	Charles E. Hughes
1941–1946	Harlan F. Stone
1946–1953	Fred M. Vinson
1953–1969	Earl Warren
1969–	Warren E. Burger

Presidents, Vice Presidents, and Cabinet Members

President and Vice President	Secretary of State	Secretary of Treasury	Secretary of War	Secretary of Navy	Postmaster General	Attorney General	Secretary of Interior
1. George Washington (1789) John Adams (1789)	Thomas Jefferson (1789) Edmund Randolph (1794) Thomas Pickering (1795)	Alexander Hamilton (1789) Oliver Wolcott (1795)	Henry Knox (1789) Timothy Pickering (1795) James McHenry (1796)		Samuel Osgood (1789) Timothy Pickering (1791) Joseph Habersham (1795)	Edmund Randolph (1789) William Bradford (1794) Charles Lee (1795)	
2. John Adams (1797) Thomas Jefferson (1797)	Timothy Pickering (1797) John Marshall (1800)	Oliver Wolcott (1797) Samuel Dexter (1801)	James McHenry (1797) John Marshall (1800) Samuel Dexter (1800) Roger Griswold (1801)	Benjamin Stoddert (1798)	Joseph Habersham (1797)	Charles Lee (1797) Theophilus Parsons (1801)	
3. Thomas Jefferson (1801) Aaron Burr (1801) George Clinton (1805)	James Madison (1801)	Samuel Dexter (1801) Albert Gallatin (1801)	Henry Dearborn (1801)	Benjamin Stoddert (1801) Robert Smith (1801) J. Crowninshield (1805)	Joseph Habersham (1801) Gideon Granger (1801)	Levi Lincoln (1801) Robert Smith (1805) John Breckinridge (1805) Caesar Rodney (1807)	
4. James Madison (1809) George Clinton (1809) Elbridge Gerry (1813)	Robert Smith (1809) James Monroe (1811)	Albert Gallatin (1809) George Campbell (1814) Alexander Dallas (1814) William Crawford (1816)	William Eustis (1809) John Armstrong (1813) James Monroe (1814) William Crawford (1815)	Paul Hamilton (1809) William Jones (1813) Benjamin Crowninshield (1814)	Gideon Granger (1809) Return Meigs (1814)	Caesar Rodney (1809) William Pinckney (1811) Richard Rush (1814)	
5. James Monroe (1817) Daniel D. Thompkins (1817)	John Quincy Adams (1817)	William Crawford (1817)	Isaac Shelby (1817) George Graham (1817) John C. Calhoun (1817)	Benjamin Crowninshield (1817) Smith Thompson (1818) Samuel Southard (1823)	Return Meigs (1817) John McLean (1823)	Richard Rush (1817) William Wirt (1817)	
6. John Quincy Adams (1825) John C. Calhoun (1825)	Henry Clay (1825)	Richard Rush (1825)	James Barbour (1825) Peter B. Porter (1828)	Samuel Southard (1825)	John McLean (1825)	William Wirt (1825)	
7. Andrew Jackson (1829) John C. Calhoun (1829) Martin Van Buren (1833)	Martin Van Buren (1829) Edward Livingston (1831) Louis McLane (1833) John Forsyth (1834)	Samuel Ingham (1829) Louis McLane (1831) William Duane (1833) Roger B. Taney (1833) Levi Woodbury (1834)	John H. Eaton (1829) Lewis Cass (1831) Benjamin Butler (1837)	John Branch (1829) Levi Woodbury (1831) Mahlon Dickerson (1834)	William Barry (1829) Amos Kendall (1835)	John M. Berrien (1829) Roger B. Taney (1831) Benjamin Butler (1833)	
8. Martin Van Buren (1837) Richard M. Johnson (1837)	John Forsyth (1837)	Levi Woodbury (1837)	Joel R. Poinsett (1837)	Mahlon Dickerson (1837) James K. Paulding (1838)	Amos Kendall (1837) John M. Niles (1840)	Benjamin Butler (1837) Felix Grundy (1838) Henry D. Gilpin (1840)	
9. William H. Harrison (1841) John Tyler (1841)	Daniel Webster (1841)	Thomas Ewing (1841)	John Bell (1841)	George E. Badger (1841)	Francis Granger (1841)	John J. Crittenden (1841)	

President	Secretary of State	Secretary of Treasury	Secretary of War	Attorney General	Postmaster General	Secretary of Navy	Secretary of Interior
10. John Tyler (1841)	Daniel Webster (1841) Hugh S. Legaré (1843) Abel P. Upshur (1843) John C. Calhoun (1844)	Thomas Ewing (1841) Walter Forward (1841) John C. Spencer (1843) George M. Bibb (1844)	John Bell (1841) John McLean (1841) John C. Spencer (1841) James M. Porter (1843) William Wilkins (1844)	John J. Crittenden (1841) Hugh S. Legaré (1841) John Nelson (1843)	Francis Granger (1841) Charles A. Wickliffe (1841)	George E. Badger (1841) Abel P. Upshur (1841) David Henshaw (1843) Thomas Gilmer (1844) John Y. Mason (1844)	
11. James K. Polk (1845) George M. Dallas (1845)	James Buchanan (1845)	Robert J. Walker (1845)	William L. Marcy (1845)	John Y. Mason (1845) Nathan Clifford (1846) Isaac Toucey (1848)	Cave Johnson (1845)	George Bancroft (1845) John Y. Mason (1846)	
12. Zachary Taylor (1849) Millard Fillmore (1849)	John M. Clayton (1849)	William M. Meredith (1849)	George W. Crawford (1849)	Reverdy Johnson (1849)	Jacob Collamer (1849)	William B. Preston (1849)	Thomas Ewing (1849)
13. Millard Fillmore (1850)	Daniel Webster (1850) Edward Everett (1852)	Thomas Corwin (1850)	Charles M. Conrad (1850)	John J. Crittenden (1850)	Nathan K. Hall (1850) Sam D. Hubbard (1852)	William A. Graham (1850) John P. Kennedy (1852)	Thomas McKennan (1850) A. H. H. Stuart (1850)
14. Franklin Pierce (1853) William R. King (1853)	William L. Marcy (1853)	James Guthrie (1853)	Jefferson Davis (1853)	Caleb Cushing (1853)	James Campbell (1853)	James C. Dobbin (1853)	Robert McClelland (1853)
15. James Buchanan (1857) John C. Breckinridge (1857)	Lewis Cass (1857) Jeremiah S. Black (1860)	Howell Cobb (1857) Philip F. Thomas (1860) John A. Dix (1861)	John B. Floyd (1857) Joseph Holt (1861)	Jeremiah S. Black (1857) Edwin M. Stanton (1860)	Aaron V. Brown (1857) Joseph Holt (1859)	Isaac Toucey (1857)	Jacob Thompson (1857)
16. Abraham Lincoln (1861) Hannibal Hamlin (1861) Andrew Johnson (1865)	William H. Seward (1861)	Salmon P. Chase (1861) William P. Fessenden (1864) Hugh McCulloch (1865)	Simon Cameron (1861) Edwin M. Stanton (1862)	Edward Bates (1861) Titian J. Coffey (1863) James Speed (1864)	Horatio King (1861) Montgomery Blair (1861) William Dennison (1864)	Gideon Welles (1861)	Caleb B. Smith (1861) John P. Usher (1863)
17. Andrew Johnson (1865)	William H. Seward (1865)	Hugh McCulloch (1865)	Edwin M. Stanton (1865) Ulysses S. Grant (1867) Lorenzo Thomas (1868) John M. Schofield (1868)	James Speed (1865) Henry Stanbery (1866) William M. Evarts (1868)	William Dennison (1865) Alexander Randall (1866)	Gideon Welles (1865)	John P. Usher (1865) James Harlan (1865) O. H. Browning (1866)
18. Ulysses S. Grant (1869) Schuyler Colfax (1869) Henry Wilson (1873)	Elihu B. Washburne (1869) Hamilton Fish (1869)	George S. Boutwell (1869) William A. Richardson (1873) Benjamin H. Bristow (1874) Lot M. Morrill (1876)	John A. Rawlins (1869) William T. Sherman (1869) William W. Belknap (1869) Alphonso Taft (1876) James Cameron (1876)	Ebenezer R. Hoar (1869) Amos T. Akerman (1870) G. H. Williams (1871) Edwards Pierrepont (1875) Alphonso Taft (1876)	John A. J. Creswell (1869) James W. Marshall (1874) Marshall Jewell (1874) James N. Tyner (1876)	Adolph E. Borie (1869) George M. Robeson (1869)	Jacob D. Cox (1869) Columbus Delano (1870) Zachariah Chandler (1875)

President and Vice President	Secretary of State	Secretary of Treasury	Secretary of War	Secretary of Navy	Postmaster General	Attorney General	Secretary of Interior
19. Rutherford B. Hayes (1877) William A. Wheeler (1877)	William M. Evarts (1877)	John Sherman (1877)	George W. McCrary (1877) Alexander Ramsey (1879)	R. W. Thompson (1877) Nathan Goff, Jr. (1881)	David M. Key (1877) Horace Maynard (1880)	Charles Devens (1877)	Carl Schurz (1877)
20. James A. Garfield (1881) Chester A. Arthur (1881)	James G. Blaine (1881)	William Windom (1881)	Robert T. Lincoln (1881)	William H. Hunt (1881)	Thomas L. James (1881)	Wayne MacVeagh (1881)	S. J. Kirkwood (1881)
21. Chester A. Arthur (1881)	F. T. Frelinghuysen (1881)	Charles J. Folger (1881) Walter Q. Gresham (1884) Hugh McCulloch (1884)	Robert T. Lincoln (1881)	William E. Chandler (1881)	Timothy O. Howe (1881) Walter Q. Gresham (1883) Frank Hatton (1884)	B. H. Brewster (1881)	Henry M. Teller (1881)
22. Grover Cleveland (1885) T. A. Hendricks (1885)	Thomas F. Bayard (1885)	Daniel Manning (1885) Charles S. Fairchild (1887)	William C. Endicott (1885)	William C. Whitney (1885)	William F. Vilas (1885) Don M. Dickinson (1888)	A. H. Garland (1885)	L. Q. C. Lamar (1885) William F. Vilas (1888)
23. Benjamin Harrison (1889) Levi P. Morgan (1889)	James G. Blaine (1889) John W. Foster (1892)	William Windom (1889) Charles Foster (1891)	Redfield Procter (1889) Stephen B. Elkins (1891)	Benjamin F. Tracy (1889)	John Wanamaker (1889)	W. H. H. Miller (1889)	John W. Noble (1889)
24. Grover Cleveland (1893) Adlai E. Stevenson (1893)	Walter Q. Gresham (1893) Richard Olney (1895)	John G. Carlisle (1893)	Daniel S. Lamont (1893)	Hilary A. Herbert (1893)	Wilson S. Bissel (1893) William L. Wilson (1895)	Richard Olney (1893) Judson Harmon (1895)	Hoke Smith (1893) David R. Francis (1896)
25. William McKinley (1897) Garret A. Hobart (1897) Theodore Roosevelt (1901)	John Sherman (1897) William R. Day (1897) John Hay (1898)	Lyman J. Gage (1897)	Russell A. Alger (1897) Elihu Root (1899)	John D. Long (1897)	James A. Gary (1897) Charles E. Smith (1898)	Joseph McKenna (1897) John W. Griggs (1897) Philander C. Knox (1901)	Cornelius N. Bliss (1897) E. A. Hitchcock (1899)
26. Theodore Roosevelt (1901) Charles Fairbanks (1905)	John Hay (1901) Elihu Root (1905) Robert Bacon (1909)	Lyman J. Gage (1901) Leslie M. Shaw (1902) George B. Cortelyou (1907)	Elihu Root (1901) William H. Taft (1904) Luke E. Wright (1908)	John D. Long (1901) William H. Moody (1902) Paul Morton (1904) Charles J. Bonaparte (1905) V. H. Metcalf (1906) T. H. Newberry (1908)	Charles E. Smith (1901) Henry Payne (1902) Robert J. Wynne (1904) George B. Cortelyou (1905) George von L. Meyer (1907)	Philander C. Knox (1901) William H. Moody (1904) Charles J. Bonaparte (1907)	E. A. Hitchcock (1901) James R. Garfield (1907)
27. William H. Taft (1909) James S. Sherman (1909)	Philander C. Knox (1909)	Franklin MacVeagh (1909)	Jacob M. Dickinson (1909) Henry L. Stimson (1911)	George von L. Meyer (1909)	Frank H. Hitchcock (1909)	G. W. Wickersham (1909)	R. A. Ballinger (1909) Walter L. Fisher (1911)

President and Vice President	Secretary of State	Secretary of Treasury	Secretary of War	Secretary of Navy	Postmaster General	Attorney General	Secretary of Interior
36. Lyndon B. Johnson (1963) Hubert H. Humphrey (1965)	Dean Rusk (1963)	C. Douglas Dillon (1963) Henry H. Fowler (1965) Joseph W. Barr (1968)	Robert S. McNamara (1963) Clark M. Clifford (1968)		John A. Gronouski (1963) Lawrence F. O'Brien (1965) W. Marvin Watson (1968)	Robert F. Kennedy (1963) N. deB. Katzenbach (1965) Ramsey Clark (1967)	Stewart L. Udall (1963)
37. Richard M. Nixon (1969) Spiro T. Agnew (1969) Gerald R. Ford (1973)	William P. Rogers (1969) Henry A. Kissinger (1973)	David M. Kennedy (1969) John B. Connally (1970) George P. Schultz (1972) William E. Simon (1974)	Melvin R. Laird (1969) Elliot L. Richardson (1973) James R. Schlesinger (1973)		Winton M. Blount (1969)	John M. Mitchell (1969) Richard G. Kleindienst (1972) Elliot L. Richardson (1973) William B. Saxbe (1974)	Walter J. Hickel (1969) Rogers C. B. Morton (1971)
38. Gerald R. Ford (1974) Nelson A. Rockefeller (1974)	Henry A. Kissinger (1974)	William E. Simon (1974)	James R. Schlesinger (1974) Donald H. Rumsfeld (1975)			William B. Saxbe (1974) Edward H. Levi (1975)	Rogers C. B. Morton (1974) Stanley K. Hathaway (1975) Thomas D. Kleppe (1975)
39. James E. Carter, Jr. (1977) Walter F. Mondale (1977)	Cyrus R. Vance (1977) Edmund S. Muskie (1980)	W. Michael Blumenthal (1977) G. William Miller (1979)	Harold Brown (1977)			Griffin B. Bell (1977) Benjamin R. Civiletti (1979)	Cecil D. Andrus (1977)
40. Ronald W. Reagan (1981) George H. Bush (1981)	Alexander M. Haig, Jr. (1981) George P. Schultz (1982)	Donald T. Regan (1981)	Caspar W. Weinberger (1981)			William French Smith (1981)	James G. Watt (1981) William Clark (1983)
41. Ronald W. Reagan (1985) George H. Bush (1985)	George P. Schultz (1985)	James B. Baker III (1985)	Caspar W. Weinberger (1985)			Edwin Meese III (1985)	Donald P. Hodel (1985)

Writing About History   Dr. Robert Weiss

What is "history"? We employ the word constantly to refer to everything from the "history" of the world to an individual's "history." But how often do we stop to think about what the word means? The following essay addresses this question, and provides some fundamental principles for reading, researching, and writing historical reports and essays.

WHAT IS HISTORY?

History can best be defined as a record and interpretation of past events. This statement is not very complicated, yet it is not as simple as it may appear. Let us examine it more carefully.

The "record" part is straightforward. Since the purpose of history is to inform us about what happend in the past, it must include substantial data, or "facts" (a troublesome word that some social scientists avoid). Names, dates, places, and events are the essence of history. But historical writing is not a compendium of facts. It consists of facts placed in a sequence to tell a connected story. A work of history is not merely a story, however. It also must analyze what happened and *why*—that is, it must interpret the past for the reader in a useful and informative manner. It is not sufficient, for example, to state that the American Revolution began in 1775–76, and then give an account of the relevant individuals and events, such as George Washington, Thomas Jefferson, Lexington and Concord, and the Declaration of Independence. The historian must proceed to the next step: Why did the Revolution occur in 1776? Here again, historians must resort to concrete data, including the Proclamation of 1763, the Boston Massacre, the Boston Tea Party, and the Intolerable Acts. Rather than simply composing a catalog of events, however, the historian must weave the material into a well-integrated narrative that analyzes the *process* whereby the American colonies severed their political ties to the mother country. To accomplish this task, historians must make certain value judgments concerning the role and significance of these events. Which were more important, and which were less important? What was the relationship of each event to the others, and what does each tell us about the behavior of the American colonists?

To address questions like these, historians must place their material within an appropriate historical context. An account of a past event is not very instructive unless it is analyzed as a component of a larger sequence of events within a specific social, political, and economic setting. The Boston Tea Party, for example, would be analyzed in relation to such factors as British financial expenses incurred during the French and Indian War, colonial views regarding commerce and taxation, Britain's relationship with its empire, and the role of merchants in American colonial society. Only by examining such factors can we hope to understand why both sides behaved as they did.

Historical interpretation takes place on many levels. Some historians focus on the "larger forces" in history, such as the industrial revolution of the nineteenth century and the communications revolution of the twentieth century. Obviously these developments exerted a profound effect on the way we live. The emphasis on context, however, also acknowledges the human element in history. Human beings are the actors in the historical drama, and an effective historical work attempts to explain why people behaved as they did. A history of the American Revolution, for example, would be incomplete if it documented the events leading up to American independence, but offered no insights as to *why* formerly loyal subjects of the British crown took up arms against their mother country. To understand human behavior, the historian, like the psychologist or psychiatrist, must examine the effects of "larger forces" and specific events on people as well as the ways in which the people themselves perceived these forces and events. To appreciate the American desire for independence in 1776, one must view the events of the 1700s through eighteenth-century, not twentieth-century, eyes.

A note of caution should be introduced here. To understand the behavior of various groups is not necessarily to endorse it. By using the proper resources, the historian can understand such phenomena as the Reign of Terror during the French Revolution, the development of slavery in the American South, and the ascendancy of Hitler in Germany. But this claim does not imply that the historian approves of guillotines, slavery, or Nazism. Rather, it asserts the historian's responsibility to analyze all facets of history, even those that he or she finds personally reprehensible.

The preceding paragraphs indicate the "subjective" nature of the interpretive process. When historians make the transition from recording data to interpreting that data, they are imposing an order and a meaning on a set of circumstances that they usually did not experience firsthand. Moreover, historians' interpretations often differ from those of various parties who *did* experience the events. While historians' interpretations should always be based on evidence, there comes a point at which they must transcend that evidence and rely on their own insights, values, and experiences in forming conclusions. Historians collect facts, and when they feel they have mastered them, they draw conclusions as to their significance and their relationship to one another. This process is not unique to the history profession, but is characteristic of all the natural and social sciences. Like all scientists, historians must pursue the maximum feasible "objectivity" in forming their conclusions, while acknowledging the impossibility of total objectivity. Historians must be aware of their personal biases and values so they can monitor the effects of these biases on their interpretations of the past. At the same time, writers of history should never allow the fear of "subjectivity" to stifle the creative process.

READING HISTORY

An understanding of the fundamentals of historical writing will make the student of history a more discerning and selective reader. Although no two historical works are identical, most contain the same basic elements and can be approached in a similar manner by the reader. When reading a historical monograph, concentrate on the two basic issues discussed in the preceding section: facts and interpretation.

Interpretation. The first question the reader should ask is: What is the author's argument? What is his theme, his interpretation, his thesis? A theme is not the same as a topic. An author may select the Civil War as a *topic*, but he then must propose a particular theme or argument regarding some aspect of the war. (The most common, not surprisingly, is *why* the war occurred.)

Discovering the author's thesis is usually easy enough because most writers state their arguments clearly in the preface to their book. Students often make the crucial error of skimming over the preface—if they read it at all—and then moving on to the "meat" of the book. Since the preface indicates the manner in which the author has used his data to develop his arguments, students who ignore it often find themselves overwhelmed with details without understanding *what* the author is attempting to say. This error should be avoided always.

The more history you read, the more you will appreciate the diversity of opinions and approaches among historians. While each author offers a unique perspective, historical works fall into general categories, or "schools," depending on their thesis and when they were published. The study of the manner in which different historians approach their subjects is referred to as *historiography*. Every historical subject has a historiography, sometimes limited, sometimes extensive. As in the other sciences, new schools of thought sup-

plant existing ones, offering new insights and challenging accepted theories. Below are excerpts from two monographs dealing with the American Revolution. As you read them, note the contrast in the underlying arguments.

1. "Despite its precedent-setting character, however, the American revolt is noteworthy because it made no serious interruption in the smooth flow of American development. Both in intention and in fact, the American Revolution conserved the past rather than repudiated it. And in preserving the colonial experience, the men of the first quarter century of the Republic's history set the scenery and wrote the script for the drama of American politics for years to come."*

2. "The stream of revolution, once started, could not be confined within narrow banks, but spread abroad upon the land. Many economic desires, many social aspirations were set free by the political struggle, many aspects of colonial society profoundly altered by the forces thus set loose. The relations of social classes to each other, the institution of slavery, the system of landholding, the course of business, the forms and spirit of the intellectual and religious life, all felt the transforming hand of revolution, all emerged from under it in shapes advanced many degrees nearer to those we know."†

What you have just read is nothing less than two conflicting theories of the fundamental nature of the American Revolution. Professor Jameson portrays the Revolution as a catalyst for major social, economic, and political change, while Professor Degler views it primarily as a war for independence that conserved, rather than transformed, colonial institutions. The existence of such divergent opinions makes it imperative that the reader be aware of the argument of every book and read a variety of books and articles to get different perspectives on a subject.

All historical works contain biases of some sort, but a historical bias is not in itself bad or negative. As long as history books are composed by human beings, they will reflect the perspectives of their authors. This need not diminish the quality of historical writing if historians remain faithful to the facts. Some historians, however, have such strong biases that they distort the evidence to make it fit their precon-

* Carl N. Degler, *Out of Our Past,* rev. ed. (New York: Harper and Row, Harper Colophon Books, 1970), p. 73.
† J. Franklin Jameson, *The American Revolution Considered As a Social Movement* (Boston: Beacon Press, 1956), p. 9.

ceived notions. This type of history writing (which is the exception rather than the rule) is of limited value, but when properly treated can contribute to the accumulation of knowledge by providing new insights and challenging the values—and creative abilities—of other historians.

Evidence. Once you are aware of the author's central argument, you can concentrate on his use of evidence—the "facts"—that buttress that argument. There are several types of questions that you should keep in mind as you progress through a book. What types of evidence does the author use? Is his evidence convincing? Which sources does he rely on, and what additional sources might he have consulted? One strategy you might adopt is to imagine that *you* are writing the monograph. Where would you go for information? What would you look at? Then ask yourself: Did the author consult these sources? Obviously no writer can examine *everything*. A good historical work, however, offers convincing data extracted from a comprehensive collection of materials.

As you begin to ask these questions, you will develop the skill of critical reading. Used in this sense the word *critical* does not mean reading to discern what is *wrong* with the narrative. Rather, it refers to analytic reading, assessing the strengths and weaknesses of the monograph, and determining whether the argument ultimately works. All historical works should be approached with a critical—but open—mind.

One important point to remember is that you need not accept or reject every aspect of a historical monograph. In fact, you most likely will accord a "mixed review" to most of the books you read. You may accept the author's argument but find his evidence inadequate, or you may be impressed by his data but draw different conclusions from it. You may find some chapters tightly argued, but others unconvincing. Even if you like a particular book, almost inevitably you will have some comments, criticisms, or suggestions.

RESEARCHING HISTORY

Most history courses, especially advanced ones, require some type of research project. Research skills are vital to history, and can be developed by observing certain rules.

The first rule is to know exactly what you are researching. Every history project begins with a question or problem. Thus the first step is to select a manageable question. Remember, a question is different from a topic. You may choose the American Revolution as a topic, for example, but you then must choose some aspect of the Revolution that interests you. Obviously a project such as "Discuss the American Revolution in all its aspects" is not realistic. You may be interested in the causes of the Revolution. This is a legitimate question, but still a broad one, more appropriate for a book than a paper. You would do better to select a more specific question, such as "Was the American Revolution really a revolution?" This question poses a specific problem, which will require you to collect data and then formulate a definite argument.

Once you have chosen the question, you begin the search for information. There are several possible sources you may wish to explore. First, you might want to consult your professor, who should be familiar with the relevant literature. This approach could be productive; on the other hand, the professor may want you to develop research skills on your own. In that case, a good encyclopedia, such as the *Encyclopaedia Britannica,* will provide a brief but useful overview of a topic and will cite the works from which the information was collected. Even more valuable is an American history textbook. The bibliography section for the appropriate chapters—and, if included, a list of recommended readings—will direct you toward the appropriate literature.

The library card catalog constitutes another vital source of information. It contains three types of cards, which may be filed separately or together, but are always in alphabetical order: author, title, and subject cards. Author cards are filed according to the author's last name; title cards, according to the book's title (excluding "the"); and subject cards by major topical groupings. Obviously subject cards are the most appropriate when you are looking for sources and ideas. If you are uncertain as to *how* your particular topic is filed, choose a heading that sounds appropriate. To come back to our sample topic, possibilities include: "American Revolution"; "Revolution—United States"; "United States—History—Revolution." If you should pick the wrong heading, the catalog will usually have one card under that heading referring you to the proper subject category. If you already have compiled a list of names and/or authors, you can save much time by going directly to the author and title cards.

The following is the card for a famous work in American history. Note the diversity of information that the card contains. (See p. 430.)

This information not only helps you to locate a book, but can indicate whether the book is relevant to your topic. Often, however, you cannot determine a book's usefulness until you have examined its table of contents and perhaps skimmed through a chapter or two.

As you search for materials, you should be aware that historical sources are divided into two

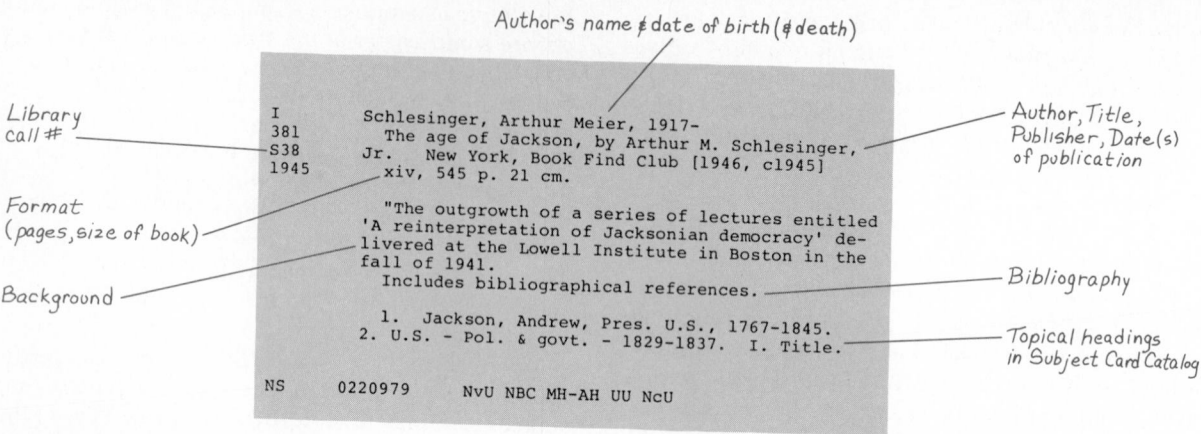

Author's name # date of birth (# death)

Library call #

Format (pages, size of book)

Background

```
I
381
S38
1945
```

Schlesinger, Arthur Meier, 1917-
   The age of Jackson, by Arthur M. Schlesinger,
Jr.   New York, Book Find Club [1946, c1945]
   xiv, 545 p. 21 cm.

   "The outgrowth of a series of lectures entitled
'A reinterpretation of Jacksonian democracy' delivered at the Lowell Institute in Boston in the
fall of 1941.
   Includes bibliographical references.

   1. Jackson, Andrew, Pres. U.S., 1767-1845.
2. U.S. - Pol. & govt. - 1829-1837. I. Title.

NS   0220979   NvU NBC MH-AH UU NcU
```

Author, Title, Publisher, Date(s) of publication

Bibliography

Topical headings in Subject Card Catalog

general categories: primary and secondary. Primary sources are those produced by the historical characters themselves or their contemporaries: correspondence, diaries and journals, autobiographies, government publications, newspapers, and similar documents. Secondary sources include books, magazine articles, and Ph.D. dissertations written by later scholars or writers. In most cases, primary sources are more impressive, since they provide a firsthand account of the events in question. Unfortunately they are often more difficult to locate. In the case of the American Revolution, for example, much primary information does exist, including correspondence, newspapers, and government materials. While some of these materials, such as the letters of Washington and Jefferson, are available in printed form in many university libraries, other materials exist only in the original manuscripts and are confined to special libraries, state historical societies, and similar institutions. Fortunately primary materials are not required for all assignments. Consult your professor and use your own judgment to determine what types of sources are most appropriate for your project.

Once you have selected your sources, the task of note taking begins. Thorough notes are the key to successful research. When you locate a source on the library shelves, the first step is to fill out a note card listing the author, title, publisher, and publication date. You might also note the library call number, in case you need to consult the book again. Once you have recorded this information, the next step is to read the appropriate sections of the book or article, and to jot down any information that may be helpful to you on additional cards. The general rule is one idea per card. Following this procedure allows you to arrange and rearrange your notes in the course of your writing. As you are taking notes, rephrase the data in your own words. Or, if you use the author's language, be sure to put quotation marks around it to indicate it is a direct quote. Always include on your card the author, title, and the page(s) on which you found the information. This will be useful when you wish to cite the material in a footnote. Remember, if

you are using a book, you need not read the entire book, but only those sections relevant to your topic. Magazine articles generally should be read in their entirety.

## WRITING HISTORY

Once you have collected your data, you face the often difficult task of putting your ideas on paper. Composing a history essay allows for few legitimate shortcuts. By adhering to a particular set of procedures, however, you can minimize difficulties while enhancing the quality of your writing.

The first step in writing a paper is to create an outline. Although students often avoid this stage in their haste to "get started" on their project, the outline performs a critical role in the creative process. Not only does it contribute to a more logical and coherent development of ideas, but it also helps you see and eliminate many structural problems before you become engrossed in the actual writing. As a general rule, the earlier you can spot any problem, the easier it is to resolve. The outline may be as general or as specific as you wish. It serves not as an ironclad script for you to follow, but as a general framework to provide direction for the narrative. It can be modified later to accommodate ideas that occur to you as you proceed.

After you complete the outline, you should begin your paper with a clear statement of your argument. For example, if you are addressing the question of whether the American Revolution really was a revolution, you should begin by taking a clear position on the question. It is important to note that the position need *not* be a simple "yes" or "no"; it may be more complicated than that. History is seldom black and white; most often it consists of many gray areas. Whatever position you take, it should be made explicit. If you fail to do this, the effectiveness of your writing will be diminished, since your readers may not be aware of the point of your essay. A common mistake students make is to treat a paper like a
```

mystery story, giving readers the "clues" first and supplying the "solution" at the end. This style is not conducive to good history. State your argument in the beginning so that your readers will be able to follow—and assess—your narrative.

From your introduction you should move smoothly into your narrative. It is here that you develop your argument, using your evidence in a convincing manner. The narrative should exhibit a logical sequence of ideas, not a random collection of data. While evidence is crucial, the key to successful writing is in the elaboration of evidence. Contrary to a popular slogan, the facts do not speak for themselves. Rather, the author must explain the relevance of his facts to his central argument. Few people, for example, would dispute the statement that George Washington crossed the Delaware River to surprise the Hessians at Trenton. The author, however, must explain why this event was significant to his topic. Otherwise it becomes a mere fact of passing interest, without any greater meaning.

History involves the process of change over time, and an effective narrative must illustrate this process. To do so, the narrative must connect diverse facts so that they form a cohesive story. Each sentence should follow logically from the preceding one, and lead into the next one; each paragraph should do the same. To accomplish this, you must pay particular attention to *transition*; that is, moving from one topic to a related topic. Too often students shift from one topic to another without explaining the connection between the two. A historical essay that shifts immediately from Washington's crossing of the Delaware to Jefferson's authorship of the Declaration of Independence creates confusion as to the course of the narrative. A successful transition can be effected by inserting a sentence such as "While some individuals fought for independence on the battlefield, others pursued it in the halls of the Continental Congress." This sentence establishes a concrete relationship between the two events.

In addition to elaborating your evidence, you must cite the sources of this evidence. Any information that is not "common knowledge" should be demarcated by a footnote. If you are uncertain as to proper footnote use and form, consult a stylistic manual such as Kate Turabian's *A Manual for Writers*. Although some footnotes can be complicated, the basic forms for books and articles are illustrated below.

For books:

Robert E. Brown, *Middle-Class Democracy and the Revolution in Massachusetts, 1691–1780* (Ithaca, N.Y.: Cornell University Press, 1955), p. 27.

Notice that the footnote includes the author, title, publisher, date, and page on which the information was found. As mentioned earlier, it is essential that you record this information when taking notes.

Articles are footnoted as follows:

Jesse Lemisch, "Jack Tar in the Streets: Merchant Seamen in the Politics of the American Revolution," *William and Mary Quarterly*, 3rd Series 25 (July, 1968): 374–381.

This footnote includes the author, title, the journal in which the article appears, and the date and edition of publication. The pages indicated are those from which the information was taken. Note that the title of the book or journal is underlined, while the title of the article is placed within quotation marks.

For an article by one author appearing in a work edited by another:

Gordon S. Wood, "Rhetoric and Reality in the American Revolution," in *Essays on the American Revolution*, ed. David L. Jacobsen (New York: Holt, Rinehart and Winston, 1970), pp. 50–52.

This form combines various elements of the previous two styles. (All forms are based on Turabian's *Manual*.)

In addition to knowing *how* to footnote, you must learn *when* to footnote. All specific data that are not common knowledge, as well as all direct quotes, should be cited. Never use historians' words or ideas without giving them credit in a footnote. To do so constitutes plagiarism, which is a serious offense within the academic world. For stylistic purposes, most readers prefer one comprehensive footnote at the end of a paragraph to a footnote at the end of each individual sentence. (A single footnote may cite several sources.) In the case of a direct quote, however, a footnote must appear at the end of a sentence. If you use a series of quotations, one multiple footnote may suffice. The word *footnote* implies that the citations should appear on the bottom of the page on which the cited material appears. While this is the most convenient arrangement for the reader, it complicates the typing of the paper substantially. Therefore, most professors will accept a separate footnote section at the end of the narrative.

One final word regarding footnotes. While you must cite a source every time you take data from it, you need only give the full citation the *first* time you cite the source. After that, an abbreviated footnote form is acceptable. For example:

Brown, *Middle-Class Democracy*, p. 11.

Adopting this form can save you considerable time in the typing of your paper.

Although all individuals must develop their own style of presenting evidence, a few basic rules should be observed. Keep your language clear and succinct. Avoid wordiness and redundancies. Expressions such as "a determined, headstrong, ambitious, unyielding, perservering individual" are repetitious and stylistically unacceptable. Make sure you have command of your vocabulary; do not employ "impressive" words if you are unsure of their precise meaning. Avoid excessive quoting. Quotes are a highly effective means of illustrating ideas and attitudes, but when used excessively, they *become* the narrative, rather than highlighting the narrative. Let your characters speak for themselves, but remember that the final argument must be yours.

Learn to employ active rather than passive verbs in your writing. "Congress passed a law" reads better than "A law was passed," and is also more informative since it reveals *who* passed the law. Since history is a record of the past, it should be written in the past tense.
Incorrect: "Hitler invad*es* Russia in June of 1941."
Correct: "Hitler invad*ed* Russia in June of 1941."
Since you are, in a sense, telling a story, humorous anecdotes and interesting asides, when used properly, can make your narrative more readable. If your writing includes extensive quantitative (numerical) data, you might want to incorporate the information into charts or appendices to avoid interrupting the flow of your narrative.

When you have completed the actual narrative, you should summarize your argument *briefly* in your conclusion. Just as your introductory paragraph prepares your readers for your argument, your conclusion reaffirms the major ideas that you want to communicate to your readers.

After the narrative comes the bibliography, which is a list of all the sources you have used in the course of your work. Several differences distinguish a bibliography from footnotes. While the sequence of footnotes is determined by your narrative, the bibliography is arranged in alphabetical order. Most bibliographies are divided into primary and secondary sources, and subdivided into general categories, such as books, articles, newspapers, and government documents. Moreover, the bibliographic form differs slightly from that of footnotes. Examples of proper bibliographic forms follow:

Brown, Robert E. *Middle-Class Democracy and the Revolution in Massachusetts, 1691–1780*. Ithaca, N.Y.: Cornell University Press, 1955.

Lemisch, Jesse. "Jack Tar in the Streets: Merchant Seamen in the Politics of the Revolutionary America." *William and Mary Quarterly*. 3rd Series 25 (July, 1968): 371–407.

Wood, Gordon S. "Rhetoric and Reality in the American Revolution." In *Essays in the American Revolution*, pp. 43–65. Edited by David L. Jacobsen. New York: Holt, Rinehart and Winston, 1970.

Although the form differs from that of footnotes, most of the information is the same. Note that in the case of articles, however, the bibliography gives the page numbers for the entire article, while the footnote gives only those pages from which information has been extracted. Note also the way the authors' last names stand out in a bibliography, enabling the reader to see at a glance which sources you have used. (The bibliographic form used here comes from Turabian's manual. If you have any questions regarding the bibliography, consult Turabian or some other manual.)

The final stage in writing a paper is proofreading. Ideally, you should compose a first draft, proofread it carefully, and then rewrite the paper where necessary. If you write only one draft, make your corrections as neatly as possible. Unless otherwise instructed, papers should be typed, double-spaced.

Finally, pay strict attention to deadlines. Allot adequate time for each project, including time for typing and proofreading. If you encounter any difficulties, inform your professor immediately. Do not wait until the due date to reveal that you cannot submit your paper on time.

Index

Architecture:
in antebellum period, 292
in colonial America, 71–72
Arista, Mariano, 269
Aristocracy:
entrepreneurs, 25
natural, 160
settlement of colonies, 24, 25–26
Arkansas, 357
Army, in War of 1812, 193
Arnold, Benedict, 108, 114, 118–19
Aroostook War, 264
Articles of Confederation, 115–17, 128, 132 (*See also* Constitution, U.S.)
Arts:
antebellum, 287–92
architecture, 292
literature, 287–90
painting, 291–92
in colonial society, 70–72
Asbury, Francis, 293
Ashanti, 32
Ashburton, Alexander, 264
Ashley, William, 254
Assistance, writ of, 88
Astor, John Jacob, 187, 212, 251, 254
Asylums, 294–95
Atahualpa, 15
Atlanta Cotton States Exposition, 301
"Atlantis" (Simms), 321
Auburn system, 294
Audubon, John, 292
Auld, Hugh, 300
Auld, Sophia, 300
Austin, Stephen F., 260
Autobiography (Douglass), 316
Aztecs, 2–3, 14

B

Bache, Benjamin Franklin, 166, 169, 171
Bacon, Nathaniel, 52
Bacon's Rebellion, 52
Balance of trade, colonial, 79–80
Balboa, Vasco Nuñez de, 14
Balloon-frame house, 292, 292
Baltimore, Lord, 25, 45
Baltimore and Ohio Railroad, 219
Bancroft, George, 268, 271

Banking:
Bank of the United States, First, *157*, 157–58
Civil War and, 364
growth of, 208–11
Hamilton and, 156, 157–58
Bank note, 156, *210*, 210
Bank of North America, 115
Bank of the United States, First, *157*, 157–58, 178, 187, 193
Bank of the United States, Second, 210, 241–43, 245
Baptists, 37, 160
Barbary pirates, 135, 176
Barbé-Marbois, François, 181
Barclay, Robert, 195
Barnburners, 331
Barron, James, 186
Barton, Clara, 372–73
Bastille, fall of, 161
Bates, Edward, 34
Bayard, James, 173
Beard, Charles A., 128, 132
Beauregard, Pierre, 350, 358
Becker, Carl, 117
Beckley, John, 166
Beecher, Catharine, 205
Beecher, Henry Ward, 341
Beecher, Lyman, 335
Beecher's Bibles, 341
Bell, John, 347
Bell, Luther, 295
Beni, 32
Bent, Charles, 274
Benton, Thomas Hart, 215, 243, 270–71, 333
Berkeley, George, 185–86
Berkeley, William, 52
Berlin Decree, 185, 190
Bernard, Francis, Sir, 93
Biddle, Nicholas, 241, 243
Billings, William, 71
Billington, Ray, 138–39
Bill of Rights, 150 (*See also* Constitution, U.S.)
Bingham, George Caleb, 291
Birney, James G., 265, 299, 318, 331
Birthrate, 55–56, 203
Black Codes, 387–88
Blacks (*See also* Reconstruction; Slavery)
as Civil War soldiers, 375–76
in colonial society, 53–55, 58
culture of, 397
education of, 397
free, 285–86
Jim Crow laws against, 285
marriages, 387

Reconstruction, 384
in Revolution, 108–9, 118–19, *120*
social structure of, *311*, 311
suffrage, 386, 390–91
Blackstone, William, 68
Blackwell, Elizabeth, 372
Blackwell, Henry B., 297
Bladensburg, Md., 196
Bleeding Kansas, 340
Blessing of the Bay, 79
Blithedale Romance, The (Hawthorne), 290
Blockade, naval, 359–61
Bloody shirt, waving the, 401
Blue-Backed Speller (Webster), 133
Board of Trade, 83, 88
Boleyn, Anne, 37
Bondsman or bondswoman, 31
Bonus Bill, 230
Boone, Daniel, 112
Booth, Anne, 255
Booth, John Wilkes, 377
Boston, 288
Boston Committee of Safety, 99
Boston Manufacturing Company, 220
Boston Massacre, 94–95, 118
Boston Tea Party, 97
Boudinot, Elias, 133, 134
Bounties, 82
Bowdoin, James, 141–42
Bowen, Francis, 204
Braddock, Edward, 87
Bradford, William, 38
Bradstreet, Anne, 70
Brant, Joseph, 112
Breckinridge, John C., 347
Breed's Hill, Battle of (1775), 108
Bremer, Fredrika, 277
Brent, Margarett, 61
"Brer Rabbit," 313
Bridger, Jim, 254
Bright, John, 362
British Empire, 74–102 (*See also* Revolution)
annexation of Texas and, 265
Boston massacre, 94–95
Canadian boundary and, 264
Civil War diplomacy and, 361–62
colonial economy and, 75–83
costs and benefits from American colonies before 1763, 81–83
crisis of, 83–100
difficulties prior to Revolution, 104

powers of, 145
public domain administration in 1780s, 135–39
ratification of Constitution, 146–50, *149*
Reconstruction and, 390–94
Shays' Rebellion and, 141
Connecticut, 40, 75
Conquistadors, 14–15
Conscription, Civil War, 362–64
Conservatives, Northern and Southern, 383
Constitution, "compact theory" of, 171
Constitution, U.S., 127–51, 408–17
checks and balances, 145
Constitutional Convention, 127, 128, 139–46
democratic features, 145
foreign affairs and, 134–135
government's power, 145–46
public domain administration and, 135–39
ratification of, 146–50, *149*
Shay's Rebellion and, 140–42
state of nation in 1780s, 128–34
Constitution, U.S.S., *194*, 195
Constitutional convention, innovation of, 122–23
Constitutional Conventions, 67, 123, 128, 139–46
Constitutional Union party, 347
Continental Army, 105–6, 113–14, 118, 132, 133
Continental Association, 97
Continental Congress, 105, 115–17, 128
Continental Navy, 106
"Continentals," 106
Convention of 1800, 169, 171
Conventions of 1860, 345–47
Convicts, colonial settlement by, 32, *33*
Cook, James, 253
Cooke, Jay, 364
Cooper, James Fenimore, 288
Cooper, Thomas, 171
Copley, John Singleton, 71
Copperheads, 366–67
Corn, 307
Cornwallis, Charles, 109, 111, 113, 114, 123
Coromantin, 32
Coronado, Francisco Vásquez de, 18
Corporations, 207–8

Corrupt bargain, 234
Corsairs, Barbary, 135, 176
Cortés, Hernando, *3*, 14
Corwin, Thomas, 252
Cotton:
Confederate diplomacy and, 355
economic growth and, 212–13
growing areas, *214*
Old South agriculture and, 307
Reconstruction South's economy and, 395
Cotton, John, 39–40, 62
Cotton gin, 206, *213*, 213
Court, General, 92
Crafts in colonial America, 72
Crawford, William H., 229, 233
Creditors in 1780s, 131–32, 134
Creek War, 195
Creoles, 182
Crèvecoeur, J. Hector St. John de, 48, 49
"Crime against Kansas, The," 342
Crime in Northeast, 282–83
"Critical Period," 128, 168 (*See also* Constitution, U.S.)
Crittenden, John J., 349
Croghan, George, 87
Crop-lien system, 396
Crusades, 7
Cuba, 336–37
Cult:
of chivalry, 319
of domesticity, 205, 295
"of true womanhood," *287*, 287
Culture:
black, 53, 397
nationalism of 1780s and, 133
in Reconstruction South, 397
slave, 313–14
Currencies, Revolutionary, 106–7, *107*
Currency Act (1764), 91
Curti, Merle, 99
Cushing, William, 121
Custer, George A., *374*

D

da Gama, Vasco, 12
Dale, Thomas, Sir, 28
Dare, Virginia, 25
"Dark Ages," 6
Dartmouth College, 68, 230

Davis, Jefferson, 310, 328, 336, 349, 355, *356*, 356–57, 365
Davis, Varina, 370
Davis Bend, 395
Dawes, William, 99
Dead books, 400
Deane, Silas, 111
Death rates in colonial society, 55–56
De Bow, J. D. B., 323, 327
DeBow's Review, 323
Debt:
confronted by 1789 government, 153–54
funded, 155–56, 176
Debtors:
immigration of, 30–31
in 1780s, 131–32
"De Camptown Races" (Foster), 319
Decatur, Stephen, 176
Declaration of Independence, 67, 94, 110, 405–7
Declaration of Rights and Grievances, 97
Declaration of Sentiments, 296
Declaratory Act (1766), 92
Deer Island, 51
Defeat, The (Warren), 99
Defense, colonial, 82
Deflation in 1780s, 132
de Grasse, Count, 114
Deism, 65
Delaware, 43, 147
Delaware Indians, 4, 112, 137, 191
Demand side perspective, 200
Democracy (*See also* Jacksonian democracy)
colonial society and, 58
Constitution's features of, 145
politics after Revolution and, 122–23
reforms of, 233
Democracy in America (Tocqueville), 277
Democratic party:
breakup of (1860), 345–47
racism of, 400–401
Democratic-Republican party (*See* Republican party)
Democratic Review, 263
Democratic Vistas (Whitman), 290
Democrats:
Jacksonian democracy and, 243–45
War and Peace, 366–67

Demos, John, 56
Depression:
  of 1836, 246
  of 1857, 343
d'Estaing, Admiral, 113
Detroit, Fort, 89
Dial, The, 289
Diary from Dixie (Chesnut), 370–71
Dias, Bartolomeu, 12
Dias, Dinis, 10
Dickens, Charles, 221, 280
Dickinson, John, 94, 99, 104, 140, 142
Diedrich Knickerbocker's A History of New York (Irving), 288
Diet, 20, *21*
Dinwiddie, Robert, 87
Diplomacy, cotton and, 355 (*See also* Foreign affairs)
Discourse Concerning Westerne Planting (Hakluyt), 26–27
Discrimination:
  against free blacks, 285–86
  against immigrants, 284–85
  against women, 286–87
  in Northeast, 284–85
Disease, 19, 203
Diversity of European settlers, 49–50
Divorce laws, 122
Dix, Dorothea, 294–96, *295*, 372
Domesticity, cult of, 205, 295
Dominion of New England, 83
Dongan, Thomas, 85
Doolittle, Amos, *100*
Dotey, Edward, 98
Doughfaces, 327
Douglas, Stephen A., 267, *333*, 333–34, 336, 337–39, 343, 346–47, 366
Douglass, Frederick, 296, 299–301, 316, 369
Dow, Neal, 295
Drake, Edwin L., 202
Drake, Francis, 27
Dred Scott decision, 339, 343
Drumgoole, Kizi, 312
Dryden, John, 70
Dürer, Albrecht, *20*
Dunmore, Lord, 108–9
Duquesne, Fort, 87
Duquesne, Marquis, 87
Durand, Asher B., 291
Dutch:
  Calvinists, 67
  colonial settlement, 26
Dutch East India Company, 17

Dutch Revolution, support of, 112
Dutch West India Company, 30
Dwight, Louis, 294
Dyer, Mary, *43*

E

East, Revolution in, 111–13
East India Company, 96, 97
East-West tensions in colonial society, 52–53
Economy, 199–226
  banks, banking and, 208–11, 363–64
  canals and, 216–19
  capital and, 206–8
  Civil War causes and, 327–28
  colonial, 75–83
  cotton and, 212–13
  course of growth in, 212–21
  factory system and, 219–21
  first party system and division in, 158
  government actions and, 211–12
  industrial workers and, 221–25
  during Jacksonian democracy, 245–46
  labor and, 203–4, 225
  land policy and, 215–16
  market growth and, 206
  modern national finance beginnings, 363–64
  production factors in, 200–212
  public schools and, 204–6
  railroads and, 219, 220
  of Reconstruction South, 394
  resources and, 200–203
  roads and, 216, 217
  sacrifice and, 212
  in 1780s, 128–33
  steamboats and, 216
  technology and, 206
  wages and, 222–25
  wheat and, 213–15
  working conditions and, 222–25
Education:
  of blacks, 397
  in colonial America, 67–68
  economic growth and, 204–6
  family's role in, 56
  for girls, 122
Edwards, Jonathan, 63, *64*, 65
Egalitarianism, 280
Elastic clause, 146

Election(s), presidential, 418–20
  of 1796, 166–67, *167*
  of 1800, 171–77, *172*
  of 1808, 189
  of 1812, 195
  of 1824, 233–34, *235*
  of 1828, *236*, 236–37
  of 1832, *245*, 245
  of 1840, *248*
  of 1844, 265
  of 1860, *348*
  of 1864, 376
  voter interest in, *246*
Electoral college, 145
Eliot, John, 50, *51*
Elite, planter, 310
Elizabeth I, 27, 28, 37
Ellsworth, Oliver, 142, 146
Emancipation Proclamation, 301, 368–70
Embargo Act (1807), 188–89
Emerson, Joseph, 205
Emerson, Ralph Waldo, 241, 288–89, *289*, 292, 366
Emerson School for Young Ladies, *205*
Employment in 19th century, 223 (*See also* Labor force)
Empress of China (ship), *129*, 130
England (*See* British Empire)
English-French Confrontation, 84–86, *86*
Enlightenment, 64–65
Entailing, 123
Entrepreneurs, aristocratic, 25
Enumeration, 82
Environment, colonial society, 48–49
Episcopalians, 133, 160, 293
Era of Good Feelings, 228–33
Ericsson, Leif, 5, 7
Erie Canal, 211, 216–18, *218*
Erskine, David M., 190
Essex decision, 185
Essex Junto, 184
Europe (*See also* specific countries)
  benefits from New World, 20–21
  contact with New World, impact of, 18–21
  diversity of settlers from, 49–50
  expansionism, 10–18
  medieval, 5–7
  revival of trade and commerce, 7–10
  Rise of Modern, 5–7

French Revolution (1789), 117, 161, 169–70
French settlers, 49
Frontier type, 279–81
Fugitive Slave Act (1850), 271, *335*, 335–36
Fuller, Margaret, 289
Fulton, Robert, 206, 216
Fundamental Orders, 40
Funded debt, 155–56, 176
Funding Act (1790), 156–57
Fur trade, 84, 134, 253–54

G

Gadsden, James, 328
Gadsden Purchase, 328
Gage, General, 98–99, 108
Gage, Thomas, 93
Gag rule, 299, 318
Galileo, 66
Gallatin, Albert, *162*, 178, 186–87, 193, 197
Gardoqui, Don Diego de, 134
Garnet, Henry Highland, 299
Garrison, William Lloyd, 239, 296, 298, 300, 301
Gaspee Incident, 95–96
Gates, Horatio, 111, 113
Gazette of the United States, 163
Gazlay, James, 229
Genêt, "Citizen" Edmond, 161–62
General Advertiser, 169
Genovese, Eugene, 252, 315
George III, King, 87, 95, 104, 110, 112, 129
Georgia, 76, 147
Georgian architecture, 72
German immigration to Northeast, 384
German settlers, 49
Gerry, Elbridge, 99, 146, 167
Gettysburg, Battle of (1863), 374–75
Ghent, Peace of (1814), 187, 197
Gibbons v. *Ogden*, 216
Gibraltar, Spanish seige of, 124, 125
Giles, Anna Malcolm, 320
Giles Enforcement Act (1809), 189
Girard, Stephen, 212
Gladstone, William, 128
Glaser, Elizabeth, *287*

Glorious Revolution (1688–89), 83
Godey's Lady's Book, 205
Gold, 207
"Gold Bug, The" (Poe), 288
Gold Rush, California (1848), 332
Gonzales, Luis de Onís, 231
Gordon, Adam, Lord, 81
Goshen, Connecticut, 81
Gothic style of antebellum architecture, 292
Government(s):
   as big business, 365
   in colonial society, 58–61
   economic growth and, 211–12
   English model of, 58–59
   powers given by Constitution to, 145–46
   Radical, 398–99
   during Revolution, 106
Governors, colonial, 59–60
Grace Church, 292
Graduation Act (1854), 216
Graham, Catherine Macaulay, 99
Grant, Ulysses S., 356, 358, 374–75, 377, 389, 394
Gray, Robert, 253
Great American Desert, 254
Great Awakening, First, 63–64
Great Awakening, Second, 293, *294*
Great Britain (*See* British Empire)
Great Lakes, War of 1812 and, 195
Greek revival style of antebellum architecture, 292
Greeley, Horace, 340, 345, 347, 349, 368, 369
"Greenbacks," 364
Greene, John, *129*
Greene, Nathanael, 113
Greenville, Treaty of (1795), 165
Greenwood, John, *80*
Gregg, William, 323, 327
Grenville, George, 89–93
Greven, Philip, 58
Grey, Charles, 118
Grimké, Angelina, 296, 299, 318
Grimké, Sarah, 296, 299, 318
Group, The (Warren), 99
Grundy, Felix, 191
Guadalupe Hidalgo, Treaty of (1848), 274
Guerrière, H.M.S., *194*, 195
Gunpowder, discovery of, 10
Gutenberg, Johann, 9
Guy Rivers (Simms), 321

H

Hacker, Louis, 75
Haiti, 168
Hakluyt the Younger, Richard, 26–27
Hale, Sarah Josepha, 205
Half-Way Covenant, 62–63
Halifax, Earl of, 83
Hall, Basil, 295
Halleck, Henry W., 358
Hamilton, Alexander, 139, 140, 142, 146, 148, 153–54, *156*, 159, 193, 228
   Burr's duel with, 184–85
   foreign relations with France and, 161–62
   as secretary of treasury, 154–58
   Whiskey Rebellion and, 165–66
Hamlin, Hannibal, 347
Hammond, James, 319
Hancock, John, 97, 99, 147, *148*
Hannibal (ship), 36
Harlan, James, 342
Harmar, Josiah, 164
Harpers Ferry, 345, 346
Harrison, Benjamin, 301
Harrison, William Henry, 190–91, 195, 229, 246, 247–49, 262
Harrisse, Henry, 322
Hartford Convention, 169, 194
Harvard College, 68
Harvey, William, 66
Hat Act (1732), 82
Hawkins, John, 27
Hawthorne, Nathaniel, 289–91
Hayes, Rutherford B., 402
Health, 203
Helper, Hinton R., 310
Henderson, Richard, 112
Henry, Joseph, 209
Henry, Patrick, 92, 148
Henry of Portugal, (Henry the Navigator), Prince, 10–12
Henry VII, King, 16
Henry VIII, King, 37
Henson, Josiah, 316
Herjulfsson, Bjarni, 5
Herkimer, Nicholas, 112
Hermandad (brotherhood), 16–17
Hermitage, *322*,
Hessians, 105, 109, 111
Higginson, Thomas Wentworth, 392
Hispaniola, 168

History, 427–32

History of the Rise, Progress and Termination of the American Revolution (Warren), 98, 99

History of the World (Raleigh), 98

Holland, explorations of New World, 17–18

Holy Alliance, 231

Homestead act, 328

Homesteading, 215–16

Hood, J. B., 377

Hooker, Joseph, 359

Hooker, Thomas, 40

Horseshoe Bend, Battle of (1814), 195

House, balloon-frame, *292*, 292

House of Commons, 58

House of Representatives, 144, 145

House of the Seven Gables, The (Hawthorne), 290

House Ways and Means Committee, 187

Housing problems, 281

Howe, Richard, 110–11

Howe, Samuel Gridley, 295

Howe, William, 108–11

Howells, William Dean, 203

Hudson, Henry, 17–18

Hudson River school, 291

Hudson's Bay Company, 254, 256

Huguenots, 45, 49, 84

Hull, William, 194

Human capital, 204

Humanism, 9

Hunkers, 331

Hurons, 4, 85

Hussey, Obed, 214

Hutchinson, Anne, 41

Hutchinson, Thomas, 61, 92, 94, 96, 98, 99

I

Ibo, 32

Icaria, 302

Ideology:
as cause of Civil War, 327
first party system and division in, 158–60
Southern, 322–24

Ill health, 203

Immediatism, 298

Immigrants
capital from, 207
discrimination against, 284–85

Immigration (*See also* Colonies, settlement of)
1820–1860, *204*
labor shortage and, 203–4
to Northeast, 283–84

Impeachment, 180, 389–90, 392–94

Impending Crisis of the South, The (Helper), 310

Import taxes, 130–31

Impost, 133

Impressment, 163, 185–87, 192

Incas, 3, 14–15

Indentured servants, 31–32, 35

Independence, Declaration of, 67, 94, 110, 405–7

Independence (*See* Revolution)

Independence Hall, 142, *143*

Independent Treasury System, 247

Indiana Territory, 191

Indian policy:
under British, 163–64
under Jackson, 239–41
of Jefferson, 182–84
in 1780s, 135–37

Indians, 2–5, *4*, 19–20, 50–52
(*See also* specific tribes)
Albany Congress and, 88–89
colonial society, treatment of, 50–52
East-West tensions over, 52–53
European contact, effect of, 20
French and Indian War, *86*, 86–89
Jamestown settlement and, 28, 29
Lewis and Clark expedition, 182–84
Madison administration and, 190–92
of New Mexico, 260
Revolution in West and, 112
in Southwest territories, 256–59
Spanish conquests of, 14–15
in War of 1812, 195

Indigo, *76*, 128

Individualism, 277, 279

Industrial workers, 221–25 (*See also* Labor)

Industry:
colonial, 78–79
Hamilton's focus on, 154, 156
in 1780s, 130–31

Inequality in colonial economy, 81

Infant mortality, 258

Inflation during Revolution, 106–8

Ingraham, Joseph Holt, 290

Intellectual America, colonial, 65–70

Intermarriage, 49

Internal Revenue, Bureau of, 363

Internal Revenue Act (1862), 389

Intolerable or Coercive Acts (1774), 97, 99

Investment in colonies, 27–28

Involuntary immigrants, 32–36

Irish immigrants, 283–85

Iron Act (1750), 82

Iron Industry, 79

Iroquois Confederacy, 4, 50, 85, 112, 137, 168

Irving, Washington, *190*, 288

Isabella and Ferdinand, 12, 13

Isabella of Castile, Queen, 16–17

Islamic civilization, 7

J

Jackson, Andrew, 169, 195, 196–97, *239*, 266, 299, 310, 320, 338 (*See also* Jacksonian democracy)
administration of, 237–46
rise to power, 233–37
style of, 238

Jackson, Fort, 195

Jackson, Rachel, 236

Jackson, Thomas J. ("Stonewall"), 272, 358

Jacksonian democracy, 227–50
democratic reforms and, 233
Democrats and, 243–45
economy during, 245–46
1828 election and, 236–37
1824 election and, 233–34, *235*
Era of Good Feelings and, 228–33
foreign affairs and, 231–33
Indian policy under, 239–41
Marshall and, 230
Nullification crisis and, 238–39
Second Bank of the United States and, 241–43
spoils system and, 237–38
Tariff of Abominations and, 235–36

Lieber, Francis, 322, 366
Lincoln, Abraham, 336, 339, 340, 343–45, *344*, 347–48, 349–50 (*See also* Civil War)
  Douglass and, 301, 344–45
  Frémont and, 271–72
  leadership skills of, 355–56
  on Polk, 252
  on slavery, 368–70
  ten-percent plan of, 385
Lincoln, Benjamin, 141
Lippard, George, 290
Literature:
  in antebellum period, 287–90
  New England Renaissance in, 288–90
  popular, 290–91
Little Belt, 192
Livingston, Robert, 110, 181
Löwenstern, Isidor, 277
Locke, John, 83, 94, 110, 159
"Log Cabin and Hard Cider" campaign, 248
London Company, 28, 29, 38
Long, Stephen, 254
López de Gómara, Francisco, 18–19
Loudon, Lord, 88
Louisbourg, Fort, *85*
Louisiana, 86, 348
Louisiana Purchase, 169, 180–82, *183*, 187
Louis XVI, King, 161
L'Ouverture, Toussaint, 168, 181
Lovejoy, Elijah, 299
Low, Nathaniel, *70*
Lowell, Francis Cabot, 220
Lowell, James Russell, 252
Lowell Mills, 220–21, *222*, 225
Lowndes, William, 191
Loyalists, 104, 105, 108, 112, *117*, 117–20, 125, 134
Loyal Publication Societies, 366
Lucas, Eliza, 76
Lusk, James, 400
Luther, Martin, 37
Lyell, Charles, 277
Lynds, Elam, 294
Lyon, Mary, 205
Lyon, Matthew, 169, 171

M

Macedonian (ship), 195
Macon's Bill Number Two, 190
Madison, Dolley, *190*, 196

Madison, James, 140, 142, 143, 146, 148, 153, 156–57, 160, 161, 171, 176, 179, *190*, 228, 229–30
  presidency, 189–97
Magellan, Ferdinand, 14
Magnetic Telegraph Company, 209
Maine, 264, 295, 330
Maize, 20, *21*
Majority, concurrent, 324
Majority rule:
  critique of, 322
  Federalists vs. Republicans on, 159–60
Mallory, Stephen R., 356
Mandan Indians, 183
Manifest Destiny, 263, 266
Mann, Horace, 204–6, 295
Manorial system, feudal, 6, 8
Manufacturers in 1780s, 130–31
Marbury, William, 180
Marbury v. *Madison*, 180
Marcy, William L., 238
Mardi (Melville), 290
Marion, Francis, 320
Markets, growth of, 206
Marriages, black, 387
Marshall, John, 148, 167, 168, 179–80, *180*, 185, 230, 239, 241
Martin, Luther, 143, 146
Martin, Martha, 338
Martineau, Harriet, 277, 321
Martin Faber (Simms), 321
Mary, Queen, 83
Maryland, 25, 32, 45
  agriculture in colonial, 76
  Articles of Confederation and, 116
  birth and death rates in colonial, 56
  navigation rights agreement, 139–40
  ratification of Constitution and, 147
Mason, George, 142, 143, 146, 148
Mason, James M., 361
Mason, John Y., 336
Massachusetts, 83, 121, 140–42, 147, 204–5
Massachusetts Antislavery Society, 300
Massachusetts Bay Colony, 38–43
  offshoots of, 39–43
  settlement, 38–39
Massachusetts Bay Company, 40

Massachusetts Spy, 98
"Massacre," Boston, 94–95, 118
Massasoit, 38, 50, 51
Materialism, 287
Mather, Cotton, 63, 70
Mayas, 2, 15
Mayflower, 38, 98
Mayflower Compact, 38
Maysville Road bill, 243
McCauley, Mary Ludwig Hays, 122
McClellan, George B., 358, 376, 389
McCormick, Cyrus, 214
McCulloch v. *Maryland*, 230
McDowell, Irvin, 358
McHenry, Fort, 196
McIntosh, Fort, 137
McLean, John, 344
McLoughlin, John, 254, 256
Meade, George G., 374
Medicine, colonial, 68–70
Medieval Europe, 5–7
Melville, Herman, 290
Mercantilism, 20–27, 81–83
Mercer, John, 146
Merchants, English, profit motive of, 27–28
Merrimac (ship), 359–60
Methodists, 133, 160
Metzer, Jacob, 308
Mexican War, 266–75, 272 (*See also* Expansionism)
  borderland capture, 269
  debate on expansionism and, 266–68
  declaration of, 252
  Great Britain and, 268
  Manifest Destiny and, 266
  moving toward, 266–69
  peace settlement, 272–74
  Slidell Mission and, 268–69
  theories on causes of, 252
  victory, 269–72
Mexico, 2–3, 14
Middle class, mid-19th century prosperity of, 222
"Midnight appointees," 179
Migration to West, 278–79
Milan Decree, 185, 190
Military forces:
  Civil War, 362–63, 375–76
  revolutionary, 105–6
  in War of 1812, 193
Miller, Stephen Decatur, 370
Milligan case, 391
Mill Springs, Battle of, 358
Mims, Forst, 195
Minerals, 200

free blacks in, 285–86
immigration to, 283–84
urbanization problems in, 281–82
Northern Conservatives, 383
North Star, 299, 301
Northup, Solomon, 316
North West Company, 254
Northwest Ordinance (1787), *137,* 137–39, *138,* 266
Norton, Charles Eliot, 366
Norwich University, 206
Noyes, John Humphrey, 302
Nuclear family of colonial society, 55–56
Nullification, theory of, 324
Nullification crisis, 238–39
Nursing profession, 372

O

Oberlin College, 297–99
Observations on the New Constitution (Warren), 99
Ogden, Peter, 254
Oglethorpe, James, 30
Ohio, 181
Ohio Indians, 137
"Old Black Joe" (Foster), 319
Olive Branch Petition, 104, 106, 109
Olmsted, Frederick Law, 309
Omaha, *278*
Omnibus Bill, 333
Omnibuses, 281
Omoo (Melville), 290
Oneida community, 302, *303*
Opechancanough, 29
Order of the Star-Spangled Banner (Know Nothings), 285, 340–41, 343
Ordinance of 1787, *137,* 137–39, *138*
Oregon, 253–56, *265,* 268, 330
Oregon Trail, 255
Orient, lure of, 7–8
Orthodox Calvinists, 293
Ostend Manifesto, 336
O'Sullivan, John L., 263, 266
Oswald, Richard, 125
Oswego, Fort, 86
Otis, Harrison Gray, 88, 159
Ottawa Indians, 137
Owen, Robert, 302
Owsley, Frank, 309

P

Pacific railroad, 328
Pacific Railway Act (1862), 364
Paine, Thomas, 65, 110
Painting:
    in antebellum period, 291–92
    in colonial America, 71
Pakenham, Edward, 196–97
Pale Faces, *399*
Pamphleteers, 94
Panama Conference (1826), 234
Panic:
    of 1836, 246
    of 1857, 343
Paper money, 106–8, 132, 156, *210,* 210
Paredes, Mariano, 268
Paris, Peace of (1763), 88
Paris, Treaty of (1783), *124,* 125, 134
Parliament, 58
Partisan, The (Simms), 321
Partisan press, 162–63
Party system, 152–74 (*See also* Federalist party; Republican party)
    Alien and Sedition Acts, 168, 170–71, 178
    beginnings of, 158–61
    economic division in, 158
    election of 1796, 166–67, *167*
    election of 1800, 171–73, *172*
    foreign relations and, 161–69
    French Revolution and, 161, 169–70
    ideological division in, 158–60
    Jay Treaty and, 164–65
    partisan press and, 162–63
    religion, role in, 160–61
    spoils system and, 238
    Washington's farewell and, 166
    XYZ affair, 167–69
Paterson, William, 142, 144
Patriarchal system, 56–57
Patriot Ideology, 94
"Patroons," 26
Pawpaw, 32
"Paxton Boys," 53
Peabody, Elizabeth, 289
Peace after Revolution, 123–25
Peace Democrats, 366–67
Pendelton, George H., 367, 376
Peninsular Campaign, 358
Penitentiaries, 294
Penn, William, 31, 43–45, 50
Pennsylvania:
    agriculture in colonial, 75

creditors and debtors in 1780s, 132
diversity of settlers in, 49, 50
East-West tensions in colonial, 52–53
French and Indian War in, 87
Gallatin as legislator, 186
Glorious Revolution's effect on, 83
political system after Revolution, 122
ratification of Constitution, 147
settlement, 43–45
slavery prohibitions after Revolution, 121
War of 1812 and, 192
Pennsylvania, University of, 68
Pennsylvania Gazette, The, 66
Pequot War, 50
Perceval, Spencer, 192
"Perfectionist" doctrine, 293 (*See also* Reform, social, during antebellum period)
Periauger, 53
Perkins, Bradford, 192
Perry, Oliver Hazard, 195
"Personal liberty" laws, 335
Personal savings, 207–8
Peru, 3, 14–15
Peters, Samuel, 117
Philadelphia, College of, 68
Philadelphia, Pa., 45, 52, 53
    Congress' flight in 1783 from, 133–34
    Constitutional Convention in, 142–46
    First Continental Congress, 97–100, 118
Philadelphia-Lancaster Road, 216
Philippines, 14
Phillips, Thomas, 36
Pickens, Fort, 350
Pickering, John, 180
Pickering, Timothy, 168–69, *170,* 171
Pickett, George, 374
Pickett's charge, 374
Pierce, Franklin, 328, 336, 339–41
Pietist Amana Society, 303
Pike, Zebulon, 254
Pilgrims of Plymouth, 38
Pinckney, Charles Cotesworth, 142, 167, 168, 171, 189
Pinckney, Thomas, 166
Pinckney Treaty (1795), 181
Pioneers, The (Cooper), 288
Pirate of the Gulf, The (Ingraham), 290

ratification of Constitution and, 147

seccession of, 348

slaves in colonial, 55

Southern Conservatives, 383

Southern Homestead Act (1866), 395

Southern Literary Messenger, 321

Southern Quarterly Review, 321

Sovereignty, popular, 337, 339

Spain:
American relations in 1780s with, 134–35
conquests of Indian civilizations, 14–15
control of Mississippi River mouth, 129
explorations from, 13–15, *15*
Ferdinand and Isabella's reign, 16–17
French and Indian War and, 87, 88
Gibraltar, siege of, 124, 125
Pinckney Treaty, *165*, 166
religious dissenters, 45
rivals, 15–18
San Ildefonso, Treaty of, 180, 181
U.S. Revolution, support of, 109–10
West Florida and, 231

Specie, 211

Specie Circular (1836), 246

Spice trade, 7, 8, 12, 13

Spoils system, 237–38

Sprague, Kate Chase, *359*

Squanto, 38

Squatters, 215

Stamp Act (1763), 91–92, 96

Stamp Act Congress, 92

Stanbery, Henry, 393

Stand-up voting, 233

Stanton, Edwin, 289, 356, 393

Stanton, Elizabeth Cady, *296*, 296, 301, 392

Stanwix, Fort, 112, 137

Star of the West (steamer), 350

States (*See also* specific states)
economic warfare in 1780s, 130–31
jurisdiction, 146

Steamboats, *203*, 206, 216

Steele, Richard, Sir, 70

Stephens, Alexander H., 387

Steuben, Friedrich Wilhem von, 105

Stevens, Sarah, 388

Stevens, Thaddeus, 386, 388–91, 395

Stiegel, Henry William, 72

Stockton, Robert, 269, 271

Stone, Lucy, 297, 392

Stono Rebellion, 55

Stowe, Harriet Beecher, 314, 335–36

Strike, Lowell Mill, 225

Sturtevant, Julian, 366

Style and Arrangement, Committee of, 146

Sublette, Milton, 254

Sublette, William, 254

Suffolk Resolves, 97

Suffrage, black, 386, 390–91

Sugar Act (1764), 90–91, 98, 118

Sullivan, John, 112

Sumner, Charles, 333, 341–42, *342*, 386, 389, 390

Sumner-Brooks incident, 341–42

Sumter, Fort, 349–50, *350*

Supply side perspective, 200

Supreme Court, 145, 179
Chief Justices of, 421
under Marshall, 230

Surinam, *80*

Sutch, Richard, 396

Sutter, John Augustus, 259, 271, 332

"Swanee River" (Foster), 319

Swartwout, Samuel, 238

Syphilis spread, from New World, 19, *20*

T

Talleyrand, Charles, 167, 181

Tallmadge, James, Jr., 329

Taney, Roger, 343

Tariff Act (1789), 153

Tariff Act (1816), 228

Tariff Act (1842), 263

Tariff of Abominations (1828), 235–36

Tariffs, 211, 327–28

Tarrytown, N.Y., 114

Taxes, 211
British, 89–93
colonial trade and, 82
government's constitutional power to impose, 145
on imports in 1780s, 130–31
Whiskey Rebellion and, 165–66

Taylor, John, 158, 159

Taylor, Sarah Knox, *323*

Taylor, Zachary, 268, 269, 331

Tea Act (1773), 96–97

Technology:
economic growth and, 206
European revival in trade and, 9–10

Tecumseh, 191, 195

Telegraph, 208–9

Temperance movement, 295

Tenantry, 395–97

Tennessee, 181, 357

Ten-percent plan, 385

Tenure of Office Act (1867), 389, 392–93

Territorial growth (*See* Expansionism)

Texas, 260–62, *262*, 264–65, 330, 332, 348

Texas and Pacific Railroad, 402

Thames, Battle of the (1813), 195

Thirteenth Amendment, 390

Thomas, George H., 358, 375, 377

Thomas, Jesse B., 330

Thoreau, Henry, 252, 289, 345

"Three-fifths compromise," 144, 146

Ticonderoga, Fort, 108, 111, 118

Tilden, Samuel J., 401–2

Tilton, James, 134

Tippecanoe, Battle of (1811), 191

Tithes, 45

Tobacco cultivation, 28–29, 76

Tocqueville, Alexis de, 277

Toleration, religious, 45

Tonnage Act (1789), 153

Tordesillas, Treaty of (1494), 15

Tories, 89, 93, 113, 117–20

Tory Rangers, 112

Townshend, Charles, 92

Townshend Acts (1967), 92–93, 95

Trade and commerce:
colonial economy and, 78, 79–81, 82
Embargo Act (1807), 188–89
foreign, 207
with France in 1790s, 163
during French and Indian War, 88
fur, 253–54
governments constitutional power to control, 145
Jay Treaty and, 164